Praise for *Professional Excel Development, Second Edition*

"As Excel applications become more complex and the Windows development platform more powerful, Excel developers need books like this to help them evolve their solutions to the next level of sophistication. *Professional Excel Development* is a book for developers who want to build powerful, state-of-the-art Excel applications using the latest Microsoft technologies."

—Gabhan Berry, Program Manager, Excel Programmability, Microsoft

"The first edition of *Professional Excel Development* is   ulted and most-recommended book on Office development   both the depth and range. It shines because it takes   ou expect. The book relies on the authors' current, rea   how a feature works, but also the practical implication

—Shauna Kelly, Director, Thendara Gre

"This book illustrates techniques that will result in well-designed, robust, and maintainable Excel-based applications. The authors' advice comes from decades of solid experience of designing and building applications. The practicality of the methods is well illustrated by the example timesheet application that is developed step-by-step through the book. Every serious Excel developer should read this and learn from it. I did."

—Bill Manville, Application Developer, Bill Manville Associates

"This book explains difficult concepts in detail. The authors provide more than one method for complex development topics, along with the advantages and disadvantages of using the various methods described. They have my applause for the incorporation of development best practices."

—Beth Melton, Independent Contractor and Microsoft Office MVP

"*Professional Excel Development* is THE book for the serious Excel developer. It reaches far beyond object models and worksheet layouts and code syntax, to the inner workings of a professional developer's mind. The book covers Excel in great depth, but more important it explores the thought processes and logistics behind successful Excel development."

—Jon Peltier, Microsoft Excel MVP and President of Peltier Technical Services, Inc.

"The authors have done what I deemed impossible: improve a book that I already considered the best book ever on Excel development!"

—Jan Karel Pieterse, Excel MVP and owner of www.jkp-ads.com

PROFESSIONAL
EXCEL DEVELOPMENT
SECOND EDITION

PROFESSIONAL
EXCEL DEVELOPMENT
SECOND EDITION

THE DEFINITIVE GUIDE TO DEVELOPING APPLICATIONS USING MICROSOFT® EXCEL, VBA®, AND .NET

Rob Bovey
Dennis Wallentin
Stephen Bullen
John Green

✦✦ Addison-Wesley

Upper Saddle River, NJ • Boston • Indianapolis • San Francisco
New York • Toronto • Montreal • London • Munich • Paris • Madrid
Capetown • Sydney • Tokyo • Singapore • Mexico City

Many of the designations used by manufacturers and sellers to distinguish their products are claimed as trademarks. Where those designations appear in this book, and the publisher was aware of a trademark claim, the designations have been printed with initial capital letters or in all capitals.

The authors and publisher have taken care in the preparation of this book, but make no expressed or implied warranty of any kind and assume no responsibility for errors or omissions. No liability is assumed for incidental or consequential damages in connection with or arising out of the use of the information or programs contained herein.

The publisher offers excellent discounts on this book when ordered in quantity for bulk purchases or special sales, which may include electronic versions and/or custom covers and content particular to your business, training goals, marketing focus, and branding interests. For more information, please contact:

U.S. Corporate and Government Sales
(800) 382-3419
corpsales@pearsontechgroup.com

For sales outside the United States please contact:

International Sales
international@pearson.com

Visit us on the Web: informit.com/aw

Library of Congress Cataloging-in-Publication Data:

Professional Excel development : the definitive guide to developing applications using Microsoft Excel, VBA, and .NET / Rob Bovey ... [et al.]. — 2nd ed.

   p. cm.

   Rev. ed. of: Professional Excel development : the definitive guide to developing applications using Microsoft Excel and VBA / Stephen Bullen, Rob Bovey, John Green. 2005.

   ISBN 978-0-321-50879-9 (pbk. : alk. paper) 1. Microsoft Excel (Computer file) 2. Microsoft Visual Basic for applications. I. Bovey, Rob. II. Bullen, Stephen. Professional Excel development.

   HF5548.4.M523B85 2009

   005.54—dc22

                                2009005855

ISBN-13: 978-0-321-50879-9
ISBN-10: 0-321-50879-3
Text printed in the United States on recycled paper at Edwards Brothers in Ann Arbor, Michigan.
Third printing August 2009

TABLE OF CONTENTS

Chapter 27 **XLLs and the C API**

Chapter 28 **Excel and Web Services**

Chapter 29 **Providing Help, Securing, Packaging, and Distributing**

ACKNOWLEDGMENTS

First and foremost, this book would never have been written without the support of our partners and families, who have graciously put up with our insatiable computer habits and many late nights over the past year. Neither would it have been done without our dogs, who kept our feet warm while we worked and forced us to get out of the house at least once each day.

We all owe a debt of gratitude to the Excel group at Microsoft, past and present, for making Excel the amazing development platform it is today. It is their dedication and commitment to us that makes Excel application development possible and enjoyable. They have repeatedly demonstrated their willingness to listen to and implement our suggestions over the years.

There are many people we want to thank at Addison-Wesley Professional, particularly our editor Joan Murray for her support while writing the book, Anne Goebel for steering us through the production process, and Curt Johnson for getting it on the shelves.

The quality of a technical book depends as much on the reviewers as the authors, so we want to thank all our technical reviewers. Most of your suggestions were implemented. At the risk of offending the others, we would particularly like to thank Bill Manville, John Peltier, and Gabhan Berry for the quality and rigor of their reviews.

Finally, we want to thank you for buying this book. Please tell us what you think about it, either by e-mail or by writing a review at Amazon.com.

Thank you,

Rob Bovey
Dennis Wallentin
Stephen Bullen
John Green

ABOUT THE AUTHORS

Rob Bovey (robbovey@appspro.com) is president of Application Professionals, a software development company specializing in Microsoft Office, Visual Basic, and SQL Server applications. He brings many years of experience creating financial, accounting, and executive information systems for corporate users to Application Professionals. You can visit the Application Professionals Web site at www.appspro.com.

Rob developed several add-ins shipped by Microsoft for Microsoft Excel, co-authored the *Microsoft Excel 97 Developers Kit* and contributed to the *Excel 2002 and 2007 VBA Programmer's References*. He earned his Bachelor of Science degree from The Rochester Institute of Technology and his MBA from the University of North Carolina at Chapel Hill. Microsoft has awarded him the title of Most Valuable Professional each year since 1995.

Dennis Wallentin (dennis@excelkb.com) is located in Östersund, Sweden, where he lives with his wife and two daughters. Dennis has been developing Excel business solutions since the 1980s and he has a Master's degree in business management and accounting.

He is the founder of XL-Dennis, which delivers solutions for all sizes of companies including the public sector both in Sweden and internationally. He also writes reviews about new Excel versions, books, and other related Excel articles for Swedish magazines. For the last few years he has specialized in creating Excel business solutions based on .NET technologies, including Visual Studio Tools for Office System (VSTO).

Stephen Bullen (stephen@oaltd.co.uk) lives in Woodford Green, London, England, with his partner Clare, daughter Becky, and their dogs, Fluffy and Charlie. A graduate of Oxford University, Stephen has an MA in engineering, economics, and management, providing a unique blend of both business and technical skills.

He is now an employee of Merrill Lynch in London, managing a global spreadsheet development team producing Front Office pricing and risk management tools.

Stephen's Web site, www.oaltd.co.uk, provides a number of helpful and interesting utilities, examples, tips, and techniques to help in your use of Excel and development of Excel applications.

Stephen contributed chapters to John Green's *Excel 2000 VBA Programmer's Reference* and co-authored subsequent editions, published by Wrox Press.

He has been active in various Excel-related online communities for more than 15 years. In recognition of his knowledge, skills, and contributions, Microsoft has awarded him the title of Most Valuable Professional each year since 1996.

John Green (greenj@bigpond.net.au) lives and works in Sydney, Australia, as an independent computer consultant, specializing in integrating Excel, Access, Word, and Outlook using VBA. He has more than 30 years of computing experience, a chemical engineering degree, and an MBA.

He wrote his first programs in FORTRAN, took part in the evolution of specialized planning languages on mainframes, and, in the early 1980s, became interested in spreadsheet systems, including 1-2-3 and Excel.

John established his company, Execuplan Consulting, in 1980, developing computer-based planning applications and training users and developers.

John has had regular columns in a number of Australian magazines and has contributed chapters to a number of books, including *Excel Expert Solutions* and *Using Visual Basic for Applications 5*, published by Que. He is the principal author of *Excel 2000 VBA Programmer's Reference* and its subsequent editions, published by Wrox Press.

Between 1995 and 2006 he was accorded the status of Most Valuable Professional by Microsoft for his contributions to the CompuServe Excel forum and MS Internet newsgroups.

CHAPTER 1

INTRODUCTION

About This Book

Microsoft Excel is much more than just a spreadsheet. With the introduction of the Visual Basic Editor in Excel 97, followed by the significantly improved stability of Excel 2000, Excel became a respected development platform in its own right. Excel applications are now found alongside those based on C++, Java, and the .NET development platform, as part of the core suite of mission-critical corporate applications.

Unfortunately, Excel is still too often thought of as a hobbyist platform, that people only develop Excel applications in their spare time to automate minor tasks. A brief look at many Excel VBA books seems to confirm this opinion. These books focus on the basics of automating Excel tasks using VBA. This book is the first of its kind in providing a detailed explanation of how to use Excel as the platform for developing professional quality applications.

While most other major development platforms seem to have a de facto standard text that explains the commonly agreed best practices for architecting, designing, and developing applications using that platform, until now Excel has not. This book attempts to fill that gap. The authors are professional Excel developers who create Excel-based applications for clients ranging from individuals to the largest multinational corporations. This book explains the approaches we use when designing, developing, distributing, and supporting the applications we write for our clients.

Who Should Read This Book

This is not a beginner-level book. If you do not already have a clear understanding of the core Excel object model and a basic understanding of Excel VBA development this is not the place to start. We assume that readers of this book have already read and (mostly) understood our *Excel 2002 or 2007 VBA Programmer's Reference*, John Walkenbach's *Excel Power Programming*, or similar titles. This book begins where other Excel VBA books end.

Owners of the first edition of *Professional Excel Development* have a different decision to make. Should you purchase the second edition? We have made numerous corrections and improvements throughout this edition as well as expanding it with over 300 pages of new material that you simply will not find anywhere else.

In the interest of full disclosure, however, we want to be very clear that the bulk of the new material is aimed at Excel developers who are working with Excel 2007 and Visual Studio 2008. If you own the first edition of this book and your primary focus is developing VBA applications in Excel 2003 and earlier, you will see incremental rather than revolutionary improvements in this edition. We don't want to discourage you from upgrading to the second edition and would welcome it if you choose to do so. But most of all we want you to be satisfied with our work, so we state the pros and cons of upgrading honestly to help you make an informed decision.

Excel Developer Categories

Excel developers can be divided into five general categories based on their experience and knowledge of Excel and VBA. This book has something to offer each of them, but with a focus on the more advanced topics. Putting yourself into one of these categories might help you decide whether this is the right book for you.

Basic Excel **users** probably don't think of themselves as developers at all. Excel is no more than a tool to help them get on with their job. They start off using Excel worksheets as a handy place to store lists or perform simple repetitive calculations. As they discover more Excel features their workbooks may begin to include more complex worksheet functions, pivot tables, and charts. There is little in this book for basic Excel users, although Chapter 4, "Worksheet Design," details the best practices to use when designing and laying out a worksheet for data entry; Chapter 20, "Data Manipulation Techniques," explains how to structure a worksheet and which functions and features to use to manipulate their lists; and Chapter 21, "Advanced Charting Techniques," explains how to get the most from Excel's chart engine. The techniques suggested in these chapters should help the basic Excel user avoid some of the pitfalls often encountered as their experience and the complexity of their worksheets increase.

Excel **power users** have a broad understanding of Excel's functionality and they know which tool or function is best used in a given situation. Power users create complex workbooks for their own use and are often called on to help develop workbooks for their colleagues, or to identify why their colleagues' workbooks don't work as intended. Power users occasionally use snippets of VBA, either found on the Internet or created with the macro recorder, but struggle to adapt the code to their needs. As a result, their code tends to be messy, slow, and hard to maintain. While this book is not a VBA tutorial, power users have much to gain from following the best practices we suggest for both worksheets and code modules. Most of the chapters in the book are relevant to power users who have an interest in improving their Excel and VBA development skills.

VBA developers make extensive use of VBA code in their workbooks—often too much. They are typically either power users who started to learn VBA too early or Visual Basic developers who switched to Excel VBA development. While they may be proficient with VBA they believe every problem must have a VBA solution. They tend to lack the experience required to know when a problem is best solved using Excel, when a problem is best solved using VBA, and when the best solution is a combination of the two. Their solutions are often cumbersome, slow, and make poor use of the Excel object model. This book has much to offer VBA developers to improve their use of Excel itself, including best practices for designing worksheets and how to use Excel's features for data entry, analysis, and presentation. The book also seeks to improve their Excel VBA development skills by introducing advanced coding techniques, detailing VBA best practices, and explaining how to improve VBA code performance.

Excel developers realize that the most efficient and maintainable applications are those that make the most of Excel's built-in functionality, augmented by VBA where appropriate. They are confident in developing Excel-based applications for their colleagues or as part of an in-house development team. While their knowledge of Excel is put to good use in their applications, their design techniques tend to be limited, and they are reluctant to use other languages and applications to augment their Excel solutions. They have probably read John Walkenbach's *Excel 2003 or 2007 Power Programming* and/or our own *Excel 2002 or 2007 VBA Programmer's Reference*. Now they need a book to take them to the highest level of Excel application development—that of the professional developer. This is the book to do that.

Professional Excel developers design and develop for their clients or employer Excel-based applications and utilities that are robust, fast, easy to use, maintainable, and secure. While Excel forms the core of their solutions, they use other applications and languages where appropriate, including third-party ActiveX controls, Office automation, Windows API calls, external databases, various standalone programming languages, and XML. This book teaches all of those skills. If you are already a professional Excel developer, you will know that learning never stops and will appreciate the knowledge and best practices presented in this book by four of your peers.

Excel as an Application Development Platform

If we look at Excel as a development platform rather than just a spreadsheet, we find that it provides five fundamental components we can use in our applications:

- The worksheets, charts, and other objects used to create a user interface and presentation layer for data entry and reporting
- The worksheets used as simple data stores for lists, tables, and other information required by our application
- VBA code and UserForms for creating business logic and advanced user interfaces
- Worksheet formulas used as a declarative programming language for high-performance numerical processing
- The Excel object model, allowing programmatic control of (nearly) all of Excel's functionality, both from within Excel and from outside it

The Worksheet as a Presentation Layer for Data Entry and Reporting

Most people think about Excel in terms of typing numbers into cells, having some calculations update, and seeing a result displayed in a different cell or on a chart. Without necessarily thinking in such terms, they are using the worksheet as a user interface for their data entry and reporting and are generally comfortable with these tasks. The in-cell editing, validation, and formatting features built in to Excel provide a rich and compelling data entry experience, while the charting, cell formatting, and drawing tools provide a presentation-quality reporting mechanism.

It is hard to imagine the code that would be required if we tried to reproduce this experience using the tools available in most other development environments, yet Excel provides these features right out of the box for use in our Excel-based applications. The biggest problem we face is how to add structure to the free-form worksheet grid to present a simple and easy-to-use interface, while leveraging the rich functionality of Excel. Chapter 4 introduces some techniques and best practices for developing worksheet-based data entry forms, while Chapter 21 covers charting capabilities.

The Worksheet as a Simple Data Store

What is a worksheet when it's never intended to be shown to the end user? At its simplest, it's no more than a large grid of cells in which we can store just about anything we want, including numbers, text, lists, tables, and pictures. Most applications use some amount of static data or graphical resources. Storing that information in a worksheet makes it both easy to access using VBA and simple to maintain. Lists and tables in worksheets can directly feed Excel's data validation feature (as shown in Chapter 4), greatly simplify the creation and maintenance of command bars (Chapter 8, "Advanced Command Bar Handling"), and allow us to construct dynamic UserForms (Chapter 13, "UserForm Design and Best Practices").

VBA Code and UserForms

We expect most readers of this book have at least some familiarity with VBA. If not, we suggest you read one of the resources mentioned at the beginning of this chapter before continuing much further. Many people see the "A" in VBA as meaning the language is somehow less than Visual Basic itself. In fact, both VB6 and Office use exactly the same DLL to provide the keywords, syntax, and statements we program with.

Most beginner and intermediate VBA developers use VBA as a purely procedural language, with nearly all their code residing in standard modules. VBA also allows us to create applications using an object oriented programming (OOP) approach, in which class modules are used to create our own objects. Chapter 7, "Using Class Modules to Create Objects," and Chapter 14, "Interfaces," explain how to use VBA in this manner, while basic OOP concepts (such as encapsulation) are used throughout the book.

Most of this book is dedicated to explaining advanced VBA techniques and a professional approach to application design and development that can put VBA in Excel on par with, and sometimes in front of, VB6 or VB.Net for application development. In Chapters 23 through 26 we show that Excel developers can achieve the best of both worlds by combining Excel with VB6 or VB.Net in a seamless application.

The Worksheet as a Declarative Programming Language

Take the following code:

```
dSales = 1000
dPrice = 10.99
dRevenue = dSales * dPrice
```

That could easily be a few lines of VBA. We give the variable dSales a value of 1000, the variable dPrice a value of 10.99, and then calculate the revenue as sales times price. If we change the names of the variables and adjust the spacing, the same code could also be written as

```
D1    =1000
D2    =10.99
D3    =D1*D2
```

This looks much more like worksheet cell addresses and formulas than lines of VBA code, showing that worksheet formulas are in fact a programming language of their own if we choose to think of it in those terms. The `IF()` worksheet function is directly equivalent to the `If...Then...Else` VBA statement, while the judicious use of circular references and iteration can be equivalent to either the `For...Next` or `Do...Loop` structures.

Instead of stating a set of **operations** that are executed line-by-line, we "program" in this language by making a set of **declarations** (by typing formulas and values into worksheet cells), in any order we want:

> "D3 is the product of D1 and D2"
> "D1 has the value 1000"
> "D2 has the value 10.99"

To "run" this program, Excel first examines all the declarations and builds a **precedence tree** to identify which cells depend on the results of which other cells and thereby determine the most efficient order in which the cells must be calculated. The same precedence tree is also used to identify the minimum set of calculations that must be performed whenever the value in a cell is changed. The result is a calculation engine that is vastly more efficient than an equivalent VBA program, and one that should be used whenever complex numerical computations are required in your application.

Microsoft Excel is unique among application development platforms in providing both a procedural (VBA) and a declarative (worksheet functions) programming language. The most efficient Excel application is one that makes appropriate use of both these languages.

It is assumed the reader of this book has a basic understanding of worksheet functions, so Chapter 20 focuses on using advanced worksheet functions (including best-practice suggestions for handling circular references) and Excel's other data analysis features.

The Excel Object Model

While the other four components of the Excel platform are invaluable in the development of applications, it is probably the rich Excel object model that provides the most compelling reason to base our applications in Excel. Almost everything that can be accomplished through the Excel user interface can also be accomplished programmatically using the objects in the Excel object model. (Accessing the list of number formats and applying a digital signature to a workbook are perhaps the most notable exceptions.)

The vast feature set exposed by these objects makes many complex applications fairly simple to develop. Unlike most other development platforms, there is no need to figure out how to program these features from scratch. Excel provides them ready-made, so all we need to do is determine how to plug them together most effectively. This book does not attempt to explore and document every obscure niche of the Excel object model. Instead, we demonstrate the best way to use the objects we most commonly use in our own application development.

Structure

Over the course of this book we cover both the concepts and details of each topic and apply those concepts to a time sheet reporting and analysis application that we will build in stages as we move along. The chapters are therefore arranged approximately in the order in which we would design and develop an Excel application:

- **Chapter 2** discusses the different styles of application we might choose to create.
- **Chapter 3** identifies some general best practices for working with Excel and VBA. These are followed throughout the book.
- **Chapter 4** explains how to design and structure a worksheet for data entry and analysis.
- **Chapters 5 and 6** introduce two specific types of application—the add-in and the dictator application, which form the basis of our time sheet reporting and analysis application.
- **Chapter 7** introduces the use of class modules in our Excel applications.
- **Chapters 8 to 11** discuss topics relevant to building command bar and Ribbon user interfaces as well as designing applications that must run in all current Excel versions using a single code base.
- **Chapters 12 to 17** discuss advanced techniques for a range of VBA topics.
- **Chapters 18 and 19** cover database development for Excel developers.
- **Chapters 20 and 21** explain how to efficiently use Excel's features to analyze data and present results.
- **Chapters 22 to 27** look outside Excel, by explaining how to automate other applications and extend Excel with Visual Basic 6, VB.NET, and C.
- **Chapter 28** focuses on how Excel applications can make use of Web Services.
- **Chapter 29** completes the development by explaining how to provide help for, secure, and deploy an Excel application.

Examples

As mentioned previously, throughout the book, we illustrate the concepts and techniques we introduce by building a time sheet data entry, consolidation, analysis, and reporting application. This consists of a data entry template to be completed by each employee, with the data sent to a central location for consolidation, analysis, and reporting. At the end of most chapters we show an updated working example of the application that incorporates ideas presented in those chapters, so the application grows steadily more complex as the book progresses.

In Chapter 4, we start with a simple data entry workbook and assume that each employee would e-mail the completed file to a manager who would analyze the results manually—a typical situation for a company with just a few employees.

By the end of the book, the data entry workbook will use XML to upload the data to a Web site, where it will be stored in a central database. The reporting application will extract the data from the database, perform various analyses, and present the results as reports in Excel worksheets and charts.

Along the way we rewrite some parts of the application in a number of different ways to show how easy it can be to include other languages and delivery mechanisms in our Excel-based applications. Most chapters also include specific concept examples to illustrate key points that are important to understand but would be too artificial if forced into the architecture of our time sheet application.

Supported Versions of Excel

When we develop an Excel application for a client, that client's upgrade policy usually determines the version of Excel we must use. Few clients agree to upgrade just so we can develop using the latest version of Excel unless there is a compelling business requirement that can only be satisfied by using features the latest version introduces. At the time of this writing, an extremely unscientific poll (based on postings to the Microsoft support newsgroups) seems to indicate the following approximate usage distribution for each current version of Excel:

Excel 2000	10%
Excel 2002	15%
Excel 2003	50%
Excel 2007	25%

There are still a small number of users on Excel 97 and earlier versions, but for various reasons we no longer consider these versions of Excel to be viable development platforms. We therefore decided to use Excel 2000 as our lowest supported version. Many features we discuss, especially when we cover XML and the .NET development platform, are only supported in Excel 2002 or 2003 and higher. Whenever we discuss a feature that is only supported in a later version of Excel we state which version(s) it applies to.

Typefaces

The following text styles are used in this book:

Menu items and dialog text are shown as *Tools > Options > Calculation > Manual*, where the ">" indicates navigation to a submenu or dialog tab.

```
Sub SomeCode()
   'Code listings are shown like this
End Sub
```

Code within the text of a paragraph is shown in a fixed-width font like `Application.Calculation = xlManual`.

Paths on the CD are shown as *\Concepts\Ch14 - Interfaces*.

New terms introduced or defined appear **like this**.

Important points or emphasized words appear ***like this***.

On the CD

Most of the code listings shown in the book are also included in example workbooks on the accompanying CD. For clarity, the code shown in the printed examples may use shorter line lengths, reduced indent settings, fewer code comments, and less error handling than the corresponding code in the workbooks. The CD has three main directories, containing the following files:

- *\Tools* contains a number of tools and utilities developed by the authors that we have found to be invaluable during our application development. The MustHaveTools.htm file contains details about each of these tools and links to other third-party utilities.
- *\Concepts* has separate subdirectories for each chapter, each one containing example files to support the text of the chapter. For best results, we suggest you have these workbooks open while reading the corresponding chapter.

■ **\Application** has separate subdirectories for the chapters where we have updated our time sheet example application. These chapters end with a Practical Example section that explains the changes made to implement concepts introduced in that chapter.

Help and Support

By far the best place to go for help with any of your Excel development questions, whether related to this book or not, are the Microsoft support newsgroup archives maintained by Google at http://groups.google. com. A quick search of the archives is almost certain to find a question similar to yours, already answered by one of the many professional developers who volunteer their time helping out in the newsgroups, including all the authors of this book. On the rare occasions that the archives fail to answer your question, you're welcome to ask it directly in the newsgroups by connecting a newsreader (such as Outlook Express) to msnews.microsoft.com and selecting an appropriate newsgroup, such as

microsoft.public.excel.misc for general Excel questions

microsoft.public.excel.programming for VBA-related questions

microsoft.public.excel.worksheet.functions for help with worksheet functions

For assistance with Excel and VB.NET integration issues we recommend the MSDN VSTO Web forum located here:

http://social.msdn.microsoft.com/Forums/en-US/vsto/threads/

A number of Web sites provide a great deal of information and free downloadable examples and utilities targeted towards the Excel developer, including

www.appspro.com

www.excelkb.com

www.oaltd.co.uk

http://peltiertech.com

www.cpearson.com

http://msdn.microsoft.com/office

The Professional Excel Development Web Site

As an experiment for the second edition of *Professional Excel Development*, we are introducing a new Web site to accompany the book at www.ProExcelDev.net.

As of this writing the site does not yet exist, so it is difficult to say exactly what you will find there. However, at a minimum you will find the latest corrections, bug fixes, and clarifications related to this book. Our hope is to eventually expand the site to provide more in-depth coverage of popular topics than we were able to fit into our publishing deadline as well as blogs and possibly even interactive technical forums.

Feedback

We have tried very hard to present the information in this book in a clear and concise manner, explaining both the concepts and details needed to get things working as well as providing working examples of everything we cover. We have tried to provide sufficient information to enable you to apply these techniques in your own applications without getting bogged down in line-by-line explanations of entire code listings.

We'd like to think we've been successful in our attempt, but we encourage you to let us know what you think. Constructive criticism is always welcomed, as are suggestions for topics you think we may have overlooked. Please send feedback to the following authors:

Rob Bovey: robbovey@appspro.com
Dennis Wallentin: dennis@excelkb.com

CHAPTER 2

APPLICATION ARCHITECTURES

One of the first decisions to be made when starting a new project is how to structure the application. This chapter explains the various architectures we can use, the situations where each is most applicable, and the pros and cons of each choice.

Concepts

The choice of where to put the code for an Excel application is rarely straightforward. In anything but the simplest of situations there is a trade-off among numerous factors, including

- **Complexity**—How easy will the chosen architecture be to create?
- **Clarity**—How easy will it be for someone other than the author to understand the application?
- **Development**—How easy will it be to modify the code, particularly in a team environment?
- **Extensibility**—How easy is it to add new features?
- Reliability—Can the results be relied on? How easily can calculation errors be introduced into the application?
- **Robustness**—How well will the application be able to handle application errors, invalid data, and other problems?
- **Security**—How easy will it be to prevent unauthorized changes to the application?
- **Deployment**—How easy will it be to distribute the application to the end user?
- **Maintainability**—How easy will it be to modify the application once it has been distributed to the end user?

Codeless Applications

The most basic application architecture is one that only uses Excel's built-in functionality. Everyone creates this type of application without knowing it, simply by using Excel. Codeless applications are typically created by beginning to intermediate Excel users who have not yet learned to use VBA. All the custom formatting, validation, formulas, and so on are placed directly on the same worksheet where data entry will be performed. There are some major problems with this approach when it is applied to non-trivial Excel applications, so totally codeless applications are rarely a good choice.

To avoid VBA, the worksheet functions and data validation criteria tend to become convoluted and hard to follow. The equivalent VBA often is easier to understand and maintain. The same worksheet is normally used for data entry, analysis, and presentation. This tends to result in a cluttered appearance that is difficult to understand, unintuitive to use, and almost impossible for anyone except the author to modify reliably.

Codeless applications have to rely on Excel's worksheet protection to prevent users from making unauthorized changes. Worksheet passwords are notoriously easy to break, and a simple copy and paste will wipe out any cell data validation. Codeless applications are therefore neither secure nor robust.

Without code, we are unable to provide much assistance to users; we have to rely on them to do everything themselves—and do it correctly—instead of providing reliable helper routines that automate some of their tasks. The more complex the application, the less likely it is that all the tasks will be performed correctly.

If we consider the definition of a "program" to be "anything that isn't the data," we see that all the conditional formatting, data validation, worksheet functions, and so on are really part of the "program," so codeless applications break the basic tenet of keeping the program and data physically separate. Once users have started to enter data it is difficult to distribute an updated workbook to them without losing the data they've already entered. You have to either hope the user can copy the existing data to the new workbook correctly or write a conversion program to copy the data from the old workbook to the new workbook for them.

Codeless applications can work well in the following situations:

- There will only be one copy of the application workbook, so any changes can be made directly to that workbook.
- Each copy of the workbook will have a short lifetime. In this case, the assumption is that the workbooks will not need updating after they have been distributed.

- The end users will maintain the workbook themselves or the workbook will not require any maintenance at all.
- There is a small number of relatively sophisticated end users who can be trained well enough to ensure the application is used correctly and not inadvertently broken.

A good example of a codeless application would be a simple survey or data collection form that requires the end user to fill in the details and e-mail the completed workbook to a central address for consolidation and analysis. The main benefit of a codeless application in such a situation is the avoidance of Excel's macro security warnings and the corresponding assurance that there is nothing malicious in the file.

Self-Automated Workbooks

A self-automated workbook is one in which the VBA code is physically contained within the workbook it acts upon. The automation code can be as simple as ensuring the workbook always opens with Sheet1 active or as complex as an entire application. This is usually the first type of application a beginning VBA developer produces, by adding helper routines to a workbook that get progressively numerous and more complex over time.

Once we introduce VBA into the workbook we acquire much more flexibility in how we provide the features required by the application. We can make a considered choice whether to use Excel's built-in functions or write our own equivalents to avoid some of Excel's pitfalls. For example, Excel's data validation feature may not operate correctly when entries are made in multiple cells simultaneously, and data validation is usually cleared when data is pasted onto a range that uses it. We can work around these limitations by trapping the Worksheet_Change event and performing our own validation in code, making the application more robust, reliable, and secure.

The Workbook and Worksheet code modules provided by Excel allow us to trap the events we want to use. Any ActiveX controls we add to a worksheet are automatically exposed in that worksheet's code module. This is the simplest application architecture to create and probably the simplest to understand—most VBA developers have written an application of this type and therefore understand, for example, how the code within a worksheet code module is triggered.

The biggest advantage of the self-automated workbook application architecture is its ease of deployment. There is only one file to distribute. There is no need to install or configure anything, and because the code is physically stored within the workbook, it is available and working as soon as the workbook is opened.

Unfortunately, the self-automated workbook's clearest advantage is also its biggest problem. When the code is physically inside the workbook, how do you update the code without affecting the data that has been entered on the worksheets? While it is possible to write VBA that modifies the code within another workbook, the user has to make a specific macro security setting to allow that to happen (in Excel 2002 and above). Also, it is only possible to unprotect and reprotect the VBA project using SendKeys, which cannot be relied on to work in foreign-language versions of Excel or if Excel doesn't have the focus. Even if the project could be unprotected and reprotected, saving the updated project would remove any digital signature that had been applied, resulting in macro virus warnings every time the workbook was subsequently opened. The only reliable way self-automated workbooks can be updated is to provide a completely new workbook with VBA code (or instructions) to copy the data from the old workbook. Self-automated workbooks are a good choice if the following conditions apply:

- The VBA code contained within the workbook provides functionality specific to that workbook (as opposed to general purpose utilities).
- There will only be one copy of the application workbook, so any changes can be made directly to that workbook.
- The workbook will have a short lifetime or will be distributed to a large audience, in which case ease of deployment becomes a significant consideration.
- The workbook does not contain any data that will need to be retained during an update, such as one that obtains its data from an external data source or saves the data entered into it to an external data repository.

General Purpose Add-ins

An add-in is a specific type of application, usually used to add features to Excel. The worksheets in an add-in are hidden from the user, so the user never interacts directly with the workbook. Instead, the add-in exposes its features by adding items to Excel's menus and toolbars or Ribbon, hooking key combinations, trapping Excel events, and/or exposing functions to be used from worksheets in other workbooks. VBA procedures in an add-in can also be executed by typing their fully qualified name (for example, MyAddin.xla!MyProcedure) in the *Tools > Macro > Macros* dialog, even though they do not appear in the list of available macros.

The procedures in a general purpose add-in will always be available to the Excel user, so this application architecture is most appropriate for utility functions that are designed to work with any file, typically using the `ActiveWorkbook`, `ActiveSheet`, or `Selection` objects to identify the items to operate on.

Care should be taken to handle potential user errors, where procedures in the add-in may be called from a context in which they won't work. For example, if your add-in changes the case of the text in the selected cell, you must verify that a cell is selected, isn't locked, and doesn't contain the result of a formula. Similarly, if your code applies custom formatting to the active worksheet, you must verify that there is an active sheet (there may be no workbooks open), it's a worksheet (not a chart or macro sheet, for example), and it's not protected.

An add-in is just a much hidden workbook, so it doesn't appear in the list of workbooks or the VBA `Workbooks` collection. It is, however, just like any other workbook in almost every other respect and should therefore be easy for an intermediate Excel/VBA developer to understand and maintain. In fact you can toggle between having the add-in workbook behave like an add-in or a normal workbook by simply changing the `IsAddin` property of its `ThisWorkbook` object in the VBE Properties window between True and False.

Because add-ins never expose their worksheets to the user, all user interaction is done with UserForms (although the VBA `InputBox` and `MsgBox` functions can be used in simple situations). This gives us a high level of control over user inputs, allowing us to create applications that are robust and reliable—assuming we include data validation code and good error handling.

If the add-in needs to persist any information, such as the most recent selections made by the user in a UserForm, that information should be kept separate from the add-in file, either by storing it in the registry (using `SaveSetting`/`GetSetting`) or in a separate file such as an INI file. By following this practice you ensure the add-in will never need to be saved by the end user and can simply be replaced by a new version if an update is required.

If you are willing to trust the end user to install the add-in correctly, it is also easy to deploy—just send the XLA file with instructions to either copy it into their Library folder or to use the Browse button in the *Tools > Add-Ins* dialog to locate the file. The alternative is to use an installation routine to write the registry entries Excel uses to maintain its add-ins list, such that the add-in is automatically opened and installed when the client next starts Excel. These registry entries are covered in detail in Chapter 29, "Providing Help, Securing, Packaging, and Distributing."

Structure of a General Purpose Add-in

Most general purpose add-ins use the same basic structure:

- Code in an Auto_Open or Workbook_Open procedure that creates the add-in's menu items and sets up the keyboard hooks. Each menu item has its OnAction property set to call the appropriate procedure in the add-in file.
- Procedures associated with each menu item that are located in a standard code module.
- (Optionally) Public functions located in a standard code module that are exposed for use in worksheet formulas.
- Code in an Auto_Close or Workbook_Close procedure that removes the add-in's menu items and clears its keyboard hooks.

Application-Specific Add-ins

As mentioned previously, the main problem with both codeless and self-automated workbooks is that the program is physically stored in the same file as the data it works with. It is difficult to reliably update the program part of those workbooks without affecting or destroying the data.

The alternative is to structure the application such that all the code is contained within one workbook, while a separate workbook is used for data entry, analysis, and so on. One such architecture is that of an application-specific add-in. These are similar to general purpose add-ins, but instead of immediately setting up their menu items, keyboard hooks, and so on, they stay invisible until the user opens a workbook the add-in can identify as one that it should make itself available for.

In a typical application-specific add-in architecture, the user would be supplied with at least two workbooks: the XLA workbook containing the program and a template workbook used for data entry. The template workbook(s) contains some kind of indicator the add-in can use to identify it, usually either a hidden defined name or a custom document property.

The key benefit of using an application-specific add-in is that we can safely distribute updates to the code, knowing we will not cause any harm to the user's data. There is, however, a small price to pay for this convenience:

- Splitting the application into two (or more) workbooks makes it slightly harder to manage, because we have to keep the correct versions of both workbooks synchronized during the development process. Simple version control is discussed in more detail in Chapter 3, "Excel and VBA Development Best Practices."

- The application is slightly harder for other developers to understand, particularly if they are used to single-workbook applications or do not understand the technique of using class modules to hook application-level events, as explained in Chapter 7, "Using Class Modules to Create Objects."
- Deployment is more complicated, because we need to distribute multiple files. Deployment strategies are covered in Chapter 29.

Structure of an Application-Specific Add-in

Application-specific add-ins are similar in structure to general purpose add-ins, but with extra code to identify when to enable or disable the menu items:

- A class module used to trap the application-level events.
- Code in an Auto_Open or Workbook_Open procedure adds the add-in's menu items. Each menu item has its OnAction property set to call the appropriate procedure in the add-in file, but these menu items are all initially either disabled or hidden. It then creates an instance of the class module and initializes application event hooks.
- Procedures associated with each menu item that are located in a standard code module.
- (Optionally) Public functions located in a standard code module that are exposed for use in worksheet formulas.
- Code in the class module that hooks the application-level WorkbookActivate event, checks whether the workbook "belongs" to the add-in and if so enables the menu items and sets up the keyboard hooks.
- Code in the class module hooks the application-level WorkbookDeactivate event, to disable the menu items and remove the keyboard hooks when no application workbook is active.
- Code in an Auto_Close or Workbook_Close procedure removes the add-in's menu items.

General purpose and application-specific add-ins are discussed in more detail in Chapter 5, "Function, General, and Application-Specific Add-ins."

2. APPLICATION ARCHITECTURES

Dictator Applications

All the architectures considered so far have sought to enhance Excel in some way to improve the end user's experience when they're using our application. In contrast, dictator applications attempt to take over the Excel user interface completely, replacing Excel's menus with their own and exercising a high level of control over the user interface. In the ideal dictator application, users will not be able to tell they are working inside Excel.

These applications are created in Excel to use the features Excel provides, but those features are entirely controlled by the application. The user interface is made up of tightly controlled data entry worksheets and/or UserForms designed to appear like any other Windows application. These applications require large amounts of code to provide that degree of control, but that control allows us to write large-scale, fully functional Windows applications on par with any that can be written in Visual Basic or other "mainstream" application development platforms. In fact, by building our application within Excel, we have a head start over other development platforms because we are immediately able to utilize the incredible amount of functionality Excel provides.

As dictator applications become more complex, they will often start to use functionality that only exists in the most recent versions of Excel (such as the XML import/export introduced in Excel 2003), so we need to decide what should happen if the application is opened in an older version of Excel. If the functionality being used is a core part of the application, it is unlikely the application will be usable at all in older versions of Excel. If the use of the new features can be limited to a small part of the application, it may make more sense to just disable user interface access to those features when running in older versions of Excel or provide separate procedures for older versions to use.

Making use of new Excel features often results in compile errors if the application workbook is opened in an older version of Excel, so many dictator applications use a "front-loader" workbook to do an initial version check, verify that all external dependencies are available, and then open and run the main application workbook if all the checks are okay. If the checks fail, we can provide meaningful error messages to the end user (such as "This application requires Excel 2003 or higher and will not work in Excel 2000").

There's no escaping the fact that dictator applications are much more complicated than either self-automated workbooks or application-specific add-ins and will require an intermediate to advanced level Excel/VBA developer to create and maintain them. The complexity of dictator applications can be mitigated by following the best practices advice discussed in Chapter 3 (general advice) and Chapter 6, "Dictator Applications" (specific advice for dictator applications).

Once the decision to build a dictator application has been made, we have an incredible amount of flexibility in terms of physically creating the application. The data can be stored in one or more separate workbooks, local databases such as Access, or a central database such as SQL Server. We can put all the code into a single add-in workbook or have a small core add-in with numerous applets that plug into the core, each performing a specific task. The decision will probably be a trade-off between (at least) the following considerations:

- A single-workbook structure tends to be easier for a single developer to maintain, because everything is in the one place.
- A multiworkbook structure is easier for a team of developers to create, because each developer can work on her own applet without conflicting with another team member.
- If a multiworkbook structure is built so each plug-in applet is not loaded until it is first used, the initial opening of the "core" add-in will be faster than loading the full application of the single-workbook structure—though modern PCs may make that difference appear immaterial.
- A single-workbook structure must be updated in its entirety, but the applets of a multiworkbook structure can be updated and deployed independently.
- The code required to implement a multiworkbook plug-in architecture is complex, and may be too complex for the intermediate VBA developer to fully understand—though we explain it in Chapter 14, "Interfaces."

Requirements of a Dictator Application

To look and operate like a standalone Windows application, a dictator application needs to modify many Excel application properties, from turning on IgnoreOtherApplications (so double-clicking an XLS file in Explorer will not use our instance of Excel) to turning off ShowWindowsInTaskBar (because we may have multiple workbooks open and do not want each of them to spawn new TaskBar buttons), as well as hiding all the built-in command bars. Unfortunately, Excel will remember many of these settings the next time it is started, so every dictator application must first record the existing state of all the settings it changes and restore them all when it closes. If the code to do this is written as two separate procedures that are assigned shortcut keys, they also provide an easy way to switch between the application user interface and the Excel user interface during development.

Once a snapshot of the user's settings has been taken, the dictator application can set the application properties it requires. It then needs to lock down Excel to prevent the user from doing things we don't want them to do. This includes

- Hiding and disabling all built-in command bars or Ribbon tabs (including shortcut command bars), and then setting up our own.
- Protecting our command bars and disabling access to the command bar customization dialog.
- Disabling all the shortcut key combinations that Excel provides, and then optionally reenabling the few we want to be exposed to the user.
- Setting `Application.EnableCancelKey` to `xlDisabled` at the start of every entry point to prevent users from stopping the code.
- When using worksheets as data entry forms, we don't want the user to be able to copy and paste entire cells, since that would include all formatting, data validation, and so on, so we need to turn off drag-and-drop (which does a cut and paste), redirect both Ctrl+X and Shift+Delete to do a Copy instead of a Cut, and redirect Ctrl+V and Shift+Insert to paste only values.

Having locked down the Excel environment while our application is running, we need to provide a mechanism to access the code so that we can debug the application. One method is to set a global IsDevMode Boolean variable to True if a particular file exists in the application directory or (more securely) depending on the Windows username. This Boolean can then be used throughout the application to provide access points, such as enabling the Alt+F11 shortcut to switch to the VBE, adding a Reset menu item and/or shortcut key to switch back to the Excel environment, and not setting the `EnableCancelKey` property, to allow the developer to break into the code. This variable can also be used within error handlers, to control whether to display a user- or developer-oriented error message.

Structure of a Dictator Application

A typical dictator application uses the following logical structure:

- A front-loader/startup procedure to perform version and dependency checks as well as any other validation required to ensure the application can run successfully.
- A core set of procedures to
  - Take a snapshot of the Excel environment settings and to restore those settings.
  - Configure and lock down the Excel application.
  - Create and remove the application's command bars.
  - Handle copying and pasting data within the worksheet templates.
  - Provide a library of common helper procedures and classes.
  - (Optionally) Implement a plug-in architecture using class modules, as described in Chapter 14.
- A backdrop worksheet, to display within the Excel window while UserForms are being shown, usually with some form of application-specific logo (if we're primarily using forms for the user interface).
- Multiple independent applets that provide the application's functionality.
- Multiple template worksheets used by the applets, such as data entry forms or preformatted report templates.

Physically, all the elements that make up a typical dictator application can reside in a single workbook or can be distributed across multiple workbooks. Dictator applications are discussed in more detail in Chapter 6.

Technical Implementations

In our discussion of the main types of application architecture there has been an underlying assumption that the application will be written using VBA. That need not be the case, as we discuss in Chapters 23 through 27, where we examine how we can use the C API to create XLL add-ins and use Visual Basic 6 and/or VB.Net to support our VBA procedures and create COM add-ins.

Any of these architectures can be implemented using either a traditional procedural design, where most of the functionality is implemented using helper procedures in standard code modules, or an object-oriented approach, where the functionality is implemented as properties and methods of class modules, as discussed in Chapter 7.

Summary

The five main types of application architecture each have their pros and cons and each is the most applicable to certain situations. The choice of architecture should be made carefully, with appropriate consideration given to ongoing maintenance (probably by a different person than the original author) as well as just the ease with which the application can be created initially. Table 2-1 lists each architecture and the advantages and disadvantages of each.

Table 2-1   Summary of Application Architectures

Architecture	Pros	Cons	Applicable To
Codeless Workbook	No VBA requirement. No macro security issues. Easy to deploy.	Usually cluttered and hard to use. Neither robust nor reliable. Doesn't provide much assistance to the user. Difficult to update.	Simple data entry forms, surveys, etc.
Self-automated workbook	Simple application, easy for a beginner VBA developer to understand. VBA can be used to improve robustness and reliability. Provides a lot of extra functionality for the user. Easy to deploy.	If the VBA needs to be updated, it will be difficult or impossible to do so once deployed.	More complex data-entry forms, where the VBA can be used to improve the quality of the data being entered, but there is little data stored in the workbook long-term.

Table 2-1 Summary of Application Architectures

Architecture	Pros	Cons	Applicable To
General purpose add-in	Designed to extend Excel's functionality. Simple application, only slightly more complex than an automated workbook. Easy to deploy (though not as simple as a workbook).	Must include robust context checks and error handling. Harder to deploy if it should be automatically ready for use.	Ideal for adding custom functionality to Excel, designed for use with any workbook.
Application-specific add-in	Separates the code from the data, so the code can be updated without affecting the user's work. Removing the code from the data workbooks makes them smaller and avoids the macro security warning.	Slightly more technically complex than the general add-in, requires an intermediate level VBA developer. Slightly harder to deploy, as it requires at least two workbooks to be installed, sometimes to separate locations.	Suitable for applications of any size and complexity.
Dictator application	Can write fully functional applications that appear to be applications in their own right. High degree of control over the user interaction allows you to write very robust and reliable applications. Functionality can be split over multiple workbooks, making them easier for a team to develop and easier to deploy updates.	Much more complex than other architectures. Care must be taken to restore the user's Excel environment. Harder to deploy, typically requiring an installation routine.	Best suited to complex applications or those that require a high degree of control over user interaction.

CHAPTER 3

EXCEL AND VBA DEVELOPMENT BEST PRACTICES

This chapter appears early in the book because we want you to understand why we do certain things the way we do in later chapters. Unfortunately, this also means we'll have to cover a few topics in this chapter that don't get full coverage until later. For best results, you may want to review this chapter after you've read the rest of the book.

As you read this chapter, you should also keep in mind that even though the practices described here are generally accepted best practices, there will always be certain cases where the best thing to do is not follow the best practice. We try to point out the most common examples of this here and in the best practices discussions in the chapters that follow.

Naming Conventions

The term "naming convention" refers to the system you use to name the various parts of your application. Whenever you declare a variable or create a UserForm, you give it a name. You implicitly name objects even when you don't give them a name directly by accepting the default name provided when you create a UserForm, for example. One of the hallmarks of good programming practice is the consistent use of a clearly defined naming convention for all parts of your VBA application.

Let's look at an example that may help demonstrate why naming conventions matter. In the following line of code:

```
x = wksDataSheet.Range("A1").Value
```

What do you know about x? From its usage you can reasonably assume it's a variable. But what data type is it designed to hold? Is its scope public, module-level, or private? What is its purpose in the program? As it stands, you can't answer any of these questions without searching through the rest of the code. A good naming convention conveys the answers to these questions with a simple visual inspection of the variable name. Here's a revised example (we cover the specifics in detail in the next section):

```
glListCount = wksDataSheet.Range("A1").Value
```

Now you know the scope of the variable (g stands for global or public scope), what data type it was designed to hold (l stands for the Long data type), as well as having a rough idea of the purpose of the variable (it holds the number of items in a list).

A naming convention helps you to immediately recognize the type and purpose of the building blocks used in an application. This allows you to concentrate on what the code is doing rather than having to figure out how the code is structured. Naming conventions also help make your code self-documenting, which reduces the number of comments required to make the purpose of your code clear.

We present one example of a well-structured naming convention in the following section. This is the naming convention we use throughout the book. You may or may not decide to use the naming convention we present here; this is not important. What is important is that you do pick some naming convention and use it consistently. As long as everyone involved in a project understands the naming convention, it doesn't matter exactly what prefixes it uses or what its conventions are for capitalization in variable names. When it comes to the use of a naming convention, consistency rules, both across projects and over time.

A Sample Naming Convention

A good naming convention applies not just to variables, but to all the elements of your application. The sample naming convention we present here covers all the elements in a typical Excel application. We begin with a discussion of variables, constants, and related elements, since these are the most common elements in any application. The general format of the naming convention is shown in Table 3-1. The specific elements of the naming convention and their purposes are described afterwards.

Table 3-1 A Naming Convention for Variables, Constants, UDTs, and Enumerations

Element	Naming Convention
Variables	`<scope><array><data type>DescriptiveName`
Constants	`<scope><data type>DESCRIPTIVE_NAME`

User-defined types	`Type DESCRIPTIVE_NAME`
	    `<data type>DescriptiveName`
	`End Type`

Enumeration types	`Enum <project prefix>GeneralDescr`
	    `<project prefix>GeneralDescrSpecificName1`
	    `<project prefix>GeneralDescrSpecificName2`
	`End Enum`

The Scope Specifier (<scope>)

g—Public

m—Module-level

(nothing)—Procedure-level

The Array Specifier (<array>)

a—Array

(nothing)—Not an array

The Data Type Specifier (<data type>)

There are so many data types that it's difficult to provide a comprehensive list of prefixes to represent them. The built-in data types are easy. The most frequently used built-in data types get the shortest prefixes. Problems arise when naming object variables that refer to objects from various applications. Some programmers use the prefix "obj" for all object names. This is not acceptable. However, devising consistent, unique, and reasonably short prefixes for every object type you will ever use is also too much to ask. Try to find reasonably meaningful one- to three-letter prefixes for the object variables you use most frequently and reserve the "obj" prefix for objects that appear infrequently in your code.

Make your code clear, and above all, be consistent. Keep data type prefixes to three or fewer characters. Longer prefixes, in combination with scope and array specifiers, make for unwieldy variable names. Table 3-2 shows some suggested prefixes for the most commonly used data types.

Table 3-2 Suggested Naming Convention Prefixes

Prefix	Data Type	Prefix	Data Type	Prefix	Data Type
b	Boolean	cm	ADODB.Command	cbo	MSForms.ComboBox*
byt	Byte	cn	ADODB.Connection	chk	MSForms.CheckBox
cur	Currency	rs	ADODB.Recordset	cmd	MSForms. CommandButton
dte	Date			ddn	MSForms.ComboBox**
dec	Decimal	cht	Excel.Chart	fra	MSForms.Frame
d	Double	rng	Excel.Range	lbl	MSForms.Label
i	Integer	wkb	Excel.Workbook	lst	MSForms.ListBox
l	Long	wks	Excel.Worksheet	mpg	MSForms.MultiPage
obj	Object			opt	MSForms.OptionButton
sng	Single	cbr	Office.CommandBar	spn	MSForms.SpinButton
s	String	ctl	Office. CommandBarControl	txt	MSForms.TextBox
u	User-Defined Type				

Table 3-2 Suggested Naming Convention Prefixes

Prefix	Data Type	Prefix	Data Type	Prefix	Data Type
v	Variant	cls	User-Defined Class Variable	ref	RefEdit Control
		frm	UserForm Variable	col	VBA.Collection

*Used for ComboBox controls with a DropDownCombo Style setting.

**Used for ComboBox controls with a DropDownList Style setting.

Using Descriptive Names

VBA gives you up to 255 characters for each of your variable names. Use a few of them. Don't try to save yourself a little effort by making your variable names very short. Doing so will make your code difficult to understand in the long run, both for you and for anyone else who has to work on it.

The Visual Basic IDE provides an auto-complete feature for identifiers (all the names used in your application). You typically need to type only the first few characters to get the name you want. Enter the first few characters of the name and press Ctrl+Spacebar to activate an auto-complete list of all names that begin with those characters. As you type additional characters, the list continues to narrow down. In Figure 3-1 the Ctrl+Spacebar shortcut has been used to display a list of message string constants available to add to a message box.

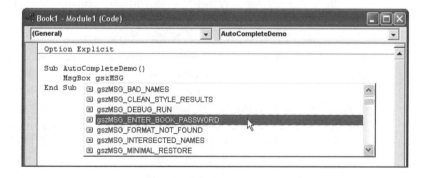

FIGURE 3-1 Using the Ctrl+Spacebar shortcut to auto-complete long names

A Few Words about Enumeration Types

Enumerations are a special type of constant available in Excel 2000 and higher. They allow you to group a list of related values together using similar, logical friendly names. VBA and the Excel object model make extensive use of enumerations. You can see these in the auto-complete list that VBA provides for the values of many properties. For example if you type

```
Sheet1.PageSetup.PaperSize =
```

into a VBA module, you'll be prompted with a long list of `XlPaperSize` enumeration members that represent the paper sizes available to print on. Figure 3-2 shows this in action.

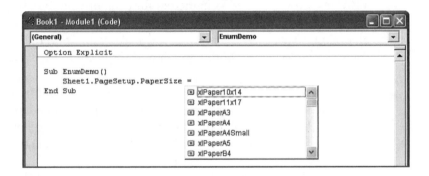

FIGURE 3-2   The Excel paper size enumeration list

These names actually represent numeric constants whose values you can examine by looking them up in the Object Browser, discussed in Chapter 16, "VBA Debugging." Notice the structure of these enumeration names. First, they all begin with a prefix identifying the application they are associated with, in this case "xl," which obviously stands for Excel. Next, the first part of their name is a descriptive term that ties them together visually as belonging to the same enumerated type, in this case "Paper." The last part of each enumeration name is a unique string describing the specific value. For example, `xlPaper11x17` represents 11x17 paper and `xlPaperA4` represents A4 paper. This system for naming enumerated constants is common and is the one we use in this book.

Naming Convention Examples

Naming convention descriptions are difficult to connect to real-world names, so we show some real-world examples of our naming convention in this section. All these examples are taken directly from commercial-quality applications written by the authors.

Variables

- **gsErrMsg**—A public variable with the data type String used to store an error message.
- **mauSettings()**—A module-level array of user-defined type that holds a list of settings.
- **cbrMenu**—A local variable with the data type CommandBar that holds a reference to a menu bar.

Constants

- **gbDEBUG_MODE**—A public constant of type Boolean that indicates whether the project is in debug mode.
- **msCAPTION_FILE_OPEN**—A module-level constant of data type String that holds the caption for a customized file open dialog (`Application.GetOpenFilename` in this instance).
- **lOFFSET_START**—A local constant of data type Long holding the point at which we begin offsetting from some Range object.

User-Defined Types

The following is a public user-defined type used to store the dimensions and location of an object. It consists of four variables of data type Double that store the top, left, width, and height of the object and a variable of data type Boolean used to indicate whether the settings have been saved.

```
Public Type DIMENSION_SETTINGS
    bSettingsSaved As Boolean
    dValTop As Double
    dValLeft As Double
    dValHeight As Double
    dValWidth As Double
End Type
```

The variables within a user-defined type definition are called member variables. These can be declared in any order. However, our naming convention suggests you sort them alphabetically by data type unless there is a strong reason to group them in some other fashion.

Enumeration Types

The following is a module-level enumeration type used to describe various types of days. The "sch" prefix in the name of the enumeration stands for the application name. This enumeration happens to come from an application called Scheduler. DayType in the enumeration name indicates the purpose of the enumeration, and each of the individual enumeration elements has a unique suffix that describes what it means.

```
Private Enum schDayType
    schDayTypeUnscheduled
    schDayTypeProduction
    schDayTypeDownTime
    schDayTypeHoliday
End Enum
```

If you don't indicate what values you want to give your enumeration member elements, VBA automatically assigns a value of zero to the first element in the list and increments that value by one for each additional element. You can easily override this behavior and assign a different starting point from which VBA will begin incrementing. For example, to make the preceding enumeration list begin with one instead of zero you would do the following:

```
Private Enum schDayType
    schDayTypeUnscheduled = 1
    schDayTypeProduction
    schDayTypeDownTime
    schDayTypeHoliday
End Enum
```

VBA continues to increment by one for each element after the last element for which you've specified a value. You can override automatic assignment of values to all your enumeration elements by simply specifying values for all of them.

Figure 3-3 shows one of the primary advantages of using enumeration types. VBA provides you with an auto-complete list of potential values for any variable declared as a specific enumeration type.

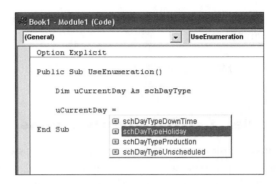

FIGURE 3-3 Even custom enumeration types get a VBA auto-complete listing.

Procedures

Subroutines and functions are grouped under the more general term procedure. Always give your procedures very descriptive names. Once again, you are allowed up to 255 characters for your procedure names. Procedure names are included in the Ctrl+Spacebar auto-complete list, so don't sacrifice a name that makes the purpose of a procedure obvious for one that's simply short.

It is not a common practice to do so, but we find that giving functions a prefix indicating the data type of their return value to be helpful in understanding code. When calling a function, always place open and closed parentheses after the function name to distinguish it from a variable or subroutine name, even if the function takes no arguments. Listing 3-1 shows a well-named Boolean function being used as the test for an If...Then statement.

Listing 3-1 An Example of Naming Conventions for Function Names

```
If bValidatePath("C:\Files") Then
    ' The If...Then block is executed
    ' if the specified path exists.
End If
```

Subroutines should be given a name that describes the task they perform. For example, a subroutine named ShutdownApplication leaves little doubt as to what it does. Functions should be given a name that describes the value they return. A function named sGetUnusedFilename() can reasonably be expected to return an available filename.

The naming convention applied to procedure arguments is exactly the same as the naming convention for procedure-level variables. For example, the bValidatePath function shown in Listing 3-1 would be declared in the following manner:

```
Function bValidatePath(ByVal sPath As String) As Boolean
```

Modules, Classes, and UserForms

In our sample naming convention, the names of standard code modules should be prefixed with an uppercase "M," class modules with an uppercase "C," and UserForms with an upper case "F." This has the advantage of neatly sorting these objects in the VBE Project Window if you don't care for the folder view, as shown in Figure 3-4.

FIGURE 3-4 Class modules, UserForms, and standard modules sorted in the Project window

This convention also makes code that uses classes and UserForm objects much clearer. In the following code sample, for example, this naming convention makes it very clear that you are declaring an object variable of a certain user-defined class type and then creating a new instance of that class:

```
Dim clsMyClass As CMyClass
Set clsMyClass = New CMyClass
```

In each case, the name on the left is a class *variable* and the object on the right is a *class*.

Worksheets and Chart Sheets

Because the CodeNames of worksheets and chart sheets in your project are treated by VBA as intrinsic object variables that reference those sheets, the CodeNames given to worksheets and chart sheets should follow variable naming conventions. Worksheet CodeNames are prefixed with "wks" to identify them in code as references to Worksheet objects. Similarly, chart sheets are prefixed with "cht" to identify them as references to Excel Chart objects.

For both types of sheets, the prefix should be followed by a descriptive term indicating the sheet's purpose in the application. In Figure 3-4 for example, wksCommandBars is a worksheet that contains a table defining the command bars created by the application. For sheets contained within an add-in or hidden in a workbook and not designed to be seen by the user, the sheet tab name should be identical to the CodeName. For sheets that are visible to the user, the sheet tab name should be a friendly name, and one that you should be prepared for the user to change. Wherever it is reasonably possible to do so, you should rely on sheet CodeNames rather than sheet tab names within your VBA code.

The Visual Basic Project

In Figure 3-4, you'll notice the Visual Basic Project has been given the same name as the workbook it's associated with. You should always give your VBProject a name that clearly identifies the application it belongs to. There's nothing worse than having a group of workbooks open in the VBE with all of them having the same default name "VBAProject." If you plan on creating references between projects you will be required to give them unique names.

Excel UI Naming Conventions

Excel user interface elements used in the creation of an application should also be named using a consistent and well-defined naming convention. We covered worksheets and chart sheets in a previous section. The three other major categories of Excel UI elements that can be named are shapes, embedded objects, and defined names.

Shapes

The term "shapes" refers to the generic collection that can contain the wide variety of objects you can place on top of a worksheet or chart sheet. Shapes can be broadly divided into three categories: controls, drawing objects and embedded objects. Shapes should be named similarly to object variables, which is to say they should be given a prefix that identifies what type of object they are followed by a descriptive name indicating what purpose they serve in the application.

Many controls that can be placed on UserForms can be placed on worksheets as well. Worksheets can also host the old Forms toolbar controls, which are similar in appearance to the ActiveX MSForms controls but with their own unique advantages and disadvantages. We'll talk more about these in Chapter 4, "Worksheet Design." Controls placed on worksheets should be named using exactly the same conventions you'd use for controls placed on UserForms.

Worksheets can also host a wide variety of drawing objects (technically known as Shapes) that are not strictly controls, although you can assign macros to all of them. These fall into the same naming convention category as the wide variety of objects that you can use in VBA. It would be very difficult to devise unique prefixes for all of them, so use well-defined prefixes for the most common drawing objects and use a generic prefix for the rest. Here are some sample prefixes for three of the most commonly used drawing objects:

pic	Picture
rec	Rectangle
txt	TextBox (not the ActiveX control)

Embedded Objects

The term "embedded object" is used here to refer to Excel objects such as PivotTables, QueryTables, and ChartObjects, as well as objects created by applications other than Excel. Worksheets can host a variety of embedded objects. Common examples of non-Excel embedded objects would include equations created with the Equation Editor and WordArt drawings. Sample prefixes for embedded objects are as follows:

cht	ChartObject
eqn	Equation
qry	QueryTable
pvt	PivotTable
art	WordArt

Defined Names

Our naming convention for defined names is a bit different than for other program elements. In the case of defined names, the prefix should indicate the broad purpose of the defined name, as opposed to the data type it's expected to hold. This is because non-trivial Excel applications typically have many defined names that are much easier to work with if they are grouped together by purpose within the Define Name dialog. When a worksheet contains dozens or hundreds of defined names, there are significant efficiencies to be gained by having names with related functions grouped together in the defined name list by prefix.

The descriptive name portion of a defined name is used to specify exactly what purpose the name serves within its broader category. The following list shows some examples of purpose-prefixes for defined names.

cht	Chart Data Range
con	Named Constant
err	Error Check
for	Named Formula
inp	Input Range
out	Output Range
ptr	Specific Cell Location
rgn	Region
set	UI Setting
tbl	Table

Exceptions—When Not to Apply the Naming Convention

Two specific situations are commonly encountered in which you want to break the general rule and not apply your naming convention. The first is when you are dealing with elements related to Windows API calls. These elements have been named by Microsoft and the names are well known within the programming community. The Windows API constants, user-defined types, procedure declarations, and procedure arguments should appear in your code exactly as they appear in the Windows API

Reference, which can be viewed on the MSDN Web site at http://msdn2.microsoft.com/en-us/library/aa383749(VS.85).aspx. Note that this reference is provided in C/C++ format only.

The second situation where you want to avoid applying your own naming conventions is when you use plug-in code from an outside source to perform a specific task. If you modify the names used in this code and refer to those modified names from code elsewhere in your application, you make it very difficult to upgrade the plug-in code when a newer version becomes available.

Best Practices for Application Structure and Organization

Keeping your applications well structured and well organized makes them much easier to maintain and upgrade. In this section, we examine a number of best practices for improving the structure and organization of your application.

Application Structure

The first decision you must make when designing your application structure is how many separate workbooks should it be divided into. The number of workbooks used in an Excel application is driven primarily by two factors: the complexity of the application itself and the limitations imposed by application distribution issues.

Simple applications and those for which you cannot impose a formal installation sequence demand the fewest number of workbooks. Complex applications and those over which you have complete control of the installation process allow division into multiple workbooks or other file types such as DLLs. Chapter 2, "Application Architectures," discusses the various types of Excel applications and the structure suited to each.

When you have the liberty to divide your application across multiple files, there are a number of good reasons to do so. These include separation of the logical tiers in your application, separation of code from data, separation of user-interface elements from code elements, encapsulating functional elements of the application, and managing change conflicts in a team development environment.

Separation of Logical Tiers

Almost every non-trivial Excel application has three distinct logical tiers or sections (see Figure 3-5):

- **User-interface tier**—Consists of all the code and visible elements required for your application to interact with the user. In an Excel application, the user-interface tier consists of visible elements such as worksheets, charts, command bars, UserForms, and the code required to directly manage those visible elements. The user-interface tier is the only logical tier that contains elements visible to the user.
- **Business logic or application tier**—Completely code-based, this tier performs the core operations the application was designed to accomplish. The business logic tier accepts input from the user-interface tier and returns output to the user-interface tier. For long-running operations, the business logic tier may transmit periodic updates to the user-interface tier in the form of status bar messages or progress bar updates.
- **Data access and storage tier**—Responsible for the storage and retrieval of data required by the application. This can be as simple as reading from and writing data to cells on a local, hidden worksheet or as complex as executing stored procedures in a SQL Server database across a network. The data access and storage tier communicates directly only with the business logic tier.

The Excel Application

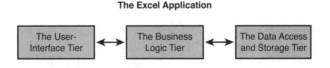

FIGURE 3-5 The relationships among the three tiers of an Excel application

As Figure 3-5 shows, all three tiers are necessary for a complete application, but they must not be inextricably linked. The three tiers of your application should be loosely coupled, such that a significant change in one tier does not require significant changes to the other two. Strongly coupled application tiers inevitably lead to maintenance and upgrade difficulties.

For example, if your data access and storage tier needs to move from using an Access database for storage to using a SQL Server database for storage you want the changes required to be isolated within the data access and storage tier. In a well-designed application, neither of the other two tiers would be affected in any way by such a change. Ideally, data should be transferred between the business logic tier and the data access and storage tier in the form of user-defined types. These provide the best trade-off between efficiency and loose coupling. Alternatively, ADO Recordset objects can be used, but these introduce subtle linkage issues that it would be better if the business logic layer didn't rely on, such as the order of fields returned from the database.

Similarly, if you need to provide an alternate Web-based presentation interface for your application, loose coupling between the user-interface tier and the business logic tier will make it much easier to accomplish. This is because no implicit assumptions will be built into the business logic tier regarding how the user interface is constructed. Elements that accept data input from the user should be completely self-contained. The business logic tier should pass the user-interface tier the data it requires for initialization as simple data types. The user-interface tier should collect the user input and pass it back to the business logic tier as simple data types, or as a UDT for more complex interfaces. Because the business logic tier should have no intrinsic knowledge of how the user-interface is constructed, referencing controls on a UserForm directly from a business logic tier procedure is expressly forbidden.

Separation of Data/UI from Code

Within the user-interface tier of many Excel applications lie two unique subtiers. These consist of the workbook and sheet elements used to construct the user interface and the code supporting those elements. The concept of separation should be applied rigorously to these subtiers. A workbook-based interface should contain no code, and the UI code that controls a workbook-based interface should reside in an add-in completely separated from the workbook it controls.

The reasoning for this separation is the same as the reasoning described previously for separating the main application tiers: isolating the effects of change. Of all the application tiers, the user-interface tier tends to undergo the most frequent changes. Therefore it's not sufficient to simply isolate user interface changes to the user-interface tier, you should also isolate changes to the visible elements of the user interface from the code that controls the user interface.

We provide real-world examples of application tier separation in the chapters that follow, so don't be concerned if what we've discussed here is not totally obvious to you at this point.

Application Organization for Procedural Programming

Procedural programming is the programming methodology most developers are familiar with. It involves dividing an application into multiple procedures, each of which is designed to perform a specific task within the application. An entire application can be written in procedural fashion, procedural elements can be combined with object oriented elements, or an entire application can be written in object oriented fashion. This section focuses on best practices for procedural programming. We discuss object oriented programming techniques in Chapter 7, "Using Class Modules to Create Objects."

Organizing Code into Modules by Function/Category

The primary purpose of separating code into modules is to improve the comprehensibility and maintainability of the application. In a procedural application, procedures should be organized into separate code modules in a logical fashion. The best way to do this is to group procedures that perform similar functions into the same code module.

TIP VBA has an undocumented "soft limit" on the maximum size of any single standard code module. A single standard code module should not exceed 64KB as measured by its text file size when exported from the project. (The VBETools utility included on the CD reports module sizes for you automatically.) Your project will not crash immediately upon a single module exceeding this 64KB limit, but consistently exceeding this limit will almost invariably lead to an unstable application.

Functional Decomposition

Functional decomposition refers to the process of breaking your application into separate procedures such that each procedure is responsible for a single task. In theory, you could write many applications as one large, monolithic procedure. However, doing so would make your application extremely difficult to debug and maintain. By using functional decomposition you design your application such that it consists of multiple procedures that are each responsible for a well-defined task that is easy to understand, validate, document, and maintain.

Best Practices for Creating Procedures

A comprehensive set of guidelines for creating good procedures could easily fill a chapter of its own. We cover the most important guidelines in the following list:

- **Encapsulation**—Whenever possible, a procedure should be designed to completely encapsulate the logical operation it performs. Ideally, your procedures should have no linkages to anything outside them. This means, for example, that a properly encapsulated procedure can be copied into a completely different project and work just as well there as it did in the project where it originated. Encapsulation promotes code reuse and simplifies debugging by isolating different logical operations from each other.
- **Elimination of duplicate code**—When writing a non-trivial Excel application, you will frequently discover you are writing code to perform the same operation in multiple places. When this occurs, you should extract this duplicated code and place it in a separate procedure. Doing so reduces the number of places where that operation needs to be validated or modified from many to one. The common procedure can also be optimized in one place and the benefits will be felt throughout your application. All this leads to a significant improvement in code quality. It also serves a second important purpose: making your code more reusable. As you factor common operations into dedicated procedures, you will discover that you can often reuse these procedures in other applications. This type of code forms the basis of a code library that you can use to increase your productivity when writing new applications. The more logical operations you have available as complete, fully tested library procedures, the less time it will take you to develop a new application.
- **Isolation of complex operations**—In many real-world applications you will find that some sections of the business logic are both complex and specific to the application for which they were designed (that is, not reusable). These sections of business logic should be isolated into separate procedures for ease of debugging and maintenance.
- **Procedure size reduction**—Procedures that are overly long are difficult to understand, debug, and maintain, even for the programmer who wrote them. If you discover a procedure containing more than 150 to 200 lines of code, it is probably trying to accomplish multiple goals and therefore should be factored into multiple single-purpose procedures.

- **Limiting the number of procedure arguments**—The more arguments a procedure accepts, the more difficult it will be to understand and the less efficient it will be to execute. In general, you should limit the number of procedure arguments to five or fewer. And don't simply replace procedure arguments with public or module-level variables. If you find yourself requiring more than five procedure arguments it's probably a good sign that your procedure, or your application logic, needs to be redesigned.

General Application Development Best Practices

Each chapter in this book explains the best development practices related specifically to the subject of that chapter. This section covers best development practices common to all application development areas.

Code Commenting

Good code commenting is one of the most important practices in Excel application development. Your code comments should provide a clear and complete description of how your code is organized, how each object and procedure should be used, and what you are trying to accomplish with your code. Comments also provide a means of tracking changes to your code over time, a subject we cover later in this chapter.

Code comments are important to both you and other developers who may need to work on your code. The value of code comments to other developers should be self-evident. What you may not realize until the cruel fist of experience has pounded it into you is that your comments are very important to you as well. It is very common for a developer to write an initial version of an application and then be asked to revise it substantially after a long period of time has passed. You would be surprised at how foreign even your own code looks to you once it has been out of sight and out of mind for a long period of time. Code comments help solve this problem.

Comments should be applied at all three major levels of your application's code: the module level, the procedure level, and individual sections or lines of code. We discuss the types of commenting appropriate to each of these levels in the following sections.

Module-Level Comments

If you used the module naming conventions described previously in this chapter, anyone examining your code will have a rough idea of the purpose of the code contained within each module. You should supplement this with a brief comment at the top of each module that provides a more detailed description of the purpose of the module.

NOTE For the purposes of code commenting, when we use the term "module," we mean it to include standard modules, class modules, and code modules behind UserForms and document objects like worksheets and the workbook.

A good module-level comment should be located at the top of the module and look something like the example shown in Listing 3-2.

Listing 3-2 A Sample Module-Level Comment

```
'
' Description:    A brief description of the purpose of the code in
'                 this module.
'
Option Explicit
```

Procedure-Level Comments

Procedure-level comments are typically the most detailed comments in your application. In a procedure-level comment block you describe the purpose of the procedure, usage notes, a detailed list of arguments and their purposes, and a description of expected return values in the case of functions.

Procedure-level comments can also serve a rudimentary change-tracking purpose by providing a place to add dates and descriptions of changes made to the procedure. A good procedure-level comment like the one shown in Listing 3-3 would be placed directly above the first line of the procedure. The procedure-level comment in Listing 3-3 is designed for a function. The only difference between a comment block for a function and a comment block for a subroutine is the subroutine comment block does not contain a Returns section, obviously because subroutines do not return a value.

Listing 3-3   A Sample Procedure-Level Comment

```
' ' ' ' ' ' ' ' ' ' ' ' ' ' ' ' ' ' ' ' ' ' ' ' ' ' ' ' ' ' ' ' ' ' ' ' ' ' ' ' ' ' ' ' ' ' ' ' ' ' ' ' ' ' ' '
' Comments:       Locates the chart to be operated on or asks the
'                 user to select a chart if multiple charts are
'                 located.
'
' Arguments:      chtChart      Returned by this function. An object
'                               reference to the chart to be
'                               operated on, or Nothing on user
'                               cancel.
'
' Returns:        Boolean       True on success, False on error or
'                               user cancel.
'
' Date            Developer     Action
' - - - - - - - - - - - - - - - - - - - - - - - - - - - - - - - - - -
' 07/04/02        Rob Bovey     Created
' 10/14/03        Rob Bovey     Error trap for charts with no series
' 11/18/03        Rob Bovey     Error trap for no active workbook
'
```

Internal Comments

Internal comments appear within the body of the code itself. These comments should be used to describe the purpose of any code where the purpose is not self-evident. Internal comments should describe the ***intent*** of the code rather than the operation of the code. The distinction between intent and operation is not always clear, so Listing 3-4 and Listing 3-5 show two examples of the same code, one with a bad comment and the other with a good comment.

Listing 3-4   Example of a Bad Internal Code Comment

```
' Loop the asInputFiles array.
For lIndex = LBound(asInputFiles) To UBound(asInputFiles)
    '...
Next lIndex
```

The comment in Listing 3-4 is monumentally unhelpful. First of all, it describes only the line of code directly below it, giving you no clue about the purpose of the loop structure as a whole. Second, the comment is simply an exact written description of that line of code. This information is easy enough to determine by simply looking at the line of code. If you removed the comment, you would not lose any information at all.

Listing 3-5 Example of a Good Internal Code Comment

```
' Import the specified list of input files into the working area
' of our data sheet.
For lIndex = LBound(asInputFiles) To UBound(asInputFiles)
    '...
Next lIndex
```

In Listing 3-5, we have a comment that adds value to the code. Not only does it describe the intent, rather than the operation of the code, it also explains the entire loop structure. After reading this comment you know what you're looking at as you delve into the code within the loop.

As with most rules, there are exceptions to the internal comment guidelines specified previously. The most important exception concerns comments used to clarify control structures. If...Then statements and Do...While loops can make code difficult to understand as they become wider, because you can no longer see the entire control structure in a single code window. At that point, it becomes difficult to remember what the applicable control expression was. For example, when evaluating a lengthy procedure we have often found ourselves looking at something like the code snippet shown in Listing 3-6.

Listing 3-6 Inscrutable Control Structures

```
    End If

    lNumInputFiles = lNumInputFiles - 1

  Loop

End If
```

In Listing 3-6, what are the logical tests being made by the two If...Then statements and what expression controls the Do...While loop? Once these structures have been filled with a substantial amount of code, you simply can't tell without scrolling back and forth within the procedure, because the entire block is no longer visible within a single code window. This problem can be alleviated easily by using the end of control block commenting style shown in Listing 3-7.

Listing 3-7 Understandable Control Structures

```
        End If   ' If bContentsValid Then

        lNumInputFiles = lNumInputFiles - 1

    Loop          ' Do While lNumInputFiles > 0

End If            ' If bInputFilesFound Then
```

The comments in Listing 3-7, although they simply restate the code at the top of each control structure, make it completely obvious what you are looking at. These types of comments should be used anywhere you have a control structure within your code that is too large to fit completely into one code window.

Avoiding the Worst Code Commenting Mistake

It may seem obvious, but the most frequent and damaging mistake related to code commenting is not keeping the comments updated as you modify the code. We have frequently seen projects that appeared at first glance to implement good code commenting practices, but upon closer examination discovered the comments were created for some ancient version of the project and now bore almost no relationship to the current code.

When attempting to understand a project, bad comments are worse than no comments at all because bad comments are actively misleading. Always keep your comments current. Old comments can either be deleted or retained as a series of change tracking records. We recommend removing obsolete in-line comments, or they will quickly clutter your code, making it difficult to understand simply due to the number of lines of inapplicable comments that accumulate. Use procedure-level comments as a change tracking mechanism where necessary.

Code Readability

Code readability is a function of how your code is physically arranged. Good visual layout of code allows you to infer a significant amount of information about the logical structure of the program. This is a key point. Code layout makes not one bit of difference to the computer. Its sole purpose is to assist humans in understanding the code. Like naming conventions, the consistent use of good code layout conventions makes your code self-documenting. The primary tool of code layout is white space. White space includes space characters, tabs, and blank lines. In the following paragraphs we discuss the most important methods of using white space to create a well-designed code layout.

Group related code elements together and separate unrelated code elements with blank lines. Sections of code separated by blank lines within a procedure can be thought of as serving a similar function to paragraphs within the chapters of a book. They help you determine what things belong together. Listing 3-8 shows an example of how blank lines can improve code readability. Even without the code comments, it would be obvious which lines of code were related.

Listing 3-8   Using Blank Lines to Group Related Sections of Code

```
' Reset Application properties.
Application.ScreenUpdating = True
Application.DisplayAlerts = True
Application.EnableEvents = True
Application.StatusBar = False
Application.Caption = Empty
Application.EnableCancelKey = xlInterrupt
Application.Cursor = xlDefault

' Delete all custom CommandBars
For Each cbrBar In Application.CommandBars
    If Not cbrBar.BuiltIn Then
        cbrBar.Delete
    Else
        cbrBar.Enabled = True
    End If
Next cbrBar

' Reset the Worksheet Menu bar.
With Application.CommandBars(1)
    .Reset
```

```
    .Enabled = True
    .Visible = True
End With
```

Within a related section of code, horizontal alignment is used to indicate which lines of code belong together. Indentation is used to show the logical structure of the code. In Listing 3-9 we show a single section from Listing 3-8 where alignment and indentation have been used to good effect. You can look at this section of code and understand immediately which elements go together as well as deduce the logical flow of the code's execution.

Listing 3-9 Proper Use of Alignment and Indentation

```
' Delete all custom CommandBars
For Each cbrBar In Application.CommandBars
    If Not cbrBar.BuiltIn Then
        cbrBar.Delete
    Else
        cbrBar.Enabled = True
    End If
Next cbrBar
```

Line continuation can be used to make complex expressions and long declarations more readable. Keep in mind that breaking code into continued lines solely for the purpose of making the entire line visible without scrolling is not necessarily a good practice and can often make code more confusing. Listing 3-10 shows examples of judicious use of line continuation.

Listing 3-10 Judicious Use of Line Continuation

```
' Complex expressions are easier to understand
' when properly continued
If (uData.lMaxLocationLevel > 1) Or _
    uData.bHasClientSubsets Or _
    (uData.uDemandType = bcDemandTypeCalculate) Then

End If


' Line continuations make long API declarations easier to read.
Declare Function SHGetSpecialFolderPath Lib "Shell32.dll" _
    (ByVal hwndOwner As Long, _
    ByRef szBuffer As String, _
```

```
ByVal lFolder As Long, _
ByVal bCreate As Long) As Long
```

General VBA Programming Best Practices

In this section, we examine a number of VBA programming best practices that help you write code that is more robust and easier to maintain and update.

Use of Module Directives

Module directives are statements at the top of a code module that instruct VBA how to treat the code within that code module. Although these directives are not required, you should always use at least one or two of them, as explained in the following list:

- **Option Explicit**—Always use the Option Explicit statement in every module. The importance of this practice cannot be overstated. Without Option Explicit, any typographical error you make results in VBA automatically creating a new Variant variable. This type of error is insidious because it may not cause an immediate run-time error, but it will almost certainly cause your application to eventually return incorrect results. Errors caused by the lack of an Option Explicit statement often pass without notice until your application is distributed, and they are difficult to debug under any circumstances.

  The Option Explicit statement forces you to explicitly declare all the variables you use. Option Explicit causes VBA to throw a compile-time error (initiated by selecting *Debug > Compile* from the VBE menu) whenever an unrecognized identifier name is encountered. This makes it easy to discover and correct typographical errors. You can ensure that Option Explicit is automatically placed at the top of every module you create by choosing *Tools > Options > Editor* from the VBE menu and checking the *Require Variable Declaration* check box. This setting is strongly recommended.

- **Option Private Module**—The Option Private Module statement makes all procedures within the module where it is used unavailable from the Excel user interface or from other Excel projects. Use this statement to hide procedures that should not be called from outside your application.

TIP The `Application.Run` method can circumvent the `Option Private Module` statement and run private procedures in modules where this statement has been used. Also, if a user knows the exact name of your procedure and your procedure does not require any arguments, the user can type the name of your procedure into the Macro dialog and run it manually. These scenarios can be made much less likely by protecting your project so that your private procedure names are not visible in the Object Browser.

- **Option Base 1**—The `Option Base 1` statement causes all array variables whose lower bound has not been specified to have a lower bound of 1. Do not use the `Option Base 1` statement. Instead, always specify both the upper and lower bounds of every array variable you use. A procedure created in a module that uses `Option Base 1` may malfunction if copied to a module in which this statement isn't used. This behavior inhibits one of the most important procedure design goals, that of reusability.
- **Option Compare Text**—The `Option Compare Text` statement forces all string comparisons within the module where it is used to be text-based rather than binary. In a text-based string comparison, upper- and lowercase versions of the same character are treated as identical, whereas in a binary comparison they are different. The `Option Compare Text` statement should be avoided for the same reason `Option Base 1` should be avoided. It makes procedures behave differently when placed in modules with the statement versus modules without it. Text-based comparisons are also much more computationally expensive than binary comparisons, so `Option Compare Text` slows down all string comparison operations in the module where it's located. Most Excel and VBA string comparison functions provide an argument you can use to specify binary or text-based comparison. It's much better to use these arguments to provide text-based comparisons only where you need them.

  There are some rare cases where `Option Compare Text` is required. The most frequent case occurs when you need to do case-insensitive string comparisons with the VBA `Like` operator. The only way to get the `Like` operator to perform in a case-insensitive manner is to use the `Option Compare Text` statement. In this case, you should isolate the procedures that require this statement in a separate code module so that other procedures that don't require this option aren't adversely affected. Be sure to document why you have done this in a module-level comment.

3. EXCEL AND VBA DEVELOPMENT BEST PRACTICES

Best Practices for Variables and Constants

Variables and constants are the most fundamental building blocks of an application. We can become so used to them that we forget they are active pieces of our application that must be used properly or the quality of our application will suffer. In this section, we cover a number of best practices to follow when using variables and constants.

Avoid Reusing Variables Each variable declared in your program should serve one purpose only. Using the same variable for multiple purposes saves you only one variable declaration line but introduces massive potential for confusion within your program. If you are trying to determine how a procedure works and you have figured out what a certain variable does in a certain place, you will naturally assume the variable serves the same purpose the next time you see it. If this is not the case, the code logic will become difficult to understand.

Avoid the Variant Data Type Avoid the use of the Variant data type whenever possible. Unfortunately, VBA is not a strongly typed programming language. Therefore, you can simply declare variables without specifying their data type and VBA will create these variables as Variants. The main reasons not to use Variants are

- **Variants are inefficient**—This is because internally, a Variant is a complex structure designed to hold any data type in the VBA programming language. Variant values cannot be accessed and modified directly as can fundamental data types such as Long and Double. Instead, VBA must use a series of complex Windows API calls behind the scenes whenever it needs to perform any operation on a Variant.
- **Data stored in a variant can behave unexpectedly**—Because Variants are designed to hold any type of data, the data type that goes into a Variant is not necessarily the data type that will come out of it. When accessing the data in a Variant, VBA attempts to coerce the data into whatever data type it thinks makes the most sense in the context of the operation. If you must use Variants, convert them explicitly to the data type you want when using their values using one of the VBA functions provided for this purpose (CStr, CLng, CDate, and so on).

Variants do have one valuable characteristic that you can take advantage of, which is if you assign a multicell range to them using the

Range.Value property they automatically become a two-dimensional array containing all the values in that range. When you need to manipulate large numbers of values contained in a range of cells, it is faster to dump them into a Variant array, loop the Variant array, and perform your operations on it, and then dump the Variant array back into the range of cells. Listing 3-11 shows an example of how to do this.

Listing 3-11   Using a Variant Array to Manipulate Range Values

```
Sub UseVariantArray()

    Dim lRow As Long
    Dim lCol As Long
    Dim vaArray As Variant

    vaArray = Sheet1.Range("A1:E5").Value

    For lRow = LBound(vaArray, 1) To UBound(vaArray, 1)
        For lCol = LBound(vaArray, 2) To UBound(vaArray, 2)
            vaArray(lRow, lCol) = vaArray(lRow, lCol) * 2
        Next lCol
    Next lRow

    Sheet1.Range("A1:E5").Value = vaArray

End Sub
```

Beware of Evil Type Coercion   Evil Type Coercion (ETC) is another symptom that results from VBA not being a strongly typed programming language. ETC occurs when VBA automatically converts one data type to another data type in a way you did not intend. The most frequent examples are Strings that hold numbers being converted to Integers and Booleans being converted to their String equivalents. Don't mix variables of different data types in your VBA expressions without using the explicit casting functions (`CStr`, `CLng`, `CDate`, and so on) to tell VBA exactly how you want those variables to be treated.

Avoid the As New Declaration Syntax   Never declare object variables using the As New syntax. For example, the following form of an object variable declaration should never be used:

```
Dim rsData As New ADODB.Recordset
```

If VBA encounters a line of code that uses this variable and the variable has not been initialized, VBA automatically creates a new instance of the variable. This is **never** the behavior you want. Good programming practice implies that the programmer should maintain complete control over the creation of all the objects used in the program. If VBA encounters an uninitialized object variable in your code, it is almost certainly the result of a bug, and you want to be notified about it immediately. Therefore, the proper way to declare and initialize the object variable shown previously is the following:

```
Dim rsData As ADODB.Recordset
Set rsData = New ADODB.Recordset
```

Using this style of declaration and initialization, if the object variable is destroyed somewhere in your procedure and you inadvertently reference it again after that point, VBA immediately throws the runtime error "Object variable or With block variable not set," notifying you of the problem.

Always Fully Qualify Object Names   Always fully qualify object names used in variable declarations and code with their class name prefix. This is because many object libraries share the same object names. If you simply declare a variable with an object name alone and there are multiple object libraries with that object name being referenced by your application, VBA creates a variable from the first library in the *Tools > References* list where it finds the object name you used. This is often not what you want.

UserForm controls present the most common situation where problems result from object variable declarations that aren't fully qualified. For example, if you wanted to declare an object variable to reference a TextBox control on your UserForm, you might be inclined to do the following:

```
Dim txtBox As TextBox
Set txtBox = Me.TextBox1
```

Unfortunately, as soon as VBA attempted to execute the second line of code, a "Type mismatch" error would be generated. This is because the Excel object library contains a TextBox object that is different from the object you are trying to reference and the Excel object library comes before the MSForms object library in the *Tools > References* list. The correct way to write this code is as follows:

```
Dim txtBox As MSForms.TextBox
Set txtBox = Me.TextBox1
```

Never Hard-Code Array Bounds   When you are looping the contents of an array variable, never hard-code the array bounds in the loop. Use the LBound and UBound functions instead, as shown in the Listing 3-12.

Listing 3-12   The Correct Way to Loop an Array

```
Dim lIndex As Long
Dim alListItems(1 To 10) As Long

' Load the array here.

For lIndex = LBound(alListItems) To UBound(alListItems)
    ' Do something with each value.
Next lIndex
```

The reason for this is because array bounds frequently change over the course of creating and maintaining an application. If you hard-code the array bounds 1 and 10 in the loop shown in Listing 3-12, you will have to remember to update the loop any time the bounds of the alListItems array change. Failure to do so is a frequent source of errors. By using LBound and UBound you make the loop self-adjusting.

Always Specify the Loop Counter after a Next Statement   Listing 3-12 demonstrates another good coding practice. You should always specify the loop counter variable after a Next statement. Even though this is not strictly required by VBA, doing so makes your code much easier to understand, especially if the distance between the For and Next statements is long.

Make Use of Constants   Constants are useful programming elements. They serve the following purposes in your code, among others:

- Constants eliminate "magic numbers," replacing them with recognizable names. For example, in the following line of code, what does the number 50 mean?

  ```
  If lIndex < 50 Then
  ```

  There is no way of knowing unless you wrote the code and you still remember what 50 represents. If instead you saw the following, you would have a very good idea of what the `If...Then` test was look-ing for:

```
Const lMAX_NUM_INPUT_FILES As Long = 50
```

```
' More code here.
```

```
If lIndex < lMAX_NUM_INPUT_FILES Then
```

If you need to know the value of a constant at design time, you can simply right-click over the constant name in the VBE and choose *Definition* from the shortcut menu. You will be brought directly to the line where the constant is defined. In break mode at runtime it's even easier. Simply hover your mouse over the constant and a ToolTip window containing its value appears.

■ Constants improve coding efficiency and avoid errors by eliminat-ing duplicate data. In the preceding example, assume you refer-ence the maximum number of input files in several places through-out your program. At some point you may need to upgrade your program to handle more files. If you hard-coded the maximum number of input files everywhere you've needed to use it, you will have to locate all these places and change the number in each one. If you used a constant, all you need to do is modify the value of the single constant declaration and the new value automatically is used wherever the constant has been used in your code. This situation is a frequent source of errors that can be eliminated by simply using constants instead of hard-coded numbers.

Public variables are dangerous. They can be modified anywhere in your application without warning, making their values unpredictable. They also work against one of the most important programming principles—encapsulation. Always create variables with the minimum scope possible. Begin by creating all your variables with local (procedure level) scope and only widen the scope of a variable when it is absolutely necessary.

As with most rules, there are a few cases where the variable scope rule should be broken because the use of public variables is useful and/or necessary:

■ When data must be passed deep into the call stack before it is used. For example, if procedure A reads some data and then passes that data to procedure B, which passes it to procedure C, which passes it to procedure D where the data is finally used, a good case can be made that the data should be passed directly from procedure A to procedure D by way of a public variable.

- Certain inherently public classes, such as an application-level event handling class, require a public object variable so they never go out of scope while your application is running.

Early Binding Versus Late Binding   The distinction between early binding and late binding is widely misunderstood and often confused with how an object is created. The **only** thing that affects whether an object is early bound or late bound is how the object variable holding the reference to the object was declared. Variables declared as a specific object data type are always early bound. Variables declared with the Object or Variant data type are always late bound. Listing 3-13 shows an example of a late bound reference, while Listing 3-14 shows an example of an early bound reference.

Listing 3-13   A Late Bound Reference to an ADO Connection Object

```
Dim objConnection As Object

' It doesn't matter how you create the object, it's still
' late bound due to the As Object variable declaration.
Set objConnection = New ADODB.Connection
Set objConnection = CreateObject("ADODB.Connection")
```

Listing 3-14   An Early Bound Reference to an ADO Connection Object

```
Dim cnConnection As ADODB.Connection

' It doesn't matter how you create the object, it's still early
' bound due to the data type used in the variable declaration.
Set cnConnection = New ADODB.Connection
Set cnConnection = CreateObject("ADODB.Connection")
```

Note that to use early binding with objects outside the Excel object model you must set a reference to the appropriate object library using the *Tools > References* menu in the Visual Basic Editor. For example, to create early bound variables referencing ADO objects, you must set a reference to the Microsoft ActiveX Data Objects 2.X Library, where X is the version of ADO you intend to use. You should use early bound object variables wherever possible. Early bound object variables provide the following advantages over late bound variables:

- **Improved performance**—When you use an object variable whose data type is known to VBA at compile time, VBA can look up the memory locations of all property and method calls you use with this object and store them with your code. At runtime, when VBA encounters one of these early bound property or method calls, it simply executes the code located at the stored location. (This is a bit of an oversimplification. What VBA actually stores is a numeric offset to the code to be executed from a known starting point in memory, which is the beginning of a structure called the object's Vtable.)

  When you use a late bound object variable, VBA has no way of knowing in advance what type of object the variable will contain. Therefore, it cannot optimize any property or method calls at compile time. This means that each time VBA encounters a late bound property or method call at runtime, it must query the variable to determine what kind of object it holds, look up the name of the property or method being executed to determine where in memory it is located, and then execute the code located at that memory address. This process is significantly slower than an early bound call.

- **Strict type checking**—In the late bound example shown previously in Listing 3-13, if you accidentally set your object variable to reference an ADO Command object instead of a Connection object, VBA would not complain. You would only discover you had a problem later in your code when you tried to use a method or property not supported by the Command object. With early binding, VBA immediately detects that you are trying to assign the wrong type of object reference to your object variable and notifies you with a "Type mismatch" error. Incorrect property and method calls can be detected even earlier, before the code is ever run. VBA attempts to look up the name of the property or method being called from within the appropriate object library at compile time and throws a compile-time error if the name cannot be located.

- **IntelliSense availability**—Early bound object variables make for much easier programming as well. Since VBA knows exactly what type of object a variable represents, it can parse the appropriate object library and provide a drop-down list of all available properties and methods for the object as soon as you type a dot operator after the variable's name.

As you might expect, there are some cases where you need to use late binding rather than early binding. The two most common reasons for using late binding instead of early binding are

- When a newer version of an application's object library has broken compatibility with an earlier version.
  This is an all too common situation. If you set a reference to the later version of the application's object library in your application and then attempt to run it on a computer that has the earlier version, you will get an immediate compile-time error "Can't find project or library," and the reference on the target machine will be prefixed with "MISSING." The worst problem with this error is that the line of code flagged as being the source of the error often has nothing to do with the object library actually causing the problem.
  If you need to use objects from an application that exhibits this problem and you can't develop against the earliest possible version of the application that you might encounter, you need to use late binding for all variables referencing objects from the application. If you are creating new objects, you also need to use the CreateObject function with the version independent ProgID of the object you want to create, rather than the = New ObjectName syntax.
- When you want to use an application that you cannot be sure will exist on the user's computer and that you cannot install yourself.
  In this case, you need to use late binding to avoid the compile-time error that would immediately result from attempting to run an application that referenced an object library that did not exist on the user's computer. Your application can then check for the existence of the object library in question and exit gracefully if that library is not installed on the user's computer.

TIP   Even if you will eventually use late binding in your code, early binding offers such a great increase in productivity while coding that you should write and test the application using early binding. Convert your code to late binding only for the final round of testing and distribution.

Defensive Coding

Defensive coding refers to various programming practices designed to help you prevent errors rather than having to correct them after they occur.

Write Your Application in the Earliest Version of Excel That You Expect It to Run In Although the Microsoft Excel team has done a better job than most of maintaining backward compatibility with earlier versions of Excel, there are many subtle differences between the versions. If you do not write your application in the earliest version of Excel that you expect it to run in you can easily write an application that will not run on earlier versions of Excel because some feature you used did not exist in those versions.

The solution to this problem is to always develop your applications in the earliest version of Excel that you expect them to run in. This may force you to do one of the following in order of worst to best practice:

- Maintain multiple versions of Excel on one computer (not recommended).
- Maintain separate computers for each version of Excel.
- Use virtualization software such as VMWare or Virtual PC to maintain as many separate development environments as you need on a single computer.

Developing in the earliest version of Excel you expect to run in is essential. If you develop an application in Excel 2003 and then discover it doesn't run properly in Excel 2000, you will have much debugging and rewriting ahead. You will save considerable time and stress by simply developing the application using Excel 2000 to begin with.

Explicitly Use ByRef or ByVal If a procedure takes arguments, there are two ways to declare those arguments: ByRef or ByVal.

- **ByRef**—This convention means you are passing the memory address of the variable rather than the value of the variable. If the called procedure modifies a ByRef argument, the modification will be visible in the calling procedure.
- **ByVal**—This convention means you are passing a value to the procedure. A procedure can make changes to a ByVal argument but these changes will not be visible to the calling procedure. In fact, a procedure can use ByVal arguments exactly as if they were locally declared variables.

Always explicitly declare your procedure arguments as ByRef or ByVal. If you do not specify this, all arguments are created ByRef by default. You should declare procedure arguments ByVal unless you have a specific need for the calling procedure to see changes made to the arguments. Declaring arguments ByVal prevents changes made to those arguments from being propagated back to the calling procedure.

The only exceptions are when you are passing large strings (very large strings), which are far more efficiently passed ByRef, or when your procedure argument is of a data type, such as an array, that cannot be passed ByVal. Be aware that declaring procedure arguments ByVal does leave you more exposed to Evil Type Coercion. A ByRef procedure argument **_must_** be passed exactly the same data type as it is declared to accept; otherwise a compile-time error will result. By contrast, VBA attempts to coerce a value passed to a ByVal procedure argument into a compatible data type.

Explicitly Call the Default Property of an Object   With the possible exception of the Item property of a Collection object, it's never a good idea to implicitly invoke the default property of an object by simply using the object's name in an expression. Listing 3-15 shows the right way and the wrong way of accessing the default property of an object using an `MSForms.TextBox` control for demonstration purposes (the Text property is the default property of an `MSForms.TextBox` control).

Listing 3-15   Default Properties

```
' The right way.
txtUsername.Text = "My Name"

' The wrong way
txtUsername = "My Name"
```

By avoiding the implicit use of default properties, you make your code much more readable and protect yourself from errors if the default behavior of the object changes in some future version of Excel or VBA.

Validate Arguments before Using Them in Procedures   If your procedure accepts input arguments that must have certain properties to be valid—for example, if they must be within a specific range of values—verify that the values passed to those arguments are valid before attempting to use them in your procedure. The idea is to catch erroneous input as soon as possible so you can generate a meaningful error message and simplify your debugging.

Wherever possible, create a test harness to validate the behavior of your procedure. A test harness is a wrapper procedure that can call the procedure being tested multiple times, passing it a wide range of arguments, and test the result to be sure it is correct. We discuss test harnesses in detail in Chapter 16.

Use Guard Counters to Protect Against Infinite Loops   Program your loops to automatically handle infinite loop conditions. One of the most common mistakes made when using Do...While or While...Wend loops is to create a situation where the loop control condition is never satisfied. This causes the loop to run forever (or until you can force your code to break by pressing Ctrl+Break if you are lucky, or the Windows Task Manager to shut down your application if you are not). Always add a counter that automatically bails out when the number of loops executed is known to be more than the highest number that should ever occur in practice. Listing 3-16 shows a Do...While loop with an infinite loop guard structure.

Listing 3-16   Guard Against Infinite Loops

```
Dim bContinueLoop As Boolean
Dim lCount As Long

bContinueLoop = True
lCount = 1

Do

    ' The code that goes here should set the
    ' bContinueLoop variable to False once the
    ' loop has achieved its purpose.

    ' This infinite loop guard exits the loop
    ' with an error after 10000 iterations.
    lCount = lCount + 1
    If lCount > 10000 Then Err.Raise _
        Number:=9999, Description:="Infinite Loop Error!"

Loop While bContinueLoop
```

The only purpose of the lCount variable within the loop is to force the loop to exit if the code within the loop fails to set the control variable to exit within 10,000 iterations (the appropriate number would depend on the particular situation). This type of construct adds very little overhead to your loop, but if performance is a significant concern, use the infinite loop guard until you are sure all the code within the loop is functioning properly; then delete it or comment it out.

Use Debug > Compile Early and Often   Never let your code stray more than a few changes away from being able to run a flawless *Debug > Compile*. Failing to adhere to this practice will lead to long, inefficient debugging sessions.

Use CodeNames to Reference Sheet Objects   Always reference worksheets and chart sheets in your application by their CodeName. Depending on sheet tab names to identify sheets is risky because you or your users may change these tab names, breaking any code that uses them.

Validate the Data Types of Selections   If you write a procedure designed to operate on a specific type of object the user has selected, always check the object type of the selection using either the `TypeName` function or the `If TypeOf...Is` construct. For example, if you need to operate on a range selected by the user, ensure the selection really is a Range object before continuing, as shown in Listing 3-17.

Listing 3-17   Verify That the Selection Is the Correct Object Type

```
' Code designed to operate on a range.
If TypeOf Application.Selection Is Excel.Range Then
    ' OK, it's a Range object.
    ' Continue code execution.
Else
    ' Error, it's not a Range object.
    MsgBox "Please select a range.", vbCritical, "Error!"
End If
```

Change Control

Change control, also known as version control, at the most basic level involves two practices: maintaining a set of prior versions of your application that you can use to recover from various programming or technical errors and documenting changes made to your application over time.

Saving Versions

When most professional programmers talk about version control, they mean the use of dedicated version control software, like Microsoft Visual Source Safe. However, this type of software is expensive, has a steep learning curve, and doesn't integrate well with applications built in Excel. This is because Excel doesn't store its modules natively as separate text files. The version control method we suggest here is quick, simple, requires no special software, and delivers the most crucial benefits of a traditional version control system.

The most important objective of a version control system is to allow you to recover an earlier version of your project if you have encountered some significant problem with the version you are currently working on. If a significant code modification has gone terribly wrong or you suddenly find yourself with a corrupt file, you will be in a very difficult position if you do not have a recent backup to help you recover.

A simple version control system that can save you from these problems would be implemented in a fashion similar to the following. First create a folder named Backup as a subfolder to the folder in which your project is stored. Each time you prepare to make a significant addition or modification to your project, or once a day at minimum, use a file compression utility such as WinZip to zip all the files in your project folder into a file with the following name format: **Backup_YYYYMMDDHH.zip**, where Y stands for year, M stands for month, D stands for day, and H stands for hour. This naming format gives your backup file a unique name that will sort in correct sequential order when viewed in Windows Explorer. Move this file into your Backup folder and continue working.

If you encounter a problem, you can recover your project from the most recent backup. You will obviously lose some work, but if you save backup versions diligently you can minimize the loss. Each time you are sure you have a fully tested build of your project you can delete most of the intermediate files from your Backup folder. It is advisable to retain at least weekly backups throughout the life of a project.

Documenting Changes with Comments

When you are maintaining code, if you make a significant change to the logic of a procedure you should also make a note with a brief description of the change, the date it was made and your name in the procedure-level comment block (refer to Listing 3-3). All non-trivial modifications to your code should be noted with an internal comment that includes the date the change was made and the name of the developer who made the change if multiple developers are working on the application.

Summary

Whether you use the naming convention proposed here or create your own, use a naming convention consistently across all your applications and over time. It makes your code self-documenting and easy to follow. Code the separate logical tiers of your application as independent entities. This prevents changes in one logical tier from forcing you to rebuild much of your application. Comment your code liberally at all levels. When trying to understand the purpose of a section of code, it's a lot easier if that purpose is explained by a code comment than if you have to figure it out yourself. Following these and all the other best practices presented in this chapter will result in robust, understandable, maintainable applications.

3. EXCEL AND VBA DEVELOPMENT BEST PRACTICES

CHAPTER 4

WORKSHEET DESIGN

A tremendous amount of Excel user interface design can and should be accomplished using the built-in features of Excel alone, with no VBA required. One of the guiding principles of Excel development is "let Excel be Excel." Don't try to reinvent the wheel. Excel provides a wide variety of prepackaged, performance-optimized features you can use to build your application's user interface. In this chapter we examine how you can produce a fully functional user interface with just the features Excel provides for this purpose.

There are two fundamental sections of an Excel worksheet user interface: those designed to be visible to the user and through which the user operates your application, and those designed to be hidden from the user and used only by your application to perform the tasks required of it. We cover each of these sections in more detail in this chapter.

Principles of Good Worksheet UI Design

The following list provides some design guidelines that apply to all worksheet user interfaces:

1. Use formatting to create visual contrast among cells designed to serve different purposes, input cells versus formula cells for example, as well as visual separation among different sections of your user interface.
2. Use consistent formatting based on the purpose of each cell. For example, don't format input cells with a white background in one area and a green background in another.
3. Don't use garish colors. Your choice of formatting should not distract from the task at hand. Do try to use colors with enough contrast that people with color-impaired vision will be able to recognize the different sections of your user interface.

4. Create a logical, well-structured flow through your user interface. Your user interface should flow from left to right and then top to bottom within a worksheet and from left to right among multiple worksheets.

5. Make your user interface as uncluttered as possible. Provide sufficient space between and around the various sections of your user interface. Leave an empty row at the top and an empty column at the far left to separate your worksheet user interface from the Excel container (this is in addition to the program rows and columns we cover in the next section).

6. Make it obvious to users what they are supposed to do each time they are required to perform some action. Techniques for doing this include the use of cell comments, validation lists, validation input messages, default values, good descriptive field names, and so on.

7. Use dynamic input verification techniques to provide feedback as quickly as possible if the user has done something wrong. Waiting until the user has completed the entire form before pointing out data entry errors should be viewed as a last resort, to be used only when there are no good alternatives.

8. Don't create an environment that potentially allows the user to make catastrophic mistakes. Protect all user interface worksheets, leaving only cells that require data entry unlocked. This prevents critical formulas from being accidentally overwritten.

9. Don't allow the user to get lost. Restrict the area of the worksheet within which the user can navigate to just the working area of your user interface.

Program Rows and Columns: The Fundamental UI Design Technique

When you design a user interface on an Excel worksheet, one of the first things you should do is leave row 1 and column A empty. This section of the worksheet will be hidden from the user and will allow your application to perform many tasks associated with an advanced Excel UI, including error checking, storing validation lists, and calculating intermediate values. In complex worksheet user interfaces it is not uncommon to have several initial rows and/or columns used as hidden work areas. These are called **program rows** and **program columns**.

An Excel worksheet user interface is typically laid out in a table format: left to right, top to bottom. Implementing design principle #6 described previously is most easily accomplished if you have a hidden area you can use to automatically examine each of the user's entries and determine whether they meet all the criteria that are enforceable using worksheet-based constructs. The result of these tests can then be used by conditional formatting and/or VBA-based validation to signal users when they have entered data incorrectly.

In the simple time sheet example shown in Figure 4-1, the user completes the first three columns of the table. The last column of the table is calculated by the worksheet. The first column of the worksheet itself is designed to be a hidden column. It performs a simple validation check on each row of the time sheet table. It counts the number of entries made by the user in each row and returns True if the number of entries is incorrect (which is to say the user has not completed all of the required entries for that row).

A6	▼		*fx*	=IF(COUNTA(C6:E6)=0,FALSE,COUNTA(C6:E6)<>3)		
	A	B	C	D	E	F
1						
2						
3	errHasError		Activity	Start Time	Stop Time	Total Hours
4	FALSE		General Programming	8:00 AM	12:00 PM	4:00
5	FALSE		Phone Conference	1:00 PM	2:00 PM	1:00
6	TRUE		Technical Support	2:00 PM		
7	FALSE					
8	FALSE					
9	FALSE					

FIGURE 4-1   An example of hidden column data validation

Here there are only two possible valid conditions. Either a row has not yet been used, and therefore has zero entries, or a row has been completely filled out, in which case there will be three entries. Any other condition is an error. Notice the error checking formula for row 6 indicates there is a data entry error in that row. This is because the user has not yet entered a Stop Time. The user may very well eliminate this error by entering a Stop Time after he completes this task. If he doesn't, it is a simple matter for your application to examine the validation range in column A and determine there is an error.

Defined Names

Defined names are an integral part of worksheet user interface design. Defined names are a superset of the more commonly understood named range feature. Defined names include named constants, named ranges, and named formulas. Each type of defined name serves an important purpose, and all non-trivial Excel worksheet user interfaces use some or all of the defined name types. The naming conventions used for the defined names in this chapter are described in Chapter 3, "Excel and VBA Development Best Practices."

Named Constants

A defined name can refer to a constant value. For example, the setHiddenCols defined constant shown in Figure 4-2 refers to the value 1.

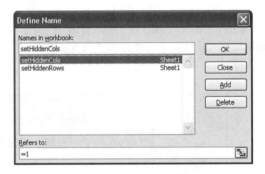

FIGURE 4-2 A sample named constant

This name illustrates a typical use of defined constants: storing settings that will be made to a user interface worksheet. In this case it indicates the number of initial columns that will be hidden. Named constants can also serve all of the same purposes on a worksheet that VBA constants serve in a VBA program, as discussed in Chapter 3.

Other common uses of named constants are worksheet identification, workbook identification, and version identification. It is common to have several broad classes of worksheet in your Excel application, such as input worksheets, analysis worksheets, reporting worksheets, and so on. You can use named constants to specify the type of each worksheet so that your application code can determine the type of the active worksheet and respond correctly, displaying the appropriate worksheet type-specific toolbar, for example.

Each user-interface workbook you create should have a unique named constant that identifies it as belonging to your application. The add-in for your application can then use this constant to determine whether the

4. WORKSHEET DESIGN

currently active workbook belongs to it. You should also include a version constant so you can pinpoint exactly what version of your application a given workbook belongs to. This becomes important when you upgrade the application such that prior version user interface workbooks must be updated or handled differently than current version user interface workbooks in some way.

Named Ranges

Named ranges allow you to reference a location on a worksheet with a friendly name that conveys information about the location rather than using a range address that cannot be interpreted without following it back to the cell or cells it refers to. As we see in the following example, named ranges also allow you to accomplish things you cannot accomplish with directly entered cell addresses.

Everyone reading this book should be familiar with fixed named ranges, those referring to a fixed cell or group of cells on a worksheet. This section concentrates on the less well-understood topic of relative named ranges. A relative named range is called relative because the location it references is determined relative to the cell in which the name is used. Relative named ranges are defined in such a way that the cell or cells they refer to change depending on where the name is used. There are three types of relative named ranges:

- **Column-relative**—The referenced column can change but the referenced row remains fixed. These can be identified because the absolute reference symbol ($) only prefixes the row number. The address A$1 is an example of a column-relative address.
- **Row-relative**—The referenced row can change but the referenced column remains fixed. These can be identified because the absolute reference symbol ($) only prefixes the column letter. The address $A1 is an example of a row-relative address.
- **Fully relative**—Both the referenced row and the referenced column can change. In fully relative named ranges, neither the row nor the column is prefixed with the absolute reference symbol ($). The address A1 is an example of a fully relative address.

To create a relative named range you must first select a cell whose position you will define the name relative to. This cell is your **starting point**. This cell is not the only cell where the name can be used; it simply gives you a point from which to define the relative name.

In the next example we demonstrate how to define and use a fully relative named range that allows you to create formulas that automatically adjust the range they refer to when a row is inserted directly above them. First let's see why this is important.

Figure 4-3 shows a simple table of sales for three hypothetical regions. The total sales for all three regions are calculated using the built-in SUM worksheet function, which you can see displayed in the formula bar.

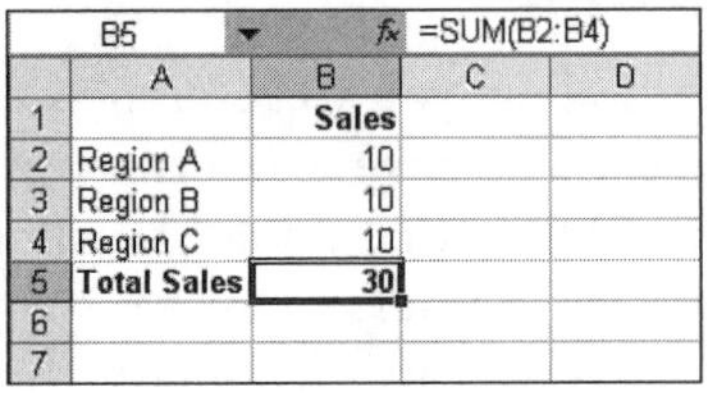

	B5	▼	*fx* =SUM(B2:B4)	
	A	B	C	D
1		Sales		
2	Region A	10		
3	Region B	10		
4	Region C	10		
5	Total Sales	30		
6				
7				

FIGURE 4-3   Total sales using a standard formula

Now assume we need to add a fourth region to our list. We insert a new row directly above the Total Sales row and add Region D. Figure 4-4 shows the result.

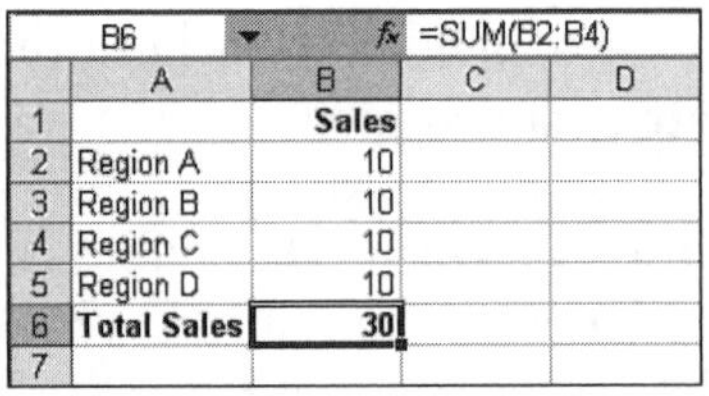

	B6	▼	*fx* =SUM(B2:B4)	
	A	B	C	D
1		Sales		
2	Region A	10		
3	Region B	10		
4	Region C	10		
5	Region D	10		
6	Total Sales	30		
7				

FIGURE 4-4   Insert an additional region to the list

Because the new region was inserted at the bottom of the list, the SUM function range did not adjust and the Total Sales number reported by the function is now wrong. This example is overly simplistic and designed to make the problem blindingly obvious. In real-world worksheets, this type of mistake is frequent and rarely so obvious. In fact it is one of the most common errors we discover when auditing malfunctioning worksheets.

This error is easy to avoid by defining a fully relative named range that always refers to the cell directly above the cell where the name is used. To do this, choose *Insert > Name > Define* to display the Define Name dialog (or better yet, use the Ctrl+F3 keyboard shortcut). In Excel 2007 select the *Formulas tab > Define Name*. As you can see in Figure 4-5, our starting point is cell B6 and we have defined a fully relative, sheet-level named range called ptrCellAbove that refers to cell B5.

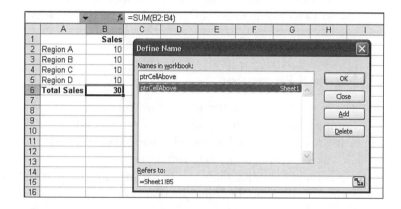

FIGURE 4-5   Creating a fully relative named range

Next we modify our SUM function so it references the ptrCellAbove named range rather than a specific ending cell address, as shown in Figure 4-6. We've also changed the first cell entry to B1.

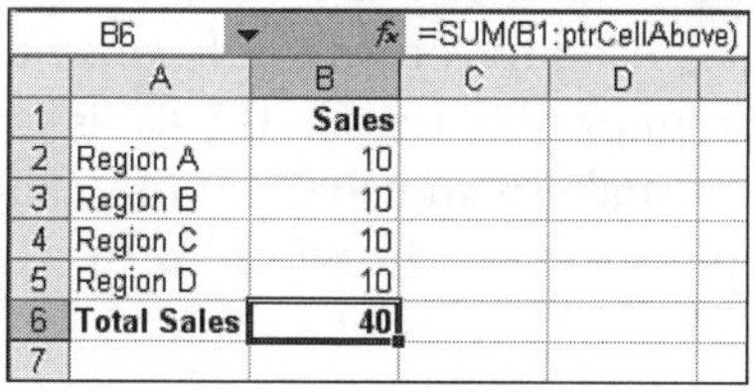

FIGURE 4-6   Using a fully relative named range in a worksheet function

Not only does our SUM function now display the correct answer, you can insert as many rows as you want directly above it or directly below the header, and it will always sum the correct area. We use relative named ranges extensively in our sample application.

NOTE In Excel 2002 and higher there is a feature that attempts to automatically detect when you have invalidated a formula by inserting rows directly above it as shown in the previous example. This feature works well for simple scenarios like the one we describe here, but it can be confused by more complex scenarios as well as turned off completely in the *Tools > Options > Edit* settings. It is always better to construct your worksheets to be self-correcting in the first place.

Named Formulas

The least understood and most powerful defined name type is the named formula. Named formulas are built from the same Excel functions as regular worksheet formulas, and like worksheet formulas they can return simple values, arrays, and range references.

Named formulas allow you to package up complex but frequently used formulas into a single defined name. This makes the formula much easier to use, because all you need to do is enter the defined name you've assigned to it rather than the entire formula. It also makes the formula easier to maintain because you can modify it in one place (the Define Name dialog) and the changes automatically propagate to every cell where the defined name is used.

In the "Practical Example" section of this chapter we show an example of how to use a named formula to package a complex worksheet formula into a defined name to make it more maintainable and easier to use.

Named formulas can also be used to create **dynamic lists**. A dynamic list formula is used to return a reference to a list of entries on a worksheet when the number of entries in the list is variable. Worksheet user interface development makes extensive use of dynamic lists for data validation purposes, a topic we cover in depth in the "Data Validation" section later in the chapter, but let's revisit the time sheet from Figure 4-1 to show a quick example.

In this type of user interface, we wouldn't want the user to enter arbitrary activity names in the Activity column. To make our data consistent from user to user we would define a data validation list of acceptable activity names and the user would pick the activity that most closely described what they were doing from our predefined data validation list. We put our activity list on a background worksheet (one not designed to be seen by the user) and create a dynamic list named formula that refers to it. This named formula is shown in Figure 4-7.

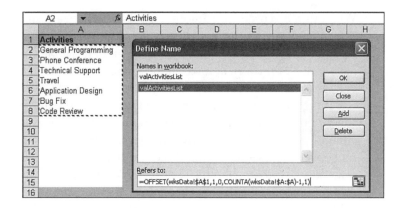

FIGURE 4-7   A dynamic named formula

The valActivitiesList named formula can now be used as the data validation list for the time sheet Activity column. A dynamic list named formula
consists of the following parts:

- **Starting point**—The point at which the list begins. In this case our
  starting point is cell wksData!$A$1.
- **Data area**—The full range in which items of our list might be located. This includes not only cells that are currently being used, but
  also cells that might be used in the future. In this case our data area
  is the entire column A, or wksData!$A:$A.
- **List formula**—A formula that determines the number of items currently in the list and returns a range reference to just those items. This
  is a combination of the OFFSET and COUNTA worksheet functions.

Scope of Defined Names

Defined names can have one of two scopes: worksheet-level or workbook-
level. These are roughly analogous to private and public variables. Like
variables, defined names should be given the most limited scope possible.
Always use worksheet-level defined names unless you must make a name
workbook-level.

When your workbook contains a large number of defined names, using
worksheet-level defined names helps reduce the number of names you
have to manage in the Define Name dialog at the same time. Worksheet-
level defined names can be used from other worksheets in most cases.

When they are used from another worksheet they are simply prefixed with the name of the worksheet from which they originated. This makes auditing worksheets that use defined names much simpler because you don't have to look up every defined name you come across in the Define Name dialog to determine which worksheet it references.

It is also often useful to have the same defined name on multiple worksheets in your user interface workbook. Two good examples of this are general-purpose, fully relative range names such as the ptrCellAbove range we discussed earlier and names that hold the values of settings you want to make to each worksheet using VBA code. We cover the latter in more detail in Chapter 5, "Function, General, and Application-Specific Add-ins."

Some circumstances require you to use workbook-level defined names. The most common case is demonstrated in Figure 4-7. A defined name that refers to a range located on a different worksheet that you want to use in a data validation list must be a workbook-level defined name. This is a limitation inherent in Excel's data validation feature.

In some cases a workbook-level defined name is simply appropriate, such as when the name truly refers to the entire workbook rather than to any individual worksheet. This would be the case with a named constant used to identify the version number of a workbook. In the "Practical Example" section of Chapter 7, "Using Class Modules to Create Objects," we demonstrate the use of a workbook-level defined constant to identify workbooks that belong to our application.

Styles

Styles provide a number of advantages that make them an integral part of any worksheet user interface. They provide a simple, flexible way to apply similar formatting to all the cells in your worksheet user interface that serve a similar purpose. The consistent use of styles also gives the user clear visual clues about how your user interface works. Using our time sheet example from Figure 4-1, Figure 4-8 shows how different styles define different areas of the worksheet user interface.

Styles allow you to apply the multiple formatting characteristics required for each user interface range all at once. Formatting characteristics commonly applied through the use of styles include number format, font type, background shading, and cell protection. Other style properties, such as text alignment and cell borders, are less commonly used because they tend to be different, even within cells of the same

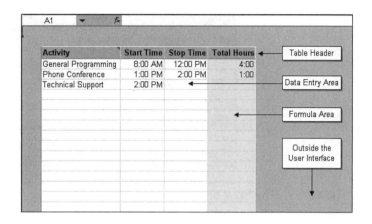

FIGURE 4-8   Using styles as visual indicators of the structure of your user interface

style. Custom styles, which we discuss in the next section, can be configured to ignore the formatting characteristics you don't want to include in them.

If you need to change the format of a certain area of your user interface, you can simply modify the appropriate style and all the cells using that style will update automatically. Here's an all too common real-world example of where this is very useful.

You've created a complex, multisheet data entry workbook using white as the background color for data entry cells. When you show this to your client or boss, they decide they want the data entry cells to be shaded light yellow instead of white. If you didn't use styles to construct your user interface you would have to laboriously reformat every data entry cell in your workbook. If you did use styles, all that's required is to change the pattern color of your data entry style from white to light yellow and every data entry cell in your workbook will update automatically. Given the frequency with which people change their minds about how their applications should look, using styles throughout an application can save you a significant amount of time and effort.

Creating and Using Styles

Adding custom styles is not the most intuitive process in Excel, but once you've seen the steps required, you'll be creating styles like an expert in no time. Custom styles are created using the *Format > Style* menu (select the *Home tab > Cell Styles > New Cell Style* in Excel 2007). This opens the Style dialog, shown in Figure 4-9, from which all style confusions originate.

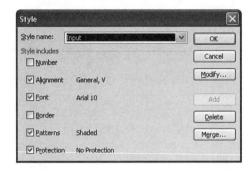

FIGURE 4-9   The Excel Style dialog

When the Style dialog first opens in Excel 2003 and earlier, it automatically displays the formatting characteristics of the cell that was selected when the dialog was invoked. In Figure 4-9, the Style dialog was invoked while the selected cell was in the Start Time column shown in Figure 4-8. As you can see, this cell was formatted with the Input style, so this is the style displayed by the Style dialog.

To create a new style, enter the name of the style you want to create in the *Style name* combo box as shown in Figure 4-10.

FIGURE 4-10   A new style is always based on the style of the cell selected when the Style dialog is displayed.

Once you do this you will encounter one of the more confusing aspects of the Style dialog. All of the *Style Includes* check boxes will be checked and their values will be set to the format of the cell that was selected when the Style dialog was invoked. This occurs even if those format characteristics are not part of the style currently applied to that cell.

NOTE In Excel 2007 the Style dialog opens with a default style name and default style settings regardless of the style applied to the selected cell when the dialog was displayed.

For example, Number, Alignment and Border attributes were excluded from the Input style that was displayed in the Style dialog immediately before we created our new style. All three of those attributes are included in our new style, however, and their specific values are drawn from the format applied to the cell that was selected when the Style dialog was first invoked. This is what the *By Example* in parentheses after the *Style Includes* title means. Don't worry; all of these attributes can easily be changed.

First, remove the check mark from beside any format option that you don't want to include in your style. When a style is applied to a range, only the format options you checked will be applied. Next, click the Modify button (or the Format button in Excel 2007) to define the properties of your new style. This displays the Format Cells dialog, shown in Figure 4-11.

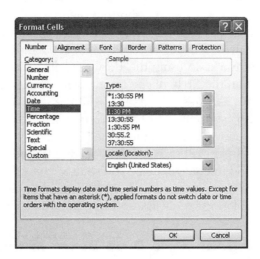

FIGURE 4-11   The Format Cells dialog as invoked from the Style dialog Modify button

Notice that the six tabs on the Format Cells dialog correspond exactly to the six *Style Includes* options shown in Figure 4-10. This is no accident. Styles are simply a way of grouping multiple cell format characteristics under a single name so they can be applied and maintained simultaneously through that name.

NOTE If you remove the check mark from a *Style Includes* option but then change any of the characteristics of that option in the Format Cells dialog, the option automatically becomes checked again in the Style dialog.

Modifying Styles

Modifying an existing style in Excel 2003 and earlier is exactly like creating a new style except that after selecting the *Format > Style* menu, you pick the style you want to modify from the *Style name* combo box rather than entering a new style name. Each time you select a style in the *Style name* combo box, that style will have its settings summarized and displayed for you in the *Style Includes* section of the dialog. Click the Modify button to display the Format Cells dialog and change any of the format options for the currently selected style. In Excel 2007 you modify an existing style by selecting the *Home tab > Cell Styles* drop-down, then right-click on the style sample button that displays the style name you want to modify, and choose *Modify* from the shortcut menu.

There is one minor caution to keep in mind when creating new styles or modifying existing styles in Excel 2003 and earlier. Once you have configured the style using the Format Cells dialog, be sure to click the Add button on the Style dialog to save your changes. If you click the OK button, your changes will be saved, but the style you have created or modified will also be applied to the currently selected cell. This is often not the result you want. Getting into the habit of using the Add button to add and update styles will save you from having to undo changes to a cell you didn't intend to change. Once you've used the Add button to create or modify a Style, you can safely use the Cancel button to dismiss the Style dialog without losing your work or formatting the currently selected cell.

Adding the Style Drop-Down to the Toolbar

If you're familiar with Word, you'll notice styles there are considered so important that a special style drop-down is automatically present on the Formatting toolbar. This not only allows you to quickly apply a style to a selection but also displays the style associated with the section of the document where your cursor is located. Excel 2003 and earlier has a similar toolbar control, but for some reason styles in Excel were not deemed important enough by Microsoft to have this control appear by default. You can add this control to one of your Excel toolbars manually, however, and if you plan on making full use of styles in Excel you should do so. Here's how:

1. Start by selecting *View > Toolbars > Customize* from the Excel menu.
2. In the Customize dialog select the *Commands* tab.
3. In the *Commands* tab select the Format item from the *Categories* list. As shown in Figure 4-12, the Style drop-down is the fifth item in the *Commands* list box.

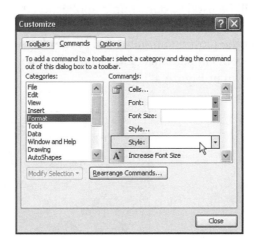

FIGURE 4-12 Selecting the Style drop-down from the list of format controls

4. Drag this control from the *Commands* list box and drop it onto one of your existing toolbars. You will now have a Style control that provides most of the same benefits as the Style control in Word. (It does not show the style names using their format as the Word Style control does.)

You can select a group of cells and apply a style to all of those cells by simply selecting the style name from the Style drop-down. And when you select a cell, the name of the style applied to that cell automatically is displayed in the Style drop-down. This feature is very helpful when creating complex worksheet user interfaces that utilize many different styles.

User Interface Drawing Techniques

Excel provides built-in tools with a surprising amount of flexibility for customizing worksheet user interfaces. In this section, we examine how to use these tools to improve the appearance and functionality of your worksheet user interface.

Using Borders to Create Special Effects

To keep the user focused on the elements of your worksheet user interface, it is often helpful to modify the normal style so that all unused areas of the worksheet have a consistent, light gray background color. This practice has been demonstrated in most of the user interface examples shown so far and will be used in our sample application. On top of this light gray background you can use cell borders to create some interesting special effects. One of the most commonly used border-based special effects gives a range of cells a 3D appearance, either raised or sunken. Examples of both effects are shown in Figure 4-13.

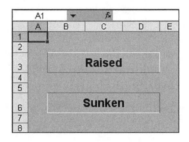

FIGURE 4-13   Using borders to create 3D visual effects

To create a raised effect you simply add a white border to the top and right sides of your range and add a 50% gray border to the left and bottom sides of your range. To create a sunken effect you do exactly the opposite. The width of the borders can be used to control the degree of the effect.

When you apply a background color to a worksheet, as we did in the previous example, Excel's standard gridlines are obscured. In many cases gridlines are a useful visual guide for the user, so you want to put them back. While there is no way to force Excel's standard gridlines to display over a background color, you can easily simulate gridlines by adding 25% gray borders with the lightest width to the area where you want the gridlines to appear. This effect is shown in Figure 4-14.

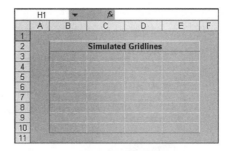

FIGURE 4-14   Using borders to simulate gridlines

Creating Well-Formatted Tables

Tables used within an Excel worksheet user interface typically have one or more of the following elements:

- Table description
- Row and column descriptions
- Data entry area
- Formula result area

Each section of your table should be formatted with a unique style that you use consistently throughout your user interface. Figure 4-15 shows a sample table with all four of the elements described previously.

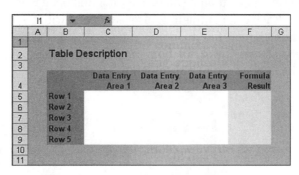

FIGURE 4-15   A basic worksheet user interface table layout

As you can see, in its simplest form the table is not very attractive. You can give your tables a much more professional appearance by using borders to provide a 3D effect, adding simulated gridlines, and increasing the row heights and column widths to provide more visual separation. Turning off row and column headers and the formula bar completes the effect. The table now looks like a completely custom user interface. Figure 4-16 shows the table with these added effects.

Table Description			
	Data Entry Area 1	Data Entry Area 2	Data Entry Area 3	Formula Result
Row 1				
Row 2				
Row 3				
Row 4				
Row 5				

FIGURE 4-16   A fully formatted worksheet user interface table

Cell Comments for Help Text

Cell comments are one of the most important user interface features provided by Excel. Their utility stems from the fact that in many cases they can serve the same purpose as a help file without requiring the user to do anything more complicated than hover the mouse cursor over the commented cell. Note that cell comments have several limitations that may make them inappropriate in certain situations:

If you are using the freeze panes feature on a worksheet and the worksheet is scrolled beyond the freeze point, if the comment window overlaps the frozen row and/or column it will be cut off at the point where the window is frozen.

Each cell comment is also associated with a specific status bar message whose structure cannot be modified. The status bar message displayed when a user hovers the mouse over a comment has the following structure, which is shown graphically in Figure 4-17.

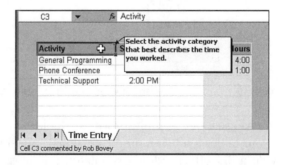

FIGURE 4-17   The format of an Excel comment status bar message

Cell **address** commented by **user name at the time the comment was created**.

The only part of this message you can modify is the **user name at the time the comment was created** section, which displays the contents of the *User name* entry located under the *Tools > Options > General* tab of the Excel menu (in Excel 2007 this is located under *Office Button > Excel Options > Popular*). If you are a consultant creating a worksheet user interface for a client, it's unlikely your client wants to see your name in the status bar each time she views a cell comment. In that case, one of the best workarounds is to change the *User name* setting on your machine to your client's company name while you create the comments for their client's user interface. Once the comments have been created, the user name displayed in the status bar is fixed and will not be affected when you change your *User name* setting back to your own name.

Remember that cell comments can be rich-text formatted. This means you can use formatting such as bold and italic fonts within the comment text as well as multiple fonts. Rich-text formatting allows you to create some sophisticated help messages. Figure 4-18 shows a rich-text formatted cell comment from a real-world worksheet user interface.

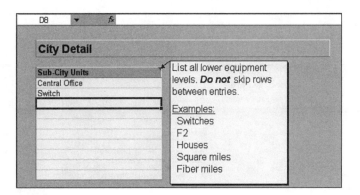

FIGURE 4-18   A rich-text formatted cell comment

Using Shapes

The ability to use shapes (objects drawn using the various options on the Drawing or Forms toolbars) on an Excel worksheet is a powerful user interface technique. Shapes are located in a special drawing layer that floats above the cells on a worksheet, so shapes cover (and obscure) worksheet cells. Shapes are also connected to the underlying worksheet through their properties, which allow them to

- Move and size with the worksheet cells they cover
- Move but don't size with the worksheet cells they cover
- Don't move or size with the worksheet cells they cover

Almost all shapes can contain text. A shape's text can either be manually entered or it can be linked dynamically to a specific cell on a worksheet by selecting the shape and entering the address of that cell as a formula in the formula bar. As you can imagine, the ability to assign formulas to shapes opens up a wide array of options for creating dynamic user interfaces. Shapes can also be given a macro assignment that causes them to execute the specified macro whenever the user clicks them. Simply right-click over the shape and choose *Assign Macro* from the shortcut menu. Figure 4-19 shows an excellent example of how shapes can be used to create a custom toolbar-like area across the top of a worksheet user interface.

These simulated toolbar buttons were created using professionally drawn clip-art images. These types of images can be found in many different places on the Web and using them in a situation like this is much preferable to laboriously drawing your own images.

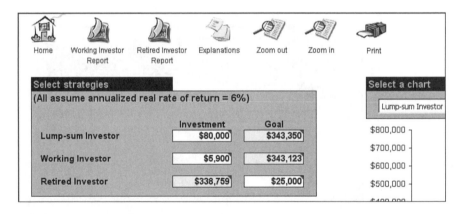

FIGURE 4-19   A custom on-sheet toolbar created with shapes

Data Validation

Data validation is one of the most useful yet underutilized features for worksheet user interface design. It allows you to ensure that most, if not all, of the inputs in your user interface are made correctly by disallowing input that does not match the rules you specify. Data validation can be as simple as restricting cell entries to whole numbers or as complex as restricting cell entries to items on a list whose contents are conditionally determined based on an entry made in a previous cell.

We assume you understand the basic use of data validation and instead demonstrate two of the more complex validation scenarios that can be created with this feature. Most complex data validation scenarios involve data validated lists or custom data validation formulas.

Unique Entries

If you need the user to enter only unique item names in a data entry list you can use a custom data validation formula to enforce uniqueness. First select the entire data entry area you need to validate. Next, choose *Data > Validation* from the menu (*Data tab > Data Validation* in Excel 2007) and select the *Custom* option from the *Allow* list. The basic syntax of the formula you need to enter is the following:

```
=COUNTIF(<entire range>,<relative reference to input cell>)=1
```

The first argument to the COUNTIF function is a fixed reference to the entire data entry area that must contain unique entries. The second argument to the COUNTIF function is a relative reference to the currently selected cell in the data input range.

If each entry is unique, the COUNTIF function evaluates to 1 and the entire formula evaluates to True, meaning the data is valid. If the COUNTIF function locates more than one instance of an entry in the data entry area, the entire formula will evaluate to False and data validation will prevent that entry from being made. Figure 4-20 shows an example of this validation setup and Figure 4-21 shows it in action.

NOTE The enforce unique entries data validation technique described previously only works correctly if the range being examined is entered into the Data Validation dialog as a hard-coded range address. If you try to use an equivalent defined name, this data validation technique will fail. This is a bug in the Excel data validation feature.

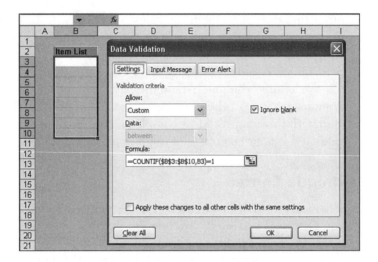

FIGURE 4-20   Data validation configuration to force unique entries in a list

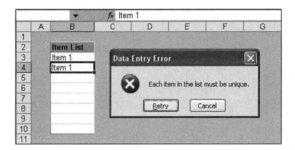

FIGURE 4-21   Unique entries data validation in action

Cascading Lists

In this type of validation, the specific data validation list that is displayed for a cell is determined by the entry selected in a previous cell. In Figure 4-22, the data validation list for the Item column is determined by the selection in the Category column. All of the data validation lists are located in the hidden column A.

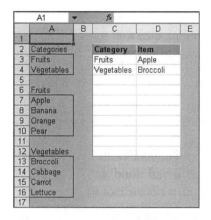

FIGURE 4-22 Initial setup for cascading data validation lists

The Categories list is the data validation list for the Category column. The Fruits list is the data validation list for the Item column when the Category selected is Fruits. The Vegetables list is the data validation list for the Item column when the Category selected is Vegetables. Each of these lists has been given the worksheet-level defined name shown in the caption above their border. Figure 4-23 shows all of the defined names used in this example.

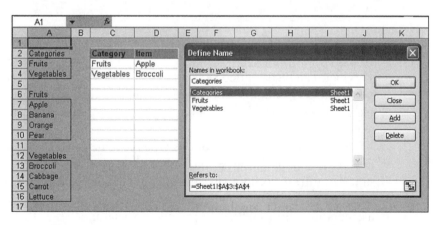

FIGURE 4-23 Defined names used for cascading data validation lists

The data validation list formula for the Category column is simple: =Categories. The data validation list formula for the Item column is a bit more complicated. It has to check the value of the corresponding Category entry and do one of three things: display no list if the Category entry has not been selected, display the list of fruits if Fruits has been selected, or display the list of vegetables if Vegetables has been selected. The formula that does this is shown here:

```
=IF(ISBLANK(C3),"",INDIRECT(C3))
```

If the cell in the Category column is blank, the formula returns an empty string, which removes the data validation list from the Item cell next to it. If the cell in the Category column has an entry, the formula uses the INDIRECT worksheet function to coerce that Category column entry into a range reference. The range reference refers to either the Fruits list or the Vegetables list depending on which item the user selected in the Category column. As Figure 4-24 shows, this formula successfully displays two completely different data validation lists depending on the category selection.

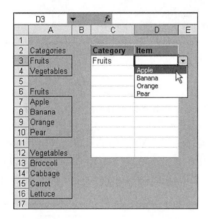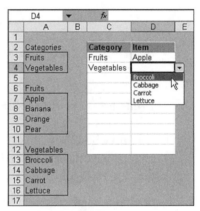

FIGURE 4-24 Cascading list validation in action

This logic can be extended to as many categories as you need. However, for cases with large numbers of categories, a table-driven approach that you'll see used in our sample time sheet application is much easier to set up and maintain.

Note that one drawback of this type of validation is that it doesn't work in both directions. In the scenario described previously, there is nothing to stop a user from accidentally changing the category entry in a row where a specific item has already been selected. In the next section you see how to use conditional formatting to provide a visual indication that this kind of error has been made.

Conditional Formatting

Conditional formatting is one of the most powerful features available for Excel user interface development. It allows you to use simple worksheet formulas to accomplish things that would otherwise require many lines of VBA code. Conditional formatting works by modifying the appearance of cells it has been applied to only if one or more conditions that you specify have been met. Conditional formatting overrides any style setting when the condition is triggered. Once the condition that triggered the conditional formatting is no longer true, the affected cell reverts to its original format. The two most common uses of conditional formatting in Excel user interface development are the creation of dynamic tables and calling out error conditions.

Creating Dynamic Tables

When building non-trivial worksheet-based user interfaces, you will often be faced with the problem of providing a table that in extreme cases will allow the entry of some large number of rows but the most common scenarios will only require a few. Rather than hard-coding a visible table with the maximum possible number of rows, you can use conditional formatting to create a table that expands dynamically as data is entered into it. We demonstrate how this is done beginning with the sample table shown in Figure 4-25.

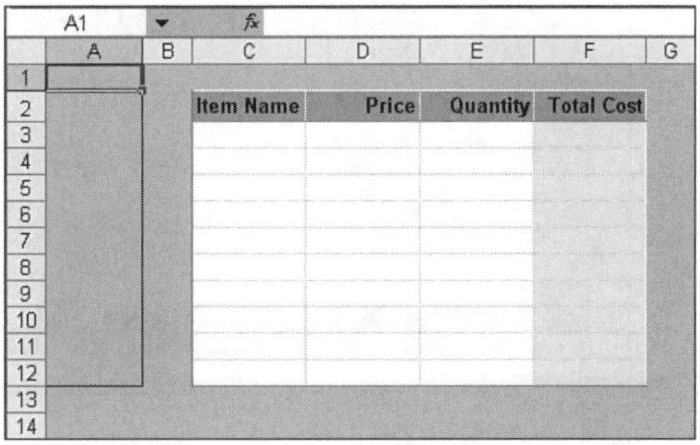

FIGURE 4-25 Data entry table prior to the addition of dynamic formatting

Let's assume this table really requires 200 rows for the largest projects but most users only need a few rows of input. Therefore, you'd like to hide the unused area of the table. As you can see, the first step in creating a dynamic table is to draw the entire table on the worksheet. You then use conditional formatting to hide the unused area of the table and reveal rows dynamically as needed. The trigger for displaying a data entry row is the user entering a new name into the Item Name column. For that reason, we always need to leave an empty Item Name entry cell at the bottom of the table.

When creating a dynamic table, it's a good idea to also create an outline showing the extent of the table in one of your hidden columns. Once we've added the conditional formatting the table disappears. This makes the table difficult to maintain if you haven't provided yourself with a visual marker indicating its extent. The empty bordered area in column A serves this purpose in our example. This area doesn't need to be empty. It could include error-checking formulas, for example. As long as it gives you a visual indication of the extent of the hidden area of the table it serves its purpose.

Our dynamic table requires three different conditionally formatted sections. Referring back to Figure 4-25, the first section encompasses range C3:C12, the second section encompasses range D3:F12, and the third range encompasses range G3:G12. We add the conditional formats one step at a time so you can see the results as they occur. To make the operation of the conditional formats more obvious we add data to the first row of the table. Keep in mind that the purpose of all three conditional formatting sections is the same: to simulate the appearance of a table that is just large enough to hold the data that has been entered into it. Figure 4-26 shows the table with the first section of conditional formatting completed.

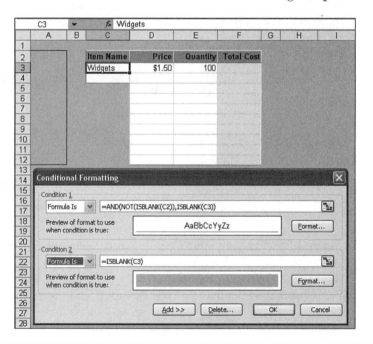

FIGURE 4-26 Conditional formatting for the first column

In addition to the purpose described previously, the first conditional format serves to leave a blank cell in front of the first unused table row to help prompt the user to enter the next item. The second conditional format is shown in Figure 4-27. It clears all unused rows in columns D through F and draws a bottom border below the first unused row in the table, thereby helping to complete the table outline.

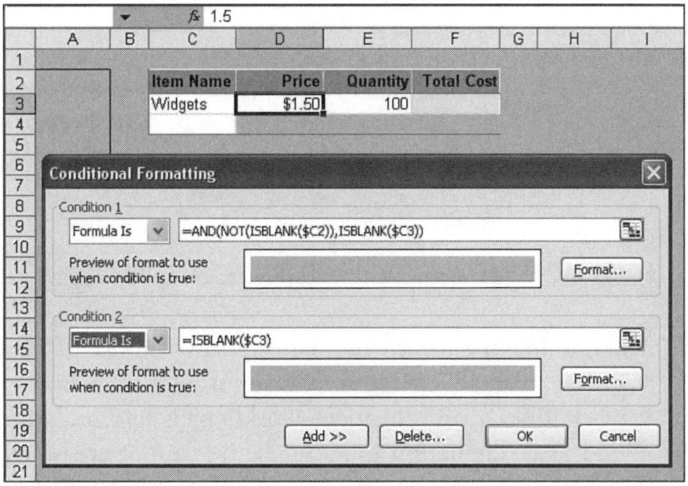

FIGURE 4-27 Conditional formatting for the remaining columns within the table

You can see the white border on the far right side of the table is missing in Figure 4-27. The purpose of the third conditional format is to complete the simulated table by drawing this border. Figure 4-28 shows the third conditional format.

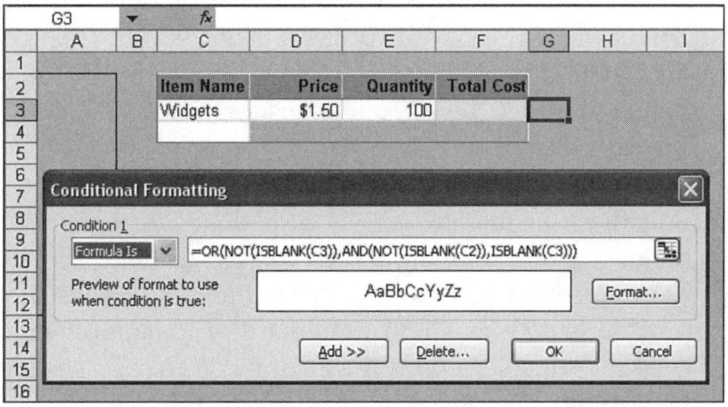

FIGURE 4-28 Conditional formatting outside the table to create the right-hand border

Figure 4-29 shows the fully formatted table with some additional entries. Each time a new entry is made, the conditional format reveals the row in which the entry was placed and adds a new prompt row below it.

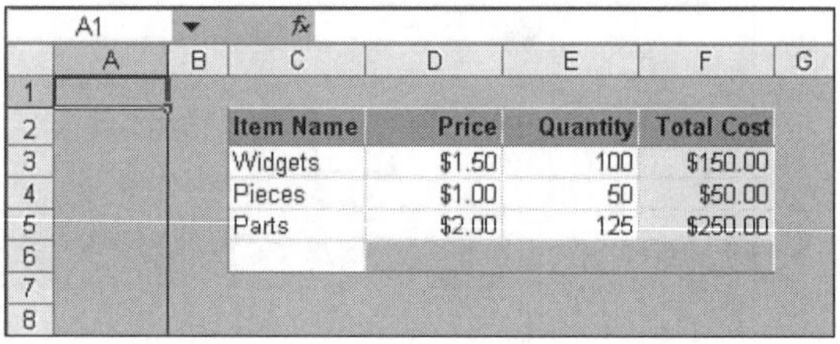

FIGURE 4-29 The complete dynamically formatted table

The one major caveat when considering the use of conditional formatting to create dynamic tables is that calculation must be set to automatic for it to work. If your user interface workbook is so calculation intensive that you need to set calculation to manual, you cannot create dynamic tables using this method (or use any other type of formula-based conditional formatting for that matter).

Calling Out Error Conditions

Conditional formatting can also work alone or in concert with formulas in hidden rows and columns to highlight invalid entries as soon as they are made. This should not be your method of first choice for pointing out data entry errors. Always try to use data validation to prevent data entry errors from being made in the first place.

A common situation where errors cannot be prevented by data validation is when you have two data entry columns such that the entry in the first column determines the allowable entries in the second column. In Figure 4-30 we revisit our cascading data validation list example from Figure 4-22.

Even though both columns' lists are data validated, an error can creep in if the user initially selects a valid category and item combination but then accidentally changes the category name at some later point in time. This type of mistake cannot be prevented by data validation, so we need to provide some visual indication that there is a mismatch between the category and item selections if this error occurs. This is a task for conditional formatting.

As you can see in Figure 4-30, we inserted a second hidden column. In this column we created an error check for each row that verifies the entry selected in the Item column is valid for the selection in the Category column.

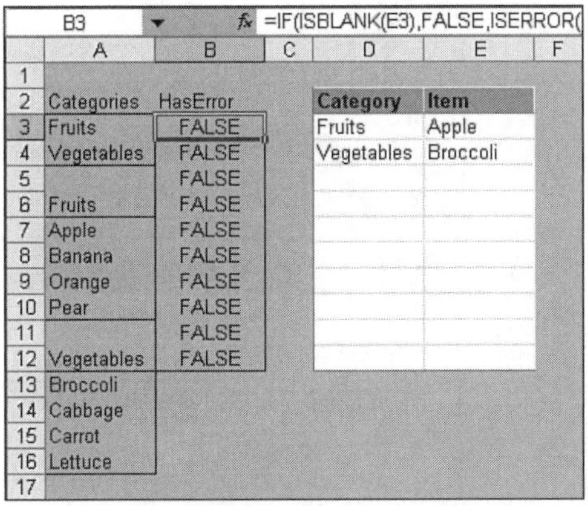

	B3			fx	=IF(ISBLANK(E3),FALSE,ISERROR(
	A	B	C	D	E	F
1						
2	Categories	HasError		Category	Item	
3	Fruits	FALSE		Fruits	Apple	
4	Vegetables	FALSE		Vegetables	Broccoli	
5		FALSE				
6	Fruits	FALSE				
7	Apple	FALSE				
8	Banana	FALSE				
9	Orange	FALSE				
10	Pear	FALSE				
11		FALSE				
12	Vegetables	FALSE				
13	Broccoli					
14	Cabbage					
15	Carrot					
16	Lettuce					
17						

FIGURE 4-30   The error check formula column for the conditional format

The error check formula is as follows. Keep in mind that the purpose of the error check formula is to return True if the corresponding row in the table has a data entry error and False otherwise.

```
=IF(ISBLANK(E3),FALSE,ISERROR(MATCH(E3,INDIRECT(D3),0)))
```

The only type of error that can occur in this situation is the Item column entry not matching the Category column entry. If there is no Item column entry, the row is not complete and we cannot determine the validity of the Category column entry. The ISBLANK function checks for this condition and returns FALSE if this is the case. Once there is an entry in the Item column, the formula uses the INDIRECT function to return a reference to the list of valid entries (recall that the Category column entry is the same as the range name of the corresponding Item list). The formula then uses the MATCH function wrapped in the ISERROR function to return TRUE if the Category entry is located in the list or FALSE if it isn't.

The next thing we do is add a conditional format to the table that checks the value of the HasError column. If the HasError column indicates there is an error in one of the table rows, our conditional format will give that row a bright red shade. Error condition highlighting is one exception to the rule of not using garish colors in your user interface. We do recommend using red, however, as this is almost universally recognized as a warning color. The conditional format required to accomplish this is shown in Figure 4-31.

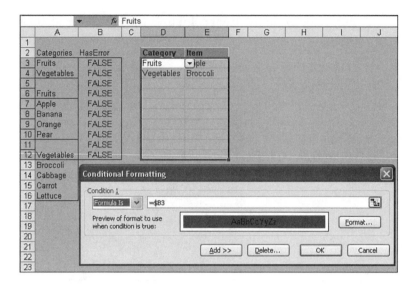

FIGURE 4-31   Setting up conditional formatting to flag an error condition

The result of the conditional format in response to an error condition is shown in Figure 4-32, where we've changed the Category column entry in the second table row from Vegetables to Fruits so it no longer matches the entry in the Item column.

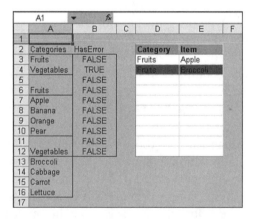

FIGURE 4-32   Conditional formatting flagging a bad entry in the table

Using Controls on Worksheets

Making extensive use of controls placed directly on worksheets is typically not the best user interface design. For most Excel application development, we recommend you use custom command bars (or Ribbon controls in Excel 2007) as entry points into your code and substitute data validation lists for combo box controls on worksheets. Command bars are covered in Chapter 8, "Advanced Command Bar Handling," while the Ribbon is covered in Chapter 10, "The Office 2007 Ribbon User Interface." There are circumstances where placing controls directly on your worksheet user interface is the best option, so in this section we cover some of the things you need to watch out for when you do this.

When you do need to use controls on a worksheet you have to make the choice between ActiveX controls and controls from the Forms toolbar. Generally we recommend you use Forms controls unless you absolutely need ActiveX controls. Forms controls are very lightweight and don't exhibit the many quirks you'll run into when using ActiveX controls on worksheets. Figure 4-33 shows a worksheet in which Forms controls have been used to great effect.

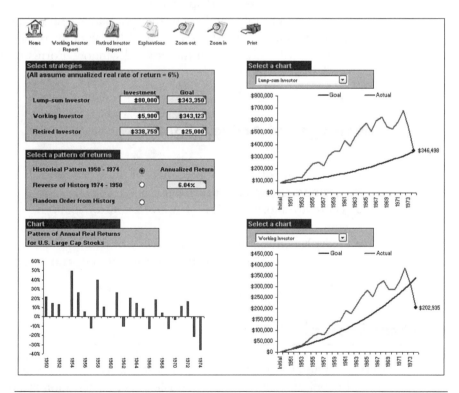

FIGURE 4-33 Good use of forms controls on a worksheet

Since everyone reading this chapter should be familiar with how controls work, we simply cover the details critical to deciding whether you can use

Forms controls in your worksheet user interface or whether you need ActiveX controls.

Advantages of Forms Controls

- Forms controls can be used on Chart sheets; ActiveX controls cannot.
- Forms controls are more tightly linked to Excel. You can select a Label or Button control and enter a formula in the formula bar that dynamically sets the captions of those controls. And unlike its ActiveX counterpart, a Forms control Listbox updates its contents in response to changes to a dynamic named range that has been assigned to its Input range property.
- It is easy to assign multiple Forms controls to run the same VBA procedure. Doing the same with ActiveX controls requires a more complicated class-based approach.
- If you use multiple windows or the split panes feature in your application to show two different views of the same worksheet, ActiveX controls will only work in the original window. Forms controls will work in any window.

Advantages of ActiveX Controls

- You can modify the appearance of ActiveX controls to a much greater degree than Forms controls.
- There are more varieties of ActiveX controls than there are Forms controls.
- ActiveX controls have a wide variety of event procedures that you can respond to, while Forms controls can only run a single macro.

Practical Example

In this chapter, we begin building a real-world Excel application that illustrates the points made in the chapter text. Our application is a time tracking system that starts as a simple, no-frills time sheet and works its way up to being a full-featured Excel application as we progress through the book. Due to space constraints we do not show every detail involved in creating this application. We demonstrate the major features and allow you to examine the rest by perusing the finished sample of the application available on the accompanying CD. This time sheet application will henceforth be referred to by its acronym PETRAS, which stands for Professional Excel Timesheet Reporting and Analysis System.

The first version of PETRAS is a simple workbook containing a time entry table on one worksheet and data validation lists on a second hidden worksheet. The user is expected to complete the time entry table each week and manually copy the workbook to a central location for consolidation. This version of PETRAS can be located on the accompanying CD in the *\Application\Ch04-Worksheet Design* folder. It is displayed in Figure 4-34.

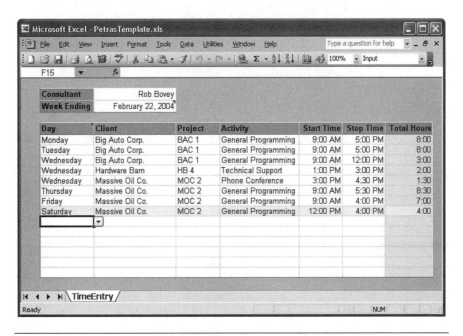

FIGURE 4-34 The first version of the PETRAS application

Most of the user interface design techniques discussed in this chapter have been used in the PETRAS application, including all variations of defined names, styles to differentiate areas by purpose, table formatting techniques, use of comments for help text, data validation, and conditional formatting. Let's quickly cover examples of how each of these techniques is used in practice.

Hidden Rows and Columns

We've taken advantage of hidden rows and columns in the PETRAS application for two purposes: error checking and background data processing. An open version of the PETRAS user interface workbook is shown in Figure 4-35.

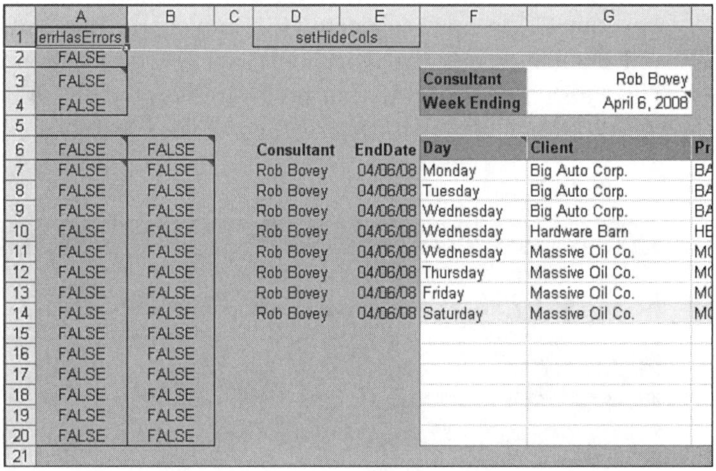

FIGURE 4-35 The PETRAS application with all rows and columns visible

There are two types of hidden columns in this worksheet. The two initial hidden columns are what we called program columns early in the chapter. We also have two hidden columns in the middle of the user interface. These two columns are used to create a data table that makes the process of automatically consolidating data simpler, while not requiring the user to enter duplicate data for each row. As we soon see in Chapter 5, we have special purpose code that uses the setHideCols named range, shown in the first row, to ensure these columns are hidden.

Defined Names

The Total Hours column in Figure 4-34 is calculated using a named formula called `forTimeDiff`. We used a defined formula for this purpose because the logic required is complex and therefore it makes sense to encapsulate it. The `forTimeDiff` named formula makes use of relative defined names to reference each part of the row from which it needs to gather the data required to perform its calculation. This defined formula is shown in Listing 4-1.

Listing 4-1   The forTimeDiff Named Formula

```
=IF(COUNTA(inpEntryRow)<6,"",
    IF(inpStop>inpStart,
        inpStop-inpStart,
        (1+inpStop)-inpStart
    )
)
```

The input-type defined names (those with the "inp" prefix) are all row relative defined names that refer to fixed columns on the TimeEntry worksheet, as follows:

- inpEntryRow = TimeEntry!$F3:$K3
- inpStart = TimeEntry!$J3
- inpStop = TimeEntry!$K3

If the number of entries in the current row is fewer than six, the formula simply returns an empty string. We cannot allow total hours to be calculated for a row that has not been completed. Once all the entries in a row have been completed, we must compare the start and stop times. These times are entered as Excel date serial time values; therefore, they are decimal values less than or equal to 1 that have no indication of the date worked. We set up the time sheet in this manner as a convenience to the user. It allows the user to simply enter a start time and a stop time without also having to enter a specific date for each time.

If the stop time is greater than the start time we know both entries refer to the same day. We can then simply subtract the start time from the stop time to calculate the amount of time worked. If the stop time is less than or equal to the start time, we know the user began working prior to midnight on one day and finished working after midnight on the next day. In this case we add 1 to the stop time, which is equivalent to adding one day in the Excel date serial format, to force it to be greater than the start time. We then subtract the start time from the result. This allows us to account for situations in which users work over midnight.

Styles

Note that PETRAS uses the same styles we introduced previously in Figure 4-8. We use separate styles to identify row and column headers, input areas, formula results, and areas outside the user interface. The

TimeEntry worksheet shown back in Figure 4-34 is designed to be protected, and once protected, the only cells that can be modified by the user are those having the Input style (the style with the white background).

User Interface Drawing Techniques

The PETRAS application demonstrates two of our recommended user interface drawing techniques. As shown in Figure 4-34, we used borders to give the time entry table a 3D appearance and a simulated grid to help guide the user. We also provided cell comments to answer the most common questions the user may have about the user interface. The cell comment describing the Day column is shown in Figure 4-36.

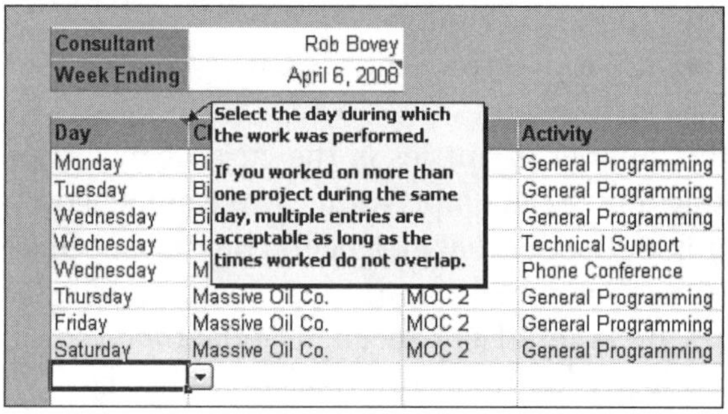

FIGURE 4-36 A cell comment used as help text

Data Validation

Data validation has been used in every input cell in the PETRAS user interface. Most of the data validation derives from dynamic lists stored on the hidden wksProgramData worksheet, part of which is shown in Figure 4-37.

The Consultants column on the wksProgramData worksheet provides the data validation list for the Consultant entry on the TimeEntry worksheet. Similarly, the Activities column on the wksProgramData worksheet provides the data validation list for the Activity column on the TimeEntry worksheet and so on. A complete picture of the various data validation techniques used on the TimeEntry worksheet can be gained by examining the sample application. Note that a more complex example of the cascading lists data validation technique described earlier in this chapter is used to connect the Client and Project columns on the TimeEntry worksheet.

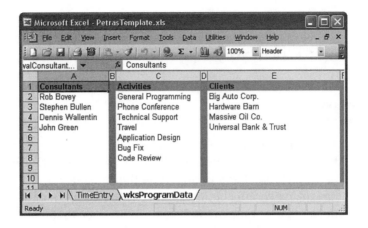

FIGURE 4-37   The hidden wksProgramData worksheet

Conditional Formatting

In Figure 4-34, you can see that conditional formatting was used to provide a clear visual indication of time entries made on a weekend. This is because work done on weekend days typically costs a higher hourly rate than work done on a weekday. Conditional formatting is also used to call out the error condition created when the user changes the first column entry of a cascading validation list pair if the second entry has already been made. In Figure 4-38, the user mistakenly changed a Client entry to a client that

Day	Client	Project	Activity	Start Time	Stop Time	Total Hours
Monday	Big Auto Corp.	BAC 1	General Programming	9:00 AM	5:00 PM	8:00
Tuesday	Big Auto Corp.	BAC 1	General Programming	9:00 AM	5:00 PM	8:00
Wednesday	Big Auto Corp.	BAC 1	General Programming	9:00 AM	12:00 PM	3:00
Wednesday	Hardware Barn	HB 4	Technical Support	1:00 PM	3:00 PM	2:00
Wednesday	Universal Bank & Trust	MOC 2	Phone Conference	3:00 PM	4:30 PM	1:30
Thursday	Massive Oil Co.	MOC 2	General Programming	9:00 AM	5:30 PM	8:30
Friday	Massive Oil Co.	MOC 2	General Programming	9:00 AM	4:00 PM	7:00
Saturday	Massive Oil Co.	MOC 2	General Programming	12:00 PM	4:00 PM	4:00

Consultant Rob Bovey
Week Ending April 6, 2008

FIGURE 4-38   Conditional formatting notifies the user of a data entry error.

does not match the Project entry previously made. Note how conditional formatting makes it instantly recognizable that changing the client entry was the wrong thing to do in this case.

Summary

We discussed many user-interface building techniques in this chapter; all of them implemented using Excel's built-in features. However, don't lose sight of the fact that the most important thing about an Excel user interface is not how many cool techniques you've used. Users don't care about cool techniques. They want an intuitive user interface that makes it easy for them to get their job done. Ideally your user interface should not draw attention to itself at all. It should simply be so well designed and constructed that users can dive right in and start working without having to spend any significant time figuring things out. Adhering to the principles described at the beginning of this chapter can help you design user interfaces that do their job so well no one notices them. This is the best user interface design of all.

CHAPTER 5

FUNCTION, GENERAL, AND APPLICATION-SPECIFIC ADD-INS

Add-ins are the primary constituents of well-designed Excel applications. In this chapter we discuss the most important duties add-ins perform within an Excel application, as well as details about the activities various types of add-ins must perform. This chapter does not cover dictator applications, as that is the subject of the next chapter.

The Four Stages of an Application

Every Excel application passes through four distinct stages, regardless of the type of add-in used to implement it. These stages are development/maintenance, startup, runtime, and shutdown. In this section we briefly discuss all four stages and identify the activities and services that must be provided by the application during each stage. Some of the topics covered do not apply to all types of applications, but we cover them all to give you a complete overview of what an application must accomplish. We do not go into great detail on the topics covered in this section. Some will be obvious to readers of this book and others will be covered extensively either later in this chapter or in later chapters of the book.

Development/Maintenance

During this stage you are either writing the application's code for the first time or updating existing code in the application. Either way, the purpose of this stage is to build or fix the application rather than to run it. You can make your life easier during this stage by using VBA to help automate the tasks required to build and maintain the application you are writing. There are two major categories of code designed to help build code:

- **Code templates**—These can be as simple as basic subroutine and function frameworks manually copied from an ad hoc storage module, or as complex as third-party code generation tools. The Excel Visual Basic Editor (VBE) provides a rudimentary tool for creating template subroutines, functions, and property procedures through the *Insert > Procedure* menu.
- **Development utilities**—You should strive to automate as many routine development processes as possible. Your application should contain a dedicated code module, or even a separate utility application, for VBA utilities that assist you in creating and maintaining the application. In the "A Table-Driven Approach to UI Worksheet Management" section later in the chapter, we demonstrate a utility for automatically managing the settings on your user interface worksheets.

Startup

When your application is starting up it must perform a number of tasks depending on what type of application it is and the conditions it finds during the startup process.

- **Check the environment**—Check any conditions that must be satisfied for your application to run. This might include verifying that the appropriate versions of Windows and Excel are installed as well as verifying the existence of any additional programs and files your application depends on. If the startup check fails, you can exit gracefully with a clear error message to the user rather than allowing your application to continue until it encounters a runtime error.
- **Save all settings that must be restored on exit**—If your application modifies the user's Excel environment, it must save the original settings so they can be restored prior to exiting. This topic is covered extensively in Chapter 6, "Dictator Applications."
- **Build or open any dynamic user interface elements**—These include application-specific command bars, Excel application settings, workbook templates, and so on.
- **Register any user-defined functions**—If your add-in contains user-defined functions (UDFs) that you want to expose to the user, you need to add some basic information about them to the Excel Function Wizard. We cover this topic in the "Function Library Add-ins" section later in the chapter.

- **Set the initial user interface configuration**—The specific settings made will depend on the type of add-in and the conditions discovered at startup. For example, if an application workbook was open that belonged to your application when the add-in was opened, you would enable your application's menus and toolbars. Otherwise you would probably disable most of them. This type of dynamic command bar modification is covered in the "Practical Example" section of Chapter 7, "Using Class Modules to Create Objects."

Runtime

Runtime is the stage during which your application performs the operations that constitute its primary purpose.

- **Handle requests from the user**—These include calls generated by command bar controls, Forms controls on worksheets, ActiveX controls on UserForms and worksheets and any keyboard shortcuts your application has provided for the user.
- **Handle Excel application events**—During runtime your application must also be prepared to respond to (and in some cases suppress) events generated by Excel itself. Excel application event handling is covered extensively in Chapter 7.
- **Handle runtime errors**—Although we would like our applications to run flawlessly all the time, every application eventually encounters a runtime error. These errors cannot be allowed to stop your application dead in its tracks. Rather they must be handled gracefully and in such a way that the user has some idea of what went wrong. Error handling is covered extensively in Chapter 15, "VBA Error Handling."
- **Call code located in other add-ins**—If you have set a reference to another add-in using the *Tools > References* menu in the VBE during development you can call public procedures located in standard modules in the referenced add-in directly by name. Without references you can accomplish the same thing by using the `Application.Run` function.
- **Provide other services**—Add-ins also provide other services at runtime, the most common being UDFs. We cover UDFs in detail in the "Function Library Add-ins" section later in the chapter.

Shutdown

The shutdown stage is when your application is exiting, either normally at
the request of the user or abnormally as the result of an error condition.
Either way there are activities that must be performed at this stage.

- **Remove all application-specific user interface components—**
  This means removing all the application-specific items created during
  the startup phase (command bars, application-specific workbooks,
  and so on).
- **Unregister any user-defined functions—**If your add-in registered any UDFs with the Excel Function Wizard on startup then it
  should unregister these functions on shutdown.
- **Restore the original environment—**If your application made any
  persistent changes to the Excel environment, it must save the original settings on startup and restore them on shutdown. This process
  is generically known as saving and restoring the user's workspace.
  This topic is covered extensively in Chapter 6.

Function Library Add-ins

One common class of VBA add-ins serves no other purpose than to provide a library of user-defined functions. These add-ins are called function
library add-ins. Add-ins are the best container for hosting general purpose UDFs, because as long as the user has the add-in containing the
functions open, those functions can be made available to all currently
open workbooks in a manner similar to the built-in Excel worksheet
functions.

A function library add-in is the simplest type of add-in from the perspective of the operational tasks it must accomplish. Although the functions it contains may be complex, the function library add-in itself has only
one responsibility: registering its UDFs with the Excel Function Wizard on
startup. In this section we first create a sample UDF and then show the
options available to the add-in for handling its registration duties.

An Example UDF

A common situation encountered when creating worksheet models is the
need to use a combination of the IF and ISERROR worksheet functions

to test the result of another function for an error condition. If the function being tested evaluates to an error value you construct the IF function to return some default value in its place. If the function being tested does not evaluate to an error value you construct the IF function to execute the function being evaluated a second time and return its result.

When the function being tested is very long and/or complex, the resulting formula is doubly long and/or complex because you must evaluate the function being tested twice. This situation can be generalized by the following pseudo-formula:

```
=IF(ISERROR(<long_function>),<default>,<long_function>)
```

In this section, we write a UDF that performs this operation with just one pass of the function being evaluated. We call our UDF IFERROR, and its syntax is the following:

```
=IFERROR(<long_function>,<default>)
```

NOTE Excel 2007 was released between the first edition of this book and the second edition that you're reading now. In Excel 2007, Microsoft has implemented a built-in IFERROR function that operates exactly like the function we demonstrate here and in subsequent chapters. We like to think this is the result of our influence. We will continue to use this function as an example because most users are still working with versions of Excel prior to 2007 where this function is not available.

The VBA code required to implement our IFERROR function is shown in Listing 5-1.

Listing 5-1 The IFERROR User-Defined Function

```
Public Function IFERROR(ByRef ToEvaluate As Variant, _
                        ByRef Default As Variant) As Variant
    If IsError(ToEvaluate) Then
        IFERROR = Default
    Else
        IFERROR = ToEvaluate
    End If
End Function
```

The ToEvaluate argument is a value, cell reference, or directly entered function expression to be evaluated. If ToEvaluate contains an error value, the Default argument is returned; otherwise, ToEvaluate is returned. The Default argument can also be a value, cell reference, or directly entered expression.

Both arguments and the function return value of the IFERROR function are specified as Variant data types to provide the maximum flexibility in the types of arguments the function can accept and return. As discussed in Chapter 3, "Excel and VBA Development Best Practices," the Variant data type can have a negative impact on performance. If you know, for example, that you will always be passing cell references to both IFERROR arguments, you can significantly improve the performance of the function by changing its arguments to the Range data type.

UDF Naming Conventions

Custom worksheet functions and their arguments (if any) should be given reasonably short descriptive names. You should do your best to make your UDFs look and feel like built-in Excel worksheet functions. This is one situation where you should not apply the naming conventions described in Chapter 3.

Making Your UDF Appear Native

You can make your user-defined functions appear more like native Excel functions by registering them with the Excel Function Wizard. This involves giving them descriptions and assigning them to categories that will assist the user in figuring out how to use them. There are two ways to do this. The first is simple but limited; the second complex but complete.

The first way is to use the `Application.MacroOptions` method. The major advantages of the `Application.MacroOptions` method are the relatively lengthy function description allowed and the fact that it removes your UDF from the default User Defined category and places it under the category you specify. The disadvantages of this method are that the function description and category are the only options you can specify, and you cannot create categories that don't already exist in the Function Wizard.

Listing 5-2 shows a procedure that uses the `Application.MacroOptions` method to register our IFERROR function. This procedure must be run prior to turning your function library into an add-in, and it must contain one call to the `Application.MacroOptions` method for each function your add-in contains.

Listing 5-2 Registering a UDF with `Application.MacroOptions`

```
Sub RegisterFunction()
    Dim sDescription As String
    sDescription = "Provides a short-cut replacement " & _
        "for the common worksheet function construct:" & _
        vbLf & "=IF(ISERROR(<function>),<default>,<function>)"
    Application.MacroOptions Macro:="IFERROR", _
                             Description:=sDescription, _
                             Category:=9
End Sub
```

Note the Category argument to the `Application.MacroOptions` method. Excel's function categories are specified by numeric values that correspond to the position of the category in the Excel Function Wizard category list, where All = 0, Financial = 1, and so on. If you do not specify a category number your UDF will be assigned to category 14 - User Defined by default. If you specify a category number that does not exist, a runtime error will occur.

The complete list of available category numbers along with their corresponding category names is shown in Table 5-1. Not all of these categories are commonly used.

Table 5-1 UDF Function Category Numbers and Names

Category Number	Category Name
0	All
1	Financial
2	Date & Time
3	Math & Trig
4	Statistical
5	Lookup & Reference
6	Database
7	Text
8	Logical
9	Information

Table 5-1   UDF Function Category Numbers and Names

Category Number	Category Name
10	Commands
11	Customizing
12	Macro Control
13	DDE/External
14	User Defined

The second way to provide descriptions for your UDFs requires you to execute an XLM macro function to register them. XLM is the native Excel programming language that predates VBA but is still supported in Excel. More than ten years after it supposedly became obsolete, there are still things that XLM does better than VBA, and this is a good example.

The advantage of this method is it gives you complete control over all aspects of the description and categorization of your function. The disadvantage of this method is the XLM macro string, which must contain all names, descriptions, and other information, is limited to 255 characters in length. This means your descriptions must be kept short. Your UDF will also continue to appear in the default User Defined category even though it also appears in any new category that you specify. Credit for originally devising this technique goes to worksheet function expert Laurent Longre.

The code required to demonstrate this method will not fit within the limited confines of a printed page, so you will need to examine the MRegister module in the Function.xla workbook located on the CD in the *Concepts* folder for this chapter to see how it works. The code in this module is commented extensively to help you understand it and is designed so that the entire module can be copied into another project and work correctly. You simply need to modify the function descriptions and add room for additional functions to suit your needs. One procedure call placed in your add-in's Auto_Open procedure will register all of your UDFs, and one procedure call placed in your add-in's Auto_Close procedure will unregister all of your UDFs.

NOTE   If you do not do anything to prevent it, any public function in your add-in will automatically be listed in the User Defined category in the Excel Function Wizard. This will occur even if your function isn't designed to be used as a worksheet function at all. The solution to this problem is to add the `Option Private`

`Module` directive to the top of any module that contains public functions. This will not prevent public worksheet functions from being used as such, but it will prevent them from being automatically added to the User Defined functions category.

Creating a Friendly Name and Description for Your Function Library Add-in

Function library add-ins are typically installed so they appear in the add-ins list of the Excel Add-Ins dialog accessed through the *Tools > Add-Ins* menu. This allows the user to easily load and unload them as the need arises. We discuss the various ways of making your add-in appear in the *Tools > Add-Ins* dialog in Chapter 29, "Providing Help, Securing, Packaging, and Distributing." You should provide a friendly name and a short description for any add-in that appears in the Add-Ins dialog. These can be made to appear when the add-in's entry is selected by setting two specific file properties of the add-in workbook.

First, set the IsAddin property of the add-in's ThisWorkbook object to False so you can access the add-in workbook from the Excel user interface. Next, choose *File > Properties* from the Excel menu. On the *Summary* tab of the resulting Properties dialog you provide a friendly name for your add-in using the *Title* entry. The description for your add-in is entered in the *Comments* field. The name and description for our sample function library add-in are shown in Figure 5-1.

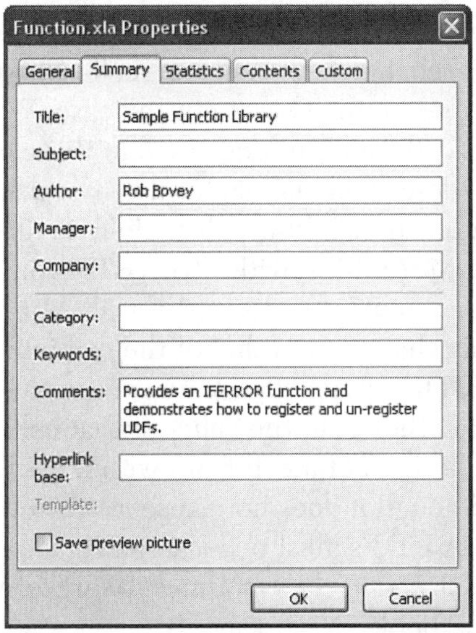

FIGURE 5-1 Adding a name and description to an add-in

Figure 5-2 shows how the name and description added in the Properties dialog appear in the Add-Ins dialog.

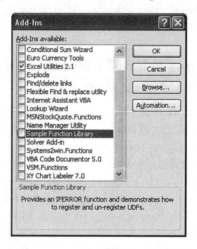

FIGURE 5-2   The add-in name and description in the Add-Ins dialog

Critical UDF Details

The following are some critical details you need to understand to develop VBA user-defined functions.

- One of the most common mistaken beliefs about UDFs is that they can change the value of cells other than the one they've been entered into. This is not the case. Whether a UDF is programmed in a VBA add-in (described in this chapter), a VB6 automation add-in (described in Chapter 23, "Excel and Visual Basic 6"), a VB.NET automation add-in (described in Chapter 25, "Writing Managed COM Add-ins with VB.NET"), or a C/C++ XLL (described in Chapter 27, "XLLs and the C API"), a user-defined function can only change the value of the cell into which it has been entered.
- A UDF cannot change any properties of the cell it has been entered into other than the value of that cell. Attempting to set the pattern or borders of a cell from within a UDF, for example, will not work (although it does not cause a VBA or function return value error).
- VBA UDFs must be located in standard code modules. They cannot be placed in class modules, UserForms, or the code modules behind workbooks or worksheets.

■ Do not attempt to change the values of UDF arguments that are declared ByRef. As we noted earlier, UDFs can only change the value of the cell into which they have been entered. Attempting to modify the value of a ByRef argument violates this principle and causes your UDF to return a #VALUE! error if you attempt to modify a ByRef argument, or any argument that has been declared as a Range object.

■ Put all range references used by your function in the function's argument list. If you refer to ranges not in the argument list from within your UDF, changes to those ranges will not cause your UDF to recalculate, possibly leading to incorrect results being displayed. You can use the `Application.Volatile` method to force your UDF to recalculate whenever calculation is triggered anywhere in Excel, but this can cause serious degradation of calculation performance and should be used only as a last resort.

VBA UDF Problems

The biggest problem with most VBA UDFs is that using them creates hard-coded links from the workbooks where they are used to the add-in that contains them. If you physically move the source add-in, workbooks that use the functions it contains will not be able to locate it, even if the add-in is opened prior to opening any workbooks that use its functions.

VBA functions also do not automatically capitalize correctly when you enter them into a worksheet cell. Capitalization will not affect the operation of the function, but it gives the function a strange appearance. And once you have entered a UDF in all lowercase characters you will find it almost impossible to get it to convert to uppercase characters even when it is defined that way in the source code in the add-in.

General Add-ins

General add-ins, also known as utility add-ins, are designed to enhance Excel by extending its feature set or providing connections between it and other programs. All of the add-ins you will find in the *Tools* folder of the CD that accompanies this book fall into this category. Like function library add-ins, general add-ins are designed to work with any workbook the user opens. General add-ins are usually contained within a single .xla workbook, although larger examples may be distributed across multiple files. General add-ins are typically placed in the add-ins list of the Excel Add-Ins dialog so the user can easily load and unload them as the need arises. They are provided with a friendly name and description in exactly the same way as described for a function library add-in in the previous section.

The most common method for providing the user access to features in a general add-in is through menus and toolbar buttons (or Ribbon controls in Excel 2007). Event handling is also frequently used to respond to user actions, and keyboard shortcuts can be provided to run commonly used features.

Because general add-ins must operate correctly no matter what state Excel is currently in, any event handling class you use must respond to changes in the Excel environment that would prevent your add-in from operating correctly. An example would be the user closing the last open workbook. In response to this situation your event handler should disable access to the features of your add-in that require an open workbook in order to function correctly. Event handling is covered in more detail in Chapter 7.

The individual entry point procedures of your add-in must also verify that the current state of Excel is valid for them to run. For example, if a procedure is designed to operate on a chart, but no chart is currently active, the procedure must detect this and provide the user with an explanatory error message rather than cause a runtime error by blindly attempting to reference a nonexistent chart.

Application-Specific Add-ins

Application-specific add-ins are different from the previous two add-in types in that they are designed to implement self-contained Excel applications. They may integrate with the standard Excel user interface, as does the add-in shown in the "Practical Example" section later in the chapter, or they may take over the Excel user interface entirely, as demonstrated in Chapter 6. In either case, an application-specific add-in is designed to operate only on workbooks specifically designed for it. Still, most of the same operations and requirements apply to application-specific add-ins as apply to function libraries and general add-ins. Application-specific add-ins simply add an additional element, the worksheet user interface.

A Table-Driven Approach to UI Worksheet Management

A significant part of the responsibility of an application-specific add-in is to manage the user interface workbook and worksheet settings. It's possible to store, apply, and remove these settings on an ad hoc basis, but when dealing with large and/or complex user interfaces it is much better to let VBA do the work for you. In this section we demonstrate a table-driven approach to managing worksheet user interface settings.

Typically a number of settings must be made prior to your application being run by the end user. However, these settings will get in your way during development. The solution is to create an automated system for defining, applying, and removing these settings. This is just one of many areas in Excel development that lends itself to a table-driven methodology.

Table-Driven Methodology Defined

In a nutshell, table-driven methods use a worksheet table to store data that describes the task you are trying to accomplish. One or more VBA procedures reads the data from the table and automatically performs that task. The biggest advantage of a table-driven method for accomplishing a specific task is that it tends to be easily reusable from project to project.

Common tasks that lend themselves to table-driven solutions are managing workbook and worksheet user interface setup, building command bars, and saving and restoring the user's workspace. We even demonstrate a table-driven method for creating UserForms in Chapter 13, "UserForm Design and Best Practices."

Typical Worksheet User Interface Settings

There are a number of settings or configuration details that tend to be common to all worksheet user interfaces. These include

- **Hidden rows and columns**—As we discussed in Chapter 4, "Worksheet Design," having hidden rows and columns at your disposal is a valuable user interface construction technique. However, you don't want these rows and columns to be hidden when you are performing development or maintenance work on the user interface.
- **Protection**—Workbook and worksheet protection are fundamental to good user interface design. Protecting the user interface prevents users from modifying areas that should not be modified.
- **Scroll area**—Setting a scroll area for each user interface worksheet prevents the user from getting lost by scrolling beyond the area of the worksheet used by your application.
- **Enable selection**—This property works with the scroll area property to keep the user focused on your user interface. It prevents the user from even selecting cells outside the boundaries of your UI.

- **Row and column headers**—Although there are some exceptions, you typically do not want to display Excel's row and column headers on your user interface worksheets. Row and column headers serve as guidelines for constructing and maintaining a user interface, so they should be visible during that process. In most well-designed user interfaces, however, they will simply be a distraction to the user. Therefore, you want them visible during development and hidden at runtime.

- **Sheet visibility**—In most non-trivial workbook-based user interfaces you will have one or more worksheets that are designed to perform background tasks and should not be seen or modified by the user. Once again, however, you want these sheets to be visible during development and maintenance.

The Settings Table

Let's see how a table-driven methodology can help us create and manipulate the user interface settings described in the preceding section. The first thing we need is a settings table. This table lists the names of the user interface worksheets in the first column and the names of the settings in the first row. At the intersection of each row and column is the value that will be applied to the specific worksheet for that setting. Figure 5-3 shows an example of a user interface settings table.

	A	B	C	D	E	F	G
1	Worksheets	setProgRows	setProgCols	setScrollArea	setEnableSelect	setProtection	setVisible
2	wksSplash	1	1	$A$1:$L$25	-4142	TRUE	-1
3	wksProgramData	0	0		0	FALSE	2
4	wksLookupTables	0	0		0	FALSE	2
5	wksAllInputs	0	0		0	FALSE	2
6	wksTableRollup	0	0		0	FALSE	2
7	wksCostDev	0	0		0	FALSE	2
8	wksCostDevAudit	0	0		0	FALSE	2
9	wksRationality	0	0		0	FALSE	2
10	wksPlanPrefModel	0	0		0	FALSE	2
11	wksPlanPrefOutput	0	0		0	FALSE	2
12	wksSelection	0	0		0	FALSE	2
13	wksFundingStatusAnalysis	1	1	$A$1:$H$20	-4142	TRUE	-1
14	wksY1FIPricingAudit	1	3	$A$1:$J$100	-4142	TRUE	-1
15	wksY1SFPricingAudit	1	3	$A$1:$J$100	-4142	TRUE	-1
16	wksInsurerProfitAnalysis	1	1	$A$1:$H$20	-4142	TRUE	-1
17	wksFundingStatusAnalysis	1	1	$A$1:$H$20	-4142	TRUE	-1
18	wksPremiumsSummary	2	2	$A$1:$I$20	-4142	TRUE	-1

FIGURE 5-3 A user interface settings table

This table would typically be located on a worksheet in your add-in. The VBA code used to manage these settings would be located in a utility module in the add-in. A utility module is a standard code module that holds code designed to assist the programmer during development and not used by the application itself. In situations where add-in size needs to be minimized, this table and its associated code could be located in a separate utility workbook that is only used during development and maintenance. However, you still need to have some user interface management code located in the add-in to set the properties of your user interface when your application is run.

NOTE There has been some confusion about exactly when the settings table and its associated code are used. The settings table described here is designed purely to assist the programmer during development and maintenance of an application. The programmer uses this table and associated code to easily remove and reapply the appropriate values for large numbers of worksheet settings that will be used by the application at runtime. However, the settings table itself serves no purpose at runtime.

There are two things to note about this table. First, you can see that all the worksheet names in the first column follow our worksheet naming convention. This is because they are the CodeNames of the worksheets, not their sheet tab names. As we mentioned in Chapter 3, you should do your best not to rely on sheet tab names because they may be changed unexpectedly by the user. A worksheet's CodeName provides a permanent, unique name by which you can identify the worksheet.

Second, beginning in column B you can see that the column headers are defined names (remember that the "set" prefix identifies a defined name that represents a setting). This is because all of these settings will be stored as sheet-level defined names on the worksheets to which they apply. This allows all of the information required to manage a worksheet to be encapsulated within that worksheet.

Also notice that some of the settings in the body of the table are blank. This indicates the setting does not apply to that worksheet and the setting name will not be defined on that worksheet. Later we see that the VBA code that implements these settings ignores settings whose defined names are missing.

The Utility Code

The settings table requires support procedures to accomplish two objectives. One procedure needs to read the settings table and add the specified defined names with the specified values to each worksheet listed in the table. A second procedure needs to loop each worksheet in the user interface workbook, read the value of each defined name listed in the settings table, and record the value of that setting in the appropriate cell of the settings table.

If we have code to create the settings defined in the settings table, you may be asking yourself, why do we also need code to read these settings back into the table? Good question. The answer is that you will often find it easier to manually update the value of the defined name for a setting on a worksheet you have just modified. For example, if you need to add additional hidden program columns to several sheets, it's very easy to update their respective setProgCols defined names as you go along. Once you've made these adjustments you can quickly synchronize the settings table and the user interface workbook by reading the values of all the defined names from the workbook back into the settings table.

As you can see in Listing 5-3, the code required to write the defined names from the settings table to the worksheets in the user interface workbook is relatively simple. As part of the structure of the settings table we have provided dynamic defined names that reference the list of worksheets and the list of settings to create. If you add worksheets or settings, these names automatically expand to include them.

Listing 5-3   Code to Write Settings to the User Interface Worksheets

```
Private Const msFILE_TEMPLATE As String = "PetrasTemplate.xlt"
Private Const msRNG_NAME_LIST As String = "tblRangeNames"
Private Const msRNG_SHEET_LIST As String = "tblSheetNames"

Public Sub WriteSettings()

    Dim rngSheet As Range
    Dim rngSheetList As Range
    Dim rngName As Range
    Dim rngNameList As Range
    Dim rngSetting As Range
    Dim sSheetTab As String
    Dim wkbTemplate As Workbook
    Dim wksSheet As Worksheet

    ' Turning off screen updating and calculation
    ' will speed the process significantly.
    Application.ScreenUpdating = False
    Application.Calculation = xlCalculationManual
```

```vba
' The time entry workbook.
Set wkbTemplate = Application.Workbooks(msFILE_TEMPLATE)
' The list of worksheets in the first column.
Set rngSheetList = wksUISettings.Range(msRNG_SHEET_LIST)
' The list of setting names in the first row.
Set rngNameList = wksUISettings.Range(msRNG_NAME_LIST)

' The outer loop processes all the worksheets in the
' first column of the table.
For Each rngSheet In rngSheetList

    ' We need an object reference to the worksheet so we
    ' can easily add a sheet-level defined name to it.
    ' The sSheetTabName() function converts a CodeName
    ' into its corresponding sheet tab name.
    sSheetTab = sSheetTabName(wkbTemplate, rngSheet.Value)
    Set wksSheet = wkbTemplate.Worksheets(sSheetTab)

    ' The inner loop adds each setting to the current sheet.
    ' If the setting already exists it will be replaced.
    For Each rngName In rngNameList

        ' The value of the setting is contained in the cell
        ' where the worksheet row and range name column
        ' intersect.
        Set rngSetting = Intersect(rngSheet.EntireRow, _
                                    rngName.EntireColumn)

        ' We only create defined names for settings that
        ' have been given a non-zero-length value.
        If Len(rngSetting.Value) > 0 Then
            wksSheet.Names.Add rngName.Value, _
                    "=" & rngSetting.Value
        End If

    Next rngName

Next rngSheet

Application.ScreenUpdating = True
Application.Calculation = xlCalculationAutomatic

End Sub
```

Keep in mind that this code does not actually **apply** any settings in the user interface workbook. It simply records the settings we want to apply in worksheet-level defined names on each worksheet. In the "Practical Example" section later in the chapter we demonstrate how to create a procedure that applies these settings to the user interface workbook. This procedure will be called as part of the application startup code so that the settings are always applied by the time the user sees the user interface workbook. The MUtility module provided with the sample application also contains a procedure that automatically removes all settings from the user interface workbook to make it easier to maintain.

Using VBA to Dynamically Modify Your Worksheet User Interface

There are many ways you can leverage the power of VBA to improve your user interface. Many of them, including techniques such as context-specific command bar enabling and dynamic hiding and unhiding of rows and columns, require the use of Excel event trapping that we cover in Chapter 7.

A simple example that we add to our sample application in this chapter is a feature that clears the data entry cells on a worksheet. A one-click method for clearing all input cells on the current user-interface worksheet is often helpful to users. To do this, simply create a named range on each data entry worksheet that includes all the data input cells and give it an obvious name such as rgnClearInputs. This must be a sheet-level defined name created on all data entry worksheets in your workbook. Listing 5-4 shows the VBA implementation of our clear data entry area feature.

Listing 5-4   VBA Implementation of a Clear Data Entry Area Feature

```
Public Sub ClearDataEntryAreas()

    Dim rngToClear As Range

    ' Make sure the active worksheet has the rgnClearInputs
    ' defined name (i.e. it's an input worksheet).
    On Error Resume Next
        Set rngToClear = ActiveSheet.Range("rgnClearInputs")
    On Error GoTo 0

    ' If the worksheet is an input worksheet, clear the contents
```

```
' of the input area.
If Not rngToClear Is Nothing Then rngToClear.ClearContents

End Sub
```

Practical Example

We illustrate some of the concepts presented in this chapter by creating an application-specific add-in for the Professional Excel Timesheet Reporting and Analysis System (PETRAS) Time Sheet application that began as a single Excel workbook in Chapter 4.

Features

The add-in for our PETRAS time sheet application will perform the following operations:

- Open and initialize the application
- Build a toolbar that gives the user access to each feature of the application
- Open and initialize the time entry workbook
- Allow the user to save a copy of the time entry workbook to a pre-defined consolidation location
- Allow the user to add more data entry rows to the time entry worksheet
- Allow the user to clear the data entry area so the time sheet can easily be reused
- Allow the user to close the PETRAS application
- Add a custom property that allows the consolidation application to locate all instances of our time entry workbook

Let's look at how the add-in accomplishes these tasks. We assume the WriteSettings utility procedure shown in Listing 5-3 has been run on the time entry workbook and the settings saved prior to running the add-in.

Open and Initialize the Application

The first operation the add-in performs when it is opened is to initialize the application and then open and initialize the user interface workbook. This is accomplished by the Auto_Open procedure, shown in Listing 5-5.

Listing 5-5   The PETRAS Add-in Auto_Open Procedure

```
Public Sub Auto_Open()

    Dim wkbBook As Workbook

    ' The very first thing your application should do upon
    ' startup is attempt to delete any copies of its
    ' command bars that may have been left hanging around
    ' by an Excel crash or other incomplete exit.
    On Error Resume Next
        Application.CommandBars(gsBAR_TOOLBAR).Delete
    On Error GoTo 0

    ' Initialize global variables.
    InitGlobals

    ' Make sure we can locate our time entry workbook before we
    ' do anything else.
    If Len(Dir$(gsAppDir & gsFILE_TIME_ENTRY)) > 0 Then

        Application.ScreenUpdating = False
        Application.StatusBar = gsSTATUS_LOADING_APP

        ' Build the command bars.
        BuildCommandBars

        ' Determine if the time entry workbook is already open.
        ' If not, open it. If so, activate it.
        On Error Resume Next
        Set wkbBook = Application.Workbooks(gsFILE_TIME_ENTRY)
        On Error GoTo 0

        If wkbBook Is Nothing Then
            Set wkbBook = Application.Workbooks.Open( _
                            gsAppDir & gsFILE_TIME_ENTRY)
        Else
            wkbBook.Activate
        End If

        ' Make the worksheet settings for the time entry
        ' workbook
        MakeWorksheetSettings wkbBook

        ' Reset critical application properties.
```

```
        ResetAppProperties

    Else

        MsgBox gsERR_FILE_NOT_FOUND, vbCritical, gsAPP_NAME
        ShutdownApplication
    End If

End Sub
```

The first thing the add-in does is blindly attempt to delete any previous instance of its toolbar. This should be considered a best practice. Application toolbars can be left behind due to an incomplete shutdown, which will then cause an error when your code tries to create them again the next time your application is run. Next, the add-in initializes any global variables. In this case we have two: a variable that holds the full path where the add-in is located and a variable that indicates when the add-in is in the process of shutting down.

As we mentioned in Chapter 3, you should use as few global variables as possible. When you do use them you must make sure they are in a known state at the beginning of every procedure where they might be accessed. Encapsulating this logic in an InitGlobals procedure that can be called wherever it's needed is a good way to manage this process.

After the add-in has performed these two basic tasks it checks to see if it can locate the user interface workbook. If the user interface workbook is located, execution continues. Otherwise, an error message is displayed and the application exits. This makes sense because there is nothing the add-in can do without the user interface workbook.

Build a Toolbar That Gives the User Access to Each Feature

Next the add-in builds its toolbar. We accomplish this with basic, hard-coded VBA command bar building techniques that should be familiar to all readers of this book. Therefore, we don't go into any detail on them. We cover more complex command bar building techniques in Chapter 8, "Advanced Command Bar Handling."

The add-in exposes four distinct features to the user through the application toolbar, as shown in Figure 5-4. Each of these features is discussed in the sections that follow.

FIGURE 5-4   The PETRAS application toolbar

Open and Initialize the Time Entry Workbook

After the command bars have been built, the add-in checks to see if the user interface workbook is open. If this workbook is not open the Auto_Open procedure opens it. If this workbook is already open the Auto_Open procedure activates it. The next step is to initializes the user interface workbook. During this process all the settings that were saved to the user interface worksheets by the WriteSettings procedure in Listing 5-3 are read and applied by the MakeWorksheetSettings procedure. This procedure is shown in Listing 5-6.

Listing 5-6   The MakeWorksheetSettings Procedure

```
Public Sub MakeWorksheetSettings(ByRef wkbBook As Workbook)

    Dim rngCell As Range
    Dim rngSettingList As Range
    Dim rngHideCols As Range
    Dim sTabName As String
    Dim vSetting As Variant
    Dim wksSheet As Worksheet

    Set rngSettingList = wksUISettings.Range(gsRNG_NAME_LIST)

    For Each wksSheet In wkbBook.Worksheets

        ' The worksheet must be unprotected and visible in order
        ' to make many of the settings. It will be protected and
        ' hidden again automatically by the settings code if it
        ' needs to be protected and/or hidden.
        wksSheet.Unprotect
        wksSheet.Visible = xlSheetVisible

        ' Hide any non-standard columns that need hiding.
        Set rngHideCols = Nothing
        On Error Resume Next
        Set rngHideCols = wksSheet.Range(gsRNG_SET_HIDE_COLS)
        On Error GoTo 0
        If Not rngHideCols Is Nothing Then
            rngHideCols.EntireColumn.Hidden = True
        End If

        For Each rngCell In rngSettingList
```

```
' Determine if the current worksheet requires the
' current setting.
vSetting = Empty
On Error Resume Next
If rngCell.Value = "setScrollArea" Then
     ' The scroll area setting must be treated
     ' differently because it's a range object.
     Set vSetting = Application.Evaluate( _
         "'" & wksSheet.Name & "'!" & rngCell.Value)
Else
     vSetting = Application.Evaluate( _
         "'" & wksSheet.Name & "'!" & rngCell.Value)
End If
On Error GoTo 0

If Not IsEmpty(vSetting) Then
    If rngCell.Value = "setProgRows" Then
        If vSetting > 0 Then
            wksSheet.Range("A1").Resize(vSetting) _
                .EntireRow.Hidden = True
        End If
    ElseIf rngCell.Value = "setProgCols" Then
        If vSetting > 0 Then
            wksSheet.Range("A1").Resize(, _
                vSetting).EntireColumn.Hidden = True
        End If
    ElseIf rngCell.Value = "setScrollArea" Then
        wksSheet.ScrollArea = vSetting.Address
    ElseIf rngCell.Value = "setEnableSelect" Then
        wksSheet.EnableSelection = vSetting
    ElseIf rngCell.Value = "setRowColHeaders" Then
        wksSheet.Activate
        Application.ActiveWindow _
            .DisplayHeadings = vSetting
    ElseIf rngCell.Value = "setVisible" Then
        wksSheet.Visible = vSetting
    ElseIf rngCell.Value = "setProtect" Then
        If vSetting Then
            wksSheet.Protect , True, True, True
        End If
    End If
End If

Next rngCell
```

```
Next wksSheet

' Leave the Time Entry worksheet active.
sTabName = sSheetTabName(wkbBook, gsSHEET_TIME_ENTRY)
wkbBook.Worksheets(sTabName).Activate

End Sub
```

The MakeWorksheetSettings procedure loops through all the work-sheets in the specified workbook and applies all the settings that we defined for each worksheet. We designed this procedure to accept a reference to a specific workbook object as an argument rather than having it assume it needs to operate on the user interface workbook because this design will allow us to generalize the application to handle multiple user interface workbooks if we need to at some time in the future. The settings table on which these settings were defined can be seen on the wksUISettings worksheet of the PetrasAddin.xla workbook.

After the user interface workbook has been initialized, the last thing we do is run a procedure that ensures all Excel application properties are set to their default values. This is the ResetAppProperties procedure shown in Listing 5-7.

Listing 5-7   The ResetAppProperties Procedure

```
Public Sub ResetAppProperties()
    Application.StatusBar = False
    Application.ScreenUpdating = True
    Application.DisplayAlerts = True
    Application.EnableEvents = True
    Application.EnableCancelKey = xlInterrupt
    Application.Cursor = xlDefault
End Sub
```

This procedure is useful because we can make whatever application settings we like during the code execution required for a feature, and as long as we call this procedure before we exit we know that all critical application properties will be left in known good states. If we didn't happen to use one of the properties reset by this procedure it doesn't matter. The values set by the ResetAppProperties procedure are the default values for each property. Therefore we aren't changing them if they weren't used.

Save a Copy of the Time Entry Workbook to a Predefined Consolidation Location

The first toolbar button saves a copy of the time entry workbook to a centralized consolidation location. The procedure that implements this feature is shown in Listing 5-8. From here, a procedure in the PETRAS Reporting Application consolidates the time entry workbooks from all of the consultants into a single report.

Listing 5-8   The PostTimeEntriesToNetwork Procedure

```
Public Sub PostTimeEntriesToNetwork()

    Dim sSheetTab As String
    Dim sWeekEndDate As String
    Dim sEmployee As String
    Dim sSaveName As String
    Dim sSavePath As String
    Dim wksSheet As Worksheet
    Dim wkbBook As Workbook
    Dim vFullName As Variant


    ' Don't do anything unless our time entry workbook is active
    ' wkbBook will return a reference to it if it is.
    If bIsTimeEntryBookActive(wkbBook) Then

        ' Make sure the TimeEntry worksheet does not have any
        ' data entry errors.
        sSheetTab = sSheetTabName(wkbBook, gsSHEET_TIME_ENTRY)
        Set wksSheet = wkbBook.Worksheets(sSheetTab)
        If wksSheet.Range(gsRNG_HAS_ERRORS).Value Then
            MsgBox gsERR_DATA_ENTRY, vbCritical, gsAPP_NAME
            Exit Sub
        End If

        ' Create a unique name for the time entry workbook.
        sWeekEndDate = Format$( _
                wksSheet.Range(gsRNG_WEEK_END_DATE).Value, _
                "YYYYMMDD")
        sEmployee = wksSheet.Range(gsRNG_EMPLOYEE_NAME).Value
        sSaveName = sWeekEndDate & " - " & sEmployee & ".xls"

        ' Check the registry to determine if we already have a
```

```
    ' consolidation path specified. If so, save the time
    ' entry workbook to that location. If not, prompt the
    ' user to identify a consolidation location, save that
    ' location to the registry and save the time entry
    ' workbook to that location.
    sSavePath = GetSetting(gsREG_APP, gsREG_SECTION, _
            gsREG_KEY, "")
    If Len(sSavePath) = 0 Then
        ' No path was stored in the registry. Prompt the
        ' user for one.
        vFullName = Application.GetOpenFilename( _
                Title:=gsCAPTION_SELECT_FOLDER)
        If vFullName <> False Then
            ' NOTE: The InStrRev function was not available
            ' in Excel 97.
            sSavePath = Left$(vFullName, _
                InStrRev(vFullName, "\"))
            SaveSetting gsREG_APP, gsREG_SECTION, _
                gsREG_KEY, sSavePath
        Else
            ' The user cancelled the dialog.
            MsgBox gsMSG_POST_FAIL, vbCritical, gsAPP_NAME
            Exit Sub
        End If
    End If

    wkbBook.SaveCopyAs sSavePath & sSaveName
    MsgBox gsMSG_POST_SUCCESS, vbInformation, gsAPP_NAME

Else
    MsgBox gsMSG_BOOK_NOT_ACTIVE, vbExclamation, gsAPP_NAME
End If

End Sub
```

This procedure shows the safety mechanism we use to prevent runtime errors from occurring if the user clicks one of our toolbar buttons without the user interface workbook being active. Prior to performing any action we verify that this workbook is active using the bIsTimeEntryBookActive() function. This function returns True if the time entry workbook is active and False if it is not. If the time entry workbook is active, the function also returns an object reference to the time entry workbook via its ByRef Workbook argument. If the time entry workbook is not active we display an error message to the user and exit.

Once we verify the time entry workbook is active we check the error flag in the hidden column on the time entry worksheet to determine if the time sheet has any data entry errors. If the flag indicates there are errors we display a message to the user and exit. If there are no data entry errors, the next task is to create a unique name for the workbook and look for our consolidation path in the registry. If the consolidation path has not yet been saved to the registry, we prompt the user to specify the path that should be used.

Finally, we use the SaveCopyAs method of the Workbook object to post a copy of the workbook to the central consolidation location. We then display a message to the user indicating that the process succeeded.

Allow the User to Add More Data Entry Rows to the Time Entry Worksheet

In the version of the time entry workbook demonstrated in Chapter 4, the number of data entry rows was fixed. In this version, the second toolbar button allows the user to add additional rows to the time entry table as needed. The procedure that implements this feature is shown in Listing 5-9.

Listing 5-9 The AddMoreRows Procedure

```
Public Sub AddMoreRows()

    Const lOFFSET_COLS As Long = 5
    Const lINPUT_COLS As Long = 6

    Dim rngInsert As Range
    Dim wkbBook As Workbook
    Dim wksSheet As Worksheet

    ' Don't do anything unless our time entry workbook is active
    If bIsTimeEntryBookActive(wkbBook) Then

        ' Get a reference to the TimeEntry worksheet and the
        ' insert row range on it. All new rows will be inserted
        ' above this range.
        Set wksSheet = wkbBook.Worksheets(sSheetTabName( _
                            wkbBook, gsSHEET_TIME_ENTRY))
        Set rngInsert = wksSheet.Range(gsRNG_INSERT_ROW)

        ' Add a new row to the time entry table.
        wksSheet.Unprotect
        wksSheet.ScrollArea = ""
        rngInsert.EntireRow.Insert
```

```
        rngInsert.Offset(-2, 0).EntireRow.Copy _
            Destination:=rngInsert.Offset(-1, 0)
        rngInsert.Offset(-1, lOFFSET_COLS) _
            .Resize(1, lINPUT_COLS).ClearContents
        wksSheet.ScrollArea = _
            wksSheet.Range(gsRNG_SET_SCROLL_AREA).Address
        wksSheet.Protect , True, True, True

    Else
        MsgBox gsMSG_BOOK_NOT_ACTIVE, vbExclamation, gsAPP_NAME
    End If

End Sub
```

In the AddMoreRows procedure we use the same method to determine if a time entry workbook is active as we used in the PostTimeEntriesToNetwork procedure. Once we've determined we have a valid workbook active, inserting a new row is a three-step process:

1. Insert a new row directly above the last row in the table. The last row in the table is marked by the gsRNG_INSERT_ROW defined name.
2. Copy the row above the newly inserted row and paste it onto the newly inserted row. This ensures all functions, formatting, and validation required to make the table operate and appear correctly are transferred to the newly inserted row.
3. The contents of the data entry area of the newly inserted row is cleared of any data that may have been transferred to the new row by the previous step. The new data entry row is now clean and ready to be used.

We remove the scroll area setting from the worksheet prior to inserting the new row and add it back after the new row has been inserted. If we didn't do this the worksheet scroll area would not adjust correctly as additional rows were inserted into the table.

Allow the User to Clear the Data Entry Area so the Time Sheet Can Be Reused

The third toolbar button, Clear Data Entries, simply clears the values from all of the data entry areas on the time sheet. The code to implement this feature was discussed in the "Using VBA to Dynamically Modify Your Worksheet User Interface" section earlier in the chapter, so we won't repeat it here.

Allow the User to Close the PETRAS Application

The fourth and last toolbar button simply closes the PETRAS application workbooks and removes its toolbar. The ExitApplication procedure that implements this feature is shown in Listing 5-10.

Listing 5-10 The ExitApplication Procedure

```
Public Sub ExitApplication()
    ShutdownApplication
End Sub
```

This is a one-line stub procedure that simply calls the ShutdownApplication procedure, which actually performs the tasks required to shut down the application. We place the shutdown logic in a separate procedure because it must be called from the ExitApplication procedure as well as from the Auto_Close procedure. These two procedures reflect the two ways the user could exit our application: selecting the Exit PETRAS toolbar button or using one of Excel's built-in exit features. The code for the ShutdownApplication procedure is shown in Listing 5-11.

Listing 5-11 The ShutdownApplication Procedure

```
Public Sub ShutdownApplication()

    ' Ignore any errors on application shutdown.
    On Error Resume Next

    ' This flag prevents this procedure from being called a
    ' second time by Auto_Close if it has already been called
    ' by the ExitApplication procedure.
    gbShutdownInProgress = True

    ' Delete command bar.
    Application.CommandBars(gsBAR_TOOLBAR).Delete

    ' Close the time entry workbook, allowing the user to
    ' save changes.
    Application.Workbooks(gsFILE_TIME_ENTRY).Close

    ' If there are no workbooks left open, quit Excel
    ' Otherwise just close this workbook.
    If lCountVisibleWorkbooks() = 0 Then
        ThisWorkbook.Saved = True
```

5. FUNCTION, GENERAL, AND APPLICATION-SPECIFIC ADD-INS

```
        Application.Quit
    Else
        ThisWorkbook.Close False
    End If

End Sub
```

The ShutdownApplication procedure is an example of a procedure where you want to ignore any errors that might occur during code execution. The application is closing down, so there isn't anything useful that could be done about any errors that did occur. Therefore, we tell VBA to ignore any errors in the procedure by using the On Error Resume Next statement. We cover this statement in detail in Chapter 15.

The first thing the ShutdownApplication procedure does is set a global flag variable that prevents it from being called twice if the user initiated shutdown by clicking the Exit PETRAS toolbar button. The process of closing the add-in workbook causes the Auto_Close procedure to fire. The Auto_Close procedure also calls ShutdownApplication, but it checks the value of the gbShutdownInProgress variable first and simply exits if shutdown is already in progress.

Next, the ShutdownApplication procedure deletes the application toolbar. It then closes the user's time entry workbook. If this workbook has not been saved, we allow Excel to prompt the user to save the workbook. Once the time entry workbook has been closed, we check to see if any other *visible* workbooks are open. If no visible workbooks are open then we can assume the user started Excel just to run our application and therefore we can close Excel. If there are still visible workbooks open we assume the user was working with Excel before opening our application and therefore we simply close our add-in and leave Excel open for the user to continue working with.

The *visible* workbooks distinction is important because many users have a hidden Personal.xls workbook or other utility workbook that is always open. We want to ignore these hidden workbooks when trying to determine whether we should close Excel or leave Excel open on exit. The procedure that counts the number of visible workbooks is shown in Listing 5-12.

Listing 5-12   The lCountVisibleWorkbooks Procedure

```
Public Function lCountVisibleWorkbooks() As Long
    Dim lCount As Long
    Dim wkbBook As Workbook
    For Each wkbBook In Application.Workbooks
        If wkbBook.Windows(1).Visible Then
```

```
        lCount = lCount + 1
      End If
   Next wkbBook
   lCountVisibleWorkbooks = lCount
End Function
```

Add a Custom Property to Allow the Consolidation Application to Locate All Instances of Our Time Entry Workbook

Once all employees have saved their time entry workbooks to the centralized consolidation location, the consolidation application needs to be able to definitively locate these workbooks. There may be other files located in the consolidation directory that the consolidation application needs to ignore. We solve this problem by adding a custom document property called PetrasTimesheet to our time entry workbook. This allows the consolidation application to uniquely identify any time entry workbooks created by our application.

To add a custom document property, activate the PetrasTemplate.xls workbook and choose *File > Properties* from the Excel menu. In the Properties dialog select the *Custom* tab. Enter PetrasTimesheet in the *Name* box, select Yes or no in the *Type* drop-down and choose the Yes option in the *Value* section. Click the Add button to add this property to the workbook. The result is shown in Figure 5-5.

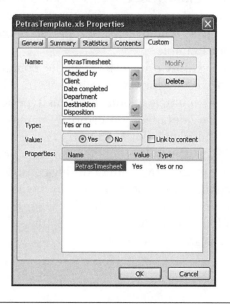

FIGURE 5-5   Adding the custom document property

Application Organization

We briefly cover the way in which the PETRAS add-in has been organized into code modules. The PetrasAddin.xla workbook is a simple, entirely procedural application at this point. It consists of six standard code modules whose names provide a reasonable indication of the type of code they contain. These modules are the following:

- **MEntryPoints**—This module contains the procedures called from the toolbar buttons of our toolbar. These procedures are entry points in the sense that they are the only way for the user to execute code in the application. The ClearDataEntryAreas procedure shown in Listing 5-4, the PostTimeEntriesToNetwork procedure shown in Listing 5-8, the AddMoreRows procedure shown in Listing 5-9, and the ExitApplication procedure shown in Listing 5-10 are all located in this module.
- **MGlobals**—This module contains the definitions of all public constants and variables used by our application as well as an InitGlobals procedure used to ensure our global variables are always properly initialized.
- **MOpenClose**—This module contains the code required to start up and shut down the application. The Auto_Open procedure shown in Listing 5-5 is located in this module.
- **MStandardCode**—This module contains standard code library procedures that are reused without modification in many different projects. The ResetAppProperties procedure shown in Listing 5-7 is one example.
- **MSystemCode**—This module contains core procedures written specifically for this application. In a larger application you would have multiple modules of this type, each of which would have a more detailed descriptive name—for example, MPrinting, MCalculation, or MExport.
- **MUtilities**—This module contains procedures designed solely for use by the programmer during construction and maintenance of the application. Procedures in this module will never be run by the end user, and in fact are hidden from the user by the Option Private Module directive. The WriteSettings procedure shown in Listing 5-3 is located in this module.

Summary

This chapter covered a complete list of stages all Excel applications go through. It described the various types of add-ins and the types of operations that each is required to perform. It demonstrated a table-driven method for maintaining and applying critical settings in a user interface workbook and demonstrated a simple example of an application-specific add-in application.

CHAPTER 6

DICTATOR APPLICATIONS

Dictator applications take control of the entire Excel session, modifying the Excel user interface to make it appear and behave like an independent Windows application. By doing this, dictator applications can leverage Excel's rich feature set while maintaining a high degree of control over the actions that can be performed by the end user. This chapter explains how to create a simple dictator application and provides a basic template from which you can build your own dictator applications. Subsequent chapters add more features to the basic application structure we present here.

Structure of a Dictator Application

As mentioned in Chapter 2, "Application Architectures," most dictator applications have the following logical structure:

- A startup routine to perform version and dependency checks as well as any other validation required to ensure the application can run successfully.
- A core set of procedures to
  - Take a snapshot of the Excel environment settings and to restore those settings.
  - Configure and lock down the Excel application.
  - Create and remove the application's command bars.
  - Handle copying and pasting data within the worksheet templates.
  - Provide a library of common helper routines and classes.
- A backdrop worksheet to display within the Excel window while UserForms are being shown, usually with some form of application-specific logo (if we're primarily using forms for the user interface)
- Multiple independent applets that provide the application's functionality

- Multiple template worksheets used by the applets, such as data entry forms or preformatted report templates

Each of these elements is discussed in more detail in the following sections in the order in which they occur within a typical dictator application. In the simplest dictator applications these elements are all contained within a single workbook, although spreading them across multiple workbooks can make maintenance easier when a team of developers works on a large application.

Startup and Shutdown

During startup, our dictator application must perform version checks and any other validation required to ensure the application can run properly. It must then store the current state of the user's Excel environment so that the state can be restored during shutdown. After this, our application builds its user interface. During shutdown, our application removes its user interface and restores Excel to its original state. In this section, we describe these activities in detail.

Version and Dependency Checks

All versions of Excel from 97 to 2003 share the same file format, so if our application requires a minimum Excel version, Excel 2000 in our case, we need to verify that our user hasn't just opened the application in Excel 97. The easiest way to do this is to check the value of the `Application.Version` property.

Each major release of Excel increments the version number, so Excel 2000 is version 9.0, Excel 2002 is version 10.0, Excel 2003 is version 11.0, and so on. In Listing 6-1 we verify that the user is running Excel 2000 or later. Because the `Application.Version` property returns a string, we use the VBA Val function to convert it into an unambiguously numeric value.

Listing 6-1 Checking the Excel Version

```
'Check that the version is at least Excel 2000
If Val(Application.Version) < 9 Then
    MsgBox "The PETRAS Reporting application " & _
           "requires Excel 2000 or later.", _
           vbOKOnly, gsAPP_TITLE

    ThisWorkbook.Close False
    Exit Sub
End If
```

Once we know we're running in an appropriate version of Excel we have to verify that the user installed any extra components we require, such as the Analysis Toolpak or Solver add-ins, or other applications that we're automating, such as Word or Outlook. For add-ins, we can either check the `Application.Addins` collection, or verify that the add-in workbook exists in the `Application.LibraryPath`. To check that other applications are installed, we can either look directly in the Registry (using API calls) or use CreateObject to try and create a new instance of the application and test for failure. This is covered in more detail in Chapter 22, "Controlling Other Office Applications."

Storing and Restoring Excel Settings

To take full control of the Excel session, dictator applications typically customize the interface to a high degree. This includes replacing the default toolbars, hiding the formula bar and changing numerous application settings. Unfortunately (and despite repeated requests to Microsoft), Excel assumes these changes are the user's choice of settings and should be preserved for the next session. There is no way to tell Excel these are temporary settings that should be used for this session only.

To solve this problem, we have to take a snapshot of the Excel settings when our application starts, store them somewhere, and reset them as part of our application shutdown processing. The easiest place to store the settings is on a worksheet in the add-in, in a plain text file located in the application folder, or in the registry. In the "Handling Crashes" section later in the chapter, we demonstrate how the user's settings can be recovered if the application crashes using a registry storage scenario.

The biggest problem with using the registry is that many companies implement security policies that block access to the registry. In that case, Excel won't be able to store any user settings, so it doesn't matter that we won't be able to store/restore them either. Listing 6-2 shows a typical procedure that stores the user's Excel settings during the startup processing of our application.

Listing 6-2 Storing Excel Settings in the Registry

```
Public Const gsREG_APP As String = "Company\Application"
Public Const gsREG_XL_ENV As String = "Excel Settings"

Sub StoreExcelSettings()

  Dim cbBar As CommandBar
```

```
Dim sBarNames As String
Dim objTemp As Object
Dim wkbTemp As Workbook

'Skip errors in case we can't use the Registry
On Error Resume Next

'Check if we've already stored the settings
'(so don't want to overwrite them)
If GetSetting(gsREG_APP, gsREG_XL_ENV, "Stored", "No") _
    = "No" Then

  'Some properties require a workbook open, so create one
  If ActiveWorkbook Is Nothing Then
    Set wkbTemp = Workbooks.Add
  End If

  'Indicate that the settings have been stored.
  'This key will be deleted in RestoreSettings.
  SaveSetting gsREG_APP, gsREG_XL_ENV, "Stored", "Yes"

  'Store the current Excel settings in the registry
  With Application
    SaveSetting gsREG_APP, gsREG_XL_ENV, _
        "DisplayStatusBar", CStr(.DisplayStatusBar)

    SaveSetting gsREG_APP, gsREG_XL_ENV, _
        "DisplayFormulaBar", CStr(.DisplayFormulaBar)

    'etc.

    'Which commandbars are visible
    For Each cbBar In .CommandBars
      If cbBar.Visible Then
        sBarNames = sBarNames & "," & cbBar.Name
      End If
    Next
    SaveSetting gsREG_APP, gsREG_XL_ENV, _
        "VisibleCommandBars", sBarNames
    SaveSetting gsREG_APP, gsREG_XL_ENV, _
        "ShowWindowsInTaskbar", _
        CStr(.ShowWindowsInTaskbar)

    'Special items for Excel 2002 and up
    If Val(.Version) >= 10 Then
```

```
      Set objTemp = .CommandBars
      SaveSetting gsREG_APP, gsREG_XL_ENV, _
          "DisableAskAQuestion", _
          CStr(objTemp.DisableAskAQuestionDropdown)

      SaveSetting gsREG_APP, gsREG_XL_ENV, _
          "AutoRecover", CStr(.AutoRecover.Enabled)
    End If
  End With

  'Close up the temporary workbook
  If Not wkbTemp Is Nothing Then wkbTemp.Close False
End If

End Sub
```

Listing 6-3 shows the corresponding procedure used to restore the user's settings. This should be called during the shutdown processing of our application.

Listing 6-3   Restoring Excel Settings During Shutdown

```
Sub RestoreExcelSettings()

  Dim vBarName As Variant
  Dim objTemp As Object

  'Restore the original Excel settings from the registry
  With Application

    'Check that we have some settings to restore
    If GetSetting(gsREG_APP, gsREG_XL_ENV, "Stored", "No") _
        = "Yes" Then

      .DisplayStatusBar = CBool(GetSetting(gsREG_APP, _
          gsREG_XL_ENV, "DisplayStatusBar", _
          CStr(.DisplayStatusBar)))

      .DisplayFormulaBar = CBool(GetSetting(gsREG_APP, _
          gsREG_XL_ENV, "DisplayFormulaBar", _
          CStr(.DisplayFormulaBar)))

      'etc.
```

```
'Show the correct toolbars
On Error Resume Next
For Each vBarName In Split(GetSetting(gsREG_APP, _
    gsREG_XL_ENV, "VisibleCommandBars"), ",")

  Application.CommandBars(vBarName).Visible = True
Next
On Error GoTo 0
.ShowWindowsInTaskbar = CBool(GetSetting(gsREG_APP, _
    gsREG_XL_ENV, "ShowWindowsInTaskbar", _
    CStr(.ShowWindowsInTaskbar)))

'Specific stuff for Excel 2002 and up
If Val(.Version) >= 10 Then
  Set objTemp = .CommandBars
  objTemp.DisableAskAQuestionDropdown = _
      CBool(GetSetting(gsREG_APP, gsREG_XL_ENV, _
      "DisableAskAQuestion", _
      CStr(objTemp.DisableAskAQuestionDropdown)))

  .AutoRecover.Enabled = CBool(GetSetting(gsREG_APP, _
      gsREG_XL_ENV, "AutoRecover", _
      CStr(.AutoRecover.Enabled)))
End If

'Once restored, delete all the registry entries
DeleteSetting gsREG_APP, gsREG_XL_ENV
  End If
End With

'Restore the Excel menus
RestoreMenus


End Sub
```

Note the use of the objTemp variable to store a generic reference to the CommandBars collection in both Listing 6-2 and Listing 6-3. Our application is designed to run in Excel 2000 and higher, but we need to store the status of the DisableAskAQuestionDropdown property. If we queried this property directly using the CommandBars collection, our code would no longer run in Excel 2000, where this property does not exist.

The objTemp variable hides the fact that we are referencing a nonexistent property from the Excel 2000 VBA compiler. As long as we never actually execute the line of code that reads the `DisableAskAQuestionDropdown` property under Excel 2000 there will be no problem having it there. We ensure this line of code is only executed in Excel 2002 and later by wrapping it in an `If...Then` block that first performs a version check.

Excel toolbar customizations are stored in a file with a .xlb extension, where the filename differs with each version of Excel. Each time a change is made to the toolbars, information about the change is added to the .xlb file. By their very nature, dictator applications usually make many changes to the toolbars, resulting in the .xlb file growing rapidly (though it can be reduced by creating the toolbars with the `temporary` parameter set to True). This slows Excel's startup processing and can eventually cause Excel to crash at startup. To avoid this, the best way to restore the user's toolbar configuration is to find and open the .xlb file just before the application closes. This hides toolbar changes from Excel and prevents it from attempting to modify the .xlb file. The RestoreMenus procedure to do this is shown in Listing 6-4.

Listing 6-4   Restoring Excel Toolbars During Shutdown

```
Public Const gsMENU_BAR As String = "PETRAS Menu Bar"

Sub RestoreMenus()

    Dim cbCommandBar As CommandBar
    Dim sPath As String
    Dim sToolbarFile As String
    Dim vBarName As Variant

    On Error Resume Next

    'Reopen the xlb toolbar customisation file
    '(if it exists), to avoid it growing in size
    sPath = Application.StartupPath

    'Work out the name of the correct toolbar file to open,
    'depending on the version of Excel
    If Val(Application.Version) = 9 Then
        sToolbarFile = Left$(sPath, InStrRev(sPath, "\")) & _
            "Excel.xlb"
    Else
```

```
    sToolbarFile = Left$(sPath, InStrRev(sPath, "\")) & _
        "Excel" & Val(Application.Version) & ".xlb"
End If


'If there is one, reopen the toolbar file
If Dir$(sToolbarFile) <> "" Then
  Workbooks.Open sToolbarFile, ReadOnly:=True
Else
  'If not, we have to tidy up ourselves

  'ReEnable all the toolbars
  For Each cbCommandBar In Application.CommandBars
    cbCommandBar.Enabled = True
  Next

  'Delete our Application's toolbar
  Application.CommandBars(gsMENU_BAR).Delete
End If


End Sub
```

Handling Crashes   It is an unfortunate fact of Excel application development that at some point Excel might crash while our application is being used. If/when that happens, our normal shutdown processing will not have the chance to run, so Excel will restart with the settings left by our application rather than the user's settings.

We can handle this by placing a copy of the `RestoreExcelSettings` procedure in a separate add-in that we distribute with our application. Our `StoreExcelSettings` procedure can be modified to copy this add-in to the `Application.StartupPath`, and our `RestoreExcelSettings` procedure can be modified to delete it. By doing this, we ensure the add-in will be left behind if Excel crashes and will be opened and run by Excel when it restarts, properly resetting the Excel environment.

Configuring the Excel Environment

Once we have taken the snapshot of the user's environment settings, we can modify the Excel environment to suit our application. These modifications can include

- Setting the application caption and icon
- Hiding the formula bar and status bar

- Setting calculation to manual (so recalculation will be under program control)
- Setting `Application.IgnoreRemoteRequests` = `True`, so double-clicking a workbook in Explorer opens a new instance of Excel instead of reusing our instance
- Switching off Windows in TaskBar, as we're likely to have multiple processing workbooks open that we don't want the user to be able to switch to
- Switching off the Ask a Question drop-down from the command bars
- Preventing the ability to customize the command bars
- Switching off auto-recover in Excel 2002 and later

Supporting a Debug Mode When developing and debugging our dictator application, we need a mechanism to allow us to access the VBE, hidden sheets, and so on and allow quick and easy switching between the Excel interface and our application interface, yet prevent users from doing the same. A simple method is to check for the existence of a specific file in a specific directory at startup and set a global `gbDebugMode` Boolean variable accordingly.

We can then configure the Excel environment differently for debug and production modes. In debug mode we keep all Excel shortcut keys active and set up an extra shortcut to switch back to the Excel user interface by calling the `RestoreExcelSettings` routine from Listing 6-3. In production mode we disable all Excel shortcut keys and ensure the VBE window is hidden. Listing 6-5 shows a typical procedure to configure the Excel environment for a dictator application. We recommend you test this procedure with the debug.ini file present.

Listing 6-5 Configuring the Excel Environment for a Dictator Application

```
Public gvaKeysToDisable As Variant
Public gbDebugMode As Boolean

Sub InitGlobals()

    gvaKeysToDisable = Array("^{F6}", "+^{F6}", "^{TAB}", _
        "+^{TAB}", "%{F11}", "%{F8}", "^W", "^{F4}", _
        "{F11}", "%{F1}", "+{F11}", "+%{F1}", "^{F5}", _
        "^{F9}", "^{F10}")

    'Use the existence of a debug file to set whether we're
    'in debug mode
```

```vba
  gbDebugMode = Dir(ThisWorkbook.Path & "\debug.ini") <> ""

End Sub


Sub ConfigureExcelEnvironment()

  Dim objTemp As Object
  Dim vKey As Variant

  With Application
    'Set the Application properties we want
    .Caption = gsAPP_TITLE
    .DisplayStatusBar = True
    .DisplayFormulaBar = False
    .Calculation = xlManual

    .DisplayAlerts = False
    .IgnoreRemoteRequests = True
    .DisplayAlerts = True

    .Iteration = True
    .MaxIterations = 100

    'Specific items for Excel 2000 and up
    If Val(.Version) >= 9 Then
      .ShowWindowsInTaskbar = False
    End If

    'Specific items for Excel 2002 and up
    If Val(.Version) >= 10 Then
      Set objTemp = .CommandBars
      objTemp.DisableAskAQuestionDropdown = True
      objTemp.DisableCustomize = True
      .AutoRecover.Enabled = False
    End If

    'We'll have slightly different environment states, _
    'depending on whether we're debugging or not
    If gbDebugMode Then
      'Since we have blitzed the environment, we should
      'set a hot key combination to restore it.
      'That key combination is Shift+Ctrl+R
      .OnKey "+^R", "RestoreExcelSettings"
```

```
   Else
      'Make sure the VBE isn't visible
      .VBE.MainWindow.Visible = False

      'Disable a whole host of shortcut keys
      For Each vKey In gvaKeysToDisable
         .OnKey vKey, ""
      Next
   End If
End With

End Sub
```

Note that the initial value of *every* persistent environment property changed in the configuration routine should be stored at startup and restored at shutdown, so any additional properties you need to change must be added to all three procedures. We're assuming the dictator application shuts down Excel when it closes, so there's no need to store and restore Excel settings that are not persistent, such as the application title.

Customizing the User Interface

In this section, we explain how to create a visually pleasing background for use in our dictator application when no documents are open. We then discuss the considerations surrounding the choice between a sheet-based and form-based user interface for our application.

Preparing a Backdrop Graphic

At this point, we have an empty, locked-down screen ready for us to add our application's user interface. The first UI element to add typically is some sort of background graphic to display as our application's desktop. The simplest version of this is to have a single worksheet contained in our application add-in that is copied to a new, visible workbook. The workbook is then maximized, has the appropriate worksheet display attributes set, and the display range is zoomed to fill the Excel window, as shown in Listing 6-6. The workbook windows can then be protected to remove the control box and minimize/maximize buttons.

Listing 6-6   Code to Prepare a Background Graphic Workbook

```
Public gwbkBackDrop As Workbook
Public Const gsBACKDROP_TITLE As String = "BackdropWkbk"

Sub PrepareBackDrop()

  Dim wkbBook As Workbook

  If Not WorkbookAlive(gwbkBackDrop) Then

    'See if there's already a backdrop workbook out there
    Set gwbkBackDrop = Nothing
    For Each wkbBook In Workbooks
      If wkbBook.BuiltinDocumentProperties("Title") = _
          gsBACKDROP_TITLE Then

        Set gwbkBackDrop = wkbBook
        Exit For
      End If
    Next

    If gwbkBackDrop Is Nothing Then
      'Copy the backdrop sheet out of this workbook
      'into a new one for display
      wksBackdrop.Copy
      Set gwbkBackDrop = ActiveWorkbook
      gwbkBackDrop.BuiltinDocumentProperties("Title") = _
          gsBACKDROP_TITLE
    End If
  End If

  With gwbkBackDrop
    .Activate

    'Select the full region that encompasses the backdrop
    'graphic, so we can use Zoom = True to size it to fit
    .Worksheets(1).Range("rgnBackDrop").Select

    'Set the Window View options to hide everything
    With .Windows(1)
      .WindowState = xlMaximized
      .Caption = ""
      .DisplayHorizontalScrollBar = False
```

```
      .DisplayVerticalScrollBar = False
      .DisplayHeadings = False
      .DisplayWorkbookTabs = False

      'Zoom the selected area to fit the screen
      .Zoom = True
   End With

   'Prevent selection or editing of any cells
   With .Worksheets(1)
      .Range("ptrCursor").Select
      .ScrollArea = .Range("ptrCursor").Address
      .EnableSelection = xlNoSelection
      .Protect DrawingObjects:=True, _
             UserInterfaceOnly:=True
   End With

   'Protect the backdrop workbook, to remove the
   'control menu
   .Protect Windows:=True
   .Saved = True
  End With
End Sub


'Function to test if a given workbook object variable
'points to a valid workbook
Function WorkbookAlive(wbkTest As Workbook) As Boolean

  On Error Resume Next

  If Not wbkTest Is Nothing Then
     WorkbookAlive = wbkTest.Sheets(1).Name <> ""
  End If

End Function
```

A more complex version contains multiple potential backdrop sheets, each designed for a specific screen resolution or window size. At runtime the appropriate sheet is selected based on the window's height or width.

Sheet-Based Versus Form-Based User Interfaces

There are two primary styles of user interface for dictator applications: those that use worksheets for the main data entry forms and those that use UserForms. Both styles can be combined with a custom menu structure, though it is slightly harder with a form-based user interface.

Worksheet-based user interfaces are similar to the application-specific add-ins discussed in Chapter 5, "Function, General, and Application-Specific Add-ins," and are designed to make maximum use of Excel's editing features, such as auto-complete, data validation, and conditional formatting. While the use of Excel's rich functionality is a compelling choice, you must take care to ensure the users do not accidentally destroy the data entry form. If you decide on a worksheet-based user interface, use worksheets for all your major data entry forms and reports; dialogs should only be used for minor tasks and wizards.

Form-based user interfaces are typically found in applications that use Excel primarily for its calculation and analysis features rather than the rich editing experience. The data entry forms tend to be much simpler than those in a worksheet-based user interface. This can be a benefit for both the user and the developer because the reduced functionality and tighter control that UserForms provide results in less chance for users to make mistakes and therefore a more robust solution. If you decide to use a form-based user interface, worksheets should only be used for reporting. Designing a form-based user interface is covered in detail in Chapter 13, "UserForm Design and Best Practices."

Trying to mix the two user interface styles rarely works well. It is simply too cumbersome to make worksheets behave like UserForms (such as tabbing between controls) and vice versa (such as auto-complete). When deciding which style to use, base the decision on where the user is likely to spend the majority of his time. Will the user be better served by the rich editing features of a worksheet or the tighter control of a UserForm?

Handling Cut, Copy, and Paste   The biggest issue with worksheet-based user interfaces is having to override Excel's default handling of cut, copy, paste, and drag-and-drop. As discussed in Chapter 4, "Worksheet Design," most of the editable cells in a data entry worksheet are given specific styles, data validation, and conditional formats. Unfortunately, Excel's default copy/paste behavior overwrites the formatting of the destination cell, and Excel's default cut behavior is to format the cell being cut with the Normal style, which is normally used for the worksheet background. Excel's drag-and-drop feature is the same as cut and paste and also destroys the data entry sheet if used. The only way to avoid this is to switch off drag-and-drop and code our own cut, copy, and paste replacement procedures, such as those shown in Listing 6-7.

Listing 6-7   Code to Handle Cut, Copy, and Paste for Data Entry Worksheets

```vba
Dim mbCut As Boolean
Dim mrngSource As Range

'Initialise cell copy-paste
Public Sub InitCutCopyPaste()

   'Hook all the cut, copy and paste keystrokes
   Application.OnKey "^X", "DoCut"
   Application.OnKey "^x", "DoCut"
   Application.OnKey "+{DEL}", "DoCut"

   Application.OnKey "^C", "DoCopy"
   Application.OnKey "^c", "DoCopy"
   Application.OnKey "^{INSERT}", "DoCopy"

   Application.OnKey "^V", "DoPaste"
   Application.OnKey "^v", "DoPaste"
   Application.OnKey "+{INSERT}", "DoPaste"

   Application.OnKey "{ENTER}", "DoPaste"
   Application.OnKey "~", "DoPaste"

   'Switch off drag/drop
   Application.CellDragAndDrop = False

End Sub

'Handle Cutting cells
Public Sub DoCut()

   If TypeOf Selection Is Range Then
      mbCut = True
      Set mrngSource = Selection
      Selection.Copy
   Else
      Set mrngSource = Nothing
      Selection.Cut
   End If

End Sub

'Handle Copying cells
Public Sub DoCopy()
```

```
    If TypeOf Selection Is Range Then
       mbCut = False
       Set mrngSource = Selection
    Else
       Set mrngSource = Nothing
    End If


    Selection.Copy
End Sub


'Handle pasting cells
Public Sub DoPaste()
    If Application.CutCopyMode And Not mrngSource Is Nothing Then
       Selection.PasteSpecial xlValues
       If mbCut Then
          mrngSource.ClearContents
       End If

       Application.CutCopyMode = False
    Else
       ActiveSheet.Paste
    End If
End Sub
```

Custom Command Bars

Most dictator applications include a set of menus and toolbars to provide access to the application's functionality. Dictator applications usually have complex menu structures, mixing built-in Excel menu items (such as Print and Print Preview) with custom menu items. The maintenance of these menu items can be made significantly easier by using a table-driven approach to building the command bars, as discussed in Chapter 8, "Advanced Command Bar Handling."

Processing and Analysis

Many dictator applications use Excel for its data processing, calculation, and analysis features, rather than its rich UI. All the processing should be performed using hidden sheets under program control, with only the results shown to the users. This allows us to design our processing sheets for maximum calculation efficiency without having to worry about whether they would be understood by users. This topic is covered in detail in Chapter 20, "Data Manipulation Techniques."

Presenting Results

Excel worksheets are excellent presentation vehicles for detailed reports and charts. Indeed, the requirement to use Excel for the application's reporting mechanism is often the main factor for choosing to create the application entirely in Excel. In practice, report styles and layouts are usually dictated by the client (to conform to a house style), but we explain how to get the most out of Excel's charting engine in Chapter 21, "Advanced Charting Techniques."

Practical Example

In Chapter 5, we introduced the client side of the PETRAS application with which our users enter their weekly timekeeping information and save the resulting workbook to a central location on the network. This chapter introduces the central consolidation, analysis, and reporting application, written as a simple, single-workbook dictator application.

PETRAS Reporting

In this version of the application, we're assuming the consolidation will be done weekly, once all the source time sheets have been received. The data will be extracted from each time sheet workbook and copied to a single table in a results workbook, from which we'll generate a single pivot table to provide rudimentary analysis capabilities. The results workbook can then be saved, and we will also allow previous results workbooks to be opened so the consolidation can be repeated (for example, if a time sheet arrives late). Later chapters add many more features to the application. The application can be found on the CD in the folder *\Application\Ch06 – Dictator Applications* and includes the following files:

- **PetrasTemplate.xls**—The client data entry template, unchanged from Chapter 5
- **PetrasAddin.xla**—The client data entry support add-in, unchanged from Chapter 5
- **PetrasReporting.xla**—The main reporting application
- **PetrasConsolidation.xlt**—A template results workbook, containing a destination area for time sheet data and a preformatted pivot table that references this area
- **Debug.ini**—A dummy file that tells the application to run in debug mode

The main reporting workbook, PetrasReporting.xla, contains the following items:

- **MGlobals**—Contains the declarations of our global constants and variables
- **MOpenClose**—Contains the startup and shutdown code, including code similar to Listing 6-1 to check the Excel version
- **MWorkspace**—Contains the code to store, configure, and restore the Excel environment, very similar to Listing 6-2, Listing 6-3, Listing 6-5, and Listing 6-6
- **MCommandbars**—Contains code to create and destroy our menus, including code like Listing 6-4 to restore them
- **MEntryPoints**—Contains the procedures called by our menus
- **MStandardCode**—Contains the WorkbookAlive function shown in Listing 6-6, a function to check whether a given file has a specific custom document property (as explained in the "Identifying Workbooks" section later in the chapter), and will contain more common utility routines as they're added throughout the book
- **MSystemCode**—Contains code specific to this application, including a routine to enable/disable some of our menu items and the main routine to perform the data consolidation
- **wksBackDrop**—The worksheet used for the background graphic

The example application uses the code shown in Listing 6-8 to set up the menu structure item-by-item. It is a lengthy procedure for only eight menu items. Fortunately, it will be replaced by a table-driven command bar builder in Chapter 8, allowing us to implement a much more comprehensive menu structure without adding new code for every item.

Listing 6-8   Code to Set Up the Menu Structure

```
Sub SetUpMenus()

    Dim cbCommandBar As CommandBar
    Dim oPopup As CommandBarPopup
    Dim oButton As CommandBarButton

    ' Hide all the toolbars
    On Error Resume Next
    For Each cbCommandBar In Application.CommandBars
        cbCommandBar.Visible = False
        cbCommandBar.Enabled = False
    Next
```

```vb
Application.CommandBars(gsMENU_BAR).Delete
On Error GoTo 0

'Create our menu bar
Set cbCommandBar = Application.CommandBars.Add( _
                 gsMENU_BAR, , True, True)

'The File menu
Set oPopup = cbCommandBar.Controls.Add(msoControlPopup)
With oPopup
    .Caption = "&File"

    'File > New
    Set oButton = .Controls.Add(msoControlButton)
    With oButton
        .Caption = "&New Consolidation..."
        .BeginGroup = True
        .FaceId = 18
        .ShortcutText = "Ctrl+N"
        .OnAction = "MenuFileNew"
        Application.OnKey "^N", "MenuFileNew"
        Application.OnKey "^n", "MenuFileNew"
    End With

    'File > Open
    Set oButton = .Controls.Add(msoControlButton)
    With oButton
        .Caption = "&Open..."
        .BeginGroup = False
        .FaceId = 23
        .ShortcutText = "Ctrl+O"
        .OnAction = "MenuFileOpen"
        Application.OnKey "^O", "MenuFileOpen"
        Application.OnKey "^o", "MenuFileOpen"
    End With

    'File > Close
    Set oButton = .Controls.Add(msoControlButton)
    With oButton
        .Caption = "&Close"
        .BeginGroup = False
        .FaceId = 106
        .OnAction = "MenuFileClose"
        .Enabled = False
    End With
```

```
        'File > Save
        'Use the standard Save button
        Set oButton = .Controls.Add(msoControlButton, 3)
        With oButton
             .BeginGroup = True
             .Enabled = False
        End With

        'File > Save As
        'Use the standard Save As button
        Set oButton = .Controls.Add(msoControlButton, 748)
        With oButton
             .BeginGroup = False
             .Enabled = False
        End With

        'File > Exit
        Set oButton = .Controls.Add(msoControlButton)
        With oButton
             .Caption = "&Exit"
             .BeginGroup = True
             .OnAction = "MenuFileExit"
        End With
End With

'The Processing menu
Set oPopup = cbCommandBar.Controls.Add(msoControlPopup)
With oPopup
     .Caption = "&Processing"

        'Processing > Consolidate
        Set oButton = .Controls.Add(msoControlButton)
        With oButton
             .Caption = "&Consolidate Timesheets"
             .BeginGroup = True
             .OnAction = "MenuConsolidate"
             .Enabled = False
        End With
End With

'The Help menu
Set oPopup = cbCommandBar.Controls.Add(msoControlPopup)
With oPopup
     .Caption = "&Help"
```

```
     'Help > About
     Set oButton = .Controls.Add(msoControlButton)
     With oButton
         .Caption = "&About PETRAS Reporting"
         .BeginGroup = True
         .OnAction = "MenuHelpAbout"
     End With
End With

cbCommandBar.Visible = True

'Protect the commandbars, to prevent customisation
Application.CommandBars("Toolbar List").Enabled = False

End Sub
```

Identifying Workbooks

Dictator applications often need to identify whether a particular workbook was created from a particular template or otherwise "belongs" to the application. One way to do this without needing to open the workbook first is to add a custom document property to the template file, as shown in Figure 6-1.

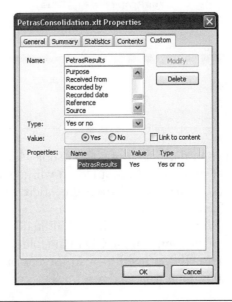

FIGURE 6-1 An identifying custom document property in a template

The dictator application can then test whether a workbook has that property using the function shown in Listing 6-9. In our example application we added the PetrasTimesheet property to the data entry template and the PetrasResults property to the consolidation results template.

Listing 6-9   Using DSOFile.dll to Check for a Custom Document Property

```
'Function to test whether a file has the given Yes/No property.
Function FileHasYesProperty(ByVal sFile As String, _
        ByVal sProperty As String) As Boolean

    Dim objDSO As DSOFile.OleDocumentProperties
    Dim objProperty As DSOFile.CustomProperty

    ' Use DSOFile to get the document properties for the
    ' specified file.
    Set objDSO = New DSOFile.OleDocumentProperties
    objDSO.Open sFile

    ' Iterate the custom document properties collection and return
    ' True if there is a Yes/No property with the specified name.
    For Each objProperty In objDSO.CustomProperties
        If (objProperty.Name = sProperty) _
            And (objProperty.Type = dsoPropertyTypeBool) Then
                FileHasYesProperty = True
                Exit For
        End If
    Next objProperty

    objDSO.Close

End Function
```

This function makes use of a COM object called DSOFile.dll to read the document properties from a closed workbook. The latest version of this DLL can be downloaded from the Microsoft Web site at http://support.microsoft.com/kb/224351.

The current version of the DSOFile.dll installation file as of this writing can also be found on the CD in the folder \Application\Ch06 – Dictator Applications. If you need to read the custom document properties from Office 2007 files, you and your users need to install the Office 2007

Compatibility Pack, which can be found at http://office.microsoft.com/en-us/products/HA101686761033.aspx.

Once you have DSOFile.dll installed and registered, a new reference will be available under the VBE *Tools > References* menu called DSO OLE Document Properties Reader 2.1, as shown in Figure 6-2. You must select this reference to use the features of DSOFile.dll.

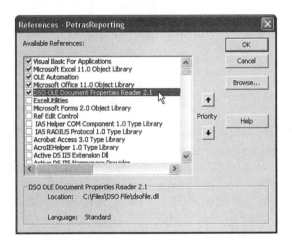

FIGURE 6-2   Reference to the DSO OLE Document Properties Reader 2.1

Using the PETRAS Reporting Application

In Chapter 5, we explained how to use the PETRAS time sheet add-in and template to create weekly time sheet workbooks and store them in a central location. The following steps can be used to consolidate and analyze your time sheets using the PETRAS Reporting dictator application:

1. Start Excel and use *File > Open* to open the PetrasReporting.xla workbook.
2. Select the *File > New Consolidation* menu as shown in Figure 6-3. This creates a new, empty consolidation workbook, and then displays a standard file open dialog.
3. Select the time sheet workbooks to include in the consolidation by multiselecting the individual files (or using Ctrl+A to select all the files in a folder) and click OK to begin the consolidation. The application extracts the time sheet data from all the selected workbooks and imports it into the consolidation workbook.
4. Review the consolidated data in the SourceData worksheet and analyze the data in the PivotTable worksheet.

6. DICTATOR APPLICATIONS

FIGURE 6-3 The PETRAS reporting application menu structure

Summary

Dictator applications allow us to leverage Excel's rich user interface, calculation engine, and analysis and presentation features while simulating the look and feel of an independent Windows program.

The Excel workspace typically requires a significant amount of configuration and customization for a dictator application. Unfortunately, Excel remembers most of these changes and tries to reuse them for the next (user) session. To work around this behavior, we must store the initial state of the user's settings when our application starts and restore them when our application shuts down.

When using a worksheet-based user interface, extreme care must be taken to prevent accidental corruption of the sheet, often as a result of a cut, copy, or paste operation.

The practical example for this chapter is a complete but simple dictator application template that you can use as a starting point for your own applications. Later chapters in this book add many more features to the application.

CHAPTER 7

USING CLASS MODULES TO CREATE OBJECTS

Class modules are used to create objects. There are many reasons for you as a developer to create your own objects, including the following:

- To encapsulate VBA and Windows API code to make it transportable and easy to use and reuse, as shown in Chapter 12, "Understanding and Using Windows API Calls"
- To trap events
- To raise events
- To create your own objects and object models

In this chapter, we assume you are already familiar with writing VBA code to manipulate the objects in Excel and are familiar with the Excel object model that defines the relationships among those objects. We also assume you are familiar with object properties, methods, and events. If you have written code in the ThisWorkbook module, any of the modules behind worksheets or charts, or the module associated with a UserForm, you have already worked with class modules. One of the key features of these modules, like all class modules, is the ability to trap and respond to events.

The goal of this chapter is to show you how to create your own objects. We begin by explaining how to create a single custom object and then show how you can create a collection containing multiple instances of the object. We continue with a demonstration of how to trap and raise events within your classes.

Creating Objects

Say we want to develop code to analyze a single cell in a worksheet and categorize the entry in that cell as one of the following:

- Empty
- Containing a label
- Containing a constant numeric value
- Containing a formula

This can be readily accomplished by creating a new object with the appropriate properties and methods. Our new object will be a Cell object. It will have an Analyze method that determines the cell type and sets the CellType property to a numeric value that can be used in our code. We will also have a DescriptiveCellType property so we can display the cell type as text.

Listing 7-1 shows the CCell class module code. This class module is used to create a custom Cell object representing the specified cell, analyze the contents of the cell, and return the type of the cell as a user-friendly text string.

Listing 7-1 The CCell Class Module

```
Option Explicit

Public Enum anlCellType
    anlCellTypeEmpty
    anlCellTypeLabel
    anlCellTypeConstant
    anlCellTypeFormula
End Enum

Private muCellType As anlCellType
Private mrngCell As Excel.Range

Property Set Cell(ByRef rngCell As Excel.Range)
    Set mrngCell = rngCell
End Property

Property Get Cell() As Excel.Range
    Set Cell = mrngCell
End Property

Property Get CellType() As anlCellType
```

```
        CellType = muCellType
End Property

Property Get DescriptiveCellType() As String
    Select Case muCellType
        Case anlCellTypeEmpty
            DescriptiveCellType = "Empty"
        Case anlCellTypeFormula
            DescriptiveCellType = "Formula"
        Case anlCellTypeConstant
            DescriptiveCellType = "Constant"
        Case anlCellTypeLabel
            DescriptiveCellType = "Label"
    End Select
End Property

Public Sub Analyze()
    If IsEmpty(mrngCell) Then
        muCellType = anlCellTypeEmpty
    ElseIf mrngCell.HasFormula Then
        muCellType = anlCellTypeFormula
    ElseIf IsNumeric(mrngCell.Formula) Then
        muCellType = anlCellTypeConstant
    Else
        muCellType = anlCellTypeLabel
    End If
End Sub
```

The CCell class module contains a public enumeration with four members, each of which represents a cell type. By default, the enumeration members are assigned values from zero to three. The enumeration member names help make our code more readable and easier to maintain. The enumeration member values are translated into user-friendly text by the DescriptiveCellType property.

NOTE The VBA `IsNumeric` function used in Listing 7-1 considers a label entry such as 123 to be numeric. `IsNumeric` also considers a number entered into a cell formatted as Text to be a number. As both these cell types can be referenced as numeric values in formulas, this has been taken to be the correct result. If you prefer to consider these cells as label entries you can use `WorksheetFunction.IsNumber` instead of `IsNumeric`.

Listing 7-2 shows the AnalyzeActiveCell procedure. This procedure is contained in the standard module MEntryPoints.

Listing 7-2   The AnalyzeActiveCell Procedure

```
Public Sub AnalyzeActiveCell()

    Dim clsCell As CCell

    ' Create new instance of Cell object
    Set clsCell = New CCell

    ' Determine cell type and display it
    Set clsCell.Cell = Application.ActiveCell
    clsCell.Analyze
    MsgBox clsCell.DescriptiveCellType

End Sub
```

If you select a cell on a worksheet and run the AnalyzeActiveCell procedure it creates a new instance of the CCell class that it stores in the clsCell object variable. The procedure then assigns the active cell to the Cell property of this Cell object, executes its Analyze method, and displays the result of its DescriptiveCellType property. This code is contained in the Analysis1.xls workbook in the *\Concepts\Ch07 – Using Class Modules to Create Objects* folder on the CD that accompanies this book.

Class Module Structure

A class module can be thought of as a template for an object. It defines the methods and properties of the object. Any public subroutines or functions in the class module become methods of the object, and any public variables or property procedures become properties of the object. You can use the class module to create as many instances of the object as you require.

Property Procedures

Rather than rely on public variables to define properties it is better practice to use property procedures. These give you more control over how properties are assigned values and how they return values. Property procedures allow you to validate the data passed to the object and to perform related actions where appropriate. They also enable you to make properties read-only or write-only if you want.

The CCell class uses two private module-level variables to store its properties internally. muCellType holds the cell type in the form of an `anlCellType` enumeration member value. mrngCell holds a reference to the single-cell Range that an object created from the CCell class will represent.

Property procedures control the interface between these variables and the outside world. Property procedures come in three forms:

- **Property Let**—Used to assign a simple value to a property
- **Property Set**—Used to assign an object reference to a property
- **Property Get**—Used to return the simple value or object reference held by a property to the outside world

The property name presented to the outside world is the same as the name of the property procedure. The CCell class uses `Property Set Cell` to allow you to assign a Range reference to the Cell property of the Cell object. The property procedure stores the reference in the mrngCell variable. This procedure could have a validation check to ensure that only single-cell ranges can be specified. There is a corresponding `Property Get Cell` procedure that allows this property to be read.

The CCell class uses two `Property Get` procedures to return the cell type as an enumeration member value or as descriptive text. These properties are read-only because they have no corresponding `Property Let` procedures.

Methods

The CCell class has one method defined by the Analyze subroutine. It determines the type of data in the cell referred to by the mrngCell variable and assigns the corresponding enumeration member to the muCellType variable. Because it is a subroutine, the Analyze method doesn't return a value to the outside world. If a method is created as a function it can return a value. The Analyze method could be converted to a function that returned the text value associated with the cell type as shown in Listing 7-3.

Listing 7-3   The Analyze Method of the Cell Object

```
Public Function Analyze() As String

    If IsEmpty(mrngCell) Then
        muCellType = anlCellTypeEmpty
    ElseIf mrngCell.HasFormula Then
        muCellType = anlCellTypeFormula
    ElseIf IsNumeric(mrngCell.Formula) Then
        muCellType = anlCellTypeConstant
    Else
        muCellType = anlCellTypeLabel
    End If

    Analyze = Me.DescriptiveCellType

End Function
```

You could then analyze the cell and display the return value with the following single line of code instead of the original two lines:

```
MsgBox clsCell.Analyze()
```

Creating a Collection

Now that we have a Cell object we want to create many instances of the object so we can analyze a worksheet or ranges of cells within a worksheet. The easiest way to manage these new objects is to store them in a collection. VBA provides a Collection object that you can use to store objects and data. The Collection object has four methods:

- Add
- Count
- Item
- Remove

There is no restriction on the type of data that can be stored within a Collection object, and items with different data types can be stored in the same Collection object. In our case, we want to be consistent and store just Cell objects in our collection.

To create a new Collection, the first step is to add a new standard module to contain global variables. This module will be called MGlobals. Next, add the following variable declaration to the MGlobals module to declare a global Collection object variable to hold the collection, as follows:

```
Public gcolCells As Collection
```

Now add the CreateCellsCollection procedure shown in Listing 7-4 to the MEntryPoints module. The modified code is contained in the Analysis2.xls workbook in the \Concepts\Ch07 – Using Class Modules to Create Objects folder on the CD that accompanies this book.

Listing 7-4 Creating a Collection of Cell Objects

```
Public Sub CreateCellsCollection()

    Dim clsCell As CCell
    Dim rngCell As Range

    ' Create new Cells collection
    Set gcolCells = New Collection

    ' Create Cell objects for each cell in Selection
    For Each rngCell In Application.Selection
        Set clsCell = New CCell
        Set clsCell.Cell = rngCell
        clsCell.Analyze
        'Add the Cell to the collection
        gcolCells.Add Item:=clsCell, Key:=rngCell.Address
    Next rngCell

    ' Display the number of Cell objects stored
    MsgBox "Number of cells stored: " & CStr(gcolCells.Count)

End Sub
```

We declare gcolCells as a public object variable so that it persists for as long as the workbook is open and is visible to all procedures in the VBA project. The CreateCellsCollection procedure creates a new instance of the collection and loops through the currently selected cells, creating a new instance of the Cell object for each cell and adding it to the collection. The address of each cell, in $A$1 reference style, is used as a key to uniquely identify it and to provide a way of accessing the Cell object later.

We can loop through the objects in the collection using a `For...Each` loop or we can access individual Cell objects by their position in the collection or by using the key value. Because the `Item` method is the default method for the collection, we can use code like the following to access a specific Cell object:

```
Set clsCell = gcolCells(3)
Set clsCell = gcolCells("$A$3")
```

Creating a Collection Object

The collection we have established is easy to use, but it lacks some features we would like to have. As it stands, there is no control over the type of objects that can be added to the collection. We would also like to add a method to the collection that enables us to highlight cells of the same type and another method to remove the highlights.

We first add two new methods to the CCell class module. The Highlight method adds color to the Cell object according to the CellType. The UnHighlight method removes the color. The new code is shown in Listing 7-5.

Note that we are applying the principle of encapsulation. All the code that relates to the Cell object is contained in the CCell class module, not in any other module. Doing this ensures that the code can be easily found and maintained and means that it can be easily transported from one project to another.

Listing 7-5   New Code for the CCell Class Module

```
Public Sub Highlight()
  Cell.Interior.ColorIndex = Choose(muCellType + 1, 5, 6, 7, 8)
End Sub

Public Sub UnHighlight()
  Cell.Interior.ColorIndex = xlNone
End Sub
```

We can now create a new class module named CCells to contain the Cells collection, as shown in Listing 7-6. The complete code is contained in the Analysis3.xls workbook in the *Concepts\Ch07 – Using Class Modules to Create Objects* folder on the CD that accompanies this book.

Listing 7-6   The CCells ClassModule

```
Option Explicit

Private mcolCells As Collection

Property Get Count() As Long
    Count = mcolCells.Count
End Property

Property Get Item(ByVal vID As Variant) As CCell
    Set Item = mcolCells(vID)
End Property

Private Sub Class_Initialize()
    Set mcolCells = New Collection
End Sub

Public Sub Add(ByRef rngCell As Range)
    Dim clsCell As CCell
    Set clsCell = New CCell
    Set clsCell.Cell = rngCell
    clsCell.Analyze
    mcolCells.Add Item:=clsCell, Key:=rngCell.Address
End Sub

Public Sub Highlight(ByVal uCellType As anlCellType)
    Dim clsCell As CCell
    For Each clsCell In mcolCells
        If clsCell.CellType = uCellType Then
            clsCell.Highlight
        End If
    Next clsCell
End Sub

Public Sub UnHighlight(ByVal uCellType As anlCellType)
    Dim clsCell As CCell
    For Each clsCell In mcolCells
        If clsCell.CellType = uCellType Then
            clsCell.UnHighlight
        End If
    Next clsCell
End Sub
```

The mcolCells Collection object variable is declared as a private, module-level variable and is instantiated in the Initialize procedure of the class module. Since the Collection object is now hidden from the outside world, we need to write our own Add method for it. We also have created Item and Count property procedures to emulate the corresponding properties of the collection. The input argument for the Item property is declared as a Variant data type because it can be either a numeric index or the string key that identifies the collection member.

The Highlight method loops through each member of the collection. If the CellType property of the Cell object is the same as the type specified by the uCellType argument, we execute the Cell object's Highlight method. The UnHighlight method loops through the collection and executes the UnHighlight method of all Cell objects whose type is the same as the type specified by the uCellType argument.

We modified the public Collection variable declaration in MGlobals to refer to our new custom collection class as shown here:

```
Public gclsCells As CCells
```

We also modified the CreateCellsCollection procedure in the MEntryPoints module to instantiate and populate our custom collection, as shown in Listing 7-7.

Listing 7-7   MEntryPoints Code to Create a Cells Object Collection

```
Public Sub CreateCellsCollection()

    Dim clsCell As CCell
    Dim lIndex As Long
    Dim lCount As Long
    Dim rngCell As Range

    Set gclsCells = New CCells

    For Each rngCell In Application.ActiveSheet.UsedRange
        gclsCells.Add rngCell
    Next rngCell

    ' Count the number of formula cells in the collection.
    For lIndex = 1 To gclsCells.Count
        If gclsCells.Item(lIndex).CellType = anlCellTypeFormula Then
            lCount = lCount + 1
        End If
```

```
Next lIndex

MsgBox "Number of Formulas = " & CStr(lCount)

End Sub
```

We declare gclsCells as a public object variable to contain our custom Cells collection object. The CreateCellsCollection procedure instantiates gclsCells and uses a For...Each loop to add all the cells in the active worksheet's used range to the collection. After loading the collection, the procedure counts the number of cells that contain formulas and displays the result.

The MEntryPoints module contains a ShowFormulas procedure that can be executed to highlight and unhighlight the formula cells in the worksheet. Several additional variations are provided for other cell types.

This code illustrates two shortcomings of our custom collection class. You can't process the members of the collection in a For...Each loop. You must use an index and the Item property instead. Also, our collection has no default property, so you can't shortcut the Item property using the standard collection syntax gclsCells(1) to access a member of the collection. You must specify the Item property explicitly in your code. We explain how to solve these problems using Visual Basic 6 or just a text editor in the next section.

Addressing Class Collection Shortcomings

It is possible to make your custom collection class behave like a built-in collection. It requires nothing more than a text editor to make the adjustments, but first we'll explain how to do it by setting procedure attributes using Visual Basic 6 (VB6) to better illustrate the nature of the changes required.

Using Visual Basic 6

In VB6, unlike Visual Basic for Applications used in Excel, you can specify a property to be the default property of the class. If you declare the Item property to be the default property, you can omit .Item when referencing a member of the collection and use a shortcut such as gclsCells(1) instead.

If you have VB6 installed you can export the code module CCells to a file and open that file in VB6. Place your cursor anywhere within the Item property procedure and select *Tools > Procedure Attributes* from the menu to display the Procedure Attributes dialog. Next, click the *Advanced >>* button and under the Advanced options select (Default) from the *Procedure ID* combo box. This makes the Item property the default property for the class.

When you save your changes and import this file back into your Excel VBA project, the attribute will be recognized even though there is no way to set attribute options within the Excel Visual Basic Editor. VB6 also allows you to set up the special procedure shown in Listing 7-8.

Listing 7-8   Code to Allow the Collection to Be Referenced in a For...Each Loop

```
Public Function NewEnum() As IUnknown
    Set NewEnum = mcolCells.[_NewEnum]
End Function
```

This procedure must be given an attribute value of 4, which you enter directly into the *Procedure ID* combo box in the Procedure Attributes dialog. Giving the `NewEnum` procedure this attribute value enables a `For...Each` loop to process the members of the collection. Once you have made this addition to your class module in VB6 and saved your changes, you can load the module back into your Excel VBA project, and once again the changes will be recognized.

Using a Text Editor

Even without VB6 you can easily create these procedures and their attributes using a text editor such as NotePad. Export the CCells class module to a file and open it using the text editor. Modify your code to look like the example shown in Listing 7-9.

Listing 7-9   Viewing the Code in a Text Editor

```
Property Get Item(ByVal vID As Variant) As CCell
Attribute Item.VB_UserMemId = 0
    Set Item = mcolCells(vID)
End Property

Public Function NewEnum() As IUnknown
Attribute NewEnum.VB_UserMemId = -4
    Set NewEnum = mcolCells.[_NewEnum]
End Function
```

When the modified class module is imported back into your project the Attribute lines will not be visible, but the procedures will work as expected. You can now refer to a member of the collection as gclsCells(1) and use your custom collection class in a `For...Each` loop as shown in Listing 7-10.

Listing 7-10   Referencing the Cells Collection in a For...Each Loop

```
For Each clsCell In gclsCells
    If clsCell.CellType = anlCellTypeFormula Then
        lCount = lCount + 1
    End If
Next clsCell
```

Trapping Events

A powerful capability built into class modules is the ability to respond to events. We want to extend our Analysis application so that when you double-click a cell that has been analyzed it will change color to indicate the cell type. When you right-click the cell the color will be removed. We also want to ensure that cells are reanalyzed when they are changed so that our corresponding Cell objects are kept up-to-date. The code shown in this section is contained in the Analysis4.xls workbook in the *\Concepts\Ch07 – Using Class Modules to Create Objects* folder on the CD that accompanies this book. To trap the events associated with an object you need to do two things:

- Declare a WithEvents variable of the correct object type in a class module.
- Assign an object reference to the variable.

For the purpose of this example we confine ourselves to trapping events associated with a single Worksheet object. You could easily substitute this with a Workbook object if you wanted the code to apply to all the worksheets in a workbook. We need to create a WithEvents object variable in the CCells class module that references the worksheet containing the Cell objects. This WithEvents variable declaration is made at the module level within the CCells class and looks like the following:

```
Private WithEvents mwksWorkSheet As Excel.Worksheet
```

As soon as you add this variable declaration to the CCells class module you can select the WithEvents variable name from the drop-down menu at the top left of the module and use the drop-down menu at the top right of the module to see the events that can be trapped, as shown in Figure 7-1.

Event names listed in bold are currently being trapped within the class, as we see in a moment.

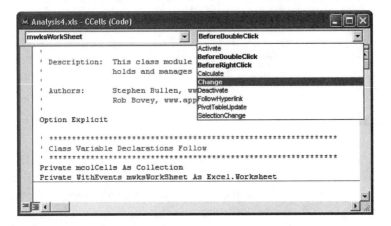

FIGURE 7-1 The Worksheet event procedures available in CCells

Selecting an event from the drop-down creates a shell for the event procedure in the module. You need to add the procedures shown in Listing 7-11 to the CCells class module. They include a new property named Worksheet that refers to the Worksheet object containing the Cell objects held by the collection, as well as the code for the BeforeDoubleClick, BeforeRightClick, and Change events.

Listing 7-11 Additions to the CCells Class Module

```
Property Set Worksheet(wks As Excel.Worksheet)
    Set mwksWorkSheet = wks
End Property



Private Sub mwksWorkSheet_BeforeDoubleClick( _
            ByVal Target As Range, Cancel As Boolean)
    If Not Application.Intersect(Target, _
            mwksWorkSheet.UsedRange) Is Nothing Then
        Highlight mcolCells(Target.Address).CellType
        Cancel = True
    End If
End Sub
```

```
Private Sub mwksWorkSheet_BeforeRightClick( _
        ByVal Target As Range, Cancel As Boolean)
    If Not Application.Intersect(Target, _
        mwksWorkSheet.UsedRange) Is Nothing Then
        UnHighlight mcolCells(Target.Address).CellType
        Cancel = True
    End If
End Sub

Private Sub mwksWorkSheet_Change(ByVal Target As Range)
    Dim rngCell As Range
    If Not Application.Intersect(Target, _
        mwksWorkSheet.UsedRange) Is Nothing Then
        For Each rngCell In Target.Cells
            mcolCells(rngCell.Address).Analyze
        Next rngCell
    End If
End Sub
```

The CreateCellsCollection procedure in the MEntryPoints module needs to be changed as shown in Listing 7-12. The new code assigns a reference to the active worksheet to the Worksheet property of the Cells object so the worksheet's events can be trapped.

Listing 7-12 The Updated CreateCellsCollection Procedure in the MEntryPoints Module

```
Public Sub CreateCellsCollection()

    Dim clsCell As CCell
    Dim rngCell As Range

    Set gclsCells = New CCells
    Set gclsCells.Worksheet = ActiveSheet

    For Each rngCell In ActiveSheet.UsedRange
        gclsCells.Add rngCell
    Next rngCell

End Sub
```

You can now execute the CreateCellsCollection procedure in the MEntryPoints module to create a new collection with all the links in place to trap the BeforeDoubleClick and BeforeRightClick events for the cells in the worksheet. Double-clicking a cell changes the cell's background to a color that depends on the cell's type. Right-clicking a cell removes the background color.

Raising Events

Another powerful capability of class modules is the ability to raise events. You can define your own events and trigger them in your code. Other class modules can trap those events and respond to them. To illustrate this we change the way our Cells collection tells the Cell objects it contains to execute their Highlight and UnHighlight methods. The Cells collection raises an event that will be trapped by the Cell objects. The code shown in this section is contained in the Analysis5.xls workbook in the \Concepts\Ch07 – Using Class Modules to Create Objects folder on the CD that accompanies this book. To raise an event in a class module you need two things.

- An Event declaration at the top of the class module
- A line of code that uses RaiseEvent to cause the event to take place

The code changes shown in Listing 7-13 should be made in the CCells class module.

Listing 7-13   Changes to the CCells Class Module to Raise an Event

```
Option Explicit

Public Enum anlCellType
    anlCellTypeEmpty
    anlCellTypeLabel
    anlCellTypeConstant
    anlCellTypeFormula
End Enum

Private mcolCells As Collection
Private WithEvents mwksWorkSheet As Excel.Worksheet

Event ChangeColor(uCellType As anlCellType, bColorOn As Boolean)

Public Sub Add(ByRef rngCell As Range)
    Dim clsCell As CCell
```

```
    Set clsCell = New CCell
    Set clsCell.Cell = rngCell
    Set clsCell.Parent = Me
    clsCell.Analyze
    mcolCells.Add Item:=clsCell, Key:=rngCell.Address
End Sub


Private Sub mwksWorkSheet_BeforeDoubleClick( _
        ByVal Target As Range, Cancel As Boolean)
    If Not Application.Intersect(Target, _
        mwksWorkSheet.UsedRange) Is Nothing Then
      RaiseEvent ChangeColor( _
          mcolCells(Target.Address).CellType, True)
      Cancel = True
    End If
End Sub


Private Sub mwksWorkSheet_BeforeRightClick( _
        ByVal Target As Range, Cancel As Boolean)
    If Not Application.Intersect(Target, _
        mwksWorkSheet.UsedRange) Is Nothing Then
      RaiseEvent ChangeColor( _
          mcolCells(Target.Address).CellType, False)
      Cancel = True
    End If
End Sub
```

Note that we moved the `anlCellType` Enum declaration into the parent collection class module. Now that we have created an explicit parent-child relationship between the CCells and CCell classes, any public types used by both classes must reside in the parent class module or circular dependencies between the classes that cannot be handled by VBA will be created.

In the declarations section of the CCells module, we declare an event named ChangeColor that has two arguments. The first argument defines the cell type to be changed, and the second argument is a Boolean value to indicate whether we are turning color on or off. The BeforeDoubleClick and BeforeRightClick event procedures have been changed to raise the new event and pass the cell type of the target cell and the on or off value. The Add method has been updated to set a new Parent property of the Cell object. This property holds a reference to the Cells object. The name reflects the relationship between the Cells object as the parent object and the Cell object as the child object.

Trapping the event raised by the Cells object in another class module is carried out in exactly the same way we trapped other events. We create a WithEvents object variable and set it to reference an instance of the class that defines and raises the event. The changes shown in Listing 7-14 should be made to the CCell class module.

Listing 7-14 Changes to the CCell Class Module to Trap the ChangeColor Event

```
Option Explicit

Private muCellType As anlCellType
Private mrngCell As Excel.Range
Private WithEvents mclsParent As CCells

Property Set Parent(ByRef clsCells As CCells)
    Set mclsParent = clsCells
End Property

Private Sub mclsParent_ChangeColor(uCellType As anlCellType, _
                                   bColorOn As Boolean)
    If Me.CellType = uCellType Then
        If bColorOn Then
            Highlight
        Else
            UnHighlight
        End If
    End If
End Sub
```

A new module-level object variable mclsParent is declared WithEvents as an instance of the CCells class. A reference to a Cells object is assigned to mclsParent in the Parent Property Set procedure. When the Cells object raises the ChangeColor event, all the Cell objects will trap it. The Cell objects take action in response to the event if they are of the correct cell type.

A Family Relationship Problem

Unfortunately, we introduced a problem in our application. Running the CreateCellsCollection procedure multiple times creates a memory leak. Normally when you overwrite an object in VBA, VBA cleans up the old version of the object and reclaims the memory that was used to hold it. You can also set an object equal to Nothing to reclaim the memory used by it. It is good practice to do this explicitly when you no longer need an object, rather than relying on VBA to do it.

```
Set gclsCells = Nothing
```

When you create two objects that store references to each other, the system will no longer reclaim the memory they used when they are set to new versions or when they are set to Nothing. When analyzing the worksheet in Analysis5.xls with 574 cells in the used range, there is a loss of about 250KB of RAM each time CreateCellsCollection is executed during an Excel session.

NOTE   If you are running Windows NT, 2000, XP, or Vista you can check the amount of RAM currently used by Excel by pressing Ctrl+Shift+Esc to display the Processes window in Task Manager and examining the memory usage column for the row where the Image Name column is EXCEL.EXE.

One way to avoid this problem is to make sure you remove the cross-references from the linked objects before the objects are removed. You can do this by adding a method such as the Terminate method shown in Listing 7-15 to the problem classes, in our case the CCell class.

Listing 7-15   The Terminate Method in the CCell Class Module

```
Public Sub Terminate()
    Set mclsParent = Nothing
End Sub
```

The code in Listing 7-16 is added to the CCells class module. It calls the Terminate method of each Cell class contained in the collection to destroy the cross-reference between the classes.

Listing 7-16   The Terminate Method in the CCells Class Module

```
Public Sub Terminate()
    Dim clsCell As CCell
    For Each clsCell In mcolCells
```

```
        clsCell.Terminate
        Set clsCell = Nothing
    Next clsCell
    Set mcolCells = Nothing
End Sub
```

The code in Listing 7-17 is added to the CreateCellsCollection procedure in the MEntryPoints module.

Listing 7-17   The CreateCellsCollection Procedure in the MEntryPoints Module

```
Public Sub CreateCellsCollection()
    Dim clsCell As CCell
    Dim rngCell As Range

    ' Remove any existing instance of the Cells collection
    If Not gclsCells Is Nothing Then
        gclsCells.Terminate
        Set gclsCells = Nothing
    End If

    Set gclsCells = New CCells
    Set gclsCells.Worksheet = ActiveSheet

    For Each rngCell In ActiveSheet.UsedRange
        gclsCells.Add rngCell
    Next rngCell

End Sub
```

If CreateCellsCollection finds an existing instance of gclsCells it executes the object's Terminate method before setting the object to Nothing. The gclsCells Terminate method iterates through all the objects in the collection and executes their Terminate methods.

In a more complex object model with more levels you could have objects in the middle of the structure that contain both child and parent references. The Terminate method in these objects would need to run the Terminate method of each of its children and then set its own Parent property to Nothing.

Creating a Trigger Class

Instead of raising the ChangeColor event in the CCells class module we can set up a new class module to trigger this event. Creating a trigger class gives us the opportunity to introduce a more efficient way to highlight our Cell objects. We can create four instances of the trigger class, one for each cell type, and assign the appropriate instance to each Cell object. That means each Cell object is only sent a message that is meant for it, rather than hearing all messages sent to all Cell objects.

The trigger class also enables us to eliminate the Parent/Child relationship between our CCells and CCell classes, thus removing the requirement to manage cross-references. Note that it is not always possible or desirable to do this. The code shown in this section is contained in the Analysis6.xls workbook in the *Concepts\Ch07 – Using Class Modules to Create Objects* folder on the CD that accompanies this book.

Listing 7-18 shows the code in a new CTypeTrigger class module. The code declares the ChangeColor event, which now only needs one argument to specify whether color is turned on or off. The class has Highlight and UnHighlight methods to raise the event.

Listing 7-18   The CTypeTrigger Class Module

```
Option Explicit

Public Event ChangeColor(bColorOn As Boolean)

Public Sub Highlight()
    RaiseEvent ChangeColor(True)
End Sub

Public Sub UnHighlight()
    RaiseEvent ChangeColor(False)
End Sub
```

Listing 7-19 contains the changes to the CCell class module to trap the ChangeColor event raised in CTypeTrigger. Depending on the value of bColorOn, the event procedure runs the Highlight or UnHighlight methods.

Listing 7-19 Changes to the CCell Class Module to Trap the ChangeColor Event of CTypeTrigger

```
Option Explicit

Private muCellType As anlCellType
Private mrngCell As Excel.Range
Private WithEvents mclsTypeTrigger As CTypeTrigger

Property Set TypeTrigger(clsTrigger As CTypeTrigger)
    Set mclsTypeTrigger = clsTrigger
End Property

Private Sub mclsTypeTrigger_ChangeColor(bColorOn As Boolean)
    If bColorOn Then
        Highlight
    Else
        UnHighlight
    End If
End Sub
```

Listing 7-20 contains the changes to the CCells module. An array variable maclsTriggers is declared to hold the instances of CTypeTrigger. The Initialize event redimensions maclsTriggers to match the number of cell types and the `For...Each` loop assigns instances of CTypeTrigger to the array elements. The Add method assigns the correct element of maclsTriggers to each Cell object according to its cell type. The result is that each Cell object listens only for messages that apply to its own cell type.

Listing 7-20 Changes to the CCells Class Module to Assign References to CTypeTrigger to Cell Objects

```
Option Explicit

Public Enum anlCellType
    anlCellTypeEmpty
    anlCellTypeLabel
    anlCellTypeConstant
    anlCellTypeFormula
End Enum

Private mcolCells As Collection
```

```vba
Private WithEvents mwksWorkSheet As Excel.Worksheet
Private maclsTriggers() As CTypeTrigger

Private Sub Class_Initialize()
    Dim uCellType As anlCellType
    Set mcolCells = New Collection
    ' Initialise the array of cell type triggers,
    ' one element for each of our cell types.
    ReDim maclsTriggers(anlCellTypeEmpty To anlCellTypeFormula)
    For uCellType = anlCellTypeEmpty To anlCellTypeFormula
        Set maclsTriggers(uCellType) = New CTypeTrigger
    Next uCellType
End Sub

Public Sub Add(ByRef rngCell As Range)
    Dim clsCell As CCell
    Set clsCell = New CCell
    Set clsCell.Cell = rngCell
    clsCell.Analyze
    Set clsCell.TypeTrigger = maclsTriggers(clsCell.CellType)
    mcolCells.Add Item:=clsCell, Key:=rngCell.Address
End Sub

Public Sub Highlight(ByVal uCellType As anlCellType)
    maclsTriggers(uCellType).Highlight
End Sub

Public Sub UnHighlight(ByVal uCellType As anlCellType)
    maclsTriggers(uCellType).UnHighlight
End Sub

Private Sub mwksWorkSheet_BeforeDoubleClick( _
            ByVal Target As Range, Cancel As Boolean)
    If Not Application.Intersect(Target, _
            mwksWorkSheet.UsedRange) Is Nothing Then
        Highlight mcolCells(Target.Address).CellType
        Cancel = True
    End If
End Sub

Private Sub mwksWorkSheet_BeforeRightClick( _
            ByVal Target As Range, Cancel As Boolean)
    If Not Application.Intersect(Target, _
            mwksWorkSheet.UsedRange) Is Nothing Then
```

```
            UnHighlight mcolCells(Target.Address).CellType
            Cancel = True
        End If
    End Sub


Private Sub mwksWorkSheet_Change(ByVal Target As Range)

    Dim rngCell As Range
    Dim clsCell As CCell

    If Not Application.Intersect(Target, _
            mwksWorkSheet.UsedRange) Is Nothing Then
        For Each rngCell In Target.Cells
            Set clsCell = mcolCells(rngCell.Address)
            clsCell.Analyze
            Set clsCell.TypeTrigger = _
                maclsTriggers(clsCell.CellType)
        Next rngCell
    End If

End Sub
```

Practical Example

We illustrate the use of class modules in our PETRAS example applications by providing both the Time Sheet and Reporting applications with Excel application-level event handlers.

PETRAS Time Sheet

The addition of an application-level event handling class to our PETRAS time sheet application will make two significant changes. First, it will allow us to convert the time entry workbook into an Excel template. This will simplify creation of new time entry workbooks for new purposes as well as allow multiple time entry workbooks to be open at the same time. Second, the event handler will automatically detect whether a time entry workbook is active and enable or disable our toolbar buttons accordingly. Table 7-1 summarizes the changes made to the PETRAS time sheet application for this chapter.

Table 7-1   Changes to PETRAS Time Sheet Application for Chapter 7

Module	Procedure	Change
PetrasTemplate.xlt		Changes the normal workbook into a template workbook
CAppEventHandler		Adds an application-level event handling class to the add-in
MEntryPoints	NewTimeSheet	New procedure to create time sheets from the template workbook
MopenClose	Auto_Open	Removes time sheet initialization logic and delegates it to the event handling class
MsystemCode		Moves all time entry workbook management code into the event handling class

The Template

When a template workbook is added using VBA, a new, unsaved copy of the template workbook is opened. To create a template workbook from a normal workbook, choose *File > Save As* from the Excel menu and select the Template entry from the *Save as type* drop-down. As soon as you select the Template option Excel unhelpfully modifies the directory where you are saving your workbook to the Office Templates directory, so don't forget to change this to the location where you are storing your application files.

Once we begin using a template workbook, the user has complete control over the workbook filename. We can determine whether a given workbook belongs to us by checking for the unique named constant "setIsTimeSheet" that we added to our template workbook for this purpose.

A template workbook combined with an application-level event handler allows us to support multiple instances of the time entry workbook being open simultaneously. This might be needed, for example, if there is a requirement to have a separate time sheet for each client or project.

Moving to a template user interface workbook also requires that we give the user a way to create new time sheet workbooks, since it is no longer a simple matter of opening and reusing the same fixed time sheet workbook over and over. In Figure 7-2, note the new toolbar button labeled *New Time Sheet*. This button allows the user to create new instances of our template.

FIGURE 7-2   The PETRAS toolbar with the New Time Sheet button

As shown in Listing 7-21, the code run by this new button is simple.

Listing 7-21   The NewTimeSheet Procedure

```
Public Sub NewTimeSheet()
    Application.ScreenUpdating = False
    InitGlobals
    Application.Workbooks.Add gsAppDir & gsFILE_TIME_ENTRY
    Application.ScreenUpdating = True
End Sub
```

We turn off screen updating and call InitGlobals to ensure that our global variables are properly initialized. We then simply add a new workbook based on the template workbook and turn screen updating back on. Rather than opening PetrasTemplate.xlt, a new copy of PetrasTemplate.xlt, called PetrasTemplate1 is created. Each time the user clicks the New Time Sheet button she gets a completely new, independent copy of PetrasTemplate.xlt.

The act of creating a new copy of the template triggers the NewWorkbook event in our event handing class. This event performs all the necessary actions to initialize the template. This event procedure is shown in the next section.

The Application-Level Event Handler

Within our application-level event handling class we encapsulate many of the tasks previously accomplished by procedures in standard modules. For example, the MakeWorksheetSettings procedure and the bIsTimeEntryBookActive function that we encountered in Chapter 5, "Function, General, and Application-Specific Add-ins," are now both private procedures of the class.

We describe the layout of the class module and then explain what the pieces do, rather than showing all the code here. You can examine the code yourself in the PetrasAddin.xla workbook of the sample application for this chapter on the CD and are strongly encouraged to do so.

Module-Level Variables

Private WithEvents mxlApp As Excel.Application

Class Event Procedures

Class_Initialize
Class_Terminate
mxlApp_NewWorkbook
mxlApp_WorkbookOpen
mxlApp_WindowActivate
mxlApp_WindowDeactivate

Class Method Procedures

SetInitialStatus

Class Private Procedures

EnableDisableToolbar
MakeWorksheetSettings
bIsTimeEntryBookActive
bIsTimeEntryWorkbook

Because the variable that holds a reference to the instance of the CAppEventHandler class that we use in our application is a public variable, we use the InitGlobals procedure to manage it. The code required to do this is shown in two locations.

In the declarations section of the MGlobals module:

```
Public gclsEventHandler As CAppEventHandler
```

In the InitGlobals procedure:

```
' Instantiate the Application event handler
If gclsEventHandler Is Nothing Then
    Set gclsEventHandler = New CAppEventHandler
End If
```

The InitGlobals code checks to see whether the public gclsEventHandler variable is initialized and initializes it if it isn't.

InitGlobals is called at the beginning of every non-trivial entry point procedure in our application, so if anything causes our class variable to lose state, it will be instantiated again as soon as the next entry point procedure is called. This is a good safety mechanism.

When the public gclsEventHandler variable is initialized, it causes the Class_Initialize event procedure to execute. Inside this event procedure we initialize the event handling mechanism by setting the class module-level WithEvents variable to refer to the current instance of the Excel Application, as follows:

```
Set mxlApp = Excel.Application
```

Similarly, when our application is exiting and we destroy our gclsEventHandler variable, it causes the Class_Terminate event procedure to execute. Within this event procedure we destroy the class reference to the Excel Application object by setting the mxlApp variable to Nothing.

All the rest of the class event procedures, which are those belonging to the mxlApp WithEvents variable, serve the same purpose. They "watch" the Excel environment and enable or disable our toolbar buttons as appropriate when conditions change.

Disabling toolbar buttons when they can't be used is a much better user interface technique than displaying an error message when the user clicks one under the wrong circumstances. You don't want to punish users (that is, display an error message in response to an action) when they can't be expected to know they've done something wrong. Note that we always leave the *New Time Sheet* and *Exit PETRAS* toolbar buttons enabled. Users should always be able to create a new time sheet or exit the application.

In addition to enabling and disabling the toolbar buttons, the mxlApp_NewWorkbook and mxlApp_WorkbookOpen event procedures detect when a time entry workbook is being created or opened for the first time, respectively. At this point they run the private MakeWorksheetSettings procedure to initialize that time entry workbook. All the mxlApp event procedures are shown in Listing 7-22. As you can see, the individual procedures are simple, but the cumulative effect is powerful.

Listing 7-22   The mxlApp Event Procedures

```
Private Sub mxlApp_NewWorkbook(ByVal Wb As Workbook)
    If bIsTimeEntryWorkbook(Wb) Then
        EnableDisableToolbar True
        MakeWorksheetSettings Wb
```

```
    Else
        EnableDisableToolbar False
    End If
End Sub

Private Sub mxlApp_WorkbookOpen(ByVal Wb As Excel.Workbook)
    If bIsTimeEntryWorkbook(Wb) Then
        EnableDisableToolbar True
        MakeWorksheetSettings Wb
    Else
        EnableDisableToolbar False
    End If
End Sub

Private Sub mxlApp_WindowActivate(ByVal Wb As Workbook, _
                                  ByVal Wn As Window)
    ' When a window is activated, check to see if it belongs
    ' to one of our workbooks. Enable all our toolbar controls
    ' if it does.
    EnableDisableToolbar bIsTimeEntryBookActive()
End Sub

Private Sub mxlApp_WindowDeactivate(ByVal Wb As Workbook, _
                                    ByVal Wn As Window)
    ' When a window is deactivated, disable our toolbar
    ' controls by default. They will be re-enables by the
    ' WindowActivate event procedure if required.
    EnableDisableToolbar False
End Sub
```

The full power of having an event handling class in your application is difficult to convey on paper. We urge you to experiment with the sample application for this chapter to see for yourself how it works in a live setting. Double-click the PetrasAddin.xla file to open Excel and see how the application toolbar behaves. Create new time sheet workbooks, open non-time sheet workbooks, and switch back and forth between them. The state of the toolbar will follow your every action.

It is also educational to see exactly how much preparation the application does when you create a new instance of the time sheet workbook. Without the PetrasAddin.xla running, open the PetrasTemplate.xlt workbook and compare how it looks and behaves in its raw state with the way it looks and behaves as an instance of the time sheet within the running application.

PETRAS Reporting

By adding a class module to handle application-level events to the PETRAS Reporting application, we can allow the user to have multiple consolidation workbooks open at the same time and switch between them using the new Window menu, as shown in Figure 7-3.

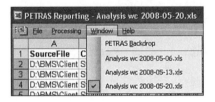

FIGURE 7-3   The PETRAS Reporting menu bar with the new Window menu

Table 7-2 summarizes the changes made to the PETRAS time sheet application for this chapter. Rather than repeat much of the previous few pages, we suggest you review the PetrasReporting.xla workbook to see exactly how the multiple-document interface has been implemented.

Table 7-2   Changes to PETRAS Reporting Application for Chapter 7

Module	Procedure	Change
CAppEventHandler		Adds an application-level event handling class to the application to manage multiple consolidation workbooks.
MCommandBars	SetUpMenus	Adds code to create the Window menu.
MSystemCode		Adds procedures to add, remove, and place a tick mark against an item in the Window menu.
MEntryPoints	MenuWindowSelect	New procedure to handle selecting an item within the Window menu. All Window menu items call this routine.

Summary

You use class modules to create objects and their associated methods, properties, and events. You can collect child objects in a parent object so that you can create a hierarchy of objects to form an object model. You can use class modules to trap the events raised by other objects including the Excel application. You can also define and raise your own events in a class module.

When you set up cross-references between parent and child objects so that each is aware of the other you create a structure that is not simple to remove from memory when it is no longer useful. You need to add extra code to remove these cross-references.

Class modules are a powerful addition to a developer's toolkit. The objects created lead to code that is easier to write, develop, maintain, and share than traditional code. Objects are easy to use because they encapsulate complex code in a form that is accessible. All you need to know to use an object are its methods, properties, and events. Objects can be shared because the class modules that define them are encapsulated (self-contained) and therefore transportable from one project to another. All you need to do is copy the class module to make the object available in another project.

As a developer you can easily add new methods, properties, and events to an object without changing the existing interface. Your objects can evolve without harming older systems that use them. Most developers find class modules addictive. The more you use them, the more you like them and the more uses you find for them. They are used extensively throughout the rest of this book.

CHAPTER 8

ADVANCED COMMAND BAR HANDLING

In this chapter, we start off by covering some best practices for command bar design. Next we introduce our table-driven command bar building methodology. This feature, which you can easily add to your own applications, removes most of the difficulties associated with building and maintaining non-trivial custom command bars. We show you how to create and use custom icon/mask file combinations in Excel 2002 and higher (a feature also supported by the command bar builder). We then finish up by explaining how to hook CommandBarControl events to intercept clicks from CommandBarControls in ways that are not possible using a simple OnAction macro assignment.

NOTE Whenever we use the noun **control** in this chapter we are referring to the generic CommandBarControl object. This noun is used whenever the topic we are currently discussing applies equally to any of the specific control objects that can be represented by a generic CommandBarControl.

Beginning with Office 2007, Microsoft began implementing a new XML-based Ribbon user interface that is completely different from the command bar-based user interface used from Office 97 until Office 2003. We say began, because as of Office 2007, significant parts of the Office user interface still use the command bars model. The plan, however, is for Office to migrate entirely to the new Ribbon UI in future versions. The new Ribbon user interface is covered in Chapter 10, "The Office 2007 Ribbon User Interface."

Command Bar Design

Before we get into command bar creation, let's cover a few best practices for command bar design. Try to follow all these practices when designing your custom command bars and controls.

- Emulate Excel's menu bar. Users are already familiar with the Excel menu structure, so if your application emulates it users will have some immediate familiarity with your application. This is especially true for dictator applications, whose menus may include many of the same features that would normally appear on Excel's menu bar.

- Don't use more than three menu sublevels. Although the table-driven command bar builder that we describe in the next section provides a means to create menus deeper than three levels, this is not something you should do unless absolutely necessary. Users tend to get lost when your menu structure exceeds three sublevels.

- If you are adding one or more top-level menus to the built-in menu bar, those menus should be located directly to the left of the Window menu. This is a longstanding user interface convention that most users are familiar with.

- Unless you have a very good reason for not doing so, always dock your custom toolbars at the top of the Excel window. There are a reasonable number of situations where it is appropriate to create floating toolbars, but remember that your users can always undock your toolbar if they want. Even less frequently, but still on occasion, it is useful to dock a toolbar at the bottom of the Excel window. Right and left docking, even though the command bar builder supports them, are never recommended. We have never seen a situation where these positions are appropriate. The vast majority of users have never encountered a toolbar docked on the right or left sides, and the necessity of doing so is almost always an indication of poor user interface design.

- Physically group controls that perform related functions. Your application will be much easier to use if similar controls are located near each other.

- Separate related groups of controls from each other using separator bars, and try not to have more than four our five menus or toolbar buttons in a row without a separator. Separator bars are created using the BeginGroup property, which we cover in the next section.

- Select or create icons whose appearance visually implies the action performed by their control. This seems obvious, but it's difficult in a custom application with a large number of features. Put as much thought and creativity into the appearance of your icons as possible. Features whose icons bear no visual resemblance to their function are much harder for users to remember than those whose icons clearly imply their function. Think, for example, how easy it is to determine which toolbar button you need to click to print a document. Do your best to emulate this close association between function and appearance.

Table-Driven Command Bars

For small-scale Excel applications with a few toolbar buttons and/or menu items it is perfectly acceptable to hard-code the creation of command bars and controls in a custom VBA procedure. We do recommend you isolate command bar building code in a separate procedure for ease of maintenance. Once you begin building large-scale applications with multiple dedicated toolbars and menus, hard-coded command bars become very time consuming to create and difficult to maintain.

The solution to this problem is a widely used technique within the Excel development community known as **table-driven** command bar building. As we discussed in Chapter 4, "Worksheet Design," table-driven is a generic term referring to any process that performs some operation guided by information stored in a dedicated table on a worksheet.

Table-driven command bar building is one of the more complex table-driven methodologies. Implemented correctly, however, it is easy to use and far superior to anything that can be accomplished using VBA alone. Even when we resort to using Visual Basic ActiveX DLLs, a technique we cover in Chapter 23, "Excel and Visual Basic 6," we use an Excel add-in workbook with a three-line stub procedure assigned to each of the command bar controls that calls the ActiveX DLL. This add-in workbook allows us to use worksheets, which would otherwise be unavailable, to implement table-driven command bars and other table-driven methodologies.

In this section, we describe the most sophisticated table-driven command bar builder available. As with all other applications described in the book, this command bar builder is included on the CD and can be integrated into any of your applications.

Introducing the Table-Driven Command Bar Builder

The table-driven command bar builder consists of three parts that form a self-contained unit you can plug directly into any application: a worksheet table that defines the command bars and controls to be built and two code modules that read this table and build the command bars and controls it specifies.

To use the command bar builder in your application you need to copy the wksCommandBars worksheet and the MCommandBars and MPastePicture modules into your project. In the "Putting It All Together" section later in the chapter we demonstrate the workbook containing the version of the command bar builder that you should use in your projects.

Once you have added definitions of the command bars and controls you want to build into the wksCommandBars worksheet, your application simply needs to call one procedure on startup and all those command bars and controls will be built to your specifications. A second procedure can be called on shutdown to dismantle the command bars and controls specified in the table. We cover this in more detail in the "Practical Example" section at the end of the chapter.

We spend most of this section explaining how to write command bar definitions in the command bar definition table. It's best to think of the code that reads and implements the command bars and controls defined by the table as a black box. This code is too lengthy and complex to cover in any detail in this chapter, but you are strongly encouraged to examine the code if you want to understand how it works. The code is open and heavily commented, so it should be reasonably approachable to the seasoned programmer.

The Command Bar Definition Table

The reason we are spending so much time describing the command bar definition table is because you will spend 99% of your command bar building time working with it. The only thing you need to do with the code, after adding it to your project, is call the build command bars procedure on startup and the reset command bars procedure on shutdown.

The command bar definition table is too wide to display entirely in a screen shot on the printed page, but we give you a taste of what it looks like with the partial example shown in Figure 8-1.

	A	B	C	D	E	F
1	Command Bar Name	Control Caption	Control Caption	Control Caption	Position	IsMenubar
2	Custom Menu Bar				1	TRUE
3		&File				
4			&New			
5			&Open			
6			&Close			
7			&Save			
8			Save &As			
9			Print Pre&view			
10			&Print...			
11			E&xit			
12		&Edit				
13			&Copy			
14			&Paste			
15			Paste &Special...			
16		&Custom				
17			Sample Submenus &1			
18				Sub Item &1		
19				Sub Item &2		
20				Sub Item &3		
21			Sample Submenus &2			
22				Sub Item &1		
23				Sub Item &2		
24				Sub Item &3		
25		&Help				
26			&About...			
27	Stop					

FIGURE 8-1   A partial command bar definition table

The custom menu bar created by this command bar definition table entry is shown in Figure 8-2.

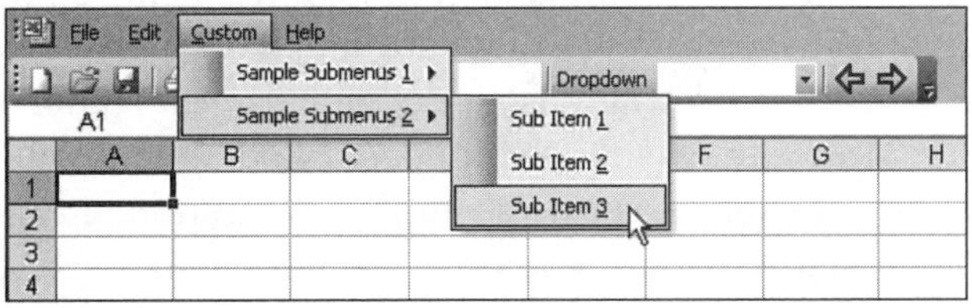

FIGURE 8-2   A custom menu bar created by the command bar builder

Keep in mind this is only a small section from the upper-left corner of the command bar definition table. The actual table contains at least 25 columns of settings and as many rows as required to define all the command bars and controls required for the application.

One of the features making the command bar definition table so easy for experienced programmers to use is that it contains sheet-level defined constants corresponding to every enumeration member used when building command bars and controls with VBA. Therefore, wherever the table calls for an enumeration member such as `msoBarTop` or `msoButtonIconAndCaption`, you can use those names exactly as you would in VBA by simply preceding them with an equal sign when you enter them into a cell. Their numeric values will appear in the cell, but if you select the cell and check the formula bar you will see the enumeration member name. An example of this is shown in Figure 8-3.

	N3	▼	*fx* =msoControlPopup		
	M	N	O	P	Q
1	Control ID	Control Type	Control Style	Face ID	Begin Group
2					
3		10			
4	1	1	3	18	
5	1	1	3	23	
6	1	1	3	106	
7	1	1	3	3	TRUE
8	1	1	3	748	
9	1	1	3	109	TRUE
10	1	1	3	4	
11	1	1	3		TRUE

FIGURE 8-3 Defined constants in the command bar definition table

In the sections that follow, we provide complete descriptions of the purpose and usage of each of the settings in the command bar definition table. In the actual table, cell comments at the top of each column give brief but reasonably complete explanations of the purpose of the column. This allows you to use the table without having to continually refer back to this chapter. The setting names in the column headers of the command bar definition table are identical or very similar to the names of the VBA properties they represent on the command bar or control being defined. This allows you to leverage all of your existing knowledge of how to build command bars and controls in VBA when using the table-driven command bar builder.

Most settings in the command bar definition table are not required. In addition, some settings apply to CommandBar objects, some to CommandBarControl objects, and some to both. Table 8-1 contains a summary of the command bar definition table settings, showing which objects each setting applies to, which settings are required, and what the default value is for each optional setting, if any.

Table 8-1 Command Bar Definition Table—Settings Summary

Setting	CommandBar	Command BarControl	Required	Default
Command Bar Name	✓		Yes	None
Control Caption		✓	Yes	None
Position	✓		No	msoBarTop

Table 8-1 Command Bar Definition Table—Settings Summary

Setting	CommandBar	Command BarControl	Required	Default
IsMenubar	✓		No	False
Visible	✓		No	False
Width	✓	✓	No	None
Protection	✓		No	msoBarNoCustomize
IsTemporary	✓	✓	No	True
IsEnabled	✓	✓	No	True
OnAction		✓	No	None
Control ID		✓	No	1 (Custom)
Control Type		✓	No	msoControlButton
Control Style		✓	No	msoButtonAutomatic
Face ID		✓	No	None
Begin Group		✓	No	False
Before		✓	No	System Default
Tooltip		✓	No	System Default
Shortcut Text		✓	No	None
Tag		✓	No	None
Parameter		✓	No	None
State		✓	No	msoButtonUp
ListRange		✓	No	None
Lists		✓	No	None

8. ADVANCED COMMAND BAR HANDLING

Beginning with the Position column and continuing through the last column in the table, the column values apply to the command bar or control whose name or caption is specified in the same row in one of the first four columns of the table. If a setting does not apply to the type of object specified in the initial columns, it will be ignored. Similarly, if the entry in the initial columns specifies an existing command bar or control object, most settings in subsequent columns are ignored.

Command Bar Name

The command bar builder has the flexibility to create new command bars as well as add controls to existing command bars. Regardless of whether you are creating a new command bar or adding controls to an existing command bar you enter the name of the command bar in this column. The command bar builder checks each command bar name specified in this column to see whether it already exists. If the specified command bar already exists, the command bar builder assumes you are adding controls to that command bar. If no command bar with the specified name exists, the command bar builder creates a new command bar with the specified name using the settings specified in later columns.

There must be two entries in the Command Bar Name column for every command bar you build or modify. The first entry must be the name or index number of the command bar being created or modified. The second entry is simply the word "Stop." The Stop entry must be placed in the row directly below the last row of the command bar definition specified by the first entry. These two entries in the first column work together to bracket the command bar definition so the command bar building code knows where the definition begins and ends.

In Figure 8-1, notice how the command bar name Custom Menu Bar is placed at the top of the Command Bar Name column in cell A2 and Stop is placed at the bottom in cell A27. As shown in this example, *there cannot be any entries between the command bar name value and the Stop keyword*. You can stack as many command bar definitions in the table as you like. The only rule is that each subsequent definition must be separated from the previous definition by at least one blank row.

Control Caption

There are three Control Caption columns by default. This is because good user interface design practice suggests you should not use more than three cascading menu levels. If you really must have additional levels you can simply insert additional Control Caption columns to the right of the existing three.

Like the Command Bar Name column, the Control Caption columns can be used to create new controls or add subcontrols to existing controls. If the command bar builder code detects that the caption in the Control Caption column refers to an existing control on the current command bar, it assumes you want to add subcontrols to it. Otherwise, it creates a new control with the specified caption using the settings specified in later columns.

Regardless of whether you are creating a single control or a cascading series of menus, each control must occupy its own row. The position of a control's caption within the series of Control Caption columns determines the level at which the control will be added. Look again at Figure 8-1. Notice that even though all three Control Caption columns have entries, no row has a Control Caption entry in more than one of the three columns. *This is an absolute requirement*.

You can provide an accelerator key for your control by placing an ampersand directly to the left of the character you want to use as the accelerator key character. The control can then be activated from the keyboard by pressing the Alt key and the specified character simultaneously. This feature only applies to controls that display their caption and are currently visible.

NOTE   When a control displays a dialog, standard user interface conventions dictate that the caption of the control, if it displays one, should be followed by an ellipsis. See the Excel *File > Print...* menu for an example of this convention.

Position

The Position setting applies only to CommandBar objects. It specifies the position on the screen where the CommandBar will appear when it is displayed. This setting must be one of the following `msoBarPosition` enumeration members:

- **`msoBarBottom`**—The command bar will be docked at the bottom of the screen.
- **`msoBarFloating`**—The command bar will not be docked but instead will float over the screen.
- **`msoBarLeft`**—The command bar will be docked on the left side of the screen.
- **`msoBarPopup`**—This setting is used to specify command bars that will be displayed when the user right-clicks with the mouse. The command bar will be displayed at the position where the user right-clicked. Command bars with this position setting must be displayed

(side tab) 8. ADVANCED COMMAND BAR HANDLING

in response to one of the BeforeRightClick event procedures using the following syntax:

```
Application.CommandBars("Name").ShowPopup
```

- **msoBarRight**—The command bar will be docked on the right side of the screen.
- **msoBarTop**—The command bar will be docked at the top of the screen. This is the default value if no position is specified.

IsMenubar

The IsMenubar setting applies only to CommandBar objects. If set to True, the specified command bar will be the menu bar when it is visible. You can define multiple command bars as menu bars for different purposes, but only one menu bar can be visible at a time. If the IsMenubar setting is False, the command bar will be a toolbar or pop-up depending on the Position setting. The IsMenubar property must be False for command bars with the Position property value msoBarPopup or a runtime error will occur. Therefore, the command bar builder code will enforce this value for msoBarPopup command bars regardless of the value actually entered in the table. The default value for the IsMenubar setting is False.

Visible

The Visible setting applies only to CommandBar objects. If set to True, the specified CommandBar will be visible, subject to the following limitations:

- If more than one command bar has both the IsMenubar and Visible settings set to True, the last such command bar in the table will be the menu bar that is actually displayed. All other menu bars will be hidden.
- The Visible property does not apply to and has no effect on command bars with the Position value msoBarPopup.

The default value of the Visible setting is False. This allows you to create a large number of command bars when your application starts up and then display them on demand as needed.

Width

The Width setting applies to CommandBar and CommandBarControl objects. The Width setting must be a positive whole number greater than zero. This setting is not required and there is no default value. If the Width setting is not specified, the width of the command bar or control is determined automatically by VBA. If the Width setting is not specified for a command bar, VBA makes the command bar wide enough to contain all of its controls on a single row. If the Width setting is not specified for a control, VBA makes the control wide enough to display its icon and/or caption.

For CommandBar objects, the Width setting applies only when the Position setting is `msoBarFloating`. The Width setting is ignored for all other command bar Position settings. You cannot make a command bar wider than its automatically calculated width. Setting the width of a floating command bar to a value narrower than its automatically calculated width allows you to stack controls in multiple rows rather than displaying a long, single-row command bar.

For CommandBarControl objects, the Width setting always applies, and you can set it to any positive whole number greater than zero. If the specified width is too narrow to display the caption and/or icon of the control, however, it will be ignored. Note that all controls on the same pop-up menu list will have the width of the widest control in the list regardless of their individual Width settings.

There are no hard-and-fast rules for deciding exactly what the Width setting should be. The best approach is to first build your command bars and controls without specifying the Width setting. Then use the Immediate window to examine the width property that has been automatically assigned by VBA. You can use that as a starting point from which to increase or decrease the width of your command bars and/or controls.

Protection

The Protection setting applies only to CommandBar objects. This setting specifies what type of modifications the user is allowed to make to the command bar. This setting must be one or more of the following `msoBarProtection` enumeration members. To apply multiple Protection values, simply add the values together in the Protection cell for the command bar in question.

- **`msoBarNoChangeDock`**—The user cannot change the position at which the command bar is docked.
- **`msoBarNoChangeVisible`**—The user cannot change the visibility status of the command bar. If the command bar is visible the user cannot hide it, and if the command bar is hidden the user cannot display it.

- **msoBarNoCustomize**—The user cannot add or remove controls on the command bar.
- **msoBarNoHorizontalDock**—The user cannot dock the command bar in any horizontal position, either top or bottom. Without any additional protection values, the command bar can still be docked vertically. To prevent a command bar from being docked anywhere, simply add the `msoBarNoHorizontalDock` and the `msoBarNoVerticalDock` enumeration member values together in the Protection cell.
- **msoBarNoMove**—The command bar cannot be moved. Be careful with this option because it will prevent the user from moving the command bar under any circumstances. For example, if you create a floating command bar whose width causes it to appear partially off-screen, the user will not be able to move the command bar into a position where they can access all of its controls.
- **msoBarNoProtection**—The user can make any changes to the command bar that they want.
- **msoBarNoResize**—The user cannot modify the width or height of the command bar.
- **msoBarNoVerticalDock**—The user cannot dock the command bar in any vertical position, either left or right.

There are two ways a user can delete your command bar regardless of its Protection setting, even if you have disabled the *View > Toolbars > Customize* menu. Both of these methods provide "back doors" to display the Customize dialog. It is particularly important to disable these options in dictator applications where deleting a custom command bar may leave the user with no way to properly exit the application.

First, if the *Toolbar List* command bar is enabled, the user can delete your custom command bar by right-clicking anywhere over the command bar area and selecting *Customize* from the shortcut menu. To disable the *Toolbar List* command bar, execute the following line of code:

```
Application.CommandBars("Toolbar List").Enabled = False
```

Second, if any empty toolbar docking surface is exposed onscreen (typically beyond the right-hand side of a toolbar), the user can double-click anywhere within this area and the Customize dialog is displayed. There is no way to directly disable this feature, so you must indirectly disable it by ensuring that no uncovered toolbar docking area is left exposed by your application. The easiest way to do this is to add a nonfunctional

CommandBarButton control (one with no Caption or OnAction assignment) at the end of each of your toolbars and set it to be wide enough so it covers the entire toolbar docking area regardless of the user's screen resolution.

IsTemporary

The IsTemporary setting applies to CommandBar and CommandBarControl objects. If set to False, the specified command bar or control will be persisted between Excel sessions. Setting this property to True causes the command bar or control to be discarded when the current session of Excel exits. The default value for this setting is True.

The command bar builder rebuilds all command bars and controls defined in the table each time your application runs, so the occasions when you want your custom command bars or controls to be persisted between Excel sessions are rare. Leave this setting blank so the default value is used unless you have a very good reason to do otherwise.

IsEnabled

The IsEnabled setting applies to CommandBar and CommandBarControl objects. This setting determines whether the command bar or control is enabled on startup. A value of True causes the command bar or control to be enabled. A value of False causes the command bar or control to be disabled. Disabled command bars are not visible to the user. The IsEnabled property overrides the Visible property for command bars in this respect. Disabled controls on a visible command bar are visible but appear grayed out. The default value for this property is True.

OnAction

This setting applies to CommandBarControl objects. It holds the name of the procedure that will be run by the control. This procedure must be a public procedure located in a standard code module. If you want to trap the Click or Change event rather than assigning a procedure to the OnAction property you can leave this setting blank. We cover control event trapping in the "Hooking Command Bar Control Events" section later in this chapter. If the Control ID setting is anything other than 1, the OnAction setting is ignored. We see why this is the case when we describe the Control ID setting next.

Control ID

This setting applies to CommandBarControl objects. A Control ID value of 1 causes the command bar builder to create a custom control whose properties are specified by the rest of the columns in the table. Any value other than 1 is interpreted as the ID of a built-in Excel control. In that case, the built-in control specified by the Control ID value is added to your command bar, along with its function and appearance. If you specify a built-in control using the Control ID setting, the following command bar definition table settings are ignored:

- OnAction
- Control Type
- Control Style
- Shortcut Text
- State
- ListRange
- Lists

You can determine the ID that you need to use to add a built-in control to your command bar in the following manner. Assume you want to add the *Print* menu item from the *File* menu on the *Worksheet Menu Bar* to your custom command bar. Enter the following into the VBE Immediate window:

```
? CommandBars("File").Controls("Print...").ID
  4
```

The Immediate window is covered in more detail in Chapter 16, "VBA Debugging," but for now, note that the ? character tells the Immediate window to print the result of the expression that follows it. In this case, the result displayed after pressing the Enter key with the cursor on the first line is the number 4, shown directly below the expression. This is the ID of the *Print* control. To add this control to your custom command bar you would simply place 4 in the Control ID column of the appropriate row in the command bar definition table.

NOTE A quirk in the Office CommandBars object model allows you to access the top-level menus of the Excel menu bar as CommandBar objects in their own right. If you loop the contents of the CommandBars collection you won't find these menus contained in it, but you can access them using the syntax shown previously just the same.

Control Type

This setting applies to CommandBarControl objects. It is used to specify what type of control you want. This setting must be one of the following `msoControlType` enumeration members:

- **`msoControlButton`**—This is a menu or toolbar button that simply executes the specified OnAction procedure when it is clicked. The majority of CommandBarControls that you see on Excel's menus and toolbars are this type of control.
- **`msoControlComboBox`**—This is a combo box control that allows the user to either select an entry from a predefined list or enter a new value of their choosing. An example of this type of control is the Zoom combo box on the Standard toolbar. You can select from a predefined list of zoom values or supply your own.
- **`msoControlDropDown`**—This control looks exactly like the msoControlComboBox control, but the only option allowed is to select an item from the predefined list.
- **`msoControlEdit`**—This is an edit box control that allows the user to enter an arbitrary text value.
- **`msoControlPopup`**—This type of control is used to create a submenu containing a list of one or more menu items. All the top-level menus on the Excel menu bar are of type `msoControlPopup`. Rather than doing anything directly they simply display their associated submenu. This is the *only* control type that can display a submenu.

For custom controls, the default value for this setting is `msoControlButton`. We examine how you use each of these control types in more detail in the "Putting It All Together" section later in the chapter.

NOTE If you look in the VBE Object Browser you will discover that there are anywhere from 21 to 27 different `msoControlType` enumeration members depending on the version of Excel you are using. Unfortunately, you are limited to one of the five members listed previously when building custom CommandBarControls.

Controls with some of the other enumeration member types can be added to a custom command bar by adding a built-in control of those types (by adding the Borders button from the Formatting toolbar, for example, whose type is `msoControlSplitButtonPopup`). Some of the `msoControlType` enumeration members simply haven't been implemented. `msoControlOCXDropdown` is one example.

Control Style

This setting applies to CommandBarControl objects. It specifies the visual layout of the control. This setting does not apply to the Control Types msoControlEdit or msoControlPopup. It applies to the other control types in the following manner:

- **msoControlButton**—Must be one of the following msoButtonStyle enumeration members:
  - **msoButtonAutomatic**—This is the default value for controls of type msoControlButton. For a menu item this is equivalent to msoButtonIconAndCaption. For a toolbar button this is equivalent to msoButtonIcon.
  - **msoButtonCaption**—This style displays only the caption assigned to the control. Any icon assigned to the control is ignored.
  - **msoButtonIcon**—This style is a bit confusing. It displays only the *icon* for toolbar buttons and only the *caption* for menu items. If no icon is specified for a toolbar button with this style a blank button is created.
  - **msoButtonIconAndCaption**—This style displays the icon and places the caption to the right of the icon for both menu items and toolbar buttons.
  - **msoButtonIconAndCaptionBelow**—This style has exactly the same effect as msoButtonIconAndCaption for menu items. For toolbar buttons it displays the caption centered below the icon.
  - **msoButtonIconAndWrapCaption**—This style is similar to the msoButtonIconAndCaption style, but it wraps long captions to the right of the icon instead of displaying them on a single line. This style gives very poor visual results when used with menu items, so we recommend against using it for that type of control.
  - **msoButtonIconAndWrapCaptionBelow**—For toolbar buttons this style is similar to the msoButtonIconAndCaptionBelow style except that long captions are wrapped beneath the button icon. For menu items this style gives exactly the same poor results as the msoButtonIconAndWrapCaption style, so we recommend against using it for that type of control.
  - **msoButtonWrapCaption**—This style is similar to the msoButtonCaption style in that it ignores any icon assigned to the

control. The difference is that it wraps long captions rather than displaying them on a single line.

- **msoControlComboBox** and **msoControlDropDown**—Must be one of the following msoComboStyle enumeration members:
  - **msoComboNormal**—This is the default value for controls of type msoControlComboBox and msoControlDropDown. It simply displays the control with no caption.
  - **msoComboLabel**—This style displays the caption directly to the left of the combo box or drop-down control.

Because the Control Style setting does not apply to controls of type msoControlPopup, you cannot modify the default appearance of this type of control. There is no workaround for this limitation. Because the Control Style setting does not apply to controls of type msoControlEdit, you cannot provide a caption for these controls. If your edit box control is located on a toolbar, you can work around this limitation by adding a nonfunctional msoControlButton with the msoButtonCaption style that displays the caption you want directly to the left of the edit box control. We demonstrate this workaround in the "Putting It All Together" section later in the chapter.

Face ID

This setting applies to CommandBarControl objects. It specifies the icon associated with the control. The Face ID setting can be specified in one of three ways:

- You can use the icon from a built-in control by specifying its FaceID as the value for the Face ID setting of your custom control. The value of the FaceID property of a control can be determined using the Immediate window in exactly the same way as we determined the ID property value in the "Control ID" section earlier in the chapter.
- You can use a custom icon by specifying its name. This icon must be a 16x16 pixel graphic that has been placed on the wksCommandBars worksheet. We demonstrate this in the "Putting It All Together" section later in the chapter.
- When operating under Excel 2002 or higher you have the option of specifying an icon and a mask. This method provides significantly superior visual results for these versions of Excel. Both the icon and the mask must be 16x16 pixel graphics that are located on the wksCommandBars worksheet. The icon and mask picture names must be entered together into the Face ID cell separated by a "/" character. We discuss this method in more detail in the "Loading

Custom Icons from Files" and "Hooking Command Bar Control Events" sections later in the chapter.

Note that the icon picture from the icon/mask pair is automatically used in versions of Excel earlier than Excel 2002, making method three equivalent to method two when running on down-level versions of Excel.

The most important characteristic of a custom icon is that its background appear transparent when applied to a control. To use custom icons under Excel 2000, you must use the *Set Transparent Color* control from the Picture toolbar to specify a transparent background color for the single picture that will become the custom icon for your control. This method is illustrated by the before and after pictures shown in Figure 8-4 and Figure 8-5.

FIGURE 8-4   An icon picture before setting the transparent background

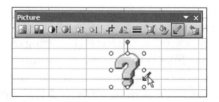

FIGURE 8-5   An icon picture after setting the transparent background

Simply place the *Set Transparent Color* control cursor over the color in your picture that you want to become transparent and click. That color disappears and the background shows through it.

We demonstrated this example with a picture that has been enlarged enough so that you can see what is happening. This is typically the way you would perform this operation in the real world as well. A 16x16 picture is too small to accurately point at the desired background color when you are dealing with a complex icon. Simply stretch the picture out to a size large enough so that you can see what you are doing, set the transparent background color, and then revert the picture to its original size in the following manner:

1. Right-click over the picture and choose *Format Picture* from the shortcut menu.
2. In the Format Picture dialog, select the *Size* tab.
3. Click the Reset button in the lower-right corner of the Size tab.

Each version of Excel uses a slightly different UI drawing technique, so picture backgrounds set to be transparent in one version of Excel do not appear transparent in other versions. As we see in the section "Loading Custom Icons from Files" later in the chapter, two new methods were added to the CommandBarButton object in Excel 2002 that allow you to load pictures directly into the control in a manner that is independent of their appearance on the worksheet.

For this reason we recommend that you use the icon/mask method described in item three in the previous list for creating custom icons in Excel 2002 and higher, while setting the transparent background color of the icon picture using Excel 2000. This gives the command bar builder an appropriately formatted icon for use in Excel 2000.

Begin Group

This setting applies to CommandBarControl objects. It is a True/False setting that specifies whether a separator bar will be placed above or to the left of the specified control depending on context. A value of True adds a separator bar. False is the default value for this setting, so if False is specified or this setting is left blank, no separator bar is created.

Before

This setting applies to CommandBarControl objects. It is used to position a new control before an existing control. If the controls are arranged horizontally, the Before setting places your control to the left of the control specified. If the controls are arranged vertically, the Before setting places your control above the control specified.

The existing control can be specified either by its name or ID number. This setting is not required and there is no default value. If this setting is left blank or if the control specified by this setting cannot be located, this setting is ignored. In this case, the control is added at the system default position, which is at the end of the current set of controls on the same level. The Before setting is typically used to position controls that are being added to built-in Excel command bars.

Tooltip

This setting applies to CommandBarControl objects. It specifies the text that will be contained in the yellow Tooltip message displayed when the user hovers the mouse pointer over the control. This setting does not apply to controls of type `msoControlPopup` or to any child control of an `msoControlPopup` control. If the Tooltip setting is not specified the system default value displayed in the Tooltip is the caption of the control.

Shortcut Text

This setting applies to CommandBarControl objects. It displays a keyboard shortcut directly to the right of the control caption. This setting applies only to controls of type `msoControlButton` that are child controls of an `msoControlPopup` control (that is, menu items on a submenu). Specifying this setting does not actually assign the keyboard shortcut to the macro specified by the OnAction setting of the control. You must do this separately in your own code. The Shortcut Text setting is not required, and there is no default value.

Tag

This setting applies to CommandBarControl objects. It allows you to store String data for your own use. The Tag setting does not modify the appearance or function of the control in any way. One common use of this setting is to differentiate among controls that have been assigned the same OnAction procedure.

Assume you have assigned the OnAction settings of three controls to the same procedure. You then assign the values 1, 2, and 3 to the Tag settings of the first, second, and third controls, respectively. When the specified OnAction procedure is called by one of these controls, you can identify the specific control that called it in the manner shown in Listing 8-1, and conditionally redirect program execution based on the result.

Listing 8-1   Distinguishing Controls Using the Tag Setting

```
Public Sub MyProcedure()

    Dim lControl As Long

    ' Retrieve the Tag value of the control that
    ' called this procedure.
    lControl = CLng(Application.CommandBars.ActionControl.Tag)
```

```
Select Case lControl
    Case 1
        ' Perform the action for control 1.
    Case 2
        ' Perform the action for control 2.
    Case 3
        ' Perform the action for control 3.
End Select

End Sub
```

As we see in the "Hooking Command Bar Control Events" section later in the chapter, the Tag setting is also used to specify the custom controls whose events you want to hook as a group.

Parameter

This setting applies to CommandBarControl objects. It is functionally identical to the Tag setting. It is a place for the programmer to store String data that will not have any effect on the appearance or function of the control.

State

This setting applies to CommandBarControl objects. It allows you to create checked menu items or depressed toolbar buttons. The value for this setting must be one of the following `msoButtonState` enumeration members:

- **msoButtonDown**—For toolbar buttons this creates the visual effect of the button being depressed. For menu items, the effect depends on whether there is an icon displayed with the menu item. For menu items with icons, the icon appears depressed in a fashion similar to the effect on toolbar buttons. For menu items without an icon, a check mark is added to the left of the menu caption.
- **msoButtonMixed**—For all current versions of Excel, this value is indistinguishable from `msoButtonDown`. It is included in the command bar builder in case it becomes supported for some different purpose in a future version of Excel.
- **msoButtonUp**—This is the default value for this setting. A State value of `msoButtonUp` has no effect on the appearance of newly created controls. This value only comes into play as a way to remove the effect of the `msoButtonDown` or `msoButtonMixed` values.

The State setting applies only to custom controls of type `msoControlButton`. Keep in mind that the State property is a dynamic property of the control. The command bar builder creates the control with whatever initial State value you specify, but once the control has been created you need to write custom code to modify the State property appropriately in response to user actions. We demonstrate this in the "Putting It All Together" section later in the chapter.

ListRange and Lists

These settings apply to CommandBarControl objects of type `msoControlComboBox` or `msoControlDropdown`. We discuss these settings together because they are, in effect, a single setting that specifies the list to be loaded into a combo box or drop-down control. The purpose of these settings is the following:

- **ListRange**—This value specifies the address of the range on the wksCommandBars worksheet that holds the list to be loaded into the control. The specified range must be located in the Lists column. Like all other settings described so far, the ListRange setting must be located on the same row as the control to which it applies.
- **Lists**—This setting is a list of values that will be loaded into the control. This is the only setting that does not have to be located on the same row as the control it applies to, and as we discuss later, it should not be located in rows that are part of any command bar or control definition.

You should always place your lists below the last command bar definition in the table. By doing this, you will not inadvertently alter one of your lists if you need to insert or delete rows in a command bar definition. For similar reasons, use a named range to specify the ListRange setting. If you were to hard-code the list address and then insert or delete rows in the command bar definition table, the list address would no longer be valid.

Post Mortem

Although it seems as if every command bar and control property under the sun has been covered here, we're not even close. Only the most frequently used properties have been included in the command bar builder. Other properties that you may find an occasional need for can always be manually coded into your application.

Examples of properties that are not included in the command bar builder are the Height and RowIndex properties of the CommandBar object, because in our experience these properties are rarely used when building command bars. Properties of the CommandBarControl object that are not supported include the DescriptionText property, because it simply duplicates the purpose of the Tag and/or Parameter properties, and the HyperLinkType property, because it is so rarely used.

There are also dynamic properties such as IsEnabled and State whose initial values are set by the command bar builder, but whose subsequent values must be managed by custom code in your application as the need to change them arises.

Putting It All Together

In this section, we create several common variations of command bars that are not associated with any application. We use these examples to demonstrate many of the settings described in the previous section.

In this example we use the version of the command bar builder code that has been integrated with the error handling system to be described in Chapter 15, "VBA Error Handling." Since the primary focus of this section is creating a valid command bar definition table, this should not cause any problems. All the error handling techniques you see in the code for this example are fully explained in Chapter 15.

The error handled command bar builder is the one we strongly recommend you use in your own projects, so bear with us if you're looking at the code and it isn't clear what all of it does. If you do use this version of the command bar builder you need to import one additional module besides the three listed at the beginning of the chapter. This is the MErrorHandler module containing all the error handling code referenced by the command bar builder.

The code for this example is located in the CommandBarDemo.xls workbook that can be found on the CD in the *Concepts\\Ch08 – Advanced Command Bar Handling* folder. We strongly recommend that you open this workbook and follow along while you read this section. The command bar definition table is physically too large to enable us to use screen shots to display all of the important information we discuss. The command bars in the CommandBarDemo.xls workbook are built automatically whenever the workbook is opened. Three types of custom command bar are demonstrated:

- A custom menu containing submenus added to the existing Worksheet Menu Bar
- A custom toolbar
- A custom right-click command bar

Figure 8-6 shows the complete set of custom command bars created by the CommandBarDemo.xls workbook. To remove the custom command bars and close the workbook select *Custom > Exit* from the Excel menu.

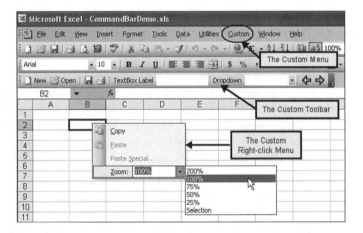

FIGURE 8-6   The custom command bars example

Adding a Custom Menu with Submenus to the Worksheet Menu Bar

Figure 8-7 shows the command bar definition table layout required to add a new top-level menu to the Worksheet Menu Bar.

	A	B	C	D
1	Command Bar Name	Control Caption	Control Caption	Control Caption
2	Worksheet Menu Bar			
3		&Custom		
4			Sub Menu &1	
5			Sub Menu &2	
6				Sub Menu Item &1
7				Sub Menu Item &2
8				Sub Menu Item &3
9			&Exit	
10	Stop			

FIGURE 8-7   Adding a custom menu to the Worksheet Menu Bar

Notice that "Worksheet Menu Bar" has been entered for the Command Bar Name. The command bar builder recognizes that this command bar already exists and adds all subsequently defined controls to the existing command bar. As explained in the "Command Bar Name" section earlier in the chapter, there can be no entries between the name of the command bar and the Stop keyword.

The new top-level menu we are adding to the Worksheet Menu Bar is located in the first of the three Control Caption columns. Its name is "Custom." The ampersand character in front of the first letter of the control caption indicates the letter "C" is the shortcut key for this menu. We also used the Before setting (not shown here) in the command bar definition table to specify that the Custom menu will be added directly to the left of the Window menu. This is the standard position for custom menus added to the Worksheet Menu Bar.

All subsequent controls will be constructed as child menus at some level below the Custom menu. You can verify this is the case because the Control Caption column entries visually display the menu hierarchy. In this case, no Control Caption entries exist below the Custom entry, so all subsequent controls must be children of this menu. The full Custom menu is shown in Figure 8-8.

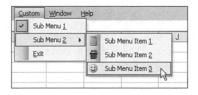

FIGURE 8-8   The Custom menu

Unless specified otherwise, all the custom controls in this example have their OnAction settings assigned to the GeneralDemo procedure shown in Listing 8-2. When a menu or toolbar button with this OnAction assignment is clicked, a message box containing the caption of the control that called the procedure is displayed. This is a simple example of how you can use a single procedure to handle multiple controls.

Listing 8-2   The GeneralDemo Procedure

```
Public Sub GeneralDemo()
    Dim sCaller As String
    sCaller = Application.CommandBars.ActionControl.Caption
    MsgBox sCaller & " was clicked.", vbInformation, gsAPP_TITLE
End Sub
```

The Custom menu has three submenus:

- **Sub Menu 1**—We use this control to demonstrate the use of the State setting. This control is initially created with its State set to msoButtonDown, as demonstrated by the depressed check mark displayed to the left of the control in Figure 8-8. Sub Menu 1 is assigned to a special procedure called StateDemo that toggles the State of the control between msoButtonDown and msoButtonUp each time it is clicked. The StateDemo procedure is shown in Listing 8-3.

Listing 8-3 The StateDemo Procedure

```
Public Sub StateDemo()
    Dim ctlCaller As Office.CommandBarButton
    Dim sMsg As String
    Set ctlCaller = Application.CommandBars.ActionControl
    If ctlCaller.State = msoButtonDown Then
        ' Switch to msoButtonUp.
        ctlCaller.State = msoButtonUp
        sMsg = "The state has been switched to up."
    Else
        ' Switch to msoButtonDown.
        ctlCaller.State = msoButtonDown
        sMsg = "The state has been switched to down."
    End If
    MsgBox sMsg, vbInformation, gsAPP_TITLE
End Sub
```

- **Sub Menu 2**—We use this control to demonstrate third-level submenus (often referred to as submenu items). Sub Menu 2 is a control of type msoControlPopup. As shown in Figure 8-7, it contains three submenu items. Each of these submenu items has had its FaceID setting assigned to the FaceID of a built-in control. As explained in the "Face ID" section earlier in the chapter, assigning the FaceID number of a built-in control to the FaceID setting of a custom control allows you to give your control the appearance of the built-in control without taking on any of its other characteristics.

- **Exit**—This is just a plain vanilla submenu control that is used to exit the demo application. Its OnAction setting is assigned to the AppExit procedure, which initiates shutdown of the application.

Adding a Custom Toolbar

Figure 8-9 shows the command bar definition table layout required to create our custom toolbar. Because the toolbar requires only a single level of Control Caption settings, we used the freeze panes feature to scroll the table over to show some of the additional settings used to create the controls on the toolbar.

O13	▼	_fx_ =msoButtonIconAndCaption				
	A	B	L	M	N	O
1	Command Bar Name	Control Caption	OnAction	Control ID	Control Type	Control Style
12	Custom Toolbar					
13		New	GeneralDemo			3
14		Open	GeneralDemo			3
15		Save		3		
16		Print		2521		
17		TextBox Label				2
18		Textbox	HandleTextBox		2	
19		Dropdown	HandleDropDown		3	1
20		Previous	GeneralDemo			
21		Next	GeneralDemo			
22	Stop					

FIGURE 8-9   Adding a custom toolbar

If you're following along with the actual workbook example, you'll see that the row in the command bar definition table used to specify the toolbar required only a single setting: Visible = TRUE. This lack of a requirement for explicit settings in most of the command bar definition table columns is pervasive, and it represents one of the primary strengths of this system.

The default values for all settings are designed to be the values you will use most frequently when building command bars and controls. Therefore, the command bar definition table requires very few entries for the majority of command bars and controls you will build with it. Just be sure you understand what the default entries are. If you're ever unsure, read the cell comment at the top of the column. Any defaults are listed there as well as any other critical information required to use the setting controlled by that column correctly. The toolbar built by the command bar definition in Figure 8-9 is shown in Figure 8-10.

FIGURE 8-10   The custom toolbar

The controls on the custom toolbar are used to demonstrate a number of features of the command bar builder:

- **New and Open**—As you can see in Figure 8-9, there is no Control ID value specified for the New or Open buttons. This means they will be created as custom controls. Both OnAction settings use the GeneralDemo procedure shown in Listing 8-2, and their FaceID settings (not shown) are the FaceID numbers of the built-in New and Open controls, respectively.

  What makes these controls different from your average toolbar buttons are their Control Style settings. As shown in Figure 8-9, these controls have a Control Style of `msoButtonIconAndCaption`. Rather than simply displaying an icon alone, this style displays the controls with their captions to the right of their icons. This is a somewhat unusual but often useful display technique when you have room on your toolbar to apply it. The meanings of toolbar buttons often tend to be obscure based on the icon alone. Adding a caption to a toolbar button can make its purpose much more obvious.

- **Save and Print**—As you can see in Figure 8-9, these buttons have Control ID values other than 1. The Control ID values are the ID values for the built-in Save and Print controls, respectively. This means the built-in Save and Print controls have been added to our custom toolbar with all of their appearance and function intact. These controls have no OnAction setting because the command bar builder would ignore it. Clicking either one of these controls causes them to perform the same action they would perform as built-in controls.

- **TextBox Label and TextBox**—This set of controls is used to demonstrate how you can add a textbox control to your toolbar and fake a caption for it by placing a nonfunctional CommandBarButton control with the desired caption to the left of the textbox control. In Figure 8-9 you can see that the OnAction setting of the textbox control is assigned to a special-purpose procedure called HandleTextBox, shown in Listing 8-4.

Listing 8-4 The HandleTextBox Procedure

```
Public Sub HandleTextBox()
    Dim ctlCaller As Office.CommandBarControl
    Set ctlCaller = Application.CommandBars.ActionControl
    MsgBox "You entered: '" & ctlCaller.Text & "'."
End Sub
```

This procedure performs exactly the same function as the GeneralDemo procedure except it displays the value entered into the textbox control.

- **Dropdown**—This control demonstrates how to add a control of type `msoControlComboBox` or `msoControlDropdown` to your toolbar. This specific example demonstrates an `msoControlDropdown` control, but the two types of controls are almost identical. Everything you see in this example can be applied to a control of type `msoControlComboBox`.

  In Figure 8-9, note that the Control Style setting for the drop-down control has a value of 1. This is the value of the `msoComboLabel` style. It causes the caption of the drop-down to be displayed to the left of the control itself. The OnAction setting of the drop-down control is assigned to the custom HandleDropDown procedure shown in Listing 8-5.

Listing 8-5 The HandleDropDown Procedure

```
Public Sub HandleDropDown()
    Dim ctlCaller As Office.CommandBarComboBox
    Set ctlCaller = Application.CommandBars.ActionControl
    MsgBox "You selected: '" & ctlCaller.Text & "'."
End Sub
```

After you select an entry from the drop-down list, this procedure displays the text of the list item you selected

- **Previous and Next**—These controls demonstrate how to apply custom icons to your controls. In Figure 8-11 you can see the Previous and Next Control Caption settings, their Face ID settings that specify named pictures, and the pictures named by the Face ID settings (we cover the meaning of the mask pictures in the "Loading Custom Icons from Files" section later in the chapter).

8. ADVANCED COMMAND BAR HANDLING

	A	B	O	P
	picPrev ▼	ƒx		
1	**Command Bar Name**	**Control Caption**	**Control Style**	**Face ID**
12	Custom Toolbar			
13		New	3	18
14		Open	3	23
15		Save		
16		Print		
17		TextBox Label	2	
18		Textbox		
19		Dropdown	1	
20		Previous		picPrev/picPrevMask
21		Next		picNext/picNextMask
22	Stop			

FIGURE 8-11   Custom icons on the toolbar

In Figure 8-11, the picture for the Previous button is selected and you can see that its name, as shown in the name box directly to the left of the formula bar, is exactly the same as the name specified for the Previous control in its Face ID setting (cell P20).

Adding a Custom Right-Click Command Bar

Figure 8-12 shows the command bar definition table layout required to create our custom right-click command bar. If you examine the Position setting for this command bar you see that its value has been set to msoBarPopup.

	A	B	L	M	N
1	**Command Bar Name**	**Control Caption**	**OnAction**	**Control ID**	**Control Type**
24	Custom Popup				
25		Copy		19	
26		Paste		22	
27		Paste Special		755	
28		Zoom		1733	
29	Stop				

FIGURE 8-12   Adding a custom right-click command bar

The only control setting on this command bar with values assigned to it is the Control ID setting. This is because all the controls on our custom right-click menu are built-in controls. Not just built-in controls by appearance, but the actual built-in controls specified by the ID numbers in the Control ID column, including all their features and attributes. The right-click command bar built by this command bar table definition is shown in Figure 8-13.

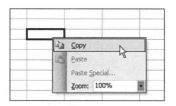

FIGURE 8-13 The custom right-click command bar

We replaced the built-in command bar normally invoked by right-clicking over a worksheet cell with our custom right-click command bar. This was accomplished using the workbook-level SheetBeforeRightClick event as shown in Listing 8-6.

Listing 8-6 The Workbook_SheetBeforeRightClick Event Handler

```
Private Sub Workbook_SheetBeforeRightClick(ByVal Sh As Object, _
               ByVal Target As Range, Cancel As Boolean)

    Dim cbrBar As Office.CommandBar

    ' Only attempt to display the custom right-click
    ' command bar if it exists.
    On Error Resume Next
        Set cbrBar = Nothing
        Set cbrBar = Application.CommandBars("Custom Popup")
    On Error GoTo 0

    If Not cbrBar Is Nothing Then
        ' Show our custom right-click command bar.
        cbrBar.ShowPopup
        ' Cancel the default action of the right-click.
        Cancel = True
    End If

End Sub
```

As Figure 8-13 shows, the controls on our custom right-click menu are behaving exactly like their corresponding Excel controls. Because we have not yet copied anything, both the Paste and Paste Special menus are disabled. The Copy menu is enabled, allowing us to copy a range. The Zoom control is enabled because we can modify the zoom at any time.

We do not need to take any action to make these controls behave in this manner because we are using the built-in controls themselves. Excel ensures they behave appropriately. In the "Hooking Command Bar Control Events" section later in the chapter we show you how to have the best of both worlds. By hooking command bar control events, we can utilize the dynamic appearance of built-in controls provided by Excel while also having them run the custom code of our choice rather than perform their normal actions.

Loading Custom Icons from Files

As explained in the "Face ID" section earlier in the chapter, each version of Excel from 2000 onward uses a slightly different user interface drawing technique. This means custom icons stored as pictures on a worksheet only appear correctly in the version of Excel in which they were optimized.

For applications running under Excel 2002 or higher there is a second method for applying custom icons to command bar controls that eliminates the problems associated with the different drawing techniques used by different versions of Excel. The command bar builder supports this method automatically, but in this section we explain how to program it manually so you can take advantage of it in an application that does not use the command bar builder.

Beginning with Office XP, two new properties were added to the CommandBarButton object. These two properties allow you to load icons directly into the control. The Picture property specifies the bitmap to be used as the foreground of the icon, and the Mask property specifies the bitmap that indicates which areas of the icon should be rendered as transparent background. In the next section we show you how to create these bitmaps.

This method requires two bitmap files for each icon, so if you have a large number of custom icons it can become unwieldy due to the number of files you must distribute. In Chapter 23 we show how you can package up all your custom icons into a single DLL resource file. Alternatively, if you are using the command bar builder, you can host both the icon and mask picture files on the wksCommandBars worksheet.

Creating Bitmap Files for Icons and Masks

If you plan to create custom icons on a regular basis, it probably makes sense to purchase a special-purpose icon creation program. For the occasional custom icon, however, every version of Windows comes with a perfectly serviceable icon creation tool: Microsoft Paint.

The type of file you need to create for use as a CommandBarButton icon is a 16x16 pixel 16-color bitmap. The icon file contains the artistic foreground picture you think of as your icon. The mask file is an overlay for the icon file in which the foreground area is colored black and everything you want to be transparent background is colored white.

To create a custom icon, open Microsoft Paint. Paint opens with a blank default image canvas. Select *Image > Attributes* from the Paint menu. In the Attributes dialog, set *Width* and *Height* to 16, *Units* to Pixels and *Colors* to Colors. These settings are shown in Figure 8-14.

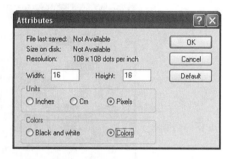

FIGURE 8-14   The icon attributes settings

Click OK on the Attributes dialog and select *View > Zoom > Custom* from the Paint menu. Select 800% as your *Zoom to* setting. The resulting image canvas is shown in Figure 8-15.

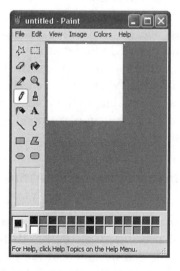

FIGURE 8-15   The blank icon canvas in Paint

You are now ready to draw your icon. Drawing icons well requires much practice. The appearance of a 16x16 pixel image at 800% magnification is often nothing like its appearance at normal size. We've provided a simple custom icon image you can use for testing purposes. This icon is called Arrows.bmp and is located on the CD in the \Concepts\Ch08 – Advanced Command Bar Handling folder. This icon is shown loaded into Paint in Figure 8-16.

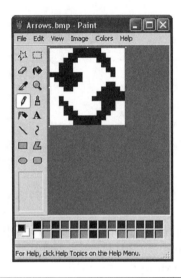

FIGURE 8-16 The arrows icon

The mask file for the arrows icon is called ArrowsMask.bmp and is located in the same CD folder as the Arrows.bmp file. As you can see in Figure 8-17, this file simply replaces the blue foreground color of the original icon with black. When loaded into the CommandBarButton, the areas of the icon corresponding to the black areas of the mask will be displayed, while the areas of the icon corresponding to the white areas of the mask will be transparent.

Using Bitmap Files as CommandBarButton Icons

Now that we have our icon and mask bitmaps, it's a simple matter to apply them to a CommandBarButton. The procedures shown in Listing 8-7 build a command bar with a single button that uses our custom arrow icon and mask. This code can be found in the LoadPictureAndMask.xls workbook located on the CD in the \Concepts\Ch08 – Advanced Command Bar Handling folder. Note that this example works only in Excel 2002 or higher.

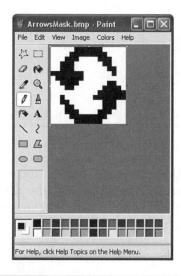

FIGURE 8-17 The mask file for the arrows icon

Listing 8-7 Adding a Custom Icon to a CommandBarButton

```
Public Sub CreateBar()

    Dim cbrBar As Office.CommandBar
    Dim ctlControl As Office.CommandBarButton
    Dim sPath As String

    ' Make sure any previously created version of our demo
    ' command bar is deleted.
    RemoveBar

    ' We're assuming that the bitmap files used to create the
    ' custom icon are located in the same path as this workbook.
    sPath = ThisWorkbook.Path
    If Right$(sPath, 1) <> "\" Then sPath = sPath & "\"

    ' Create a toolbar-type command bar.
    Set cbrBar = CommandBars.Add("Demo", msoBarTop, False, True)
    cbrBar.Visible = True

    ' Add the command bar button control.
    Set ctlControl = cbrBar.Controls.Add(msoControlButton)
    ' Load the foreground bitmap file.
    ctlControl.Picture = LoadPicture(sPath & "Arrows.bmp")
    ' Load the mask bitmap file.
```

```
        ctlControl.Mask = LoadPicture(sPath & "ArrowsMask.bmp")

End Sub

Public Sub RemoveBar()
    On Error Resume Next
    Application.CommandBars("Demo").Delete
End Sub
```

To create the command bar button with the custom icon, run the CreateBar procedure. To remove the demo command bar and its button, run the RemoveBar procedure. The resulting custom icon appears as shown in Figure 8-18.

FIGURE 8-18   The arrows custom icon

Hooking Command Bar Control Events

In Office 2000, Microsoft added the Click event to the CommandBarButton object and the Change event to the CommandBarComboBox object to provide an event-based mechanism for working with command bar controls in addition to the OnAction property. The primary reason for this was to allow controls to be used by non-VBA projects such as COM add-ins, which were introduced at the same time. There are, however, subtle differences in the behavior of a control when using an event hook compared to using the OnAction property. We can exploit this behavior to our advantage in VBA.

Why Use an Event Hook

Setting the OnAction property is usually the easiest option for custom command bar controls; when the control is clicked, the procedure specified by the OnAction property is called. Using an event hook allows us to interact with controls in three additional ways that can't be accomplished using the OnAction property:

- Hook the Click events of the built-in controls, giving us a Before_xxx event for any control that we hook.
- Hook the Click events of both built-in and custom controls in other Office applications, including the VBE. For example, if we're using

Excel to automate Word, our Excel code can respond to the user clicking a control in Word—either a built-in Word control or one we have created.

■ Hook the Click events of both built-in and custom controls from outside VBA, such as when automating Excel from Visual Basic, within COM Add-ins, or in VSTO solutions. These scenarios are covered in detail in Chapters 23 through 26.

What an Event Hook Can Do

When hooking custom controls, event hooks behave exactly like OnAction procedures. They run when the control is clicked. When hooking built-in controls, however, the event hook is called **before the built-in process**, effectively giving us a Before_xxx event in which to run any code we want and/or cancel the built-in processing.

For example, in Chapter 6, "Dictator Applications," we used an OnKey assignment to ensure that the Ctrl+V keyboard shortcut pasted only values into our data entry forms. By hooking the *Edit > Paste* menu instead, we could check to see whether the cell being pasted into was within our data entry form. If so, we'd replace it with a *Paste Special > Values* and cancel Excel's default paste behavior using the CancelDefault argument supplied by the Click event procedure. Otherwise we'd let Excel perform a normal paste operation.

Within the Click event procedure we could also use the Application.OnTime method to run a routine immediately after Excel has done its normal process, effectively giving us an After_xxx event. This method only works within an Excel-based add-in.

We can also use event hooks to implement custom controls that are enabled and disabled automatically as the environment changes. For example, the built-in *Paste Values* control is only enabled when there is something on the Clipboard to paste and a cell selected to paste into. We can use event hooks to create our own custom buttons that are enabled and disabled in the same way. All we need to do is create a copy of the *Paste Values* control, give it a different icon, add our own code to the click event, and cancel the default behavior. Because our custom controls are based on a built-in control, Excel handles their enable/disable behavior for us. We demonstrate this in "The Paste Special Command Bar" section later in the chapter.

The Importance of the Tag Property

When you use a WithEvents object declaration to hook a CommandBarButton or CommandBarComboBox, you're not actually

8. ADVANCED COMMAND BAR HANDLING

hooking that specific instance of the control, but rather that control ID for built-in controls or that ID/Tag property combination for custom controls. This means when you hook one of the built-in controls, your event will be fired whenever *any* instance of that control is clicked—a big advantage over having to search for every instance of the control and hook each one (including having to determine whether the user has dragged a new one on to his toolbar at some point during your application's operation).

Custom controls with an ID of 1 and no Tag assignment are treated as unique, individual controls for the purposes of a WithEvents assignment. This is a safety mechanism built into the event hooking system. If hooking any custom control with an ID/Tag combination of 1/<blank> meant hooking all custom controls with that ID/Tag combination you might be hooking a very large number of controls indeed, including many that didn't even belong to your application.

To take advantage of multiple simultaneous event hooks for our custom controls, we need to assign the same Tag value to all the custom controls we want to hook together. We can then use the Parameter value of the Ctrl argument passed to the event to identify which control was clicked and decide what to do with it.

We can also have a custom control emulate the enabled/disabled behavior of a built-in control automatically. We do this by assigning the ID value of the built-in control whose behavior we want to emulate to the Control ID value of our custom control. We then give that control a unique Tag value and set up the event hook. Excel manages the enabled/disabled behavior of our custom control, but the control runs the code we assign to it in the event handler.

This is actually just a special case of hooking a built-in control. And because we are hooking the ID of a built-in control, that built-in control will also activate our event handler. We can use the Tag value of the Ctrl argument passed to the event procedure to determine whether the event was fired by our custom control or the built-in control whose behavior our custom control emulates. If there is no Tag, we know the built-in control called the event. In this case we simply do nothing and allow Excel to perform its default process for the control. If the Tag property is set, we know our custom control called the event. In this case we cancel Excel's default action and run our own code in its place.

If we want to have multiple custom controls, all with the same enabled/disabled behavior but each with different actions, we can give these controls the same Control ID and Tag values so they all fire the same event hook, and then use the Parameter value to uniquely identify each control to conditionally execute the correct code for it in the event handler.

This is all very confusing, but it will become clear once you see the example in the next section.

The Paste Special Command Bar

After you have copied a range, Excel provides a number of useful paste special options buried under the *Edit > Paste Special* menu. Built-in toolbar buttons are provided for two commonly used paste special options: *Paste Values* and *Paste Formatting*. What we want, however, is a toolbar that exposes *all* of the most commonly used paste special options.

All the buttons on this toolbar should have the same enabled/disabled behavior exhibited by the built-in *Paste Values* button, but they should run the operation-specific code that we assign to them. In this section we take advantage of command bar control event hooking to create this toolbar. The workbook that implements this example is called PasteSpecialBar.xls and is located on the CD in the *\Concepts\Ch08 – Advanced Command Bar Handling* folder. We strongly recommend that you open this workbook and examine it while you read this section.

The Paste Special Toolbar Definition

The first step in creating our Paste Special toolbar is to write the correct definition for it in the command bar definition table. The complete command bar definition table for this toolbar is too wide to fit within a single screen shot, so we show a series of screen shots that utilize the Excel freeze panes feature to display several of the most important sections of the definition table. Showing the entire command bar definition table for our Paste Special toolbar would require more screen shots than we have room for, so please follow along with the example workbook provided on the CD. Figure 8-19 shows the basic structure and definition of the Paste Special toolbar and its controls.

	A	B	L	M	N
1	Command Bar Name	Control Caption	OnAction	Control ID	Control Type
2	Paste Special				
3		All		370	
4		Formulas		370	
5		Values		370	
6		Formatting		370	
7		Comments		370	
8		Validation		370	
9		Column Widths		370	
10	Stop				

FIGURE 8-19 The basic Paste Special toolbar definition

Our Paste Special toolbar will be constructed as an `msoBarFloating` CommandBar with seven controls of type `msoControlButton`. Note that all the controls on the toolbar have been assigned the same built-in Control ID value 370. This number is the ID of the built-in *Paste Values* CommandBarButton. What we are doing is creating seven identical copies of the built-in *Paste Values* control that we will later modify to perform different actions. We do this because even after our modifications, Excel will enable and disable these controls automatically as if they were still identical copies of the *Paste Values* control. This is exactly what we want. In Figure 8-20, we demonstrate how we are setting the appearance of our seven controls.

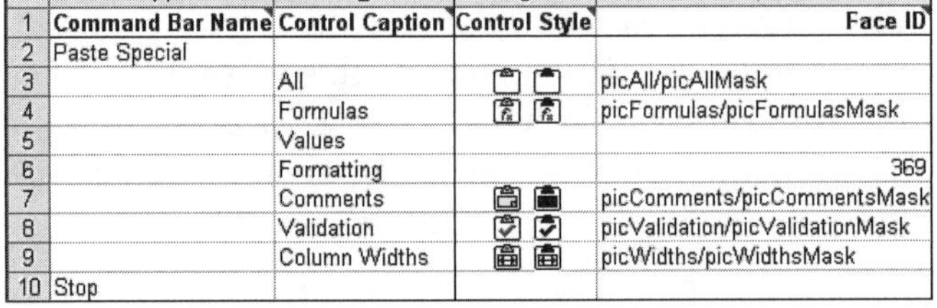

	A	B	O	P
1	Command Bar Name	Control Caption	Control Style	Face ID
2	Paste Special			
3		All		picAll/picAllMask
4		Formulas		picFormulas/picFormulasMask
5		Values		
6		Formatting		369
7		Comments		picComments/picCommentsMask
8		Validation		picValidation/picValidationMask
9		Column Widths		picWidths/picWidthsMask
10	Stop			

FIGURE 8-20   The Paste Special toolbar Face ID assignments

Let's start with the Values button. Because all the controls on our toolbar are copies of the built-in *Paste Values* control, and this control is actually included on our toolbar, we don't have to specify anything for its Face ID setting. It takes on the appearance of the *Paste Values* control by default. Next, look at the Face ID setting for the Formatting control. Because Excel provides a built-in *Paste Formatting* control, we can simply use its Face ID rather than having to create a custom icon for our Formatting control.

For all the other controls on our toolbar we have provided custom icons and masks. The purpose and usage of icons and masks have been covered extensively in the "Face ID" and the "Loading Custom Icons from Files" sections earlier in the chapter, so we do not repeat that information here. What we do describe is how this feature has been implemented on the command bar definition table shown in Figure 8-20.

The pictures for the icons and masks have been placed in the unused Control Style column. This column is unused because the default value msoButtonIcon is exactly what we want for our controls. These pictures could theoretically be located anywhere on the wksCommandBars worksheet, but for ease of maintenance we generally recommend that you place your icon and mask pictures on the same row as the control to which they apply and as close as possible to the Face ID column in which they are named. Although it is somewhat difficult to differentiate when looking at a black-and-white screen shot, in all cases the icon is the picture on the left and the mask is the picture on the right.

If you examine the value of the Face ID setting for each of the controls utilizing an icon and mask you see that it consists of the icon picture name and the mask picture name separated by a "/" character. For Excel versions 2002 and higher, both of these pictures are used to create the icon for the control. For Excel versions 2000 and lower, only the icon picture is used, and its appearance on the control is exactly the same as its appearance on the worksheet. Therefore, if your application will be run on Excel 2000, you should set the transparent background color of the icon picture in Excel 2000 and save the workbook in that version of Excel. In Figure 8-21, we show the Tag and Parameter settings for our controls.

	A	B	U	V
1	Command Bar Name	Control Caption	Tag	Parameter
2	Paste Special			
3		All	pxlPasteSpecial	All
4		Formulas	pxlPasteSpecial	Formulas
5		Values		
6		Formatting	pxlPasteSpecial	Formatting
7		Comments	pxlPasteSpecial	Comments
8		Validation	pxlPasteSpecial	Validation
9		Column Widths	pxlPasteSpecial	ColWidths
10	Stop			

FIGURE 8-21 The Paste Special toolbar Tag and Parameter assignments

Except for the Values control, all the controls have been assigned the same Tag setting value. This is what allows all these controls' events to be trapped by the same event handler. The Tag value is not required for the Values control because it is a built-in copy of the Excel *Paste Values* control. Since all our controls are copies of this control, our event handler will trap its event automatically. In the event code that we show in a moment, event calls from the built-in *Paste Values* control are ignored, and Excel is allowed to handle them as if they had not been trapped at all. When the Paste Special toolbar is first created, there is nothing on the Clipboard and therefore all the controls are in the disabled state as shown in Figure 8-22.

FIGURE 8-22 The Paste Special toolbar with all controls disabled

Achieving this effect requires absolutely no work on our part. By using the *Paste Values* control as the basis for all the custom controls on the Paste Special toolbar, Excel manages enabling and disabling the controls appropriately for us. Once a range has been copied, Excel automatically enables all our controls, as shown in Figure 8-23.

FIGURE 8-23 The Paste Special toolbar with all controls enabled

Now let's look at the code required to manage these controls. A WithEvents class module called CControlEvents is used to trap the events for our controls. A reference to this class must be created in and held by a global variable so that event trapping continues throughout the life of our application. Therefore, we must add the following object variable declaration to the MGlobals module of our example workbook:

```
Public gclsControlEvents As CControlEvents
```

It seems obvious, but bears mentioning, that the global class variable can't be instantiated until after we have built the command bars specified in the command bar definition table. Otherwise, there would be no controls to hook. Both of these tasks are accomplished in the Auto_Open procedure, a fragment of which is shown in Listing 8-8. As in the example in the "Putting It All Together" section earlier in the chapter, the version of the command bar builder code used here has been integrated with the error handling system to be described in Chapter 15.

Listing 8-8 Instantiating the Event Handler in the Auto_Open Procedure

```
' Initialize global variables.
InitGlobals

' Build the custom commandbars specified in the
' wksCommandBars table.
If Not bBuildCommandBars() Then Err.Raise glHANDLED_ERROR

' Instantiate the control event handler class variable.
Set gclsControlEvents = New CControlEvents
```

The complete code from the CControlEvents class module that actually traps and handles the control events is shown in Listing 8-9.

Listing 8-9 The CControlEvents Class Module

```
Private WithEvents mctlPasteSpecial As Office.CommandBarButton

Private Sub Class_Initialize()
    ' Find and hook one of our custom buttons.
    ' The Click event will fire when *any* of the controls with
    ' the same ID and Tag are clicked, as well as when the
    ' built-in control whose ID we're using is clicked.
    ' We've given all our controls the same ID and Tag, so
    ' we're handling the click events for all our controls
    ' using a single hook and event handler.
    Set mctlPasteSpecial = _
            Application.CommandBars.FindControl(Tag:=gsMENU_TAG)
End Sub

Private Sub Class_Terminate()
    Set mctlPasteSpecial = Nothing
End Sub

Private Sub mctlPasteSpecial_Click( _
                ByVal Ctrl As Office.CommandBarButton, _
                CancelDefault As Boolean)

    Dim uPasteType As XlPasteType

    ' This is called for all instances of the built-in
    ' Paste Special > Values button as well as our custom
    ' Paste Special buttons, so check if it's one of ours.
    ' If the button is not one of ours, we'll do nothing
    ' and Excel will perform its normal action for that
    ' button.
    If Ctrl.Tag = gsMENU_TAG Then

        ' It is one of ours, so set the appropriate paste type.
        Select Case Ctrl.Parameter
            Case gsMENU_PS_ALL
                uPasteType = xlPasteAll
            Case gsMENU_PS_FORMULAS
                uPasteType = xlPasteFormulas
            Case gsMENU_PS_VALUES
```

```
                uPasteType = xlPasteValues
        Case gsMENU_PS_FORMATS
                uPasteType = xlPasteFormats
        Case gsMENU_PS_COMMENTS
                uPasteType = xlPasteComments
        Case gsMENU_PS_VALIDATION
                uPasteType = 6  ' xlPasteValidation in 2002+
        Case gsMENU_PS_COLWIDTHS
                uPasteType = 8  ' xlPasteColumnWidths in 2002+
    End Select

    ' If the paste special doesn't succeed, fail silently.
    On Error Resume Next
        Selection.PasteSpecial uPasteType
    On Error GoTo 0

    ' We handled the event, so cancel its default behavior.
    CancelDefault = True

    End If

End Sub
```

When the global gclsControlEvents class variable is instantiated by the Auto_Open procedure, the first thing that happens is the Class_Initialize event fires. This event locates a single instance of a control on our Paste Special toolbar and assigns it to the internal WithEvents class variable. As we explained previously, this is enough to cause **all** the controls on our toolbar to be hooked by our event handler (as well as any built-in *Paste Values* controls on which our custom controls are based).

Because Excel is managing whether our controls are enabled or disabled, when our mctlPasteSpecial_Click event does fire, we know the user has clicked one of our controls **and** there is something on the Clipboard that can potentially be pasted. The first item of business is then to determine whether the control that fired the click event is one of our custom controls. We do this by comparing the Tag property exposed by the Ctrl argument to the Tag value that we assigned to each of our custom controls. If the Tag property of the Ctrl argument doesn't match the Tag value we assigned to our custom controls, we know that a built-in Excel control fired the event procedure. In this case we simply exit the procedure without doing anything. This allows Excel to perform the default action for that built-in control, which is the behavior we want.

If the Tag property of the control that fired the event matches the Tag value we assigned to our custom controls then we know we're dealing with one of our custom controls. In this case we continue processing. The action we take depends on the value of the Parameter property of the control that fired the event. The Parameter property is used to distinguish among our custom controls because the Control ID and Tag properties are identical for all of them. This is what allows them all to fire the same event procedure.

In this case, the Parameter value is used to specify the type of paste special operation that should be performed. Within the event procedure we convert the Parameter value into one of the `xlPasteType` enumeration values. Once we have the correct paste special enumeration value, we attempt to perform the specified operation. This paste special operation is wrapped in `On Error Resume Next`/`On Error GoTo 0` so no error will be generated if the paste special operation being attempted is not valid for the current version of Excel or the contents of the Clipboard. We explain the use of the various permutations of the `On Error` statement in more detail in Chapter 15.

Practical Example

Since we have not yet introduced the topic of error handling, the command bar builder that we integrate into the sample application at this point does not make use of any error handling techniques. This is not the preferred method, but we are using it to avoid confusing the addition of an automated command bar builder, discussed in this chapter, with the addition of error handling, to be covered in Chapter 15.

PETRAS Time Sheet

The toolbar for our PETRAS add-in is a simple one compared to the examples that we've seen already. We show it again in Figure 8-24 to refresh your memory.

FIGURE 8-24 The PETRAS add-in toolbar

All five buttons on the toolbar are custom buttons, and all of them use built-in Excel command bar control Face ID values, so there is no need to attach external pictures to them (see the section on the command bar builder Control ID column for an easy method to determine the ID values for built-in controls). A partial view of the command bar definition table is shown in Figure 8-25. We've frozen panes at column B and scrolled the right pane to column O to show some of the more interesting control settings. To see the entire table, simply set the IsAddin property of the PetrasAddin.xla workbook to False so the wksCommandBars worksheet is visible in the Excel user interface.

	O3	▼	ƒ𝑥 =msoButtonIconAndCaption		
	A	B	O	P	Q
1	Command Bar Name	Control Caption	Control Style	Face ID	Begin Group
2	PETRAS Toolbar				
3		New Time Sheet	3	2520	
4		Post to Network	3	107	TRUE
5		Add More Rows	3	296	TRUE
6		Clear Data Entries	3	47	TRUE
7		Exit PETRAS	2		TRUE
8	Stop				

FIGURE 8-25 The PETRAS add-in command bar definition table

The code within the add-in looks exactly like it did when we last saw it except for the addition of two code modules: MCommandBars and MPastePicture. These hold the code that reads the command bar definition table and builds the command bars it specifies. The procedure call used to create the command bar in the Auto_Open procedure is exactly the same as before. The difference is now it calls the BuildCommandBars procedure in the MCommandBars module instead of our previous, hard-coded command bar building procedure of the same name that was located in the MSystemCode module. There has been one simple change in the Auto_Close procedure. Rather than removing our custom toolbar with the line

```
Application.CommandBars(gsBAR_TOOLBAR).Delete
```

we are now calling the following MCommandBars procedure that is designed to work backwards through the command bars table and remove the command bars and controls it specifies:

```
ResetCommandBars
```

We've done this for illustration purposes only. In the simple case of a single, fully custom toolbar, the first line of code is the more efficient method for removal. When you begin building complex applications that use a combination of modified built-in and fully customized command bars, however, you will find it much easier to let the command bar builder remove your application's command bars based on the command bar definition table that defined them in the first place. A summary of the changes made to the PETRAS time sheet application to implement the table-driven command bar builder is shown in Table 8-2.

Table 8-2   Changes to the PETRAS Time Sheet Application for Chapter 8

Module	Procedure	Change
MCommandBars (new module)		New module containing the command bar building code.
MPastePicture (new module)		New module to support the command bar builder. Used to add a picture to and retrieve a picture from the Clipboard.
MOpenClose	Auto_Open	The BuildCommandBars procedure is now called from the new MCommandBars module instead of MSystemCode.
MSystemCode	BuildCommandBars	This procedure was removed because the task of building the command bars is now handled by the table-driven command bar builder.

PETRAS Reporting

Previous versions of the PETRAS reporting application have had a simple menu structure, little more than the usual *File > New, Open, Close, Save,* and *Exit* menus and a *Window* menu to switch between results workbooks. When we're displaying a results workbook, however, we would really like to provide most (but not all) of Excel's built-in menus, to allow our users to work directly with the workbook. Adding the command bar builder to the application makes this a trivial task of including the appropriate built-in menu IDs. In the definition table shown in Figure 8-26, for example, we include Excel's entire Edit menu (and all its submenus) just by specifying its control ID of 30003.

	A	B	C	L	M	N
1	Command Bar Name	Control Caption	Control Caption	OnAction	Control ID	Control Type
2	Petras Menu Bar					
3		&File				10
4			&New Consolidation...	MenuFileNew		
5			&Open...	MenuFileOpen		
6			&Close	MenuFileClose		
7			&Save		3	
8			Save &As...		748	
9			Page Set&up...		247	
10			Prin&t Area		30255	
11			Print Pre&view		109	
12			Print...		4	
13			&Exit	MenuFileExit		
14		&Edit			30003	10
15		&View			30004	10
16		&Insert			30005	10
17		F&ormat			30006	10
18		&Data			30011	10
19			&Consolidate Timesheets	MenuConsolidate		
20		&Window				10
21			&Arrange...		298	
22			Split		302	
23			&Freeze Panes		443	
24			Petras &Backdrop	MenuWindowSelect		
25		&Help				10
26			Microsoft Excel &Help		984	
27			&About Petras Reporting	MenuHelpAbout		
28	Stop					

FIGURE 8-26 The PETRAS reporting command bar definition table

If you look at the *OnAction* and *Control ID* columns of the table, you'll see we added a lot of rich functionality to our application just by borrowing Excel's standard menus. In fact all these features were added without us having to write ***any*** code to implement them.

Application Contexts

As dictator applications become more and more complex, we need an easier way to handle the enabling and disabling of the menu items than coding them individually. One approach is to introduce the concept of an application context, which is an identifier to specify what part of the application is being displayed. Typical contexts in Excel dictator applications include

- **Backdrop**—The static backdrop sheet is being displayed, so almost all menus not related to beginning work or exiting the application are disabled.
- **DataEntry**—We're in a data entry worksheet, so a limited set of editing menus are enabled.
- **Results**—We're in a results workbook, so all the editing and formatting menus are enabled.

We can specify the contexts in which each menu item (or an entire pop-up toolbar) should be enabled by listing the applicable contexts in the Parameter column of the definition table. In the PETRAS reporting application, we're only using the Backdrop and Results contexts.

Since the context is usually determined by the worksheet currently being displayed, we can use the application WindowActivate event to trigger the enabling/disabling by using code like that shown in Listing 8-10.

Listing 8-10   The Code to Implement Application Contexts

```
Private Sub mxlApp_WindowActivate(ByVal Wb As Workbook, _
                                  ByVal Wn As Window)

  'Set the correct context, depending if we have a results
  'workbook or not.
  If IsResultsWorkbook(Wb) Then
     EnableDisableMenus gsCONTEXT_RESULTS
  Else
     EnableDisableMenus gsCONTEXT_BACKDROP
  End If
End Sub


'Enable/disable menu items, depending on the
'application context.
Sub EnableDisableMenus(ByVal sContext As String)

    Dim cbCommandbar As CommandBar

    On Error Resume Next

    'Enable/disable key menu items, by calling the
    'EnableDisableMenuBar procedure, which recursively operates
    'on all Menu items in the structure
    EnableDisableMenuBar Application.CommandBars(gsMENU_BAR), _
        sContext, ""

    'Enable/disable all the toolbars
    For Each cbCommandbar In Application.CommandBars
        If cbCommandbar.Type <> msoBarTypeMenuBar Then
            cbCommandbar.Enabled = (sContext = gsCONTEXT_RESULTS)
        End If
    Next
```

```vb
        'Enable/disable the associated shortcut keys
        If sContext = gsCONTEXT_RESULTS Then
            Application.OnKey "^s"
            Application.OnKey "^S"
        Else
            Application.OnKey "^s", ""
            Application.OnKey "^S", ""
        End If

End Sub

'Recursive routine to process the menu bar hierarchy,
'enabling/disabling items based on their context.
Private Sub EnableDisableMenuBar(cbBar As CommandBar, _
            sContext As String, sBarContext As String)

    Dim ctlControl As CommandBarControl

    On Error Resume Next

    'Loop through all the controls on this bar
    For Each ctlControl In cbBar.Controls

        If TypeOf ctlControl Is CommandBarPopup Then
            'If it's a popup, recurse down to process its menus
            EnableDisableMenuBar ctlControl.CommandBar, _
                            sContext, ctlControl.Parameter

        ElseIf ctlControl.Parameter = "" Then
            'If the control doesn't have a parameter, use the
            'commandbar's parameter. This allows us to add entire
            'Excel builtin commandbars to our app, without
            'specifying every menu item on them
            ctlControl.Enabled = InStr(1, sBarContext, _
                                    sContext) > 0
        Else
            'Otherwise enable/disable the bar
            ctlControl.Enabled = InStr(1, ctlControl.Parameter, _
                                    sContext) > 0
        End If
    Next

End Sub
```

Adding the table-driven command bar builder required a number of relatively minor changes throughout the PETRAS reporting application, detailed in Table 8-3.

Table 8-3 Changes to the PETRAS Reporting Application for Chapter 8

Module	Procedure	Change
MOpenClose	Auto_Open	Set initial application context at end of routine.
MCommandBars		Replaced the entire module with the table-driven command bar builder.
MPastePicture (new module)		New module to support the command bar builder. Used to add a picture to and retrieve a picture from the Clipboard.
MGlobals		Added constants for application contexts.
MEntryPoints	MenuWindowSelect	We were using the Parameter to test for the PETRAS Backdrop menu item. Changed to use the caption instead, as the Parameter is now used for the application context.
CAppEventHandler	mxlApp_WindowActivate	Identify the application context and pass it to EnableDisableMenus, as shown in Listing 8-10.
MSystemCode	EnableDisableMenus	Implemented Listing 8-10, to enable/disable the menus based on application context instead of hard-coding each menu item.
MSystemCode	AddToWindowMenu	Set the Parameter value to Backdrop, Results when adding the workbook window menu items.
MWorkspace	RestoreExcelSettings	Moved the code to reenable the toolbars to here, from the old RestoreMenus routine (which has been replaced by the command bar builder).

Table 8-3 Changes to the PETRAS Reporting Application for Chapter 8

Module	Procedure	Change
wksCommandBars (new worksheet)		New worksheet to hold the command bar definition table.

Summary

The purpose of this chapter is to simplify command bar building in your applications to save time and allow you to focus more effort on good design. To assist in that effort we covered a number of best practice design principles that you should follow. Command bars are the user's entry point into your application. Make them easy to discover, easy to use, and easy to remember.

We introduced you to a table-driven command bar building methodology that removes most of the work associated with building and maintaining command bars for your application. We showed you how to create custom icon and mask pictures that allow you to avoid the problems associated with divergent appearance of custom command bar button icons among various current versions of Excel. We also explained how to hook the events generated when the user clicks on command bar controls so that you can control the behavior of those controls in a more granular fashion.

CHAPTER 9

INTRODUCTION TO XML

Microsoft has gradually added features that enable Excel applications to work with XML. Saving a workbook as XML was introduced in Excel 2002, the ability to read and write arbitrary XML schemas was introduced in Excel 2003, and XML became the native file format in Excel 2007. This chapter introduces XML and explains the most common ways we might want to use it within our Excel applications. The use of XML to create custom Excel 2007 Ribbon user interfaces is covered in Chapter 10, "The Office 2007 Ribbon User Interface."

XML

If you're primarily an Excel developer, you're probably also wondering what all the XML fuss is about. XML is a format used for the textual expression of data. In that respect it's no different from the fixed-width, comma-delimited or tab-delimited text formats we've been using for years. There are, however, a number of key factors that differentiate XML from all the other text formats that have come before it. These make it much more appealing to developers.

- XML is a **structured** format, which means that we can define exactly how the data is arranged, organized, and expressed within the file. When we are given an XML file we can validate that it conforms to a specific structure prior to importing the data. Because we know the structure of the file in advance, we know what it contains and how to process each item. Prior to XML, the only structure in a text file was positional. We knew the bit of text after the fourth comma should be a date of birth, for example, and we had no way to validate whether it was a date of birth, or even a date, or whether it was in day/month/year or month/day/year order.

- XML is a **described** format, which means that within the text file every item of data has a name that is both human and machine readable as well as being uniquely identifiable. We can open these files, read their contents, and understand the data they contain without having to refer back to another document to find out what the text after the fourth comma represents. Similarly, we can edit these documents with a fairly high level of confidence that we're making the correct changes.
- XML can easily describe **hierarchical** data and the *relationships* between data. If we want to import and export a list of authors with their names, addresses, and the books they've written, deciding on a reasonable format for a CSV file is by no means straightforward. Using XML, we can define what an Author item is and that it has a name, address, and multiple Book items. We can also define what a Book item is and that it has a title publisher and ISBN. The hierarchy and relationships are a natural consequence of the definition.
- XML can be **validated**, which means we can provide a second XML file called an XML Schema Definition file, or XSD, that describes exactly how the XML data file should be structured. Before processing an XML file we can compare it with the schema to ensure it conforms to the structure we expect to receive.
- XML is a **discoverable** format, which means programs (including Excel 2003 and later) can parse an XML data file and infer the structure and relationships between the items. This means we can read an XML file, infer its structure, and generate new XML data files that conform to the same structure with a high degree of confidence that the new XML data files will pass validation.
- XML is a **strongly typed** format, which means the schema definition file specifies the data type of each element. When importing the data, the application can check the schema definition to identify the data type to import it as. We no longer run the risk of the product code 01-03 being imported as a date.
- XML is a **global** format. There is only one way to express a number in an XML file (with US number formats) and only one way to express a date. We no longer have to check whether a CSV file was created with US or French settings and adjust our processing of it accordingly.
- XML is a **standard** format. The World Wide Web Consortium (W3C) has specified the way in which the content of an XML file is defined. This allows applications (including Excel 2003 and later) to read, understand, and validate the structure of an XML file, as well as create files that conform to the specified structure. It also allows *different* applications to read, write, understand, and validate the

same XML files, allowing us to share data between applications in an extremely robust manner.

Since the earliest computers, we've been storing data and sharing it between applications. If we control both ends of the dialogue it doesn't matter what's passed between them, so long as each end knows what to supply and what to expect and nothing goes wrong. If the format of a file is documented, any application can (in theory) be programmed to read and write the same data files. With XML files an application can read (or infer) the structure definition and join in any conversation without extra programming. Using XML just makes some things much easier and more reliable.

An Example XML File

Listing 9-1 shows an example XML file for an author, including his name, e-mail address, and some of the books he has been involved with.

Listing 9-1   An Example XML File

```
<?XML version="1.0" encoding="utf-8" ?>
<Author>
  <Name>Rob Bovey</Name>
  <Email>robbovey@appspro.com</Email>
  <Book>
    <Title>Professional Excel Development</Title>
    <Publisher>Addison Wesley</Publisher>
    <ISBN>0321262506</ISBN>
  </Book>
  <Book>
    <Title>Excel 2007 VBA Programmer's Reference</Title>
    <Publisher>Wrox</Publisher>
    <ISBN>0470046430</ISBN>
  </Book>
</Author>
```

If XML lives up to its hype, you should be able to read and understand all the items of data in that file and understand the relationships between the elements. Just in case, we highlight the main items.

- The first line identifies the contents of the file as XML. Every XML file starts with this line.
- The file consists of both data and pairs of tags surrounding the data, which are together called an **element**. Our file consists of Author,

Name, Email, Book, Title, Publisher, and ISBN elements. A tag is identified by text enclosed within angle brackets, like <Tag>. All the tags come in pairs, with an opening tag like <Tag> and a closing tag like </Tag>; all the text between the opening and closing tags in some way "belongs" to the tag. However, if nothing is contained within the opening and closing tags, they can be combined so that <Tag></Tag> can be shown as <Tag/>. This is often used when the data for an element is provided as an **attribute** of the element, using a syntax like <Publisher name="Addison Wesley"/>. There is little difference between using elements or attributes, though our preference is to use elements. Note that tags and attributes are case-sensitive, so <Author> does not match with </author>.

- The second line identifies a **root element**, which in this file represents an Author. Every XML file must have one and only one root element; all other elements in the file belong to the root element.
- The third and fourth lines identify the author's name and e-mail address. We know it's the author's name and e-mail address because they're both within the same <Author> element.
- The fifth line is the start of a Book element, with the next three lines giving the book's details (as they're contained within the Book element). The ninth line closes the Book element, telling us we've finished with that book.
- Lines 10 to 14 show a second Book element, with the book's details.
- Line 15 closes the Author element, telling us we've finished with that author.

That example hopefully demonstrates the main attributes of an XML file. It is structured, described, hierarchical, and relational. Next we show how an XML file is validated.

An Example XSD File

The structure of an XML file is specified using an XML Schema Definition file, which usually has the extension XSD and contains sets of XML tags that have been defined by the World Wide Web Consortium (W3C). The XSD file for the Author XML data is shown in Listing 9-2.

Listing 9-2 An Example XSD File

```
<?XML version="1.0" ?>
<xs:schema xmlns:xs="http://www.w3.org/2001/XMLSchema">
```

```
<xs:element name="Author">
 <xs:complexType>
  <xs:sequence>
   <xs:element name="Name" type="xs:string"/>
   <xs:element name="Email" type="xs:string"
              minOccurs="0" maxOccurs="unbounded"/>
   <xs:element name="Book"
              minOccurs="0" maxOccurs="unbounded">
    <xs:complexType>
     <xs:sequence>
      <xs:element name="Title" type="xs:string"/>
      <xs:element name="Publisher" type="xs:string"/>
      <xs:element name="ISBN" type="xs:string"/>
     </xs:sequence>
    </xs:complexType>
   </xs:element>
  </xs:sequence>
 </xs:complexType>
</xs:element>
</xs:schema>
```

This is slightly less readable XML. We explain how to create an XSD file later in the chapter, but it's helpful to understand how this file describes the structure of the XML data file shown in Listing 9-1.

- Like all XML files, the first line identifies the contents as XML.
- The second line identifies the namespace http://www.w3.org/2001/XMLSchema and gives it the alias, xs. This is the namespace defined by the W3C that contains all the XML tags used in XML Schema Definition files. When we need to use a tag from that namespace, we precede it with the xs: alias identifier so the XML processor can correctly identify it. This mechanism of using namespace aliases is often encountered in XML files that contain elements from multiple namespaces (such as Excel workbook files, which contain tags from both the Excel and Office namespaces).
- The third line defines an Author element that must occur once and only once in the file (unless otherwise specified, the default occurrence of a tag is "must occur once and only once"), so our XML data file can only be for one author.
- The fourth line states that the Author element is a complexType, which means it contains other elements.

- The fifth line states that all the items within the Author element must be listed in the sequence shown in the XSD file, that is, Name then Email then Book.
- The sixth line defines an element within Author called Name of type string, and there must be one and only one of them. The use of the "/>" at the end of the element tag is a shorthand for creating a self-closing tag, so <Tag/> is equivalent to <Tag></Tag>.
- The seventh and eighth lines define an element within Author called Email of type string, which doesn't have to occur (minOccurs="0"), or there can be any number of them (maxOccurs="unbounded").
- Lines 9-15 define an element within Author called Book, of which there can be any number. If provided, each Book element must contain a single Title, Publisher, and ISBN string element in that order.
- Lines 16-22 close out the tags.

Before we import any data files we can verify that they conform to these rules (assuming we have the XSD file to check them against) and reject any files that can't be validated.

Overview of Excel 2003's XML Features

NOTE The XML features added to Excel 2003 are only available in the Professional version of Office and standalone version of Excel. They have been disabled in the Standard and Student versions of Office. In practice, this means that if we want to utilize the new XML features, all our users must be running Office 2003 Professional or higher.

Throughout this book, we stress the importance of physically separating our data from our code so we can easily update our code without affecting the data. The only separation boundary we've been able to define so far is the boundary between VBA and our data entry templates. When it comes to our data entry template files, however, it's not necessarily obvious what we should consider our "code" to be and hence where to put the break between application and data.

Whenever we've had a new set of data to store, we've stored it inside a copy of our template. That leaves us a little concerned that we don't have to change anything in the template. If we discovered a bug in the data validation settings, for example, we would have to open and update every copy of every workbook created using that template (or choose to ignore it for archived files). We haven't really separated our data from our logic. Within each of our data files we're storing a lot of formatting, validation, and ancillary information as well as the data entered by the users.

What we'd really like to do is to completely separate the raw data from the formatting and data validation so we would only need one copy of the data entry workbook on each machine that could import and export the raw data. That's exactly what Excel 2003's XML features allow us to do.

Using Excel 2003's new *XML Source* Task Pane we can import an XML Schema Definition file into a workbook and link the elements defined in that file to cells (for the single elements) or Lists (for the multiple-occurring elements) in the workbook. A List is a new feature in Excel 2003 that allows us to tell Excel that a range contains a table or list of data. Lists are covered in more detail in Chapter 20, "Data Manipulation Techniques." Excel can then treat the range more intelligently, by adding AutoFilter drop-downs, automatic totals, and automatically adjusting formulas that refer to columns in the list as new rows are added.

We can then import any XML data file that conforms to the schema into our workbook. Excel parses the XML data file, verifies that it conforms to the schema, reads the data from all the elements, and populates the linked cells and lists. Figure 9-1 shows an Excel workbook containing the XSD from Listing 9-2 and having imported the XML data from Listing 9-1.

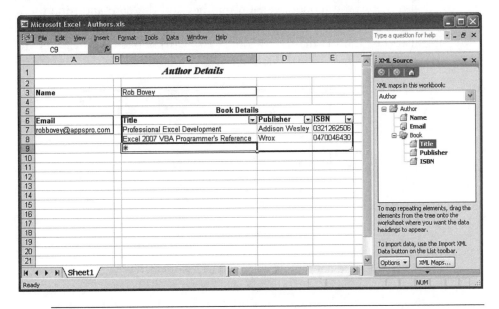

FIGURE 9-1   An Excel workbook linked to an XML schema

We can also type data into the linked cells and Lists and export the data as an XML file. Excel creates an XML data file that conforms to the schema and contains the data from the linked cells and lists.

Excel's XML features can greatly help with the maintenance of our financial models. Until Excel 2003, if we wanted to use our model to analyze different data sets we'd have to use a separate copy of the model workbook for each set. If we subsequently found an error in our model we would have to open and update all the copies. In Excel 2003 we can create a schema for our model's input variables and another schema for its results, include them both in the workbook and link them to the relevant cells or Lists. We can then use a single copy of the model workbook to import the input variables, calculate the model, and export the results.

These XML features are all exposed to VBA, so we can easily identify which cells are linked to which elements of which schemas (and vice versa), read and write the XML to and from strings as well as (or instead of) importing and exporting files, and respond to events raised both before and after XML data is imported or exported.

A Simple Financial Model

To demonstrate how Excel 2003 uses XML, we create a simple financial model that calculates the Net Present Value of a list of cash flows, giving us the number of flows, the total cash flow, and the net present value. We also record the model's version number and the date and time the model was calculated. Figure 9-2 shows the spreadsheet for the model, which can also be found in the Model1.xls workbook on the CD in the \Concepts\Ch09 – Introduction to XML folder.

	A	B	C	D	E
1	Net Present Value Calculation Model				
2					
3	Control Information			Processing Details	
4	Submitted by:	Rob Bovey		Version:	1.0
5	Email:	robbovey@appspro.com		Date:	22 Dec 2008
6	Comment:	Fee Fi Fo Fum			
7					
8	Input Data			Results	
9	Rate	Flows		Flows:	4
10	5%		10	Total:	100.00
11			20	NPV:	86.49
12			30		
13			40		

FIGURE 9-2 The net present value calculation model

Note that the flows data in B9:B13 is in an Excel 2003 List, so as data is typed into it the references used in the functions in cells E9:E11 are automatically updated. This is obviously a very simple financial model to demonstrate the principles. In practice there may be many sets of input data, many worksheets of calculations, pivot tables, and a large set of results.

Let's assume for now that we want to analyze many sets of data, in this case different combinations of rates and cash flows, and we want to store each set of data so we can review it at a later date. Let's also imagine this is a large and complex model, so we'd prefer not to have multiple copies of it to keep in sync.

What we'd really like to do is tell Excel what bits of the file are the raw data and be able to import and export just that data in a form we could edit and even create offline. With Excel 2003, we can do exactly that.

Creating an XML Schema Definition

The first step is to create an XML Schema Definition (XSD) file to define our raw data. If we already have an XML file containing some data we want to import, Excel can infer an XSD from it. Excel generally does a good job at inferring the structure, but we have more control over the details if we define it ourselves.

For example, in the Authors XML file in Listing 9-1 the data file included a single e-mail address. In this case Excel would infer that the schema only allows one e-mail address, but the real schema allows multiples. Excel also always assumes data is optional, while we've made the author name mandatory. In our financial model, all the input data is shown with a light shading in Figure 9-2. From this we can see the structure we'd like to emulate.

- There is a single block of control information, which must exist.
- Within the control information, we have a name, e-mail address, and comment. For this example we make the name and e-mail required but the comment optional. Each item can occur only once (if at all), and they are all strings.
- We also have a single block of data information that must exist.
- The data information contains a single Rate number and multiple Flows numbers, all of which are Doubles. Though not required by the NPV function, we require a minimum of two cash flow amounts.

The XSD for this data is shown in Listing 9-3, which includes a root NPVModelData element to contain our data types.

Listing 9-3 The XSD File for the NPV Model Data

```xml
<?XML version="1.0" ?>
<XSD:schema xmlns:XSD="http://www.w3.org/2001/XMLSchema">
 <XSD:element name="NPVModelData">
  <XSD:complexType>
   <XSD:sequence>
    <XSD:element name="ControlInformation">
     <XSD:complexType>
      <XSD:sequence>
       <XSD:element name="SubmittedBy" type="XSD:string" />
       <XSD:element name="Email" type="XSD:string" />
       <XSD:element name="Comment" type="XSD:string"
                    minOccurs="0" maxOccurs="1" />
      </XSD:sequence>
     </XSD:complexType>
    </XSD:element>
    <XSD:element name="InputData">
     <XSD:complexType>
      <XSD:sequence>
       <XSD:element name="Rate" type="XSD:double" />
       <XSD:element name="Flows" type="XSD:double"
                    minOccurs="2" maxOccurs="unbounded" />
      </XSD:sequence>
     </XSD:complexType>
    </XSD:element>
   </XSD:sequence>
  </XSD:complexType>
 </XSD:element>
</XSD:schema>
```

You should be able to read Listing 9-3 and see the direct correlation to the data in our worksheet and the previous statements about the structure we want to emulate. A few noteworthy points are

- We always start an XSD file with the same first two lines.
- Every element that is a container of other elements must be followed by the <XSD:complexType> tag and a tag to identify how the elements are contained. In this example (and in most cases) we use the <XSD:sequence> tag to say that the elements are contained in the sequence shown.
- The Comment element includes the attributes minOccurs="0" maxOccurs= "1", which is how we specify an optional item. It doesn't

have to occur (minOccurs="0"), but if it does occur there can only be one of them (maxOccurs="1").

■ The Flows element includes the attributes minOccurs="2" maxOccurs="unbounded", which is how we specify that there must be at least two cash flows, but there can be any number. Theoretically, we should put maxOccurs="65527", as that is the maximum number of flows that will fit on our model worksheet.

XML Maps

Now that we have an XSD file describing our data we need to tell Excel to use it and to link each element in the XSD file to a worksheet cell or range. Importing the schema and linking it to cells is known as **mapping**, and Excel refers to these as **XML Maps** (which is Excel's terminology, not an industry standard). To map our XSD to our model, first open the Model1.xls file; then click the *View > Task Pane* menu and select the *XML Source* task pane from the drop-down in the task pane title bar, as shown in Figure 9-3.

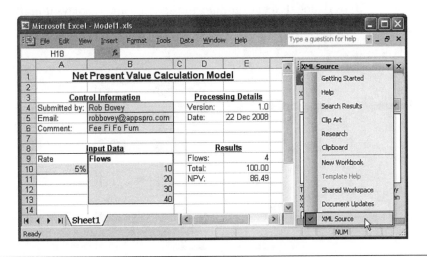

FIGURE 9-3 Selecting the XML Source task pane

Next, click the *XML Maps...* button at the bottom of the *XML Source* task pane to bring up the *XML Maps* dialog. Click the *Add* button on the dialog and browse to the XSD file. If the XSD is valid, Excel imports the schema and creates an XML Map using it, as shown in Figure 9-4.

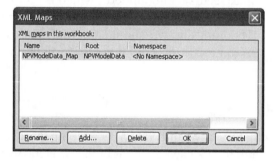

FIGURE 9-4   The XML Maps dialog after adding the NPVModelData Schema

If there is an error in the XSD, Excel shows you where it thinks the error is. Note that if we selected an XML data file instead of the XSD file Excel would infer a schema from the XML data. It is definitely best practice, though, to create and use an XSD file. When we click OK on the *XML Maps* dialog, Excel examines the schema and displays it in the *XML Source* task pane, as shown in Figure 9-5.

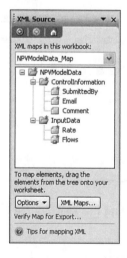

FIGURE 9-5   The XML Source task pane showing the NPVModelData Schema

Note that Excel has identified the hierarchical structure of the schema, the elements that are required (shown with an asterisk in the icon), and the elements that are repeating (shown by the arrow at the bottom of the Flows icon).

The final step is to associate the elements in the schema with the data entry cells in our model worksheet. We do this by selecting each element from the tree in the task pane, dragging it to the worksheet, and dropping it on the cell that we want to link it to. In Figure 9-6, we're dragging the SubmittedBy element and dropping it on cell B4.

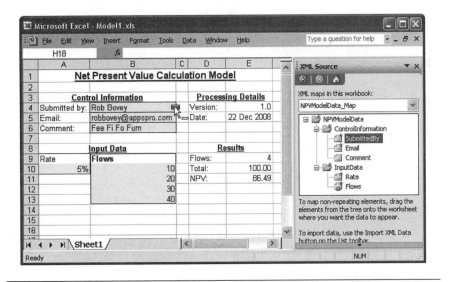

FIGURE 9-6 Drag and drop the elements from the task pane to the worksheet

We map the rest of the schema to our worksheet by dropping the Email element on cell B5, the Comment element on cell B6, the Rate element on cell A10, and the Flows element on cell B10 (or anywhere inside the Flows List).

As we do this, Excel annoyingly adjusts the column widths of each cell to fit the data it contains. We'd prefer the default behavior to not do this, and we can switch it off by right-clicking one of the mapped cells and choosing *XML > XML Map Properties* from the pop-up menu. This displays the *XML Map Properties* dialog shown in Figure 9-7, in which we've set the properties that we recommend using.

9. INTRODUCTION TO XML

FIGURE 9-7 The XML Map Properties dialog

The first check box *Validate data against schema for import and export* defaults to off, but in our opinion is the most important setting in the whole of Excel's XML support. With it turned on, Excel verifies that the XML data files we import conform to the format defined in the schema, and that any data we've entered conforms to the schema before allowing us to export it.

We've now defined the raw data our financial model uses, created an XSD file to formally specify it, added the schema to the model, and linked the elements in the schema to the model's data entry cells. The completed workbook can be found in the Model2.xls workbook.

Exporting and Importing XML Data

The menu items to import and export our XML data can be found on the *Data > XML* menu, with toolbar buttons also located on the List toolbar. Using the *Export XML* menu results in the XML data file for our model shown in Listing 9-4.

Listing 9-4 The XML Data File Produced from our Model

```
<?XML version="1.0" encoding="UTF-8" standalone="yes"?>
<NPVModelData>
  <ControlInformation>
    <SubmittedBy>Rob Bovey</SubmittedBy>
    <Email>robbovey@appspro.com</Email>
    <Comment>Fee Fi Fo Fum</Comment>
  </ControlInformation>
```

```
<InputData>
   <Rate>0.05</Rate>
   <Flows>10</Flows>
   <Flows>20</Flows>
   <Flows>30</Flows>
   <Flows>40</Flows>
</InputData>
</NPVModelData>
```

Hopefully everything in this file makes sense by now, particularly the multiple <Flows> elements. If we delete the <Comment> element, add a few more <Flows> elements to the bottom, save it with a different name, and use the *Import XML* menu to import it back into our model, we get the worksheet shown in Figure 9-8. Remember that our XSD file specified the <Comment> tag as optional, so our file passes the schema validation even though the comment data is missing. The extra <Flows> elements have been included in the List, which has automatically extended to accommodate them, and the formulas in cells E9:E11 have also automatically been adjusted to encompass the extended data range.

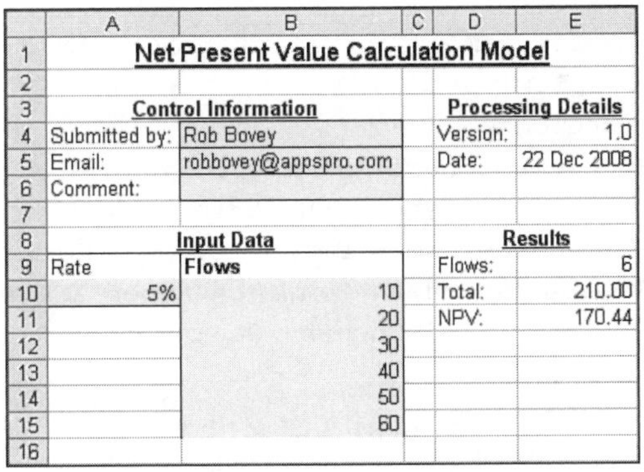

FIGURE 9-8 Importing an XML data file adjusts the ranges as required.

We have achieved our goal of being able to completely separate our data from our model, importing and exporting the data as we choose, with the model automatically updating to use the new data as we import it.

The XML Object Model and Events

Now that we can import and export the raw data for the model, the next step is to export the results, with the export file also containing a copy of the input data and details about the model itself, such as the version number and when the calculation was performed. Listing 9-5 shows the XSD file for the full set of our NPVModel data, which can be found on the CD in the NPVModel.xsd file.

The definition for the NPVModelData schema from Listing 9-3 has been included inside the new root NPVModel tag, and we've added elements for the model details and results. It may look complicated, but it really isn't. Just remember that when we want to nest one element inside another we have to include a pair of <XSD:complexType> and <XSD:sequence> tags between them.

Listing 9-5 The Full XSD File for our Model

```
<?XML version="1.0" ?>
<XSD:schema xmlns:XSD="http://www.w3.org/2001/XMLSchema">
 <XSD:element name="NPVModel">
  <XSD:complexType>
   <XSD:sequence>
    <XSD:element name="NPVModelData">
     <XSD:complexType>
      <XSD:sequence>
       <XSD:element name="ControlInformation">
        <XSD:complexType>
         <XSD:sequence>
          <XSD:element name="SubmittedBy"
                       type="XSD:string" />
          <XSD:element name="Email" type="XSD:string" />
          <XSD:element name="Comment" type="XSD:string"
                       minOccurs="0" maxOccurs="1" />
         </XSD:sequence>
        </XSD:complexType>
       </XSD:element>
       <XSD:element name="InputData">
        <XSD:complexType>
         <XSD:sequence>
          <XSD:element name="Rate" type="XSD:double" />
          <XSD:element name="Flows" type="XSD:double"
                       minOccurs="2" maxOccurs="unbounded" />
         </XSD:sequence>
        </XSD:complexType>
       </XSD:element>
      </XSD:sequence>
     </XSD:complexType>
    </XSD:element>
```

```
<XSD:element name="NPVModelDetails">
  <XSD:complexType>
    <XSD:sequence>
      <XSD:element name="ModelVersion" type="XSD:string" />
      <XSD:element name="CalcDate" type="XSD:dateTime" />
    </XSD:sequence>
  </XSD:complexType>
</XSD:element>
<XSD:element name="NPVModelResults">
  <XSD:complexType>
    <XSD:sequence>
      <XSD:element name="FlowCount" type="XSD:double" />
      <XSD:element name="FlowTotal" type="XSD:double" />
      <XSD:element name="FlowNPV" type="XSD:double" />
    </XSD:sequence>
  </XSD:complexType>
</XSD:element>
        </XSD:sequence>
      </XSD:complexType>
    </XSD:element>
</XSD:schema>
```

We can add this schema to our model as a second XML Map and map the NPVModelDetails and NPVModelResults elements to the appropriate cells in column E. When we try to map the ControlInformation elements to the cells in column B, however, Excel displays the error message "The operation cannot be completed because the result would overlap an existing XML mapping" and prevents us from doing the mapping. This is because Excel limits us to a one-to-one relationship between cells and XML elements. Any one cell can only map to one element from one XML Map and vice versa.

We want all our input data to map to both the NVPModelData map (so we can import it) and the NVPModel map (so we can include it in the export). The only way we can achieve our objective is to have a copy of the input data that we include in our NPVModel map, as shown in Figure 9-9. All the single-cell inputs such as the e-mail address and rate can be linked using standard worksheet formulas, but the Lists will have to be synchronized through VBA.

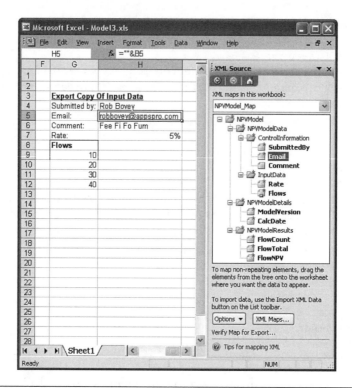

FIGURE 9-9 Mapping the NPVModel elements to a copy of the input data

Fortunately, Excel 2003 includes a rich object and event model for working with XML Maps. We can use the Workbook_BeforeXMLExport event to copy the Flows data from the input range (B9 and below) to the export range (G8 and below), using the mapping to identify the ranges in each case, as shown in Listing 9-6.

Listing 9-6 Copying the Input Flows List to the Export Copy

```
'Run before any XML is exported
Private Sub Workbook_BeforeXMLExport(ByVal Map As XMLMap, _
    ByVal Url As String, Cancel As Boolean)

  Dim rngSource As Range
  Dim rngTarget As Range

  'Are we exporting the full Model data?
  If Map.RootElementName = "NPVModel" Then

    'Find the data part of the target List
```

```
Set rngTarget = Sheet1.XMLDataQuery( _
    "/NPVModel/NPVModelData/InputData/Flows")

'If there is any existing data in the target List,
'remove it.
If Not rngTarget Is Nothing Then rngTarget.Delete

'Find the data part of the source List
Set rngSource = Sheet1.XMLDataQuery( _
    "/NPVModelData/InputData/Flows")

'Is there any source data to copy?
If Not rngSource Is Nothing Then

  'Find the header part of the target List
  Set rngTarget = Sheet1.XMLMapQuery( _
      "/NPVModel/NPVModelData/InputData/Flows")

  'Copy the data to the cell below the target List header
  rngSource.Copy
  rngTarget.Cells(1).Offset(1, 0).PasteSpecial xlValues

End If

End If

End Sub
```

Within the object model, ranges and XML schema elements are linked using XPaths. The XPath is a concatenated string of all the element names in an element's hierarchy. To get to the Flows element in the NPVModelData map we start at the root NPVModelData, go down to the InputData element, and then to the Flows element, so the XPath for the Flows element in that map is /NPVModelData/InputData/Flows. This path is stored in the XPath property of the Range object, so we can use the XPath property to determine which element a Range is mapped to.

To find the range mapped to a given element we use the XMLMapQuery and XMLDataQuery methods, passing the XPath of the element. It's a curiosity of the object model that while XML Maps are workbook-level items and an element can be mapped to any range in any sheet in the workbook, the XMLMapQuery and XMLDataQuery methods are worksheet-level methods. If we didn't know which sheet the range was on, we'd have to scan through them all, repeating the XMLMapQuery for each.

Both XMLMapQuery and XMLDataQuery return the range that is mapped to a given XPath string. The only difference between them is when the mapped range is a List. In this case, the XMLMapQuery returns the full range of the List, including the header row, while the XMLDataQuery returns only the data in the List or Nothing if the List is empty. With just a few mouse clicks, we can now import some raw data for our financial model, recalculate it, and export the results. This produces an XML data file like the one shown in Listing 9-7.

Listing 9-7   The XML Data File From Our NPV Model

```
<?XML version="1.0" encoding="UTF-8" standalone="yes"?>
<NPVModel>
  <NPVModelData>
    <ControlInformation>
      <SubmittedBy>Rob Bovey</SubmittedBy>
      <Email>robbovey@appspro.com</Email>
      <Comment>Fee Fi Fo Fum</Comment>
    </ControlInformation>
    <InputData>
      <Rate>0.05</Rate>
      <Flows>10</Flows>
      <Flows>20</Flows>
      <Flows>30</Flows>
      <Flows>40</Flows>
    </InputData>
  </NPVModelData>
  <NPVModelDetails>
    <ModelVersion>1.0</ModelVersion>
    <CalcDate>2008-12-22T13:44:04.430</CalcDate>
  </NPVModelDetails>
  <NPVModelResults>
    <FlowCount>4</FlowCount>
    <FlowTotal>100</FlowTotal>
    <FlowNPV>86.49</FlowNPV>
  </NPVModelResults>
</NPVModel>
```

It's not hard to imagine our financial model being used as a "black box" service, whereby individuals (or other applications) submit XML files containing the raw data for the model, and we import it, calculate, export the results, and send them back.

Notice the very specific format used for the date and time in the CalcDate element. This is how XML avoids the issue of identifying different date formats. It doesn't, however, account for different time zones.

By adding the ability to export results directly from our model we also created a vulnerability. Users could import data into the NPVModel map, which would overwrite our formulas. We can prevent this using the Workbook_BeforeXMLImport event, as shown in Listing 9-8.

Listing 9-8   Prevent Importing of the Results XML

```
'Run before any XML is imported
Private Sub Workbook_BeforeXMLImport(ByVal Map As XMLMap, _
     ByVal Url As String, ByVal IsRefresh As Boolean, _
     Cancel As Boolean)

  'Are we importing to the full Model data?
  If Map.RootElementName = "NPVModel" Then

     'Yes, so disallow it
     MsgBox "The XML file you selected contains the " & _
            "results for this model, and can not be imported."

     'Cancel the import
     Cancel = True

  End If

End Sub
```

XML Support in Earlier Versions

Excel 2003 has made the handling of arbitrary XML files very easy, but we don't *have* to upgrade to Excel 2003 to use XML. As we mentioned at the start of the chapter, XML is just another text file format, so in theory we can read and write XML files using standard VBA text handling and file I/O code. When Excel 2003 imports an XML data file, it uses the MSXML library to perform the validation and parsing of the file, and there's nothing stopping us from referencing and using the same library from VBA. Of course, we also have to write our own procedures to import the data from the MSXML structure to the worksheet and export the data from the worksheet to an XML file.

Using Namespaces

All the examples shown so far in this chapter have ignored the use of namespaces. This means the XML files we use and produce are only identified by the root elements of NPVModel and NPVModelData. There is nothing in the file to identify them as the data for *our* NPV model. This means that in theory, someone else could create an XML file that uses a similar structure to ours and we could import it without knowing it was not intended for our application.

To avoid this, we can include a namespace identifier both in the XSD and XML files to uniquely identify all the tags in the file and hence the data they contain. When the file is processed the namespace is prefixed to all the tags, allowing the parser to distinguish between, say, the Name element in this file denoting the author's name and the Name element in a workbook file denoting an Excel Defined Name.

The text of the namespace can be any string, but should be globally unique. It is general practice to use a URL, which has the advantage that the viewer of the file could browse to the URL in the hope of finding a description of the namespace. We tell Excel the namespace to use by including it within the <XSD:schema> tag at the top of our XSD file, as shown in Listing 9-9.

Listing 9-9 Providing Excel with a Namespace

```
<?XML version="1.0" ?>
<XSD:schema xmlns:XSD="http://www.w3.org/2001/XMLSchema"
   targetNamespace="http://www.appspro.com/NPVModelData"
   xmlns:md="http://www.appspro.com/NPVModelData"
   elementFormDefault="qualified" >
   <XSD:element name="NPVModelData">
   . . .
```

When this schema is added to a workbook, Excel will remember the namespace, create an alias for it, such as ns0, ns1, ns2, and so on, and prefix that alias to all the elements in the file, as shown in Figure 9-10.

FIGURE 9-10 All the XML elements are prefixed with the namespace alias

When the XML is exported, Excel includes the namespace in the file and qualifies all the elements with the namespace alias, as shown in Listing 9-10.

Listing 9-10 Providing Excel with a Namespace

```
<?XML version="1.0" encoding="UTF-8" standalone="yes"?>
<ns1:NPVModelData xmlns:ns1="http://www.appspro.com/NPVModelData">
  <ns1:ControlInformation>
    <ns1:SubmittedBy>Rob Bovey</ns1:SubmittedBy>
    <ns1:Email>robbovey@appspro.com</ns1:Email>
    <ns1:Comment>Fee Fi Fo Fum</ns1:Comment>
  </ns1:ControlInformation>
  <ns1:InputData>
    <ns1:Rate>0.05</ns1:Rate>
    <ns1:Flows>10</ns1:Flows>
    <ns1:Flows>20</ns1:Flows>
    <ns1:Flows>30</ns1:Flows>
    <ns1:Flows>40</ns1:Flows>
  </ns1:InputData>
</ns1:NPVModelData>
```

It is definitely a good practice to use namespaces in our XML files to avoid any chance of Excel importing erroneous data into our applications. The only reason we haven't used them so far in this chapter is to avoid over-complicating our explanation of Excel's XML features.

Summary

By representing our data as XML we are able to define its structure, content, data types, and other rules and validate any data file against those rules before we attempt to process it. This can greatly increase the robustness of our data processing code while also reducing its complexity, making it much easier to maintain.

XML adds names, data types, and hierarchies to our data, allowing us to think of our data in terms of individual elements and the data they contain, in the same way that class modules allow us to think of our application in terms of objects and their properties and methods. Indeed, Visual Studio.NET displays XML data in Intellisense Lists, for example, in almost the same way as it does the content of object libraries.

Excel 2003's XML-handling features can perform most of the processing we would otherwise have to code, including checking for completeness and consistency and removing unwanted data such as header and footer records.

CHAPTER 10

THE OFFICE 2007 RIBBON USER INTERFACE

Ever since Office 2007 was released, **RibbonX** and its user interface (**Ribbon UI**) have been widely discussed in the Office developer community. As you would expect from a version 1.0 technology, RibbonX comes with limitations that prevent us from fully leveraging its UI capabilities. However, even at this early stage we need to understand the new UI paradigm so we can use it to create well-designed custom user interfaces.

Another challenge is to work in parallel with command bar and RibbonX UI technologies on a daily basis. This includes creating solutions that work with both the UIs, so called cross-version applications. In this chapter we discuss best practices for designing a Ribbon UI and coding RibbonX, while cross-version applications are discussed in Chapter 11, "Creating Cross-Version Applications." We also cover some advanced problems, especially for dictator applications. The table-driven process for building command bar user interfaces is a widely accepted de facto standard. This implies we also should use it with RibbonX, so we also cover that topic here.

Office 2007 also introduced a new file format called **Office Open XML** (**OOXML** or just **Open XML**). It provides the framework for RibbonX, and they are tightly associated with each other. The new file format also makes it possible to create and manipulate Office documents without using any software in the Office suite. This chapter also provides a short introduction to the Open XML file format.

The RibbonX Paradigm

For more than a decade, command bars have been the only UI technology we have needed to target. With RibbonX we have a new technology and a new UI paradigm, which together have a major impact on the way we work. At first glance it may appear the challenge is to learn and manipulate RibbonX. However, in our experience the real challenge is to work in parallel on a daily basis with both command bars and RibbonX.

RibbonX has advantages as well as disadvantages when compared to command bars. Although RibbonX is only in its first version, its foundation is set and the characteristics of the RibbonX paradigm can be summarized in the following way:

- Customizations are defined at design-time. They are defined using XML and stored as a custom part of the XML file format. But most of the controls' attributes can be modified at runtime using VBA (such as enabled, label, visible, and so on).
- When a workbook that contains Ribbon customization is opened, Excel automatically reads the Ribbon XML definition and creates the Ribbon UI that it specifies. No VBA code is required to initiate this process, and in fact there is no way to prevent it from occurring if you don't want it to happen.
- When a workbook is open and active, its Ribbon customizations are applied and visible. When the workbook is closed its Ribbon customizations are automatically removed.
- When an add-in of any kind is loaded, its Ribbon customizations are applied and visible for all open workbooks.
- In a custom Ribbon UI, all the built-in Ribbon controls can be incorporated, overridden, executed, or queried for their captions, images, and so forth.

An Introduction to the Office 2007 Open XML File Format

XML was first introduced with Office 2002, and since then Microsoft has continued to expand and improve the XML part of the Office suite. With the release of Office 2007 we have a new file format solely based on XML, the Open XML file format. The Open XML file format provides the ability to work with Office documents and their contents without requiring the use of an Office application. This leads to an increase in the alternatives available for generating server-side Office documents. It can also simplify the data exchange between different systems and Office documents.

Each Open XML based Office document is stored in a **ZIP archive**. This archive is a container that holds the user data in XML format as well as other files with style information, images, and so on. When a document is saved in the Open XML format it is compressed, which results in a smaller file size when compared to the binary file format. Microsoft claims we can get up to a 75% file size reduction, although we have typically seen file size reductions closer to 60% to 65%.

Because an Open XML document consists of several parts that are placed together in a ZIP container, it results in Office documents that are more robust than with the binary file format. This reduces the risk of lost information due to damaged or corrupted files.

It is a common requirement that solutions we develop target several versions of Excel. This raises the question of which file format we should use. The solution providing the smoothest interoperability is the .xls file format (Excel 97-2003 file format in Excel 2007). However, it is possible to use the Open XML file format with older versions of Office if the target computers have the *Microsoft Office Compatibility Pack for Word, Excel, and PowerPoint 2007 File Formats* package installed. This package is free and can be downloaded from the Microsoft Web site. Note that Office 2000 can only convert Open XML files to binary via the Windows Explorer.

The Structure of the Open XML File Format

The Open XML file format can be described as a structure made up of building blocks (parts) and connections (relationships) that are used to compose, package, distribute, and render the document content. The core of the file format is the use of XML reference schemas and a ZIP archive. When we save an Office document in the Open XML file format, a ZIP archive is created that contains the following components:

- **Part items**—Most part items consist of XML files that describe the application data and metadata. This modularity is an important characteristic of the file format as it enables us to locate a specific part and to work directly with just that part.
- **Content Type items**—These describe what file types are stored in a document part. For example, image/png denotes a PNG image. This information enables applications to determine the contents of any part in the package and to process its contents accurately.
- **Relationship items**—These specify how the collection of document parts comes together to form a document. While the parts make up the content of the file, the relationships describe how the pieces work together.

Let us examine the composition of an Excel file on our own. For this operation we need to have a ZIP program like WinZip or 7-Zip available. First we create an Excel file, create a chart in it, and save it under the name PED.xlsm. For the next step we need the **Office 2007 CustomUI Editor**, which is a free tool available for download from the Microsoft Web site. Open the file in the CustomUI Editor and add a RibbonX customization shown in Listing 10-1 to the workbook.

Listing 10-1   Sample RibbonX Customization

```
<customUI xmlns="http://schemas.microsoft.com/office/2006/01/customui">
    <ribbon startFromScratch="false">
        <tabs>
            <tab id="customTab" label="Custom Tab">
                <group id="customGroup" label="Custom Group">
                    <button id="customButton" label="Custom Button"
                    imageMso="HappyFace" size="large"
                    onAction="Callback" />
                </group>
            </tab>
        </tabs>
    </ribbon>
</customUI>
```

Finally, open the PED.xlsm file in a ZIP program. Its content should be similar to that shown in Figure 10-1. Some ZIP programs may require that you temporarily rename the file extension of the workbook to .zip to open it.

As we can see in Figure 10-1, an Excel file may consists of a great number of folders and XML files. These make it possible to work with individual parts of a file in great detail, but it is beyond the scope of this chapter to cover all the parts. We include both the Excel file (PED.xlsm) and the ZIP file (PED.zip) on the companion CD in the \Concepts\Ch10 – The Office 2007 Ribbon User Interface\Open XML File Format folder.

NOTE   If we have access to Visual Studio 2008 Professional or higher and have installed the free Microsoft Visual Tools for the Office System Power Tools, we can review and edit Ribbon customizations within Excel files using the Open XML Editor tool.

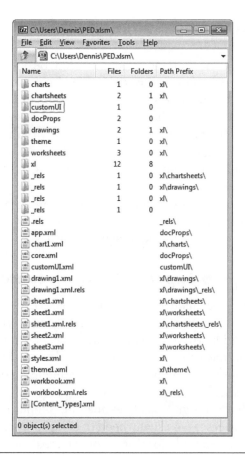

Figure 10-1 The content in a ZIP container

Whenever we add a Ribbon UI customization to a workbook or an add-in, a folder named `customUI` is created within the Open XML file structure. Inside the customUI folder, an XML file named customUI.xml is created, which holds all the required information to customize the Ribbon UI. When we update the customization of the Ribbon UI, the customUI.xml file is updated accordingly. All customization of the Ribbon UI using the CustomUI Editor tool affects the `customUI` part in the Excel file. Later in this chapter we discuss table-driven Ribbon UI customization with VBA.

Ribbon Design and Coding Best Practices

Many of the general recommended design approaches in Chapter 8, "Advanced Command Bar Handling," can also be applied to designing the Ribbon UI. As of this writing, Excel 2007 has only been available for about two years and still has a relatively small share of the market. As a consequence, the best practices for working with the Ribbon UI are only beginning to be agreed upon within the Excel developer community.

The following practices have been formulated based on our real-world development experiences and should be considered as just the start of a framework for best practices for designing and coding the Ribbon UI. Whenever a graphical user interface is involved the general best approach is to keep it simple and straightforward.

Design to Support the Work Processes

The major challenge in custom Ribbon UI design is to create a user interface that actually supports the underlying work processes. This means we need to identify the major work processes for a solution and implement them in the Ribbon UI design. We also need to identify the elements for each work process where those elements need to be implemented in a hierarchical structure.

These design objectives may be simple to achieve in theory, but in practical cases we usually need to compromise when designing the Ribbon UI. As an example for discussion we create a Ribbon UI design for a solution to track the budgets for various departments, projects, and clients, as shown in Figure 10-2.

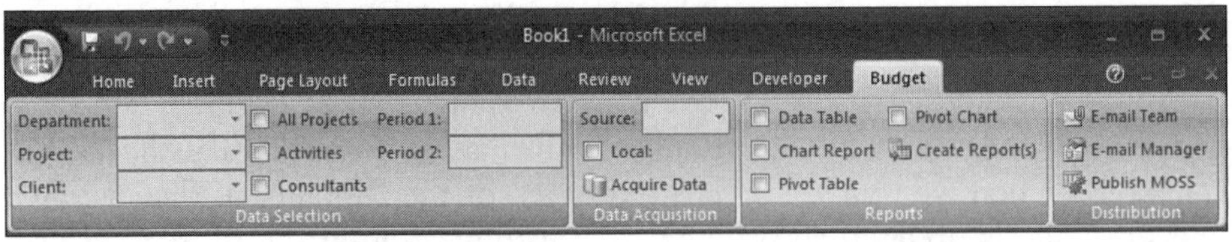

FIGURE 10-2   Ribbon UI design

In this example, we identified four major horizontal work processes that we have divided into four separate Ribbon groups:

1. **Data Selection**—Specify the parameters that identify the desired data.

2. **Data Acquisition**—Select the data source to be used and acquire the data.
3. **Reports**—Specify the desired reports and create them.
4. **Distribution and Publishing**—E-mail a report to a fixed recipient list or publish a report to a Microsoft Office SharePoint Service (MOSS).

As Figure 10-2 also shows, within each work process we identified the elements necessary to be implemented in a vertical hierarchical structure.

Using the Add-Ins Tab

In our experience the Add-Ins tab is the preferred location for the user interface of general add-ins. Using the Add-Ins tab for simple utility interfaces keeps the number of tabs down and the overall Excel user interface clean.

The Add-Ins tab should be used when an add-in requires only a few visible controls. Because add-ins that only create command bar based user interfaces are automatically placed under this tab, we can control whether individual add-ins should be placed here. Many third-party tools like SnagIt, which targets several versions of Excel, are intentionally placed under this tab.

Sharing Custom Tabs and Groups among Multiple Add-ins

In most cases we create individual solutions where each of them adds their own custom tabs, groups, and controls to the Ribbon UI. However, in some cases we want to share those items among several add-ins. For example, we have a main add-in that creates a basic tab, group, and menu structure to which other associated add-ins add their own specific items. Figure 10-3 shows an add-in that provides a tab that is designed to be shared.

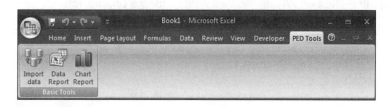

FIGURE 10-3   A shared tab

When an associated add-in is loaded, it uses the shared tab to host its group of controls, as shown in Figure 10-4.

FIGURE 10-4   Another add-in's controls added to the shared tab

This can be a handy approach for large-scale solutions. The key attribute required to create and manage a shared tab is the **namespace** attribute. Any time we create a custom Ribbon UI we use a namespace. The first line in all Ribbon XML includes the namespace http://schemas.microsoft.com/office/2006/01/customui, as shown in the next line:

```
<customUI xmlns="http://schemas.microsoft.com/office/2006/01/
customui">
```

The prefix `xmlns` is an abbreviation for XML namespace. Microsoft decided to use a URL as the namespace identifier for all Ribbon XML definitions. This namespace allows us to customize the Ribbon UI in all Office programs. In the next example we create our own custom namespace that allows us to identify and add controls to a custom tab from multiple files. This type of solution is called a **shared tab**.

A solution that shares a tab requires at least two Excel files. In this example we use two add-ins, one that acts as the host for the shared tab and another that adds a group with controls to the shared tab. First we create an add-in named Shared Tab.xlam and add the Ribbon XML to it that is shown in Listing 10-2.

Listing 10-2   Ribbon XML in the First Add-in for the Shared Tab

```
<customUI xmlns="http://schemas.microsoft.com/office/2006/01/customui"
        xmlns:nsPED="PED Namespace">
    <ribbon startFromScratch="false">
    <tabs>
            <tab idQ="nsPED:rxtabPED" label="PED Tools" visible="1">
            <group id="rxgrpBasic" label="Basic Tools" visible="1">
                    <button id="rxbtnImportData"
```

```
                    label="Import data"
                    screentip="Import Data."
                    imageMso="DatabaseAccessBackEnd"
                    size="large"
                    tag="Import_Data"
                    onAction="Shared_Basic_Tools_Click"/>
                <button id="rxbtnDataReport"
                    label="Data Report"
                    screentip="Create a data report."
                    imageMso="ImportExcel"
                    size="large"
                    tag="Data_Report"
                    onAction="Shared_Basic_Tools_Click"/>
                <button id="rxbtnChartReport"
                    label="Chart Report"
                    screentip="Create a chart report."
                    imageMso="PivotChartType"
                    size="large"
                    tag="Chart_Report"
                    onAction="Shared_Basic_Tools_Click"/>
        </group>
        </tab>
    </tabs>
    </ribbon>
</customUI>
```

At the top of Listing 10-2, we create a new namespace, nsPED. We also add a new attribute to the custom tab, idQ, which stands for **Qualified ID**. We prefix the tab's idQ attribute value with our custom nsPed namespace. By specifying the value of the idQ attribute in this way we make it possible to reference this specific tab object from any file that uses our namespace. The approach we show here for creating a shared tab can also be applied to shared groups and shared controls.

Next we add a global callback handler to a code module in the add-in, as shown in Listing 10-3. The Shared_Basic_Tools_Click callback handler uses the tag attribute of the calling control to determine which button triggered the callback.

Listing 10-3 The Callback Handler in the First Add-in

```
Option Explicit

Sub Shared_Basic_Tools_click(control As IRibbonControl)
```

```
Const sMESSAGE As String = "You want to "

Dim sActivity As String

Select Case control.Tag

    Case "Import_Data": sActivity = "import data."

    Case "Data_Report": sActivity = "create a data report."

    Case "Chart_Report": sActivity = "create a chart report."

End Select

MsgBox sMESSAGE & sActivity

End Sub
```

When the Shared Tab.xlam add-in is loaded, it creates the PED Tools tab previously shown in Figure 10-3. To illustrate the shared nature of this tab we create a second add-in and name it Add Group Shared Tab.xlam. We then add the Ribbon XML shown in Listing 10-4 to the second add-in.

Listing 10-4 Ribbon XML in the Second Add-in for the Shared Tab

```xml
<customUI xmlns="http://schemas.microsoft.com/office/2006/01/customui"
        xmlns:nsPED="PED Namespace">
    <ribbon startFromScratch="false">
    <tabs>
            <tab idQ="nsPED:rxtabPED" label="PED Tools" visible="1">
            <group id="rxgrpDistribution" label="Distribution">
                    <button id="rxbtnEmailTeam"
                            label="E-mail Team"
                            screentip="E-mail Team."
                            imageMso="AttachItem"
                            size="large"
                            tag="Email_Team"
                            onAction="Shared_Distribution_Click"/>
                    <button id="rxbtnEmailManager"
                            label="E-mail Manager"
                            screentip="E-mail Manager."
                            imageMso="FileManageMenu"
```

```
                               size="large"
                               tag="Email_Manager"
                               onAction="Shared_Distribution_Click"/>
                   <button id="rxbtnPublishMoss"
                           label="Publish MOSS"
                           screentip="Publish to MOSS."
                           imageMso="ExportSharePointList"
                           size="large"
                           tag="Publish_MOSS"
                           onAction="Shared_Distribution_Click"/>
            </group>
            </tab>
        </tabs>
        </ribbon>
</customUI>
```

When comparing the Ribbon XML in Listing 10-4 with the Ribbon XML previously shown in Listing 10-3, we see that they share the same namespace, nsPED and use the same idQ attribute and label name for the shared tab. This is required to share a tab among multiple files. Finally, we add the global callback handler to the second add-in shown in Listing 10-5.

Listing 10-5   The Callback Handler in the Second Add-in

```
Option Explicit

Sub Shared_Distribution_Click(control As IRibbonControl)

Const sMESSAGE As String = "You want to "
Dim sActivity As String

Select Case control.Tag

    Case "Email_Team": sActivity = "mail the report to the team."

    Case "Email_Manager": sActivity = "mail the report to the manager."

    Case "Publish_MOSS": sActivity = "publish the report on MOSS."

End Select

MsgBox sMESSAGE & sActivity

End Sub
```

When both add-ins are loaded, the Ribbon controls created by both of them appear on the same PED Tools shared tab shown previously in Figure 10-4. We can also load these two add-ins independently. Each of them is capable of creating the shared tab and placing its controls on that tab. However, this leads to a minor problem.

Because we lack a native mechanism to control the sequence of groups on our shared tab the order in which groups appear on the tab will vary depending on the sequence in which the add-ins that use the shared tab are opened. The best solution to this problem is to use a master file that controls the loading sequence of the associated files.

The add-ins we created in this example are available on the companion CD in the folder \Concepts\Ch10 – The Office 2007 Ribbon User Interface\Sharing Tab.

The keytip Attribute

We have seen some impressive Ribbon UI solutions where no **keytips** have been provided for the user interface. This is a serious limitation. When we press the Alt key it puts the keyboard into **keyboard navigation mode**. In this mode users can easily navigate the Excel Ribbon UI by just pressing characters on the keyboard.

The biggest problem with keytips is not the process of adding them to the Ribbon XML; that's easy. Rather the problem is determining the relevant characters to use. So many character combinations have already been taken by built-in Excel features that not many are left to choose from. In a dictator application this is less of a problem, but for general add-ins and workbooks it can be difficult to find good solutions.

Managing Control Custom Images

Office 2007 ships with a larger number of built-in images that can be used for custom controls. So before considering the use of custom images you should explore the built-in images available. Using built-in images also helps keep your user interface as familiar as possible. For example, instead of using a custom image for your Print button, use the same built-in picture that Excel uses. Using a large number of custom images may also have a negative impact on performance.

Microsoft has made an Excel file, Office2007IconsGallery.xlsm, available for download. This file adds a set of image galleries to the Developer tab that makes it easy to find the names of built-in images for use in your custom RibbonX. Another useful file available for download is 2007OfficeControlIDsExcel2007.exe, which lists all the built-in Control IDs.

If we decide it is necessary to use custom images, then the preferred image file format is **PNG**. The Ribbon drawing engine is designed to work best with full-color (24-bit) images that also have an alpha channel to control each pixel's transparency. Since the PNG file format supports an alpha channel and produces relatively small files, it is the best alternative. The preferred sizes of custom icons are either 16x16 (small size) or 32x32 (large size).

With the CustomUI Editor we can add custom images to workbooks, but we cannot refer to them in Ribbon XML. This means we need to use standalone image files. The Ribbon XML to use for PNG images is shown in Listing 10-6, where we specifically use the attribute `getImage`.

Listing 10-6 Ribbon XML for a PNG Image

```
<customUI xmlns="http://schemas.microsoft.com/office/2006/01/customui">
    <ribbon startFromScratch="false">
        <tabs>
            <tab id="rxtabPED" label="PED Tools" visible="1">
            <group id="rxgrpPED" label="PED Toolset" visible="1">
                <button id="rxbtnReport"
                label="Report"
                screentip="Create a report."
                getImage="GetImage"
                size="large"
                onAction="rxbtnReport_Click"/>
            </group>
            </tab>
        </tabs>
    </ribbon>
</customUI>
```

The callback handler for the `getImage` attribute is shown in Listing 10-7. The only problem with the PNG file format is that we need to have a custom solution to load them. This is because the built-in LoadPicture function in Excel 2007 does not support the PNG file format. In Listing 10-7 we use a custom function LoadPictureGDI, which takes one argument, the full path and filename of the PNG file to be loaded.

Listing 10-7 The Callback for the getImage Attribute

```
Sub GetImage(control As IRibbonControl, ByRef returnedVal)

    Set returnedVal = _
    LoadPictureGDI(ThisWorkbook.Path & "\Report.png")

End Sub
```

The custom function uses some **GDI+ (Graphics Device Interface)** APIs to convert the PNG image to an **IPicture** object. It is beyond the scope of this chapter to cover this process in detail. However, we include this custom function in the Load PNG pictures.xlsm workbook on the companion CD in the \Concepts\Ch10 – The Office 2007 Ribbon User Interface\Loading Custom PNG file folder.

Using Global Callback Handlers

By using global callback handlers we can handle several control objects at the same time. Having related control objects use a single callback handler makes our code better structured and less time consuming to maintain. In the RibbonX shown in Listing 10-8, the onAction attributes of all three buttons are assigned to a common callback handler, PED_Click.

Listing 10-8 Using One Callback Handler for Several Control Objects

```
<customUI xmlns="http://schemas.microsoft.com/office/2006/01/customui">
    <ribbon startFromScratch="false">
    <tabs>
        <tab id="rxtabPED" label="PED Tools" visible="1">
            <group id="rxgrpPED" label="PED Toolset" visible="1">
                <button id="rxbtnImportData"
                    label="Import data"
                    screentip="Import Data."
                    imageMso="DatabaseAccessBackEnd"
                    size="large"
                    tag="ImportData"
                    onAction="PED_click" />
                <button id="rxbtnDataReport"
                    label="Data Report"
                    screentip="Create a data report."
                    imageMso="ImportExcel"
```

```
                        size="large"
                        tag="DataReport"
                        onAction="PED_click" />
                <button id="rxbtnChartReport"
                        label="Chart Report"
                        screentip="Create a chart report."
                        imageMso="PivotChartType"
                        size="large"
                        tag="ChartReport"
                        onAction="PED_click" />
            </group>
        </tab>
    </tabs>
    </ribbon>
</customUI>
```

The `PED_Click` callback handler uses the `tag` attribute of the calling control to determine which button triggered the callback. This callback handler is shown in Listing 10-9.

Listing 10-9 The Common Callback Handler

```
Sub PED_click(control As IRibbonControl)

    Select Case control.Tag

        Case "ImportData": Import_Data

        Case "DataReport": Create_Data_Report

        Case "ChartReport": Create_Chart_Report

    End Select

End Sub
```

Invalidating

Invalidating is a resource-intensive process, and we need to be careful when to use it. Wherever possible we should invalidate specific controls rather than the whole Ribbon UI, as the latter may have a significant negative impact on performance. Invalidating controls does not reload them, it only refreshes them.

There appears to be a bug related to the getEnabled callback in the current version of the Ribbon. If you use the getEnabled callback to dynamically enable and disable specific Ribbon controls the callback may not fire correctly unless you invalidate the entire Ribbon rather than the individual controls.

Let us take a closer look at the invalidation part in the Ribbon XML and its requirements in VBA. We first need a variable in VBA to represent the IRibbonUI object. To get it we need to specify a callback procedure for the onLoad attribute, as shown in Listing 10-10.

Listing 10-10 Ribbon XML to Invalidate a Button

```
<customUI xmlns="http://schemas.microsoft.com/office/2006/01/customui"
    onLoad="rxRibbonUI_onLoad">
        <ribbon>
            <tabs>
                <tab id="rxtabInvalidate" label="PED">
                    <group id="rxgrpPed" label="Invalidate">
                        <button id="rxbtnPED"
                            getLabel ="rxbtn_GetTime"
                            screentip="Show the time."
                            imageMso="DateAndTimeInsert"
                            size="large"
                            onAction="rxbtn_Invalidate_Click"/>
                    </group>
                </tab>
            </tabs>
        </ribbon>
</customUI>
```

In this example, we refresh the date and time displayed by the button control every time it is clicked. We therefore need a callback procedure that invalidates the button control so we can refresh its content and a callback procedure to populate the button control with the current date and time. In Listing 10-10, we use the getLabel attribute to get the date and time, and we use the onAction attribute to invalidate the button control. The onLoad callback as well as the two button callbacks are shown in Listing 10-11.

Listing 10-11   Callbacks to Invalidate a Button

```
Private m_rxRibbonUI As IRibbonUI

'Callback for customUI.onLoad
Sub rxRibbonUI_onLoad(Ribbon As IRibbonUI)
    Set m_rxRibbonUI = Ribbon
End Sub

'Callback for rxbtnPED onAction
Sub rxbtn_Invalidate_Click(control As IRibbonControl)

    m_rxRibbonUI.InvalidateControl control.ID

End Sub

'Callback for rxbtnPED getLabel
Sub rxbtn_GetTime(control As IRibbonControl, ByRef returnedValue)

    returnedValue = CStr(Now())

End Sub
```

An example file containing this code is available on the companion CD in the folder \Concepts\Ch10 – The Office 2007 Ribbon User Interface\Validating Individual Controls. Microsoft has also made a document available that discusses design of the Ribbon UI. Search for 2007 Office System Document: UI Style Guide for Solutions and Add-Ins on the Microsoft Web site.

Table-Driven Ribbon UI Customization

When building command bar user interfaces the table-driven building process is the de facto standard, especially for large-scale solutions. We might assume there is no reason we cannot apply the same approach for customization of the Ribbon UI.

However, two major technical limitations prevent us from creating a table-driven Ribbon UI: In VBA we have no access to an object model to manipulate the Ribbon UI, and at runtime VBA cannot provide the XML for the Ribbon definition. It would have been useful to see a standard

GetCustomUI event added to the Workbook object and a CreateCustomUI method added to the Commandbars object.

In Visual Studio Tools for Office System (VSTO), we have access to a Visual Designer tool for the Ribbon UI that allows us to visually manipulate the Ribbon for our solution. This tool automatically generates the Ribbon XML file, callbacks, images, and other UI components based on our visual layout. In other words, in VSTO we have full support for customizing the Ribbon UI while in VBA we have no support at all.

In light of this situation, we can only conclude that Microsoft has relegated VBA to the status of second-class citizen. In the following section we discuss what we can do at present to work with the **customUI XML part** in individual Excel files using VBA.

Get Access to the customUI XML Part

To access the customUI XML part in Excel files we need to temporarily change the file extension to .zip, make the customization, and then change the file extension back to its original value. The temporary change to the .zip file extension makes all the new file format's XML parts visible and accessible in Windows Explorer, as shown in Figure 10-5. When we manually add a Ribbon UI customization to a file using the CustomUI Editor, the folder customUI is automatically created. The folder must exist if we want a customization to work properly. If the folder does not exist, it must be created before we create and save the customUI.xml file into it.

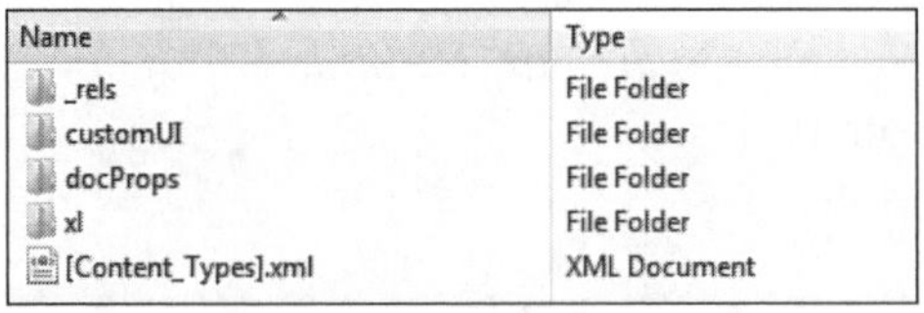

Name	Type
_rels	File Folder
customUI	File Folder
docProps	File Folder
xl	File Folder
[Content_Types].xml	XML Document

FIGURE 10-5 The content of a ZIP file

All the Ribbon XML must reside in the customUI.xml file. The Ribbon XML must also follow the **XML Schema Definition (XSD)** in the customUI.xsd. An XML file is simply a text file that uses the file extension .xml instead of .txt. Because of this we can create customUI.xml files in the same manner as regular text files. If we have enough knowledge to work with an **XML parser** like **Microsoft XML**, then that may be a better choice. As for updating a customUI.xml file, it is much simpler and faster to overwrite the current file with a complete new version than to write code to update it in place.

It is technically possible to create a tool in Excel to generate Ribbon XML based on entries in a worksheet table, similar to the table-driven setup for building command bar user interfaces. A far better option would be to develop such a tool on the .NET platform, mainly because of its extensive support for working with XML and the Ribbon UI.

Advanced Problem Solving

In addition to the lack of a Ribbon UI object model in VBA, the major criticism of the Ribbon UI is that it is less flexible than the old command bar user interface. Many commands are too deeply embedded in the UI to be easily accessible, and from a process point of view commands are not accessible in a logical way.

Custom Ribbon UI solutions can solve some of these limitations, while some other limitations, such as using additional controls, can only be solved with .NET and third-party tools. The remaining limitations, such as not being able to create custom or floating toolbars, are built into the Ribbon UI architecture and cannot be resolved. Here we discuss some of the more frequent issues that developers face and how to solve them.

Creating Ribbon UI for Dictator Applications

In a dictator application we completely remove the default Ribbon UI and replace it with a custom Ribbon UI. The standard approach is to set the attribute `startFromScratch="true"` in the Ribbon XML, which gives us the interface shown in Figure 10-6.

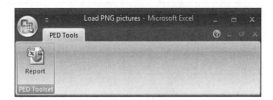

FIGURE 10-6 A basic dictator application Ribbon UI

The major advantage of this approach is that we do not need to use VBA code to set up our Ribbon UI when the workbook is opened. We also do not need VBA code to restore it to its default settings when our application closes. All this is done automatically when opening and closing the workbook.

As Figure 10-6 shows, the **Office button** is still available, including some basic commands, together with the **Quick Access Toolbar (QAT)**. Two of the items that remain under the Office button in a `startFromScratch="true"` Ribbon UI are the *Excel Options* button and the *Exit Excel* button. In a dictator application we may want to prevent access to these features.

Unfortunately, it is not possible to hide these two controls, so the best approach is to disable them. Although they are physically located on the Office menu, RibbonX does not allow us to manipulate them from the `officeMenu` element in the Ribbon XML. Instead we do it using the `command` element, as shown in Listing 10-12.

Listing 10-12 Ribbon XML to Disable the Excel Options and Exit Excel Commands

```
<customUI xmlns="http://schemas.microsoft.com/office/2006/01/customui">
...
    <commands>
        <command idMso="FileExit" enabled="false"/>
        <command idMso="ApplicationOptionsDialog" enabled="false"/>
    </commands>
...
</customUI>
```

Under the Office button menu the commands New, Open, and Save are also still available. If we want to hide these as well we do so using the `officeMenu` element as shown in Listing 10-13.

Listing 10-13 Ribbon XML to Hide the New, Open, and Save Commands

```
<officeMenu>
    <button idMso="FileNew" visible="false" />
    <button idMso="FileOpen" visible="false" />
    <button idMso="FileSave" visible="false" />
</officeMenu>
```

The remaining part to hide in the Office button menu is the **Recent documents list**, also known as the **Most Recently Used (MRU)** file list. This cannot be done using Ribbon XML, and in VBA we can only clear the list but not remove it. To clear the list on startup we use the first code block in Listing 10-14. When the application is closed we need to restore the maximum number of available files, which is done with the second code block in Listing 10-14.

Listing 10-14 Code to Clear the Most Recently Used File List

```
'A module variable to hold the maximum number of recently used files.
Dim miNumberOfFiles As Integer

    '...
    With Application.RecentFiles
        'Get the maximum number of available files.
        miNumberOfFiles = .Maximum
        'Clear the list.
        .Maximum = 0
    End With


    '...
    'To restore the maximum number of recently used files.
    Application.RecentFiles.Maximum = miNumberOfFiles
```

After running this code, the resulting Office button menu is shown in Figure 10-7.

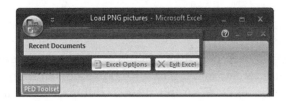

FIGURE 10-7 The Office button menu

Keep in mind that setting the maximum number of recent files to zero permanently clears the MRU list. Many users rely on this list and will not be very happy if it is not restored. This presents a problem. The MRU file list (as well as the maximum number of files setting) is stored in the Windows Registry in the key:

```
HKEY_CURRENT_USER\Software\Microsoft\Office\12.0\Excel\File MRU
```

It is technically possible to save and restore this registry key so we do not destroy the user's MRU list. However, it is common, especially in corporate environments, for our programs to be denied access to the registry. This prevents us from developing a truly robust solution to the problem of permanently clearing the MRU list.

Usually we also want to remove the default shortcut menu that is displayed by right-clicking on the worksheet surface. This is easy to do with VBA, as shown in Listing 10-15.

Listing 10-15 Remove the Right-Click Menu in Excel 2007

```
Private Sub Workbook_SheetBeforeRightClick(ByVal Sh As Object, _
                                 ByVal Target As Range, _
                                 Cancel As Boolean)

    Cancel = True

End Sub
```

We then substitute the default shortcut menu with our own custom command bar. We did not make a mistake when we said "command bar" in the previous sentence. Even in Excel 2007, the shortcut menus are still the same command bars as in previous versions of Excel.

They have been enhanced with some additional features we do not have access to, but they are still fundamentally command bars, and in a custom application we still replace them with our own custom command bars using:

```
Application.CommandBars("CustomMenu").ShowPopup
```

We can only guess that Microsoft intended to merge this part of the Excel user interface into the new Ribbon model, but simply ran out of time to do it in Excel 2007, so this may be different in future versions of Excel. All that is left to do now is customize Excel in the same manner as we did in Chapter 6, "Dictator Applications."

Hide the Ribbon UI

In some situations, we may need to completely hide the Ribbon UI. We can accomplish this by using VBA to execute the first XLM macro shown in Listing 10-16. To restore the Ribbon we use VBA to execute the second XLM macro shown in Listing 10-16.

Listing 10-16 Hide and Unhide the Ribbon UI

```
'To hide the Ribbon UI.
Application.ExecuteExcel4Macro "Show.Toolbar(""Ribbon"", False)"
```

```
'To restore the Ribbon UI.
Application.ExecuteExcel4Macro "Show.Toolbar(""Ribbon"", True)"
```

Figure 10-8 shows the result of using this technique to hide the Ribbon UI.

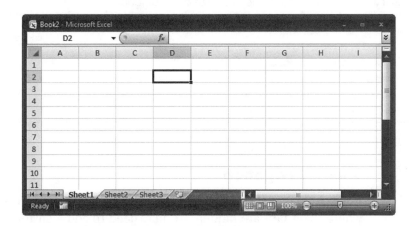

FIGURE 10-8   The Excel UI with a completely hidden ribbon

Two implications of this technique require further clarification. First, executing this XLM macro to hide the Ribbon UI affects all open workbooks in that Excel session. Second, this technique relies on continued support for XLM macros in Excel. XLM was the macro language used to develop Excel macros and applications prior to the introduction of VBA. It has been more than 15 years since XLM was officially replaced by VBA, and Microsoft is very likely to eliminate support for XLM within the next version or two of Office. Therefore, if you use this technique you cannot rely on it to work in future versions of Excel.

Determine the Size of comboBox, dropDown, and editBox Controls

In some cases, we may want to control the size of a `comboBox` and its related controls `dropDown` and `editBox`. To do so we use the `sizeString` attribute, but instead of using a number like 10 or 20 we enter a text string that contains the maximum number of characters we want to display. The specific characters we use in this text string are not important, but the font type used in the control does affect the actual width of the control.

If we need to limit the number of characters entered in the control, we use the `maxLength` attribute together with a number like 5 or 8. In Listing 10-17 we set the width of the `comboBox` to seven characters and the maximum number of characters to eight.

Listing 10-17   Ribbon XML to Set the Size of a comboBox Control

```
<comboBox id="rxcboName"
    label="Name:"
    sizeString="xxxxxxx"
    maxLength="8"
    screentip="Enter the name."
    onChange="rxcboName_OnChange"/>
```

Sheet Navigation

For solutions with many worksheets in the user interface workbook, or where sheet tabs are hidden, we may need to add a custom sheet navigation function. In this example we have six worksheets of which one is hidden. Therefore, we need to create a worksheet list containing the five visible worksheets.

In this example, we use the dropDown control instead of the comboBox control, mainly because the latter allows users to type new entries into the control, which we do not want to allow. However, one problem with the dropDown control is that unlike the comboBox control, it does not explicitly give us the name of the selected item, only its ID and index number.

Although we should strive to create fully dynamic applications, they come with the price of having to write code for all possible scenarios. In real-world applications we therefore tend to create semifixed applications where some parts are fixed and some parts are dynamic. That is how we build the solution in this example. Because we have a fixed list of worksheets whose names will not change during runtime we do not need to invalidate the dropDown control during runtime. On the other hand, we will not hardcode the worksheet names in order to ease future maintenance.

The worksheet "Hidden" is supposed to be hidden and therefore should always be excluded from the list. The Ribbon XML for this example is shown in Listing 10-18. The `getItemCount` attribute is used to retrieve the number of worksheet names, while the `getItemLabel` attribute populates the dropDown control with the list of names. By using these two attributes we get a more dynamic solution.

Listing 10-18 Ribbon XML for Sheet Navigation

```
<customUI xmlns="http://schemas.microsoft.com/office/2006/01/customui">
    <ribbon startFromScratch="false">
        <tabs>
            <tab id="rxtabPED" label="Sheet Navigation">
                <group id="rxgrpDropDowns" label="Navigation">
                    <dropDown id="rxddSheetNavigation"
                        label="Navigate to:"
                        getItemCount="rxdd_ItemCount"
                        getItemLabel="rxdd_ListItem"
                        onAction="rxdd_Item_Selected"/>
                </group>
            </tab>
        </tabs>
    </ribbon>
</customUI>
```

The required callback procedures are shown in Listing 10-19. The
rxdd_ItemCount callback returns a count of the number of visible worksheets in the workbook. This tells Excel how many times it should execute
the rxdd_ListItem callback. The rxdd_ListItem callback adds the names
of each visible worksheet to the dropDown control. When retrieving the
name of the selected worksheet we add 1 to the list index passed to VBA.
This is because the index array of the worksheet collection is one-based,
while VBA operates with zero-based arrays.

Listing 10-19 Callbacks for Sheet Navigation

```
Option Explicit

'Callback for rxddSheetNavigation getItemCount.
Sub rxdd_ItemCount(control As IRibbonControl, ByRef returnedVal)

    Dim lCount As Long
    Dim wksSheet As Worksheet

    Set mwkbNavigation = ThisWorkbook

    'Get the count of visible worksheets.
    For Each wksSheet In mwkbNavigation.Worksheets
        If wksSheet.Visible = xlSheetVisible Then
            lCount = lCount + 1
```

```
            End If
        Next wksSheet

        'Dimension the array of sheets.
        returnedVal = lCount

End Sub


'Callback for rxddSheetNavigation getItemLabel.
Sub rxdd_ListItem(control As IRibbonControl, index As Integer, _
        ByRef returnedVal)

        'Populate the dropDown control with sheet names.
        If mwkbNavigation.Worksheets(index + 1).Visible = _
            xlSheetVisible Then

            returnedVal = mwkbNavigation.Worksheets(index + 1).Name

        End If

End Sub


'Callback for rxddSheetNavigation onAction.
Sub rxdd_Item_Selected(control As IRibbonControl, id As String, _
        index As Integer)

    Dim sSheetName As String

    'Get the name of the selected worksheet.
    sSheetName = mwkbNavigation.Worksheets(index + 1).Name

    'Activate the selected name.
    mwkbNavigation.Worksheets(sSheetName).Activate

End Sub
```

When the workbook is launched, a new Sheet Navigation tab is created. Users can navigate to the desired sheet by selecting its name from the dropDown control, as shown in Figure 10-9.

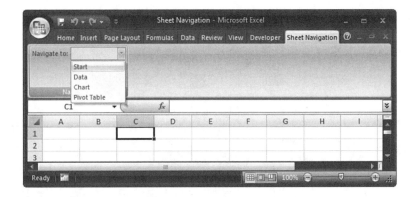

FIGURE 10-9   Sheet navigation

The workbook containing this example can be found on the companion CD in the folder *Concepts\Ch10 – The Office 2007 Ribbon User Interface\Sheet Navigation*.

Using Templates

By using templates, we save time during the development stage. The Custom UI Editor makes it easy to create and use customized Ribbon XML templates.

1. Create the Ribbon XML in the Custom UI Editor and validate that it is well formed.
2. Copy the XML into a text editor like NotePad and save it to the folder ...*Program Files\CustomUIEditor\Samples*\ with the file extension .XML.

Figure 10-10 shows how the Sample menu in the Custom UI Editor looks after we have added several templates. Selecting a template copies its Ribbon XML to the Custom UI tab.

FIGURE 10-10   Custom templates in the Custom UI Editor

Further Reading

RibbonX: Customizing the Office 2007 Ribbon

Authored by Robert Martin, Ken Puls, and Teresa Hennig
ISBN# 978-0-470-191111-8
Because the new Ribbon UI is an Office-wide feature, there are no books that cover only the Ribbon UI for Excel. This book covers Ribbon UI customization for Excel, Word, and Access. It is written in a straightforward, easy to understand way and should be considered the RibbonX "bible."

Related Portals

XML in Office Developer Portal

The XML in Office Developer Portal at Microsoft is a good starting point for more information about Open XML. Visit this site: http://msdn.microsoft.com/sv-se/office/aa905545(en-us).aspx.

OpenXMLDeveloper.org

Another good site on Open XML is the OpenXMLDeveloper.org site at http://openxmldeveloper.org/default.aspx.

The Office Fluent User Interface Developer Portal

The Office Fluent User Interface Developer Portal at Microsoft provides access to extensive information about RibbonX at this site: http://msdn. microsoft.com/en-us/office/aa905530.aspx.

Summary

In this chapter, we singled out some of the most important best practices for designing and coding RibbonX. As more experience is gained in these fields, the more these best practices will evolve. RibbonX is in many ways a new and interesting technology, but at the same time it has some serious limitations when working with it from VBA. Perhaps the major limitation is that we cannot use the table-driven building approach, especially for dictator applications.

CHAPTER 11

CREATING CROSS-VERSION APPLICATIONS

With the introduction of Office 2007 and Windows Vista, the life of Excel developers everywhere became much more complicated. As with each previous version of Office and Windows, we have to be sure our existing applications continue to run on these new platforms. Unlike the version updates of Office and Windows we have seen since the year 2000, however, Office 2007 and Windows Vista often require significant changes to our applications for them to continue to run correctly.

If at all possible we want to avoid writing applications that are version-specific to Office or Windows. As of this writing, it is still rare to encounter companies that have upgraded to Office 2007 or Vista across the board. Therefore, we need to determine how to modify our applications so they continue to work across all versions of Office and Windows using a common code base to the greatest extent possible. In this chapter we introduce techniques that allow you to accomplish this goal.

NOTE Throughout this book we attempt to present the well-accepted best practices for professional Excel development. However, the area of cross-version Excel application development is not yet mature, and there is not yet complete agreement within the Excel community on what the best practices are in this area. The authors have used the solutions presented here to create real-world applications and found them useful in most situations.

Command Bar and Ribbon User Interfaces in a Single Application

The primary problem facing us when we want to make our existing applications compatible with Excel 2007 and higher is the fact that the Excel user interface has changed to a completely different model. Although Microsoft constructed these newer versions of Excel so they do not technically break applications that attempt to create a command bar user interface, the results of this backward compatibility are primitive and unacceptable for professional applications.

There are a number of methods that can be used to develop applications that display a native user interface in both Excel 2003 and earlier (command bars) and Excel 2007 and later (the Ribbon). We focus on the two methods that we have found to be most useful. We refer to these methods as light weight and heavy weight.

Light Weight

Our light weight cross-version user interface design uses what is fundamentally a command bar based application. When it detects that it is being opened in Excel 2007 or later, however, it bypasses the construction of its command bar user interface and instead opens an Excel 2007 add-in that contains a Ribbon user interface.

The Ribbon UI add-in contains no features of its own. Its only purpose is to build the Ribbon user interface in Excel 2007 and later. The onAction attribute of each Ribbon control is assigned to a single callback procedure. This callback procedure determines which Ribbon control called it and then runs the same entry point procedures that would normally have been run by the corresponding command bar control in Excel 2003 and earlier.

The light weight user interface model is the best choice for applications that have relatively simple user interfaces. This method is not well suited to applications that need to dynamically modify the user interface in response to different situations.

To demonstrate this user interface design we created a simple example application that can be found on the companion CD in the folder *\Concepts\Ch11 - Creating Cross-Version Applications\LightWeight*. When opened in Excel 2003 or earlier, this application builds a toolbar with three buttons. When opened in Excel 2007 or later the application creates a custom tab on the Ribbon that contains the same three buttons.

The Excel 2003 version of the UI is shown in Figure 11-1, while the Excel 2007 version of the UI is shown in Figure 11-2.

FIGURE 11-1 The Excel 2003 toolbar UI

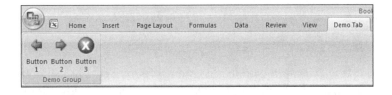

FIGURE 11-2 The Excel 2007 Ribbon UI

To run the example application, open the LightWeightUI.xla add-in in either Excel 2003 or Excel 2007. The Auto_Open procedure from this add-in is shown in Listing 11-1.

Listing 11-1 The LightWeightUI.xla Auto_Open Procedure

```
Public Sub Auto_Open()
    If Application.Version < 12 Then
        ' Build a command bar for Excel 2003 and earlier.
        BuildToolbar
    Else
        ' Open the file that creates a Ribbon UI for Excel 2007.
        Application.Workbooks.Open _
            ThisWorkbook.Path & "\" & gsFILE_2007_UI
    End If
End Sub
```

The entry point procedures that are assigned to the command bar buttons in our demonstration application are simple one-line macros that display message boxes to identify themselves. These entry point procedures are shown in Listing 11-2.

Listing 11-2 The LightWeightUI.xla Entry Point Procedures

```
Public Sub EntryPoint1()
    MsgBox "You clicked button 1.", vbInformation, gsAPP_NAME
End Sub

Public Sub EntryPoint2()
    MsgBox "You clicked button 2.", vbInformation, gsAPP_NAME
End Sub

Public Sub EntryPoint3()
    MsgBox "You clicked button 3.", vbInformation, gsAPP_NAME
End Sub
```

In a real application, these entry points can be as simple or complex as required, as long as they don't require any modifications to the user interface to function correctly.

The RibbonX markup used to create the Excel 2007 UI for the example application is located in the RibbonUI.xlam add-in. The RibbonX from this add-in is shown in Listing 11-3.

Listing 11-3 The RibbonX Markup for the Demonstration Application

```
<?xml version="1.0" encoding="UTF-8" standalone="yes"?>
<customUI xmlns="http://schemas.microsoft.com/office/2006/01/customui">
    <ribbon>
        <tabs>
            <tab id="pedTab" label="Demo Tab" insertAfterMso="TabView">
                <group id="pedGroup" label="Demo Group">
                    <button id="pedButton1"
                        label="Button 1"
                        size="large"
                        onAction="PED_CallBack"
                        imageMso="LeftArrow2"/>
                    <button id="pedButton2"
                        label="Button 2"
                        size="large"
                        onAction="PED_CallBack"
                        imageMso="RightArrow2"/>
                    <button id="pedButton3"
                        label="Button 3"
                        size="large"
                        onAction="PED_CallBack"
                        imageMso="CancelRequest"/>
```

```
        </group>
      </tab>
    </tabs>
  </ribbon>
</customUI>
```

As you can see, all three buttons are assigned to the same callback procedure. This callback procedure is shown in Listing 11-4.

Listing 11-4   The RibbonX Callback Procedure

```
Public Const gsFILE_MAIN_ADD_IN As String = "LightWeightUI.xla"

' All three Ribbon buttons call back to this procedure.
' Here we determine which button was clicked and reroute
' the code to the appropriate entry point in the main add-in.
Public Sub PED_CallBack(ByRef ctlButton As IRibbonControl)

    Dim sEntryPoint As String

    Select Case ctlButton.ID
        Case "pedButton1"
            sEntryPoint = "EntryPoint1"
        Case "pedButton2"
            sEntryPoint = "EntryPoint2"
        Case "pedButton3"
            sEntryPoint = "EntryPoint3"
    End Select

    Application.Run gsFILE_MAIN_ADD_IN & "!" & sEntryPoint

End Sub
```

This procedure uses a `Select...Case` statement to translate the ID property of the button that triggered the callback into the name of the entry point procedure that should be executed in the main add-in. It then uses the `Application.Run` method to call this entry point procedure.

Heavy Weight

Our heavy weight cross-version user interface design is for applications that require significant interaction between the application code and its user interface or have a user interface with a large number of complex controls. This design requires that all user interface logic be factored out into two separate front-loader add-ins, one for Excel 2003 and earlier and one for Excel 2007 and later.

The application is run by opening the front-loader add-in designed for the version of Excel being used. The front-loader builds the user interface and opens the main add-in containing the application business logic. This design requires an installer to determine which version of Excel is being used on the target computer so only the front-loader appropriate to that version of Excel is installed.

Our PETRAS time sheet application makes a good demonstration project for the heavy weight user interface design concept. It is relatively simple but does dynamically enable and disable some of its toolbar buttons based on whether a time sheet workbook is open. In this section we modify the time sheet application to implement the heavy weight user interface design concept. The modified version of the PETRAS time sheet application can be found on the companion CD in the folder *Concepts\Ch11 - Creating Cross-Version Applications\HeavyWeight*.

Extracting the Command Bars Logic

Our first task is to take the current version of the time sheet application and extract all the command bars logic into a new loader add-in called LoadPETRAS.xla. This add-in also is responsible for opening and closing PetrasAddin.xla, which contains the business logic for the application, so the Auto_Open and Auto_Close procedures also are moved into the new loader add-in. Table 11-1 summarizes the modifications required to create the LoadPETRAS.xla add-in.

Table 11-1   Changes to the PETRAS Time Sheet Application Required to Create LoadPETRAS.xla

Module	Change
MCommandBars	Moved to the new LoadPETRAS.xla add-in.
MPastePicture	Moved to the new LoadPETRAS.xla add-in.
wksCommandBars	Moved to the new LoadPETRAS.xla add-in.

Table 11-1 Changes to the PETRAS Time Sheet Application Required to Create LoadPETRAS.xla

Module	Change
CAppEventHandler	The EnableDisableToolbar procedure was moved to the MEntryPoints module in the LoadPETRAS.xla add-in. The event procedures in the PetrasAddin.xla CAppEventHandler module check the version of Excel they are running under and call either this procedure to manage command bars in Excel 2003 and earlier or a procedure to manage the new Ribbon UI in Excel 2007 and later.
MOpenClose	Auto_Open and Auto_Close were moved to the LoadPETRAS.xla add-in. Application initialization and destruction functions were created in the main PetrasAddin.xla add-in. These are called from the loader add-in after it has opened PetrasAddin.xla and before it is about to close PetrasAddin.xla, respectively.
MEntryPoints	The code in the PetrasAddin.xla entry point procedures remains the same, but the procedure names were changed. They are all now prefixed with the string "PETRAS_" to prevent name clashes. An MEntryPoints module was created in the new LoadPETRAS.xla add-in. This module contains stub procedures with the same names as all of the original entry point procedures. These stub procedures contain a single line of code that simply uses Application.Run to delegate code execution to the corresponding true entry point in PetrasAddin.xla. The Ribbon callback procedure in the Excel 2007 version of the loader does the same.
MSystemCode	This module was empty at this point in the PETRAS time sheet application development process, so we removed it to improve the clarity of the application.

Let's clarify a few points from Table 11-1 that may be confusing. The time sheet application is now run by opening the new LoadPETRAS.xla add-in (the loader add-in), so most of the application startup logic has been moved to that add-in from the original PetrasAddin.xla add-in (the main add-in). The only startup logic that remains in the main add-in is a short procedure to initialize variables and application state that do not depend on what particular user interface the application is running under.

The new LoadPETRAS.xla Auto_Open procedure is shown in Listing 11-5. We also included the definitions of two filename constants from MGlobals to improve the clarity of the example.

Listing 11-5   The LoadPETRAS.xla Auto_Open Procedure

```
' Constants from MGlobals
Public Const gsFILE_MAIN_ADDIN As String = "PetrasAddin.xla"
Public Const gsFILE_TIME_ENTRY As String = "PetrasTemplate.xlt"

' From MOpenClose
Public Sub Auto_Open()

    ' The very first thing your application should do upon
    ' startup is attempt to delete any copies of its
    ' command bar that may have been left hanging around
    ' by an Excel crash or other incomplete exit.
    On Error Resume Next
        Application.CommandBars(gsBAR_TOOLBAR).Delete
    On Error GoTo 0

    ' Initialize global variables.
    InitGlobals

    ' Make sure we can locate our application workbooks before we
    ' do anything else.
    If (Len(Dir$(gsAppDir & gsFILE_TIME_ENTRY)) > 0) _
            And (Len(Dir$(gsAppDir & gsFILE_MAIN_ADDIN)) > 0) Then

        Application.ScreenUpdating = False
        Application.EnableEvents = False
        Application.StatusBar = gsSTATUS_LOADING_APP

        ' Build the command bars.
        BuildCommandBars

        ' Open and initialize the main add-in.
        Application.Workbooks.Open gsAppDir & gsFILE_MAIN_ADDIN
        Application.Run gsFILE_MAIN_ADDIN & "!InitializeApplication"

        ' Reset critical application properties.
        ResetAppProperties

    Else
```

```
      MsgBox gsERR_FILE_NOT_FOUND, vbCritical, gsAPP_NAME
      ShutdownApplication
   End If

End Sub
```

After the Auto_Open procedure in the loader add-in validates the startup conditions, it builds the command bar user interface and then opens and initializes the main add-in. Initialization of the main add-in is accomplished by using the `Application.Run` method to execute the new InitializeApplication procedure we created in the main add-in. The code for this procedure is shown in Listing 11-6.

Listing 11-6   The PetrasAddin.xla InitializeApplication Procedure

```
Public Sub InitializeApplication()

   ' Initialize global variables.
   InitGlobals

   ' Set the initial state of the application.
   gclsEventHandler.SetInitialStatus

End Sub
```

As you can see, very little code is required to initialize the main add-in. This is because most of the code run during startup of the time sheet application is user interface logic, and this logic was moved to the new loader add-in.

The loader add-in builds the command bars for the application and sets the OnAction property of each command bar control to the same MEntryPoints procedure name as before. However, these entry point procedures in the loader add-in no longer perform any actions themselves. They simply use `Application.Run` to delegate code execution to the corresponding entry point procedures in the main add-in that still contain the application logic required to implement each feature. This is illustrated in Listing 11-7, where we show the entry point procedure used to create a new time sheet workbook in the loader add-in and the main add-in.

Listing 11-7 Entry Point Handling in the New Application Structure

```
'  In LoadPETRAS.xla
Public Sub NewTimeSheet()
    Application.Run gsFILE_MAIN_ADDIN & "!PETRAS_NewTimeSheet"
End Sub

' In PetrasAddin.xla
Public Sub PETRAS_NewTimeSheet()
    Application.ScreenUpdating = False
    InitGlobals
    Application.Workbooks.Add gsAppDir & gsFILE_TIME_ENTRY
    Application.ScreenUpdating = True
End Sub
```

The loader add-in simply passes calls from the user interface directly to the main add-in. The main add-in still performs all the work. Because the code required to implement this feature happens to be short, you may wonder why we go to all this trouble. The reason is because the code for other features is more complex, and we do not want to duplicate it in the two versions of the loader add-ins that we need to create to support both command bar and Ribbon user interfaces.

Creating a Ribbon User Interface Loader

Now that we have cleanly separated the command bar user interface logic into a new loader add-in we can use it as a template for building a version that creates a Ribbon user interface. The first step is to use Excel 2007 to save the LoadPETRAS.xla add-in in the Excel 2007 add-in file format. The Excel 2007 file is named LoadPETRAS.xlam. Table 11-2 summarizes the modifications required to convert a copy of LoadPETRAS.xla into LoadPETRAS.xlam.

Table 11-2 Changes to LoadPETRAS.xla Required to Create LoadPETRAS.xlam

Module	Change
MCommandBars	Removed.
MPastePicture	Removed.
wksCommandBars	Removed. Because we must have at least one worksheet in the add-in, we replace this with a blank Sheet1.

Table 11-2 Changes to LoadPETRAS.xla Required to Create LoadPETRAS.xlam

Module	Change
customUI.xml	This Ribbon definition file is incorporated into LoadPETRAS.xlam using the Custom UI Editor.
MOpenClose	All command bar handling code is removed from Auto_Open and Auto_Close.
MEntryPoints	All the command bar entry point procedures from LoadPETRAS.xla were replaced by Ribbon callback procedures. The EnableDisableToolbar procedure was replaced by an InvalidateButtons procedure that serves a similar purpose in the Ribbon UI.

Before we begin to discuss the code changes in detail, let's take a look at the XML that defines our Ribbon user interface. This is shown in Listing 11-8.

Listing 11-8 The Ribbon XML for the PETRAS Time Sheet Application

```xml
<?xml version="1.0" encoding="UTF-8" standalone="yes"?>
<customUI xmlns="http://schemas.microsoft.com/office/2006/01/customui"
          onLoad="pedCustomUI_onLoad">
    <ribbon>
        <tabs>
        <tab id="pedPetrasTimesheetTab"
            label="PETRAS Timesheet"
            insertAfterMso="TabView">
                <group id="pedPetrasTimesheetGroup" label="Timesheet">
                    <button id="pedNewTimesheet"
                        label="New Timesheet"
                        size="large"
                        onAction="PETRAS_CallBack"
                        imageMso="FileNew"/>
                    <button id="pedPostToNetwork"
                        label="Post To Network"
                        size="large"
                        onAction="PETRAS_CallBack"
                        getEnabled="pedSetControlState"
                        imageMso="ExportExcel"/>
```

```
                        <button id="pedAddMoreRows"
                            label="Add More Rows"
                            size="large"
                            onAction="PETRAS_CallBack"
                            getEnabled="pedSetControlState"
                            imageMso="CellsInsertDialog"/>
                        <button id="pedClearDataEntries"
                            label="Clear Data Entries"
                            size="large"
                            onAction="PETRAS_CallBack"
                            getEnabled="pedSetControlState"
                            imageMso="InkEraseMode"/>
                        <button id="pedExitPETRAS"
                            label="Exit PETRAS"
                            size="large"
                            onAction="PETRAS_CallBack"
                            imageMso="CancelRequest"/>
                </group>
            </tab>
            </tabs>
        </ribbon>
</customUI>
```

In this Ribbon definition, we create a new tab and group for our time sheet application buttons, but we have exactly the same five buttons in this user interface as we do in the command bar version. There are a few things to note about the plumbing of the Ribbon user interface:

- We defined an `onLoad` callback for our custom Ribbon. This allows us to retrieve and store a reference to the `IRibbonUI` object for later use.
- Each of the buttons in our ribbon is assigned to the same `onAction` callback procedure. As we see in a moment, this callback procedure redirects code execution to the appropriate entry point in the main add-in.
- The three buttons that must be enabled and disabled dynamically have a callback procedure assigned to their `getEnabled` attribute. This callback allows us to dynamically modify the Ribbon user interface.

Next we examine the contents of the LoadPETRAS.xlam MEntryPoints module. The contents of this module are shown in Listing 11-9. We included the declaration of the IRibbonUI object variable from the MGlobals module to improve the clarity of the example.

Listing 11-9   The LoadPETRAS.xlam MEntryPoints Module

```
' In MGlobals
Public grxRibbonUI As IRibbonUI


' In MEntryPoints
Public Sub pedCustomUI_onLoad(ribbon As IRibbonUI)
    Set grxRibbonUI = ribbon
End Sub


Public Sub PETRAS_CallBack(control As IRibbonControl)
    Dim sProcName As String
    Select Case control.ID
        Case "pedNewTimesheet"
            sProcName = "PETRAS_NewTimeSheet"
        Case "pedPostToNetwork"
            sProcName = "PETRAS_PostTimeEntriesToNetwork"
        Case "pedAddMoreRows"
            sProcName = "PETRAS_AddMoreRows"
        Case "pedClearDataEntries"
            sProcName = "PETRAS_ClearDataEntryAreas"
        Case "pedExitPETRAS"
            ShutdownApplication
    End Select
    If Len(sProcName) > 0 Then
        Application.Run gsFILE_MAIN_ADDIN & "!" & sProcName
    End If
End Sub


Public Sub pedSetControlState(control As IRibbonControl, _
                ByRef returnedVal)
    ' If one of our time sheet workbooks is active then we enable
    ' the dynamic buttons.
    If Not Application.ActiveWorkbook Is Nothing Then
        returnedVal = bIsTimeEntryWorkbook(Application.ActiveWorkbook)
    End If
End Sub


Public Sub InvalidateButtons()
    ' The Is Nothing check is required because the Ribbon reference
```

```
' will not yet have been set when we receive the first call from
' the main add-in.
   If Not grxRibbonUI Is Nothing Then grxRibbonUI.Invalidate
End Sub
```

The first procedure shown in Listing 11-9 is the onLoad callback procedure triggered when our Ribbon UI is created. This callback procedure provides us with a reference to the IRibbonUI object that represents our custom Ribbon. We will need this object later to implement dynamic control over our Ribbon, so we store a reference to it in the global variable shown at the top of the listing.

The second procedure shown in Listing 11-9 is the common onAction callback procedure. This procedure uses a Select...Case statement to translate the ID property of the button that triggered the callback into the name of the entry point procedure that should be executed in the main add-in. This entry point procedure is then executed using the Application.Run method.

The third procedure shown in Listing 11-9 is the getEnabled callback procedure for the buttons that must be enabled and disabled dynamically. By default, the returnedVal argument is False, and if its value is not changed to True the button that triggered the callback will be disabled. The callback procedure first checks whether a workbook is active. If there is an active workbook it sets the returnedVal argument to True if that workbook is a time sheet workbook (using the value returned by the bIsTimeEntryWorkbook function).

The bIsTimeEntryWorkbook function is a case where we put the same code in both the XLAM version of the loader workbook and the main add-in. This is because this function is very simple and unlikely to change. If the function were more complicated or potentially variable we would keep a single copy of it in the main add-in and call it from the loader add-in. As we explain shortly, the need to call this function from the callback procedure is a result of our inability to directly modify Ribbon control attributes.

The fourth procedure shown in Listing 11-9, InvalidateButtons, is not a Ribbon callback procedure. This procedure replaces the EnableDisableToolbar procedure from the XLA version of our loader add-in. The InvalidateButtons procedure uses the grxRibbonUI object reference that we stored in the onLoad callback to invalidate our custom Ribbon. Invalidating the Ribbon causes each of the controls to trigger their callback functions.

As we see in a moment, the event handling class in the main add-in determines which version of Excel it is running under and then calls either the EnableDisableToolbar procedure or the InvalidateButtons procedure in response to changes in the Excel user interface. These procedures then enable and disable the appropriate command bar or Ribbon buttons, either directly, by setting command bar button properties in the case of the EnableDisableToolbar procedure, or indirectly, by invalidating the Ribbon in the case of the InvalidateButtons procedure.

We use the WindowActivate event handler from the PetrasAddin.xla CAppEventHandler module to illustrate how the Excel version-specific user interface handling works. This event procedure is shown in Listing 11-10. We included two constant declarations from the MGlobals module to improve the clarity of the example.

Listing 11-10   The PetrasAddin.xla CAppEventHandler WindowActivate Event Procedure

```
' In MGlobals
Public Const gsFILE_LOADER_2003 As String = "LoadPETRAS.xla"
Public Const gsFILE_LOADER_2007 As String = "LoadPETRAS.xlam"


' In CAppEventHandler
Private Sub mxlApp_WindowActivate(ByVal Wb As Workbook, _
                                     ByVal Wn As Window)
    ' When a window is activated, check to see if it belongs
    ' to one of our workbooks. Enable all our toolbar controls
    ' if it does.
    If CLng(Application.Version) < 12 Then
        Application.Run gsFILE_LOADER_2003 & "!EnableDisableToolbar", _
                            bIsTimeEntryBookActive()
    Else
        Application.Run gsFILE_LOADER_2007 & "!InvalidateButtons"
    End If
End Sub
```

Although this event procedure is simple, it contains all the basic logic required to make a custom user interface respond correctly in different versions of Excel.

When the WindowActivate event is fired, it first checks the version number of the Excel application it is running under. If the version number is less than 12, the application is running under Excel 2003 or earlier and the EnableDisableToolbar procedure in the XLA version of the loader workbook is called. If the version number is greater than or equal to 12, the application is running under Excel 2007 or higher and the

InvalidateButtons procedure in the XLAM version of the loader workbook is called.

Notice that when we call the EnableDisableToolbar procedure we pass it an argument that tells it whether to enable or disable the dynamic buttons (using the result of the bIsTimeEntryBookActive function). The situation with the Ribbon is a bit more complicated. Because the Ribbon does not provide a COM object module like the command bars user interface does, we cannot directly modify the properties of Ribbon controls.

Instead, we must call a procedure that invalidates the Ribbon. This causes each Ribbon control to execute any callback procedures assigned to its "get" attributes (getEnabled, getVisible, and so on). These callback procedures must then run the code required to determine the correct state of the control attribute. We saw this illustrated in the pedSetControlState callback procedure from Listing 11-9.

The result of all this in our Ribbon user interface is shown in Figures 11-3 and 11-4. Figure 11-3 shows the partially disabled appearance of our PETRAS Timesheet tab when there is no time sheet workbook active. Figure 11-4 shows the fully enabled set of controls triggered by activating or opening a time sheet workbook.

FIGURE 11-3   The PETRAS time sheet application Ribbon at startup

FIGURE 11-4   The PETRAS time sheet application Ribbon after opening a time sheet workbook

Other Considerations

As we mentioned at the beginning of this section, the heavy weight user interface design requires you to have some method of supplying the user with just one version of the loader add-in appropriate to their version of Excel. The types of applications that require a heavy weight user interface design are also the types of applications that typically require a custom installer. Therefore, the best solution is to have the installer detect which version of Excel the user is running and install only the loader add-in appropriate to that version of Excel. We cover installers in more detail in Chapter 29, "Providing Help, Securing, Packaging, and Distributing."

A second consideration with this user interface design is how to prevent the user from trying to start the application by opening the main add-in instead of the loader add-in. This can be accomplished by having your installer create a desktop icon that points to the loader add-in or registry entries that tell Excel to open the loader add-in automatically. It is also a good practice to apply a workbook open password to the main add-in so the user can't open it directly. This password can then be supplied by the loader add-in when it opens the main add-in automatically.

Other Excel 2007 Development Issues

After more than a decade of almost complete backward compatibility in each new version of Excel, the release of Excel 2007 introduced significant changes that force us to reevaluate how we develop applications in Excel. Excel 2007 is significantly less backward compatible in a number of areas than previous Excel releases, so we must take care to avoid these areas if our applications are to run smoothly across all current versions of Excel.

The Inability to Add Code to Macro-Free Excel Files

Among the new file formats in Excel 2007 we can save workbooks in the **macro-free** file format "Excel Workbook"—.xlsx. Workbooks saved in this format cannot contain any VBA code, and in fact any VBA code they may contain is discarded when they are saved. The idea is that workbooks saved in this format can be safely downloaded as well as accepted in e-mail file attachments because they are known to be free of any malicious VBA code. The intention was good, but the result has serious limitations from a developer's point of view.

Suppose we have a situation where a worksheet containing code needs to be copied into a workbook that has been saved in the XLSX file format. In Listing 11-11 we show a procedure that copies a worksheet containing VBA code from a macro-enabled workbook to a macro-free workbook.

Listing 11-11 Code to Copy a Worksheet

```
Sub Copy_Worksheet()

    Dim wksSource As Worksheet
    Dim wkbTarget As Workbook

    With Application
        Set wksSource = .Workbooks("Code.xlsm").Worksheets("Data")
        Set wkbTarget = .Workbooks("Free.xlsx")
    End With

    wksSource.Copy before:=wkbTarget.Worksheets(1)

End Sub
```

When the code in Listing 11-11 is executed the worksheet is copied, but the code it contains is dropped from the copy without any notification. In another scenario we may use Forms Controls in a worksheet where the file is saved in the macro-free file format. If we want to assign these Forms Controls to macros in an add-in it cannot be done without resaving the workbook in a macro-enabled format.

Working with the File System

With the release of Excel 2007 the `Application.FileSearch` feature was disabled. If we used this feature in our applications we need to find a replacement. In our experience the best option is to use the **Microsoft Scripting Runtime** object library. This gives us access to drives, folders, and files in the file system.

In the versions of Windows commonly used as of this writing we can assume the scripting runtime object library is installed and available. To use it we need to set a reference to the library by selecting *Tools > References...* from the VBE menu and placing a check mark beside the Microsoft Scripting Runtime entry, as shown in Figure 11-5.

The top-level objects in the scripting runtime object library are the **Dictionary** object and the **FileSystemObject (FSO)** object. The Dictionary object is similar to the VBA Collection object, while the FSO object is the root object in a hierarchy of objects designed to allow us to work with the file system.

The FSO object is the only creatable object in its hierarchy—that is to say, can be declared using the `New` keyword—while the other objects in the

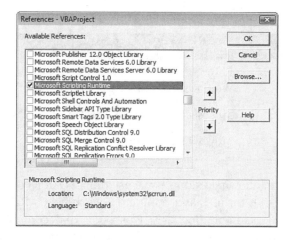

FIGURE 11-5   Set a reference to the Microsoft Scripting Runtime

hierarchy are dependent objects derived from the FSO object and are exposed in the form of methods or properties. Table 11-3 lists the most common methods exposed by the FSO object.

Table 11-3   Common Methods of the FSO Object

Methods	Descriptions
CopyFile	Copies one or more files.
CopyFolder	Copies entire folders with their contents.
CreateFolder	Creates a new folder.
DeleteFile	Deletes one or more files.
DeleteFolder	Deletes one or more folders together with their contents.
DriveExists	Returns True if a logical drive exists.
FileExist	Returns True if a given file exists.
FolderExist	Returns True if a given folder exists.
GetExtensionName	Extracts the file extension from a filename.
GetFileName	Extracts the filename.
GetFolder	Returns the Folder object that is related to the directory passed as the argument.

Table 11-3 Common Methods of the FSO Object

Methods	Descriptions
GetSpecialFolder	Returns a folder to one of the special Windows directories; 0 - WindowsFolder, 1 - SystemFolder and 2 -TemporaryFolder.
MoveFile	Moves a file from one directory to another.
MoveFolder	Moves a folder and its content.

In the following example, we use the FSO object and the Dictionary object to search for files and populate a worksheet with the retrieved filenames. The Documentation.xlsm workbook that contains this example can be found on the companion CD in the *Concepts\Ch11 – Creating Cross-Version Applications\File Documentation* folder. The result of running the example is shown in Figure 11-6.

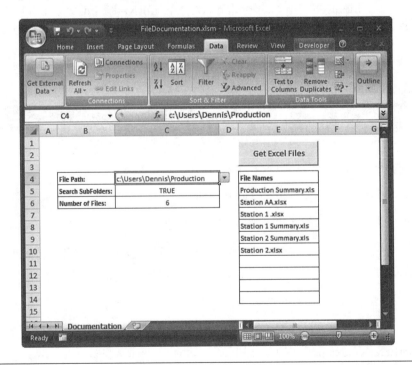

FIGURE 11-6 The list of files found

This example uses one main procedure, shown in Listing 11-12, and a file search utility function shown in Listing 11-13. Because the FSO object does not include a search function we need to create our own.

Listing 11-12   The Main Procedure

```vba
Sub File_Documentation()

    'Search criteria which includes all Excel file types.
    Const sSEARCH_CRITERIA As String = "*.xl*"

    'Variables for the Excel objects.
    Dim rngFileNames As Range
    Dim rngFileCount As Range
    Dim lRowCount As Long

    'Variable for the path string.
    Dim sFilePath As String

    'Variable to indicate if subfolders
    'also be part of the search.
    Dim bSearchSubFolders As Boolean

    'Variable for the Dictionary object.
    Dim dctFileNames As Scripting.Dictionary

    'Variable to be used when we iterate through
    'the Dictionary collection.
    Dim vFileName As Variant

    Set rngFileCount = wksDocumentation.Range("C6")
    Set rngFileNames = wksDocumentation.Range("E4")

    'Get the path which can be chosen from a list
    'in the cell.
    sFilePath = wksDocumentation.Range("C4").Value

    'Get the boolean value to decide to include or
    'to exclude the subfolders. It can be left
    'empty.
    bSearchSubFolders = wksDocumentation.Range("C5").Value

    'Instantiate a new Dictionary collection object.
    Set dctFileNames = New Scripting.Dictionary

    lRowCount = 1

    Application.ScreenUpdating = False
```

```
'Get the file names.
If bGet_Excel_Files(sFilePath, dctFileNames, _
                    sSEARCH_CRITERIA, _
                    bSearchSubFolders) Then

    'Retrieve the number of located files.
    rngFileCount.Value = dctFileNames.Count

    'Iterate the Dictionary collection.
    For Each vFileName In dctFileNames

        'Write the retrieved file names into the worksheet.
        rngFileNames.Offset(lRowCount, 0).Value = vFileName

        lRowCount = lRowCount + 1

    Next vFileName

End If

wksDocumentation.Columns("E:E").EntireColumn.AutoFit

'Release object from the memory.
Set dctFileNames = Nothing

End Sub
```

At the top of the main procedure, we create a search criteria constant that targets all Excel files. We use a string variable, sFilePath, to hold the path to the folder being searched and a Boolean variable, bSearchSubFolders, to indicate whether subfolders should be included in the search. The values for both of these variables are retrieved from the worksheet with the CodeName wksDocumentation.

The file search function is called to populate a Dictionary object with the retrieved filenames. The filenames are then written to a table on the wksDocumentation worksheet. The file search function is shown in Listing 11-13.

Listing 11-13 The File Search Function

```
Private Function bGet_Excel_Files( _
                ByVal sPath As String, _
                ByRef dctDictionary As Scripting.Dictionary, _
```

```vba
                    ByVal sSearchCriteria As String, _
                    Optional ByVal bRecursive As Boolean) As Boolean

Dim fsoFileSystem As Scripting.FileSystemObject
Dim fsoFolder As Scripting.Folder
Dim fsoSubFolder As Scripting.Folder
Dim fsoFile As Scripting.File

'Instantiate a new FSO object.
Set fsoFileSystem = New Scripting.FileSystemObject

'Check to see if the folder exist or not.
If fsoFileSystem.FolderExists(sPath) Then

    Set fsoFolder = fsoFileSystem.GetFolder(sPath)

Else

    MsgBox "The folder: " & vbNewLine & _
            sPath & vbNewLine & _
            "does not exist.", vbCritical

    bGet_Excel_Files = False

    GoTo ExitFunction

End If

'Iterate through the files in the folder and add the files
'that meet the search criteria.
For Each fsoFile In fsoFolder.Files

    If fsoFile.Name Like sSearchCriteria Then

            'Add the file name to the Dictionary.
            dctDictionary.Add Key:=fsoFile.Name, Item:="File List"

    End If

Next fsoFile

If bRecursive Then

    'The function is called recursively to return the file
```

```
        'names in each subfolder.
        For Each fsoSubFolder In fsoFolder.SubFolders
            bGet_Excel_Files fsoSubFolder.Path, _
                            dctDictionary, _
                            sSearchCriteria, _
                            bRecursive:=True
        Next fsoSubFolder

    End If

    bGet_Excel_Files = True

ExitFunction:

    'Release objects from the memory.
    Set fsoFile = Nothing
    Set fsoSubFolder = Nothing
    Set fsoFolder = Nothing
    Set fsoFileSystem = Nothing

End Function
```

The file search function requires that we pass the path to the folder we want to search, a Dictionary object to be populated with filenames, and a search criteria string. The function also takes an optional Boolean argument that specifies whether to include subfolders in the search.

We instantiate a new FSO object and then verify that the specified search folder exists. Next, we loop through the search folder and add any files that match the criteria to the Dictionary object. If any subfolders should be included in the search the function calls itself recursively, passing the path to the subfolder to be searched.

Although the file system methods provided by the scripting runtime object library are convenient and easy to use, where performance is critical the preferred approach is to use the methods built into VBA for this purpose.

Windows Vista Security and Folder Structure

With Windows Vista we have a new security paradigm, **User Account Control (UAC)**, which introduces a new technology and a new infrastructure. This includes a new folder structure for all the user accounts that have logged into a computer running Vista. The new folder structure may cause existing Excel applications to break when running on Vista. Therefore, we must take into consideration the changes in Vista when we need to develop Excel applications that run on both Windows XP and Vista.

User Account Control (UAC)

The aim of UAC is to improve the security of Windows. When UAC is enabled, standard users are prohibited from

- Installing and uninstalling applications, including ActiveX controls
- Changing files in the system root (C:\) and in the Program Files folder
- Changing system settings, including settings for Windows Firewall, UAC settings, and running the Task Scheduler

If a standard user attempts to do something that requires administrator rights he is notified that the task is prohibited or that administrative credentials are required to proceed. Even if we are logged into Vista as an administrator these operations trigger a UAC prompt, as shown in Figure 11-7.

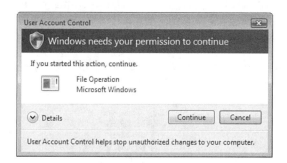

FIGURE 11-7 The UAC prompt

Just because a user has administrative privileges, the applications run by the user do not have those privileges unless they are approved in advance or the user explicitly authorizes them when prompted by UAC.

The restrictions Vista places on standard user accounts have a major impact on where we locate the files for our Excel applications. If we want to install an Excel application under the Program Files folder in Vista it requires the following:

- Administrative privileges to create the folder.
- Administrative privileges to place the files in the folder.
- The folder must be added to the list of trusted locations in Excel.

Placing and removing applications in the XLStart directory or in an Alternate Startup directory for Excel also require administrative privileges, although administrative privileges are not required when running applications from these locations.

Many developers we know have turned off UAC on their development computer because they find the UAC prompts annoying. Instead of turning it off it is possible to run UAC in quiet mode. This mode suppresses all UAC prompts for the administrator. To do this you can download the free tool TweakUAC from www.tweakuac.com.

Standard User Accounts

In Windows Vista the Document and Settings folder has been replaced with the Users folder. All user accounts are located in this folder, and the path to it is C:\Users\. As Figure 11-8 shows, we have several fixed folders available and accessible in a user account. Some of them are new folders while others are familiar from the Windows XP environment.

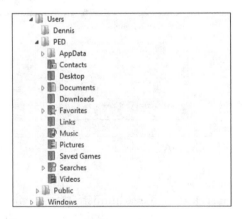

FIGURE 11-8   Folders in a User account

Notice in Figure 11-8 that the My Documents folder no longer exists in Windows Vista. Instead we have the Documents folder. If we expand the

AppData folder under the PED user account we see the folder structure shown in Figure 11-9.

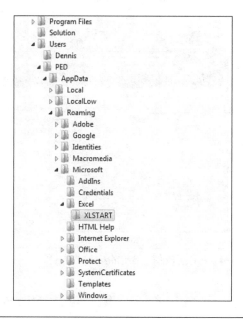

FIGURE 11-9   The AppData folder structure

In Windows Vista the Local folder, shown in Figure 11-9, replaces the Local Settings folder. Vista uses the Local and LocalLow folders for application data that does not roam with the user. Usually this data is either machine specific or too large to roam.

Also shown in Figure 11-9 is the Roaming folder. A roaming user profile is a network profile set up on a server. When we log on for the first time to a computer on the same domain as the server, we are authenticated by the server and our complete user profile is sent down to the computer, where it is saved as a local user profile. When we log off the computer, any changes we made to the settings in the profile are saved both on that computer and on the server. This ensures that the client data follows users as they roam the environment. The Roaming folder in Windows Vista replaces the \Documents and Settings\username\Application Data folder in Windows XP.

Public Profile

In Windows XP, we have the All Users profile, which Windows Vista replaced with the Public profile. Its folder structure is the same as all other

Vista profiles. The Public folder can be seen in Figure 11-8, and its contents are shown in Figure 11-10. All information stored in the Public profile is available for all users of that computer.

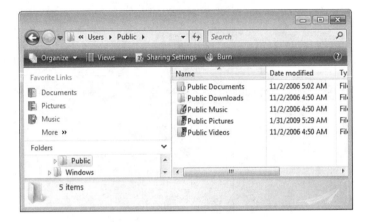

FIGURE 11-10   The Public profile

Targeting Windows XP and Windows Vista

The changes in the folder structure in Windows Vista create problems with where to install our Excel applications when targeting both Windows XP and Windows Vista. In some scenarios where we have standalone Excel files, templates, add-ins, or workbooks, these can be mailed to the client together with instructions on where to install them. Other scenarios may require a custom installer that detects the operating system in use on the target computer and installs the files in correct folders based on that operating system. We discuss installers in more detail in Chapter 29.

Summary

The introduction of Office 2007 and Windows Vista represents a platform change that Excel developers have not experienced since the change from Office 95 to Office 97 or Windows 3.1 to Windows 95. In this chapter we tried to explain the most common challenges faced by Excel developers needing to support Office 2007 and Vista in addition to previous versions of Office and Windows and suggest solutions that we have found useful in our own experience. However, best practices in this area are still evolving, so what we present here may not be the final word on these subjects.

CHAPTER 12

UNDERSTANDING AND USING WINDOWS API CALLS

In the "Programming with the Windows API" chapter of our *Excel 2007 VBA Programmers Reference*, we approach the subject of using Windows API calls by explaining how to locate the definitions for various functions on the MSDN Web site and translate those functions for use in VBA. The idea was to give readers the ability to browse through the API documentation and be able to use anything of interest they found.

In reality, few people use Windows API calls in that manner. Instead, most of us go to Google and search the Web or the newsgroups for the answer to a problem and find the solution requires the use of API calls. We copy the solution into our application and hope it works, usually without really understanding what it does. This chapter shines a light on many of those solutions, explaining how they work, what they use the API calls for, and how they can be modified to better fit our applications. Along the way, we fill in some of the conceptual framework of common Windows API techniques and terminology.

By the end of the chapter, you will be comfortable including API calls in your applications, understand how they work, and be able to modify them to suit your needs.

Overview

When developing Excel-based applications we can accomplish most of the things we need to do using the Excel object model. Occasionally, though, we need some information or a feature that Excel doesn't provide. In those cases, we can usually go directly to the files that comprise the Windows operating system to find what we're looking for.

To do this, we must first tell VBA the Windows API function exists, where to find it, what arguments it takes, and what data type it returns. This is done using the `Declare` statement, such as that for the `GetSystemMetrics` function:

```
Declare Function GetSystemMetrics Lib "user32" _
                (ByVal nIndex As Long) As Long
```

This statement tells the VBA interpreter there is a function called GetSystemMetrics located in the file user32.dll (or user32.exe, it checks both if they both exist) that takes one argument of a Long data type and returns a value in a Long data type. Once defined, we can call GetSystemMetrics in exactly the same way as if it were the VBA function:

```
Function GetSystemMetrics(ByVal nIndex As Long) As Long
End Function
```

Declare statements can be used in any type of code module. They can be Public or Private (just like standard procedures) but must always be placed in the declarations section at the top of the module.

Finding Documentation

All the functions in the Windows API are fully documented in the "Windows API Reference" section of the MSDN Library on Microsoft's Web site at http://msdn.microsoft.com/en-us/library/aa383749(VS.85).aspx.

Although the terminology used and the code samples provided tend to be targeted at the C++ developer, a Google search will usually locate documentation more appropriate for the VBA developer. However, the documentation provided for VBA is unlikely to be as complete as MSDN. If you're using API calls found on a Web site, the Web page hopefully explains what they do, but it is a good idea to always check the official documentation to see whether there are any limitations or other remarks that may affect your usage.

Unfortunately, the MSDN library's search engine is significantly worse than using Google to search the MSDN site. We find that Google always gives us more relevant pages than MSDN's search engine. To use Google to search MSDN, browse to www.google.com and click the Advanced Search link, type in the search criteria, and in the *Domain* edit box, type msdn.microsoft.com to restrict the search to MSDN.

Finding Declarations

It is not uncommon to encounter code snippets on the Internet that include incorrect declarations for API functions, such as declaring an argument's data type as Integer or Boolean when it should be Long. While using the declaration included in the snippet may work with the example provided, it may not work for the full range of possible arguments that the function accepts and in rare cases may cause memory corruption and data loss.

The official VBA-friendly declarations for many of the more commonly used API functions can be found in the win32api.txt file, which is included with a viewer in the Developer Editions of Office as well as VB6 and is available for download from http://support.microsoft.com/?kbid=178020.

You'll notice that this file hasn't been updated for some time. It therefore doesn't include the declarations and constants added in recent versions of Windows. If you're using one of those newer declarations, you'll have to trust the Web page author, examine a number of Web pages to check that they all use the same declaration, or create your own VBA-friendly declaration by following the steps we describe in the *Excel 2007 VBA Programmers Reference*.

Finding the Values of Constants

Many API functions are passed constants to modify their behavior or specify the type of value to return. For example, the GetSystemMetrics function shown previously accepts a parameter to specify which metric we want, such as SM_CXSCREEN to get the width of the screen in pixels or SM_CYSCREEN to get the height. All the appropriate constants are shown on the MSDN page for that declaration. For example, the GetSystemMetrics function is documented at http://msdn.microsoft.com/en-us/library/ms724385.aspx. This page shows more than 80 valid constants for the nIndex argument.

While many of these constants are included in the win32api.txt file mentioned earlier, it does not include constants added for recent versions of Windows. The best way to find these values is by downloading and installing the core Platform SDK. Navigate to www.microsoft.com/downloads/Browse.aspx?displaylang=en.

Select Developer Tools from the *Search* drop-down at the top of the page, enter "SDK" as the search term, and click the *Go* button. Browse the list of results for the Windows SDK that applies to the most recent version of Windows Server.

The SDK includes the C++ header files that include the declarations of all Windows API functions and constants in a subdirectory called *include*.

These are plain text files that can be searched using normal Windows file searching to find the file that contains the constant we're interested in. For example, searching for SM_CXSCREEN gives the file winuser.h. Opening that file with a text editor and searching within it produces the following lines:

```
#define SM_CXSCREEN             0
#define SM_CYSCREEN             1
```

These constants can then be included in your VBA module by declaring the following:

```
Const SM_CXSCREEN As Long = 0
Const SM_CYSCREEN As Long = 1
```

Sometimes constant values are shown in hexadecimal (hex) form, such as 0x8000, which can be converted to VBA by replacing the 0x with &h and adding a trailing & character, such that

```
#define KF_UP                  0x8000
```

becomes

```
Const KF_UP As Long = &h8000&
```

The trailing & character is required to force VBA to recognize the hex value as a Long (32-bit) data type. VBA assumes constant integral values have an Integer (16-bit) data type by default. Because the hex value &h8000 is a very different number when interpreted as an Integer versus a Long, we have to force VBA to interpret this value as a Long by appending an ampersand character. The reason for this difference in interpretation has to do with the way negative numbers are represented in binary, which is beyond the scope of this chapter to discuss in detail.

Understanding Handles

Within VBA we're used to setting a variable to reference an object using code like

```
Set wkbBackDrop = Workbooks("Backdrop.xls")
```

and releasing that reference by setting the variable to Nothing (or letting VBA do that for us when it goes out of scope at the end of the procedure). Under the covers, the thing that we see as the Backdrop.xls workbook is just an area of memory containing data structured in a specific way that only Excel understands. When we set a variable equal to that object, it is just given the memory location of that data structure.

The Windows operating system works similarly, but at a much more granular level. Almost everything within Windows is maintained as a data structure somewhere. If we want to work with the item that is represented by that structure (such as a window), we need to get a reference to it and pass that reference to the appropriate API function. These references are known as **handles** and are just ID numbers that Windows uses to identify the data structure. Variables used to store handles are usually given the prefix "h" and are declared As Long.

When we ask for the handle to an item, some functions—such as FindWindow—give us the handle to a shared data structure. There is only one data structure for each window so every call to FindWindow with the same parameters returns the same handle. In these cases, we can just discard the handle when we're finished with it.

In most situations, however, Windows allocates an area of memory, creates a new data structure for us to use, and returns the handle to that structure. In these cases we ***must*** clean up after ourselves by explicitly telling Windows that we've finished using the handle (and by implication, the memory used to store the data structure that the handle points to). If we fail to clean up correctly, each call to our procedure uses another bit of memory until Windows crashes. This is called a **memory leak**. The most common cause of memory leaks is forgetting to include cleanup code within a procedure's error handler. The MSDN documentation will tell you whether you need to release the handle and which function to call to do it.

Encapsulating API Calls

GetSystemMetrics is one of the few API calls that can easily be used in isolation. It has a meaningful name, takes a single parameter, returns a simple result, and doesn't require any preparation or cleanup. So long as you can remember what SM_CXSCREEN is asking for, it's very easy to call this function; GetSystemMetrics(SM_CXSCREEN) gives us the width of the screen in pixels.

In practice, however, we recommend that you wrap your API calls inside their own VBA functions and place those functions in modules dedicated to specific areas of the Windows API, for the following reasons:

- The VBA procedure can run validity checks before trying to call the API function. Passing invalid data to API functions often results in a crash.

- Most of the textual API functions require string variables to be preallocated before they are passed in. The allocated string is then populated and returned by the API function. Using a VBA procedure hides this complexity and ensures it is done properly every time.
- Many API functions accept parameters that we don't need to use. A VBA procedure can expose only the parameters that we need in our application.
- Few API functions can be used in isolation. Most require extra preparatory and cleanup calls. Using a VBA procedure hides this complexity and ensures it is done properly every time.
- The API declarations themselves can be declared Private to the module in which they're contained, so they can be hidden from use by other developers who may not understand how to use them. Instead, their functionality can then be exposed through more friendly VBA procedures.
- Some API tasks, such as those using the encryption or Internet functions, require an initial set of preparatory calls to open resources, a number of functions that use those resources, and a final set of functions to close the resources and clean up. These tasks are ideally encapsulated in a class module, with the Class_Initialize and Class_Terminate events used to ensure the resources are opened and closed properly.
- By using dedicated modules for specific areas of the Windows API, we can safely copy API procedures between applications in the knowledge that they are self-contained.

Once we start to include a lot of API calls in our application, it quickly becomes difficult to keep track of which constants belong to which functions. We can make the constants much easier to manage if we encapsulate them in an enumeration and use that enumeration for our VBA function's parameter, as shown in Listing 12-1.

Listing 12-1 Encapsulating the GetSystemMetrics API Function and Related Constants

```
'Declare all the API-specific items Private to the module
Private Declare Function GetSystemMetrics Lib "user32" _
        (ByVal nIndex As Long) As Long
Private Const SM_CXSCREEN As Long = 0
Private Const SM_CYSCREEN As Long = 1 .

'Wrap the API constants in a public enumeration,
'so they appear in the Intellisense dropdown
```

```
Public Enum SystemMetricsConstants
   smScreenWidth = SM_CXSCREEN
   smScreenHeight = SM_CYSCREEN
End Enum

'Wrapper for the GetSystemMetrics API function,
'using the SystemMetricsConstants enumeration
Public Function SystemMetrics( _
        ByVal uIndex As SystemMetricsConstants) As Long

   SystemMetrics = GetSystemMetrics(uIndex)
End Function
```

By doing this, the applicable constants are shown in the IntelliSense list when the VBA function is used, as shown in Figure 12-1. The ability to define enumerations was added in Excel 2000.

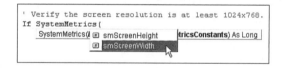

FIGURE 12-1   Enumeration members in the IntelliSense drop-down

Working with the Screen

The procedures included in this section all relate to the Windows screen and can be found in the *MScreen* module of the *API Examples.xls* workbook located in the *\Concepts\Ch12 – Understanding and Using Windows API Calls* folder on the CD that accompanies this book.

Reading the Screen Resolution

The GetSystemMetrics API function was used to illustrate the general concepts discussed earlier. It can be used to discover many of the simpler aspects of the operating system, from whether a mouse or network is present to the height of the standard window title bar. Its most common use in Excel development is to determine the screen resolution, either to check that it is at least a minimum size or to work out which UserForm to display if you have different layouts optimized for different resolutions. The code

in Listing 12-2 wraps the GetSystemMetrics API function, exposing it as
separate ScreenWidth and ScreenHeight functions.

Listing 12-2   Reading the Screen Resolution

```
'Declare all the API-specific items Private to the module
Private Declare Function GetSystemMetrics Lib "user32" _
        (ByVal nIndex As Long) As Long
Private Const SM_CXSCREEN = 0      'Screen width
Private Const SM_CYSCREEN = 1      'Screen height

'The width of the screen, in pixels
Public Function ScreenWidth() As Long
   ScreenWidth = GetSystemMetrics(SM_CXSCREEN)
End Function

'The height of the screen, in pixels
Public Function ScreenHeight() As Long
   ScreenHeight = GetSystemMetrics(SM_CYSCREEN)
End Function
```

Finding the Size of a Pixel

In general, Excel measures distances in points while most API functions use
pixels and many ActiveX controls (such as the Microsoft Flexgrid) use twips.
A point is defined as being 1/72 (logical) of an inch, while a twip is defined
as 1/20th of a point. To convert between pixels and points we need to know
how many pixels Windows is displaying for each logical inch. This is the DPI
(dots-per-inch) set by the user in *Control Panel > Display > Settings >
Advanced > General > Display*, which is usually either Normal size (96 DPI)
or Large size (120 DPI). In versions of Windows prior to XP this was known
as Small Fonts and Large Fonts. The value of this setting can be found using
the GetDeviceCaps API function, which is used to examine the detailed
capabilities of a specific graphical device such as a screen or printer.

Device Contexts

One of the fundamental features of Windows is that applications can interact with all graphical devices (screens, printers, or even individual picture
files) in a standard way. This is achieved by operating through a layer of
indirection called a device context that represents a drawing layer. An
application obtains a reference (handle) to the drawing layer for a specific

device (for example, the screen), examines its capabilities (such as the size of a dot, whether it can draw curves, and how many colors it supports), draws onto the drawing layer, and then releases the reference. Windows takes care of exactly how the drawing layer is represented on the graphical device. In this example, we're only examining the screen's capabilities.

The code to retrieve the size of a pixel is shown in Listing 12-3. Remember that when adding this code to an existing module, the declarations must always be placed at the top of the module.

Listing 12-3 Finding the Size of a Pixel

```
Private Declare Function GetDC Lib "user32" _
        (ByVal hwnd As Long) As Long

Private Declare Function GetDeviceCaps Lib "gdi32" _
        (ByVal hDC As Long, ByVal nIndex As Long) As Long

Private Declare Function ReleaseDC Lib "user32" _
        (ByVal hwnd As Long, ByVal hDC As Long) As Long

Private Const LOGPIXELSX = 88      'Pixels/inch in X

'A point is defined as 1/72 inches
Private Const POINTS_PER_INCH As Long = 72

'The size of a pixel, in points
Public Function PointsPerPixel() As Double

    Dim hDC As Long
    Dim lDotsPerInch As Long

    hDC = GetDC(0)
    lDotsPerInch = GetDeviceCaps(hDC, LOGPIXELSX)
    PointsPerPixel = POINTS_PER_INCH / lDotsPerInch
    ReleaseDC 0, hDC

End Function
```

The first thing to notice about this routine is that we can't just call GetDeviceCaps directly; we need to give it a handle to the screen's device context. This handle is obtained by calling the GetDC function, where the zero parameter conveniently gives us the device context for the screen. We then call the GetDeviceCaps function, passing it the LOGPIXELSX constant, which asks for the number of pixels per logical inch horizontally. For screens, the horizontal and vertical DPI is the same, but this might not be true for printers, which is why circles onscreen sometimes print out as ovals.

With Normal Size chosen, we get 96 dots per inch. We divide the 72 points-per-inch by the 96 dots-per-inch, telling us that a dot (that is, pixel) is 0.75 points. Therefore, if we want to move something in Excel by one pixel we need to change its Top or Left by 0.75. With Large Size selected a pixel is 0.6 points.

Every time we use GetDC to obtain a handle to a device context, we use up a small amount of Windows' graphical resources. If we didn't release the handle after using it, we would eventually use up all of Windows' graphical resources and crash. To avoid that, we have to be sure to release any resources we obtain, in this case by calling ReleaseDC and passing it the handle that Windows gave us in the GetDC call.

Working with Windows

Everything that we see on the screen is either a window or is contained within a window, from the Windows Desktop to the smallest pop-up Tooltip. Consequently, if we want to modify something on the screen we always start by locating its window.

Windows are organized into a hierarchy, with the desktop at the root. The next level down includes the main windows for all open applications and numerous system-related windows. Each application then owns and maintains its own hierarchy of windows. Every window is identified by its window handle, commonly referred to as **hWnd**. The best tool for locating and examining windows is the Spy++ utility included with Visual Studio. Figure 12-2 shows the Spy++ display for the window hierarchy of a typical Excel session.

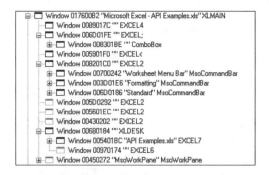

FIGURE 12-2 The Spy++ display of the Excel window hierarchy

Window Classes

As well as showing the hierarchy, the Spy++ display shows three key attributes for each window: the handle (in hexadecimal), the caption, and the class. Just like class modules, a window class defines a type of window. Some classes, such as the ComboBox class, are provided by the Windows operating system, but most are defined as part of an application. Each window class is usually associated with a specific part of an application, such as XLMAIN being Excel's main application window. Table 12-1 lists the window classes shown in the Spy++ hierarchy and their uses, plus some other window classes commonly encountered during Excel application development.

Table 12-1   Excel Window Classes and Their Uses

Window Class	Usage
XLMAIN	The main Excel application window
EXCEL4	The status bar
EXCEL;	The left half of the formula bar, including the Name drop-down
ComboBox	A standard Windows combo box (in this case, it's the Name drop-down)
EXCEL<	The edit box section of the formula bar
EXCEL2	The four command bar docking areas (top, left, right, and bottom)
MsoCommandBar	A commandbar
XLDESK	The Excel desktop
EXCEL7	A workbook window
EXCEL6	A window used to provide in-cell editing
EXCELE	A window used to provide in-sheet editing of embedded charts
MsoWorkPane	A window for the TaskPane in Excel 2002 and higher

Finding Windows

The procedures shown in the sections that follow can be found in the *MWindows* module of the *API Examples.xls* workbook located in the *\Concepts\Ch12 – Understanding and Using Windows API Calls* folder on the CD that accompanies this book.

To work with a window we first need to find its handle. In Excel 2002 the hWnd property was added to the Excel Application object, giving us the handle of the main Excel application window directly. In previous versions of Excel, and for all other top-level windows (that is, windows that are direct children of the desktop), we can use the FindWindow API call, which is defined as

```
Declare Function FindWindow Lib "user32" Alias "FindWindowA" _
    (ByVal lpClassName As String, _
      ByVal lpWindowName As String) As Long
```

To use the FindWindow function, we need to supply a class name and/or a window caption. We can use the special constant vbNullString for either, which tells the function to match on any class or caption. The function searches through all the immediate children of the desktop window (known as **top-level windows**), looking for any that have the given class and/or caption that we specified. To find the main Excel window in versions prior to Excel 2002, we might use

```
hWndExcel = FindWindow("XLMAIN", Application.Caption)
```

ANSI Versus Unicode and the Alias Clause

You might have noticed that the declaration for FindWindow contains an extra clause that we haven't used before—the **Alias** clause. All Windows API functions that have textual parameters come in two flavors: ANSI and Unicode. Those that operate on ANSI strings have an A suffix, while those that operate on Unicode strings have a W suffix. While all the documentation on MSDN refers to the "FindWindow" function, the Windows user32.dll does not actually contain a function by that name. It contains two functions called FindWindowA and FindWindowW. We use the Alias statement to provide the actual name (case-sensitive) of the function we want to use. As long as we provide the correct name in the Alias clause, we can give the declared function any name we want:

```
Declare Function Foo Lib "user32" Alias "FindWindowA" _
    (ByVal lpClassName As String, _
```

```
        ByVal lpWindowName As String) As Long

ApphWnd = Foo("XLMAIN", Application.Caption)
```

Although VBA stores strings as Unicode internally, it always converts them to ANSI when passing them to API functions. This is usually sufficient, and it is rare to find examples of VB6 or VBA calling the Unicode versions. In some cases, though, we need to support the full Unicode character set and can work around VBA's conversion behavior by calling the W version of the API function and using the VBA StrConv function to force an ANSI-to-Unicode conversion within our API function calls:

```
Declare Function FindWindow Lib "user32" Alias "FindWindowW" _
        (ByVal lpClassName As String, _
        ByVal lpWindowName As String) As Long

ApphWnd = FindWindow(StrConv("XLMAIN", vbUnicode), _
        StrConv(Application.Caption, vbUnicode))
```

Finding Related Windows

The problem with using FindWindow to get the main Excel window handle is that if we have multiple instances of Excel open that have the same caption there is no easy way to tell which one we get. This is a common problem if the user typically doesn't have their workbook windows maximized, in which case all instances of Excel will then have the same caption "Microsoft Excel."

A more robust and foolproof method is to use the FindWindowEx function to scan through all children of the desktop window, stopping when we find one that belongs to the same process as our current instance of Excel. FindWindowEx works in exactly the same way as FindWindow, but we provide the parent window handle and the handle of a child window to start searching after (or zero to start with the first). Listing 12-4 shows a specific ApphWnd function that calls a generic FindOurWindow function. The FindOurWindow function uses the following API functions:

- GetCurrentProcessID to retrieve the ID of the instance of Excel running the code
- GetDesktopWindow to get the handle of the desktop window that we pass to FindWindowEx to iterate the children of the desktop window (all application windows are children of the desktop window)
- GetWindowThreadProcessID to retrieve the ID of the instance of Excel that owns the window that FindWindowEx found

Listing 12-4 Foolproof Way to Find the Excel Main Window Handle

```
'Get the handle of the desktop window
Declare Function GetDesktopWindow Lib "user32" () As Long

'Find a child window with a given class name and caption
Declare Function FindWindowEx Lib "user32" _
        Alias "FindWindowExA" _
        (ByVal hWnd1 As Long, ByVal hWnd2 As Long, _
        ByVal lpsz1 As String, ByVal lpsz2 As String) _
        As Long

'Get the process ID of this instance of Excel
Declare Function GetCurrentProcessId Lib "kernel32" () _
        As Long

'Get the ID of the process that a window belongs to
Declare Function GetWindowThreadProcessId Lib "user32" _
        (ByVal hWnd As Long, ByRef lpdwProcessId As Long) _
        As Long

'Foolproof way to find the main Excel window handle
Function ApphWnd() As Long

  'Excel 2002 and above have a property for the hWnd
  If Val(Application.Version) >= 10 Then
    ApphWnd = Application.hWnd
  Else
    ApphWnd = FindOurWindow("XLMAIN", Application.Caption)
  End If

End Function

'Finds a top-level window of the given class and caption
'that belongs to this instance of Excel, by matching the
'process IDs
Function FindOurWindow( _
        Optional sClass As String = vbNullString, _
        Optional sCaption As String = vbNullString)

  Dim hWndDesktop As Long
  Dim hWnd As Long
  Dim hProcThis As Long
  Dim hProcWindow As Long

  'Get the ID of this instance of Excel, to match to
```

```
hProcThis = GetCurrentProcessId

'All top-level windows are children of the desktop,
'so get that handle first
hWndDesktop = GetDesktopWindow

Do
    'Find the next child window of the desktop that
    'matches the given window class and/or caption.
    'The first time in, hWnd will be zero, so we'll get
    'the first matching window. Each call will pass the
    'handle of the window we found the last time,
    'thereby getting the next one (if any)
    hWnd = FindWindowEx(hWndDesktop, hWnd, sClass, _
                        sCaption)

    'Get the ID of the process that owns the window
    GetWindowThreadProcessId hWnd, hProcWindow

    'Loop until the window's process matches this process,
    'or we didn't find a window
Loop Until hProcWindow = hProcThis Or hWnd = 0

'Return the handle we found
FindOurWindow = hWnd

End Function
```

The FindOurWindow function can also be used to safely find any of the top-level windows that Excel creates, such as UserForms.

Once we've found Excel's main window handle we can use the FindWindowEx function to navigate through Excel's window hierarchy. Listing 12-5 shows a function to return the handle of a given Excel workbook window. To get the window handle we start at Excel's main window, find the desktop (class XLDESK), and then find the window (class EXCEL7) with the appropriate caption.

Listing 12-5 Function to Find a Workbook Window Handle

```
Private Declare Function FindWindowEx Lib "user32" _
        Alias "FindWindowExA" _
        (ByVal hWnd1 As Long, ByVal hWnd2 As Long, _
        ByVal lpsz1 As String, ByVal lpsz2 As String) _
        As Long
```

```
'Function to find the handle of a given workbook window
Function WorkbookWindowhWnd(wndWindow As Window) As Long

    Dim hWndExcel As Long
    Dim hWndDesk As Long

    'Get the main Excel window
    hWndExcel = ApphWnd

    'Find the desktop
    hWndDesk = FindWindowEx(hWndExcel, 0, _
                        "XLDESK", vbNullString)

    'Find the workbook window
    WorkbookWindowhWnd = FindWindowEx(hWndDesk, 0, _
                        "EXCEL7", wndWindow.Caption)

End Function
```

Windows Messages

At the lowest level, windows communicate with each other and with the operating system by sending simple messages. Every window has a main message-handling procedure (commonly called its wndproc) to which messages are sent. Every message consists of four elements: the handle of the window to which the message is being sent, a message ID, and two numbers that provide extra information about the message (if required). Within each wndproc a huge case statement works out what to do for each message ID. For example, the system sends the WM_PAINT message to a window when it requires the window to redraw its contents.

We can also send messages directly to individual windows using the SendMessage function. The easiest way to find which messages can be sent to which window class is to search the MSDN library using a known constant and then look in the See Also list for a link to a list of related messages. Look down the list for a message that looks interesting and then go to its details page to see the parameters it requires. For example, if we look again at Figure 12-1 we can see that the EXCEL; window contains a combo box. This combo box is actually the Name drop-down to the left of the formula bar. Searching the MSDN library (using Google) with the search term "combo box messages" gives us a number of relevant hits.

One of them takes us to http://msdn.microsoft.com/en-us/library/ bb775792(VS.85).aspx.

Looking down the list of messages, we find the CB_SETDROPPEDWIDTH message that we can use to change the width of the drop-down portion of the Name box. In Listing 12-6, we use the SendMessage function to make the Name drop-down 200 pixels wide, allowing us to see the full text of lengthy defined names. As of Excel 2007, the Name drop-down can be widened manually, so the procedure shown in Listing 12-6 is no longer necessary even though it still works.

Listing 12-6 Changing the Width of the Name Drop-down List

```
Private Declare Function FindWindowEx Lib "user32" _
        Alias "FindWindowExA" _
        (ByVal hWnd1 As Long, ByVal hWnd2 As Long, _
        ByVal lpsz1 As String, ByVal lpsz2 As String) _
        As Long

Private Declare Function SendMessage Lib "user32" _
        Alias "SendMessageA" _
        (ByVal hwnd As Long, ByVal wMsg As Long, _
        ByVal wParam As Long, Byval lParam As Long) _
        As Long

'Not included in win32api.txt, but found in winuser.h
Private Const CB_SETDROPPEDWIDTH As Long = &H160&

'Make the Name dropdown list 200 pixels wide
Sub SetNameDropdownWidth()

  Dim hWndExcel As Long
  Dim hWndFormulaBar As Long
  Dim hWndNameCombo As Long

  'Get the main Excel window
  hWndExcel = ApphWnd

  'Get the handle for the formula bar window
  hWndFormulaBar = FindWindowEx(hWndExcel, 0, _
                "EXCEL;", vbNullString)

  'Get the handle for the Name combobox
  hWndNameCombo = FindWindowEx(hWndFormulaBar, 0, _
```

```
        "combobox", vbNullString)

    'Set the dropdown list to be 200 pixels wide
    SendMessage hWndNameCombo, CB_SETDROPPEDWIDTH, 200, 0

End Sub
```

Changing the Window Icon

When creating a dictator application, the intent is usually to make it look as though it is a normal Windows application and not necessarily running within Excel. Two of the giveaways are the application and worksheet icons. These can be changed to our own icons using API functions. We first use the ExtractIcon function to get a handle to an icon from a file and then send that icon handle to the window in a WM_SETICON message, as shown in Listing 12-7. The SetIcon procedure takes a window handle and the path to an icon file as arguments, so it can be used to set either the application icon or a workbook window icon. For best use, the icon file should contain both 32x32 and 16x16 pixel versions of the icon image. When you set a new icon for a workbook window, Excel doesn't refresh the image to the left of the menu bar until a window is maximized or minimized/restored. Therefore, you may need to toggle the WindowState to force an update.

Listing 12-7   Setting a Window's Icon

```
Private Declare Function ExtractIcon Lib "shell32.dll" _
        Alias "ExtractIconA" _
        (ByVal hInst As Long, _
        ByVal lpszExeFileName As String, _
        ByVal nIconIndex As Long) As Long

Private Declare Function SendMessage Lib "user32" _
        Alias "SendMessageA" _
        (ByVal hwnd As Long, ByVal wMsg As Long, _
        ByVal wParam As Long, Byval lParam As Long) _
        As Long

Private Const WM_SETICON As Long = &H80

'Set a window's icon
Sub SetIcon(ByVal hWnd As Long, ByVal sIcon As String)
```

```
Dim hIcon As Long

'Get the icon handle
hIcon = ExtractIcon(0, sIcon, 0)

'Set the big (32x32) and small (16x16) icons
SendMessage hWnd, WM_SETICON, 1, hIcon
SendMessage hWnd, WM_SETICON, 0, hIcon

End Sub
```

Changing Windows Styles

If you look at all the windows on your screen, you might notice that they all look a little different. Some have a title bar, some have minimize and maximize buttons, some have an [x] to close them, some have a 3D look, some are resizable, some are a fixed size, and so on. All these things are individual attributes of the window and are stored as part of the window's data structure. They're all on/off flags stored as bits in two Long data type values associated with the window. We can use the GetWindowLong function to retrieve a window's style settings, switch individual bits on or off, and write them back using SetWindowLong. Modifying windows styles in this way is most often done for UserForms and is covered in Chapter 13, "Userform Design and Best Practices."

Working with the Keyboard

The behavior of many Excel toolbar buttons and some of its dialog buttons changes if the Shift key is held down when the button is clicked. For example, the Increase Decimal toolbar button normally increases the number of decimal places shown in a cell, but decreases the number of decimal places if it is clicked with the Shift key held down. Similarly, when closing Excel, if you hold down the Shift key when clicking the *No* button on the *Save Changes* dialog, it acts like a "No to All" button.

We can do exactly the same in our applications by using API functions to examine the state of the keyboard. The procedures included in this section can be found in the MKeyboard module of the API Examples.xls workbook located in the *Concepts\Ch12 – Understanding and Using Windows API Calls* folder on the CD that accompanies this book.

Checking for Shift, Ctrl, Alt, Caps Lock, Num Lock, and Scroll Lock

The GetKeyState API function tells us whether a given key on the keyboard is currently held down or "on" (in the case of Caps Lock, Num Lock, and Scroll Lock). We pass this function a code representing the key we're interested in, and it returns whether that key is being held down or is "on." Listing 12-8 shows a function to determine whether one of the six "special" keys is currently pressed. Note that we have again encapsulated the key code constants inside a more meaningful enumeration.

Listing 12-8   Checking if a Key Is Held Down

```
Private Declare Function GetKeyState Lib "user32" _
     (ByVal vKey As Long) As Integer

Private Const VK_SHIFT As Long = &H10
Private Const VK_CONTROL As Long = &H11
Private Const VK_MENU As Long = &H12
Private Const VK_CAPITAL = &H14
Private Const VK_NUMLOCK = &H90
Private Const VK_SCROLL = &H91

Public Enum GetKeyStateKeyboardCodes
  gksKeyboardShift = VK_SHIFT
  gksKeyboardCtrl = VK_CONTROL
  gksKeyboardAlt = VK_MENU
  gksKeyboardCapsLock = VK_CAPITAL
  gksKeyboardNumLock = VK_NUMLOCK
  gksKeyboardScrollLock = VK_SCROLL
End Enum

Public Function IsKeyPressed _
     (ByVal lKey As GetKeyStateKeyboardCodes) As Boolean

  Dim iResult As Integer

  iResult = GetKeyState(lKey)

  Select Case lKey
  Case gksKeyboardCapsLock, gksKeyboardNumLock, _
     gksKeyboardScrollLock

    'For the three 'toggle' keys, the 1st bit says if it's
```

```
   'on or off, so clear any other bits that might be set,
   'using a binary AND
   iResult = iResult And 1

Case Else
   'For the other keys, the 16th bit says if it's down or
   'up, so clear any other bits that might be set, using a
   'binary AND
   iResult = iResult And &H8000
End Select

IsKeyPressed = (iResult <> 0)

End Function
```

Bit Masks

The value obtained from the call to GetKeyState should not be interpreted as a simple number, but as a series of bits where each individual bit specifies whether a particular attribute is on or off. This is also one of the few functions that return a 16-bit Integer value, rather than the more common 32-bit Long.

The MSDN documentation for GetKeyState says, "If the high-order bit is 1, the key is down, otherwise the key is up. If the low-order bit is 1, the key is on, otherwise the key is off." The first sentence is applicable for all keys (down/up), while the second is only applicable to the Caps Lock, Num Lock, and Scroll Lock keys. It is possible for both bits to be set, for example, if the Caps Lock key is held down while it is "on."

The low-order bit is the rightmost bit, while the high-order bit is the leftmost (16th) bit. To examine whether a specific bit has been set, we have to apply a **bit mask**, to zero-out the bits we're not interested in. This is accomplished by performing a binary AND between the return value of the function and a binary value that has a single 1 in the position we're interested in. In the first case, we're checking for a 1 in the first bit, which is the number 1. In the second case, we're checking for a 1 in the 16th bit, that is, the binary number 1000 0000 0000 0000, which is easiest to represent in code as the hexadecimal number &h8000. Once we've isolated that bit, a zero value means off/up and a nonzero value means on/down.

Testing for a Key Press

As we mentioned earlier, at the lowest level, windows communicate through messages sent to their wndproc procedure. When an application is busy (such as Excel running some code), the wndproc only processes critical messages (such as the system shutting down). All other messages get placed in a queue and are processed when the application next has some spare time. This is why using SendKeys is so unreliable; it's not until the code stops running (or issues a DoEvents statement) that Excel checks its message queue to see if there are any key presses to process.

We can use Excel's message queuing to allow the user to interrupt our code by pressing a key. Normally, if we want to allow the user to stop a lengthy looping process, we can either show a modeless dialog with a Cancel button (as explained in Chapter 13), or allow them to press the Cancel key to jump into the procedure error handler (as explained in Chapter 15, "VBA Error Handling"). An easier way is to check the Excel message queue during each iteration of the loop to see whether the user has pressed a key. This is achieved using the PeekMessage API function:

```
Declare Function PeekMessage Lib "user32" _
        Alias "PeekMessageA" _
        (ByRef lpMsg As MSG, _
        ByVal hWnd As Long, _
        ByVal wMsgFilterMin As Long, _
        ByVal wMsgFilterMax As Long, _
        ByVal wRemoveMsg As Long) As Long
```

Structures

If you look at the first parameter of the PeekMessage function, you see it is declared As MSG and is passed ByRef. MSG is a windows **structure** and is implemented in VBA as a user-defined type. To use it in this case, we declare a variable of that type and pass it in to the function. The function sets the value of each element of the UDT, which we then read.

Many API functions use structures as a convenient way of passing large amounts of information into and out of the function rather than having a long list of parameters. Many messages that we send using the SendMessage function require a structure to be passed as the final parameter (as opposed to a single Long value). In those cases, we use a different form of the SendMessage declaration, where the final parameter is declared As Any and is passed ByRef:

```
Declare Function SendMessageAny Lib "user32" _
        Alias "SendMessageA" _
        (ByVal hwnd As Long, ByVal wMsg As Long, _
        ByVal wParam As Long, _
        ByRef lParam As Any) As Long
```

When we use this declaration, we're actually sending a pointer to the memory where our UDT is stored. If we have an error in the definition of our UDT, or if we use this version of the declaration to send a message that is not expecting a memory pointer, the call will at best fail and possibly crash Excel. The full code to check for a key press is shown in Listing 12-9.

Listing 12-9   Testing for a Key Press

```
'Type to hold the coordinates of the mouse pointer
Private Type POINTAPI
  x As Long
  y As Long
End Type

'Type to hold the Windows message information
Private Type MSG
  hWnd As Long        'the window handle of the app
  message As Long     'the type of message (e.g. keydown)
  wParam As Long      'the key code
  lParam As Long      'not used
  time As Long        'time when message posted
  pt As POINTAPI      'coordinate of mouse pointer
End Type

'Look in the message buffer for a message
Private Declare Function PeekMessage Lib "user32" _
        Alias "PeekMessageA" _
        (ByRef lpMsg As MSG, ByVal hWnd As Long, _
        ByVal wMsgFilterMin As Long, _
        ByVal wMsgFilterMax As Long, _
        ByVal wRemoveMsg As Long) As Long

'Translate the message from a key code to a ASCII code
Private Declare Function TranslateMessage Lib "user32" _
        (ByRef lpMsg As MSG) As Long

'Windows API constants
Private Const WM_CHAR As Long = &H102
```

```
Private Const WM_KEYDOWN As Long = &H100
Private Const PM_REMOVE As Long = &H1
Private Const PM_NOYIELD As Long = &H2

'Check for a key press
Public Function CheckKeyboardBuffer() As String

    'Dimension variables
    Dim msgMessage As MSG
    Dim hWnd As Long
    Dim lResult As Long

    'Get the window handle of this application
    hWnd = ApphWnd

    'See if there are any "Key down" messages
    lResult = PeekMessage(msgMessage, hWnd, WM_KEYDOWN, _
            WM_KEYDOWN, PM_REMOVE + PM_NOYIELD)

    'If so ...
    If lResult <> 0 Then

        '... translate the key-down code to a character code,
        'which gets put back in the message queue as a WM_CHAR
        'message ...
        lResult = TranslateMessage(msgMessage)

        '... and retrieve that WM_CHAR message
        lResult = PeekMessage(msgMessage, hWnd, WM_CHAR, _
                WM_CHAR, PM_REMOVE + PM_NOYIELD)

        'Return the character of the key pressed,
        'ignoring shift and control characters
        CheckKeyboardBuffer = Chr$(msgMessage.wParam)
    End If

End Function
```

When we press a key on the keyboard, the active window is sent a WM_KEYDOWN message with a low-level code that identifies the physical key pressed. The first thing we need to do is use PeekMessage to examine the message queue and see if there is a pending WM_KEYDOWN message, removing it from the queue if we find one. If we find one, we have to translate it into a character code using TranslateMessage, which sends the translated message back into Excel's message queue as a WM_CHAR message. We then check the message queue for this WM_CHAR message and return the character pressed.

Working with the File System and Network

The procedures included in this section can be found in the MFileSys module of the API Examples.xls workbook located in the \Concepts\Ch12 – Understanding and Using Windows API Calls folder on the CD that accompanies this book.

Finding the User ID

Excel has its own user name property, but does not tell us the user's network logon ID. This ID is often required in Excel applications for security validation, auditing, logging, change history, and so on. It can be retrieved using the API call shown in Listing 12-10.

Listing 12-10   Reading the User's Login ID

```
Private Declare Function GetUserName Lib "advapi32.dll" _
        Alias "GetUserNameA" _
        (ByVal lpBuffer As String, _
        ByRef nSize As Long) As Long

'Get the user's login ID
Function UserName() As String

  'A buffer that the API function fills with the login name
  Dim sBuffer As String * 255

  'Variable to hold the length of the buffer
  Dim lStringLength As Long

  'Initialise to the length of the string buffer
  lStringLength = Len(sBuffer)

  'Call the API function, which fills the buffer
  'and updates lStringLength with the length of the login ID,
  'including a terminating null - vbNullChar - character
  GetUserName sBuffer, lStringLength
```

```
   If lStringLength > 0 Then
     'Return the login id, stripping off the final vbNullChar
     UserName = Left$(sBuffer, lStringLength - 1)
   End If

End Function
```

Buffers

Every API function that returns textual information such as a user name does so by placing the textual data into a preallocated buffer that we provide. A buffer consists of a String variable initialized to a fixed size and a Long variable holding the size of the buffer. When the function is called, it writes the text to the buffer (including a final Null character) and either updates the length variable with the number of characters actually written or returns the length as the function's result depending on the function. We can then extract the result text from the buffer.

Note that VBA stores strings in a very different way than the API functions expect, so whenever we pass strings to API functions, VBA does some conversion for us behind the scenes. For this to work properly, we **always** pass strings by value (ByVal) to API functions, even when the function updates the string. Some people prefer to ignore the buffer length information, looking instead for the first vbNullChar character in the buffer and assuming that it marks the end of the returned string, so you may encounter usage like that shown in Listing 12-11.

Listing 12-11 Using a Buffer, Ignoring the Buffer Length Variable

```
'Get the user's login ID, without using the buffer length
Function UserName2() As String
  Dim sBuffer As String * 255
  GetUserName sBuffer, 255
  UserName2 = Left$(sBuffer, InStr(sBuffer, vbNullChar) - 1)
End Function
```

Changing to a UNC Path

VBA's intrinsic ChDrive and ChDir statements can be used to change the active path prior to using Application.GetOpenFilename, such that the dialog opens with the correct path preselected. Unfortunately, that can only be used to change the active path to local folders or network folders that have been mapped to a drive letter. Note that once set, the VBA CurDir function returns a UNC path. We need to use API functions to change the folder to a network path of the form \\server\share\path, as shown in Listing 12-12. In practice, the SetCurDir API function is one of the few that can be called directly from your code.

Listing 12-12 Changing to a UNC Path

```
Private Declare Function SetCurDir Lib "kernel32" _
      Alias "SetCurrentDirectoryA" _
      (ByVal lpPathName As String) As Long

'Change to a UNC Directory
Sub ChDirUNC(ByVal sPath As String)

  Dim lReturn As Long

  'Call the API function to set the current directory
  lReturn = SetCurDir(sPath)

  'A zero return value means an error
  If lReturn = 0 Then
    Err.Raise vbObjectError + 1, "Error setting path."
  End If

End Sub
```

Locating Special Folders

Windows maintains a large number of special folders that relate to either the current user or the system configuration. When a user is logged in to Windows with relatively low privileges, such as the basic User account, it is very likely they only have full access to their personal folders, such as their *My Documents* folder. These folders can usually be found under *C:\Documents and Settings\UserName*, but could be located anywhere. We can use an API function to give us the correct paths to these special folders using the code shown in Listing 12-13. Note that this listing contains a subset of all the possible folder constants. The full list can be found by searching MSDN for "CSIDL Values." The notable exception from this list is the user's Temp folder, which can be found by using the GetTempPath function. Listing 12-13 includes a special case for this folder, so that it can be obtained using the same function.

Listing 12-13   Locating a Windows Special Folder

```
Private Declare Function SHGetFolderPath Lib "shell32" _
        Alias "SHGetFolderPathA" _
        (ByVal hwndOwner As Long, ByVal nFolder As Long, _
        ByVal hToken As Long, ByVal dwFlags As Long, _
        ByVal pszPath As String) As Long

Private Declare Function GetTempPath Lib "kernel32" _
        Alias "GetTempPathA" _
        (ByVal nBufferLength As Long, _
        ByVal lpBuffer As String) As Long


'More Commonly-used CSIDL values.
'For the full list, search MSDN for "CSIDL Values"
Private Const CSIDL_PROGRAMS As Long = &H2
Private Const CSIDL_PERSONAL As Long = &H5
Private Const CSIDL_FAVORITES As Long = &H6
Private Const CSIDL_STARTMENU As Long = &HB
Private Const CSIDL_MYDOCUMENTS As Long = &HC
Private Const CSIDL_MYMUSIC As Long = &HD
Private Const CSIDL_MYVIDEO As Long = &HE
Private Const CSIDL_DESKTOPDIRECTORY As Long = &H10
Private Const CSIDL_APPDATA As Long = &H1A
Private Const CSIDL_LOCAL_APPDATA As Long = &H1C
Private Const CSIDL_INTERNET_CACHE As Long = &H20
Private Const CSIDL_WINDOWS As Long = &H24
Private Const CSIDL_SYSTEM As Long = &H25
Private Const CSIDL_PROGRAM_FILES As Long = &H26
Private Const CSIDL_MYPICTURES As Long = &H27


'Constants used in the SHGetFolderPath call
Private Const CSIDL_FLAG_CREATE As Long = &H8000&
Private Const SHGFP_TYPE_CURRENT = 0
Private Const SHGFP_TYPE_DEFAULT = 1
Private Const MAX_PATH = 260


'Public enumeration to give friendly names for the CSIDL values
Public Enum SpecialFolderIDs
  sfAppDataRoaming = CSIDL_APPDATA
```

```vb
    sfAppDataNonRoaming = CSIDL_LOCAL_APPDATA
    sfStartMenu = CSIDL_STARTMENU
    sfStartMenuPrograms = CSIDL_PROGRAMS
    sfMyDocuments = CSIDL_PERSONAL
    sfMyMusic = CSIDL_MYMUSIC
    sfMyPictures = CSIDL_MYPICTURES
    sfMyVideo = CSIDL_MYVIDEO
    sfFavorites = CSIDL_FAVORITES
    sfDesktopDir = CSIDL_DESKTOPDIRECTORY
    sfInternetCache = CSIDL_INTERNET_CACHE
    sfWindows = CSIDL_WINDOWS
    sfWindowsSystem = CSIDL_SYSTEM
    sfProgramFiles = CSIDL_PROGRAM_FILES

    'There is no CSIDL for the temp path,
    'so we need to give it a dummy value
    'and treat it differently in the function
    sfTemporary = &HFF
End Enum

'Get the path for a Windows special folder
Public Function SpecialFolderPath( _
        ByVal uFolderID As SpecialFolderIDs) As String

    'Create a buffer of the correct size
    Dim sBuffer As String * MAX_PATH
    Dim lResult As Long

    If uFolderID = sfTemporary Then
        'Use GetTempPath for the temporary path
        lResult = GetTempPath(MAX_PATH, sBuffer)

        'The GetTempPath call returns the length and a
        'trailing \ which we remove for consistency
        SpecialFolderPath = Left$(sBuffer, lResult - 1)
    Else
        'Call the function, passing the buffer
        lResult = SHGetFolderPath(0, _
                uFolderID + CSIDL_FLAG_CREATE, 0, _
                SHGFP_TYPE_CURRENT, sBuffer)

        'The SHGetFolderPath function doesn't give us a
        'length, so look for the first vbNullChar
        SpecialFolderPath = Left$(sBuffer, _
```

```
                         InStr(sBuffer, vbNullChar) - 1)
   End If

End Function
```

The observant among you might have noticed that we've now come across all three ways in which buffers are filled by API functions:

- GetUserName returns the length of the text by modifying the input parameter.
- GetTempPath returns the length of the text as the function's return value.
- SHGetFolderPath doesn't return the length at all, so we search for the first vbNullChar character.

Deleting a File to the Recycle Bin

The VBA Kill statement can be used to delete a file, but it does not send the deleted file to the Recycle Bin for potential recovery by the user. To send a file to the recycle bin we need to use the SHFileOperation function, as shown in Listing 12-14.

Listing 12-14 Deleting a File to the Recycle Bin

```
'Structure to tell the SHFileOperation function what to do
Private Type SHFILEOPSTRUCT
   hwnd As Long
   wFunc As Long
   pFrom As String
   pTo As String
   fFlags As Integer
   fAnyOperationsAborted As Boolean
   hNameMappings As Long
   lpszProgressTitle As String
End Type

Private Declare Function SHFileOperation Lib "shell32.dll" _
      Alias "SHFileOperationA" _
      (ByRef lpFileOp As SHFILEOPSTRUCT) As Long

Private Const FO_DELETE = &H3
```

```
Private Const FOF_SILENT = &H4
Private Const FOF_NOCONFIRMATION = &H10
Private Const FOF_ALLOWUNDO = &H40

'Delete a file, sending it to the recycle bin
Sub DeleteToRecycleBin(ByVal sFile As String)

    Dim uFileOperation As SHFILEOPSTRUCT
    Dim lReturn As Long

    'Fill the UDT with information about what to do
    With FileOperation
        .wFunc = FO_DELETE
        .pFrom = sFile
        .pTo = vbNullChar
        .fFlags = FOF_SILENT + FOF_NOCONFIRMATION + _
                FOF_ALLOWUNDO
    End With

    'Pass the UDT to the function
    lReturn = SHFileOperation(FileOperation)

    If lReturn <> 0 Then
        Err.Raise vbObjectError + 1, "Error deleting file."
    End If

End Sub
```

There are two things to note about this function. First, the function uses a user-defined type to tell it what to do, instead of the more common method of having multiple input parameters. Second, the function returns a value of zero to indicate success. If you recall, the SetCurDir function in Listing 12-12 returned a value of zero to indicate failure. The only way to know which to expect is to check the Return Values section of the function's information page on MSDN.

Browsing for a Folder

All versions of Excel include the GetOpenFilename and GetSaveAsFilename functions to allow the user to select a filename to open or save. Excel 2002 introduced the common Office FileDialog object,

which can be used to browse for a folder using the code shown in Listing
12-15. This results in the dialog shown in Figure 12-3.

FIGURE 12-3 The standard Office folder picker dialog

Listing 12-15 Using the Office FileDialog to Browse for a Folder

```
'Browse for a folder, using the Office FileDialog
Sub BrowseForFolder()

    ' Use the FileDialog object
    With Application.FileDialog(msoFileDialogFolderPicker)

        ' Initialise the dialog
        .Title = "Select Folder"
        .InitialFileName = "C:\"

        ' Display the dialog
        If .Show Then
            MsgBox "You selected " & .SelectedItems(1)
        End If

    End With

End Sub
```

We consider this layout much too complicated when all we need is a
simple tree view of the folders on the computer. We can use API functions

to show the standard Windows "Browse for folder" dialog shown in Figure 12-4, which our users tend to find much easier to use. The Windows dialog also gives us the option to display some descriptive text to tell our users what they should be selecting.

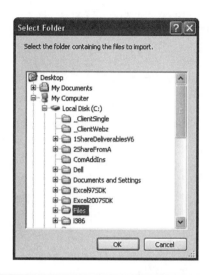

FIGURE 12-4   The standard Windows folder picker dialog

Callbacks

Every function we've encountered so far simply performs its task and returns its result. But a range of API functions (including the SHBrowseForFolder function that we're about to use) interact with the calling program while they're working. This mechanism is known as a **callback**. Excel 2000 added a VBA function called AddressOf, which provides the address in memory where a given procedure can be found. This address is passed to the API function, which calls back to the procedure found at that address as required.

For example, the EnumWindows function iterates through all the top-level windows, calling back to the procedure with the details of each window it finds. Obviously, the procedure being called must be defined exactly as Windows expects it to be so the API function can pass it the correct number and type of parameters.

The SHBrowseForFolder function uses a callback to tell us when the dialog is initially shown, allowing us to set its caption and initial selection, and each time the user selects a folder, allowing us to check the selection and enable/disable the OK button. The full text for the following example is contained in the MBrowseForFolder module of the API Examples.xls workbook, and a slightly simplified version is shown in Listing 12-16.

Listing 12-16   Using Callbacks to Interact with the Windows File Picker Dialog

```
'UDT to pass information to the SHBrowseForFolder function
Private Type BROWSEINFO
   hOwner As Long
   pidlRoot As Long
   pszDisplayName As String
   lpszTitle As String
   ulFlags As Long
   lpfn As Long
   lParam As Long
   iImage As Long
End Type


'Commonly-used ulFlags constants

'Only return file system directories.
'If the user selects folders that are not
'part of the file system (such as 'My Computer'),
'the OK button is grayed.
Private Const BIF_RETURNONLYFSDIRS As Long = &H1

'Use a newer dialog style, which gives a richer experience
Private Const BIF_NEWDIALOGSTYLE As Long = &H40

'Hide the default 'Make New Folder' button
Private Const BIF_NONEWFOLDERBUTTON As Long = &H200


'Messages sent from dialog to callback function

Private Const BFFM_INITIALIZED = 1
Private Const BFFM_SELCHANGED = 2


'Messages sent to browser from callback function
Private Const WM_USER = &H400

'Set the selected path
Private Const BFFM_SETSELECTIONA = WM_USER + 102
```

```vb
'Enable/disable the OK button
Private Const BFFM_ENABLEOK = WM_USER + 101


'The maximum allowed path
Private Const MAX_PATH = 260

'Main Browse for directory function
Declare Function SHBrowseForFolder Lib "shell32.dll" _
        Alias "SHBrowseForFolderA" _
        (ByRef lpBrowseInfo As BROWSEINFO) As Long

'Gets a path from a pidl
Declare Function SHGetPathFromIDList Lib "shell32.dll" _
        Alias "SHGetPathFromIDListA" _
        (ByVal pidl As Long, _
        ByVal pszPath As String) As Long

'Used to set the browse dialog's title
Declare Function SetWindowText Lib "user32" _
        Alias "SetWindowTextA" _
        (ByVal hwnd As Long, _
        ByVal lpString As String) As Long

'A versions of SendMessage, to send strings to the browser
Private Declare Function SendMessageString Lib "user32" _
        Alias "SendMessageA" (ByVal hwnd As Long, _
        ByVal wMsg As Long, ByVal wParam As Long, _
        ByVal lParam As String) As Long

'Variables to hold the initial options,
'set in the callback function
Dim msInitialPath As String
Dim msTitleBarText As String

'The main function to initialize and show the dialog
Function GetDirectory(Optional ByVal sInitDir As String, _
        Optional ByVal sTitle As String, _
        Optional ByVal sMessage As String, _
        Optional ByVal hwndOwner As Long, _
        Optional ByVal bAllowCreateFolder As Boolean) _
        As String
```

```vba
'A variable to hold the UDT
Dim uInfo As BROWSEINFO

Dim sPath As String
Dim lResult As Long

'Check that the initial directory exists
On Error Resume Next
sPath = Dir(sInitDir & "\*.*", vbNormal + vbDirectory)
If Len(sPath) = 0 Or Err.Number <> 0 Then sInitDir = ""
On Error GoTo 0

'Store the initials setting in module-level variables,
'for use in the callback function
msInitialPath = sInitDir
msTitleBarText = sTitle

'If no owner window given, use the Excel window
'N.B. Uses the ApphWnd function in MWindows
If hwndOwner = 0 Then hwndOwner = ApphWnd

'Initialise the structure to pass to the API function
With uInfo
   .hOwner = hwndOwner
   .pszDisplayName = String$(MAX_PATH, VbNullChar)
   .lpszTitle = sMessage
   .ulFlags = BIF_RETURNONLYFSDIRS + BIF_NEWDIALOGSTYLE _
      + IIf(bAllowCreateFolder, 0, BIF_NONEWFOLDERBUTTON)

   'Pass the address of the callback function in the UDT
   .lpfn = LongToLong(AddressOf BrowseCallBack)
End With

'Display the dialog, returning the ID of the selection
lResult = SHBrowseForFolder(uInfo)

'Get the path string from the ID
GetDirectory = GetPathFromID(lResult)

End Function


'Windows calls this function when the dialog events occur
Private Function BrowseCallBack (ByVal hwnd As Long, _
        ByVal Msg As Long, ByVal lParam As Long, _
```

```
                ByVal pData As Long) As Long

    Dim sPath As String

    'This is called by Windows, so don't allow any errors!
    On Error Resume Next

    Select Case Msg
    Case BFFM_INITIALIZED
        'Dialog is being initialized,
        'so set the initial parameters

        'The dialog caption
        If msTitleBarText <> "" Then
            SetWindowText hwnd, msTitleBarText
        End If

        'The initial path to display
        If msInitialPath <> "" Then
            SendMessageString hwnd, BFFM_SETSELECTIONA, 1, _
                              msInitialPath
        End If

    Case BFFM_SELCHANGED
        'User selected a folder
        'lParam contains the pidl of the folder, which can be
        'converted to the path using GetPathFromID
        'sPath = GetPathFromID(lParam)

        'We could put extra checks in here,
        'e.g. to check if the folder contains any workbooks,
        'and send the BFFM_ENABLEOK message to enable/disable
        'the OK button:
        'SendMessage hwnd, BFFM_ENABLEOK, 0, True/False
    End Select

End Function


'Converts a PIDL to a path string
Private Function GetPathFromID(ByVal lID As Long) As String

    Dim lResult As Long
    Dim sPath As String * MAX_PATH
```

```
    lResult = SHGetPathFromIDList(lID, sPath)

    If lResult <> 0 Then
      GetPathFromID = Left$(sPath, InStr(sPath, Chr$(0))) - 1
    End If

End Function

'VBA doesn't let us assign the result of AddressOf
'to a variable, but does allow us to pass it to a function.
'This 'do nothing' function works around that problem
Private Function LongToLong(ByVal lAddr As Long) As Long
  LongToLong = lAddr
End Function
```

Let's take a closer look at how this all works. First, most of the shell functions use things called PIDLs to uniquely identify folders and files. For simplicity's sake, you can think of a PIDL as a handle to a file or folder, and there are API functions to convert between a PIDL and the normal file or folder name.

The GetDirectory function is the main function in the module and is the function that should be called to display the dialog. It starts by validating the optional input parameters and then populates the BROWSEINFO user-defined type that is used to pass all the required information to the SHBrowseForFolder function.

The hOwner element of the UDT is used to specify the parent window for the dialog, which should be the handle of the main Excel window, or the handle of the UserForm window if showing this dialog from a UserForm. The ulFlags element is used to specify detailed behavior for the dialog, such as whether to show a Make Folder button. The full list of possible flags and their purpose can be found on MSDN by searching for the SHBrowseForFolder function. The lpfn element is where we pass the address of the callback function, BrowseCallBack. We have to wrap the AddressOf value in a simple LongToLong function, because VBA doesn't let us assign this value directly to an element of a UDT.

After the UDT has been initialized, we pass it to the SHBrowseForFolder API function. This function displays the dialog, and Windows calls back to our BrowseCallBack function, passing the BFFM_INITIALIZED message. We respond to that message by setting the dialog's caption (using the SetWindowText API function) and the initial folder selection (by sending the BFFM_SETSELECTIONA message back to the dialog with the path string).

Every time the user clicks on a folder, it triggers a Windows callback to our BrowseCallBack function, passing the BFFM_SELCHANGED message and the ID of the selected folder. All the code to respond to that message is commented out in this example, but we could add code to check whether the folder is a valid selection for our application (such as whether it contains any workbooks) and enable/disable the OK button appropriately (by sending the BFFM_ENABLEOK message back to the dialog).

When the user clicks the OK or Cancel buttons, the function returns the ID of the selected folder and execution continues back in the GetDirectory function. We then convert the folder ID into its corresponding string path and return this to the calling code.

Practical Examples

All the procedures included in this chapter are taken from actual Excel applications, so they are all truly practical examples of using API calls. The PETRAS application files for this chapter can be found on the CD in the folder *Application\Ch12 – Understanding and Using Windows API Calls*. This folder now includes the following files:

- **PetrasTemplate.xlt**—The time sheet template
- **PetrasAddin.xla**—The time sheet data entry support add-in
- **PetrasReporting.xla**—The main reporting application
- **PetrasConsolidation.xlt**—A template to use for new results workbooks
- **Debug.ini**—A dummy file that tells the reporting application to run in debug mode
- **PetrasIcon.ico**—A custom icon file to replace the default icon in Excel's main window

PETRAS Time Sheet

Prior to this chapter, the Post to Network feature used Excel's GetOpenFilename to allow the user to select the directory to save the time sheet workbook to. The problem with this method is that the directory must already contain at least one file to be selected. In this chapter we replace GetOpenFilename with the BrowseForFolder dialog, which allows empty folders to be selected.

We also added a new feature to the time sheet add-in. In previous versions you were prompted to specify the consolidation location the first time you posted a time sheet workbook to the network. When you selected a location, that location was stored in the registry, and from there on out the application simply read the location from the registry whenever you posted a new time sheet.

This didn't take into account the possibility that the consolidation location might change. If it did, you would have no way, short of editing the application's registry entries directly, of switching to the new location. Our new Specify Consolidation Folder feature allows you to click a button on the toolbar and use the Windows browse for folder dialog to modify the consolidation folder. The SpecifyConsolidationFolder procedure is shown in Listing 12-17, and the updated toolbar is shown in Figure 12-5.

Figure 12-5   The updated PETRAS time sheet toolbar

Listing 12-17   The New SpecifyConsolidationFolder Procedure

```
Public Sub SpecifyConsolidationFolder()

    Dim sSavePath As String

    InitGlobals

    ' Get the current consolidation path.
    sSavePath = GetSetting(gsREG_APP, gsREG_SECTION, _
            gsREG_KEY, "")

    ' Display the browse for folders dialog with the initial
    ' path display set to the current consolidation folder.
    sSavePath = GetDirectory(sSavePath, _
            gsCAPTION_SELECT_FOLDER, gsMSG_SELECT_FOLDER)

    If Len(sSavePath) > 0 Then
        ' Save the selected path to the registry.
        If Right$(sSavePath, 1) <> "\" Then _
            sSavePath = sSavePath & "\"
        SaveSetting gsREG_APP, gsREG_SECTION, _
```

```
        gsREG_KEY, sSavePath
    End If

End Sub
```

Table 12-2 summarizes the changes made to the time sheet add-in for this chapter.

Table 12-2   Changes to the PETRAS Time Sheet Add-in to Use the BrowseForFolder Feature

Module	Procedure	Change
MBrowseForFolder (new module)		Included the entire MBrowseForFolder module shown in Listing 12-16
MEntryPoints	PostTimeEntriesToNetwork	Added call to the GetDirectory function in MBrowseForFolder
	SpecifyConsolidationFolder	New feature to update the consolidation folder location

PETRAS Reporting

The changes made to the central reporting application for this chapter are to display a custom icon for the application and to allow the user to close all the results workbooks in one go, by holding down the Shift key while clicking the *File > Close* menu. The detailed changes are shown in Table 12-3, while Listing 12-18 shows the new MenuFileClose routine that includes the check for the Shift key.

Table 12-3   Changes to the PETRAS Reporting Application for Chapter 12

Module	Procedure	Change
MAPIWrappers (new module)	ApphWnd	Included Listing 12-4 to obtain the handle of Excel's main window
MAPIWrappers (new module)	SetIcon	Included Listing 12-7 to display a custom icon, read from the new PetrasIcon.ico file

12. UNDERSTANDING AND USING WINDOWS API CALLS

Table 12-3 Changes to the PETRAS Reporting Application for Chapter 12

Module	Procedure	Change
MAPIWrappers	IsKeyPressed	Included Listing 12-8 to check for the shift key held down when clicking *File > Close*
MGlobals		Added a constant for the icon filename
MWorkspace	ConfigureExcelEnvironment	Added a call to SetIcon
MEntryPoints	MenuFileClose	Added check for Shift key being held down, shown in Listing 12-17, doing a Close All if so

Listing 12-18 The New MenuFileClose Routine, Checking for a Shift+Close

```
'Handle the File > Close menu
Sub MenuFileClose()

  Dim wkbWorkbook As Workbook

  'Ch12+
  'Check for a shift+Close
  If IsKeyPressed(gksKeyboardShift) Then

    'Close all results workbooks
    For Each wkbWorkbook In Workbooks
      If IsResultsWorkbook(wkbWorkbook) Then
        CloseWorkbook wkbWorkbook
      End If
    Next
  Else
    'Ch12-

    'Close only the active workbook
    If IsResultsWorkbook(ActiveWorkbook) Then
      CloseWorkbook ActiveWorkbook
    End If
  End If

End Sub
```

Later chapters, particularly Chapter 13, use more of the procedures and concepts introduced in this chapter.

Summary

The Excel object model provides a rich set of tools for us to use when creating our applications. By including calls to Windows API functions, we can enhance our applications to give them a truly professional look and feel.

This chapter explained the most common API functions encountered in Excel application development. All the fundamental concepts were explained as well, so you should now be able to interpret and understand new uses of API functions as you encounter them. All the example routines included in this chapter are taken from actual Excel applications and are ready for you to use in your own workbooks.

CHAPTER 13

UserForm Design and Best Practices

Dialog boxes of various kinds are a fundamental part of most Excel application user interfaces, ranging from message boxes to complex data entry forms. This chapter explains how to get the most out of custom dialog boxes built with VBA UserForms.

Principles

When we design and code UserForms we strive to adhere to a small set of basic principles whenever possible, as explained in the following sections. By following these principles you create UserForms that are easy to use, code, and maintain. While some of these principles may seem a little artificial at first, our experience has shown that sticking to them provides long-term rewards.

Keep It Simple

A UserForm should not require a help file to explain how to use it. If a UserForm is designed properly, users will be able to determine what they need to do simply by looking at it. In practice, this means using a relatively small number of controls that are well positioned, clearly labeled, and appropriately grouped and ordered to match the task the UserForm is designed to accomplish.

When designing a UserForm to assist with a complex task, a wizard design should be used. In this design the UserForm is broken down into multiple steps, each of which adheres to the Keep it Simple principle. There are, of course, situations that require complex UserForms. In these cases, extra effort should be invested to make the UserForm as simple as possible to use. Making a complex UserForm as easy as possible for the user usually requires the most effort on the part of the programmer and often results in very complex code.

Display Canvas, Not Business Rules

A UserForm is a user interface element, not a place to implement business logic. The user interaction should always be separated from the business response to that interaction, at least logically if not physically. In practice, this means the only code that should be included in control event procedures either changes another control's properties or calls functions in the business logic layer. Conversely, the code in the business logic layer should never directly reference controls on a UserForm and ideally should not even assume that any specific display mechanism is being used (such as a set of option buttons versus a list box). So what is business logic in this context? Figure 13-1 shows a simple UserForm with a combo box to select a region and a two-column list to show sales by product:

FIGURE 13-1   A simple UserForm

If the code in the ComboBox_Click event procedure identifies the region, retrieves the products for the region, retrieves the total sales for each product, and adds them to the list box, it's implementing business logic and is doing too much.

When the user selects a new region, there are two things we need to specify: the appropriate response and the data required to satisfy that response. In our example, the appropriate response is to populate the list of products, and the data required to satisfy the response is the list of products and the total sales for each.

At a minimum, the data required to satisfy the response should be obtained from the business logic layer. In this case, we'd have a function in the business logic layer that takes a region as a parameter and returns an array of products and total sales. It does this by retrieving the underlying data from the data access layer and populating the array. Code in the combobox_click event would read the selected region from the combo box, call the business logic layer function to get the array of products and sales, and write that array to the list box. Listing 13-1 shows an example of this mechanism.

Listing 13-1 The User Interface Layer Determines the Response

```
'**********************************
'* User Interface Layer, FSimpleForm
'**********************************

'Handle selecting a different region
Private Sub cboRegion_Change()

  Dim vaProductSales As Variant

  'Get the Product/Sales array for the selected region
  'from the business logic layer
  vaProductSales = GetProductSalesForRegion(cboRegion.Value)

  'Populate the list box
  lstProducts.List = vaProductSales

End Sub
```

At the extreme, we introduce a new user interface support (UIS) layer that contains the code to determine the appropriate response for each user action. The event procedure would then contain a single line that calls a procedure in the UIS layer, passing the selected region. The UIS layer calls the function in the business logic layer to retrieve the array of products and total sales and then tells the UserForm to populate the list with the array. This mechanism treats the UserForm as nothing more than a drawing and interaction layer and is an extremely useful way to handle complex forms. An example of this technique can be found in the UISLayer.xls workbook on the in the \Concepts\Ch13 – Userform Design and Best Practices folder on the CD that accompanies this book. In Listing 13-2, the UIS layer is physically located in a separate class module that tells the UserForm what to do by raising custom events. For more details about class modules and custom events, see Chapter 7, "Using Class Modules to Create Objects."

Listing 13-2 The User Interface Support Layer Determines the Response

```
'****************************************
'* User Interface Layer in
'* UserForm FComplexForm
'****************************************


'UIS Event handler
Dim WithEvents mclsUISComplexForm As CUISComplexForm


'Initialize our UIS class
Private Sub UserForm_Initialize()
   Set mclsUISComplexForm = New CUISComplexForm
End Sub


'
' Control events, to handle the user telling us
' to do something. In most cases, we just pass it
' on to the UIS class.
'


'Handle selecting a different region
Private Sub cboRegion_Change()

   'Tell the UIS layer that the user
   'just selected a different region
   mclsUISComplexForm.RegionSelected cboRegion.Value

End Sub



'
' UIS class events, to handle the UIS layer
' telling us to do something
'


'Populate the Product Sales List
Private Sub mclsUISComplex_PopulateProductList( _
     vaProductSales As Variant)

   lstProducts.List = vaProductSales
End Sub



'**************************************************
```

```
'* User Interface Support Layer
'* in class CUISSimpleForm
'*************************************************

'Events to tell the UserForm what to do
Public Event PopulateProductList(vaProductSales As Variant)


'The user selected a different region.
Public Sub RegionSelected(ByVal sRegion As String)

    Dim vaProductSales As Variant

    'Get the Product/Sales array from the business logic layer
    vaProductSales = GetProductSalesForRegion(sRegion)

    'Tell the UserForm to populate the products list
    RaiseEvent PopulateProductList(vaProductSales)

End Sub
```

There is obviously more overhead in using an intermediate UIS layer, but it reduces most of the UserForm event procedures to one-line calls into the UIS layer, allowing us to concentrate on the detail of the user experience within the UserForm module. This makes the UserForm itself much easier to maintain. Notice also that the UIS class has no knowledge of how the information is obtained or displayed—all it knows is that when it's given a region, it should tell the UserForm that there's a new list of products. The UIS class could be used by multiple versions of the same UserForm—perhaps with each one optimized for different screen resolutions.

Use Classes Instead of the Default Instance

Whenever we add a UserForm to a project, VBA automatically gives us a default instance of the UserForm. This is effectively a global variable that has the same name as the UserForm and declared As New. This means that as soon as we refer to the UserForm, Excel creates the default instance for us (this is known as **Auto-Instantiation**). When we unload the UserForm, the default instance is destroyed, and when we refer to it again, the default instance is re-created. Consider a UserForm, FMyForm, containing a single text box, txtName. The code in Listing 13-3 shows the UserForm and then attempts to display the name entered by the user.

Listing 13-3   Using the UserForm's Default Instance

```
Sub TestDefaultInstance()

  'Show the UserForm
  FMyForm.Show

  'Show the contents of the text box
  MsgBox "The name is: " & FMyForm.txtName.Text

End Sub
```

Run the procedure, type a name into the text box, and close the UserForm using the [x] in the top-right corner. The procedure runs without any errors, but the message box doesn't show the name you typed in. This is because when the [x] was clicked, the UserForm was unloaded and anything entered into it was lost. Within the MsgBox line, the reference to FMyForm then caused VBA to create a new instance of the UserForm in which the name text box is blank.

Do not use default instances. UserForms are just a special type of class module, and they should be treated like class modules. By doing so, we gain control over when the UserForm is created and destroyed, preventing the type of bug demonstrated in Listing 13-3. The example in Listing 13-4 treats the UserForm as a class. This time the name is displayed correctly.

Listing 13-4   Treating the UserForm Like a Class

```
Sub TestClassInstance()

  'Define our object variable
  Dim frmMyForm As FMyForm

  'Set our object variable to be a new instance of the UserForm
  Set frmMyForm = New FMyForm

  'Show the UserForm
  frmMyForm.Show

  'Show the contents of the text box
  MsgBox "The name is: " & frmMyForm.txtName.Text

  'If showing the UserForm modeless, we have to unload it
  Unload frmMyForm

End Sub
```

Unfortunately, using a UserForm like this gives us a minor problem that we need to be aware of and work around: If the UserForm is unloaded while our object variable is referring to it we often get an automation error. This is easily avoided by ensuring that code within our UserForm only hides the UserForm instead of unloading it. The code in Listing 13-5 can be added to any UserForms that have the standard OK and Cancel buttons.

Listing 13-5 Hiding Instead of Unloading a UserForm

```
'Store whether the user OK'd or Cancel'd
Dim mbOK As Boolean

'Handle the OK button
Private Sub cmdOK_Click()
    mbOK = True
    Me.Hide
End Sub

'Handle the Cancel button
Private Sub cmdCancel_Click()
    mbOK = False
    Me.Hide
End Sub

'Make the [x] behave the same as Cancel
Private Sub UserForm_QueryClose(Cancel As Integer, _
                                CloseMode As Integer)

    'If CloseMode = vbFormControlMenu then we know the user
    'clicked the [x] close button or Alt+F4 to close the form.
    If CloseMode = vbFormControlMenu Then
        cmdCancel_Click
        Cancel = True
    End If

End Sub

'Return whether the OK or Cancel button was clicked
Public Property Get OK() As Boolean
    OK = mbOK
End Property
```

Expose Properties and Methods, Not Controls

Following the philosophy of treating a UserForm like a class, we should only interact with the UserForm via properties and methods that we add to the UserForm class module. We should never refer to individual controls from outside the UserForm, nor should we set any properties of the UserForm object itself.

Proper encapsulation dictates that everything to do with a UserForm should be contained within the UserForm. By adding properties and methods to isolate a UserForm's controls from external code, we gain the ability to rename or change the type of any of the controls, knowing that we won't break any code that uses the UserForm.

Imagine a UserForm with a set of three option buttons to select a level of detail for a report. If we were to allow external code to directly access the controls, we might be tempted to write code like Listing 13-6 (where we've assumed the form includes the code from Listing 13-5).

Listing 13-6   Using a UserForm's Controls Directly

```
Sub UseTheControls()

  Dim frmOptions As FOptions
  Set frmOptions = New FOptions

  'Show the UserForm
  frmOptions.Show

  If frmOptions.OK Then
    'Which option was selected?
    If frmOptions.optDetailed.Value Then
      RunDetailedReport

    ElseIf frmOptions.optNormal.Value Then
      RunNormalReport

    ElseIf frmOptions.optSummary.Value Then
      RunSummaryReport
    End If
  End If

End Sub
```

The result of doing this is that the calling code is very tightly bound to the physical layout of the UserForm. Therefore, if we wanted to change the UserForm's layout, say to use a combo box instead of the three option buttons, we have to locate code throughout our application where the UserForm is used and change that code as well as the code within the UserForm itself.

Instead, we should expose everything using property procedures so the calling code does not need to know how the property is physically represented on the UserForm. Listing 13-7 adds a DetailLevel property to the UserForm, returning the level of detail as an enumeration, which the calling code uses to decide which report to run:

Listing 13-7   Using Property Procedures

```
'
'Within the UserForm FOptions
'
'Enum for the levels of detail
Public Enum odlOptionDetailLevel
   odlDetailLevelDetailed
   odlDetailLevelNormal
   odlDetailLevelSummary
End Enum

'Property to return the level of detail
Public Property Get DetailLevel() As odlOptionDetailLevel

   'Which option was selected?
   If optDetailed.Value Then
     DetailLevel = odlDetailLevelDetailed

   ElseIf optNormal.Value Then
     DetailLevel = odlDetailLevelNormal

   ElseIf optSummary.Value Then
     DetailLevel = odlDetailLevelSummary
   End If

End Property


'
'The calling code
'
Sub UseAProperty()
```

```
Dim frmOptions As FOptions
Set frmOptions = New FOptions

'Show the UserForm
frmOptions.Show

If frmOptions.OK Then
   'Which option was selected?
   If frmOptions.DetailLevel = odlDetailLevelDetailed Then
      RunDetailedReport

   ElseIf frmOptions.DetailLevel = odlDetailLevelNormal Then
      RunNormalReport

   ElseIf frmOptions.DetailLevel = odlDetailLevelSummary Then
      RunSummaryReport
   End If
End If

End Sub
```

Now if we want to change the option buttons to a combo box, all the changes are contained within the UserForm, making maintenance much easier and much less prone to introducing new bugs. Unfortunately, all the controls on a UserForm and all the UserForm's properties are always exposed to external code, so any properties and methods we add get lost in the IntelliSense list. In Chapter 14, "Interfaces," we explain how to define and use our own interfaces, which allow us to expose only the properties and methods that we want to be called.

Control Fundamentals

There are a few fundamental details that we simply have to get right when working with controls on UserForms.

Naming

As discussed in Chapter 3, "Excel and VBA Development Best Practices," all our controls should be given meaningful names that include a two- or three-character prefix to identify the control type. This allows us to easily identify the control in code and when setting the tab order. For example, we have no idea which button CommandButton1 is, but we can easily identify cmdOK, for example.

Layering

If we include the background, UserForms have three drawing layers. When we add a control to a UserForm, it gets added to one of the top two layers, depending on the type of control. The three layers are identified as

1. The UserForm background and its scrollbar
2. The Label, CheckBox, ComboBox, CommandButton, Image, OptionButton, RefEdit, ScrollBar, SpinButton, TabStrip, ToggleButton, and TextBox controls
3. The Frame, ListBox, MultiPage, and other ActiveX controls

Controls in layer 2 can overlap each other, but are always drawn behind controls in layer 3, while all the controls in layer 3 can overlap each other. Fortunately, layer 3 includes the Frame control, so if we want to draw any of the other controls on top of a layer 3 control we can put it inside a Frame. Within a layer, we can arrange our controls' z-order using the *Format > Order* menu.

Positioning

All controls on a UserForm should be aligned both horizontally and vertically with a consistent amount of space between them. When people read UserForms they read the text of each control, so it is the text that we should align and not the edges of the controls. If we have Snap to Grid switched on and we add a text box and a label to a UserForm, the label needs to be moved down (usually by four pixels) to ensure the text of the label aligns with the text entered into the text box.

We can do this by editing Top property of the label to add four pixels. But how big is a pixel? In Chapter 12, "Understanding and Using Windows API Calls," we explained that the pixel size is dependent on the dots-per-inch setting the user has specified. It is usually 0.75 points for the Normal setting of 96 dpi and 0.6 points for the Large setting of 120 dpi. So to move a control by one pixel, we have to add 0.75 or 0.6. Moving and sizing controls pixel-by-pixel is made much easier by using the *VBE Tools Control Nudger* toolbar shown in Figure 13-2. This toolbar is part of the *VBE Tools* add-in included on the CD in the *Tools*\ folder.

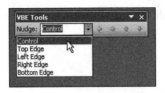

FIGURE 13-2   The VBE Tools Control Nudger toolbar

Tab Orders and Accelerator Keys

As designers of UserForms, we tend to be "mousers" and often forget that many people prefer to use the keyboard to navigate around our UserForms. We must remember to facilitate keyboard usage by ensuring we give our controls a sensible tab order and/or accelerator keys. The tab order should match the natural reading order—left-to-right and top-to-bottom—and should include labels as well as controls. If the UserForm includes container controls, such as the Frame and MultiPage controls, we must remember to set the tab order for the controls they contain as well. We do this by ensuring the container control is selected before clicking the *View > Tab Order* menu.

Accelerator keys allow us to use an Alt+key combination to jump directly to the control. The accelerator key for a control is identified by an underscore under the appropriate letter of the control's caption. If we set the accelerator key for a label and use that accelerator key, the focus jumps to the control with the next highest TabIndex value. This behavior allows us to provide keyboard access to controls that do not have a caption, such as list boxes, edit boxes, and so on.

Data Binding

Many UserForm controls have properties that allow them to be bound to worksheet cells to specify their contents and/or return their value/text. Don't use them. They are there for beginners to create simple, quick, and dirty forms, but they very quickly become more trouble than they're worth. Using VBA to set the controls' contents and handle the data entry gives us much more flexibility and allows us to validate the data before updating cells.

Event Handling

The MSForms controls used on UserForms have a fairly rich event model. Deciding which event to use for a given purpose can be daunting. Our recommendation is to follow the principle of keeping it simple and use the basic _Change or _Click events for most situations.

In particular, don't try to intercept the _KeyDown or _KeyPress events in an attempt to force numeric entry into a control. If your code prevents letters, it also prevents the valid use of exponential notation, such as 1E3 for 1000. It you try to prevent multiple decimal separators, you have to make sure you're allowing the decimal separator set in the Regional Settings applet, and if the user put the decimal in the wrong place, you're forcing him to delete the wrong one before typing the new one. It is much better (and easier for us) to allow the user to type in whatever he chooses and then validate the entry using VBA's IsNumeric() function.

Control events are fired both by user action and when the control is changed in code. We can use Application.EnableEvents to turn events on and off for Excel's objects, but that has no effect on the MSForms object model. We can get the same level of control over when UserForm and control events are handled by using a module-level variable that is checked at the start of all our event procedures, as shown in Listing 13-8.

Listing 13-8 Handling Controls' Events

```
'Module level variable to control events firing
Dim mbStopEvents As Boolean



'Handle clicking a 'Get Data' button
Private Sub btnGetNames_Click()

  Dim vaNames As Variant

  'Get a list of names from somewhere
  vaNames = Array("Rob", "Dennis", "Stephen", "John")

  'Turn off events while populating the controls
  mbStopEvents = True

  'Populate controls.
  'The Clear method triggers the Change event.
  lstNames.Clear
  lstNames.List = vaNames

  'Turn events on again
  mbStopEvents = False
```

```
'Select the first name, allowing the Change event to fire
If lstNames.ListCount > 0 Then
    lstNames.ListIndex = 0
End If

End Sub


'Handle selecting a name
Private Sub lstNames_Change()

    'Don't do anything if we've stopped events
    If mbStopEvents Then Exit Sub

    'Process selecting a name from the list
    MsgBox "You selected " & lstNames.Text

End Sub
```

Validation

Most UserForms have controls for data entry and a pair of OK and Cancel buttons. When the OK button is clicked the data is written to the sheet/database/object model. When the Cancel button is clicked the data is ignored. At some point between the user entering data and that data being stored it must be validated.

Many people are tempted to use the _BeforeUpdate event for their validation code because it has a Cancel property that can be used to force the user to enter valid data. Don't use it. UserForms should never get in the way of the user, or interrupt their work, yet should also provide feedback as soon as possible, to give them the opportunity (but not force them) to correct their mistakes. Our recommendation is to use an unobtrusive form of validation in each control's AfterUpdate event and an intrusive form of validation in the OK button's Click event. By intrusive, we mean something that stops the user from continuing, such as displaying a message box. By unobtrusive, we mean something that alerts the user to an error situation, but allows them to continue, such as turning the background red and setting the Tooltip to show the error message. Listing 13-9 shows the code to validate a simple UserForm that contains two sales figures, while Figure 13-3 shows the UserForm with an error in the first edit box.

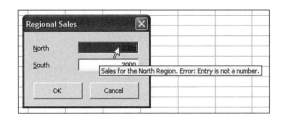

FIGURE 13-3   An unobtrusive error indicator

Listing 13-9   Validating Controls

```
Option Explicit

'Store whether the user OK'd or Cancel'd
Dim mbOK As Boolean

'When exiting the controls, we perform some
'unintrusive validation, by calling the
'CheckNumeric function
Private Sub txtSalesNorth_AfterUpdate()
  CheckNumeric txtSalesNorth
End Sub

Private Sub txtSalesSouth_AfterUpdate()
  CheckNumeric txtSalesSouth
End Sub


'In the OK button, we use the same CheckNumeric
'function to show some intrusive validation
'messages.
Private Sub btnOK_Click()

  Dim dNorth As Double
  Dim dSouth As Double
  Dim sError As String
  Dim sAllErrors As String
  Dim bFocusSet As Boolean

  'Validate the North Sales text box,
  'returning the value or some error text
  If Not CheckNumeric(txtSalesNorth, dNorth, sError) Then

    'Set the focus to the first control with an error
```

```
      If Not bFocusSet Then
        txtSalesNorth.SetFocus
        bFocusSet = True
      End If

      'Build an error string, so we display all errors on the
      'UserForm in one error message
      sAllErrors = sAllErrors & "North Sales:" & sError & vbLf
   End If

   'Validate the South Sales text box,
   'returning the value or some error text
   If Not CheckNumeric(txtSalesSouth, dSouth, sError) Then

      'Set the focus to the first control with an error
      If Not bFocusSet Then
        txtSalesSouth.SetFocus
        bFocusSet = True
      End If

      'Build an error string, so we display all errors on the
      'UserForm in one error message
      sAllErrors = sAllErrors & "South Sales:" & sError & vbLf
   End If

   'Display any errors we got
   If Len(sAllErrors) > 0 Then
      MsgBox "Please correct the following error(s):" & _
             vbLf & sAllErrors, vbOKOnly
   Else
      'No errors, so store the result
      ActiveSheet.Range("rngNorthSales").Value = dNorth
      ActiveSheet.Range("rngSouthSales").Value = dSouth

      'And hide the UserForm
      mbOK = True
      Me.Hide
   End If

End Sub

'The cancel button just hides the UserForm.
Private Sub btnCancel_Click()
    mbOK = False
    Me.Hide
```

```vba
End Sub

'Function to check a control (textbox or combobox) for
'numeric entry
'
'Parameters: txtData [in] The textbox or combobox
'            dResult [out] The numeric value from the box
'            sError [out] The text of the error message
'
Function CheckNumeric(ByRef txtData As MSForms.Control, _
    Optional ByRef dResult As Double, _
    Optional ByRef sError As String) As Boolean

  Const sERR As String = ". Error: "
  Dim lErrPos As Long

  'Remove any existing tooltip error text
  lErrPos = InStr(1, txtData.ControlTipText, sERR)
  If lErrPos > 0 Then
    txtData.ControlTipText = Left$(txtData.ControlTipText, _
        lErrPos - 1)
  End If

  'Check for valid entry
  If txtData.Text = "" Then
    'Allow empty
    dResult = 0
    sError = ""
    CheckNumeric = True

    'And give the text box its usual background
    txtData.BackColor = vbWindowBackground

  ElseIf IsNumeric(txtData.Text) Then
    'Numeric, so set the return values
    dResult = CDbl(txtData.Text)
    sError = ""
    CheckNumeric = True

    'And give the text box its usual background
    txtData.BackColor = vbWindowBackground
  Else
    'Not numeric, so set the return values
    dResult = 0
    sError = "Entry is not a number."
```

```
    CheckNumeric = False

    'Give the text box a red background
    txtData.BackColor = vbRed

    'And add the error message to the tooltip
    txtData.ControlTipText = txtData.ControlTipText & _
        sERR & sError
  End If

End Function
```

Visual Effects

UserForm Window Styles

We mentioned briefly in Chapter 12 that we can use a few API functions to modify the appearance of a window's border and/or title bar. Listing 13-10 shows the SetUserFormAppearance procedure to do just that for UserForms, allowing us to independently set the following attributes:

- Whether the UserForm has a title bar
- Whether the title bar is the normal size or the small size used for floating toolbars
- Whether the UserForm is resizable
- Whether the UserForm has a maximize button
- Whether the UserForm has a minimize button
- Whether the UserForm has a close button
- Whether the UserForm has an icon and the icon to use

Listing 13-10 Modifying a UserForm's Window Styles

```
'Windows API calls to do all the dirty work
Private Declare Function GetWindowLong Lib "user32" Alias _
    "GetWindowLongA" (ByVal hWnd As Long, _
    ByVal nIndex As Long) As Long

Private Declare Function SetWindowLong Lib "user32" Alias _
```

```
        "SetWindowLongA" (ByVal hWnd As Long, _
        ByVal nIndex As Long, ByVal dwNewLong As Long) As Long

Private Declare Function GetSystemMenu Lib "user32" _
        (ByVal hWnd As Long, ByVal bRevert As Long) As Long

Private Declare Function DeleteMenu Lib "user32" _
        (ByVal hMenu As Long, ByVal nPosition As Long, _
        ByVal wFlags As Long) As Long

Private Declare Function DrawMenuBar Lib "user32" _
        (ByVal hWnd As Long) As Long

'Window API constants
Private Const GWL_STYLE As Long = (-16)
Private Const GWL_EXSTYLE As Long = (-20)
Private Const WS_CAPTION As Long = &HC00000
Private Const WS_SYSMENU As Long = &H80000
Private Const WS_THICKFRAME As Long = &H40000
Private Const WS_MINIMIZEBOX As Long = &H20000
Private Const WS_MAXIMIZEBOX As Long = &H10000
Private Const WS_EX_DLGMODALFRAME As Long = &H1
Private Const WS_EX_TOOLWINDOW As Long = &H80
Private Const SC_CLOSE As Long = &HF060

'Public enum of our UserForm styles
Public Enum UserFormWindowStyles
  uwsNoTitleBar = 0
  uwsHasTitleBar = 1
  uwsHasSmallTitleBar = 2
  uwsHasMaxButton = 4
  uwsHasMinButton = 8
  uwsHasCloseButton = 16
  uwsHasIcon = 32
  uwsCanResize = 64
  uwsDefault = uwsHasTitleBar Or uwsHasCloseButton
End Enum


'Routine to set a UserForm's window style,
'called from UserForm_Initialize event
Sub SetUserFormAppearance(ByRef frmForm As Object, _
        ByVal lStyles As UserFormWindowStyles, _
        Optional ByVal sIconPath As String)
```

```
Dim sCaption As String
Dim hWnd As Long
Dim lStyle As Long
Dim hMenu As Long

'Find the window handle of the form
sCaption = frmForm.Caption
frmForm.Caption = "FindThis" & Rnd
hWnd = FindOurWindow("ThunderDFrame", frmForm.Caption)
frmForm.Caption = sCaption

'If we want a small title bar, we can't have an icon,
'max or min buttons as well
If lStyles And uwsHasSmallTitleBar Then
  lStyles = lStyles And Not (uwsHasMaxButton Or _
      uwsHasMinButton Or uwsHasIcon)
End If

'Get the normal windows style bits
lStyle = GetWindowLong(hWnd, GWL_STYLE)

'Update the normal style bits appropriately

'If we want and icon or Max, Min or Close buttons,
'we have to have a system menu
ModifyStyles lStyle, lStyles, uwsHasIcon Or _
      uwsHasMaxButton Or uwsHasMinButton Or _
      uwsHasCloseButton, WS_SYSMENU

'Most things need a title bar!
ModifyStyles lStyle, lStyles, uwsHasIcon Or _
      uwsHasMaxButton Or uwsHasMinButton Or _
      uwsHasCloseButton Or uwsHasTitleBar Or _
      uwsHasSmallTitleBar, WS_CAPTION

ModifyStyles lStyle, lStyles, uwsHasMaxButton, WS_MAXIMIZEBOX
ModifyStyles lStyle, lStyles, uwsHasMinButton, WS_MINIMIZEBOX
ModifyStyles lStyle, lStyles, uwsCanResize, WS_THICKFRAME

'Update the window with the normal style bits
SetWindowLong hWnd, GWL_STYLE, lStyle

'Get the extended style bits
lStyle = GetWindowLong(hWnd, GWL_EXSTYLE)
```

```
'Modify them appropriately
ModifyStyles lStyle, lStyles, uwsHasSmallTitleBar, _
      WS_EX_TOOLWINDOW

'The icon is different to the rest -
'we set a bit to turn it off, not on!
If lStyles And uwsHasIcon Then
   lStyle = lStyle And Not WS_EX_DLGMODALFRAME

   'Set the icon, if given
   If Len(sIconPath) > 0 Then
     SetIcon hWnd, sIconPath
   End If
Else
   lStyle = lStyle Or WS_EX_DLGMODALFRAME
End If

'Update the window with the extended style bits
SetWindowLong hWnd, GWL_EXSTYLE, lStyle

'The Close button is handled by removing it from the
'control menu, not through a window style bit
If lStyles And uwsHasCloseButton Then
   'We want it, so reset the control menu
   hMenu = GetSystemMenu(hWnd, 1)
Else
   'We don't want it, so delete it from the control menu
   hMenu = GetSystemMenu(hWnd, 0)
   DeleteMenu hMenu, SC_CLOSE, 0&
End If

'Refresh the window with the changes
DrawMenuBar hWnd

End Sub


'Helper routine to check if one of our style bits is set
'and set/clear the corresponding Windows style bit
Private Sub ModifyStyles(ByRef lFormStyle As Long, _
      ByVal lStyleSet As Long, _
      ByVal lChoice As UserFormWindowStyles, _
      ByVal lWS_Style As Long)
```

```
If lStyleSet And lChoice Then
  lFormStyle = lFormStyle Or lWS_Style
Else
  lFormStyle = lFormStyle And Not lWS_Style
End If

End Sub
```

To set the appearance for a UserForm we call the SetUserFormAppearance procedure from the UserForm_Initialize event, passing in the required set of values from the UserFormWindowStyles enum added together. This code is included on the CD in the *MFormStyles* module in the *UserFormstyles.xls* workbook and uses the FindOurWindow and SetIcon procedures previously introduced in Chapter 12.

Disabling the Close Button

Even though the procedure shown in Listing 13-10 can be used to remove the close menu from a UserForm, the standard Windows keystroke of Alt+F4 to close a window can still be used to close the form. We handle this by hooking the UserForm_QueryClose event, as shown in Listing 13-11. The QueryClose event can also be used in this manner without removing the close button, but that gives conflicting messages to the user. You're showing an enabled close button that doesn't do anything.

Listing 13-11   Preventing the User from Closing the UserForm

```
'Set the form to have a (small) title bar, but no close button
Private Sub UserForm_Initialize()

  SetUserFormAppearance Me, uwsHasSmallTitleBar

End Sub

'Prevent the form being closed using Alt+F4
Private Sub UserForm_QueryClose(Cancel As Integer, _
    CloseMode As Integer)

  Cancel = (CloseMode = vbFormControlMenu)

End Sub
```

13. UserForm Design and Best Practices

Displaying Graphics, Charts, and WordArt on UserForms

UserForms have limited graphics capabilities; while we can set the colors and fonts of the controls and use empty labels to draw rectangles, we can't draw diagonal lines, arrows, ovals, or other shapes. Neither can we embed other objects on the UserForm to display charts, WordArt, and so on. We can, however, draw our graphics on a worksheet, copy them to the Clipboard, and paste them as pictures to use for the background of many of the MSForms controls.

To set the picture, select the control (or the UserForm itself), click in the Picture property box in the Properties Window and either click the ellipsis to select an image file or just press Ctrl+V to paste a picture from the Clipboard. Most controls just stretch the picture to fill the control, but the Image, Frame, and Page controls and the UserForm background allow us to control the picture sizing (zoom, stretch, or crop), alignment (within the control), and whether the picture is tiled to fill the control.

At runtime, we can use the Excel CopyPicture method to copy a range, chart, or other drawing object to the Clipboard. We can then use our custom PastePicture function to retrieve the image from the Clipboard as a standard Picture object that can be assigned to the Picture property of any MSForms control that supports it. The PastePicture function uses a series of complex Windows API calls to extract the picture from the Clipboard, so it's best to treat it as a "black box" by just copying the entire MPastePicture module into your project. We did this in Chapter 8, "Advanced Command Bar Handling," to set a command bar button's Picture and Mask properties. The MPastePicture module can be found in the PastePicture.xls example workbook, which demonstrates how to display a chart on a UserForm, as shown in Figure 13-4. The code used to update the chart is shown in Listing 13-12.

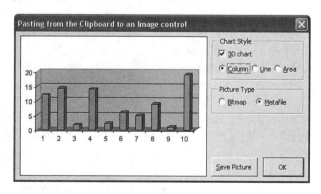

Figure 13-4 Displaying a chart on a UserForm

Listing 13-12   Displaying a Chart on a UserForm

```
'Update the chart image on the form
Private Sub UpdateChart()

  Dim chtChart As Chart
  Dim lPicType As Long

  'Find the chart object on the sheet
  Set chtChart = Sheet1.ChartObjects(1).Chart

  'Do we want a metafile or a bitmap?
  'If scaling the image, xlPicture will give better results
  'If not scaling, xlBitmap will give a 'truer' rendition.
  'obMetafile is the 'Metafile' option button on the form
  lPicType = IIf(obMetafile, xlPicture, xlBitmap)

  'Copy the chart to the clipboard, as seen on screen
  chtChart.CopyPicture xlScreen, lPicType, xlScreen

  'Paste the picture from the clipboard into our image control
  Set imgChtPic.Picture = PastePicture(lPicType)

End Sub
```

Locking Versus Disabling Controls

When text boxes and combo boxes are disabled, Excel displays the text in gray but keeps the white background. If there is no text in the box, there is no way for the user to tell whether it is disabled. An alternative is to keep the control enabled but locked and give it a gray background. Locking a text box or combo box allows the user to select the text but not change it. This can be useful when displaying information the user may want to copy to the Clipboard, such as an error message.

Figure 13-5 shows a section of a UserForm containing three text boxes, one disabled, one locked with a gray background, and one used as a label. In our opinion, the middle text box gives the best visual indicator that it is disabled, while keeping the text readable. Listing 13-13 shows the standard procedure we use to "disable" our controls by locking them. Unfortunately, we can't use the same technique with a list box because it doesn't redraw the selection indicator when the background color is changed.

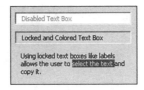

FIGURE 13-5 Three text boxes

Listing 13-13 Standard Procedure to "Disable" a Control by Locking it

```
'Enable/Disable a control by locking it and
'changing the background color
Public Sub EnableControl(ByRef ctlControl As MSForms.Control, _
                         ByVal bEnable As Boolean)

    ctlControl.Locked = Not bEnable
    ctlControl.BackColor = IIf(bEnable, vbWindowBackground, _
                                        vbButtonFace)

End Sub
```

Pop-up Menus

When designing complex UserForms there is always a trade-off between adding features that make the UserForm easier to use versus confusing the user by making the UserForm too cluttered. For example, if we have a list box with a long list of names, we could make it easier to find a name by adding options to sort by first name or last name in ascending or descending order. We could add these controls as sets of option buttons or combo boxes, but those take up valuable space on the form and make it appear too cluttered.

An alternative mechanism is to put those options in a pop-up menu. We can create a pop-up menu for a list box using a command bar with the msoBarPopup style that we display when the user right-clicks the list box. Figure 13-6 shows a list box with the pop-up menu displayed, and Listing 13-14 shows the code to trap the right-click and show the pop-up menu. This code assumes the command bar has already been created and that other procedures handle the menu item selections.

FIGURE 13-6 A list box with pop-up sort menu

Listing 13-14 Showing a Pop-up for a List Box

```
'Show a Sort Method popup when the list box is right-clicked
Private Sub lstNames_MouseDown(ByVal Button As Integer, _
    ByVal Shift As Integer, ByVal X As Single, _
    ByVal Y As Single)

  '2=Right Button
  If Button = 2 Then
    Application.CommandBars("NameSortPopup").ShowPopup
  End If

End Sub
```

UserForm Positioning and Sizing

Positioning Next to a Cell

If we display a UserForm in response to the user selecting a menu item from a cell's pop-up menu, it is a nice touch to display the UserForm directly beside the cell (assuming there's space for it on the screen). Trying to determine the exact position of a cell on the screen using the Range object's position is extremely difficult. We would have to account for the zoom factor, scroll settings, how many rows of toolbars were displayed, and whether the Excel application window is maximized. Fortunately there is an easier workaround, which is to use the window that Excel uses for editing embedded charts.

If we create a chart object over the cell and activate it, Excel moves a window with the class name EXCELE to that position. We can immediately delete the chart object, use API functions to read the position of the EXCELE window, and display our UserForm at the same position. Listing 13-15 shows a procedure to move a UserForm over a cell and an example of it being used to display a UserForm directly to the right of the active cell. This procedure can be found on the CD in the MFormPos module of

UserFormPositioning.xls. Note that the procedure uses functions in the MScreen and MWindows modules from the API Examples.xls workbook that were documented in Chapter 12.

Listing 13-15 Showing a UserForm Next to the Active Cell

```
'API Functions to find a window and read its position
Private Declare Function FindWindowEx Lib "user32" _
    Alias "FindWindowExA" (ByVal hWnd1 As Long, _
    ByVal hWnd2 As Long, ByVal lpsz1 As String, _
    ByVal lpsz2 As String) As Long

Private Declare Function GetWindowRect Lib "user32" _
    (ByVal hWnd As Long, lpRect As RECT) As Long

Private Type RECT
    Left As Long
    Top As Long
    Right As Long
    Bottom As Long
End Type



'Routine to move a form to a given cell
Public Sub MoveFormToCell(frmForm As Object, _
    rngCell As Range)

    Dim hWndDesk As Long
    Dim hWndChart As Long
    Dim uChartPos As RECT

    'Create a chart object at the cell, activate it and
    'immediately delete it. That puts the EXCELE chart
    'editing window in the correct place
    With rngCell.Parent.ChartObjects.Add(rngCell.Left, _
            rngCell.Top, 1, 1)

        .Activate
        .Delete
    End With

    'Find the EXCELE window
    hWndDesk = FindWindowEx(ApphWnd, 0, "XLDESK", vbNullString)
    hWndChart = FindWindowEx(hWndDesk, 0, "EXCELE", vbNullString)

    'Read its position
```

```
    GetWindowRect hWndChart, uChartPos

    'Move the form to the same position,
    'converting pixels to points
    frmForm.Left = uChartPos.Left * PointsPerPixel
    frmForm.Top = uChartPos.Top * PointsPerPixel

End Sub



'Test procedure to show a form next to the active cell
Sub ShowMyForm()

  Dim frmForm As FMyForm

  Set frmForm = New FMyForm

  'Set the form to show in a custom position
  frmForm.StartUpPosition = 0

  'Move the form over the cell
  MoveFormToCell frmForm, ActiveCell.Offset(0, 1)

  'Show the form
  frmForm.Show

End Sub
```

Responding to Different Resolutions

We regularly see questions in the Microsoft support newsgroups from people who designed a UserForm to fill their own screen, only to find that it's too big for a user with a lower screen resolution. The question usually ends "How do I change the user's resolution to display my UserForm?" The answer is always "You don't." Instead, we have to design our UserForms so they are usable on the lowest resolution our users have. Typically, that means a resolution of 800x600 pixels, though people with visual impairment may use 640x480 pixels. Designing our UserForms to fit on a 640x480 display gives us two main issues to solve:

■ We can't fit many controls on a 640x480 UserForm.

- UserForms that fit on a 640x480 screen often make very poor use of the space available with larger resolutions.

In practice, most of the UserForms we create are quite simple and can usually fit within the bounds of a 640x480 screen. For complex forms, we usually use pop-up menus, drop-down panes (see later), and/or a wizard design to make the most of the available space. We also may design multiple versions of the same form for use with different screen resolutions. The forms for lower resolutions use more compact controls, such as combo boxes instead of option buttons or list boxes, and have less blank space around each control, while the forms for higher resolutions have more controls directly visible, with each control using more space. If we correctly split our code between the presentation layer and business logic layer, both forms can use the same UIS class for their business logic.

Resizable UserForms

Part of the Keep it Simple principle is to avoid overwhelming the user. Our experience has shown that if a UserForm won't fit on an 800x600 resolution screen it almost certainly contains too many controls. For this reason, we design our forms to fit on an 800x600 screen but make them resizable so users can choose to make better use of the space available if they have a higher resolution screen.

For example, if our UserForm includes a list box, we allow the list box to change size with the form, allowing the user to see more items in the list. The FormResizer.xls example workbook contains a class module, CFormResizer, which can be included in a project to handle the resizing of any form. The class changes the form's window styles to make it resizable and handles the resizing and repositioning of all the controls on the form.

We define the resize behavior of each control by setting its Tag property to indicate by how much its top, left, height, and/or width should change in proportion to a change in size of the form. To make one of the properties change as the form is sized, we include the letter T, L, H, or W followed by a number giving the percentage change (or omitted for 100%).

For example, if we have an OK button in the middle-bottom of the form, we would want it to move up/down by the same amount as the change in the form's height and move left/right by half the change in the form's width. Therefore, its Tag would be TL0.5. If we have a form with a pair of list boxes side-by-side, we would want the left list box to keep its top and left constant, but grow by the full change in the form's height and half the change in the form's width. Therefore, its Tag would be HW0.5. The right-hand list box would resize the same way but should also move to the right by half the change in the form's width (so its right edge stays constant relative to the right edge of the form). Therefore, its Tag would be L0.5HW0.5.

To start including resizable UserForms in your applications, copy the CFormResizer class into the project, hook it up to a form using the code shown in Listing 13-16, and set the controls' Tag properties appropriately. It will probably take some trial and error to get the tags correct at first, but this will become much easier with practice. For best results, list boxes should have their IntegralHeight property set to False, and due to an Excel bug they may need an extra blank item added to the bottom of the list for all the items to display correctly.

Listing 13-16 Making a UserForm Resizable Using the CFormResizer Class

```
'Declare an object of our CFormResizer class to handle
'resizing for this form
Dim mclsResizer As CFormResizer

'The Resizer class is set up in UserForm_Initialize
Private Sub UserForm_Initialize()

  'Create the instance of the class
  Set mclsResizer = New CFormResizer

  'Tell it which form it's handling
  Set mclsResizer.Form = Me

End Sub


'When the form is resized, the UserForm_Resize event is
'raised, which we just pass on to the Resizer class
Private Sub UserForm_Resize()
    mclsResizer.FormResize
End Sub


'The QueryClose event is called whenever the form is closed.
'We call the FormResize method one last time, to store the
'form's final size and position in the registry
Private Sub UserForm_QueryClose(Cancel As Integer, _
    CloseMode As Integer)

  mclsResizer.FormResize
End Sub
```

Splitter Bars

If our resizable UserForms contain two or more list boxes, it may not always be desirable to let them both grow or shrink at the same rate. We can allow our users to decide how much space to give each list box by adding a splitter bar between them. We don't actually have a splitter bar control, but we can fake one using a Label.

The UserForm shown in Figure 13-7 has two list boxes that are both configured so their width changes at half the rate of the form's change in width, keeping the gap between them central to the form. We also added a label to fill the gap between them. For clarity, it is shown with its caption, but it would normally be transparent and blank. The label's MousePointer property has been changed to 9 - fmMousePointerSizeWE, so we get the standard left/right sizing arrows when the mouse moves over the label. The code in Listing 13-17 uses the label's mouse events to simulate a splitter bar.

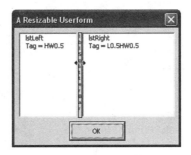

FIGURE 13-7 A splitter bar between two list boxes

Listing 13-17 The Code to Turn a Label into a Splitter Bar

```
'Module variables to handle the splitter bar
Dim mbSplitterMoving As Boolean
Dim mdSplitterOrigin As Double


'When pressing down the left mouse button,
'initiate the dragging and remember where we started
Private Sub lblSplitterBar_MouseDown( _
    ByVal Button As Integer, ByVal Shift As Integer, _
    ByVal X As Single, ByVal Y As Single)

  If Button = 1 Then
    mbSplitterMoving = True
    mdSplitterOrigin = X
```

```
   End If
End Sub

'When releasing the left mouse button,
'stop the dragging
Private Sub lblSplitterBar_MouseUp( _
    ByVal Button As Integer, ByVal Shift As Integer, _
    ByVal X As Single, ByVal Y As Single)

   If Button = 1 Then mbSplitterMoving = False
End Sub

'When moving the mouse over the label
'and we're in 'drag' mode (i.e. dragging the splitter),
'move all the controls appropriately
Private Sub lblSplitterBar_MouseMove( _
    ByVal Button As Integer, ByVal Shift As Integer, _
    ByVal X As Single, ByVal Y As Single)

   Dim dChange As Double

   'Are we doing a drag?
   If mbSplitterMoving Then

      'Find where we moved to
      dChange = (X - mdSplitterOrigin) / PointsPerPixel

      'Adjust the control sizes and positions
      If (lstLeft.Width + dChange > 0) And _
         (lstRight.Width - dChange > 0) Then

         'The left list changes size
         lstLeft.Width = lstLeft.Width + dChange

         'The splitter bar in the middle moves
         lblSplitterBar.Left = lblSplitterBar.Left + dChange

         'The right list moves and changes size
         lstRight.Left = lstRight.Left + dChange
         lstRight.Width = lstRight.Width - dChange
      End If
   End If

End Sub
```

Wizards

Wizard dialogs are normally used when we need to collect a reasonably large amount of data from the user. The only absolute requirement this data must fulfill to be a candidate for a wizard dialog is that the bits of data being collected must be logically related to each other in some way. Wizard dialogs are particularly useful when the data being collected has the following characteristics in addition to being logically related:

- The information is complex and varied.
- The information must be supplied in a defined order because earlier selections alter the allowable parameters of later selections.
- The user does not need to understand the relationship between earlier and later choices. The wizard dialog can then abstract this decision-making process away from the user.

The primary purpose of a wizard dialog is to reduce the number of choices the user must make at any one time to a manageable level. An important secondary purpose of a wizard dialog is to allow us to alter the parts of the user interface that depend on the selections the user is currently making without having to do so in a way that is visible to the user and thereby potentially distract them from the task at hand. We cover the scenario in more detail in the "Dynamic UserForms" section later in the chapter.

Design Rules for Wizard Dialogs

1. The first page of a wizard dialog should explain the purpose of the wizard and the steps involved, but always have a "Don't show this again" check box to automatically skip the first page in the future if the user wants.
2. The last page of a wizard dialog should confirm everything the user entered, and no action should be taken until the user clicks the Finish button.
3. Always display the step number the user is currently working on within the wizard as well as the total number of steps to complete. This information is typically displayed in the title bar, although we've seen perfectly acceptable designs that display it elsewhere.

4. Wizard navigation is typically controlled by a series of four buttons: Cancel, Back, Next, and Finish. The enabled state of these buttons should be used to provide visual clues to the user about how they're doing. Track the user's progress through the wizard and watch their input during each step of the wizard. Based on where the user is and what data they've entered, enable only the navigation buttons that make sense, such as

   - First step with no data entered—If this is the explanation page, both the Cancel and Next buttons should be enabled. If the user opted not to display the explanation page and this is the first data entry step, the Cancel button should be the only button enabled (Cancel is always enabled).
   - The Next button is only enabled when the page passes all validation checks. Be sure the user can easily identify invalid entries as described in the "Validation" section earlier in this chapter.
   - Last step with all data entered and validated—Cancel enabled, Back enabled, Next disabled, Finish enabled.
   - The user has completed all wizard steps correctly but then used the Back button to revisit an earlier step—All buttons enabled until the user makes an entry that invalidates the ability of the wizard to finish or move forward.
   - In, say, a 5-step wizard where steps 4 and 5 allow the user to enter optional information, the Finish button can be enabled after step 3. Excel's Chart Wizard is a good example of this.

5. The user should be able to move back and forth through a wizard dialog to their heart's content. Therefore, you must always keep track of the status of all steps in the wizard to properly set the status of the navigation buttons. It is perfectly appropriate for the user to click Finish from step 2 of a 5-step wizard as long as they've completed all five steps and have just moved back to step 2 to make a minor change.

6. In some wizard designs, selections made in a step affect other selections on that same step. If a selection in a step makes another selection in that same step unnecessary, do not **hide** the controls for the unnecessary selection. Simply disable them. Controls that pop in and out of existence in front of the user's face tend to confuse them.

Creating a Wizard Dialog

The easiest way to create a wizard dialog is to use a MultiPage control, with each page of the control used for a separate step of the wizard and a common set of buttons at the bottom. Figure 13-8 shows the wizard UserForm template included on the CD in the *WizardDemo.xls* workbook, with the MultiPage tabs showing on the right-hand side. Prior to distributing the wizard, the MultiPage should be formatted to not have any tabs showing by setting its Style property to 2 - `fmTabStyleNone` and reducing both the MultiPage's and UserForm's width accordingly.

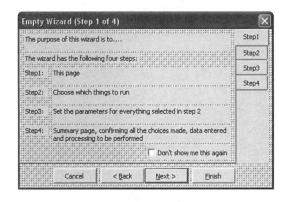

FIGURE 13-8   An empty wizard UserForm using a MultiPage control for the steps

Unfortunately, the MultiPage control is not without its problems, particularly when using non-MSForms controls within a page. If you intend to use the RefEdit control or any of the Windows Common Controls (such as the TreeView and ListView control), you should use a separate Frame control for each step of the wizard instead of a MultiPage control. If using a Frame control, it's easiest to develop the wizard with all the frames visible at the same time on a UserForm much larger than the final version. When the wizard is complete, change the frames' left and top so they all overlap and reduce the UserForm to its correct size.

Listing 13-18 shows the code for the four navigation buttons, which each call further procedures to initialize and validate the controls in each step. The content of the InitializeStep and bValidateStep procedures obviously depend on the contents of the step, so they have not been shown here. As well as initializing the controls on each page, the InitializeStep procedure should update the UserForm's caption to show the step number and enable/disable the navigation buttons. Note that the MultiPage value for any given step is one less than its step number. For example, MultiPage.Value = 0 displays step 1, MultiPage.Value = 1 displays step 2, and so on.

Listing 13-18 The Navigation Code for a Wizard Dialog

```
Private Sub cmdCancel_Click()
  mbUserCancel = True
  Me.Hide
End Sub

Private Sub cmdBack_Click()
  ' Can't go back from step 1.
  If mlStep > 1 Then
    ' No validation is required when moving back.
    mlStep = mlStep - 1
    mpgWizard.Value = mlStep - 1
    InitializeStep mlStep
  End If
End Sub

Private Sub cmdNext_Click()
  ' Can't go forward from the last step.
  If mlStep <= mlNumSteps Then
    ' We validate the controls on the current step
    ' before allowing the user to move forward.
    If bValidateStep(mlStep) Then   ' Validation succeeded.
      mlStep = mlStep + 1
      mpgWizard.Value = mlStep - 1
      InitializeStep mlStep
    Else                 ' Validation failed.
      MsgBox gsErrMsg, vbCritical, gsAPP_TITLE
      gsErrMsg = gsEMPTY_STRING
    End If
  End If
End Sub

Private Sub cmdFinish_Click()
  ' The last step must be validated before the user
  ' is allowed to complete the wizard.
  If bValidateStep(mlStep) Then   ' Validation succeeded.
    mbUserCancel = False
    Me.Hide
  Else                ' Validation failed.
```

```
    MsgBox gsErrMsg, vbCritical, gsAPP_TITLE
    gsErrMsg = gsEMPTY_STRING
  End If
End Sub
```

Dynamic UserForms

Most UserForms that we create are static, which is to say they have a fixed number of controls that are always visible (although they may be disabled at certain times). Dynamic UserForms can display different controls each time the form is shown.

Subset UserForms

The easiest way to create a dynamic UserForm is to start with a form that has more controls of all types than we'll ever need. When the form is shown, we set the position, caption, and so on of all the controls we need, hide the extra controls that we don't use, and set the size of the UserForm to encompass only the controls we use. This method is ideal when the upper limit on the number of controls is known and when each control is a known type. An example would be a survey, where each question might have between two and five responses. We create the form with five option buttons, set their captions with the applicable responses for each question, and hide the unused buttons.

Code-Created and Table-Driven UserForms

If we can't predict a reasonable upper limit on the number of controls or if there could be many different types of control, having a pre-prepared set of controls on the form becomes increasingly difficult to maintain. Instead, we can add controls to the UserForm at runtime. It's rare to find a situation that requires a UserForm to be created dynamically at runtime. We can usually either design the form directly or use the "subset" technique to hide the controls we don't need to use.

The one situation where dynamic UserForms make our development much easier is the use of table-driven dynamic wizards. Imagine a wizard used to generate a batch of reports, with each report using check boxes to set its options. In step 2 of the wizard, we could display a multiselect list box of the available reports, where the list of reports is read from a table in a worksheet. When the user clicks the Next > button, we populate step 3 of the wizard with the check boxes appropriate for the selected report(s), where again the check boxes are read from a worksheet table. By implementing a table-driven report wizard we can add new reports to the wizard by simply adding rows to the appropriate lists in the definition table. An example of this technique can be found on the CD in the *ReportWizard.xls* workbook and is explained in the following sections.

Figure 13-9 shows an extract of the wksReportOptions worksheet containing the lists of the available reports and their options, while Figure 13-10 shows step 3 of the report wizard dialog, where the Client Detail report has been selected to run.

Report	Report Options			
List	Report	Name	Caption	Default
Client Detail	Client Detail	CDIncProjects	Include Project Details	Y
Client Summary	Client Detail	CDIncTasks	Include Task Details	Y
Staff Detail	Staff Detail	SDIncHolidays	Include Holidays	N
Staff Summary	Staff Detail	SDGroupByClient	Group Results by Client	Y

FIGURE 13-9   A list of reports and their options

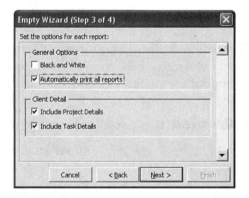

FIGURE 13-10   The table-driven step 3 of the report wizard

In this wizard step, the *General Options* panel is a permanent part of the wizard and contains options common to all the reports. The report-specific panes, such as the *Client Detail* pane, are created each time this step is initialized. A separate pane is created for each selected report that has options (note that the two summary reports have no options) using the code in Listing 13-19.

Listing 13-19 Code to Create the Report Options Panels

```
'Procedure to create the Report Option panels in Step 3
Private Sub CreateReportOptions()

    Dim vaOptions As Variant
    Dim lReport As Long
    Dim lOption As Long
    Dim sReport As String
    Dim fraFrame As MSForms.Frame
    Dim chkControl As MSForms.CheckBox
    Dim ctlControl As MSForms.Control
    Dim dFraTop As Double
    Dim dCtlTop As Double

    'Constants for each column in the Report Options table
    Const clREPORT = 1
    Const clPARAM = 2
    Const clCAPTION = 3
    Const clDEFAULT = 4

    'Read the report options table into an array
    vaOptions = wksReportLists.Range("rngReportOptions").Value

    'Clear out existing frames
    For Each ctlControl In fraReportOptions.Controls
        If TypeOf ctlControl Is MSForms.Frame And _
            ctlControl.Name <> "fraGeneral" Then

            fraReportOptions.Controls.Remove ctlControl.Name
        End If
    Next ctlControl

    'Get the position of the top of the first frame
    dFraTop = fraGeneral.Top + fraGeneral.Height + 6

    'Loop through the reports
    For lReport = 0 To lstReports.ListCount - 1

        'Was this one selected to run?
        If lstReports.Selected(lReport) Then

            'Get its name from the list box
            sReport = lstReports.List(lReport)
```

```
'A new report, so clear the frame
Set fraFrame = Nothing

'Loop through the options array
For lOption = 1 To UBound(vaOptions)


  'Is the option for the selected report?
  If vaOptions(lOption, clREPORT) = sReport Then

    'If we don't have a frame for this report,
    'create one
    If fraFrame Is Nothing Then

      'Add a new frame to the dialog
      Set fraFrame = fraReportOptions.Controls.Add( _
          "Forms.Frame.1", "fraRpt" & lReport, True)

      'Set the frame's size and position
      With fraFrame
        .Caption = sReport
        .SpecialEffect = fmSpecialEffectSunken
        .Top = dFraTop
        .Left = fraGeneral.Left
        .Width = fraGeneral.Width
      End With

      'Where to put the first control in the frame
      dCtlTop = chkBlackWhite.Top
    End If

    'Add a check box to the report's frame
    Set chkControl = fraFrame.Controls.Add( _
          "Forms.CheckBox.1", _
          vaOptions(lOption, clPARAM), True)

    'Set its size and position, caption and value
    With chkControl
      .Top = dCtlTop
      .Left = chkBlackWhite.Left
      .Width = chkBlackWhite.Width
      .Height = chkBlackWhite.Height

      .Caption = vaOptions(lOption, clCAPTION)
```

```
            .Value = GetSetting(gsREG_APP, gsREG_SECTION, _
                    vaOptions(lOption, clPARAM), _
                    vaOptions(lOption, clDEFAULT)) = "Y"
        End With

        'Move to the next control position
        dCtlTop = dCtlTop + chkAutoPrint.Top - _
                chkBlackWhite.Top
      End If
    Next lOption

    If Not fraFrame Is Nothing Then
      'If we have a frame for this report, work out how
      'high it needs to be
      fraFrame.Height = fraGeneral.Height - _
          chkAutoPrint.Top + dCtlTop - _
          (chkAutoPrint.Top - chkBlackWhite.Top)

      'Calculate the position for the next report's frame
      dFraTop = fraFrame.Top + fraFrame.Height + 6
    End If
  End If
Next lReport

'Set the scroll area of the Report Options frame,
'in case our report options don't fit
fraReportOptions.ScrollHeight = dFraTop

End Sub
```

To keep this example simple, we used only check boxes for the report options and we forced each check box to be shown on a different row. A real-world version of this technique would have many more columns for the report options, allowing all control types to be used and having more control over their position and style.

Scroll Regions

The observant reader will have noticed that the last line of the procedure shown in Listing 13-19 sets the ScrollHeight of the fraReportOptions frame. This is the frame in Figure 13-10 that contains all the report option panels and was formatted to show a vertical scrollbar. Setting the frame's ScrollHeight allows us to add more controls to the frame than can be seen at one time. When the ScrollHeight is greater than the frame height the user can use the scrollbars to bring the additional controls into view. While this should be considered a last resort in most UserForm design situations it can be very useful when creating dynamic forms that might extend beyond the visible area.

Dynamic Control Event Handling and Control Arrays

The downside to adding controls at runtime is that we can't add procedures to the UserForm's code module to handle their events. In theory, we could use the VBA Extensibility library to create a UserForm in a new workbook, add both controls and event procedures to it, and then show the form, but we've yet to encounter a situation that requires such a cumbersome solution. We can, however, use a separate prefabricated class module to handle most events of the controls we add to the form.

The class module shown in Listing 13-20 uses a WithEvents variable to trap the events of any TextBox it's connected to. We use the Change event to validate that the entry is a number, using the CheckNumeric function discussed earlier. We'd prefer to use the BeforeUpdate or AfterUpdate events for this, so we could trigger validation only when the user left the control instead of every time its value was changed. Unfortunately, those events belong to the generic MSForms.Control object and are not exposed to us when we declare a WithEvents object in this manner.

Listing 13-20   Class to Handle a TextBox's Events

```
'Class CTextBoxEvents

'Withevents variable to hook the events for a text box
Private WithEvents mtxtBox As MSForms.TextBox

'Allow the calling code to set the control to hook
Public Property Set Control(txtNew As MSForms.TextBox)
  Set mtxtBox = txtNew
End Property

'Validate the text box with each change.
'Ideally, we'd using the AfterUpdate event, but
'we don't get it through the WithEvents variable
Private Sub mtxtBox_Change()
  CheckNumeric mtxtBox
End Sub
```

Every time we add a text box to the form, we also create a new instance of the class to handle its events. We store all the class instances in a module-level collection as shown in Listing 13-21.

Listing 13-21   Assigning Event-Handler Classes to Controls Created at Runtime

```
'Module-level collection to store instances of our
'event handler class
Dim mcolEvents As Collection

'Build the UserForm in the initialize routine
Private Sub UserForm_Initialize()

  Dim sBoxes As String
  Dim lBoxes As Long
  Dim lBox As Long
  Dim lblLabel As MSForms.Label
  Dim txtBox As MSForms.TextBox
  Dim clsEvents As CTextBoxEvents

  'Ask the user how many boxes to show
  sBoxes = InputBox("How many boxes (1-5)?", , "3")

  'Validate the entry
  If sBoxes = "" Then Exit Sub
  If Not IsNumeric(sBoxes) Then Exit Sub

  lBoxes = CLng(sBoxes)
  If lBoxes < 1 Then lBoxes = 1
  If lBoxes > 5 Then lBoxes = 5

  'Initialize the collection of event handler classes
  Set mcolEvents = New Collection

  'Create the required number of boxes
  For lBox = 1 To lBoxes

    'Add a label to the form
    Set lblLabel = Me.Controls.Add("Forms.Label.1", _
          "lbl" & lBox)

    With lblLabel
```

```
      .Top = (lBox - 1) * 21.75 + 9
      .Left = 6
      .Width = 50
      .Height = 9.75
      .WordWrap = False
      .Caption = "Text Box " & lBox
    End With

    'Add the text box to the form
    Set txtBox = Me.Controls.Add("Forms.TextBox.1", _
            "txt" & lBox)

    With txtBox
      .Top = (lBox - 1) * 21.75 + 6
      .Left = 56
      .Width = 50
      .Height = 15.75
    End With

    'Create a new instance of the event handler class
    Set clsEvents = New CTextBoxEvents

    'Tell it to handle the events for the text box
    Set clsEvents.Control = txtBox

    'Add the event handler instance to our collection,
    'so it stays alive during the life of the form
    mcolEvents.Add clsEvents
  Next

End Sub
```

We can use the same technique to handle the events of controls in static UserForms as well. Imagine a form with 50 text boxes, all requiring numeric validation. We could include all 50 Change event procedures in our code and accept the maintenance overhead it brings, or we could use the class module from Listing 13-20 to handle the validation for all our text boxes. The code in Listing 13-22 does this by iterating through all the controls on the form and hooking up new instances of the event handler class for every text box it finds.

Listing 13-22   Class to Handle a TextBox's Events

```
'Collection to store instances of our event handler class
Dim mcolEvents As Collection

'Hook the events for all the Text Boxes
Private Sub UserForm_Initialize()

  Dim ctlControl As MSForms.Control
  Dim clsEvents As CTextBoxEvents

  'Initialize the collection of event handler classes
  Set mcolEvents = New Collection

  'Loop through all the controls
  For Each ctlControl In Me.Controls

    'Check if it's a text box
    If TypeOf ctlControl Is MSForms.TextBox Then

      'Create a new instance of the event handler class
      Set clsEvents = New CTextBoxEvents

      'Tell it to handle the events for the text box
      Set clsEvents.Control = ctlControl

      'Add the event handler instance to our collection,
      'so it stays alive during the life of the form
      mcolEvents.Add clsEvents
    End If
  Next

End Sub
```

Modeless UserForms

Most of the dialogs we come into contact with are modal, which is to say that neither the application nor the user can do anything until the form is dismissed. When the Show statement is processed, the application window is disabled by default, then the form is displayed, and code execution in the procedure that displayed the form stops. Code can run in response to control and form events from within the form being displayed, but code execution does not continue in the calling procedure until after the user closes the form or an event procedure unloads or hides the form.

When a UserForm is shown modeless, however, code execution in the calling procedure continues immediately after the UserForm_Initialize and UserForm_Activate event procedures have finished, with the UserForm remaining displayed. The form remains open and both the UserForm and the application window can be used.

Splash Screens

The simplest use for a modeless UserForm is as an introductory splash screen. The UserForm is shown modeless at the start of the Auto_Open or Workbook_Open procedure and unloaded at the end of the procedure. Listing 13-23 shows a simple example, where the form uses the SetUserFormAppearance procedure introduced earlier to remove the title bar.

Listing 13-23 Showing a Splash Screen at Startup

```
Sub Auto_Open()

  Dim frmSplash As FSplashScreen

  'Show the form modelessly
  Set frmSplash = New FSplashScreen
  frmSplash.Show vbModeless

  'Process the startup code
  Application.Wait Now + TimeValue("00:00:5")

  'Unload the splash screen
  Unload frmSplash
  Set frmSplash = Nothing

End Sub

'The FSplashScreen UserForm's Code Module
Option Explicit
```

```
'Set the form to have no title bar
Private Sub UserForm_Initialize()

  'Adjust the height for the missing caption
  Me.Height = Me.InsideHeight

  SetUserFormAppearance Me, uwsNoTitleBar

End Sub

'Prevent the form being closed using Alt+F4
Private Sub UserForm_QueryClose(Cancel As Integer, CloseMode As Integer)

  Cancel = (CloseMode = vbFormControlMenu)

End Sub
```

When using a splash screen in your application, keep in mind that it may be tolerable, and even interesting, the first time the user sees it, but after many times they will probably grow tired of it. Always give the user some method of bypassing the splash screen when starting your application.

Progress Bars

A rather more interesting use of modeless forms is to display progress information to the user during lengthy operations. Figure 13-11 shows a simple progress bar UserForm, where the progress indicator is made up of two overlapping Frame controls, each containing a label. The back frame has a white background and a label with blue text, while the front frame has a blue background and a label with white text. As the progress is updated, the width of the front frame is adjusted, allowing us to see more of the blue background. This makes the bar appear to fill up as the progress increases.

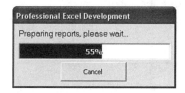

Figure 13-11 A modeless progress bar

The code for the progress bar form is too long to show here but is included on the CD in the *ModelessForms.xls* example workbook. The FProgressBar form can be copied from the example workbook into your project and controlled using code like that shown in Listing 13-24.

Listing 13-24 Using the Progress Bar UserForm

```
Sub ShowProgress()

  Dim lLoop As Long
  Dim lIterations As Long
  Dim frmProgress As FProgressBar

  lIterations = 2000

  'Initialize the progress bar
  Set frmProgress = New FProgressBar
  frmProgress.Title = "Professional Excel Development"
  frmProgress.Text = "Preparing reports, please wait..."
  frmProgress.Min = 1
  frmProgress.Max = lIterations

  'Show the progress bar
  frmProgress.ShowForm

  For lLoop = 1 To lIterations
    'Check if the user cancelled
    If frmProgress.Cancelled Then Exit For

    'Update the progress
    frmProgress.Progress = lLoop

    'Do Stuff
  Next lLoop

  'Unload the progress bar form
  Unload frmProgress

End Sub
```

Combining with Menu Items

If we display a modeless UserForm and then allow our code to finish, the form is left active on the screen and both the form and the application can be used. This behavior can be used to very good effect in forms-based dictator applications. In this application design, worksheets are only used for a backdrop display. All the interaction with the user is done through UserForms.

Most forms-based applications have a central "switchboard" form containing a set of buttons to display subforms for each functional area. Those forms have their own buttons to show other forms and so on. It is usually difficult to navigate around the application. If we use modeless UserForms, however, the menus are available, so we can implement a menu structure that allows the user to quickly switch among the various parts of the application.

To implement this design we need to be able to easily communicate with any currently active form. This allows us to notify the form when the user clicks a menu item to jump to another form, perform a save operation, or exit the application. We accomplish this by having all the forms include the same set of standard control procedures, shown in Listing 13-25, that can be called from a central form handling procedure.

Listing 13-25 Standard Procedures to Be Included in All Modeless Forms

```
' Called prior to navigating to another form.
' Allows the form to validate and store its data, then unload
' If validation fails, the navigation can be cancelled
Public Sub BeforeNavigate(ByRef Cancel As Boolean)
End Sub


' Called prior to saving the data workbook
' Allows the form to validate and store its data
' If validation fails, the navigation can be cancelled
Public Sub BeforeSave(ByRef Cancel As Boolean)
End Sub


' Called after to saving the data workbook
' Allows the form to update its display
' (e.g. if showing the file name)
Public Sub AfterSave()
End Sub
```

```
' Called when the application is about to be closed
' The form should unload itself, but could cancel the close
Public Sub AppExit(ByRef Cancel As Boolean)
End Sub
```

The central form handling procedure is shown in Listing 13-26.

Listing 13-26 The Central Control Routine to Handle Navigation Between Forms

```
' Global variable to hold the form currently being displayed
Dim gfrmActiveForm As Object

' A single OnAction procedure for most menu items, where the
' form name is obtained from the menu item's Parameter
Sub FormMenuClick()
   ShowForm Application.CommandBars.ActionControl.Parameter
End Sub

'Common routine to switch between forms
Sub ShowForm(ByVal sForm As String)

   Dim bCancel As Boolean

   'If there's an active form, tell it to save and unload
   If Not gfrmActiveForm Is Nothing Then
     gfrmActiveForm.BeforeNavigate bCancel
   End If

   'If the save/close wasn't cancelled,
   If Not bCancel Then
     'Show the next form, assuming it is in the same workbook
     Set gfrmActiveForm = VBA.UserForms.Add(sForm)
     gfrmActiveForm.Show vbModeless
   End If
End Sub

'The OnAction routine for the File > Save menu item
Sub MenuFileSave()

   Dim bCancel As Boolean

   'If there's an active form, tell it to save its data
```

```
If Not gfrmActiveForm Is Nothing Then
  gfrmActiveForm.BeforeSave bCancel
End If

If Not bCancel Then
  'Save the data workbook if not cancelled
  gwkbDataWorkbook.Save

  'If there's an active form, tell it to we saved OK
  If Not gfrmActiveForm Is Nothing Then
    gfrmActiveForm.AfterSave
  End If
End If

End Sub
```

Using this mechanism, we can add more UserForms to the application without having to add any extra code to control their display. As long as they include the standard set of control procedures shown in Listing 13-25, they will automatically plug into the central form handling procedure. All we need to do is add the form module to the workbook and add the additional rows to the command bar builder table required to include the new form in our application's menu structure.

Control Specifics

Most of the controls we use in our forms are well documented and well understood, so documenting them here would be of little benefit to the reader. Instead, this section explains how to use some of the lesser-known controls, or how to use them in innovative ways.

ComboBox

The ComboBox is the unsung hero of the MSForms toolbox. By changing the style of the drop-down button, we can use a combo box as a normal drop-down list, as a text box, as a filename entry box, or as a fully customized drop-down control. Figure 13-12 shows four combo boxes, with the bottom one shown in its dropped state, revealing a custom drop-down panel for specifying a filter.

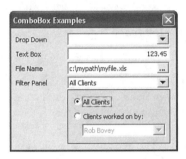

FIGURE 13-12   ComboBox styles

Drop-Down List/Combo

The default behavior for a combo box is to allow the user to select an item from a list or enter values that do not exist in the supplied list. When the drop arrow is clicked, the list is shown below the combo box. When the user clicks an item in the list, the list is hidden and the selected item is displayed in the control.

Text Box

If we set the combo box to have `ShowDropButtonWhen = fmShowDropButton Never` and `Style = fmStyleDropDownCombo`, the result is a control that looks and behaves exactly like a text box. This allows us to have a single control that can be used to select an item from a list, or allow direct entry.

For example, in the UserForm in Figure 13-12 the top drop-down may be a list of attributes about a person, such as age, sex, and so on, while the second drop-down would be used to fill in the value for the selected attribute. When Age is selected from the drop-down we want to be able to type a number directly into the control, but when Sex is selected we want to show a drop-down to choose between Male and Female.

File Name Box

By changing the DropButtonStyle to fmDropButtonStyleEllipsis, we create a control that looks like a filename box. The user would expect a File Open dialog to appear when they click the button. We can do exactly that by hooking the DropButtonClick event, as shown in Listing 13-27.

Listing 13-27   Handle the Ellipsis in the File Name Combo

```
'Handle clicking the ellipsis in the File Name combo
Private Sub cboFileName_DropButtonClick()
```

```
Dim vFile As Variant

'Get the file name
vFile = Application.GetOpenFilename()

'Write it to the control
If TypeName(vFile) = "String" Then
  cboFileName.Text = vFile
End If

'Toggle the Enabled property to move the focus
'to the next control
cboFileName.Enabled = False
cboFileName.Enabled = True

End Sub
```

One annoying aspect of hooking the DropButtonClick event is that we can't cancel it, so the control is left with an empty list displayed after we obtain the file name. One workaround for this is to toggle the Enabled property of the control, which forces the focus to move to the next control in the tab order, as shown in Listing 13-27.

Drop-down Panes

The fourth combo box in Figure 13-12 implements a fully customized drop-down pane to display a simple filter selection. This would typically be used in conjunction with a list box to filter the items in the list. The code to handle the filter pane is shown in Listing 13-28.

Listing 13-28   Code to Manage a Custom Drop-Down Panel

```
'Boolean to identify if the filter has changed
Dim mbFilterChanged As Boolean

'Set up the form
Private Sub UserForm_Initialize()
  cboFilter.AddItem "All Clients"
  cboFilter.ListIndex = 0

  cboConsultant.List = Array("Rob Bovey", "Dennis Wallentin", _
                             "Stephen Bullen", "John Green")
  cboConsultant.ListIndex = 0
```

```
End Sub

'When clicking the dropdown, show the filter frame
Private Sub cboFilter_DropButtonClick()

  mbFilterChanged = False
  fraFilter.Visible = True
  fraFilter.SetFocus

End Sub

'Changing any of the filter options
'sets the 'Filter Changed' boolean
Private Sub optAllClients_Click()
  mbFilterChanged = True
  cboConsultant.Enabled = optClientsForConsultant.Value
End Sub

Private Sub optClientsForConsultant_Click()
  mbFilterChanged = True
  cboConsultant.Enabled = optClientsForConsultant.Value
End Sub

Private Sub cboConsultant_Change()
  mbFilterChanged = True
End Sub

'When exiting the frame, check for updates to the filter
Private Sub fraFilter_Exit(ByVal Cancel As _
    MSForms.ReturnBoolean)

  CheckFilterFrame
End Sub

'When clicking outside the frame,
'check and close the filter panel
Private Sub UserForm_MouseDown(ByVal Button As Integer, _
    ByVal Shift As Integer, ByVal X As Single, _
    ByVal Y As Single)

  CheckFilterFrame
End Sub

'Handle clicking outside the frame,
'to check for updates and close the panel
```

```
Private Sub CheckFilterFrame()

  'If it's visible, update the list
  If fraFilter.Visible Then
    If mbFilterChanged Then ApplyFilter
  End If

  fraFilter.Visible = False
End Sub

'Apply the changed filter options
Private Sub ApplyFilter()
  'Update the text of the filter dropdown
  If optAllClients Then
    cboFilter.List(0) = "All Clients"
  Else
    cboFilter.List(0) = "Clients for " & cboConsultant.Text
  End If
  'Update the contents of the list box

End Sub
```

The custom drop-down panel is a standard Frame control, initially set to be invisible, containing the controls used for our filter. When the user clicks the combo box drop-down button we use the DropButtonClick event to initialize a Boolean variable mbFilterChanged. This variable is used to identify whether changes have been made within the frame. We then make the frame visible and give it the focus. This makes the frame appear to "drop down" from the combo box. We include code in the Change event for all the controls in the frame to set the mbFilterChanged variable to True, indicating that the frame's content has changed.

The user can exit the frame by tabbing to or clicking on another control (causing the Exit event to fire) or by clicking somewhere else on the UserForm (which we detect with the UserForm_MouseDown event). In both cases, we call the CheckFilterFrame procedure to hide the frame, check whether any of the controls were changed, and apply the new filter. In this case, we just update the text shown in the combo box to show the filter settings. The combo box style is set to fmStyleDropDownList, so that clicking anywhere in the combo box causes the DropButtonClick event to fire. We have a single item in the combo box list with the ListIndex set to zero to show it in the control. To update the text shown in the combo box we change the text of that item.

Windows Common Controls

There is an OCX file available on most computers called mscomctl.ocx, usually found in the *C:\windows\system32* folder that contains a set of controls collectively known as the Microsoft Windows Common Controls 6.0. Although it theoretically might not exist, we have yet to come across a computer in practice that doesn't have this file. It is so widely used that anything other than a bare Windows installation includes it. This file contains the following controls that can be used in our UserForms:

- Microsoft ImageComboBox Control 6.0
- Microsoft ImageList Control 6.0
- Microsoft ListView Control 6.0
- Microsoft ProgressBar Control 6.0
- Microsoft Slider Control 6.0
- Microsoft StatusBar Control 6.0
- Microsoft TabStrip Control 6.0
- Microsoft ToolBar Control 6.0
- Microsoft TreeView Control 6.0

To access these controls, right-click the Control Toolbox, select the *Additional Controls* menu, and put a check mark beside each of the controls you intend to use. Some of these controls, such as the TabStrip and UpDown controls, are similar to the standard MSForms controls, but the others are new and different.

For example, the ListView is similar to the File pane of Windows Explorer. It allows us to display a list of items with icons, giving us many formatting possibilities for each item in the list. The ListView report style is similar in appearance to the normal List control, but allows us to display each item using a different font, color, and so on. The TreeView control is an excellent way to display hierarchical data, and the ImageList and ImageCombo controls can be used where displaying thumbnails may be more appropriate than text.

To fully document each of the Windows Common Controls is beyond the scope of this book, but the CommonControls.xls example workbook contains the UserForm shown in Figure 13-13, with fully commented code to explain its operation.

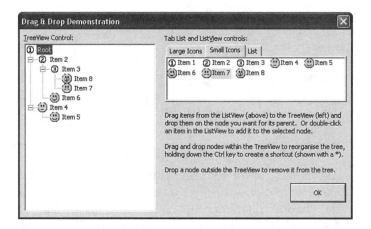

FIGURE 13-13   Using the Windows Common Controls

The official documentation for the Windows Common Controls can be found in the MSDN library within the Visual Basic 6.0 section. For example, the documentation for the TreeView control starts at http://msdn.microsoft.com/en-us/library/aa443492.aspx.

The only issue to be aware of when using the Windows Common Controls on UserForms is that they do not like to be placed inside the MultiPage control. Trying to modify a control that is not on the active page usually fails.

Drag-and-Drop

The normal MSForms controls do not support drag-and-drop operations between controls. If we want to implement drag-and-drop between controls on our forms (such as being able to drag an item from one list box and drop it on another), we have to use either the Windows Common Controls or a Visual Basic form. The CommonControls.xls workbook contains fully commented code that implements drag-and-drop between the ListView and TreeView controls as well as within the TreeView control to change its structure.

Practical Example

PETRAS Time Sheet

The PETRAS time sheet add-in has not been changed for this chapter

PETRAS Reporting

At this stage of the PETRAS reporting application, it would be artificial to add a suite of UserForms just to demonstrate the techniques discussed in this chapter. Therefore, the only change made to the reporting application for this chapter is to display a progress bar while consolidating all the time sheet workbooks. When we modify the application to use a database back end in Chapter 19, "Programming with Access and SQL Server," we add a set of UserForms to the reporting application for the user to maintain the static lists of consultants, clients, projects, and so on. The code changes required to add the progress bar are detailed in Table 13-1.

Table 13-1 Changes to the PETRAS Reporting Application for Chapter 13

Module	Procedure	Change
FProgressBar (new form)		Added the FProgressBar form shown in Figure 13-11
MSystemCode	ConsolidateWorkbooks	Modified to use the FProgressBar form instead of writing the progress to the status bar

Summary

As programmers, we tend to think that our code is the most important part of an application and dismiss the UserForms as mere eye candy. Our users, on the other hand, don't see the code, only the interface that we provide them. The UserForms are the most important part of our application to the user, and they will like or dislike our applications based primarily on how well the UserForms are designed. For this reason and more, UserForm design should be as much a priority as any other part of our application development. Taking the time to design UserForms that are easy to use and easy to maintain, and that adapt to the user's environment, can give our workbook the polished appearance expected of a professionally developed application.

CHAPTER 14

INTERFACES

In previous chapters, we explained class modules and the various parts they can play in our applications in some depth, including handling events, encapsulating functionality, and creating our own object models. We've also seen that UserForms and the workbook and worksheet code modules are just special types of class module.

This chapter takes a step further into object oriented design by explaining how one class can appear to be many different types of object and how many different classes can appear to be the same type of object. By using the techniques explained in this chapter we can improve the robustness of our solution, simplify the development experience, and reduce the amount of code we need to write. As an example, we convert our central consolidation and reporting application to use a plug-in architecture for its UserForms, allowing us to extend the application without having to add any more code to the core procedures.

What Is an Interface?

An interface is a list of public properties, methods, events, user-defined types, constants, and/or enumerations that we can use to interact with an object. When we dimension a variable to be a certain object type, we're actually specifying the **interface** the variable uses to communicate with an object. When we later make the variable refer to an object, we're specifying which **object** we want to communicate with through the interface. When the code is run, the compiler checks to see whether the object has the interface we specified and throws a *Type mismatch* error if it doesn't, as shown in Listing 14-1.

Listing 14-1   A Type Mismatch Error

```
'Declare a variable that will talk to objects through the
'Worksheet interface
Dim wksInput As Worksheet

'Sheet1 in our workbook has the Worksheet interface,
'so we can talk to it
Set wksInput = Sheet1

'The ThisWorkbook object doesn't have the Worksheet interface,
'so we get a Type Mismatch error.
Set wksInput = ThisWorkbook
```

Whenever we create a class module the VBA compiler also creates a default interface for that class. The default interface is given the same name as the class and contains a list of all the public properties, methods, and so on that we add to the class. When we dimension a variable using `Dim clsTheClass As CClassName`, we're saying that the variable uses the *interface* CClassName. When we use code like `Set clsTheClass = New CCClassName`, we're creating an object that is a new instance of the *class* CClassName, and then setting the variable to refer to the object, as in Listing 14-2.

Listing 14-2   Variables, Interfaces, and Classes

```
'Declare a variable to use the CClassName interface
Dim clsTheClass As CClassName

'Create a new instance of the CClassName class
'and set our variable to refer to it
Set clsTheClass = New CclassName
```

The code in the class module defines how the object behaves, while the interface defines how we access the code. By hiding this implementation detail from us, VBA makes it much easier to work with class modules. We don't need to care whether we're dealing with a class or an interface. Unfortunately, it also hides the useful fact that we can define our own custom interfaces and mix-and-match classes and interfaces if we want. The rest of this chapter examines a few ways that we can improve our applications by doing just that.

Code Reuse

One of the basic tenets of good programming is to write procedures that can be reused as much as possible. For example, a generic sorting procedure like the simple bubble sort shown in Listing 14-3 can be used to sort an array of any simple data type.

Listing 14-3 A Generic Bubble Sort

```
'A simple, generic, slow bubble sort, to sort a 1D array
Sub Generic1DBubbleSort(ByRef vaArray As Variant)

  Dim bDoAgain As Boolean
  Dim vTemp As Variant
  Dim iIndex As Integer

  Do
    'Assume we're done
    bDoAgain = False

    'Loop through the array, comparing the names
    For iIndex = LBound(vaArray) To UBound(vaArray) - 1

      'If we found some in the wrong order, ...
      If vaArray(iIndex) > vaArray(iIndex + 1) Then

        '... swap them ...
        vTemp = vaArray(iIndex)
        vaArray(iIndex) = vaArray(iIndex + 1)
        vaArray(iIndex + 1) = vTemp

        '... and remember to loop again.
        bDoAgain = True
      End If

    Next iIndex

  Loop While bDoAgain

End Sub
```

Unfortunately, we can't use this procedure to sort objects because there is nothing in the code to say which property to sort on; every type of object would need a specific version of the procedure. Let's assume we're writing an application for a publishing company to manage the production of a book. We're using an object-oriented design and we have a CAuthor class and a CReviewer class (among others). The CAuthor class might look something like Listing 14-4 (but with more properties than just the name).

Listing 14-4 A CAuthor Class

```
'Name:          CAuthor
'Description:   Class to represent a book's author

Option Explicit

Private msAuthName As String

Public Property Let AuthorName(sNew As String)
  msAuthName = sNew
End Property

Public Property Get AuthorName() As String
  AuthorName = msAuthName
End Property
```

At some point in the application, we have the requirement to produce a list of Authors sorted by name. Because this is a collection of objects, we can't just pass them to a generic procedure. We have to use a specific procedure such as that shown in Listing 14-5 to sort a collection of Authors using the AuthorName property.

Listing 14-5 A Bubble Sort for the CAuthor Class

```
'A simple bubble sort, to sort a collection of CAuthor objects
Sub BubbleSortAuthors(ByRef colAuthors As Collection)

  Dim bDoAgain As Boolean
  Dim iIndex As Integer
  Dim clsAuthorLow As CAuthor
  Dim clsAuthorHigh As CAuthor

  Do
    'Assume we're done
```

```
bDoAgain = False

'Loop through the collection, comparing the names
For iIndex = 1 To colAuthors.Count - 1

   'Get the Author objects from the collection at this point
   Set clsAuthorLow = colAuthors(iIndex)
   Set clsAuthorHigh = colAuthors(iIndex + 1)

   'If we found some in the wrong order, ...
   If clsAuthorLow.AuthorName > clsAuthorHigh.AuthorName Then

      '... swap them ...
      colAuthors.Remove iIndex + 1
      colAuthors.Add clsAuthorHigh, , iIndex

      '... and remember to loop again.
      bDoAgain = True
   End If

   Next iIndex

Loop While bDoAgain

End Sub
```

Similarly, we might need specific procedures to sort collections of CReviewer, CEditor, CDistributor, and so on, objects. Wouldn't it be much better if we could have a single procedure that could sort collections of any of these objects? If we use a custom interface, we can.

Defining a Custom Interface

If we want to create a generic sort procedure that works with any of our classes, we need to be able to talk to each class in the same way. We need the ability to tell each class "I don't care what specific type of class you are, just give me something to sort you by." To achieve this, we need to give each of our classes a custom interface through which we can ask for the item to sort by. Our custom interface is called ISortableObject (by convention, interfaces start with a capital I) and has a single property called

SortKey. A generic object sorting procedure can then use that interface to ask each object for its key, without caring what type of class it is.

As we mentioned before, whenever we create a class module the VBA compiler also creates an interface of the same name containing all the public properties, methods, and so on that the class implements. Therefore, all we need to do to define a custom interface is create a new class module that contains the properties and methods we want to use but without any code in those procedures. VBA creates the interface for us behind the scenes, and we can then implement this interface in our other classes.

We define our ISortableObject interface by adding a new class module to our project with the name ISortableObject and containing a public SortKey property, as shown in Listing 14-6.

Listing 14-6   An ISortableObject Interface Class

```
'Name:            ISortableObject
'Description:     Class to define the ISortableObject interface

'Get the key to use in the generic sorting procedure
Public Property Get SortKey() As Variant
End Property
```

That's all there is to it. Note that we defined the SortKey property to return a Variant data type so we can use the same generic procedure for objects that require sorting by different data types.

Implementing a Custom Interface

Once we've defined our interface we have to add it to all the classes we want to use it with. We do this by using the `Implements` keyword followed by the interface name at the top of the class module.

```
Implements ISortableObject
```

Figure 14-1 shows that as soon as we add this line of code to the class module, the interface name appears in the object drop-down at the top-left of the code pane, just like an object on a UserForm.

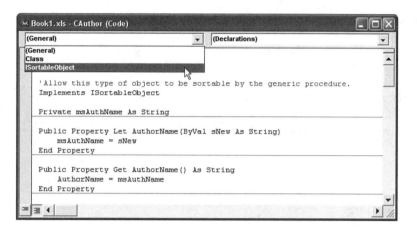

FIGURE 14-1   The interface appears in the object drop-down.

When the interface name is selected in the object drop-down, the right-hand drop-down lists the methods and properties defined for that interface, as shown in Figure 14-2.

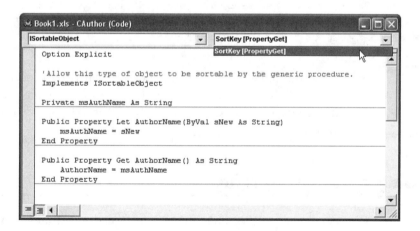

FIGURE 14-2   With the interface selected, the properties and methods appear in the right-hand drop-down.

Clicking one of the properties or methods of the interface adds an outline procedure to the code module, just as it does for any other object. We just need to add code to that procedure to return the value to use when sorting this type of object. The complete, sortable CAuthor class is shown in Listing 14-7, where the code to implement the ISortableObject interface is highlighted.

Listing 14-7 The Sortable CAuthor Class

```
'Name:          CAuthor
'Description:    Class to represent a book's author

'Allow this type of object to be sortable
'by the generic procedure
Implements ISortableObject

Private msAuthName As String

Public Property Let AuthorName(sNew As String)
  msAuthName = sNew
End Property

Public Property Get AuthorName() As String
  AuthorName = msAuthName
End Property

'Return the value to be used when sorting this object
Private Property Get ISortableObject_SortKey() As Variant
  ISortableObject_SortKey = AuthorName
End Property
```

Note that the name of the ISortableObject_SortKey procedure is a concatenation of the interface name and the property name and that it is a Private property of the CAuthor class, so it won't appear in the CAuthor interface.

Using a Custom Interface

With the custom ISortableObject interface defined and implemented in our CAuthor class, we can modify our BubbleSortAuthors procedure to be able to sort collections of any class that implements our ISortableObject interface, as shown in Listing 14-8. All we need to do is define our data types As ISortableObject instead of As CAuthor, use the SortKey property instead of AuthorName, and change the variable names to be more generic.

Listing 14-8 A Generic Bubble Sort Procedure for Classes That Implement ISortableObject

```
'A simple bubble sort, to sort an array of objects
'that implement ISortableObject
Sub BubbleSortSortableObjects(ByRef colSortable As Collection)

    Dim bDoAgain As Boolean
    Dim iIndex As Integer
    Dim clsSortable1 As ISortableObject
    Dim clsSortable2 As ISortableObject

    Do
        'Assume we're done
        bDoAgain = False

        'Loop through the collection, comparing the names
        For iIndex = 1 To colSortable.Count - 1

            'Get the objects from the collection at this point
            Set clsSortable1 = colSortable(iIndex)
            Set clsSortable2 = colSortable(iIndex + 1)

            'If we found some in the wrong order, ...
            If clsSortable1.SortKey > clsSortable2.SortKey Then

                '... swap them ...
                colSortable.Remove iIndex + 1
                colSortable.Add clsSortable2, , iIndex

                '... and remember to loop again.
                bDoAgain = True

            End If

        Next iIndex

    Loop While bDoAgain

End Sub
```

We can then use this procedure with any type of object that implements the ISortableObject interface, as shown in Listing 14-9. This technique assumes that the values provided by each object's ISortableObject_SortKey property can be used within a "greater than" comparison.

Listing 14-9 Using the Generic Sorting Procedure for a Collection of CAuthors

```
Sub AuthorSortExample()

  Dim vItem As Variant
  Dim colAuthors As Collection
  Dim clsAuthor As CAuthor

  Set colAuthors = New Collection

  'Populate the Authors collection
  For Each vItem In Array("Rob Bovey", "Dennis Wallentin", _
                          "Stephen Bullen", "John Green")
    Set clsAuthor = New CAuthor
    clsAuthor.AuthorName = CStr(vItem)
    colAuthors.Add clsAuthor
  Next vItem

  'Sort the Authors using the generic procedure
  BubbleSortSortableObjects colAuthors

  'Show the sorted list
  For Each clsAuthor In colAuthors
    Debug.Print clsAuthor.AuthorName
  Next clsAuthor

End Sub
```

That was a quick introduction to custom interfaces, so let's recap what we achieved and why we're doing it. When we create non-trivial object models, we often end up with multiple object types (that is, classes) that have a lot of properties in common, but also some significant differences. We also often need to process many of those object types in similar ways (such as sorting them). We could do this using a variable declared As Object and hope that all our classes use the same names for their common properties, but that is neither robust nor efficient. Instead, we can define a custom interface containing the properties and methods that are common to our objects and add code to each class to implement the interface. Our processes can then communicate with any of those object types through the custom interface, making our code much more robust, efficient, maintainable, and reusable.

Polymorphic Classes

The ability of a class to appear to be many different types of object is called **polymorphism** and is something that many of the classes in the Excel object model use. For example, we can access the different aspects of the various menu item types using their detailed interfaces, CommandBarPopUp, CommandBarButton, CommandBarComboBox, and so on, or iterate through them all using the more generic set of properties that they expose through the CommandBarControl interface. We can make our own classes polymorphic by simply defining and implementing multiple custom interfaces in the same way that we added the ISortableObject interface.

For example, another requirement for our fictional book-publishing application might be to generate a letter for everyone involved in the book's production. Ideally we'd like to be able to put all the CAuthor, CReviewer, CEditor, and CDistributor objects into a single collection; sort the collection; and then loop through it to generate the letters.

Putting all the objects into one collection is not a problem. The VBA Collection object can handle mixed object types. Assuming all those classes have implemented our ISortableObject interface, sorting the collection is not a problem either. Our generic sorting procedure doesn't care what type of object it operates on, so long as that object implements the correct interface.

The problem comes when we want to generate the letters. How do we iterate through the collection of mixed object types to get the contact details? The answer, of course, is to add another custom interface to those classes through which we can access the contact details and other properties common to all the objects. In the example shown in Listing 14-10 we create a new IContactDetails interface that includes Name and Address properties.

Listing 14-10 The IContactDetails Interface Class

```
'Name:          IContactDetails
'Description:    Class to define the IContactDetails interface

'Get/set the name
Public Property Get Name() As String
End Property

Public Property Let Name(sNew As String)
End Property

'Get/set the postal address
Public Property Get Address() As String
End Property

Public Property Let Address(sNew As String)
End Property
```

The extended CAuthor, CReviewer, CEditor, and CDistributor classes can then implement the IContactDetails interface. In Listing 14-11, the CAuthor class has been modified to implement and support the IContactDetails interface.

Listing 14-11 The CAuthor Class Implementing the IContactDetails Interface

```
'Name:          CAuthor
'Description:    Class to represent a book's author

'Allow this type of object to be sortable
'by the generic procedure
Implements ISortableObject

'Provide access through the IContactDetails interface
Implements IContactDetails

Dim msAuthName As String
Dim msAddress As String

'Set/get the Author name
Public Property Let AuthorName(sNew As String)
  msAuthName = sNew
End Property
```

```
Public Property Get AuthorName() As String
  AuthorName = msAuthName
End Property

'Set/Get the address
Public Property Let Address(sNew As String)
  msAddress = sNew
End Property

Public Property Get Address() As String
  Address = msAddress
End Property

'Implement the ISortableObject class
Private Property Get ISortableObject_SortKey() As Variant
  ISortableObject_SortKey = AuthorName
End Property

'Implement the IContactDetails interface,
'by calling through to the default interface's properties
Private Property Let IContactDetails_Name(RHS As String)
  Me.AuthorName = RHS
End Property

Private Property Get IContactDetails_Name() As String
  IContactDetails_Name = Me.AuthorName
End Property

Private Property Let IContactDetails_Address(RHS As String)
  Me.Address = RHS
End Property

Private Property Get IContactDetails_Address() As String
  IContactDetails_Address = Me.Address
End Property
```

When using the interface and procedure name drop-downs to add the Property Let procedures, the VB editor always uses RHS as the variable name for the new property value (because it represents the Right Hand Side of the property assignment expression). If the code will do anything other than just pass the value on to another procedure it's a good idea to give the variable a more meaningful name, in line with the best practices on naming conventions covered in Chapter 3, "Excel and VBA Development Best Practices."

Once we add the interface to all our classes, we can add the classes to a single collection, sort the collection using the ISortableObject interface, and iterate through it using the IContactDetails interface, shown in Listing 14-12. The ShowDetails procedure processes the contact details for each object in the collection, again using the IContactDetails interface, and is explained later.

Listing 14-12 Sorting and Listing Mixed Classes That Implement ISortableObject and IContactDetails

```
Sub CombinedIterateExample()

  Dim vItem As Variant
  Dim colMailList As Collection
  Dim clsAuthor As CAuthor
  Dim clsReviewer As CReviewer
  Dim clsDetails As IContactDetails

  Set colMailList = New Collection

  'Add the Authors to the collection
  For Each vItem In Array("Rob Bovey", "Dennis Wallentin", _
                          "Stephen Bullen", "John Green")
    Set clsAuthor = New CAuthor
    clsAuthor.AuthorName = CStr(vItem)
    colMailList.Add clsAuthor
  Next vItem

  'Add some Reviewers to the collection
  For Each vItem In Array("Bill Manville", "Jon Peltier")
    Set clsReviewer = New CReviewer
    clsReviewer.ReviewerName = CStr(vItem)
    colMailList.Add clsReviewer
  Next vItem

  'Sort the Mailing list using the generic procedure
  BubbleSortSortableObjects colMailList

  'Although colMailList is a collection of mixed object types,
  'they all implement the IContactDetails interface, so we can
  'process them all by using an object variable declared
```

```
'As IContactDetails
For Each clsDetails In colMailList
  ShowDetails clsDetails
Next clsDetails

End Sub
```

We can use the `TypeOf` function to test whether a class implements a certain interface. We can then switch (or cast) between interfaces by declaring a variable as the type of interface we want to look through and then setting it to refer to the object, as shown in Listing 14-13. Regardless of which interface we're looking through, the VBA `TypeName()` function always returns the object's class name.

Listing 14-13 Checking an Object's Interfaces

```
'Show the details of any given object
Sub ShowDetails(objUnknown As Object)

  'Two variables that we can use to look at the object
  'through two different interfaces
  Dim clsAuthor As CAuthor
  Dim clsDetails As IContactDetails

  'Check if this object has the full CAuthor interface
  If TypeOf objUnknown Is CAuthor Then

    'Yes, so look at the object through the CAuthor interface
    Set clsAuthor = objUnknown

    'Write a special message for the authors
    Debug.Print clsAuthor.AuthorName & " wrote the book"

  'Does the object implement the IContactDetails interface?
  ElseIf TypeOf objUnknown Is IContactDetails Then

    'Yes, so look at it through that interface
    Set clsDetails = objUnknown

    'And write a message for everyone that helped
    Debug.Print clsDetails.Name & " helped with the book"
  Else
    'An object we can't use, so write the class name
    Debug.Print "Unknown Object: " & TypeName(objUnknown)
```

```
    End If

End Sub
```

Improving Robustness

The ability to iterate through a collection of different object types could be achieved without using a custom interface by declaring the loop variable As Object and ensuring that all the classes we want to access have the same properties and methods. However, that makes the object late-bound, so it's slower and doesn't show any IntelliSense. Also, coding errors aren't caught until runtime, and all classes must use the same names for their properties. Had we tried to implement the preceding functionality with a generic Object type we would have had a few issues to resolve, including

- Having started with CAuthor.AuthorName and CReviewer.ReviewerName, we would have had to add a common .Name property to both, resulting in two properties that do the same thing. Alternatively, we could have checked the rest of the application and changed AuthorName and ReviewerName to Name wherever it was used.
- We would have to expose **all** the properties of the class on its single default interface, including those such as the SortKey property that are only used for specific internal functionality.
- We would have to rely on the **implicit** agreement that our objects have the correct property names. Any errors caused by missing, renamed, or simply mistyped properties won't be caught until runtime.

Taking the extra step to define and use a custom interface gives us all the benefits of early binding (speed, IntelliSense, and compile-time type checking) as well as **explicitly** stating how the classes and their consumers interact. This significantly improves the robustness of our applications.

Simplifying Development

One of the most useful tools in the Visual Basic Editor is the IntelliSense pop-up that appears upon typing a "." (or dot operator) after an object.

This pop-up lists all the methods and properties defined in the interface for that type of object. Unfortunately, when we try to set properties or call methods in a worksheet or UserForm class, the IntelliSense list contains so many items that it's hard to find the properties and methods we need to use.

If we follow the best practices for encapsulating our code, for example, we shouldn't set any of a UserForm's properties from outside the form. We should instead expose the form's functionality through our own properties and methods. When viewing the IntelliSense pop-up for a UserForm it shows our properties and methods mixed with those of the form. Defining and using our own interface for the form allows us to restrict the list of properties and methods to only those that we choose to expose.

A Progress Bar

Many applications include some form of progress indicator to show the status of lengthy operations. It's likely that such an indicator is used in multiple places in our application, so it makes sense to implement it as a common function that can be called from all our procedures. If we use an object-oriented design, we'd like to treat it just like any other object, using something like the code in Listing 14-14.

Listing 14-14   Using a ProgressBar Class

```
Sub LongProcedure()

  Dim pbProgBar As ProgressBar
  Dim iCounter As Integer

  Set pbProgBar = New ProgressBar

  pbProgBar.Title = "Professional Excel Development"
  pbProgBar.Text = "Preparing report, please wait..."
  pbProgBar.Min = 0
  pbProgBar.Max = 1000
  pbProgBar.Progress = 0
  pbProgBar.Show

  For iCounter = 0 To 1000
    pbProgBar.Progress = iCounter
  Next iCounter
```

```
pbProgBar.Hide

End Sub
```

There is nothing in this code to suggest that the progress indicator is a UserForm. The code is only saying that we want to display some type of progress indication to the user. The way in which it's presented is entirely encapsulated within the ProgressBar class and could easily be a UserForm, a message in the status bar, or an audible prompt.

To help other developers who might use the ProgressBar class, it would be ideal if the IntelliSense list only showed the seven properties and methods (Title, Text, Min, Max, Progress, Show, and Hide) that we should be using to control the progress bar. Unfortunately, if the ProgressBar is a UserForm class, the IntelliSense list shows our seven items lost among the other 57 properties and methods of UserForms.

As well as making it harder to pick out the correct properties and methods to use, exposing the normal UserForm properties makes it tempting for the consumer of the progress bar class to set some of the other properties of the form. At worst that could break the way in which the progress bar works, or make the progress bar appear differently in different parts of the application. At best it would make it much harder for us to modify the implementation of the progress bar itself, because our new implementation may break the nonstandard way in which the progress bar class has been used.

By using a custom interface, we can **guarantee** that all users of the progress bar class are only able to use the properties and methods that we define in that interface. Doing so removes the temptation to use the normal UserForm properties and makes it impossible for consumers of the class to use the progress bar form in nonstandard ways. This allows us to totally separate the *implementation* of the progress indicator from the *use* of the progress indicator. As long as we keep the same interface we could implement it as a UserForm or as a simple class module that just updates the status bar.

The IProgressBar Interface

As before, we define the interface to use for our progress bar form by creating a new class module, giving it the name IProgressBar, and adding empty procedures for each of the elements on the interface, as shown in Listing 14-15.

Listing 14-15 The IProgressBar Interface Class

```vb
'Set and get the title
Public Property Let Title(sNew As String)
End Property

Public Property Get Title() As String
End Property

'Set and get the descriptive text
Public Property Let Text(sNew As String)
End Property

Public Property Get Text() As String
End Property

'Set and get the minimum value for the bar
Public Property Let Min(dNew As Double)
End Property

Public Property Get Min() As Double
End Property

'Set and get the maximum value for the bar
Public Property Let Max(dNew As Double)
End Property

Public Property Get Max() As Double
End Property

'Set and get the progress point
Public Property Let Progress(dNew As Double)
End Property

Public Property Get Progress() As Double
End Property

'Show the progress bar
Public Sub Show()
End Sub

'Hide the progress bar
Public Sub Hide()
End Sub
```

The FProgressBar Form

The FProgressBar form implements the IProgressBar interface by displaying the progress indicator on a UserForm. The progress bar is made up of two superimposed Frames, each containing a label. The back frame and label is blue-on-white, while the front frame and label is white-on-blue. The progress measure controls the width of the front frame, to give the appearance of the progress bar shown in Figure 14-3.

FIGURE 14-3 A simple progress bar form

The complete FProgressBar form can be found on the CD in the workbook \Concepts\Ch14 – Interfaces\Progress Bars.xls, but is reproduced in a simple form in Listing 14-16.

Listing 14-16 The FProgressBar Form Module Implementing the IProgressBar Interface

```
'
' Name:         FProgressBar
' Description:   Displays a modeless progress bar on the screen
' Author:        Stephen Bullen

Option Explicit

' Implement the IProgressBar interface
Implements IProgressBar

' Store the Min, Max and Progress values in module variables
Dim mdMin As Double
Dim mdMax As Double
Dim mdProgress As Double
Dim mdLastPerc As Double

' Initialize the form to show blank text
Private Sub UserForm_Initialize()
  lblMessage.Caption = ""
  Me.Caption = ""
End Sub
```

```vb
'Ignore clicking the [x] on the dialog
Private Sub UserForm_QueryClose(Cancel As Integer, _
                                CloseMode As Integer)
  If CloseMode = vbFormControlMenu Then Cancel = True
End Sub


' Let the calling procedure set/get the caption of the form
Private Property Let IProgressBar_Title(RHS As String)
  Me.Caption = RHS
End Property


Private Property Get IProgressBar_Title() As String
  IProgressBar_Title = Me.Caption
End Property


' Let the calling procedure set/get the descriptive text
Private Property Let IProgressBar_Text(RHS As String)
  If RHS <> lblMessage.Caption Then
    lblMessage.Caption = RHS
  End If
End Property


Private Property Get IProgressBar_Text() As String
  IProgressBar_Text = lblMessage.Caption
End Property


' Let the calling procedure set/get the Minimum scale
Private Property Let IProgressBar_Min(RHS As Double)
  mdMin = RHS
End Property


Private Property Get IProgressBar_Min() As Double
  IProgressBar_Min = mdMin
End Property


' Let the calling procedure set the Maximum scale
Private Property Let IProgressBar_Max(RHS As Double)
  mdMax = RHS
End Property


Private Property Get IProgressBar_Max() As Double
  IProgressBar_Max = mdMax
End Property
```

```
' Let the calling procedure set the progress amount.
' Update the form to show the progress.
Private Property Let IProgressBar_Progress(RHS As Double)

  Dim dPerc As Double

  mdProgress = RHS

  'Calculate the progress percentage
  If mdMax = mdMin Then
    dPerc = 0
  Else
    dPerc = Abs((RHS - mdMin) / (mdMax - mdMin))
  End If

  'Only update the form every 0.5% change
  If Abs(dPerc - mdLastPerc) > 0.005 Then
    mdLastPerc = dPerc

    'Set the width of the inside frame,
    'rounding to the pixel
    fraInside.Width = Int(lblBack.Width * dPerc / _
                     0.75 + 1) * 0.75

    'Set the captions for the blue-on-white and
    'white-on-blue text
    lblBack.Caption = Format(dPerc, "0%")
    lblFront.Caption = Format(dPerc, "0%")

    'Refresh the form if it's being shown
    If Me.Visible Then
      Me.Repaint
    End If
  End If

End Property

Private Property Get IProgressBar_Progress() As Double
  IProgressBar_Progress = mdProgress
End Property


'Show the form modelessly
```

```
Private Sub IProgressBar_Show()
  Me.Show vbModeless
End Sub

'Hide the form
Private Sub IProgressBar_Hide()
  Me.Hide
End Sub
```

The only differences between this code and the "plain" Progress Bar form we saw in Chapter 13, "UserForm Design and Best Practices," are that the Title, Text, Min, Max, and Progress properties have been exposed via the IProgressBar interface and we added our own Show and Hide methods to show and hide the form using that interface.

The difference between the IntelliSense display when using our custom IProgressBar interface instead of the default UserForm interface can be seen in Figure 14-4 and Figure 14-5. By implementing the IProgressBar interface, the consumer of our progress bar form has a much clearer display of the properties and methods that should be used to control the progress bar. Figure 14-4 shows the IntelliSense pop-up we get if we add the progress bar properties directly to the form, while Figure 14-5 shows the much simpler IntelliSense list we get when using the custom interface.

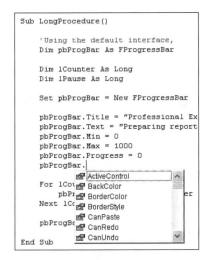

FIGURE 14-4 The default interface of the UserForm shows all properties in the IntelliSense list.

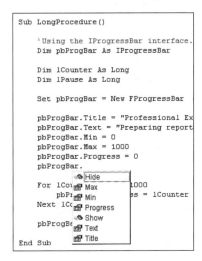

FIGURE 14-5 The custom IProgressBar interface limits the IntelliSense list to the items we want to expose.

The CProgressBar Class

Once we know the consumer of our progress indicator is accessing it through our custom interface, we are free to modify the implementation of the progress indicator any way we want. As long as we keep the interface the same we **know** the code that uses the class will continue to work. The opposite is also true. As consumers of the class we **know** that as long as the interface is kept the same, the creator of the class cannot change the name of any of the properties or methods and in doing so break our code. As an example, the code in Listing 14-17 implements the interface using a class module instead of a UserForm and displays the progress on Excel's status bar.

Listing 14-17   The CProgressBar Class Implementing the IProgressBar Interface

```
' Class to show a progress indication in the status bar.
' Implements to IProgressBar interface to allow easy switching
' between showing the progress on the statusbar (this class)
' or on a UserForm (the FProgressBar form).

Option Explicit

'Implement the IProgressBar interface
Implements IProgressBar

'Module-level variables to store the property values
Dim msTitle As String
Dim msText As String
Dim mdMin As Double
Dim mdMax As Double
Dim mdProgress As Double
Dim mbShowing As Boolean
Dim msLastCaption As String


'Assume an initial progress of 0-100
Private Sub Class_Initialize()
   mdMin = 0
   mdMax = 100
End Sub
```

```
'Set and get the title
Private Property Let IProgressBar_Title(RHS As String)
   msTitle = RHS
   If mbShowing Then UpdateStatusBar
End Property

Private Property Get IProgressBar_Title() As String
   IProgressBar_Title = msTitle
End Property


'Set and get the descriptive text
Private Property Let IProgressBar_Text(RHS As String)
   msText = RHS
   If mbShowing Then UpdateStatusBar
End Property

Private Property Get IProgressBar_Text() As String
   IProgressBar_Text = msText
End Property


'Set and get the minimum value for the bar
Private Property Let IProgressBar_Min(RHS As Double)
   mdMin = RHS
   If mbShowing Then UpdateStatusBar
End Property

Private Property Get IProgressBar_Min() As Double
   IProgressBar_Min = mdMin
End Property


'Set and get the maximum value for the bar
Private Property Let IProgressBar_Max(RHS As Double)
   mdMax = RHS
   If mbShowing Then UpdateStatusBar
End Property

Private Property Get IProgressBar_Max() As Double
   IProgressBar_Max = mdMax
End Property
```

```
'Set and get the progress point
Private Property Let IProgressBar_Progress(RHS As Double)
  mdProgress = RHS
  If mbShowing Then UpdateStatusBar
End Property

Private Property Get IProgressBar_Progress() As Double
  IProgressBar_Progress = msprogress
End Property


'Show the progress bar
Private Sub IProgressBar_Show()
  mbShowing = True
  mdLastProgress = 0
  UpdateStatusBar
End Sub


'Hide the progress bar
Private Sub IProgressBar_Hide()
  Application.StatusBar = False
  mbShowing = False
End Sub


'Private procedure to show the progress indication
'on the status bar
Private Sub UpdateStatusBar()

  Dim dPerc As Double
  Dim sCaption As String

  'Calculate the progress percentage
  If mdMax = mdMin Then
    dPerc = 0
  Else
    dPerc = Abs((mdProgress - mdMin) / (mdMax - mdMin))
  End If

  'Create the caption
  If Len(msTitle) > 0 Then sCaption = msTitle
```

```
If Len(msTitle) > 0 And Len(msText) > 0 Then
  sCaption = sCaption & ": "
End If

If Len(msText) > 0 Then sCaption = sCaption & msText

'Calculate and add the formatted percentage
sCaption = sCaption & " (" & Format$(dPerc, "0%") & ")"

'Update the status bar if it's changed
If sCaption <> msLastCaption Then
  msLastCaption = sCaption
  Application.StatusBar = sCaption
End If

End Sub
```

The calling code can very easily switch between using either the form or the status bar for the progress display, perhaps according to a user's preference, as shown in Listing 14-18.

Listing 14-18   Using the IProgressBar Interface Allows the Choice Between the Form or the Class

```
Sub LongProcedure(bProgressInForm As Boolean)

  'Always use the IProgressBar interface
  Dim pbProgBar As IProgressBar

  Dim iCounter As Integer

  If bProgressInForm Then
    'Use the progress bar form
    Set pbProgBar = New FProgressBar
  Else
    'Use the status bar class
    Set pbProgBar = New CProgressBar
  End If
```

```
'The rest of the code is unchanged
pbProgBar.Title = "Professional Excel Development"
pbProgBar.Text = "Preparing report, please wait..."
pbProgBar.Min = 0
pbProgBar.Max = 1000
pbProgBar.Progress = 0
pbProgBar.Show

For iCounter = 0 To 1000
   pbProgBar.Progress = iCounter
Next

pbProgBar.Hide

End Sub
```

A Plug-in Architecture

We saw in Chapter 13 how it is possible to create a user interface consisting of modeless UserForms, in which the interaction with the user occurs within UserForms (as opposed to worksheets) yet with the command bars still available. To allow the forms to respond to menu bar clicks we had to ensure that all our forms had the same basic set of procedures that could be called by our common menu handler. Those procedures were called BeforeNavigate, BeforeSave, AfterSave, and AppExit.

In fact, we created our own implicit interface without knowing it. By making that interface explicit, we can improve robustness and reliability and simplify the development of the application. We call this interface IPlugInForm and define it as shown in Listing 14-19, where we also add a Show method so we can show the form through this interface.

Listing 14-19 The IPlugInForm Interface Class

```
'Name:           IPlugInForm
'Description:     Interface to be implemented by each form

'The form's name
Public Property Get Name() As String
End Property

'Show the form
Public Sub Show(Optional ByVal Style As _
                FormShowConstants = vbModal)
End Sub


'The user clicked a menu item to navigate to a different form
'Save any changes on the form and unload
Public Sub BeforeNavigate(ByRef bCancel As Boolean)
End Sub

'The user clicked the Save button
'Save any changes on the form and unload
Public Sub BeforeSave(ByVal bSaveAs As Boolean, _
                ByRef bCancel As Boolean)
End Sub

'After the save completed
'Update the form with any new information
Public Sub AfterSave(ByVal bSaveAs As Boolean)
End Sub

'The user clicked the Close button to exit the application
'Tidy up and unload the form
Public Sub AppExit()
End Sub
```

If all our forms implement this interface, the central control procedure shown in Listing 13-26 in Chapter 13 can declare the gfrmActiveForm variable As IPlugInForm instead of As Object and call the same methods as before. Using the interface allows us to be explicit about what the code is doing, prevents typing errors, ensures none of our common procedures are accidentally deleted from the forms, and helps enforce a common structure throughout the application.

Practical Example

The PETRAS application files for this chapter can be found on the CD in the folder *\Application\Ch14 – Interfaces*.

PETRAS Time Sheet

The PETRAS time sheet add-in has not been updated for this chapter.

PETRAS Reporting

For this chapter, we modify the progress bar handling to display the consolidation progress unobtrusively in the status bar if we're consolidating fewer than ten time sheet workbooks, but pop up a cancelable progress bar UserForm if consolidating ten or more time sheets. We include the IProgressBar interface from Listing 14-15, the FProgressBar form from Listing 14-16, and the CProgressBar class from Listing 14-17.

In this example, the form has an extra Cancel button and the interface has been extended to include a Cancelled property that is set to True when the Cancel button is clicked. The code changes required for this enhancement are summarized in Table 14-1.

Table 14-1   Changes to the PETRAS Reporting Application for Chapter 14

Module	Procedure	Change
IProgressBar (new class)		Added class to define the IProgressBar interface, copied from Listing 14-15, adding Cancelable property.
CProgressBar (new class)		Added class to show the progress in the status bar, copied from Listing 14-17.
FProgressBar		Moved various methods to be exposed through the IProgressBar interface instead of the default interface. The resulting code is similar to Listing 14-16.
MSystemCode	ConsolidateWorkbooks	Modified to use the IProgressBar interface and test whether to use the CProgressBar class or FProgressBar form.

Summary

Whenever we create a class module in VBA, the compiler creates both the class and a default interface for it. The code in the class defines how the object behaves, while the interface defines how we access the code. With a small amount of effort we can define our own custom interfaces and implement them in our classes, allowing us to treat different classes as if they were the same type of object.

When developing UserForms we can use a custom interface to expose only the properties and methods that apply to the features we're providing, eliminating the clutter of an IntelliSense list filled with all the basic UserForm properties. By using these techniques, we can make our code more generic, robust, and reliable, as well as easier to write and maintain.

By implementing a standard custom interface in all our forms, reports, and processes, we can design an application architecture that is totally extensible, without requiring any changes to the core application. If working in a multideveloper team, this interface can be extended across workbooks, allowing each developer to work independently on the application's functions, safe in the knowledge that their work does not directly conflict with the work of any other developer.

CHAPTER 15

VBA ERROR HANDLING

Error handling is one of the most commonly omitted features in Excel applications. This is not an acceptable state of affairs. The last thing you want your users to see is an unvarnished Excel or VBA runtime error. They will most surely not understand what they are seeing, and they will often panic, lose faith in your application, or both. A good error handling system does not prevent errors from occurring, but it does make errors that do occur much less distressing to your users and much easier for you to diagnose and correct.

All the errors we talk about in this chapter are runtime errors—errors that occur while your code is executing. The other type of error, the compile-time error, should not be a factor at this point. A good developer will ensure his project cleanly passes a *Debug > Compile* in the VBE before attempting to run its code.

Error Handling Concepts

Unhandled Versus Handled Errors

Runtime errors fall into two broad categories: **unhandled errors** and **handled errors**. Simply put, an unhandled error is one that is not caught by an error handling mechanism in the procedure where it occurs, while a handled error is caught by such an error handler. This is not to imply that all unhandled errors are bad. There are situations where you can reasonably choose not to handle errors in a certain procedure, instead deferring them to an error handler further up the call stack. The error is converted from an unhandled error into a handled error at the point where it reaches an error handling mechanism. What is unacceptable is an error that remains unhandled all the way until it reaches the user. Figure 15-1 shows the result of an unhandled error.

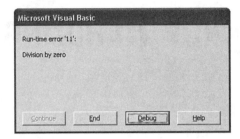

Figure 15-1 An unhandled error message

The Err Object

When any kind of runtime error occurs, the affected code is said to be in error mode. An intrinsic, global VBA object called the `Err` object is populated with information about the error. Almost every error handling mechanism makes use of the `Err` object, so it is helpful to understand its most commonly used properties and methods:

- **Err.Clear**—This method clears all the properties of the `Err` object, canceling the current error.
- **Err.Description**—This property contains a short string that describes the error.
- **Err.HelpFile**—This property contains the full path and filename of the help file containing a description of the error.
- **Err.HelpContext**—This property contains the help context ID of the topic within the help file that describes the error.
- **Err.LastDLLError**—Theoretically, this property returns any error code generated by calls to a DLL, such as a Windows API call. In practice, this value is unreliable because Windows may execute DLL functions automatically that overwrite the information in this property before your code gets a chance to look at it. This property occasionally provides useful information when you are actively debugging your code, but you should never rely on it in a production error handler.
- **Err.Number**—This property returns the number associated with the most recent runtime error. When your error handler needs to take different actions depending on the specific error that occurred, this is the property you should use to distinguish among different types of errors.
- **Err.Raise**—This method allows you to intentionally raise errors within your application. We discuss this topic in detail later in the chapter.

- **Err.Source**—This property identifies the source of the error. It is not very useful for providing information about VBA runtime errors because it simply returns the name of the project in which the error occurred. However, as we discuss later in this chapter, you can populate this property yourself with more detailed information when raising custom errors.

NOTE All contents of the Err object are cleared automatically when code execution encounters a Resume statement, an On Error statement, Exit Sub, Exit Function, Exit Property, End Sub, End Function, or End Property.

What Is an Error Handler?

An error handler is a labeled section of a procedure that you designate as the place where code execution will be redirected whenever a runtime error occurs within that procedure. An On Error Goto <Label> statement, discussed in the next section, is used to designate an error handler. The error handler must be a separate block of code within the procedure, with the only way into it being an error and the only way out of it being a Resume, Exit Sub, Exit Function, or Exit Property. Listing 15-1 shows an example of a procedure with a simple error handler.

Listing 15-1   A Procedure with a Simple Error Handler

```
Public Sub MyProcedure()

    On Error GoTo ErrorHandler

    ' Lots of code here.

    Exit Sub

ErrorHandler:
    MsgBox Err.Description, vbCritical, "Error!"
End Sub
```

In this procedure, the section of code identified by the ErrorHandler label is designated as the error handler for the procedure when the On Error GoTo ErrorHandler statement is executed. Note the Exit Sub statement prior to the ErrorHandler section. This prevents the procedure from executing the code in the ErrorHandler section if no error has occurred.

Designating a section of code as an error handler **enables** it. When a runtime error occurs and code execution is redirected to the error handler, the error handler is said to be **active**. This difference is not academic. If an error handler is active (currently in the process of handling an error) and another error occurs as a result of something the code in that error handler does, the new error cannot be handled by the same error handler. If this situation occurs, control is passed to the error handler of the next highest procedure in the call stack or an unhandled error is generated if there is no higher-level error handler available.

Why is this important? There are some circumstances in which you need to perform an operation that may generate another error inside an error handler. If this is the case, put this code into a separate procedure with its own error handler and call that procedure from the active error handler. Multiple error handlers can be active at the same time, so an error that occurs in, and is handled by, this separate procedure will not affect the error handler that called it.

NOTE There is only a single global `Err` object. Its properties are set by the error that occurred most recently. If you think you will run into an error within an error situation, as described previously, save any information about the original error in your own variables so you don't lose it.

Error Handler Scope

The scope of an error handler, which is the body of code that will activate it if a runtime error occurs, includes the procedure the error handler is defined in as well as any called procedures that do not have their own error handlers. If a calling procedure has a designated error handler but the procedures it calls do not, the error handler of the calling procedure will be activated by any errors that occur. The simple code example in Listing 15-2 illustrates this more clearly.

Listing 15-2 The Scope of an Error Handler

```
Public Sub EntryPointProcedure()

    On Error GoTo ErrorHandler
```

```
    SubProcedure1

    Exit Sub

ErrorHandler:
    MsgBox Err.Description, vbCritical, "Error!"
End Sub

Private Sub SubProcedure1()
    SubProcedure2
End Sub

Private Sub SubProcedure2()
    Dim lTest As Long
    ' This error will activate the error handler
    ' in the entry point procedure.
    lTest = 1 / 0
End Sub
```

In this example, only EntryPointProcedure has defined an error handler. EntryPointProcedure calls SubProcedure1, and SubProcedure1 calls SubProcedure2. If a runtime error occurs in **any** of these three procedures, code execution immediately branches to the error handler defined in EntryPointProcedure.

There are some cases where this is a valid and reasonable error handling technique, but usually it's not the best choice. First, you lose any information about where the error actually occurred. Second, if any of the called procedures need to perform cleanup prior to exiting (destroy objects, close connections, reset public variables, and so on), this cleanup code will be skipped. Code execution branches unconditionally to the error handler in the top-level procedure, and it cannot be made to return to the procedure where the error occurred (even with the use of the `Resume` statement, which we discuss later in the chapter). For these reasons, it is usually best if each procedure in your application handles its own errors.

The On Error Statement

The three variants of the `On Error` statement provide the foundation of VBA's error handling capability.

On Error GoTo <Label>

This statement is used to specify an error handler for a procedure. Literally, what it tells VBA to do is redirect code execution to the line in the procedure identified by <Label> when a runtime error occurs. All code below this line is considered the error handler for the procedure.

On Error Resume Next

This statement is both dangerous and useful at the same time. It tells VBA to ignore any errors that occur and continue with the next line of code until you tell it to do otherwise. First let's make it very clear what you should not do with this statement. All too often I receive code from a client where the first line in several large procedures is On Error Resume Next. Don't do this! On Error Resume Next is not a substitute for writing code correctly in the first place. If you have a large procedure that will not run unless you place On Error Resume Next at the top of it, then that procedure is almost certainly poorly written.

With that out of the way, let's talk about the circumstances in which On Error Resume Next is useful and necessary. You sometimes encounter situations where you expect an error to occur during normal program execution. In cases like this you do not want the error to activate your error handler. Instead you want code execution to continue in some conditional fashion based on whether an error occurred.

For example, assume a procedure needs to use an existing workbook that may or may not be open when the procedure is executed. In this case, you would use On Error Resume Next to temporarily bypass error handling while you determine whether the workbook is open. The moment you finish this test you would re-enable the error handler using the On Error Goto <Label> statement. Listing 15-3 shows an example of this.

Listing 15-3   When to Use On Error Resume Next

```
Public Sub OnErrorResumeNextDemo()

    Dim wkbCalcs As Workbook

    On Error GoTo ErrorHandler

    ' Lots of code here.

    ' Test if the Calcs.xls workbook is open.
    Set wkbCalcs = Nothing
    On Error Resume Next
        Set wkbCalcs = Application.Workbooks("Calcs.xls")
```

```
On Error GoTo ErrorHandler

' If the workbook wasn't open we need to open it.
If wkbCalcs Is Nothing Then
    Set wkbCalcs = Application.Workbooks.Open( _
                    ThisWorkbook.Path & "\Calcs.xls")
End If

' Lots more code here.

Exit Sub

ErrorHandler:
    MsgBox Err.Description, vbCritical, "Error!"
End Sub
```

Notice that On Error Resume Next is used to disable error handling for just the single line of code that determines whether the Calcs.xls workbook is already open. This is a best practice. Always keep the number of lines of code affected by On Error Resume Next to an absolute minimum. If you do not turn it off immediately once you no longer need it, you will very likely suppress errors you did not intend to suppress.

As with almost all rules, there are a few exceptions to the ban on entire procedures being "wrapped" in On Error Resume Next. The first situation concerns a special type of procedure in which an error is an integral part of the logic of the procedure. In the code in Listing 15-3, for example, we could substitute the in-place test for the Calcs.xls workbook being open with a general purpose function that could be used anywhere this type of test is required. The result would look like the function in Listing 15-4, which is wrapped entirely in On Error Resume Next by design.

Listing 15-4   An Entire Function Wrapped in On Error Resume Next

```
Private Function bIsBookOpen(ByVal sBookName As String, _
                ByRef wkbBook As Workbook) As Boolean
    ' Checks to see if the specified workbook is open. If it is,
    ' a reference to it is returned in the wkbBook argument.
    On Error Resume Next
    Set wkbBook = Application.Workbooks(sBookName)
    bIsBookOpen = Not wkbBook Is Nothing
End Function
```

The second situation that requires wrapping an entire procedure in `On Error Resume Next` involves application shutdown code. When your application is closing, you typically attempt to perform some cleanup. If an error occurs during this process, there really isn't anything useful an error handler can accomplish. It's typically better to use `On Error Resume Next` to bypass any errors and continue performing whatever cleanup the application can accomplish before it closes. You can see an example of this in the shutdown code for our sample add-in.

The third situation that requires wrapping an entire procedure in `On Error Resume Next` involves class Terminate events. When your class is in the process of going away, there's not much point in activating an error handler. The best choice when an error occurs in this type of procedure is usually to skip the line that caused the error and continue to execute as much of the code as possible. We cover these cases later in the chapter.

On Error GoTo 0

This statement disables any previously enabled error handler in the current procedure. It has no effect in procedures that do not contain error handling, even if they have been called by a higher-level procedure that does contain error handling. In Listing 15-2 for example, placing `On Error GoTo 0` in SubProcedure1 would not prevent errors that occurred in that procedure from being handled by the still enabled error handler in EntryPointProcedure.

The Resume Statement

The `Resume` statement is used to deactivate an error handler and cause code execution to resume at a specific location that depends on which variation of the statement is used. The `Resume` statement can only be used inside an active error handler. Using it under any other circumstance will cause a runtime error to occur.

A `Resume` statement can only cause code execution to resume at some point within the procedure where the current error handler is located. This means if the current error handler has trapped an error from a lower level procedure, `Resume` cannot cause code execution to return to that procedure.

You must be very careful with the `Resume` statement because you can easily create an infinite loop in your code with it. There are three variations of the `Resume` statement as discussed in the following sections.

Resume

This is the most dangerous `Resume` statement of them all. It causes code execution to return to the line of code that caused the error (or the call to a subprocedure where the error originated if the error did not originate in the current procedure). The implicit assumption is that your error handler has done something to correct the error condition before calling `Resume`. If this is not the case, the error simply occurs again, triggering the error handler, which resumes execution on the line of code that caused the error and so on. This is the dreaded infinite loop condition, and in many situations the only way to stop it is to use Ctrl+Alt+Del to shut down Excel.

With this warning very clear, however, the `Resume` statement can be useful. If you are attempting to make a connection to a remote database over a slow or congested network, for example, it is not uncommon to fail one or more times. When a connection failure occurs, an error is thrown and your error handler is activated. You can increment a counter in your error handler and use `Resume` to try connecting again. If you are unable to connect successfully after a certain number of attempts, you can have your error handler bail out with an error message to the user. We demonstrate this use of `Resume` in Chapter 19, "Programming with Access and SQL Server."

The `Resume` statement is also useful within the context of built-in debugging aids. When your code has a special flag that indicates it is in debug mode, your error handler can direct code execution to a branch that automatically places the code in break mode and allows you to resume code execution on the line of code that generated the error. This allows you to debug the problem much more easily. You see error handling constructs that assist debug mode in this chapter, but we do not cover debugging in detail until Chapter 16, "VBA Debugging."

Resume Next

The `Resume Next` statement causes code execution to continue on the first executable line of code after the one that generated the error. The `Resume Next` statement does not return to a lower-level procedure if that is where the error was generated. Instead, it resumes execution in the procedure that handled the error on the line of code immediately following the call to the procedure where the error was generated.

15. VBA ERROR HANDLING

Resume <Label>

The `Resume <Label>` statement causes code execution to continue on the line of code following the specified label. The label must be located in the same procedure as the error handler. Like the `Resume` statement, the `Resume <Label>` statement can cause an infinite loop in your code if the code that originally caused the error is located below the specified label.

Raising Custom Errors

Although it may seem counterintuitive, deliberately generating runtime errors in your code can be a useful technique that is fully supported by VBA. The reasons for using custom errors are better dealt with in the context of procedure error handling as a whole, so we defer a detailed discussion of this topic until later in the chapter. In this section we cover only the mechanics of raising custom errors.

Custom errors are raised using the `Raise` method of the `Err` object. The syntax of this method is the following:

```
Err.Raise Number, Source, Description, HelpFile, HelpContext
```

The arguments to the `Err.Raise` method correspond to the properties of the `Err` object, which we described above. When you raise a custom error you can set these arguments however you like. All arguments other than the Number argument are optional.

One caveat is you can't use an error number for a custom error that is already used by an Excel or VBA error (you can raise predefined errors using their error numbers). The numbers from 1024 through 65535 should be available for custom errors. VBA also provides the special constant `vbObjectError` for creating custom error numbers that are typically used with classes. Any number added to the `vbObjectError` constant is guaranteed to be an error number that is not used by any Windows process. An example of a custom error number created using the `vbObjectError` constant is shown below:

```
Err.Raise vbObjectError + 1024
```

The Source argument of the error should be set to the name of the procedure in which the error was raised. The Description of a custom error should be a reasonably brief but clear description of the reason the error was raised. The HelpFile and HelpContextID arguments allow you to provide the user with additional information about the error if your project uses a help file. Otherwise, these arguments can be ignored. Help files are covered in more detail in Chapter 29, "Providing Help, Securing, Packaging, and Distributing."

The Single Exit Point Principle

One of the best architectural practices in any procedure is to have a single exit point. This means that once your error handler finishes handling an error, it should redirect code execution back into the body of the procedure so the procedure exits at the same point under all circumstances. The practical reason for this is that it's common for some type of cleanup to be required before a procedure exits. Even if a procedure currently requires no cleanup, this may very well change as a result of some future code modification. A single exit point prevents you from having to duplicate this cleanup code in the error handler.

The mechanism for implementing a single exit point is the `Resume <Label>` statement discussed previously. In this case `<Label>` identifies the point in each procedure at which code execution resumes after an error has occurred and been handled. We give this label the name `ErrorExit`. The `ErrorExit` label has no effect on code execution when the procedure completes without error. Normal code execution simply passes this label and continues on to the end of the procedure. When an error occurs, however, this label identifies the point at which the error handler should resume code execution once an error has been handled. This guarantees that code execution completes at the same point in a procedure whether or not an error has occurred. We show examples of single exit point procedures in the sections that follow.

Simple Error Handling

In the simplest form of error handling, error handlers are placed only in **entry point procedures**. Entry point procedures are those procedures from which code execution can be initiated. They are typically the procedures assigned to menu items, toolbar buttons, or controls placed on worksheets. Most event procedures are also entry points, because they initiate execution based on some action made by the user.

If the error handler in an entry point procedure is the only error handler in its call stack, this error handler traps all errors that occur in all lower level procedures. A simple error handler displays an error message to the user and exits the procedure. An example of this is shown in Listing 15-5.

Listing 15-5 An Example of a Simple Error Handler

```
Public Sub MyEntryPoint()

    On Error GoTo ErrorHandler

    ' Your code here.

ErrorExit:

    Exit Sub

ErrorHandler:
    MsgBox Err.Description, vbCritical, "Application Name"
    Resume ErrorExit
End Sub
```

Simple error handlers are appropriate only for the most trivial applications. An example might be a utility add-in that provides a number of simple features that require a small amount of code and do not require any significant cleanup. The primary purpose of a simple error handler is to shield users from raw runtime errors like the one shown in Figure 15-1 at the beginning of the chapter.

Complex Project Error Handler Organization

There are several complex error handling designs commonly used in Excel VBA applications and minor variations on each of them. If designed correctly, all of them accomplish the same purpose: gracefully handling runtime errors encountered by your application. The complex error handing system we introduce in this section has the following characteristics:

- All non-trivial procedures contain error handlers.
- All procedure error handlers call a central error handling function. This function tracks and logs each error, decides whether to display an error message to the user, and tells the calling procedure how to proceed by way of its return value.
- All entry point procedures are subroutines. An entry point procedure is any procedure in which code execution begins. This includes

subroutines in standard modules called by toolbar buttons and event procedures executed in response to some user action.

- All non-trivial lower-level procedures (all procedures that are called by entry point procedures) are Boolean functions whose return value indicates whether the function succeeded or failed.

We cover all these points in detail as this section progresses, but we want to give you a high-level overview of how our error-handling system works.

An important point to keep in mind as you read this section is that entry point procedures must only be triggered directly by some user action. One entry point procedure must never call another entry point procedure or the error handling system described here will break down. If two entry point procedures need to run the same code, the common code should be factored out into a lower-level function that can be called by both entry point procedures.

Procedure Error Handlers

In Listing 15-6, we show two error handling procedure skeletons. The first is an example of an entry point subroutine, the second an example of a lower-level, Boolean function. We placed a call from the entry point subroutine to the lower-level function to demonstrate how the error handling system would work. We explain the purpose of the various constants shown in Listing 15-6 as well as the function call inside the error handlers in "The Central Error Handler" section later in the chapter.

Listing 15-6 Subroutine and Function Error Handlers

```
Private Const msMODULE As String = "MMyModule"

Public Sub MyEntryPointSubroutine()

    Const sSOURCE As String = "MyEntryPointSubroutine()"

    On Error GoTo ErrorHandler

    ' Call the lower level function.
    If Not bMyLowerLevelFunction() Then
        Err.Raise glHANDLED_ERROR
    End If
```

```
ErrorExit:

    On Error Resume Next
    ' Cleanup code here.

    Exit Sub

ErrorHandler:
    If bCentralErrorHandler(msMODULE, sSOURCE, , True) Then
        Stop
        Resume
    Else
        Resume ErrorExit
    End If
End Sub

Private Function bMyLowerLevelFunction() As Boolean

    Const sSOURCE As String = "bMyLowerLevelFunction()"

    Dim bReturn As Boolean ' The function return value

    On Error GoTo ErrorHandler

    ' Assume success until an error is encountered.
    bReturn = True

    ' Operational code here.

ErrorExit:

    On Error Resume Next
    ' Cleanup code here.

    bMyLowerLevelFunction = bReturn
    Exit Function

ErrorHandler:
    bReturn = False
    If bCentralErrorHandler(msMODULE, sSOURCE) Then
        Stop
        Resume
    Else
```

```
        Resume ErrorExit
    End If
End Function
```

The general layout of the error handlers is similar in both cases. The only significant difference is the function must return a value indicating success or failure without violating the single exit point principle, so we added the structure required to accomplish that to the function's error handler.

Listing 15-6 shows examples of simple error handlers. They don't try to respond to errors other than by invoking the central error handler and exiting. In many situations, you will be aware of errors that might occur but can be corrected in the error handler and allow code execution to continue. A more complex error handler, such as the one shown in Listing 15-7, allows you to accomplish this.

Listing 15-7 A More Complex Error Handler

```
ErrorHandler:

    Select Case Err.Number

    Case 58
        ' File already exists. Resolve the problem and resume.
        Resume
    Case 71
        ' Disk not ready. Resolve the problem and resume.
        Resume
    Case Else
        ' The error can't be resolved here. Invoke the central
        ' error handling procedure.
        If bCentralErrorHandler(msMODULE, sSOURCE, , True) Then
            ' If the program is in debug mode, execution
            ' continues here.
            Stop
            Resume
        Else
            Resume ErrorExit
        End If
    End Select

End Function
```

A `Select Case` statement is used to identify error numbers that can be handled within the error handler. If the error number of the trapped error is not one of those handled by a specific `Case` clause it falls through to the `Case Else` clause, which invokes the central error handler.

NOTE   In the context of error handling, the term **trap** refers to an error handler being activated by an error. It is synonymous with the word **catch**, which is commonly used in its place.

A typical error handling scenario based on the examples shown in Listings 15-6 and 15-7 would play out something like this:

- The MyEntryPointSubroutine calls bMyLowerLevelFunction to perform some operation.
- An error occurs in bMyLowerLevelFunction that cannot be handled by its error handler.
- The error handler in bMyLowerLevelFunction calls the central error handler.
- The central error handler logs the error and passes a value back to bMyLowerLevelFunction that tells it to exit.
- bMyLowerLevelFunction exits and returns False to the MyEntryPointSubroutine calling procedure.
- In MyEntryPointSubroutine, a custom error is raised (because bMyLowerLevelFunction returned False), which then calls the central error handler again.
- Because an entry point subroutine called the central error handler, an error message is displayed to the user.
- After the central error handler has completed its duties, code execution resumes in the MyEntryPointSubroutine, which then exits.

In "The Central Error Handler" section later in the chapter, we describe how the central error handler determines when an error message should be displayed and how it influences program execution after an error is handled.

Trivial Procedures

At the beginning of this section, we stated that all **non-trivial** procedures contain error handlers. That begs the question of what is a trivial procedure that wouldn't require an error handler. A trivial procedure is either so simple that an error cannot occur within it or is structured so that any errors that do occur are ignored. Listing 15-8 shows examples of both types.

Listing 15-8   Trivial Procedures Don't Require Error Handlers

```
' This subroutine is so simple that no errors
' will ever be generated within it.
Public Sub ResetAppProperties()
    Application.StatusBar = False
    Application.ScreenUpdating = True
    Application.DisplayAlerts = True
    Application.EnableEvents = True
    Application.EnableCancelKey = xlInterrupt
    Application.Cursor = xlDefault
End Sub


' Any errors that occur in this function are ignored.
Private Function bIsBookOpen(ByVal sBookName As String, _
                    ByRef wkbBook As Workbook) As Boolean
    On Error Resume Next
    Set wkbBook = Application.Workbooks(sBookName)
    bIsBookOpen = (Len(wkbBook.Name) > 0)
End Function
```

The Central Error Handler

The central error handler is the heart of any complex error handling system. It consists of a procedure designed to log errors to an error log file or other persistent location and display error messages to the user, as well as provide facilities that allow the programmer to debug errors during development (we cover debugging in detail in Chapter 16). The module that contains the central error handler also contains all error handling-related constants, making the error handling system fully encapsulated. Listing 15-9 shows an example of a complete central error handler.

Listing 15-9   A Central Error Handler

```
Public Const gbDEBUG_MODE As Boolean = False
Public Const glHANDLED_ERROR As Long = 9999
Public Const glUSER_CANCEL As Long = 18

Private Const msSILENT_ERROR As String = "UserCancel"
Private Const msFILE_ERROR_LOG As String = "Error.log"

Public Function bCentralErrorHandler( _
            ByVal sModule As String, _
            ByVal sProc As String, _
            Optional ByVal sFile As String, _
            Optional ByVal bEntryPoint As Boolean) As Boolean

    Static sErrMsg As String

    Dim iFile As Integer
    Dim lErrNum As Long
    Dim sFullSource As String
    Dim sPath As String
    Dim sLogText As String

    ' Grab the error info before it's cleared by
    ' On Error Resume Next below.
    lErrNum = Err.Number
    ' If this is a user cancel, set the silent error flag
    ' message. This will cause the error to be ignored.
    If lErrNum = glUSER_CANCEL Then sErrMsg = msSILENT_ERROR
    ' If this is the originating error, the static error
    ' message variable will be empty. In that case, store
    ' the originating error message in the static variable.
    If Len(sErrMsg) = 0 Then sErrMsg = Err.Description

    ' We cannot allow errors in the central error handler.
    On Error Resume Next

    ' Load the default filename if required.
    If Len(sFile) = 0 Then sFile = ThisWorkbook.Name

    ' Get the application directory.
    sPath = ThisWorkbook.Path
    If Right$(sPath, 1) <> "\" Then sPath = sPath & "\"

    ' Construct the fully-qualified error source name.
```

```
sFullSource = "[" & sFile & "]" & sModule & "." & sProc

' Create the error text to be logged.
sLogText = " " & sFullSource & ", Error " & _
                    CStr(lErrNum) & ": " & sErrMsg

' Open the log file, write out the error information and
' close the log file.
iFile = FreeFile()
Open sPath & msFILE_ERROR_LOG For Append As #iFile
Print #iFile, Format$(Now(), "mm/dd/yy hh:mm:ss"); sLogText
If bEntryPoint Then Print #iFile,
Close #iFile

' Do not display silent errors.
If sErrMsg <> msSILENT_ERROR Then

        ' Show the error message when we reach the entry point
        ' procedure or immediately if we are in debug mode.
        If bEntryPoint Or gbDEBUG_MODE Then
            Application.ScreenUpdating = True
            MsgBox sErrMsg, vbCritical, gsAPP_TITLE
            ' Clear the static error message variable once
            ' we've reached the entry point so that we're ready
            ' to handle the next error.
            sErrMsg = vbNullString
        End If

        ' The return value is the debug mode status.
        bCentralErrorHandler = gbDEBUG_MODE

Else
        ' If this is a silent error, clear the static error
        ' message variable when we reach the entry point.
        If bEntryPoint Then sErrMsg = vbNullString
        bCentralErrorHandler = False
End If

End Function
```

This is a lot of code to digest, so let's dissect it piece by piece. First the constant declarations:

- **gbDEBUG_MODE**—This public Boolean constant is used by the developer to set the debug mode status of the application. When you are testing your application or attempting to locate errors in your code you want your error handlers to behave differently than they do when your application is deployed to end users. Setting the gbDEBUG_MODE constant to True causes the central error handler function to display an error message immediately after an error occurs and then return True.

  As shown in Listings 15-6 and 15-7, when the central error handler function returns True, the procedure error handler drops into a VBA Stop statement that is followed by a Resume statement. The Stop statement puts the project into Break mode, and the Resume statement allows you to single-step back to the line of code in the procedure where the error occurred. You can then debug the error. Again, we discuss debugging in detail in Chapter 16.

- **glHANDLED_ERROR**—This public Long constant is an error number you can use to raise custom errors. As we discussed in the section on raising custom errors, when you raise a custom error you must supply an error number not already used by Excel or VBA. The glHANDLED_ERROR constant has a value of 9999, which is not within the range of error number values used by VBA. It also has the advantage of being easily recognizable as a custom error number for debugging purposes. In all but the most complex error handling scenarios, a single custom error number can be used for all of your custom errors.

- **glUSER_CANCEL**—This public Long constant is set to the VBA error value 18. This error value occurs when the user cancels program execution by pressing the Esc or Ctrl+Break keys. Unless it is absolutely critical that your program not be interrupted, such as during startup and shutdown, you should always allow the user to halt program execution. The best way to do this is to add the following statement at the beginning of each entry point procedure:

  ```
  Application.EnableCancelKey = xlErrorHandler
  ```

  This causes VBA to treat a user cancel as a runtime error with an Err.Number = 18 that is routed through your error handler. When the central error handler sees this error number, it converts it into a special error message string (covered next) that causes the error to be ignored.

- **msSILENT_ERROR**—This private String constant is assigned to the static error message variable in the central error handling function whenever a user cancel error (Err.Number = glUSER_CANCEL) is detected.

Because this error message variable is static, it holds its value between calls to the central error handler. This means no matter how deep in the call stack the program was when the user canceled execution, the error handler passes the error up the stack and out the entry point procedure without displaying an error message to the user. Silent errors also do not trigger the procedure debugging mechanism, even if the application is in debug mode. Silent errors are written to the error log file because experience has taught us that it is often useful to see when users have canceled code execution.

- **msFILE_ERROR_LOG**—This private String constant specifies the name of the text file to which all error messages will be written. The error log file is always located in the same directory as the workbook containing the central error handler. The information stored in the error log file is designed to help you debug errors that have occurred on a user's computer that you may not necessarily have access to. The error log file shows you the exact error message, the procedure where the error originated, and the call stack that led to the error. When combined with a brief verbal report from the user about exactly what they were doing when the error occurred, this information is usually sufficient to allow you to debug the problem.

Now we examine the code in the central error handler function line-by-line to see how an error is treated under various conditions. First let's look at the arguments to the function. The first three arguments to the bCentralErrorHandler function identify the code module, procedure, and file name from which the function was called. This information is written to the error log file for use in debugging runtime errors. The fourth argument to the bCentralErrorHandler function indicates whether it was called from an entry point procedure. If the application is not in debug mode, an error message is displayed to the user only when the error reaches the originating entry point procedure. If the application is in debug mode, the fourth argument is ignored, an error message is displayed immediately, and the central error handler returns False so that you can begin debugging the error.

Notice that within the bCentralErrorHandler function we declared a static String variable. This variable is used to store the original error message so we can display it to the user once we reach the entry point, regardless of how many procedures deep in the stack we are when the error occurs. This static variable holds its value until we explicitly change it.

As soon as code execution enters the bCentralErrorHandler function, we must read and store any information we need from the VBA Err object. The reason for this becomes apparent very shortly.

```
lErrNum = Err.Number
' If this is a user cancel, set the silent error flag
' message. This will cause the error to be ignored.
If lErrNum = glUSER_CANCEL Then sErrMsg = msSILENT_ERROR
' If this is the originating error, the static error
' message variable will be empty. In that case, store
' the originating error message in the static variable.
If Len(sErrMsg) = 0 Then sErrMsg = Err.Description
```

First we read and store the error number. Next, if the error number indicates the user canceled program execution, we store the gsSILENT_ERROR flag message in our static error message variable. If the error number does not indicate a user cancel and the static error message variable does not already contain a value, we store the error description in the static error message variable. In this way, we store only the original error message and persist it through any additional calls to the central error handler function. The static variable will be cleared after the entry point procedure has been reached and the error message displayed to the user.

The reason we must persist any necessary Err object values immediately upon entering the central error handler function is because we cannot allow any errors to occur in this function. Therefore the entire function is wrapped in On Error Resume Next:

```
' We cannot allow errors in the central error handler.
On Error Resume Next
```

As soon as code execution passes the On Error Resume Next statement, all properties of the Err object are automatically cleared. If you have not stored the original values from the Err object's properties at this point they are lost forever. In the next section of code we construct several String values the error handler requires.

```
' Load the default filename if required.
If Len(sFile) = 0 Then sFile = ThisWorkbook.Name

' Get the application directory.
sPath = ThisWorkbook.Path
If Right$(sPath, 1) <> "\" Then sPath = sPath & "\"

' Construct the fully-qualified error source name.
sFullSource = "[" & sFile & "]" & sModule & "." & sProc

' Create the error text to be logged.
sLogText = " " & sFullSource & ", Error " & _
                CStr(lErrNum) & ": " & sErrMsg
```

You will notice from Listing 15-9 that the sFile argument is optional. If no value for this argument is passed, the central error handler assumes it is being called from within the current workbook and it loads this argument's value with `ThisWorkbook.Name`. The next task is to get the path to the current workbook. This is where the error log file will be created (or updated if it has already been created). In the next line of code we construct a fully qualified location that identifies where the call to the bCentralErrorHandler function originated. This location identifier has the following format:

```
[FileName]CodeModuleName.ProcedureName
```

The last string we construct in this section is the complete error log file entry. This consists of the fully qualified location string created previously, prefixed with the date and time the error occurred and suffixed with the error number and the error message. We see examples of actual error log file entries later in this chapter.

Our next task is to write the entry to the application error log file. As shown in the following code, we use standard VBA file I/O techniques to create or append to the error log file:

```
' Open the log file, write out the error information and
' close the log file.
iFile = FreeFile()
Open sPath & msFILE_ERROR_LOG For Append As #iFile
Print #iFile, Format$(Now(), "mm/dd/yy hh:mm:ss"); sLogText
If bEntryPoint Then Print #iFile,
Close #iFile
```

We first acquire an available file number and use it to create or open the error log file specified by the `msFILE_ERROR_LOG` constant and located in the path created in the previous section. We then write the log file entry string created previously to the log file. If the bCentralErrorHandler function has been called by an entry point procedure, we write an additional blank line to the error log file to provide visual separation between this and subsequent errors. Finally, we close the error log file.

The last section of the central error handler determines if and when an error message is displayed to the user and whether to trigger debug mode behavior in the procedure that called it.

```
' Do not display or debug silent errors.
If sErrMsg <> msSILENT_ERROR Then

    ' Show the error message when we reach the entry point
```

```
' procedure or immediately if we are in debug mode.
If bEntryPoint Or gbDEBUG_MODE Then
    Application.ScreenUpdating = True
    MsgBox sErrMsg, vbCritical, gsAPP_TITLE
    ' Clear the static error message variable once
    ' we've reached the entry point so that we're ready
    ' to handle the next error.
    sErrMsg = vbNullString
End If


' The return vale is the debug mode status.
bCentralErrorHandler = gbDEBUG_MODE

Else
    ' If this is a silent error, clear the static error
    ' message variable when we reach the entry point.
    If bEntryPoint Then sErrMsg = vbNullString
    bCentralErrorHandler = False
End If
```

The value contained in the static sErrMsg variable is used to determine when to display an error message and when to ignore it. Remember that this variable holds the value of the original error message that triggered the central error handler. If the value of the sErrMsg variable indicates the original error was the result of the user canceling program execution, no error message is displayed, the static error message variable is cleared to prepare the central error handler for the next error, and the return value of the central error handler is False, so as not to trigger any debug actions.

If the static error message variable indicates any error other than a user cancel error, then an error message is displayed. If the application is in debug mode (gbDEBUG_MODE = True), an error message is displayed as soon as the error occurs and the central error handler returns True so the calling procedure can begin executing debug code. If the application is not in debug mode, an error message is displayed only when the call stack has been completely unwound and the original entry point procedure has been reached. When not in debug mode, the central error handler function returns False throughout so as not to trigger any procedure-level debug code.

Error Handling in Classes and UserForms

Classes and UserForms present some unique error handling challenges that we cover in this section. As we explained previously, event procedures in classes and UserForms should almost always be considered entry point procedures. The Initialize, Activate, and Terminate events are exceptions to this rule. The user does not directly trigger these events. Instead, they are fired as a side effect of a class being created or destroyed or a UserForm being created, shown, or destroyed.

If there are no error handlers in these event procedures, any errors that occur in the code they contain result in unhandled errors. Errors that occur in these event procedures cannot be handled by error handlers in the procedure that created the class or UserForm. This is a quirk in the way VBA error handling operates and there is no workaround.

Because of this, your best option is either not to use these event procedures at all or only to place code in them that is not critical to the functionality of the class or UserForm and then wrap that code in On Error Resume Next.

Initialize and Activate Events

Errors that occur in the Initialize or Activate events during class and/or UserForm creation are typically catastrophic errors that render the class or UserForm in which they occur unusable. These errors cannot normally be handled in any way that would mitigate them. For this reason, it is critical to be able to pass control back to the error handler of the calling procedure.

The best way to do this is to create a custom Initialize method. This is a Boolean function that would be called explicitly by your code after creation of the class or UserForm. The custom Initialize method would replace the Initialize and/or Activate event procedures for the purpose of preparing a class or UserForm for use. In the "Putting It All Together" section, we show an example of a custom Initialize method in a UserForm.

Terminate Events

Errors that occur in Terminate events are unusual in that, assuming proper programming techniques have been used, neither are they catastrophic nor can they be mitigated. Once the Terminate event is fired, the class or UserForm has performed its function and is being destroyed. If you need to place code in the Terminate event of a class or UserForm, it is best to simply ignore any errors that occur by using the On Error Resume Next statement at the beginning of the procedure.

Putting It All Together

Although we've described all the pieces of an error handling system, it may not be clear how those pieces fit together. In this section we show a small but complete program that demonstrates the basic error handling techniques. This program is admittedly contrived, but the idea behind it is to have a complete program with as little distraction from non-error handling-related code as possible. The complete program can be found in the *Concepts* folder of the CD in the workbook named ErrorHandlingDemo.xls.

The error handling demo program consists of a single entry point procedure that displays a UserForm and then calls a function that intentionally generates an error depending on whether the user clicks the OK or Cancel button on the UserForm. Figure 15-2 shows the UserForm for our error handling demo, and Listing 15-10 shows the code behind this UserForm.

FIGURE 15-2 The error handling demo UserForm

Listing 15-10 The Code Behind the Error Handling Demo UserForm

```
Private Const msMODULE As String = "FDemo"

Private bUserCancel As Boolean

Public Property Get UserCancel() As Boolean
    UserCancel = bUserCancel
End Property

Private Sub cmdOK_Click()
    bUserCancel = False
    Me.Hide
End Sub

Private Sub cmdCancel_Click()
```

```
        bUserCancel = True
        Me.Hide
End Sub

Private Sub UserForm_QueryClose(Cancel As Integer, _
                                CloseMode As Integer)
    ' Route any X-close button calls through
    ' the cmdCancel_Click procedure.
    If CloseMode = vbFormControlMenu Then
        Cancel = True
        cmdCancel_Click
    End If
End Sub

Public Function Initialize() As Boolean

    Const sSOURCE As String = "Initialize()"

    Dim bReturn As Boolean ' The function return value

    On Error GoTo ErrorHandler

    ' Assume success until an error is encountered.
    bReturn = True

    ' Set the UserForm caption.
    Me.Caption = gsAPP_TITLE

ErrorExit:

    Initialize = bReturn
    Exit Function

ErrorHandler:
    bReturn = False
    If bCentralErrorHandler(msMODULE, sSOURCE) Then
        Stop
        Resume
    Else
        Resume ErrorExit
    End If
End Function
```

The first thing to notice is the UserForm has a read-only UserCancel property. The value of this property is determined by which button the user clicks. If the OK button is clicked, the UserCancel property returns False (meaning the user did not cancel the UserForm). If the Cancel button is clicked, the UserCancel property returns True. In the code for the calling procedure we demonstrate how to raise a custom user cancel error in response to the UserCancel method returning True that causes the error handler to exit silently rather than displaying an error.

The second thing to notice is we are trapping clicks to the X-close button on the UserForm with the UserForm_QueryClose event procedure and rerouting them to the cmdCancel_Click event procedure. This makes a click on the X-close button behave exactly like a click on the Cancel button.

The last thing to notice is the UserForm contains a custom Initialize method. This method is a Boolean function that returns True if initialization succeeds and False if an error occurred during initialization. This method is called prior to showing the UserForm. The calling procedure then examines the return value of the method and does not attempt to show the UserForm if initialization failed. Listing 15-11 shows the function that purposely causes an error.

Listing 15-11   The bCauseAnError Function

```
Public Function bCauseAnError() As Boolean

    Const sSOURCE As String = "bCauseAnError()"

    Dim bReturn As Boolean ' The function return value
    Dim lTest As Long

    On Error GoTo ErrorHandler

    ' Assume success until an error is encountered.
    bReturn = True

    ' Cause a divide by zero error.
    lTest = 1 / 0

ErrorExit:

    bCauseAnError = bReturn
    Exit Function

ErrorHandler:
    bReturn = False
    If bCentralErrorHandler(msMODULE, sSOURCE) Then
        Stop
```

```
        Resume
    Else
        Resume ErrorExit
    End If
End Function
```

This function is exactly the same as the one we showed in Listing 15-6 with some code added that causes it to throw a divide by zero error. Now we can tie things together with the entry point procedure that runs the application. The code for this procedure is shown in Listing 15-12.

Listing 15-12   The EntryPoint Subroutine

```
Public Sub EntryPoint()

    Const sSOURCE As String = "EntryPoint"

    Dim bUserCancel As Boolean
    Dim frmDemo As FDemo

    On Error GoTo ErrorHandler

    Set frmDemo = New FDemo
    Load frmDemo

    ' If UserForm initialization failed, raise a custom error.
    If Not frmDemo.Initialize() Then Err.Raise glHANDLED_ERROR
    frmDemo.Show

    ' Read the property that tells us whether the user clicked
    ' the OK or Cancel button.
    bUserCancel = frmDemo.UserCancel

    ' If the user pressed the Cancel button, raise a custom
    ' user cancel error. This will cause the central error
    ' handler to exit the program without displaying an
    ' error message.
    If bUserCancel Then Err.Raise glUSER_CANCEL

    ' If the user pressed the OK button, run the function that
    ' is designed to cause an error.
    If Not bCauseAnError() Then Err.Raise glHANDLED_ERROR
```

```
ErrorExit:

    On Error Resume Next
    ' Clean up the UserForm
    Unload frmDemo
    Set frmDemo = Nothing

    Exit Sub

ErrorHandler:
    If bCentralErrorHandler(msMODULE, sSOURCE, , True) Then
        Stop
        Resume
    Else
        Resume ErrorExit
    End If
End Sub
```

The EntryPoint subroutine is run from a button located on Sheet1 of the ErrorHandlingDemo.xls workbook. This application has only two possible execution paths. Clicking the OK button on the UserForm triggers the first, and clicking the Cancel button on the UserForm triggers the second. Let's examine what happens in each case and see the resulting error log entries.

The EntryPoint subroutine first creates a new instance of the FDemo UserForm, loads it, and calls the UserForm's custom Initialize method. In this sample application the UserForm never fails to initialize. We provided this custom Initialize method to demonstrate how you would initialize a UserForm in a way that is linked into the error handling system.

Next, the EntryPoint subroutine shows the FDemo UserForm. As you can see in Figure 15-2, the only actions available to the user are clicking the OK or Cancel buttons. Clicking the OK button sets the FDemo UserForm's UserCancel property to False, meaning the user did not cancel. Clicking the Cancel button sets the UserCancel property to True, meaning the user did cancel. Clicking either button also hides the UserForm, allowing the EntryPoint subroutine to continue executing.

Because the FDemo UserForm is hidden rather than unloaded, when code execution returns to the EntryPoint subroutine the UserForm is still in memory. This allows the EntryPoint subroutine to check the value of the FDemo UserCancel property to determine what the user has asked it to do.

If the UserCancel property is True, the EntryPoint subroutine needs to exit without displaying an error message but still run its cleanup code. It accomplishes this by raising a custom user cancel error. If you recall from the discussion of the central error handler, VBA uses the error number 18 to indicate the user has canceled program execution. We defined a public constant that holds this value and when the central error handler sees this error number it exits silently. Therefore, to exit as a result of the user clicking Cancel in the FDemo UserForm, the EntryPoint subroutine raises a custom error with the error number gentlemanUSER_CANCEL. The line of code used to accomplish this follows:

```
If bUserCancel Then Err.Raise glUSER_CANCEL
```

This notifies the central error handler of the error. The central error handler logs the error and returns control to the EntryPoint procedure so it can complete its cleanup activities prior to exiting.

The central error handler records all errors, including user cancel errors, in the error log. The error.log file is located in the same directory as the ErrorHandlingDemo.xls workbook. The entry made in response to the user clicking the FDemo Cancel button is similar to the following entry except it will be written to a single line in the error log file:

```
03/30/08 20:23:37 [ErrorHandlingDemo.xls]
MEntryPoints.EntryPoint, Error 18: UserCancel
```

If the user did not cancel program execution, the EntryPoint subroutine continues with the next line of code. This line is a call to the function that is designed to intentionally throw a divide by zero error. As you can see in Listing 15-11, this function's error handler first calls the central error handler to notify it of the error and then causes the function to return False to notify the calling procedure that an error has occurred. In this case, the error is catastrophic, so the calling procedure must terminate the program. It does this by raising a custom handled error, as follows:

```
If Not bCauseAnError() Then Err.Raise glHANDLED_ERROR
```

Because this error was raised from an entry point procedure, the original error message stored by the central error handler is displayed to the user, as shown in Figure 15-3.

FIGURE 15-3 The error message displayed to the user

In this case, the central error handler logs two entries: one from the function where the error originated and one from the entry point procedure.

```
03/30/08 20:44:20 [ErrorHandlingDemo.xls]
MSystemCode.bCauseAnError(), Error 11: Division by zero
03/30/08 20:44:20 [ErrorHandlingDemo.xls]
MEntryPoints.EntryPoint, Error 9999: Division by zero
```

Note that the first error number recorded is the original VBA error number, while the second error number (and any subsequent error numbers) is the value of our predefined glHANDLED_ERROR constant. If there are multiple procedures in the call stack when an error occurs, the central error handler creates a log entry for each one. This provides helpful information when debugging an error because it provides a record of the call stack at the time the error occurred.

Once the error has been logged and the error message displayed, the central error handler returns control to the EntryPoint subroutine so it can complete its cleanup prior to exiting.

Practical Example

PETRAS Time Sheet

In the practical example section of this chapter we retrofit our time entry add-in with a complete centralized error handling system. This is the best example to examine if you want to see how a real-world error handling system is constructed.

The process of retrofitting our add-in with error handling is tedious but uncomplicated. All entry point procedures are outfitted with the entry-point version of the error handling code, and all subprocedures are converted into Boolean functions and outfitted with the function version of the error handling code.

The only code example from the new version of the PETRAS add-in that we show here is the Auto_Open procedure, in Listing 15-13. This is the entry point procedure that makes the most calls to lower-level procedures. It also has the unique requirement to shut down the application if an error occurs. This makes it the most interesting example of error handling in the add-in. You are encouraged to examine the complete revised code for the PETRAS add-in, located on the CD in the

Application folder for this chapter, for a complete view of the error handling system.

Listing 15-13 The PETRAS Add-in Auto_Open Procedure with Error Handling

```
Public Sub Auto_Open()

    Const sSOURCE As String = "Auto_Open"

    Dim bErrorOut As Boolean
    Dim wkbBook As Workbook

    ' The very first thing your application should do upon
    ' startup is attempt to delete any copies of its
    ' command bars that may have been left hanging around
    ' by an Excel crash or other incomplete exit.
    On Error Resume Next
        Application.CommandBars(gsBAR_TOOLBAR).Delete
    On Error GoTo ErrorHandler

    ' Initialize global variables.
    If Not bInitGlobals() Then Err.Raise glHANDLED_ERROR

    ' Assume False until an error is encountered.
    bErrorOut = False

    ' Make sure we can locate our time entry workbook before we
    ' do anything else.
    If Len(Dir$(gsAppDir & gsFILE_TIME_ENTRY)) = 0 Then _
        Err.Raise glHANDLED_ERROR, sSOURCE, gsERR_FILE_NOT_FOUND

    Application.ScreenUpdating = False
    Application.EnableEvents = False
    Application.StatusBar = gsSTATUS_LOADING_APP

    ' Build the command bars.
    If Not bBuildCommandBars() Then Err.Raise glHANDLED_ERROR

    ' Set the initial state of the application.
    If Not gclsEventHandler.SetInitialStatus() Then _
                                    Err.Raise glHANDLED_ERROR
```

```
ErrorExit:

    ' Reset critical application properties.
    ResetAppProperties

    ' If an error occurred during the Auto_Open procedure,
    ' the only option is to exit the application.
    If bErrorOut Then ShutdownApplication

    Exit Sub

ErrorHandler:
    ' This variable informs the clean up section when an error
    ' has occurred.
    bErrorOut = True
    If bCentralErrorHandler(msMODULE, sSOURCE, , True) Then
        Stop
        Resume
    Else
        Resume ErrorExit
    End If
End Sub
```

This version of the Auto_Open procedure is different from the version we last saw in Chapter 8, "Advanced Command Bar Handling." Notice that with the exception of the ResetAppProperties procedure and the ShutdownApplication procedure, every procedure called by Auto_Open is now a Boolean function whose return value indicates success or failure.

The ResetAppProperties procedure is an exception because it is the rare case of a procedure in which nothing can go wrong. This type of procedure was described in the "Trivial Procedures" section earlier in the chapter, and the ResetAppProperties procedure itself was shown in Listing 15-8.

The ShutdownApplication procedure is an exception because it is the last procedure run before the application closes. Similar to the bCentralErrorHandler function we examined in Listing 15-9, it doesn't make any sense to try and handle errors that occur in this procedure, so the entire ShutdownApplication procedure is wrapped in On Error Resume Next.

We also added a new bErrorOut flag variable. This is because the cleanup section for the Auto_Open procedure (the section of code between the `ErrorExit` label and the `Exit Sub` statement) needs to know whether an error occurred prior to it being executed. The error handler for the Auto_Open procedure sets the bErrorOut variable to True when an error occurs. It then calls the central error handler and, after the central error handler returns, it redirects code execution to the cleanup section, starting directly below the ErrorExit label. If the bErrorOut variable indicates to the cleanup section that an error occurred, the cleanup section initiates application shutdown by calling the ShutdownApplication procedure.

PETRAS Reporting

As we mentioned in the "Complex Project Error Handler Organization" section earlier in the chapter, there are two or three complex error handling system designs commonly used in Excel VBA applications and several minor variations on each of those. Throughout this chapter, we demonstrated the concepts of error handling using a system known as the **function return value** method. In this system, every subprocedure is written as a Boolean function whose return value indicates success or failure. If an error occurs, it is trapped in the function's error handler, which logs the error and then sets the function's return value to False. The calling procedure tests the return value and (usually) raises another error to trigger its own error handler, and so the error bubbles up the call stack. Listing 15-14 shows the order in which lines are executed in a nested set of procedures.

Listing 15-14   The Order of Execution When Using the Function Return Value System

```
Sub EntryPoint()

    Const sSOURCE As String = "EntryPoint"

1   On Error GoTo ErrorHandler

2   If Not bSubProc1() Then
20      Err.Raise glHANDLED_ERROR
    End If

ErrorExit:
    'Run some cleanup code
23 Exit Sub
```

```
ErrorHandler:
21 If bCentralErrorHandler(msMODULE, sSOURCE, , True) Then
       Stop
       Resume
   Else
22     Resume ErrorExit
   End If
End Sub

Function bSubProc1() As Boolean

   Const sSOURCE As String = "bSubProc1"
   Dim bReturn As Boolean

3  On Error GoTo ErrorHandler
4  bReturn = True

5  If Not bSubProc2() Then
14     Err.Raise glHANDLED_ERROR
   End If

ErrorExit:
   'Run some cleanup code
18 bSubProc1 = bReturn
19 Exit Function

ErrorHandler:
15 bReturn = False
16 If bCentralErrorHandler(msMODULE, sSOURCE) Then
       Stop
       Resume
   Else
17     Resume ErrorExit
   End If
End Function

Function bSubProc2() As Boolean

   Const sSOURCE As String = "bSubProc2"
   Dim bReturn As Boolean

6  On Error GoTo ErrorHandler
7  bReturn = True

   'Cause an error
```

```
8    Debug.Print 1 / 0

ErrorExit:
     'Run some cleanup code
12 bSubProc2 = bReturn
13 Exit Function


ErrorHandler:
9    bReturn = False
10   If bCentralErrorHandler(msMODULE, sSOURCE) Then
         Stop
         Resume
     Else
11       Resume ErrorExit
     End If
End Function
```

You'll notice that in the vast majority of cases, the calling procedure handles a False return value by simply raising another error to trigger its own error handler.

Error handling in VBA is designed such that any unhandled errors and any errors raised within an error handler automatically fire the error handler of the calling procedure. So if we raise an error within the sub-procedure's error handler, it automatically triggers the calling procedure's error handler, without the calling procedure having to test for a False return value and trigger the error handler itself. The same happens if we raise an error at the end of the central error handler. This is known as the **re-throw** system of error handling and has been implemented in the PETRAS reporting application. The main advantages of the re-throw system are that we can use it within Sub, Property, and Function procedures, and our functions' return values can be used for their results instead of success/failure indicators. The main disadvantages are that it becomes slightly harder for us to include complex cleanup code if an error occurs, and this system will not work properly if you need to trap errors in a procedure called using the Excel `Application.Run` method.

Listing 15-15 is taken from the MErrorHandler module of the PETRASReporting.xla workbook and shows a modified central error handler that implements the re-throw system by default but allows us to override the re-throw behavior in the exceptional cases when we need to run complex post-error cleanup code. This is similar to Listing 15-9, with the extra code to implement the re-throw method highlighted.

Listing 15-15 A Central Error Handler Implementing the Re-Throw System

```
Public Function bCentralErrorHandler( _
        ByVal sModule As String, _
        ByVal sProc As String, _
        Optional ByVal sFile As String, _
        Optional ByVal bEntryPoint As Boolean = False, _
        Optional ByVal bReThrow As Boolean = True) As Boolean

    Static sErrMsg As String

    Dim iFile As Integer
    Dim lErrNum As Long
    Dim sFullSource As String
    Dim sPath As String
    Dim sLogText As String

    ' Grab the error info before it's cleared by
    ' On Error Resume Next below.
    lErrNum = Err.Number

    ' If this is a user cancel, set the silent error flag
    ' message. This will cause the error to be ignored.
    If lErrNum = glUSER_CANCEL Then sErrMsg = msSILENT_ERROR

    ' If this is the originating error, the static error
    ' message variable will be empty. In that case, store
    ' the originating error message in the static variable.
    If Len(sErrMsg) = 0 Then sErrMsg = Err.Description

    ' We cannot allow errors in the central error handler.
    On Error Resume Next

    ' Load the default filename if required.
    If Len(sFile) = 0 Then sFile = ThisWorkbook.Name

    ' Get the application directory.
    sPath = ThisWorkbook.Path
    If Right$(sPath, 1) <> "\" Then sPath = sPath & "\"

    ' Construct the fully-qualified error source name.
    sFullSource = "[" & sFile & "]" & sModule & "." & sProc
```

```
' Create the error text to be logged.
sLogText = " " & sFullSource & ", Error " & _
           CStr(lErrNum) & ": " & sErrMsg

' Open the log file, write out the error information and
' close the log file.
iFile = FreeFile()
Open sPath & msFILE_ERROR_LOG For Append As #iFile
Print #iFile, Format$(Now(), "dd mmm yy hh:mm:ss"); sLogText
If bEntryPoint Or Not bReThrow Then Print #iFile,
Close #iFile

' Do not display or debug silent errors.
If sErrMsg <> msSILENT_ERROR Then

        ' Show the error message when we reach the entry point
        ' procedure or immediately if we are in debug mode.
        If bEntryPoint Or gbDEBUG_MODE Then
            Application.ScreenUpdating = True
            MsgBox sErrMsg, vbCritical, gsAPP_TITLE
            ' Clear the static error message variable once
            ' we've reached the entry point so that we're ready
            ' to handle the next error.
            sErrMsg = vbNullString
        End If

        ' The return vale is the debug mode status.
        bCentralErrorHandler = gbDEBUG_MODE

Else
        ' If this is a silent error, clear the static error
        ' message variable when we reach the entry point.
        If bEntryPoint Then sErrMsg = vbNullString
        bCentralErrorHandler = False
End If

'If we're using re-throw error handling,
'this is not the entry point and we're not debugging,
're-raise the error, to be caught in the next procedure
'up the call stack.
'Procedures that handle their own errors can call the
```

```
        'central error handler with bReThrow:=False to log the
        'error, but not re-raise it.
        If bReThrow Then
            If Not bEntryPoint And Not gbDEBUG_MODE Then
                On Error GoTo 0
                Err.Raise lErrNum, sFullSource, sErrMsg
            End If
        Else
            'Error is being logged and handled,
            'so clear the static error message variable
            sErrMsg = vbNullString
        End If
    End Function
```

Listing 15-16 shows the order in which lines are executed in a nested set
of procedures when the re-throw system is implemented.

Listing 15-16 The Order of Execution When Using the Re-Throw System

```
Sub EntryPoint()

    Const sSOURCE As String = "EntryPoint"

1   On Error GoTo ErrorHandler

2   SubProc1

ErrorExit:
11 Exit Sub

ErrorHandler:
    'Run simple clean-up code here

9   If bCentralErrorHandler(msMODULE, sSOURCE, , True) Then
        Stop
        Resume
    Else
10      Resume ErrorExit
    End If
End Sub

Sub SubProc1()
```

```
        Const sSOURCE As String = "SubProc1"

3       On Error GoTo ErrorHandler

4       SubProc2

        Exit Sub

ErrorHandler:
        'Run simple clean-up code here

8       If bCentralErrorHandler(msMODULE, sSOURCE) Then
            Stop
            Resume
        End If
End Sub

Sub SubProc2()

        Const sSOURCE As String = "bSubProc2"

5       On Error GoTo ErrorHandler

        'Cause an error
6       Debug.Print 1 / 0

        Exit Sub

ErrorHandler:
        'Run simple clean-up code here

7       If bCentralErrorHandler(msMODULE, sSOURCE) Then
            Stop
            Resume
        End If
End Sub
```

Using the re-throw method, we can only include cleanup code at the start of our error handlers (before the call to the central error handler), so we have to be careful to ensure that the cleanup code does not cause any more errors to occur and does not reset the Err object. In practice, this means the re-throw method is best used when no cleanup is required, or when the cleanup is trivial and cannot cause an error.

In Listing 15-15, we added an optional parameter to the central error handler, which allows us to stop the error being re-raised. This results in exactly the same behavior as the function return value system, thereby allowing us to use that method in the cases that require complex cleanup code. This parameter is used in the *ConsolidateWorkbooks* procedure to handle errors that occur while extracting the data from a time sheet workbook. In that case, we call the central error handler to log the error, and then close the problem time sheet workbook and continue with the next one.

Whether to use the function return value or re-throw system of error handling is largely a philosophical decision. Both have advantages and disadvantages, and both are more or less appropriate for different situations. Either system is better than having no error handling at all.

Summary

In this chapter, we covered a lot of ground that may be unfamiliar to many readers. Look closely at the sample applications for this chapter and read the chapter again if error handling concepts continue to be unclear. One of the best ways to discover how an error handler works is to use debugging techniques to single step through an application as it handles an error. We cover debugging techniques in detail in Chapter 16. After reading that chapter you may want to revisit this chapter and examine the sample applications in more detail using VBA debugging techniques.

CHAPTER 16

VBA DEBUGGING

Debugging is the most important and probably the least understood aspect of programming. No one writes perfect code on the first try. Being able to efficiently locate and correct the mistakes you've made is a significant part of what separates a great programmer from a skilled amateur. In this chapter we demonstrate how to use the built-in debugging features of the Visual Basic Editor (VBE) to locate and correct bugs in your code as well as provide tips and techniques that will help you become a better debugger.

Basic VBA Debugging Techniques

Run Mode Versus Break Mode

A running application can exist in one of two states. Run mode is exactly what its name suggests. The application is running normally. In break mode an application is still technically running, but execution has been interrupted. Break mode can be triggered by an unhandled runtime error, a Stop statement, or a break point placed within the code.

In the first group of topics in this section we discuss how the global VBE Error Trapping setting affects how an application enters break mode. The global error trapping settings are located under the VBE *Tools > Options* menu on the General tab in the Error Trapping section.

Break on All Errors

This setting is reasonably self-explanatory. When you select the *Break on All Errors* setting, all error handlers are ignored. The moment any runtime error occurs, an error message is displayed and you have the option to end the program or enter break mode on the line of code that caused the error.

Break in Class Module

If an error occurs within a class module procedure that contains an error handler, this setting is equivalent to the *Break on Unhandled Errors* setting that we cover next. This is to say it does not cause code execution to halt in response to the error. If an error occurs within a class module procedure that ***does not*** contain an error handler, code execution will be interrupted on the line of code in the class module procedure that generated the error. If you've ever experienced a run-time error on a line of code like `Userform1.Show`, using this setting will bring you to the line of code within the UserForm class module that actually caused the error.

Break on Unhandled Errors

This setting causes code to break on errors only where there are no error handlers anywhere in the call stack above the procedure in which the error occurred. This is an important distinction. Even if an error occurs in a procedure without an error handler, if that procedure was called by another procedure that does contain an error handler, the calling procedure's error handler will handle the error. Code execution only breaks when there are no error handlers anywhere in the call stack above the procedure where the error occurred. We cover the call stack in more detail in "The Call Stack" section later in this chapter.

Keep in mind that the error trapping setting is a persistent, application-level setting, and there is no way to detect or change this setting within your VBA code. Therefore, when you are having strange problems with the error handling behavior on a specific user's computer, the first thing you should do is determine what error trapping setting is currently specified for that instance of Excel. We recommend Break on Unhandled Errors as the appropriate setting except when debugging a difficult error that requires one of the other two options.

Debug Mode

During development you may find it useful to change the way errors are normally handled to help you diagnose a problem. We call this state of the program **debug mode**. Debug mode refers to the state of an application when error handling has been intentionally bypassed in some fashion. Debug mode is usually built into the error handling system used by the application. We covered debug mode as a design feature of an error handling system in Chapter 15, "VBA Error Handling."

Placing an application into debug mode can also be as simple as changing the VBE Error Trapping setting to *Break on All Errors*. This is not a robust solution for implementing debug mode, however, because many nontrivial applications deliberately generate runtime errors that are designed to be ignored as a normal part of program execution. The *Break on All Errors* setting doesn't distinguish between errors that are a normal part of code execution and those that are the result of bugs; it simply breaks on any of them. If you need to get past a "normal" error to reach an error caused by a bug, you need a more sophisticated debug mode implementation, such as the one described next.

User-Defined Debug Mode

A user-defined debug mode typically involves a public constant that can be used to disable or modify the behavior of error handling on an applicationwide basis. In the error handling system we demonstrated in Chapter 15, debug mode was implemented with the following public constant defined in the MErrorHandler module:

```
Public Const gbDEBUG_MODE As Boolean = False
```

When set to False, the gbDEBUG_MODE constant has no effect and application error handling proceeds normally. When set to True, the gbDEBUG_MODE constant causes the error handler within the procedure where the error occurred to drop into a Stop statement. As we see in the next section, this initiates break mode and allows us to debug the error.

The gbDEBUG_MODE constant is also used to disable error handling in other contexts. For example, some procedures may not have formal error handling. Procedures that are wrapped entirely in On Error Resume Next are the most common example. When a procedure is constructed in this manner it implies that any errors that might occur within it are expected and should be ignored. This is not always a valid assumption, so we need some way of conditionally disabling On Error Resume Next. The standard way to accomplish this is shown in Listing 16-1.

Listing 16-1 Conditionally Disabling On Error Resume Next

```
If Not gbDEBUG_MODE Then
    On Error Resume Next
End If
```

The code shown in Listing 16-1 would appear at the top of the procedure in question. If our gbDEBUG_MODE constant is set to True, all error bypassing is disabled. When the gbDEBUG_MODE constant is set to False, the procedure functions normally, ignoring any errors that occur in the course of its execution.

The Stop Statement

When VBA encounters a Stop statement in your program, code execution is halted at the statement and break mode is initiated. You can then use any of the standard debugging techniques discussed throughout this chapter to step past the Stop statement and debug your program. The Stop statement can be used as part of a larger debug mode infrastructure, as described in Chapter 15, or it can be added to your code on an ad hoc basis when you are attempting to debug errors in specific locations.

Just remember to remove any ad hoc Stop statements from your code and disable debug mode prior to shipping your application. Failing to do this is one of the most common debugging mistakes we have seen. If VBA encounters a Stop statement in an unprotected VBA application the user will be unceremoniously dumped into break mode. The vast majority of users will have no idea what has happened or what they should do about it.

Project protection disables the effect of Stop statements, but *only* the Stop statement is disabled, not any related code. This causes significant problems if the protected project was inadvertently left in debug mode. If a program with a protected VBA project uses an error handling system similar to the one we presented in Chapter 15 and it has been left in debug mode, the program enters an infinite loop any time a runtime error occurs.

This is because program flow is not affected by project protection. As shown in Listing 16-2, the program flow for a debug mode project is identical in either case, but the Stop statement is ignored in a protected project. Rather than halting at the Stop statement, VBA executes the Resume statement that immediately follows the Stop statement. This causes VBA to re-execute the line of code that generated the error, which triggers the error handler again, causing the Resume statement to be executed again, ad infinitum.

Listing 16-2 The Perils of Leaving Debug Mode Active

```
ErrorHandler:
    bReturn = False
    If bCentralErrorHandler(msMODULE, sSOURCE) Then
        Stop      ' This will be ignored in a protected project.
        Resume
```

```
    Else
        Resume ErrorExit
    End If
End Function
```

If you are lucky, the user will understand how to press Ctrl+Break to halt the infinite loop. In most cases, however, the only option the user will understand is Ctrl+Alt+Del or worse, the Power button. *Always* remember to disable debug mode prior to shipping your code.

Conditional Compilation Constants

We mention conditional compilation constants briefly in this section for the sake of completeness. Conditional compilation constants are designed to allow you to compile different versions of your code for different situations. A conditional compilation constant could also be substituted for the normal constant used to control debug mode, but there are no significant benefits to doing so.

Conditional compilation constants are useful in general application development for things like easily swapping between early and late binding. For example, if you are automating PowerPoint from your Excel application you will want to take advantage of type checking and IntelliSense during development, but you may need to avoid any dependency on a specific version of the PowerPoint object library when your application is distributed.

This can be accomplished by using conditional compilation constants to create parallel variable declarations. As shown in Listing 16-3, conditional compilation constants allow you to declare the same variable with two different data types. This is because VBA never "sees" more than one of these declarations. In this case we have an early-bound declaration for use in development and a late-bound declaration for use in the distributed version of the application.

Listing 16-3 Dual Variable Declarations Using Conditional Compilation Constants

```
#If HAS_PPT_REFERENCE Then
    Dim objPPTApp As Powerpoint.Application
#Else
    Dim objPPTApp As Object
#End If
```

Conditional compilation constants cannot be treated like standard VBA constants. They have their own special set of statements with which they must be used. The # character prefix to the programming statements used with the conditional compilation constant is required. There are only a few VBA programming language constructs designed to work with conditional compilation constants, and all of them use this prefix.

Conditional compilation constants can be defined at the module-level or globally, using the VBE *Tools > VBAProject Properties* menu (where "VBAProject" is the actual name of your project). In Figure 16-1, we create the conditional compilation constant required for the example shown in Listing 16-3.

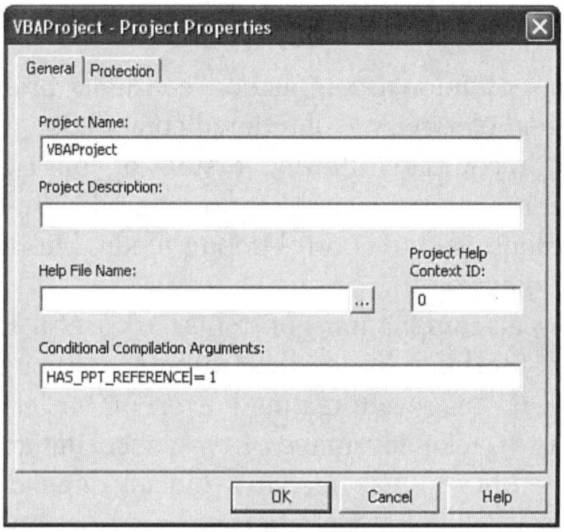

FIGURE 16-1 Creating conditional compilation constants

Conditional compilation constants are defined at the bottom of the *General* tab of the Project Properties dialog. Conditional compilation constants defined in the Project Properties dialog have public scope. These constants can only be assigned integer values. They can function as Boolean values using the rule that zero = False and non-zero = True. You can define multiple conditional compilation constants by separating each constant definition in the Project Properties dialog with a colon character.

Using Break Points (F9)

Break points are specific positions within your code at which program execution automatically stops and enters break mode. Break points are conceptually similar to the `stop` statement. The difference is that break points can be added and removed with the click of a mouse or a keyboard shortcut, and they are not saved with your code. If you set break points in your code and then save your project, those break points will disappear if you close and re-open the project. `Stop` statements will remain. Break points can be set in one of two ways: using your mouse or using keyboard shortcuts. Figure 16-2 shows a break point being set using the mouse.

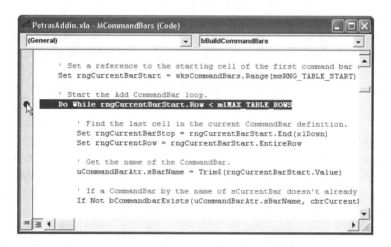

FIGURE 16-2   Setting a break point with your mouse

Each code module has a gray bar running down the left side. This is called the **margin indicator bar**. Clicking on the margin indicator bar adds a break point to your code at the position where you clicked. Clicking on an existing break point in the margin indicator bar removes that break point.

Setting break points using keyboard shortcuts is just as easy. To set a break point, place the cursor anywhere on the line of code where you want the break point to be located and press the F9 key. A break point is added to that line of code. Pressing F9 while the cursor is located on an existing break point removes that break point. Break points can only be set on executable lines of code. Code comments, blank lines, and variable declarations are examples of places where you cannot set a break point.

Once you have set a break point, run your application as you would normally. When code execution reaches the break point, it stops and enters break mode. You can then use the debugging techniques discussed in the following sections to step over the break point and debug the problem you are having with your code.

Stepping Through Code

The fundamental skill you must master to become proficient at debugging is stepping through your code. The phrase "stepping through your code" implies a one-way, deterministic process. This is not the case. Stepping through code can involve moving backward or forward through your code as well as skipping sections of code or allowing sections of code to run but then halting when they have completed.

We discuss the various techniques used to step through code in detail in this section. Keep in mind that the whole point of stepping through code is to see what the code is doing. When you step through code, you are duplicating exactly what your program does when it is running normally, but you are doing it one line of code at a time. In later sections we explain in detail how you determine what your code is doing once you are stepping through it.

Every code stepping feature in VBA has both a keyboard shortcut and a toolbar button equivalent. To become truly efficient at code debugging you **must** learn the keyboard shortcuts. For this reason we cover only the keyboard shortcuts required to initiate each technique. It is a simple matter to examine the VBE Debug toolbar and discover the equivalent toolbar buttons for each keyboard shortcut we discuss. You can display the VBE Debug toolbar by choosing *View > Toolbars > Debug* from the VBE menu. We provide a comprehensive list of debugging-related keyboard shortcuts at the end of the chapter.

Step Into (F8)

Stepping into code can be initiated in one of two ways. If you need to examine code execution from the beginning of a procedure, you can place your cursor anywhere inside that procedure and press F8 to begin stepping through its code.

Alternatively, if you want to start your debugging session deeper in the procedure, or even deeper in the call stack, you can place a break point on the first line of code you want to debug and press F5. VBA runs your code until it reaches the break point. You can then use F8 to begin executing your code one line at a time from that point.

As you are stepping through your code you will notice a yellow line that moves each time you execute one of the step commands. This line is called the **execution point**. To make it easier to follow, the execution point displays an arrow in the margin indicator bar of the code module, as shown in Figure 16-3.

The execution point indicator can be a bit confusing until you get used to it. It does not represent the line of code you have just executed; rather it shows the line of code that will be executed next.

With each press of the F8 key the line of code currently highlighted by the execution point indicator is executed and the execution point indicator moves to the line of code that logically follows based on the

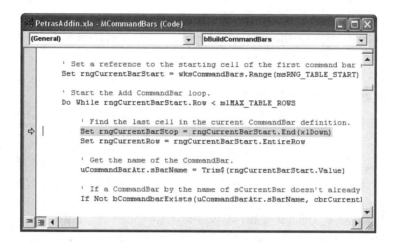

FIGURE 16-3   The execution point indicator

results of executing the previous line. This may or may not be the next physical line of code depending on how your program is structured.

Step Over (Shift+F8)

While single stepping through code you will often reach calls to subprocedures that you are sure do not contain any errors. If you continue to press F8, code execution steps into the subprocedure and begins executing its code. What you would rather do in this case is have VBA execute all code associated with the subprocedure and break again on the line of code that immediately follows it. This is accomplished using the Step Over command, whose keyboard shortcut is Shift+F8.

The Step Over command executes all code required to pass over the line currently highlighted by the execution point indicator and then breaks on the next executable line of code that logically follows the result of that execution. If the line of code currently highlighted by the execution point indicator is not a call to an outside procedure, the Step Over command is logically equivalent to the Step Into command.

Step Out (Ctrl+Shift+F8)

If you step into a subprocedure call by accident or step into it on purpose and then realize you don't need to continue stepping through it, the Step Out command is your savior. Rather than having to tediously step through the rest of the subprocedure code or physically locate the calling procedure and use the Step To Cursor command described in the next section, you can simply press Ctrl+Shift+F8. VBA runs the rest of the subprocedure automatically and breaks again on the next executable line of code in the calling procedure that logically follows the result of the subprocedure call.

Step to Cursor (Ctrl+F8)

This option would be more accurately described as "run to cursor." Whether you are already in break mode or you are just initiating a debugging session, you can simply place your cursor on the line of code where you want execution to break and press the Ctrl+F8 keyboard shortcut. VBA runs your code from the beginning until it reaches the location of your cursor, at which point it enters break mode. This option works almost exactly like placing a break point on the line. The only difference is that Step to Cursor is transient. As soon as you move the cursor, the step to cursor point changes.

This option is most useful when you are single stepping through your code and you encounter a section of code you are sure does not contain any errors. Simply use the arrow keys to move the cursor down to the first executable line of code beyond this section and press Ctrl+F8. VBA runs all the code between the current execution point and the line marked by the cursor, entering break mode again at the line marked by the cursor. This allows you to avoid tediously single stepping through sections of code where it is not necessary.

Changing the Execution Point, or Set Next Statement (Ctrl+F9)

There are times when you want to either skip lines of code that are about to be executed or retrace the execution steps that have already occurred. One of the most amazing things about the VBA debugger is that it allows you to do both of these things. You can move the execution point backward and forward as you please using the Set Next Statement command. The execution point can also be dragged to different positions using your mouse. Once you have repositioned the execution point you can resume stepping through your code from that point using the commands covered in the previous section.

The difference between changing the execution point using the Set Next Statement command and the step commands that we have previously covered is the following:

- If you reposition the execution point such that it skips lines of code that have not yet been executed, the lines you skipped *will not be executed*.

- If you reposition the execution point such that it resumes execution prior to the point where it is currently positioned, all of the lines of code between the new position of the execution point and its previous position will be executed *a second time*.

As you can imagine, you must have a firm understanding of what your code does and where it makes sense to change the execution point to avoid spurious errors or garbage results. For example, if you skip a line of code that sets an object variable and then attempt to execute a line of code that uses the object variable you will obviously get an "Object variable or with block variable not set" error. Similarly, if you move the execution point backward such that you rerun a block of code that increments a variable, the value of that variable will be incremented beyond the value it would normally reach, resulting in potentially garbage data.

The ability to change the execution point is a valuable tool. It allows you to safely skip a section of code that you know would otherwise cause an error, or rerun a section of code that you would like to examine a second time without having to restart debugging. Just be sure you are fully aware of what you are doing before you use it.

The Immediate Window (Ctrl+G)

The Immediate window is an interactive debugging tool that is always available for you to use. To display the Immediate window in the VBE, press the Ctrl+G shortcut key, or choose *View > Immediate Window* from the VBE menu. You can do almost anything in the Immediate window that you can do in your VBA project, either at design-time or while in break mode, including

- Calling procedures
- Checking or changing the value of variables
- Instantiating and testing classes
- Running single-line loops

The Immediate window is the more powerful cousin of the most basic debugging technique of all: message box debugging. Message box debugging is typically the first debugging method you learn as a VBA programmer. It involves placing message boxes at various locations within your code, each of which display the values of one or more variables and/or location information. The Immediate window allows you to do everything you can do with message box debugging and much more, without the intrusive message boxes.

Debug.Print

The `Debug.Print` statement is the Immediate window's direct equivalent of message box debugging. The `Debug.Print` statement prints the value of the expression that follows it to the Immediate window. Two sample `Debug.Print` statements are shown in Listing 16-4.

Listing 16-4   Sample Debug.Print Statements

```
Dim sSheetTab As String
Dim wkbBook As Workbook

Set wkbBook = Application.ActiveWorkbook
sSheetTab = sSheetTabName(wkbBook, gsSHEET_TIME_ENTRY)

Debug.Print wkbBook.Name
Debug.Print sSheetTab
```

The results of these `Debug.Print` statements are shown in Figure 16-4.

FIGURE 16-4   Output from the Debug.Print statements

As you can see, the output from each `Debug.Print` statement begins on a new line in the Immediate window. If you are familiar with VBA text I/O functions, note that the `Debug.Print` statement supports most of the same formatting features supported by the text I/O `Print#` statement.

It is uncommon to use extensively formatted output from the `Debug.Print` statement in the Immediate window, so we do not cover these features in any detail other than to say that you can include multiple expressions in a `Debug.Print` statement separated by commas and they will all be printed on the same line in the Immediate window separated by tabs.

Making the Best Use of the Immediate Window

There are two primary ways in which the Immediate window is used. It can be used as a simple collection point for the output of `Debug.Print` statements that post results as your code is running normally, or it can be used as an interactive tool while you are stepping through your code. There are two ways to use the Immediate window interactively:

- To evaluate a variable or expression. This is accomplished by entering a question mark character (?) followed by the variable or expression that you want to evaluate. The Immediate window is typically used for one-time evaluations. If you want to evaluate the variable or expression multiple times you should add a watch instead. We explain how to do this in "The Watch Window" section later in the chapter. Figure 16-5 shows the Immediate window being used to evaluate the value in a worksheet cell that is used in the next line of code to be executed in the module below it.

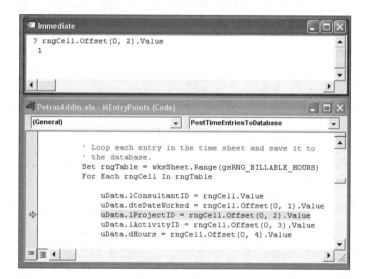

FIGURE 16-5 Using the Immediate window to evaluate an expression

- To execute code. This can include changing the value of variables that are currently being used in your application, modifying application settings, calling procedures in your code, and almost anything else you could normally do in VBA. The only difference between evaluating expressions and executing code using the Immediate window is that you leave out the question mark when executing code. Placing your cursor anywhere within the line of code and pressing Enter causes the line of code to be executed.

One common task involving code execution in the Immediate window is modifying the value of the `Application.Cursor` property. During long running VBA procedures, the Excel cursor often flickers back and forth between an hourglass and the default pointer. This can be confusing to the user, so you force the cursor to display an hourglass at the beginning of the entry point procedure and reset it at the end of the entry point procedure. The problem arises when you want to debug something within this procedure. Even in break mode the cursor setting you make is persistent, and it applies to the VBE as well as the Excel interface. The solution is to use the Immediate window to change the `Application.Cursor` property back to its default value, as shown in Figure 16-6.

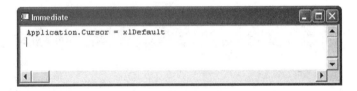

FIGURE 16-6   Executing a line of code in the Immediate window

Another excellent example of the ability to execute code in the Immediate window is running loops that print out information. Anything you can fit on a single line can be run in the Immediate window, and you can string multiple lines of VBA code together by separating them with the colon character (:). Figure 16-7 shows an example of running a loop that prints out the names of all open workbooks in the Immediate window.

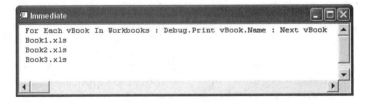

FIGURE 16-7   Executing a loop in the Immediate window

Keep in mind that the Immediate window is fully functional even during design-time. It's the perfect environment for testing specific lines of code you are unsure about. The Immediate window should become the most commonly used debugging tool in your arsenal.

The Call Stack (Ctrl+L)

The **call stack** refers to the sequential list of procedures that were executed to get you to the procedure you're currently executing in break mode. The call stack is important for two reasons:

- It shows you the execution path that got you to where you are now. This is especially important when debugging procedures that are called from multiple places within your code. It also allows you to "walk" back up the procedure stack by simply selecting the specific procedure you are interested in.
- If you want to know exactly which statements in each procedure in the call stack got you into the mess that you are currently debugging, press Ctrl+L to display the Call Stack window. Double-click the procedure name located directly below the name of the procedure you are currently in. The Call Stack window brings you to the line of code in the procedure you double-clicked that called the procedure in which the error occurred. Repeating this process allows you to walk back up the call stack until you reach the line of code in the entry point procedure where the problem call originated.

The Call Stack window is only available while executing code in break mode. A typical example of a Call Stack window you would encounter during break mode is shown in Figure 16-8.

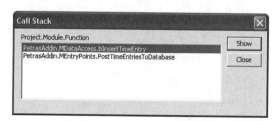

FIGURE 16-8 The Call Stack window

Notice that the procedure deepest in the stack is the first procedure listed, and the entry point procedure is at the bottom of the list. When debugging procedures that display UserForms you will see something a bit strange in the Call Stack window. An example is shown in Figure 16-9.

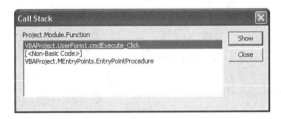

FIGURE 16-9   Non-basic code entry in the Call Stack window

The second entry, [<Non-Basic Code>], is an indication that VBA had to perform an operation "under the covers," in this case showing the UserForm. You can step back and forth to procedures above and below this entry, but you cannot step into this entry because it represents a procedure that is not running within the VBA environment.

The Watch Window

The Watch window is another amazingly multifunction debugging tool provided by the VBE. Inexplicably, there is no direct keyboard shortcut available to display the Watch window. You can, however, use the standard Windows menu hotkey sequence Alt+V followed by an h character.

The Watch window is typically used to display the value of variables or expressions that you specified while you are stepping through your code in break mode. But the Watch window contains two features that make it invaluable as a runtime debugging tool as well: *Break When Value is True* and *Break When Value Changes*. Both of these features are discussed at length later in this section. Unlike the Immediate window, the Watch window does not operate at design-time.

Setting a Basic Watch

The most fundamental feature of the Watch window is its ability to dynamically display the value of a variable or expression that you specify as you step through your code. Adding a watch is easy, but inexplicably, it is another fundamentally important operation involving the Watch window that has no keyboard shortcut. Therefore, the easiest way to add a watch is to highlight the variable or expression that you want to watch, right-click on the highlighted area, and choose Add Watch from the shortcut menu. The process of adding a watch is shown in Figures 16-10, 16-11, and 16-12.

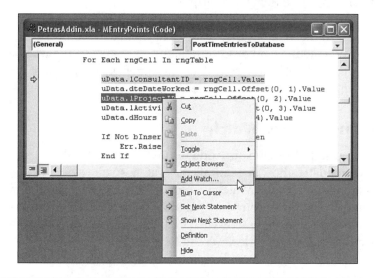

FIGURE 16-10 Specifying the watch expression

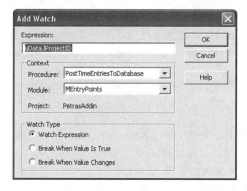

FIGURE 16-11 Configuring the watch expression

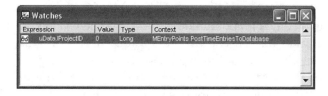

FIGURE 16-12 The completed watch expression

The watch expression added is shown in Figure 16-12. This sequence assumes that you simply accepted all the default values in the Add Watch dialog shown in Figure 16-11. We discuss why and when you might want to change these defaults later in this section.

As you can see, the Watch window displays the expression being watched, the value of the expression, the data type of the expression, and the code module and procedure name within which the watch was defined. You can add as many simultaneous watches as you want. Each watch is shown on a separate line in the Watch window.

Using a Basic Watch

As you step through your code in break mode, the Watch window continually updates the values of all the watches you've added. This is the primary purpose of the Watch window. There are typically a large number of things going on in your code, and the Watch window provides you with a method to monitor exactly what's happening to all the critical variables and expressions in the code you're debugging.

The Watch window also allows you to modify the value of any variable or expression that is an **lvalue**. This is simply a fancy computer science term meaning the variable or expression is valid when placed on the left-hand side of an assignment operator (a constant, for example, is not an lvalue because it cannot have a new value assigned to it). In the following line of code, the expression `Sheet1.Range("A1").Value` is an lvalue because it is valid for this expression to appear on the left-hand side of the assignment operation, which in this case assigns it the value of 25.

```
Sheet1.Range("A1").Value = 25
```

By contrast, the expression `ThisWorkbook.Worksheets.Count` is not an lvalue because it is a read-only property of the Workbook object that you cannot simply assign a new value to. It can only be changed by physically adding or removing worksheets in the workbook.

To modify the value of an lvalue expression in the Watch window, simply click on the Watch window Value column in the row containing the value you wish to modify. The Value column entry turns into an editable field and you can type in a new value. The new value must be a data type that is valid for the expression you are altering. Figure 16-13 shows us changing the value of the expression `Sheet1.Range("A1").Value` to 99.

You can also edit the Expression column of the watch. In the case of Figure 16-13, for example, you could change the watch to point to `Range("B1")` instead of `Range("A1")`. Feel free to experiment with

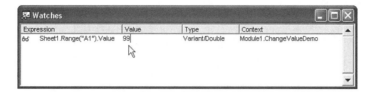

FIGURE 16-13 Modifying the value of a watch expression

modifying expressions in the Watch window for yourself. Don't be concerned about trying to determine what you're allowed to change and what you aren't. If you make a mistake, the VBE will display an error message and the Watch window will revert to its previous state. No harm will be done.

Watch Types

When you create a watch expression, you don't have to accept the default values of all the options in the Watch window. By modifying these defaults you can create watches that are much more powerful than those that simply use the default values.

There are two option categories that you can modify when you add a watch: *Watch Context* and *Watch Type*. We cover them both in following sections. Don't worry if you don't get the values of these options correct when you first add the watch. You can edit any existing watch to modify these options. The steps required to edit a watch are shown in Figures 16-14 and 16-15.

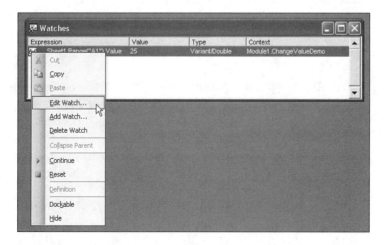

FIGURE 16-14 Right-click over a watch expression to edit it.

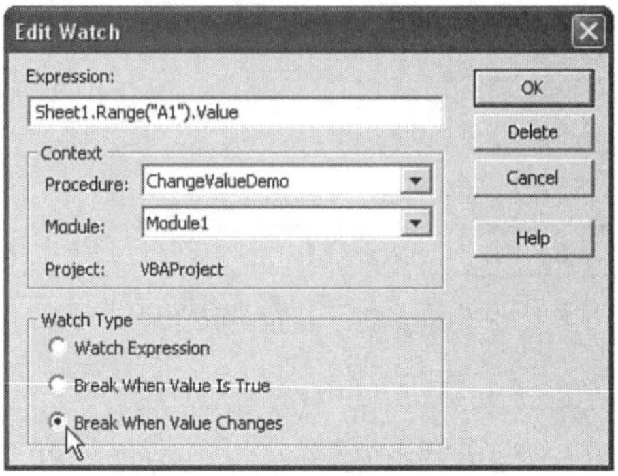

FIGURE 16-15 Change the watch type to Break When Value Changes.

Context

The *Context* options control the scope of the watch expression. Watches can be confined to code executing within a single procedure in a single module (the typical default), or they can apply to code executing anywhere within the project.

Suppose, for example, you want to place a watch on a global variable or expression. If you simply add a watch on that variable or expression from within the first procedure where you come across it, the watch will only be valid when code is executing within the procedure where the watch was added. To change this, you change the selections in the two *Context* drop-downs.

Module We are going to discuss the *Context* options in reverse order of their appearance on the Watch dialog because the *Module* setting drives the *Procedure* setting. You have two options when selecting a *Module* setting:

- **Select a Specific Module**—All standard modules, class modules, UserForm modules, and document object modules in the current project are available to be selected. Once you select a specific module, the values available in the *Procedure* setting are narrowed down to only the procedures that exist within the module you selected. The scope of the watch is then determined by the value you select in the *Procedure* drop-down.
- **Select the (All Modules) Value**—This is the first value in the *Module* drop-down. When you select this value, the value of the *Procedure* drop-down automatically changes to the corresponding (All Procedures) value. When you make this selection, the scope of

the watch becomes global. The Watch window attempts to evaluate it no matter where code is currently executing within the project.

Procedure   The *Procedure* setting determines what procedure the watch expression is valid for within the module specified by the *Module* setting. As described earlier, if the *Module* setting value is (All Modules), then you have no choice over the *Procedure* setting. In this case, its only possible value is (All Procedures). If a specific code module is selected in the *Module* setting there are two options for the *Procedure* setting:

- **Select the Name of a Specific Procedure**—In this case, the watch expression is evaluated only when code is executing within the specified procedure or one of the subprocedures called from that procedure. If code is executing in some unrelated procedure, even if it is contained within the same module, the value displayed by the Watch window for the watch expression is "<Out of context>".
- **Select the (All Procedures) Value**—Selecting this value means the scope of the watch is all procedures within the module specified by the *Module* setting. Whenever code is executing within that module, the Watch window attempts to evaluate the watch. When code is executing within a different module, the watch value displays "<Out of context>". The only exception is if code execution reaches a different module as the result of a call to a subprocedure originating in the module where the watch was created. In that case the watch continues to evaluate normally.

Watch Type

The *Watch Type* setting determines how the Watch window handles the watch. The first option is passive and used only while stepping through code in break mode. The second two options are active and used to initiate break mode.

Watch Expression   This is the default value for the *Watch Type* setting. It simply adds the specified variable or expression as a watch and displays its value while you are stepping through your code in break mode.

Break When Value Is True   This *Watch Type* setting has much in common with the Excel conditional formatting expressions we discussed in Chapter 3,

"Excel and VBA Development Best Practices." When you specify this watch type, your watch is treated as a Boolean expression, and code execution stops and enters break mode whenever the value of the expression changes from False to True or <out of context> to True.

One common use for this *Watch Type* setting is to track down rogue Application settings. For example, the `Application.EnableEvents` property is persistent from the time it is set to False until it is explicitly set back to True or Excel is closed, whichever comes first. While this property is False, all Excel events are disabled. One of the most frequent Excel programming bugs is to set `Application.EnableEvents` to False and then forget to set it back to True when you no longer need to disable events. This obviously wreaks havoc in any application that depends on trapping Excel events for its operation.

We can easily debug this problem by telling the Watch window to break code execution whenever the `Application.EnableEvents` property equals False. Once you have set this watch, each time code execution breaks you know you have turned off Excel events. You can then examine the code that follows and ensure that `Application.EnableEvents` is properly reset before this section of code exits. We demonstrate setting this watch expression in Figure 16-16.

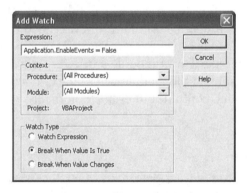

FIGURE 16-16 Setting a break when value is true watch

Note that we set the *Context* of this watch to (All Procedures) and (All Modules). This is because the `Application.EnableEvents` property setting is global to the current instance of Excel, regardless of where it was set.

Break When Value Changes Another common situation you want to watch for is when the value of an expression or variable in your code changes. In this case you are typically not concerned about the specific value to which the variable or expression changed, rather you want code execution to break whenever that value changes to anything other than its current value.

With this type of watch, code execution stops and enters break mode whenever the value of the expression changes. In Figure 16-17, we set a watch that causes code execution to stop and enter break mode whenever the value of the expression `Sheet1.Range("A1")`.Value changes.

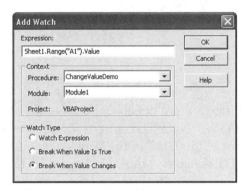

FIGURE 16-17 Setting a break when value changes expression

Note that we set the *Context* settings for this watch to a specific module and procedure. This means code execution breaks only when the value of the watch expression is changed by the specified procedure or one of its subprocedures.

Arrays, UDTs, and Classes in the Watch Window

Simple variables and expressions added to the Watch window are easy to understand on sight. But the Watch window is much more powerful than this. It can easily handle complex data types like arrays, UDTs, and classes. Watches for these data types are added in exactly the same way that watches for simple variables are added, but the results are different.

In Chapter 19, "Programming with Access and SQL Server," we create a BILLABLE_HOURS UDT to hold information about a billable hour entry from our time sheet application. Listing 16-5 shows a section of code from the PostTimeEntriesToDatabase procedure that uses this UDT.

Listing 16-5 Code That Uses the BILLABLE_HOURS UDT

```
Dim uData As BILLABLE_HOUR

For Each rngCell In rngTable
```

16. VBA DEBUGGING

```
uData.lConsultantID = rngCell.Value
uData.dteDateWorked = rngCell.Offset(0, 1).Value
uData.lProjectID = rngCell.Offset(0, 2).Value
uData.lActivityID = rngCell.Offset(0, 3).Value
uData.dHours = rngCell.Offset(0, 4).Value

If Not bInsertTimeEntry(uData) Then
    Err.Raise glHANDLED_ERROR
End If

Next rngCell
```

Let's assume that we are debugging this code and we want to watch the contents of the BILLABLE_HOURS UDT. There's no need to add each individual element of the UDT to the Watch window. Simply add a watch on the uData UDT variable as shown in Figure 16-18.

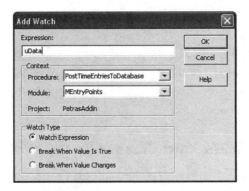

FIGURE 16-18   Adding a watch on a UDT variable

Figure 16-19 shows how the Watch window displays a UDT watch expression when you are stepping through code.

Even though we only added a watch to the uData variable, the Watch window understands this is a UDT, and it displays the member variables of the UDT in a hierarchical list below the variable the watch was defined on.

Array variables and object variables are treated the same way. The Watch window recognizes their data types and displays the current values of all their members in a hierarchical list similar to that shown in Figure 16-19. This is a great way to learn the object model of the application you're working with. Set a watch on an object variable, trigger break mode

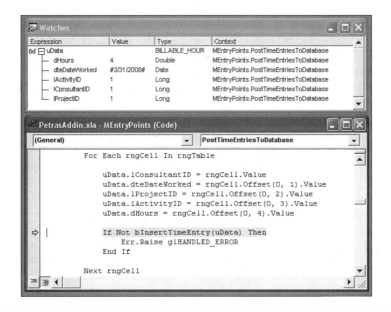

FIGURE 16-19 Using a watch on a UDT variable

once that variable has been set, and then use the Watch window to drill down through that object's properties and child collections.

Quick Watch (Shift+F9)

The Quick Watch window is the little brother of the Watch window. By highlighting a variable or expression while in break mode and pressing Shift+F9, the Quick Watch window allows you to examine all the same details that would be displayed by the Watch window except for the data type. The Quick Watch window also allows you to quickly add the selected variable or expression to the Watch window by invoking the Add button (Alt+A). Figure 16-20 shows an example of the Quick Watch window being used to display the contents of a string variable.

FIGURE 16-20 The Quick Watch window

The Quick Watch window is designed for hands-on-the-keyboard debugging. If you're using the mouse, in most cases the Quick Watch window is unnecessary. This is because the VBE dynamically displays the value of most expressions in a Tooltip when you hover your mouse cursor over them. This behavior is shown in Figure 16-21.

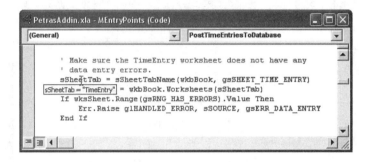

FIGURE 16-21 Tooltip expression evaluation

Even if you do make use of the Tooltip expression evaluation feature, remember how to use the Quick Watch window. You will come across many expressions that can't be evaluated by the Tooltip feature. To see the value of these expressions you need to use the Quick Watch window.

The Locals Window

The Locals window is another valuable debugging tool closely related to the Watch window that also inexplicably has no built-in keyboard shortcut that can be used to display it. In place of that you can use the standard menu hotkey sequence Alt+V followed by an s character.

The Locals window can be thought of as a specialized version of the Watch window that automatically displays the names, values, and data types of all variables and constants that are local to the procedure currently being executed. The Locals window for our debugging session in the PostTimeEntriesToDatabase procedure is shown in Figure 16-22.

Like the Watch window, you can use the Locals window to change the value of any variable in the watch list. There are also two unique features provided by the Locals window:

- **Quick access to the call stack**—The button in the upper-right corner of the Locals window directly below the X-close button displays the call stack window and allows you to change the scope of

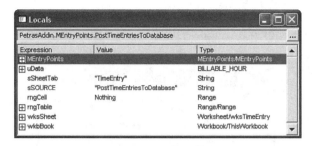

FIGURE 16-22   The Locals window in action

the variables being displayed in the Locals window to any other procedure in the call stack.

- **The Module Variables entry**—If you look closely at the first line
  in the Locals window you see that it has the same name as the module within which the current procedure is executing. If you expand
  this entry it displays a list of values for all module-level variables and
  constants.

The Object Browser (F2)

Probably the most overlooked and underused tool in the VBA programmer's arsenal is the Object Browser. This is unfortunate, because it is
also one of the most important. The Object Browser is your window into
the contents of the object libraries you're working with. For every object
library marked under the VBE *Tools > References* menu, the Object
Browser displays all the objects, methods, properties, constants, and
enumerations supported by that object library.

In addition to simply displaying these items, the Object Browser displays
a brief description of the syntax required to use each item with hyperlinks to
other items where applicable. For constants and enumerations the Object
Browser displays the actual numeric value of the constant or enumeration.

The VBA help system is also directly linked to the Object Browser. If
you need further explanation of some object, property, or method you're
looking at, you can simply select the name of the item in the Object
Browser and press F1 to bring up its help topic (specific constants and enumerations are rarely associated with help topics).

The Object Browser is packed with so many useful features that it
almost warrants a chapter in its own right. We cover the most commonly
used features of the Object Browser in this section. An example of the

Object Browser being used to display information about the ADO object library is shown in Figure 16-23.

FIGURE 16-23 The VBE Object Browser

Basic Features

The most commonly used features of the Object Browser window itself are the following:

- **Object Library box**—The drop-down in the upper-left corner of the Object Library window. It determines which object library is displayed in the Object Browser. The Object Library box contains one entry for every referenced object library in the currently active project, one entry for the currently active project itself, and a default <All Libraries> entry that causes the Object Browser to display all the contents of all the referenced libraries as well as the currently active project in one big heap. We recommend trying to narrow down the object library you want to examine by selecting it in this drop-down. Having everything displayed at once makes any one thing difficult to locate.
- **Classes list**—The list that runs down the left side of the Object Browser window. Its name is a bit of a misnomer because it displays modules, constants, and enumerations in addition to classes. This is the second level of detail you look through after you've selected the object library you want to look in.

- **Members list**—The list that runs down the right side of the Object Browser window. It displays a complete list of members for whatever item is selected in the Classes list. For example, in Figure 16-23 the Command object is selected in the Classes list, so the Members list displays all the members of the Command object.
- **Details window**—The window that occupies the bottom of the Object Browser. It provides a description of the item that is currently selected in the Members list. For example, in Figure 16-23 the Execute method of the Command object is selected in the Members List. The Details window provides a brief description of the syntax of this method with hyperlinks to related items in the object library.

Advanced Features

Once you become acquainted with the basic features of the Object Browser, you should explore two of the advanced features it provides:

- **Search combo box**—The combo box located directly below the Object Library drop-down. Using the Search combo box you can look for all occurrences of a given term within the object library or libraries currently selected in the Object Library box. Simply type the term you want to search for in the search combo box and click the Search button (the toolbar button that looks like a pair of binoculars). In Figure 16-24, for example, we searched for all occurrences of the term "ActiveConnection" within the ADO object library.
- **Show Hidden Members**—It may come as a surprise, but many elements of every object library are hidden from the default Object Browser view. There can be several reasons for this: The hidden features might not be usable from VBA, the hidden features might not be implemented at all, or the hidden features might be older features that Microsoft wants to discourage you from using. This last reason is why we can thank the Microsoft development team for providing a way to make these hidden features visible. Sometimes these older features are useful, even necessary, for top-quality Excel development. Just don't expect to find any help topics linked to these hidden features. Figure 16-25 shows an excellent example of the value of the Show Hidden Members feature.

  Notice that some of the items in the list are colored in very light gray. These are the hidden members that are revealed when you select the Show Hidden Members option. As we discussed in

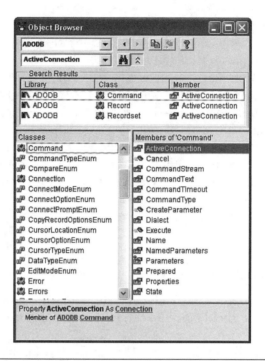

FIGURE 16-24 Using the Search feature of the Object Browser

FIGURE 16-25 Turning on Show Hidden Members

Chapter 4, "Worksheet Design," the controls from the Forms tool-bar are often the best choice for use of controls on worksheets. Unfortunately, these controls date back prior to the Excel 97 era, and even though they are fully supported by VBA it is not obvious how to find information on them unless you have a copy of Excel 5 or 95 running on a spare computer. As shown in Figure 16-25, by using the Object Browser's shortcut menu you can display these hidden objects to learn more about them.

Creating and Running a Test Harness

As we discussed in the "Functional Decomposition" section of Chapter 3, you should strive to break your application into as many single-purpose, reusable procedures as possible. Once you've done this, however, you need to verify that these procedures work under all circumstances. Testing them manually within your application is tedious, time-consuming, and not very thorough.

The proper way to test a procedure is to write a wrapper procedure that calls the procedure to be tested in a loop, passing it all possible combinations of arguments and verifying the results to ensure they are correct. This wrapper procedure is called a **test harness**, and we show you how to build one in this section. The workbook containing the procedures we're about to demonstrate is called TestHarnessDemo.xls and is located on the CD in the \Concepts\Ch16 – VBA Debugging folder.

One frequently useful task is the ability to write binary data from a string into a text file for storage and read that data from the text file for use at a later time. Procedures to write and read this data are shown in Listing 16-6.

Listing 16-6   The WriteToTextFile and ReadFromTextFile Procedures

```
Public Sub WriteToTextFile(ByRef sFullName As String, _
                           ByRef sData As String)
    Dim iFile As Integer
    ' Get an available file handle.
    iFile = FreeFile()
    ' Open the specified file for Output.
    Open sFullName For Output As #iFile
    ' Write the data to the file.
    Print #iFile, sData
    ' Close the file.
    Close #iFile
```

```
End Sub

Public Sub ReadFromTextFile(ByRef sFullName As String, _
                            ByRef sData As String)
    Dim iFile As Integer
    ' Get an available file handle.
    iFile = FreeFile()
    ' Open the specified file for Input.
    Open sFullName For Input As #iFile
    ' Return the data from the file.
    sData = Input$(LOF(iFile), #iFile)
    ' Remove the trailing vbCrLf characters.
    sData = Left$(sData, Len(sData) - 2)
    ' Close the file.
    Close #iFile
End Sub
```

To verify that these procedures work as expected, we need to create a test harness that feeds them a large number of data strings and then compares the original data string to the string we get after saving the data to a text file and retrieving it from a text file. If there are any differences between the original string and the string retrieved from the text file, then we know there is a bug in one of the procedures that needs to be fixed. The test harness that performs this operation is shown in Listing 16-7.

Listing 16-7 The Test Harness for the ReturnPathAndFilename Procedure

```
Public Sub TestHarness()

    Dim bFailure As Boolean
    Dim lTest As Long
    Dim lLength As Long
    Dim lChar As Long
    Dim sFullName As String
    Dim sInput As String
    Dim sOutput As String

    ' The full path and file name to use for testing.
    sFullName = ThisWorkbook.Path & "\ReadWriteTest.txt"

    For lTest = 1 To 1000
```

```
    Application.StatusBar = "Running test: " & lTest

    ' Generate a random binary data string.
    Randomize
    sInput = vbNullString
    lLength = CLng(Rnd() * 100)
    For lChar = 1 To lLength
        ' Start at Chr(27) so as not to embed an EOF.
        sInput = sInput & Chr(27 + CLng(Rnd() * 228))
    Next lChar

    ' Write the string to the text file.
    WriteToTextFile sFullName, sInput

    ' Read the string from the text file.
    ReadFromTextFile sFullName, sOutput

    ' Compare the returned string to the original.
    If StrComp(sInput, sOutput, vbBinaryCompare) <> 0 Then
        Debug.Print "Comparison error on test " & lTest
        Debug.Print "Input: " & sInput
        Debug.Print "Ouput: " & sOutput
        bFailure = True
    End If

Next lTest

' Delete the test file.
Kill sFullName

' Display the results.
Application.StatusBar = False
If bFailure Then
    MsgBox "Failures encountered. " & _
        "See list in the Immediate window."
Else
    MsgBox "All tests succeeded."
End If

End Sub
```

In the TestHarness procedure, we generate a random string, save the string to a text file, read the string back out of the text file, and compare the resulting string to the string we originally generated. We use a loop to perform this process on a large number of randomly generated strings. If any string read from the text file does not match the originally generated string exactly, we print the results to the Immediate window and display an error message upon completion of the test harness. Otherwise, we display a success message. Verifying as many procedures as possible using the test harness approach should be considered a best programming practice.

Using Assertions

Assertions are a way to guarantee that one or more specific conditions hold true. They can be used to test the validity of variables or expressions at specific points within your program. In VBA programming, assertions are implemented using the `Debug.Assert` method. The `Debug.Assert` method takes a Boolean expression as its single argument. If the value of the expression is False, `Debug.Assert` causes code execution to halt and enter break mode on the line of code where the assertion failed.

Assertions created using `Debug.Assert` ignore the global error trapping setting defined under the VBE *Tools > Options > General > Error Trapping* menu. A `Debug.Assert` statement causes code execution to enter break mode regardless of the global error trapping setting. Listing 16-8 shows an example of `Debug.Assert` in use.

Listing 16-8   Debug.Assert Example

```
Sub DebugAssertExample()

    Dim lRow As Long
    Dim lColumn As Long

    ' Some code here that sets lRow and lColumn.

    Debug.Assert (lRow > 0) And (lColumn > 0)

    Sheet1.Cells(lRow, lColumn).Value = True

End Sub
```

In this example, we are using two variables to store the row and column number that specifies the Range we access using the Cells method in the last line of code. Because both the row and column number must be greater than zero, we use the `Debug.Assert` statement to halt program execution if either one of them fails this test.

Note that we combine two related Boolean tests into a single `Debug.Assert` expression. You can link as many related tests into the same assertion as you want. We recommend, however, that unrelated assertions get separate lines of code. This simplifies the debugging process, especially in cases where you may be experiencing multiple errors.

Assertions are especially valuable when debugging intermittent errors or errors that are difficult to reproduce. If you can narrow down the section of code where the error is occurring, you can simply place assertions on all the important variables and expressions used in that section of code. You then run the program normally, trying various combinations of things until one of your assertions fails and halts your program.

Keep in mind that `Debug.Assert` is purely a debugging tool. It should not be used to test conditions that require validation each time your program runs (and in fact `Debug.Assert` will be ignored completely if your project is protected). For example, if your application needs a specific file to function correctly, you should write code to check for that file in your Auto_Open procedure. This is called a **permanent assertion**, because it is always performed. A permanent assertion is different from the kind created using the `Debug.Assert` statement because it throws a runtime error that can be handled by your project error handling system. An example of this is shown in the excerpt from our PetrasAddin.xla workbook's Auto_Open procedure in Listing 16-9.

Listing 16-9 A Permanent Assertion

```
' Make sure we can locate our time entry workbook before we
' do anything else.
If Len(Dir$(gsAppDir & gsFILE_TIME_ENTRY)) = 0 Then _
    Err.Raise glHANDLED_ERROR, sSOURCE, gsERR_FILE_NOT_FOUND
```

This permanent assertion verifies that we can locate our time entry template workbook and throws a custom error if we can't. Our program can never run properly without its accompanying time entry template, so this check should be performed whenever the application is run.

Debugging Shortcut Keys That Every Developer Should Know

As with most programming tasks, the fewer times you take your hands off the keyboard during debugging the faster and more productive you will be in the long term. With that in mind, what follows is a list of the most useful debugging-related keyboard shortcuts.

General

F5—Run: Runs the procedure within which the cursor is currently located. If the cursor is not currently located within a procedure that can be run directly, or if the cursor is not located within any procedure, the VBE prompts you with the Macros dialog, which displays a list of procedures that can be run. If you are already in break mode, F5 runs your code to the next break point or to completion, whichever comes first.

F9—Toggle Break Point: Toggles between setting and removing a break point on the line of code occupied by the cursor. See the section on "Using Break Points" earlier in the chapter for more details on how to effectively use break points.

Ctrl+Shift+F9—Clear All Break Points: If you have set a number of break points in your code, and then corrected the error you were looking for, you may simply want to remove all break points from your code so that you can run it normally and verify your fix. You can quickly remove all break points from your code by pressing Ctrl+Shift+F9.

Ctrl+G—Display the Immediate Window: After viewing the contents of the Immediate window, you may want to clear it. Unfortunately, there is no single shortcut key to do this, but the combination of Ctrl+G, Ctrl+A, Del gives the Immediate window focus and the cursor; select all text in the Immediate window and delete it. This process is also automated by an excellent, free set of utilities called MZTools, which also contains a host of other useful VBE utilities. You can download a copy of MZTools at www.mztools.com/v3/download.aspx.

Debug Mode Code Execution

F8—Step Into: Once in break mode, this key allows you to step through your code one line at a time. If you are not in break mode but your cursor is within a valid entry point procedure, code execution begins and break mode starts on the first line of that procedure.

Shift+F8—Step Over: Once in break mode, this steps completely over the next line of code to be executed. Whether that line is a simple statement or a complex nested function call, Shift+F8 executes all the code required to step over the line and resumes break mode at the next breakable position.

Ctrl+Shift+F8—Step Out Of: If you have stepped into a called procedure and determined that what you are looking for is not there, you don't have to continue single stepping through the rest of the procedure to get back out. Ctrl+Shift+F8 tells VBA to finish executing the procedure you are in and resume break mode on the first breakable line immediately following the call that brought you into the procedure.

Ctrl+F8—Step to Cursor: During debugging, you will often encounter a group of statements that you do not need to examine carefully. Rather than single stepping through them, you can place your cursor at the beginning of the next line of code you want to step through and press Ctrl+F8. VBA runs all the lines of code between your current position and the point where you placed the cursor, and then stops and resumes break mode at the line where you placed the cursor.

Ctrl+F9—Set Next Statement: When you are single-step debugging your code, you may see a section that you want to skip altogether. To do so, simply move the cursor down to the next line you want executed and press Ctrl+F9. VBA skips all the lines of code between the current execution point and resumes break mode on the line specified by your cursor position.

Navigation

Shift+F2—Procedure Definition: When you place your cursor on the name of a procedure and press this shortcut, you are taken to the definition of that procedure. This also works for variables, constants, and enumerations.

Ctrl+Shift+F2—Last Position: This shortcut is the reverse of Shift+F2. It returns you to the position within your code where you were located when you pressed Shift+F2.

Information

Ctrl+L—Call Stack: This shortcut displays the Call Stack window so you can see how you got to the procedure where you're currently located in a deeply nested section of code.

Shift+F9—Quick Watch: This displays the Quick Watch dialog, which displays the context (scope) of the expression you selected, the expression itself, and the value of the expression.

F2—Object Browser: This displays the Object Browser.

Summary

Excellent debugging skills are one of the primary attributes that separate professional programmers from skilled amateurs. In this chapter we covered the vast array of debugging tools and techniques that you have at your disposal in the VBA environment. If ever there were an aspect of programming to which the old adage "practice makes perfect" applies, it is surely debugging. All the dedicated debugging tools described here notwithstanding, the practice of debugging is just as much art as science.

Learning these tools is a starting point, but you must debug a significant amount of real-world code, ideally not all of it your own, before you become truly proficient. Many people have remarked to us, and we believe it to be true, that you learn more from debugging mistakes than you do from getting it right the first time. So go forth and debug!

CHAPTER 17

OPTIMIZING VBA PERFORMANCE

A common complaint about VBA in general, and particularly procedures that automate Excel, is poor performance. While there is some truth in that, say when compared to C++, it is often due to poorly structured or poorly written code. This is probably because VBA makes it easy to write code that works, but difficult to write code that works fast. As a general rule, the speed of a well-optimized procedure can often be an order of magnitude faster than the original code, and improvements of two orders of magnitude are not uncommon. This chapter explains how to achieve those savings.

Measuring Performance

The end users of your application are the final arbiters of performance, and they rarely use stopwatches to time how long something takes. Instead, they form an impression based on their expectations, past experiences, visual cues, and the activity they're performing. As a general guideline, we aim to keep within the times shown in Table 17-1.

All these targets refer to the end user experience and so must be checked using a PC similar to the average user's specification. Note also that the difference between a simple form or report and a complex one is purely the user's perception and need not have any relationship to the technical complexity.

Hopefully, you'll find that most code you write performs well within these targets, even with the largest data sets, so there will be little benefit in trying to optimize it. Undoubtedly, though, some of your code will take much longer to run and will give your application a poor reputation among users. Radically improving the few slowest procedures often gives the impression the whole application is more responsive overall. The rest of this chapter explains the steps you can take to achieve significant improvements in the performance of your slowest procedures.

Table 17-1 Target Response Times

Action	Response Time
Displaying a simple form	< 2 seconds
Displaying a complex form	< 10 seconds
Selecting items within a form	< 1 second
Typing within a form	Unnoticeable
Preparing a simple report	< 10 seconds
Preparing a complex report	< 30 seconds

Once you've optimized the application as much as possible there are a few tricks you can use to make it seem to perform better, even though it might not be doing so:

- If a procedure takes more than about a second, change the cursor to an hourglass at the start of it and back to normal at the end. This tricks the user into expecting a delay, and they're pleasantly surprised when it finishes quickly.
- If a procedure is triggered by the user typing into a text box, never show an hourglass. Showing an hourglass tells the user you expect the procedure to be lengthy and no procedures triggered by text box Change events should have a noticeable delay.
- If a procedure takes more than about 5 seconds, display a progress bar (such as the ones shown in Chapter 13, "UserForm Design and Best Practices," and Chapter 14, "Interfaces") prominently on the screen. A progress bar that quickly reaches 100% gives the impression of speed, while a progress bar for a lengthy procedure lets users know the procedure is advancing, lets them estimate how long there is left, and gives them something to concentrate on so they don't think the application is frozen and get the urge to press Ctrl+Alt+Del.

The PerfMon Utility

The PerfMon utility is a set of three DLLs that allow us to monitor and record the performance of a VBA application as it is executing. It achieves this by adding a line of code to the top and bottom of every procedure to notify the monitoring DLL when the procedure starts and finishes. The DLL records the number of times each procedure is called and the maximum, total, and average time spent in each.

The result is a complete list of all the procedures called and the detailed timings for each, either copied to the Clipboard or saved to a text file. Once imported into an Excel worksheet and sorted by total time, the result looks something like Figure 17-1. We can immediately see that the first procedure accounts for nearly the entire processing time and is therefore where we should focus our optimization efforts.

	A	B	C	D	E	F	G
1	Tot Dur	11.24252					
2							
3	Project	Module	Proc	Count	Total	Avg	Max
4	prjChapter17	MPerfMon	ALengthyProcedure2	1	11.12998	11.12998	11.12998
5	prjChapter17	MPerfMon	ALengthyProcedure1	1	0.11243	0.11243	0.11243
6	prjChapter17	MPerfMon	ALengthyProcedure	1	0.00009	0.00009	0.00009

FIGURE 17-1   An example of the PerfMon results

The three DLLs are found in the *Tools\PerfMon* directory on the CD and comprise:

- **PerfMonitor.dll**—An ActiveX DLL that uses the Windows high-performance counter to track the performance of each procedure. It is listed in the *Project > References* dialog as *PerfMon: VB/VBA Performance Monitor*.
- **PerfMonOffice.dll**—An add-in for the Office VBE to add and remove the calls to the PerfMonitor dll.
- **PerfMonVB6.dll**—An add-in for the VB6 IDE to add and remove the calls to the PerfMonitor dll.

The folder also includes the CPerfMon.cls file, which is a class module that can be included in a VB6 project to enable cross-process performance monitoring for use during development of combined Excel/VB6 solutions (see Chapter 23, "Excel and Visual Basic 6"). To install the DLLs, close Excel, copy them to your hard disk, and open each one with the Regsvr32.exe program. The easiest way to do this is to right-click the file in Windows Explorer, choose *Open With...*, and browse to the Regsvr32.exe file, usually found in *C:\Windows\System32*.

To start using the utility, click on *Add-ins > PerfMon > Add PerfMon Calls* and select which procedures to add the calls to, as shown in Figure 17-2.

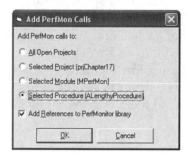

FIGURE 17-2 The Add PerfMon Calls dialog

When you click OK, the utility adds a reference to the PerfMonitor DLL and adds calling code to the top and bottom of the selected procedure(s), as shown in Listing 17-1.

Listing 17-1 A Procedure with the Automatic PerfMon Calls Added

```
Sub ALengthyProcedure()
  PerfMonProcStart "PrjChapter17.MPerfMon.AlengthyProcedure"

  'Do something lengthy

  PerfMonProcEnd "PrjChapter17.MPerfMon.AlengthyProcedure"
End Sub
```

Note that every procedure is given a unique ID consisting of the concatenation of the project name, module name, procedure name, and property type (if it is a property procedure). If you have a particularly long procedure that would be better monitored in separate blocks, you can add extra PerfMon calls manually. Just take care to match ProcStart and ProcEnd calls, as shown in Listing 17-2.

Listing 17-2 A Procedure with Manual PerfMon Calls Added

```
Sub ALengthyProcedure()
  PerfMonProcStart "PrjChapter17.MPerfMon.AlengthyProcedure"
```

```
PerfMonProcStart "PrjChapter17.MPerfMon.AlengthyProcedure1"
'Do something lengthy
PerfMonProcEnd "PrjChapter17.MPerfMon.AlengthyProcedure1"


PerfMonProcStart "PrjChapter17.MPerfMon.AlengthyProcedure2"
'Do something else lengthy
PerfMonProcEnd "PrjChapter17.MPerfMon.AlengthyProcedure2"


PerfMonProcEnd "PrjChapter17.MPerfMon.AlengthyProcedure"
End Sub
```

The last thing to do is add a line to tell the utility when to start and stop
monitoring, as shown in Listing 17-3.

Listing 17-3 Include the Calls to Start and Stop the Monitoring

```
Sub ALengthyProcedure()

'Start monitoring all procedures from here
PerfMonStartMonitoring

PerfMonProcStart "PrjChapter17.MPerfMon.AlengthyProcedure"

PerfMonProcStart "PrjChapter17.MPerfMon.AlengthyProcedure1"
'Do something lengthy
PerfMonProcEnd "PrjChapter17.MPerfMon.AlengthyProcedure1"

PerfMonProcStart "PrjChapter17.MPerfMon.AlengthyProcedure2"
'Do something else lengthy
PerfMonProcEnd "PrjChapter17.MPerfMon.AlengthyProcedure2"

PerfMonProcEnd "PrjChapter17.MPerfMon.AlengthyProcedure"

'Stop monitoring and write the results to a file
'If no file name given, the results will be put on the clipboard
PerfMonStopMonitoring "c:\MyProcedureTiming.txt"

End Sub
```

The easiest way to analyze the results is to start a new Excel session, click on *Data > Get External Data > Import Text File* (Excel 2000) or *Data > Import External Data > Import Data* (Excel XP/2003) or *Data > Get External Data > From Text* (Excel 2007), select the text file that you gave in the PerfMonStopMonitoring call, and click through the Text Import Wizard. It is better to import the data instead of just opening the file, as the latter locks the file and the PerfMon monitor will not then be able to overwrite it with new results for each subsequent run. We can also set the import to use the same filename each time, allowing us to re-import the new results by clicking the Refresh button, shown in Figure 17-3.

	A	B	C	D	E	F	G
1	Tot Dur	11.24252					
2							
3	Project	Module	Proc	Count	Total	Avg	Max
4	prjChapter17	MPerfMon	ALengthyProcedure2	1	11.12998	11.12998	11.12998
5	prjChapter17	MPerfMon	ALengthyProcedure1	1	0.11243	0.11243	0.11243
6	prjChapter17	MPerfMon	ALengthyProcedure	1	0.00009	0.00009	0.00009
7							
8			External Data				
9							
10							
11			Refresh Data				

FIGURE 17-3 Importing the file allows us to quickly refresh the data with new results.

All the timings shown in the results table are in seconds, with an accuracy of at least a millisecond. The monitoring calls themselves take a small amount of time, so the results shown are typically slightly slower than the unmonitored code. Sort the table by the Total column to quickly identify the slowest procedures. In this example, we can clearly see the second half of our procedure is taking nearly all the time. To achieve the most accurate results, the tests should be run without any other applications open, and certainly without switching to them, so Windows can dedicate all its resources to the application being tested.

Because these timings will probably be done on a developer-class computer, we need to calculate a target duration for us to work towards, by comparing the total duration shown in the top-left corner to that experienced by the user and prorating it to the user's target time. Obviously, this can only be done when you are timing "end-to-end" processes—that is, from the time the user clicked a button to when the form or report is displayed. All we need to do then is think of ways in which the speed of the procedures can be improved.

Creative Thinking

The key to improving your application's performance is to remove the bottlenecks by trying to find a different and faster way to perform the same task. Either by rethinking the entire approach, so the task that took so long is no longer needed, or by figuring out how to accomplish the task in less time.

The trick is to tap into the creative side of your brain, so rather than "analyzing" the problem and "identifying" a solution, use your imagination to conjure up sentences that start with "I wonder what would happen if I...." While this may seem like an alien concept to those of us who are normally analytical instead of artistic, there are a few exercises that can help.

Doing a Jigsaw Puzzle

On the rare occasions that we teach a class on performance optimization, we split the class into pairs, give each pair a child's six-piece jigsaw puzzle to build, and time how long they take to complete it. The rules of the game are

1. All the pieces must start face down, arranged randomly on the table.
2. The jigsaw puzzle must be completed and finish face up.
3. You are not allowed to touch any piece until the timer starts.

The first attempt usually takes about 30 seconds. Applying the rule that an optimized procedure should be an order of magnitude faster than the first attempt gives us a target of 3 seconds to do the six-piece jigsaw puzzle.

Identify the Steps

The bigger the task, the harder it is to invent a completely new way of performing it that will still work. Instead, break the task down into smaller steps and try to think how each step could be either avoided entirely or speeded up. In VBA terms, the temptation is to focus on each existing procedure, but doing so just locks in the existing design. Instead, look at the process as a whole and identify the transformations, checks, and processing that occur.

Looking at our jigsaw puzzle example, the processing could be broken down into the following steps for each piece:

Pick it up → Turn it over → Identify it → Put it down → Join it up

With six pieces and five things to do for each piece, 30 seconds is a reasonable amount of time, but can any of those steps be removed?

Think Outside the Box

"Think outside the box" is probably the most commonly used phrase of consultant jargon, urging us to come up with some new idea. But what does it really mean? The origin we like most comes from being asked to join up nine dots by drawing as few connected straight lines as possible— analogous to making a procedure run as fast as possible.

Using five lines is easy (as is our first attempt at coding a VBA procedure).

But can you connect all the dots using four straight lines? Visually, the nine dots appear to our brains as a box, which is a visual metaphor for the many rules, regulations, and norms that we work (and code) within, usually as a

result of our upbringing and education. Connecting the dots using four lines requires us to break through the boundaries of the box, and start to consider the area outside it—literally thinking outside the box.

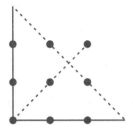

Now that you're thinking outside the box, can you solve the problem using three straight lines? You'll have to think further outside the box, and also remove a constraint that was never stated but has so far been assumed; that the lines have to pass through the center of each dot.

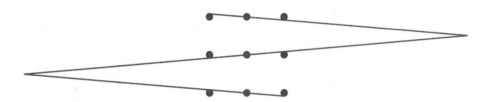

So what other unstated assumptions can we break to join the dots using even fewer lines? Just one line, perhaps? If we take the three-line solution to its extreme, we could have one line that spirals around the globe (the solution doesn't have to be physically practical). Or we could break another assumption and use a thicker pen. In fact a paintbrush could cover all the dots with one line.

But our thinking is *still* boxed in—literally. To truly think outside the box requires us to remove the box itself. Was it ever stated that we couldn't cut the paper? Doing so makes a one-line solution trivial.

The final optimization is to realize we can complete the task of joining the dots without drawing any lines at all. If we cut the paper carefully, we can have all the dots touching to begin with. Even better is to break a last assumption and think in terms of 3D, not 2D, space and stack the dots on top of each other. We've now optimized the task of joining the dots to doing nothing.

The next time you're asked to "Think outside the box," step out of your cubicle and ask "What box?"

Break the Rules

A large part of creative thinking, then, is to break the (often unstated) rules that normally govern our behavior. These rules (usually) exist for some good reasons, but performance is rarely one of them. For example, passing a variable to a procedure by value (ByVal) is the method recommended in Chapter 3, "Excel and VBA Development Best Practices." This is mainly due to defensive programming. You know the procedure being called can't change the value of the variable passed in, but is often slower than passing the variable by reference (ByRef). This is particularly true when passing large strings or Variant arrays.

The one thing we ***must*** do when breaking rules it to fully document the rules we're breaking and why we're breaking them, preferably both in the formal documentation and by commenting the affected code. It's not uncommon for a maintenance developer to think, "We shouldn't do that" and unwittingly undo your optimizations.

Returning to our jigsaw puzzle, what rules can we break to speed up the task? The five steps to completing a piece of the puzzle are

Pick it up → Turn it over → Identify it → Put it down → Join it up

One thing we can do is draw on the table. By tracing around the completed jigsaw pieces (on a piece of paper) we can tell exactly where each piece goes, allowing us to put it down in its final position. We've combined the "Put it down" and "Join it up" tasks and reduced the time accordingly. In VBA terms, a procedure that processes a set of data often has a final step that organizes the results for the next process (such as removing duplicates/blanks, sorting, and so on). Try to combine that organization into the processing of the data, so the natural output of the data processing can be passed directly to the next procedure.

We can also write on the puzzle pieces. By numbering the back of each piece and its final position on the flip chart paper, we know before we've even touched a piece exactly where it has to go, and we no longer need the "Identify it" step. The VBA equivalent is to ensure the incoming data is in a structured, predictable format before we have to process it. If the incoming data can't be obtained in such a format (by modifying the previous procedure), it is often faster to arrange it that way at the start of a procedure than to deal with the lack of structure during the data processing. For example, if the procedure does a lot of searching through a list, it is much faster to sort the list first and use a binary search algorithm than it is to search through an unsorted list each time.

By ensuring we have structured our incoming data (by numbering the jigsaw pieces) and combined the final reorganization into the main processing (by drawing and numbering an outline of each piece of the completed jigsaw), we no longer need to turn the piece over to identify it and so have reduced the processing required for each piece to a simple "Move it." One task for each of our six pieces gives us a processing time of roughly 6 seconds, which is well on the way to our target of 3 seconds.

So far we've concentrated on optimizing a procedure by changing the way in which things are done to reduce the amount of processing required. By doing these macro-scale optimizations we've achieved 80% of our target 90% saving. This is typical for many situations. The last 10% comes from making the remaining minimum processing as fast as it can be.

Know the Data

When doing a jigsaw puzzle, with everything else being equal, the second and third attempts are likely to be somewhat faster than the first. This is simply because the people assembling the puzzle start to recognize which piece is which and where it goes, shaving another few seconds off the processing time. The last second can be shaved by choosing to do the pieces in a specific order. Each person does one of the middle two pieces first, then the two pieces at opposite ends.

The equivalent VBA is in knowing the amount, format, type, and so on of the incoming data and hence the most efficient way to process most of it. Procedures are often required to handle slightly different types of data in slightly different ways, but where the differences are rarely sufficient to justify separate, dedicated procedures. But it is almost impossible for a procedure to be equally efficient at handling all the expected data types.

In most cases, the procedures we write are fastest when operating within certain limits, such as the typical size of lists. The most efficient code to handle lists with up to ten items is unlikely to be the most efficient at handling lists with thousands of items. If we know the data we'll be given and can identify which are the most common situations, we can optimize our procedures to handle those situations as efficiently as possible to maximize overall performance. If this results in poor performance for the rare cases, we may be forced to include alternative procedures optimized for those. In that case, there would be a trade-off between performance and maintainability.

Ask Questions

What if it were an elephant? What if it were a mouse? The corollary to knowing the data is to consider how you would approach the problem if you had to process significantly more or significantly less data. By forcing yourself to consider solutions to out-of-bounds situations you may think of new ways to streamline the processing.

What if I stood on my head? Instead of looking at the code from top to bottom and accepting that B follows A, look at it from bottom to top and keep asking "Does B *have to* follow A? What can I change in B to break that dependency? If I do that, can I get rid of A entirely? Is that any faster?"

Know the Tool

Once we've reduced the number of processing steps to a minimum and organized the rest to be most efficient when handling the most common situations, ensuring that we write the most efficient code can save the last few percentage points. Both in pure VBA, and when automating Excel, there are usually a number of alternative ways of doing the same thing, some faster than others. These micro-level optimizations require a good understanding of the tool being used (that is, VBA and/or Excel), are often counterintuitive, and are often different for different data types (Longs versus Strings versus Variants). Many of these alternatives are explained in the "Micro-Optimization" section later in this chapter.

Macro-Optimization

The vast majority of performance improvement comes from restructuring your code to use a more efficient algorithm. In this section we highlight some of the things to look for and provide alternative suggestions for doing the same thing more efficiently. Whether the suggestions shown here are better or worse than your existing code depends very much on the situation, particularly on the amount and type of data being processed.

The slowest parts of a procedure invariably involve either external data retrieval or repeatedly looping through sets of data. Large loops are almost always an opportunity for optimization. Any improvement that can be made inside a loop, however minor, is a gain many times over.

The performance of external data retrieval is usually dependent on server and network performance and is something we have little control over. One thing we *can* do to minimize the effect of poor database performance is to load as much data as possible (such as static lookup lists) when the application starts instead of as it is required. Users often find it more acceptable to have a longer startup time than sluggish performance once the application is running.

Pre-Process

Before reading the rest of this paragraph, start Excel and write the fastest possible VBA procedure you can to calculate how many 1's there are in the binary representation of the numbers 0 through 255. How did you do it? Did you use the Dec2Bin function from the Analysis Toolpak? Did you use a recursive procedure? Did you repeatedly divide by 2 and check if the result was odd or even? Or did you work the numbers yourself, hard-code the results in a VBA array, and just read them at runtime, as shown in Listing 17-4?

Listing 17-4   How Many 1's Are There in a Binary Number?

```
Function CountTheOnes(ByVal iValue As Integer) As Integer

    Static vaOneCount As Variant

    'Initialize the array
    If IsEmpty(vaOneCount) Then
        vaOneCount = Array(0, 1, 1, 2, 1, ... , 7, 8)
    End If

    'Read the result
    CountTheOnes = vaOneCount(iValue)

End Function
```

If we do as much processing as possible when developing an application, the application doesn't need to do the processing at runtime.

Check the Order

The best procedures are those whose performance doesn't vary significantly with the volume of data being processed. For example, if a procedure that processes an array takes approximately the same amount of time to execute whether there are ten or ten thousand elements in the array, the procedure is said to have an order of 1. This is very hard to achieve in practice.

The next best are those that vary linearly with the volume of data, such as one or more sequential For...Next loops through the data. These procedures have an order of N, so if we have ten times as much data, the procedure is likely to take approximately ten times as long. With a little thought and work, most procedures can be reduced to order N.

Nested loops result in procedures that are very sensitive to the volume of data being processed. A procedure with two nested loops has an order N^2, and each extra level of nesting adds an extra order to the procedure. If these procedures are given ten times as much data to process, they are likely to take 100 or 1,000 times as long. If a procedure with three nested loops normally takes 10 seconds to complete, it might take 15 minutes to process ten times as much data.

In most cases, nested loops are just a quick and easy way to code an algorithm that could be redesigned as multiple sequential loops through the data. Note that nested loops often are spread over many different procedures, for example, where ProcedureA loops through an array and calls ProcedureB for each element, which itself loops through another array to process the element. As an example, consider the procedure in Listing 17-5, which compares two arrays and processes any items that are in both.

Listing 17-5 Compare Two Arrays

```
Sub ProcessLists(asArray1() As String, asArray2() As String)

   Dim lIndex1 As Long
   Dim lIndex2 As Long

   'Loop through the first array
   For lIndex1 = LBound(asArray1) To UBound(asArray1)

      'Loop through the second array
      For lIndex2 = LBound(asArray2) To UBound(asArray2)

         'Do they match?
         If asArray1(lIndex1) = asArray2(lIndex2) Then
            'Yes, so process it
```

```
    End If

  Next lIndex2

Next lIndex1

End Sub
```

Without thinking too hard about how to improve this procedure, we might be tempted to just add an `Exit For` to jump out of the inner loop once we've found a match, but that still leaves the procedure essentially of order N^2. If the two arrays are sorted, we can reduce this to order N by looping through both arrays within the same loop, as shown in Listing 17-6.

Listing 17-6 Process Both Arrays within One Loop

```
Sub ProcessLists(asArray1() As String, asArray2() As String)

  Dim lIndex1 As Long
  Dim lIndex2 As Long
  Dim iComp As Integer

  lIndex1 = LBound(asArray1)
  lIndex2 = LBound(asArray2)

  'Loop through both arrays together
  Do
    'Compare the elements from both arrays
    iComp = StrComp(asArray1(lIndex1), asArray2(lIndex2))

    If iComp = 0 Then
      'A match, so process it
      Debug.Print asArray1(lIndex1)

      'And advance in both arrays
      lIndex1 = lIndex1 + 1
      lIndex2 = lIndex2 + 1

    ElseIf iComp = -1 Then
      'Item in array1 is before item in array2,
      'so move down array1 and check again
      lIndex1 = lIndex1 + 1

    ElseIf iComp = 1 Then
```

```
      'Item in array1 is after item in array2,
      'so move down array2 and check again
      lIndex2 = lIndex2 + 1
   End If
   'Stop when we reach the end of one of the arrays
 Loop Until lIndex1 > UBound(asArray1) Or _
             lIndex2 > UBound(asArray2)


End Sub
```

If the arrays are not sorted, it will probably be faster to sort them both beforehand and then use the procedure shown in Listing 17-6. If the output has to be in a specific order (preventing us from sorting both arrays), we could sort asArray2 and use a binary search procedure to see whether the string exists, or use a Dictionary object (we show an example of each later).

Tighten the Loop

Having replaced the nested loops with more efficient algorithms, the next task is to make the code within the remaining loop as tight as possible. As well as implementing all the micro-optimizations shown later in this chapter, the primary goal is to ensure that during each iteration we only execute the minimum amount of code possible. Returning to the question above "Does B have to follow A?" it is common to see loops that contain code to calculate intermediate results, followed by some tests to check whether the intermediate result should be used (as this reflects the order in which we originally thought about the procedure). If we turn the procedure on its head, we can do the tests first and only calculate the intermediate results for those elements we know we'll be using.

Fast VBA Algorithms

QuickSort

The QuickSort procedure is one of the fastest sorting algorithms and should be used whenever you want to sort an array. It works by doing the following:

1. Select one element from the array, typically taken from the middle.
2. Scan through the array moving everything that should come before the selected element to the bottom of the array and everything that should come after the selected element to the top of the array.

3. Call itself to sort the bottom half.
4. Call itself to sort the top half.

For best performance, you should have a number of QuickSort procedures for specific data types, such as that shown in Listing 17-7 for one-dimensional string arrays.

Listing 17-7 A QuickSort Procedure for One-Dimensional String Arrays

```
'''''''''''''''''''''''''''''''''''''''''''''''''''''''''''''''''
' Comments: Sorts the passed String array into required order.
'           The array must be a 1D string array of any size.
'
' Arguments:    saArray         A 1D string array to sort.
'               bSortAscending  True = ascending order.
'               lLow1           The first item to sort between.
'               lHigh1          The last item to sort between.
'
' Date          Developer       Action
' - - - - - - - - - - - - - - - - - - - - - - - - - - - - - - - -
' 02 Jun 04     Stephen Bullen  Created
'
Sub QuickSortString1D(ByRef saArray() As String, _
            Optional ByVal bSortAscending As Boolean = True, _
            Optional ByVal lLow1 As Variant, _
            Optional ByVal lHigh1 As Variant)

    'Dimension variables
    Dim lLow2 As Long
    Dim lHigh2 As Long
    Dim sKey As String
    Dim sSwap As String


    On Error GoTo ErrorExit

    'If not provided, sort the entire array
    If IsMissing(lLow1) Then lLow1 = LBound(saArray)
    If IsMissing(lHigh1) Then lHigh1 = UBound(saArray)

    'Set new extremes to old extremes
    lLow2 = lLow1
    lHigh2 = lHigh1

    'Get value of array item in middle of new extremes
```

```
sKey = saArray((lLow1 + lHigh1) \ 2)

'Loop for all the items in the array between the extremes
Do While lLow2 < lHigh2

  If bSortAscending Then
    'Find the first item that is greater than the mid-point item
    Do While saArray(lLow2) < sKey And lLow2 < lHigh1
      lLow2 = lLow2 + 1
    Loop

    'Find the last item that is less than the mid-point item
    Do While saArray(lHigh2) > sKey And lHigh2 > lLow1
      lHigh2 = lHigh2 - 1
    Loop
  Else
    'Find the first item that is less than the mid-point item
    Do While saArray(lLow2) > sKey And lLow2 < lHigh1
      lLow2 = lLow2 + 1
    Loop

    'Find the last item that is greater than the mid-point item
    Do While saArray(lHigh2) < sKey And lHigh2 > lLow1
      lHigh2 = lHigh2 - 1
    Loop
  End If

  'If the two items are in the wrong order, swap the rows
  If lLow2 < lHigh2 Then
    sSwap = saArray(lLow2)
    saArray(lLow2) = saArray(lHigh2)
    saArray(lHigh2) = sSwap
  End If

  'If the pointers are not together, advance to the next item
  If lLow2 <= lHigh2 Then
    lLow2 = lLow2 + 1
    lHigh2 = lHigh2 - 1
  End If
Loop

'Recurse to sort the lower half of the extremes
If lHigh2 > lLow1 Then
  QuickSortString1D saArray, bSortAscending, lLow1, lHigh2
End If
```

```
'Recurse to sort the upper half of the extremes
If lLow2 < lHigh1 Then
   QuickSortString1D saArray, bSortAscending, lLow2, lHigh1
End If

ErrorExit:

End Sub
```

Binary Search

A binary search is a fast way to locate an item within a sorted array. It works by doing the following:

1. Compare the item to look for with the element in the middle of the array.
2. If they match, we found it.
3. If the item to look for is less than the middle of the array, throw away the top half.
4. If the item to look for is greater than the middle of the array, throw away the bottom half.
5. Repeat steps 1 through 4, cutting the array in half each time until we find the item or run out of array.

A binary search procedure, such as that shown in Listing 17-8, is practically insensitive to the size of the array passed in. Doubling the size of the array results in only one additional iteration of the procedure.

Listing 17-8   A Binary Search Algorithm

```
''''''''''''''''''''''''''''''''''''''''''''''''''''''''''''''''
' Comments:      Uses a binary search algorithm to quickly locate
'                a string within a sorted array of strings
'
' Arguments:     sLookFor    The string to search for in the array
'                saArray     An array of strings, sorted ascending
'                lMethod     Either vbBinaryCompare or vbTextCompare
'                            Defaults to vbTextCompare
'                lNotFound   The value to return if the text isn't
'                            found. Defaults to -1
'
```

```vba
' Returns:        Long        The located position in the array,
'                             or lNotFound if not found
'
' Date            Developer        Action
' - - - - - - - - - - - - - - - - - - - - - - - - - - - - - - - --
' 02 Jun 04      Stephen Bullen   Created
'
Function BinarySearchString(ByRef sLookFor As String, _
        ByRef saArray() As String, _
        Optional ByVal lMethod As VbCompareMethod = vbTextCompare, _
        Optional ByVal lNotFound As Long = -1) As Long

    Dim lLow As Long
    Dim lMid As Long
    Dim lHigh As Long
    Dim lComp As Long

    On Error GoTo ErrorExit

    'Assume we didn't find it
    BinarySearchString = lNotFound

    'Get the starting positions
    lLow = LBound(saArray)
    lHigh = UBound(saArray)

    Do
        'Find the midpoint of the array
        lMid = (lLow + lHigh) \ 2

        'Compare the mid-point element to the string being searched for
        lComp = StrComp(saArray(lMid), sLookFor, lMethod)

        If lComp = 0 Then
            'We found it, so return the location and quit
            BinarySearchString = lMid
            Exit Do

        ElseIf lComp = 1 Then
            'The midpoint item is bigger than us - throw away the top half
            lHigh = lMid - 1
        Else
            'The midpoint item is smaller than us - throw away the bottom
half
            lLow = lMid + 1
```

```
    End If

    'Continue until our pointers cross
    Loop Until lLow > lHigh

ErrorExit:

End Function
```

Sort and Scan

The combination of a QuickSort and BinarySearch gives us an efficient way of comparing two arrays and to locate and process their common elements, as shown in Listing 17-9.

Listing 17-9 Combining a Sort and Binary Search

```
Sub ProcessLists(asArray1() As String, asArray2() As String)

    Dim lIndex As Long

    'Sort the second array
    QuickSortString1D asArray2

    'Loop through the first array
    For lIndex = LBound(asArray1) To UBound(asArray1)

        'Use the binary search procedure to
        'check if the element is in the second array
        If BinarySearchString(asArray1(lIndex), asArray2) <> -1 Then

            'A match, so process it
            Debug.Print asArray1(lIndex)
        End If
    Next

End Sub
```

This is not quite as efficient as the example shown previously that relied on both arrays being sorted, but it's an efficient and easy to understand alternative for use when the initial array must be left in its original order.

The SORTSEARCH_INDEX UDT

When dealing with large 2D arrays, arrays of objects, or multiple keys, it is usually more efficient to create a new indexing array and sort and search that than to try to sort and search the original array. An index array is an array of the SORTSEARCH_INDEX user-defined type, which is defined as

```
Public Type SORTSEARCH_INDEX
   Key As String
   Index As Long
End Type
```

The key is the string used for sorting and searching, which is typically the value from the first column of a 2D array, the name of an object, or a concatenation of the values to sort an array by multiple columns. The index is the row number in the original array. Once the UDT array is sorted, we can loop through its elements in sorted order and use the Index property to identify the corresponding item in the original array, as shown in Listing 17-10.

Listing 17-10 Using the SORTSEARCH_INDEX User-Defined Type

```
Sub UseIndexSort()

  Dim vaArray As Variant
  Dim lRow As Long
  Dim uaIndex() As SORTSEARCH_INDEX

  'Assume vaArray is a 2D Variant array
  'e.g. as read from the worksheet
  vaArray = Selection.Value

  'Create an index array of the same size
  ReDim uaIndex(LBound(vaArray) To UBound(vaArray))

  'Populate the index array with the original row number
  'and sort key
  For lRow = LBound(vaArray) To UBound(vaArray)
    uaIndex(lRow).Index = lRow
    uaIndex(lRow).Key = vaArray(lRow, 1)
```

```
Next lRow

'Sort the index array
QuickSortIndex uaIndex

'Loop through the sorted array
For lRow = LBound(uaIndex) To UBound(uaIndex)
   'The .Index element of the sorted UDT points to the
   'row in the original array
   Debug.Print vaArray(uaIndex(lRow).Index, 2)
Next lRow

End Sub
```

QuickSortIndex is a version of the QuickSort algorithm for arrays of the SORTSEARCH_INDEX user-defined type and can be found on the CD in the workbook *Concepts\Ch17 – Optimizing VBA Performance\ Algorithms.xls*. The workbook also contains a version of the binary search algorithm, BinarySearchIndex, which searches for a string in the index array and returns the row number in the original array.

Micro-Optimization

Both VBA and Excel often provide many ways to do the same thing, some of which are always faster than the others, but some of which are sometimes faster and sometimes slower depending on the data being processed. This section discusses many of the common alternatives. Before blindly using the recommended alternative you should always confirm the behavior using your own data. This can usually be done quickly using the code shown in Listing 17-11.

Listing 17-11 A Simple Procedure to Compare Two Alternatives

```
Sub CompareThem()

   Dim dStart As Double
   Dim lCounter As Long

   'We often need lots of loops to get a measurable result
```

```
Const lLOOPS As Long = 10000

dStart = Timer

For lCounter = 1 To lLOOPS
  'The code for the first alternative
Next lCounter

Debug.Print "Version 1 took " & (Timer - dStart) & " seconds"

dStart = Timer

For lCounter = 1 To lLOOPS
  'The code for the second alternative
Next lCounter

Debug.Print "Version 2 took " & (Timer - dStart) & " seconds"

End Sub
```

VBA's built-in Timer call is fairly slow and not very accurate, so we usually have to run each alternative many times to get a consistent result, proving these micro-optimizations only have a noticeable effect if they're executed many times over.

VBA

Use Matching Data Types

VBA is very forgiving when we mix data types, such as passing a Double to a procedure that expects a String or vice versa. However, there is some overhead associated with the conversion, and it can introduce subtle bugs, so it should be avoided. Whenever passing a variable to a procedure or setting one variable equal to another, always ensure the variables have the same data type.

Perform Explicit Conversions Instead of Implicit Conversions

When you are unable to match data types, always tell VBA which conversion to perform, such as CStr(), CDbl(), and so on. By being explicit about the conversion you want to perform, you avoid wasting the time required for VBA to make the decision itself.

Use Len(String)=0 Instead of String=""

VBA stores strings in memory by storing the length of the string first, followed by the characters it contains. Because the length of the string is readily available, it is much quicker to check if it is zero than to ask VBA to perform a string comparison (with all the memory allocation that involves).

Use Left$, Right$, and Mid$ Instead of Left, Right, and Mid

Most of the VBA string-handling functions have both a variant version (Left, Right, Mid) and a string version (Left$, Right$, Mid$). If you use the variant versions with string variables, VBA has to convert the inside string to a variant, pass it to the function, get the result (as a variant), and convert the result back to a string. By using the string version of the function you eliminate the two variant-to-string conversions, which can be relatively slow, particularly with large strings.

Pass Strings and Variant Arrays ByRef Instead of ByVal

Whenever strings and arrays are passed to a procedure by value (ByVal), VBA has to make a copy of the entire string or array and pass the copy to the procedure. If the string or array is passed by reference (ByRef), VBA only has to pass a pointer to the procedure, which is much faster.

Don't Use Option Compare Text

Adding `Option Compare Text` to the top of a module forces VBA to perform all string comparisons in a case-insensitive manner. In the majority of cases, this is not required and only wastes time. Instead, every module should have `Option Compare Binary` set and you should use the CompareMethod parameter of `StrComp`, `Instr`, and so on functions to specify when case-insensitive comparisons are required. If you need to use a function that doesn't have a CompareMethod parameter (such as Like), you should either force both strings to upper- or lowercase and do a normal binary compare, or have a specific procedure to do the comparison and place it in its own module with `Option Compare Text` set.

Use Early-Binding Wherever Possible

Whenever you declare a variable `As Object`, VBA doesn't know anything about it until runtime. Every time you call a property or method of the object, VBA has to check whether the method exists, check its parameters, and confirm that your code can call it. All of this takes time and should be avoided by declaring all your object variables as specific object types wherever possible. If you are using `As Object` to call the same property on a number of your own classes you should implement a custom interface in those classes instead (see Chapter 14).

Use Integer Arithmetic Where Possible

VBA can perform integer arithmetic, particularly division, much faster than floating-point arithmetic. You can tell VBA to use integer arithmetic by declaring your variables `As Long` and using the integer division operator, `\`:

```
'Slower - uses floating-point operations
dMid = (dLow + dHigh) / 2

'Faster - uses integer operations
lMid = (lLow + lHigh) \ 2
```

Use For...Each to Iterate Collections (Not by Index)

The VBA Collection object is designed to be iterated most efficiently using the `For...Each` construct, instead of `For...Next`.

Iterate Arrays by Index (Not For...Each)

VBA arrays, however, are faster to iterate by index instead of using `For...Each`.

Use Dictionaries Instead of Collections (If Order Is Not Important)

The *Microsoft Scripting Runtime Library*, scrrun.dll, contains a very fast and lightweight Dictionary object that can be used just like a VBA Collection. As well as being faster, it exposes both the items and the keys used to store them, and supports the Exists property to check whether a key exists in the collection. Its biggest drawback is it does not allow items to be inserted into the middle of the list and so can't be used when reordering is required.

Don't Use If bVariable = True Then, Just Use If bVariable Then

If you have a Boolean variable, adding the extra step of comparing it to True in an If statement is just wasting processing cycles. The redundant comparison to True should be removed.

Don't Use IIf()

The VBA IIf() function is a convenient way to choose between two alternatives. However, it is also extremely slow compared to a multiline If statement, mostly because it always evaluates both the True and False expressions.

Use Multiple If...ElseIf...End If Instead of Select Case

Similarly, Select Case is a convenient, clear, and easy to read construct for choosing between multiple alternatives but is also slower than the equivalent If...ElseIf construct.

Use With Blocks and Object Variables to Reduce Dot Operators

VBA allows us to navigate through object model hierarchies using the dot (.) operator to access an object's properties or methods. Think of every dot as a small pause in your application and reduce them by using With blocks or object variables to cache deeply buried objects for later reuse.

Excel

Turn Off ScreenUpdating and Automatic Calculation

The biggest gains when automating Excel are achieved by setting `Application.ScreenUpdating = False` and `Application.Calculation = xlManual`. This stops Excel from continually refreshing its display or recalculating everything when data is written to a worksheet.

Don't Select

The macro recorder produces very inefficient code, peppered with lines like

```
Range("A1").Select
Selection.Font.Bold = True
```

17. OPTIMIZING VBA PERFORMANCE

It is rare to ever need to select anything when controlling Excel from VBA. In most cases, these lines can be combined by removing the Select/Selection:

```
Range("A1").Font.Bold = True
```

You will occasionally need to insert an extra object between the Select and Selection, particularly when charts or drawing objects are involved, such as changing a chart's title:

```
ActiveSheet.ChartObjects("Chart 1").Activate
ActiveChart.ChartTitle.Select
Selection.Characters.Text = "Hello"
```

becomes

```
ActiveSheet.ChartObjects("Chart 1").Chart.ChartTitle _
    .Characters.Text = "Hello"
```

Use Variant Arrays

Instead of reading and writing cells one-by-one, it is much faster to read a range of cells into a Variant variable and then process the variable as a 2D array, or populate a Variant array and then write it to a range of cells, as shown in Listing 17-12.

Listing 17-12 Reading and Writing Variant Arrays

```
Sub ReadWriteVariantArrays()

    Dim vaData As Variant
    Dim lRow As Long
    Dim lCol As Long

    'Read the data from the sheet in one go
    vaData = Sheet1.Range("A1:B10").Value

    'Process the data within VBA
```

```
For lRow = LBound(vaData) To UBound(vaData)
    For lCol = LBound(vaData, 2) To UBound(vaData, 2)
        If IsNumeric(vaData(lRow, lCol)) And _
            Not IsEmpty(vaData(lRow, lCol)) Then

            vaData(lRow, lCol) = vaData(lRow, lCol) * 2
        End If
    Next lCol
Next lRow

'Write the data to the sheet in one go
Sheet1.Range("D1:E10").Value = vaData

End Sub
```

Don't Use ActiveSheet, Selection, or Worksheets() Repeatedly

Some of the more commonly used properties in the Excel object model, such as ActiveSheet, Selection, or Worksheets, return the generic Object type, so all calls that use these objects will be late-bound and slow. For best performance, you should declare a variable of the specific data type and set it to the ActiveSheet, Selection, and so on.

Test a Property Before Setting It

It is often much faster to read a property than to write it. It can save time to only update a property when it needs to change, by checking whether it has the required value first. For example, reading the value of Range.Font.Bold and only setting it to True if it isn't True already. This contradicts the general rule of reducing the amount of code you write, but it will provide a significant performance increase if it allows you to avoid setting properties unnecessarily.

Use Doubles to Talk to Excel

When passing numbers to Excel, either to populate a worksheet cell or as parameters to Excel functions, it is usually most efficient to pass variables declared As Double. Excel generally uses the Double data type internally, and so this practice eliminates type conversions. When populating a cell, Excel also tries to apply cell formatting if other data types (such as Date or Currency) are used. Using doubles throughout avoids Excel's auto-formatting and so improves performance even more.

Use the PAGE.SETUP XLM Function Instead of the PageSetup Object

Each time you change a property of the PageSetup object, Excel repaginates the page to determine whether the automatic zooming or page breaks need to change. To do this, Excel has to communicate with the printer drivers, which is extremely slow. This can be avoided by using the PAGE.SETUP XLM function, which is fully documented in the macrofun.hlp file available from http://support.microsoft.com/kb/128185. This technique is shown in Listing 17-13. Note that the PAGE.SETUP function always applies the settings to the active sheet.

Listing 17-13   Using PAGE.SETUP to Set a Page Header

```
Sub SetHeaders()

  'Set the header using the slow PageSetup object
  With Sheet1.PageSetup
    .LeftHeader = "Hello"
    .RightHeader = "World"
  End With

  'Set the header using the faster PAGE.SETUP XLM function
  Sheet1.Activate
  ExecuteExcel4Macro "PAGE.SETUP(""&LHello &RWorld"")"

End Sub
```

Summary

A highly optimized VBA procedure often executes in 1/10 or 1/100 the time taken by the first version of the procedure. In most cases VBA's performance is "good enough," in that the procedure executes within an acceptable time, such as 2 seconds to show a form, 0.5 seconds for elements within the form (for example, when typing into a text box), or 30 seconds to produce a report. Procedures that take significantly longer than this are good candidates for optimization. The CD included with this book contains an add-in for both the Excel VBE and VB6 IDE to monitor an application's performance as it runs. The data produced by the monitoring can then be used to assess the performance impact of changes to the code.

Macro-optimization looks at the structure of the procedure to ensure it uses the most efficient algorithms and minimizes the amount of code that needs to be executed. This is where most time savings are usually found.

Micro-optimization ensures the most efficient VBA statements and data types are used within the code. These account for the final few percentage points and usually only have an impact where loops are executing thousands of times.

The trade-off is complexity. A QuickSort is much faster than a bubble sort, and a binary search in a sorted array is much faster than looping through a collection, but they are also more complex and therefore harder to debug and maintain.

By using the techniques suggested in this chapter when writing new procedures, the knowledgeable VBA developer can write procedures that are already well optimized and are likely to operate within acceptable time limits.

17. OPTIMIZING VBA PERFORMANCE

CHAPTER 18

INTRODUCTION TO DATABASE DEVELOPMENT

A large percentage of non-trivial Excel applications require some sort of external data store, usually in the form of a database. In this chapter we cover the basics of database design, SQL syntax, and the ADO object model. We do not go into great detail on any of these topics, as all of them are book-length subjects in their own right. By the end of this chapter, however, you will have all the fundamental tools required to begin incorporating a database into your application. In the next chapter we demonstrate how to apply these tools to Microsoft Access and SQL Server development.

An Introduction to Databases

Working with databases is significantly different from working with Excel worksheet tables. This section covers the most important things you need to know about how databases work and why you'd want to use one.

The biggest hurdle for an Excel-centric developer making the leap to applications that utilize a back-end database is understanding the fundamental differences between how data is treated in Excel and how data is treated in a database. A database requires you to follow significantly more rigorous rules compared to an Excel worksheet. You can enter almost anything you want on a worksheet, but database tables are much more picky. Even some of the things you can enter into database tables you shouldn't.

Database tables also have a concept of being formally related to each other, a concept that doesn't exist at all in Excel. Modifications made to databases take effect immediately. There's no need to "save" the data. Unfortunately, there's also no way to undo a change made to data in a database once that change has been committed.

NOTE Those of you who are familiar with databases and the terminology surrounding them will notice that we use some nonstandard terms to describe database concepts in this section. This is intentional and is designed to explain these concepts in terms that Excel programmers with limited database experience will find easier to understand.

Why Use a Database

For many purposes Excel is a perfectly adequate data container. However, certain common circumstances may force you to use a database. These circumstances include

- **An existing database**—The data your Excel application requires may already be stored in a database. In that case you need to use the existing database, if for no other purpose than to extract the data your application requires.
- **Capacity constraints**—An Excel worksheet can hold only a limited amount of data. It is not uncommon for a large application to deal with *millions* of rows of data. You can't hope to store this much data in Excel, so you are forced to use a database, which can easily manage this volume of data.
- **Operational requirements**—Excel is not a multiuser application. It does have some unreliable sharing capabilities, but as a general rule, if one person is using an Excel workbook that contains data, anyone else who wants to use it must wait for that person to finish. Databases, by contrast, are inherently multiuser applications. They are designed from the ground up to allow many people to access the same data at the same time. If your application requires multiple users to access the same data at the same time, then you probably need a database.

Relational Databases

A relational database is a set of tables containing data organized into specific categories. Each table contains data categories in columns. Each row contains a unique instance of data for the categories defined by the columns. A relational database is structured such that data can be accessed in many different ways without having to reorganize the tables.

A relational database also has the important advantage of being easy to extend. After the original database is created, new tables can be added without requiring all existing applications that use the database to be modified. The standard method used to access relational data is structured query language (SQL), which we cover in detail later in the chapter.

File-Based Databases Versus Client-Server Databases

There are two broad categories of relational databases: file-based databases and client-server databases. The fundamental difference between them has to do with where the data access logic is executed.

In a file-based database, the database consists of one or more files that simply contain the data. When an application uses a file-based database, all the data access logic is executed on the client computer where the application resides. The advantages of file-based databases are that they are inexpensive, relatively simple, and require little ongoing maintenance. The disadvantages of file-based databases are that they can create significant network traffic, they are limited in the amount of data they can store, and are limited in the number of simultaneous users who can access them. Microsoft Access and Microsoft Visual FoxPro are two examples of file-based databases.

In a client-server database, databases are contained within a larger server application. This database server is responsible for executing the data access requests from client applications. The advantages and disadvantages of client-server databases are more or less the mirror image of those for file-based databases. Client-server databases reduce network traffic by handling the data access logic on the server. They can store very large amounts of data and handle very large numbers of simultaneous users. However, client-server databases are complex and require routine maintenance to keep them operating efficiently. They can also be expensive if you need a full-service license. Microsoft SQL Server and Oracle are two examples of client-server databases.

Normalization

Normalization is the process of optimizing the way data is stored in your database tables. The goal of normalization is to eliminate redundant data and ensure that only related data is stored in each table. Normalization can be taken to extreme lengths, but for most developers most of the time, understanding the first three rules of normalization and ensuring that your database is in third normal form is all you ever need to do. We cover the first three normal forms in detail in the sections that follow.

> **NOTE** Prior to normalizing your data you must ensure that all rows in every table are unique. A database table should not contain duplicate rows of data, and normalization will not correct this problem.

Before we can discuss normalization we need to explain the concept of a **primary key**. A primary key consists of one or more columns in a data table whose value(s) uniquely identify each row in the table. Let's take a look at a simple example. Figure 18-1 shows a database table containing a list of author information.

FirstName	LastName	City	Country
Robert	Bovey	Winchester	United States
Dennis	Wallentin	Östersund	Sweden
Stephen	Bullen	London	UK
John	Green	Sydney	Australia
Robert	Rosenburg	Los Angeles	United States

FIGURE 18-1 The Authors table

Notice there are two instances of the name Robert in the FirstName column. These names refer to different people, but if you were trying to use only this column to identify rows there would be no way to distinguish these rows from duplicate entries.

To uniquely identify rows in this table we must designate the FirstName **and** LastName columns as the primary key. If you combine the values of these two columns there is no longer any duplication, and all rows are uniquely identified. In the text that follows, primary key columns often are referred to simply as **key columns**, while any columns that do not belong to the primary key are referred to as **non-key columns**.

For our discussion of normalization we use the BillableHours table shown in Figure 18-2. This table contains data that might have been extracted from our PETRAS time entry workbooks and is in a form that is typical for data stored in Excel. In this form, however, the data is denormalized and not suitable for use in a relational database. The primary key for this table consists of a combination of the Consultant, Date, Project, and Activity columns.

First Normal Form

There are two requirements a data table must meet to satisfy the first normal form:

Consultant	Date	Client	Project	Activity	Hours	Rate	Charge
Rob Bovey	11/25/2008	Big Auto Corp.	BAC 1	General Programming	8	$150	$1,200
Rob Bovey	11/25/2008	Big Auto Corp.	BAC 1	Application Design	6	$200	$1,200
John Green	11/25/2008	Big Auto Corp.	BAC 1	Bug Fix	4	$100	$400
John Green	11/25/2008	Big Auto Corp.	BAC 1	Phone Conference	1	$75	$75
John Green	11/25/2008	Big Auto Corp.	BAC 1	Travel	4	$100	$400
Dennis Wallentin	11/25/2008	Hardware Barn	HB 2	Bug Fix	3	$100	$300
Stephen Bullen	11/25/2008	Hardware Barn	HB 2	Travel	5	$100	$500
Dennis Wallentin	11/25/2008	Hardware Barn	HB 2	Phone Conference	2	$75	$150
Dennis Wallentin	11/25/2008	Hardware Barn	HB 2	Travel	3	$100	$300
Stephen Bullen	11/25/2008	Hardware Barn	HB 2	Bug Fix	2	$100	$200
Stephen Bullen	11/25/2008	Massive Oil Co.	MOC 3	Phone Conference	2	$75	$150
Dennis Wallentin	11/25/2008	Massive Oil Co.	MOC 3	Phone Conference	1	$75	$75
John Green	11/25/2008	Massive Oil Co.	MOC 3	Code Review	2	$150	$300
Rob Bovey	11/25/2008	Massive Oil Co.	MOC 3	General Programming	5	$150	$750
John Green	11/25/2008	Massive Oil Co.	MOC 3	Travel	6	$100	$600
John Green	11/25/2008	Universal Bank & Trust	UBT 4	Application Design	4	$200	$800
Rob Bovey	11/25/2008	Universal Bank & Trust	UBT 4	General Programming	6	$150	$900

Record: 18 of 18

FIGURE 18-2 The initial BillableHours table

- All column values are **atomic**. This means there are no values that can be split into smaller meaningful parts. We have one column that obviously violates this requirement. The Consultant column consists of both the first name and the last name of each consultant. This data must be separated into two distinct columns, FirstName and LastName, to satisfy the first normal form.
- Repeating groups of data should be eliminated by moving them into new tables. The Consultant column, even after separating it into first name and last name, violates this requirement. The solution is to create a separate Consultants table to hold this data. Each consultant is assigned a unique consultant ID number that will be used in the BillableHours table to identify the consultant.

The result of transforming our BillableHours table into first normal form is two tables: the modified BillableHours table shown in Figure 18-3 and a new Consultants table shown in Figure 18-4. The first column in the BillableHours table, which previously held each consultant's name, has been replaced with a unique ConsultantID number created in the Consultants table.

This not only allows us to satisfy first normal form, but also allows us to handle the situation in which two consultants have the same first and last names. In the original table there would have been no way to distinguish between two consultants with the same name.

Before we go any further we must explain the concept of a **foreign key**. A foreign key is a column in one table that uniquely identifies records

FIGURE 18-3 The BillableHours table in first normal form

FIGURE 18-4 The new Consultants table

in some other table. In the previous case, the ConsultantID column in the BillableHours table is a foreign key column, each of whose values identifies a single unique consultant in the new Consultants table. As we see in the upcoming section "Relationships and Referential Integrity," foreign keys are used to create connections between related tables in a database.

Second Normal Form

There are two requirements a data table must meet to satisfy second normal form:

- The table must be in first normal form. Each successive normal form builds upon the previous normal form. Since our BillableHours table is already in first normal form, this requirement has been satisfied.

■ Each column in the table must depend on the whole primary key. This means that if any column in the primary key were removed, you could no longer uniquely identify the rows in any non-key column in the table.

The primary key in our BillableHours table consists of a combination of the ConsultantID, Date, Project, and Activity columns. Do we have any columns that are not dependent on all four of these key columns? Yes. The Client column depends only on the Project column because a project name uniquely identifies the client for whom the project is completed.

To solve this problem we remove the Client column from the BillableHours table and create a new Clients table. We also create a new Projects table that provides each project with a unique ID number, and use this project ID rather than the project name in the BillableHours table. This serves two purposes. The new projects table provides a link from the BillableHours table to the Clients table (which we discuss in more detail later in the chapter). It also allows us to handle the situation in which two clients have the same project name.

The result of transforming our BillableHours table into second normal form is three tables: the modified BillableHours table shown in Figure 18-5, a new Clients table shown in Figure 18-6, and a new Projects table shown in Figure 18-7. (This is in addition to the Consultants table we created in the previous step.)

ConsultantID	Date	ProjectID	Activity	Hours	Rate	Charge
1	11/25/2008	1	General Programming	8	$150	$1,200
1	11/25/2008	1	Application Design	6	$200	$1,200
4	11/25/2008	1	Bug Fix	4	$100	$400
4	11/25/2008	1	Phone Conference	1	$75	$75
4	11/25/2008	1	Travel	4	$100	$400
2	11/25/2008	5	Bug Fix	3	$100	$300
3	11/25/2008	5	Travel	5	$100	$500
2	11/25/2008	5	Phone Conference	2	$75	$150
2	11/25/2008	5	Travel	3	$100	$300
3	11/25/2008	5	Bug Fix	2	$100	$200
3	11/25/2008	11	Phone Conference	2	$75	$150
2	11/25/2008	11	Phone Conference	1	$75	$75
4	11/25/2008	11	Code Review	2	$150	$300
1	11/25/2008	11	General Programming	5	$150	$750
4	11/25/2008	11	Travel	6	$100	$600
4	11/25/2008	16	Application Design	4	$200	$800
1	11/25/2008	16	General Programming	6	$150	$900

Record: 18 of 18

FIGURE 18-5 The BillableHours table in second normal form

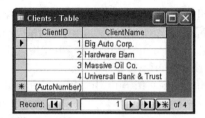

FIGURE 18-6 The new Clients table

ProjectID	ClientID	ProjectName
1	1	BAC 1
2	1	BAC 2
3	1	BAC 3
4	2	HB 1
5	2	HB 2
6	2	HB 3
7	2	HB 4
8	2	HB 5
9	3	MOC 1
10	3	MOC 2
11	3	MOC 3
12	3	MOC 4
13	4	UBT 1
14	4	UBT 2
15	4	UBT 3
16	4	UBT 4
17	4	UBT 5
18	4	UBT 6

FIGURE 18-7 The new Projects table

> **NOTE** The sharp-eyed among you may have noticed that the Rate column in the BillableHours table also violates second normal form. This is absolutely correct, so give yourself a gold star if you caught this. However, because this column makes such an excellent example for demonstrating third normal form we've decided to postpone it for that step.

Third Normal Form

There are three requirements a data table must meet to satisfy third normal form:

- The table must be in second normal form. This requirement has been met by the modifications we made in the previous step.

- Non-key columns cannot describe other non-key columns. This requirement can be memorably expressed as "Non-key columns must represent the key, the whole key, and nothing but the key." In our BillableHours table, the Rate column depends only on the Activity key column. All the other key columns could be removed from the table and the values in the Rate column could still be uniquely associated with the remaining Activity column.

  We can solve this problem by creating a new table to hold the list of Activities and their associated rates. The BillableHours table retains only an activity ID number in place of the previous Activity and Rate columns.

- The table cannot contain **derived data**. Derived data refers to a column in a data table whose values have been created by applying a formula or transformation to the values in one or more other columns in the table. In our BillableHours table, the Charge column is a derived column that is the result of multiplying the Rate column by the Hours column. Columns containing derived data should simply be removed from the table and calculated "on-the-fly" whenever their values are required.

The result of transforming our BillableHours table into third normal form is two tables: the modified BillableHours table shown in Figure 18-8 and a new Activities table shown in Figure 18-9.

ConsultantID	Date	ProjectID	ActivityID	Hours
1	11/25/2008	1	1	8
1	11/25/2008	11	1	5
1	11/25/2008	16	1	6
4	11/25/2008	1	2	1
2	11/25/2008	5	2	2
3	11/25/2008	11	2	2
2	11/25/2008	11	2	1
4	11/25/2008	1	4	4
3	11/25/2008	5	4	5
2	11/25/2008	5	4	3
4	11/25/2008	11	4	6
1	11/25/2008	1	5	6
4	11/25/2008	16	5	4
4	11/25/2008	1	6	4
2	11/25/2008	5	6	3
3	11/25/2008	5	6	2
4	11/25/2008	11	7	2

Record: 18 of 18

FIGURE 18-8 The BillableHours table in third normal form

Activities : Table		
ActivityID	ActivityName	Rate
1	General Programming	$150
2	Phone Conference	$75
3	Technical Support	$75
4	Travel	$100
5	Application Design	$200
6	Bug Fix	$100
7	Code Review	$150
(AutoNumber)		

Record: 7 of 7

FIGURE 18-9   The new Activities table

Note that our third normal form BillableHours table consists of a set of primary key columns, the ConsultantID, Date, ProjectID, and ActivityID columns, and a non-key Hours column that depends on the entire primary key and nothing but the primary key. Because there are no other non-key columns in the table, the Hours column can't possibly depend on any non-key columns. If any primary key column were removed from the table it would no longer be possible to uniquely identify any of the entries in the Hours column. Our data is now ready to be used in a relational database.

The complete set of normalized tables is depicted in the database diagram shown in Figure 18-10. We discuss the meaning of the various elements in this diagram shortly in the "Relationships and Referential Integrity" section.

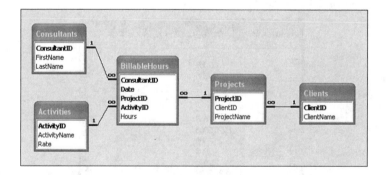

FIGURE 18-10   The complete set of normalized tables

When Not to Normalize

In the vast majority of cases you want to follow the normalization rules described previously when preparing your data for storage in a relational database. As with almost every other rule, however, there are exceptions.

The most common exception has to do with derived columns. When we transformed our BillableHours table into third normal form we eliminated the derived column that showed the total charge for each line item. This is generally a good practice because if you have derived columns you must also create logic to ensure those columns are updated correctly if the values of any of the columns they depend on change. This creates overhead that is best deferred until you actually need to query the derived value.

In some cases, however, it makes sense to store derived data. This is usually the case when the data is derived from columns that are unlikely to change. If the columns the derived data depends on are unlikely to change, then the derived data is also unlikely to change. In this case you can improve the performance of queries that access the derived data by calculating it in advance and storing the result so the query can simply retrieve its value rather than having to calculate it on-the-fly.

Relationships and Referential Integrity

The ability to take advantage of **relationships** and **referential integrity** are two of the primary advantages relational databases provide over Excel for data storage. The ability to create formal relationships between tables allows you to avoid massive repetition of data and the associated frequency of data entry errors that lead to bad or "dirty" data. Referential integrity allows you to ensure that data entered into one table is consistent with data in other related tables. Neither one of these capabilities is available to data stored in Excel.

Foreign Keys

Before we can discuss relationships and referential integrity, we need to have a firm understanding of foreign keys. A foreign key is a column in one table (the **referencing** table) containing data that uniquely identifies records from another table (the **referenced** table). The foreign key serves to connect the two tables and ensure that only valid data from the referenced table can be entered in the referencing table. For example, the ActivityID column in the BillableHours table shown in Figure 18-8 is a foreign key that refers to the ActivityID column in the Activities table in Figure 18-9.

For a column to serve as a foreign key, it must either be the primary key of the referenced table or a column on which a unique index has been defined. We cover unique indexes later in the chapter. A foreign key can also consist of multiple columns as long as the constraints discussed previously are followed. Foreign keys provide the basis for creating relationships between tables.

In this section, we use the Microsoft Access Relationships window to visually display the effect of relationships and referential integrity. Figure 18-11 shows the relationship described previously between the BillableHours table and the Activities table. Each table's primary key columns are shown in bold.

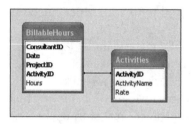

FIGURE 18-11   The relationship between the BillableHours and Activities tables

Types of Relationships

Most relationships between database tables fall into one of three categories: one-to-one, one-to-many, and many-to-many.

One-to-One   In this type of relationship, each row in one table is associated with a single row in another table. One-to-one relationships are not frequently encountered. The most common reason for creating a one-to-one relationship is to divide a single table into two tables with the most frequently accessed columns in one table and the least frequently accessed columns in another table. This is called **vertical partitioning**.

Vertical partitioning can improve performance by making the most frequently accessed table smaller. All things being equal, the rows in a small table can be accessed more quickly than the rows in a large table. A smaller table is also more likely to remain in memory or require less bandwidth to transfer to the client depending on the type of database being used. Consider the hypothetical Parts table shown in Figure 18-12.

FIGURE 18-12   The Parts table

Assume this table has a very large number of rows and the only columns you want to access in most cases are the PartNumber, PartName, UnitPrice, and Weight columns. You can improve the performance of queries against your Parts table by vertically partitioning it into two tables, with the most frequently accessed columns in one table and the rest in a second table. Each row in these two new tables is related to exactly one row in the other table, and the two tables share a primary key. The result of this partitioning is shown in Figure 18-13.

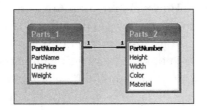

FIGURE 18-13 The Parts table partitioned into two tables with a one-to-one relationship

The Microsoft Access Relationship window indicates a one-to-one relationship by placing the number 1 on each side of the relationship line connecting the two tables.

One-to-Many This is by far the most common type of relationship. In a one-to-many relationship, a single row in one table can be related to zero, one, or many rows in another table. Every relationship created during the process of normalizing our BillableHours table is a one-to-many relationship, as shown in Figure 18-14.

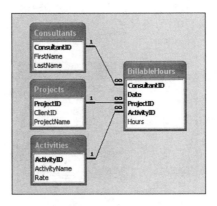

FIGURE 18-14 One-to-many relationships

The Microsoft Access Relationship window indicates a one-to-many relationship by placing the number 1 on the one side of the relationship line and the infinity symbol on the many side of the relationship line. Each row in the Consultants, Projects, and Activities table can be related to zero, one, or many rows in the BillableHours table. The one or many part of the relationship should be obvious; the zero part may require some additional explanation.

If a new consultant has joined the company but not yet logged any billable hours, that consultant would be represented by a row in the Consultants table. However, the row representing the new consultant would not be associated with any rows in the BillableHours table. The Consultants table would have a one-to-many relationship with the BillableHours table, and the row representing the new consultant in the Consultants table would be associated with zero rows in the BillableHours table.

NOTE Some of you may be thinking that Excel's data validation list feature provides the same benefit as a one-to-many database relationship. Unfortunately, this is not true. While it's a useful feature, a data validation list only enforces a one-time relationship check, at the time an entry is selected from the list. Unlike a database relationship, once an entry has been selected from a data validation list, it does not maintain any connection to the list from which it was selected.

Many-to-Many In a many-to-many relationship each row in one table can be related to multiple rows in the other table. This concept can be a bit difficult to visualize. We demonstrate it by extending the example we used in the "Normalization" section earlier in the chapter to include the role each consultant plays on each project. Our list of roles might look like the Roles table shown in Figure 18-15.

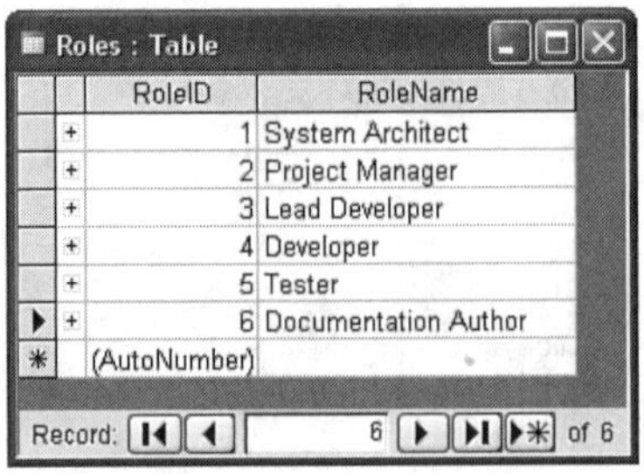

FIGURE 18-15 The Roles table

Each project requires multiple roles, and consultants serve in different roles on different projects. For example, a consultant might be a developer on one project and a tester on another. On a small project, in fact, one consultant could very well have multiple roles. This means that role information cannot be attached to either the Projects table or the Consultants table because there are many-to-many relationships between projects and roles as well as consultants and roles. Each project requires multiple roles, and each role applies to multiple projects. Likewise, each consultant can have multiple roles, and each role can be served by multiple consultants.

Most relational databases cannot directly represent a many-to-many relationship. When this type of relationship is encountered, however, it can always be broken up into multiple one-to-many relationships, each linked by an intermediate table. In our projects, consultants, and roles example, the many-to-many relationships would be represented in the database as shown in Figure 18-16.

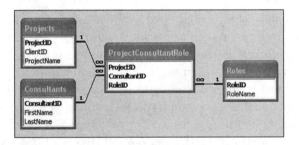

FIGURE 18-16 Many-to-many relationships resolved into one-to-many relationships

The ProjectConsultantRole table serves as the intermediate table that allows us to convert the many-to-many relationships between the Projects and Roles tables and the Consultants and Roles tables into one-to-many relationships with the ProjectConsultantRole table in the middle. The Projects, Consultants, and Roles tables now have one-to-many relationships with the ProjectConsultantRole table, allowing the many-to-many relationships between the Projects and Roles tables and the Consultants and Roles tables to be implemented.

Referential Integrity

Once your database has been fully normalized and you have established relationships among your tables, referential integrity ensures that the data in those tables remains valid when data is added, modified, or deleted. In

Figure 18-14 for example, referential integrity ensures that invalid rows cannot be added to the BillableHours table by enforcing the fact that the ConsultantID, ProjectID, and ActivityID foreign key columns all refer to valid rows in their respective source tables. The validity of the Date and Hours columns is ensured by domain constraints that can be added to those columns. The topic of domain constraints is beyond the scope of this chapter.

NOTE   All modern relational databases support the concept of referential integrity, but the steps required to implement it are completely different from one database to the next. Consult the documentation for your database to determine how to implement referential integrity.

Natural Versus Artificial Primary Keys

There is an ongoing debate within the database community over whether the primary key for a table should be natural, which is to say it should consist of one or more columns that naturally occur in the table, or whether it should be artificial. An artificial key is a unique but otherwise meaningless number that is automatically added to each row in a table. Most modern relational databases provide a special column type that automatically generates a unique number for every row added to a table.

To oversimplify the debate, natural keys tend to be advocated by people who primarily design databases, while artificial keys tend to be advocated by people who must live and work with databases. The argument really comes down to two points: providing easily usable foreign keys and ensuring the true uniqueness of records in a table.

The formal task of a primary key can be divided into two similar but subtly different tasks: uniquely identifying each row in a table and ensuring every row in a table is unique. The first task provides a foreign key that can be used by other tables to uniquely identify a specific row in a table while the second task enforces data integrity by ensuring that you cannot create duplicate records in a table.

When a table has a primary key that performs both tasks simultaneously, problems begin to arise when you need to reference that table from another table through the use of a foreign key. Take for example our BillableHours table. This table requires the use of four columns to construct a natural primary key. If you need to reference the BillableHours table from another table in your database, you need to add a foreign key to that table consisting of all four of these columns. This is because all four columns are required to uniquely identify a row in the BillableHours table. As you can imagine, this can become unwieldy. Assume we have an Invoices table that needs to reference the BillableHours table. An example of how this would be accomplished using a natural key is shown in Figure 18-17.

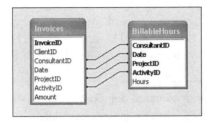

FIGURE 18-17 Using a natural key for the BillableHours table

The alternative is to separate the two tasks of the primary key between two different constructs. The task of uniquely identifying a row in the table can be accomplished with a single column that provides a unique number for each row. This column becomes the primary key for the table. When you need to reference this table from another table, the only column you need to import as the foreign key is the single numeric primary key column. In Figure 18-18, we added an artificial primary key to the BillableHours table. This is simply a number that uniquely identifies each row in the table. This makes the task of referencing a record in the BillableHours table from the Invoices table much simpler.

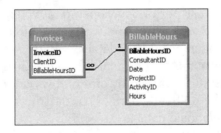

FIGURE 18-18 Using an artificial key for the BillableHours table

If all we did was create an artificial primary key consisting of an automatically generated unique value that had no real meaning, you could easily enter two completely identical rows in the BillableHours table and the database would make them artificially unique by creating a unique value in the artificial primary key column. The task of ensuring data uniqueness can be accomplished with a unique index.

A unique index is a special construct you can create that includes one or more columns in a table. The combination of values in the column(s) on which the unique index is defined must be unique within the table. The index will not allow duplicate values to be entered. In the case of our BillableHours table, we would create a unique index that included the ConsultantID, Date, ProjectID, and ActivityID columns. Note that these columns are the columns that originally formed the natural primary key.

NOTE All modern relational databases support the creation of unique indexes, but the method used to create them is completely different from one database to the next. Consult the documentation for your database to determine how to create unique indexes on a table.

At the risk of antagonizing those on the opposite side of this debate, we recommend the use of artificial primary keys. Artificial primary keys make database construction and use much simpler in practice, and you can easily enforce true uniqueness in every table by creating a unique index on the columns that would otherwise form the natural primary key.

An Introduction to SQL

Structured query language, most commonly referred to by its acronym SQL, is the native programming language of all relational databases. Using SQL you can perform any operations you require on the data stored within a database as well as modify the structure of the database itself and perform any maintenance the database might require. Although SQL has technically been an ANSI standard for more than 20 years, each relational database uses its own slightly different variation of SQL. In this section we focus on the ANSI standard SQL constructs that should work correctly across all relational databases.

The most common use of SQL is to operate on data in a database that has already been designed and constructed for use in your application. There are four fundamental operations that you need to perform on data stored in a database. You need to retrieve data for use in your application, add new data to the database, modify data that already exists in the database, and delete data that is no longer needed. Data manipulation is implemented in SQL by the SELECT, INSERT, UPDATE, and DELETE statements. In this section we cover these four statements in detail.

The SELECT Statement

The SQL SELECT statement is used to retrieve data from the database. The SELECT statement can also be used to create derived data by performing operations on the data being retrieved. For example, two columns can be multiplied or their results concatenated. The basic syntax of the SELECT statement is shown in Listing 18-1.

Listing 18-1   The SQL SELECT Statement

```
SELECT    <column list>
FROM      <table list>
WHERE     <criteria>
GROUP BY  <column list>
HAVING    <criteria>
ORDER BY  <column list>
```

We've placed each clause of the SELECT statement on a separate line for the purpose of clarity. In reality, white space has no effect on a SQL statement, and you can arrange it on a single line or multiple lines as you see fit. Just make sure that at least one space separates each element in the statement from the next and that the clauses appear in the order shown in Listing 18-1. The meaning of each clause is the following:

- **SELECT**—This clause is a comma-delimited list of columns you want to retrieve.
- **FROM**—This clause contains the names of one or more tables that contain the data you want to retrieve. If multiple tables are specified you need to perform a **join**. Various types of joins are available in SQL, and a discussion of them all is beyond the scope of this chapter. However, the most common join type is the INNER JOIN, which uses the following syntax:

```
FROM table1 INNER JOIN table2 ON table1.IDColumn =
table2.IDColumn
```

- **WHERE**—This clause contains any criteria that restrict what data should be returned. It is typically expressed as a Boolean condition in the form of `column_name = value`. The WHERE clause is optional and can be omitted if you simply want to retrieve all the data in a table.

- **GROUP BY**—This is used when you want to calculate an aggregate expression in the SELECT list.
- **HAVING**—This clause can only be used in conjunction with a GROUP BY clause. It restricts the values returned after the aggregation has been performed. This is in contrast to the WHERE clause, which eliminates records before any aggregation is performed.
- **ORDER BY**—This clause indicates which columns you want the data sorted by. The ORDER BY clause is optional if you are not concerned about the order in which the data is returned to you.

The INSERT Statement

The SQL INSERT statement is used to add new data to the database. The basic syntax of the INSERT statement is shown in Listing 18-2. An explanation of each clause of the statement follows.

Listing 18-2   The SQL INSERT Statement

```
INSERT INTO <table name> (<column list>)
VALUES (<value list>)
```

- **INSERT INTO**—This clause includes the name of the table into which you are inserting the data and a comma-delimited list of columns that will be receiving data enclosed in parentheses. You are not required to list the columns if you will be supplying data in the VALUES clause for every required column in the table in the same order in which they appear in the table. Certain types of columns cannot be included in the INSERT clause. These include AutoNumber columns in an Access database table or IDENTITY columns in a SQL Server database table.
- **VALUES**—This clause includes a comma-delimited list of values to be inserted into the table enclosed in parentheses. The VALUES clause must provide a value for every column listed in the INSERT INTO clause. Text strings must typically be surrounded by single quotes (with embedded single quotes doubled up). The syntax used to support date/time values varies among databases. For

example, data/time values are surrounded by single quotes when using SQL Server but must be surrounded by # characters when using Access.

The UPDATE Statement

The SQL UPDATE statement is used to modify data that already exists in the database. The basic syntax of the UPDATE statement is shown in Listing 18-3. An explanation of each clause of the statement follows.

Listing 18-3 The SQL UPDATE Statement

```
UPDATE   <table name>
SET      <column name> = <value>
WHERE    <criteria>
```

- **UPDATE**—This clause contains the name of the table that holds the data to be updated.
- **SET**—This clause provides the column name to be updated and the value it will be updated with. Multiple columns can be updated in a single SQL statement by providing a comma-delimited list of column name - value pairs in the SET clause.
- **WHERE**—This clause contains the criterion that identifies the row to be updated. It is expressed as a Boolean condition, typically in the form of `column_name = value`. The WHERE clause is technically optional, but beware. If you do not supply a WHERE clause in the UPDATE statement, every row in the table will be updated with the specified value. This is rarely what you want to do, and it is impossible to reverse.

The DELETE Statement

The SQL DELETE statement is used to delete data from the database. The basic syntax of the DELETE statement is shown in Listing 18-4. An explanation of each clause of the statement follows.

Listing 18-4 The SQL DELETE Statement

```
DELETE FROM <table name>
WHERE <criteria>
```

- **DELETE FROM**—This clause contains the name of the table that holds the data to be deleted.
- **WHERE**—This clause contains the criterion that identifies the row to be deleted. It is expressed as a Boolean condition in the form of column_name = value. The WHERE clause is technically optional, but beware. If you do not supply a WHERE clause in the DELETE statement, every row in the table will be deleted. This is rarely what you want to do, and it is impossible to reverse.

Data Access with ADO

An Introduction to ActiveX Data Objects (ADO)

ADO is the data access technology designed by Microsoft to make data access as simple and transparent as possible, regardless of how or where the data is stored. Previous data access technologies such as DAO and ODBC are still in use, but Microsoft has made it clear that ADO is the data access technology for the future, so we recommend that all new applications be based on it. As we see in Chapter 24, "Excel and VB.NET," classic ADO has a counterpart called ADO.NET in the .NET development environment.

Data Access Technology Defined

A data access technology like ADO can be thought of as a connector between your application and the data storage mechanism it uses. ADO allows your application to "talk" to databases in the VBA programming language. You still need to understand the use of SQL, but you do not need to understand the low-level APIs required to translate SQL-based requests between VBA and the target data storage application. ADO abstracts these low-level requirements into a set of common objects, properties, and methods that are used in the same way no matter what data storage application you're working with.

NOTE For simple applications where the data is stored entirely within open Excel workbooks, you will rarely need to use a separate data access technology like ADO. VBA will do the job quite nicely. However, your data access code should still be separated into its own logical tier to minimize the number of problems you'll encounter if you need to move to a data storage mechanism that does require the use of ADO.

How does ADO accomplish this? It operates through a lower-level technology called OLE DB. You can think of OLE DB as ADO for C++ programmers. OLE DB can't be used directly from VBA, but ADO translates the OLE DB data access mechanisms into a form VBA understands.

The root of OLE DB's ability to make all data storage applications look the same is a component called a **provider**. There is an OLE DB provider for each data storage application. This provider translates the unique, low-level APIs of that application into a common OLE DB interface (the concept of interfaces is covered extensively in Chapter 14, "Interfaces"). Providers for the most commonly used databases are packaged with ADO.

If you need to use ADO to access a database for which a provider has not been supplied, there are two potential options. You can obtain a native OLE DB provider for that database from a third-party vendor if one is available. If no third-party provider is available you can fall back on the OLE DB provider for ODBC. ODBC was an early industry standard low-level data access technology pioneered by Microsoft. Any database application that supports ODBC can be accessed by ADO using the OLE DB provider for ODBC. We demonstrate how providers are used in ADO later in this section.

The ADO Object Model

ADO is built on a simple yet flexible object model. For the vast majority of purposes you will require only three top-level objects: Connection, Command, and Recordset, along with the three collections that belong to these top-level objects: Errors, Parameters, and Fields. The top-level objects are not organized hierarchically. Each object can be created and used along with or independently of the others. As shown in Figure 18-19, the core ADO object model can be visualized as a triangle among the three top-level objects with the associated collections attached to the top-level object they belong to.

In the sections that follow, we cover the most commonly used properties and methods of the ADO objects shown in Figure 18-19 in a relatively generic manner. In Chapter 19, "Programming with Access and SQL Server," we demonstrate how ADO is used specifically to work with data stored in Access and SQL Server.

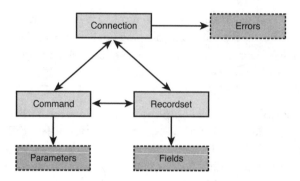

FIGURE 18-19   The core ADO object model

The Connection Object

The primary purpose of the Connection object is exactly what its name implies: connecting to a database. In keeping with the flexibility of ADO, however, a Connection object can be used to execute plain text SQL statements or stored queries directly. In this section we cover the most commonly used properties and methods of the Connection object.

The ConnectionString Property   This property provides the Connection object with the information required to connect to the database. The connection string consists of a semicolon-delimited series of arguments in the form of "name=value;" pairs. The only argument we cover in this chapter is the Provider argument.

The Provider argument tells ADO which OLE DB provider to use and by extension which database you are trying to connect to. All arguments in the connection string after the provider argument are specific to the OLE DB provider being used. ADO passes these arguments directly through to the provider.

We cover provider-specific connection string arguments for Access and SQL Server in Chapter 19. Some common provider arguments are shown in the following list. If no provider is specified, ADO uses the OLE DB provider for ODBC by default.

- `Provider=Microsoft.Jet.OLEDB.4.0`—Microsoft Jet 4.0 OLE DB Provider (for Access 2003 and earlier)
- `Provider=Microsoft.ACE.OLEDB.12.0`—Microsoft Office 12 Access Database Engine OLE DB Provider (for Access 2007)
- `Provider=SQLOLEDB`—The Microsoft OLE DB Provider for SQL Server

- **Provider=SQLNCLI**—SQL Native Client (supports features introduced in SQL Server 2005 and later)
- **Provider=MSDASQL**—The Microsoft OLE DB Provider for ODBC Drivers

The ConnectionTimeout Property   This property specifies the number of seconds ADO waits for a connection attempt to succeed before canceling the attempt and raising an error. The default value is 15 seconds. If you have a situation where connections normally take a long time to complete, you can use this property to increase the number of seconds ADO waits so that connection attempts are not terminated prematurely. The following code sample changes the ConnectionTimeout value of a Connection object to 30 seconds:

```
cnConn.ConnectionTimeout = 30
```

The State Property   The State property allows you to determine whether a connection is currently open, closed, connecting, or executing a command. The value is a bit mask containing one or more of the following ObjectStateEnum constants:

- **adStateClosed**—The connection is closed.
- **adStateOpen**—The connection is open.
- **adStateConnecting**—The process of making a connection is in progress.
- **adStateExecuting**—The connection is executing a command.

If you attempt to close a Connection object that is already closed, you cause an error. You can prevent this from occurring by testing the state of the Connection object before attempting to close it, as shown here:

```
If CBool(cnConn.State And adStateOpen) Then cnConn.Close
```

The Close Method   This method closes the connection to the database. Simply closing the connection does not destroy the Connection object. To destroy the Connection object and free its memory, you need to set the Connection object variable to Nothing. For example, to ensure that a Connection object variable is closed and removed from memory you would execute the following code:

18. INTRODUCTION TO DATABASE DEVELOPMENT

```
If CBool(cnConn.State And adStateOpen) Then cnConn.Close
Set cnConn = Nothing
```

The Open Method This method opens a connection to a database. It has the following syntax:

```
Connection.Open ConnectionString, UserID, Password, Options
```

The ConnectionString argument serves the same purpose as the ConnectionString property discussed earlier. ADO allows you to set this property in advance or pass it when you open the connection. The UserID and Password arguments can be passed separately from the connection string if you want.

The Options argument is particularly interesting. This argument allows you to make your connection asynchronously. That is, you can tell your Connection object to go off and open the connection in the background while your code continues to run. You do this by setting the Options argument to the `ConnectOptionEnum` value `adAsyncConnect`. The following code sample demonstrates making an asynchronous connection:

```
cnConn.Open Options:=adAsyncConnect
```

This can be useful in situations where you have lengthy connection times, because it allows you to make a connection without freezing the rest of your application during the connection process.

The Execute Method This method executes the string passed to its CommandText argument. In the following syntax examples, the first example is for an action query (a query that does not return a recordset), while the second is for a select query (a query that returns a recordset).

```
Connection.Execute CommandText, [RecordsAffected], [Options]
```

```
Set Recordset = Connection.Execute(CommandText, _
                        [RecordsAffected], [Options])
```

The CommandText argument can contain any executable string recognized by the OLE DB provider used to open the connection. This can be a SQL statement or the name of a stored procedure, table, or view. The optional RecordsAffected argument is a return value that tells you how many records the CommandText operation affected. It's a good idea to check this value against the number of records that you expect to be affected so you can detect potential errors in your command text.

The Options argument can significantly optimize the execution efficiency of your command, so you should always use it even though it's technically optional. The Options argument allows you to relay two different types of information to the OLE DB provider: what type of command is contained in the CommandText argument and how the provider should execute the contents of the CommandText argument.

To execute the CommandText the OLE DB provider must know what type of command it contains. If you don't use the Options argument to specify the type, the provider has to determine that information for itself. This slows down the execution of your query. You can avoid this by specifying the CommandText type using one of the following CommandTypeEnum values:

- **adCmdText**—The CommandText is a raw SQL string.
- **adCmdTable**—The CommandText is the name of a table. This sends an internally generated SQL statement to the provider that looks something like `"SELECT * FROM table_name"`.
- **adCmdStoredProc**—The CommandText is the name of a stored procedure (stored procedures are covered in Chapter 19).
- **adCmdTableDirect**—The CommandText is the name of a table, but unlike the adCmdTable option, this option does not generate a SQL statement and therefore returns the contents of the table more efficiently. Use this option if the provider supports it.

You can also provide specific execution instructions to the provider by including one or more of the ExecuteOptionEnum constants, including

- **adAsyncExecute**—Tells the provider to execute the command asynchronously, which returns execution to your code immediately.
- **adExecuteNoRecords**—Tells the provider not to construct a Recordset object. ADO always constructs a recordset in response to a command, even if your CommandText argument is an action query that does not return any data. To avoid the overhead required to create an unnecessary recordset, use this value in the Options argument whenever you execute an action query.

The `CommandTypeEnum` and `ExecuteOptionEnum` values are bit masks that can be combined together in the Options argument using the logical Or operator. For example, to execute a plain text SQL command and tell ADO not to construct a Recordset object you would use the following syntax:

```
sSQL = "DELETE FROM Projects WHERE ProjectID = 99"
cnConn.Execute sSQL, lNumAffected, adCmdText Or adExecuteNoRecords
If lNumAffected <> 1 Then MsgBox "Error executing SQL statement."
```

Connection Object Events   To trap Connection object events, you must declare a module-level WithEvents Connection object variable in a class module. Trapping these events is required whenever you are using a Connection object asynchronously, because these events are what notify your application that the Connection object has completed its task.

Covering asynchronous connections is beyond the scope of this chapter. However, they are important enough to deserve mention so you can pursue them further if you like. The two most commonly used Connection events are

- **ConnectComplete**—Triggered when an asynchronous connection attempt has completed. You can examine the arguments passed to this event to determine whether the connection was successful.
- **ExecuteComplete**—Triggered when an asynchronous command has finished executing.

The Errors Collection   This collection contains a set of Error objects, each of which represents an OLE DB provider-specific error (ADO itself generates runtime errors). The Errors collection may contain not just errors but also warnings and even status messages. The Errors collection can be helpful in providing extra detail when something in your data access code has malfunctioned. When debugging ADO problems, you can dump the contents of the Errors collection to the Immediate window with the following code:

```
For Each objError In cnConn.Errors
    Debug.Print objError.Description
Next objError
```

The Command Object

The Command object is typically used to execute SQL statements or stored procedures that require parameters or do not return data. In this section we cover the most commonly used properties and methods of the Command object.

The ActiveConnection Property   Prior to executing a Command object, you can use the ActiveConnection property to assign an existing Connection object or a connection string for the command to use to connect to the database. If you assign a connection string, the Command object creates a Connection object for itself. The following code assigns a Connection object to the ActiveConnection property:

```
Set cmCmd.ActiveConnection = cnConn
```

The following code assigns a connection string to the ActiveConnection property:

```
cmCmd.ActiveConnection = _
              "Provider=Microsoft.Jet.OLEDB.4.0;" & _
              "Data Source=C:\Files\MyDatabase.mdb;"
```

The CommandText Property   The CommandText property is identical to the CommandText argument to the Connection object's Execute method covered earlier in the chapter. This property is used to set the command string that will be executed by the data provider. It can be a SQL statement or the name of a stored procedure, table, or view.

The CommandType Property   The CommandType property is identical to the Options argument to the Connection object's Execute method covered earlier in the chapter. It is used to tell the provider how to interpret and execute the Command object's CommandText.

The CreateParameter Method   This method is used to manually create Parameter objects that can then be added to the Command object's Parameters collection. The CreateParameter method has the following syntax:

```
Set Parameter = Command.CreateParameter([Name], [Type], [Direction], _
                                        [Size], [Value])
```

Name is the name of the parameter object. You can use this name to reference the Parameter object through the Command object's Parameters
collection. When working with SQL Server the name of a Parameter
should be the same as the name of the stored procedure argument that it
corresponds to.

Type indicates the data type of the parameter. It is specified as one of the
DataTypeEnum constants. There are several dozen possible data types, so we
do not go into them in any detail here. Check the ADO help file or the use
the Object Browser to view these constants in the ADO object library.

Direction is a ParameterDirectionEnum value that indicates whether
the parameter will be used to pass data to an input argument, receive data
from an output argument, or accept a return value from a stored procedure. Direction can be one of the following values:

- **adParamInput**—The parameter represents an input argument.
- **adParamInputOutput**—The parameter is both an input and an output argument.
- **adParamOutput**—The parameter represents an output argument.
- **adParamReturnValue**—The parameter represents a return value.

Size is used to specify the size of Parameter in bytes and is dependent on
Parameter's data type. Value is used to provide an initial value for the
Parameter.

The following code sample demonstrates how you can use the
CreateParameter method in conjunction with the Parameters collection
Append method to create a Parameter and append it to the Parameters
collection with one line of code:

```
cmCmd.Parameters.Append _
    cmCmd.CreateParameter("MyParam", adInteger, adParamInput, 0)
```

The Execute Method This method executes the text contained in the
Command object's CommandText property. In the following syntax examples,
the first example is for an action query (a query that does not return a recordset), while the second is for a select query (a query that returns a recordset).

```
Command.Execute [RecordsAffected], [Parameters], [Options]
```

```
Set Recordset = Command.Execute([RecordsAffected], [Parameters], _
[Options])
```

The RecordsAffected and Options arguments are identical to the corresponding arguments for the Connection object's Execute method. If you are executing a SQL statement that requires one or more parameters you can supply an array of values to the Parameters argument, one for each parameter required.

The Parameters Collection   This collection contains all the Parameter objects associated with the Command object. Parameters are used to pass arguments to SQL statements and stored procedures as well as to receive output and return values from stored procedures. We demonstrate the use of the Parameters collection in the "Data Access with SQL Server" section of Chapter 19.

The Recordset Object

The Recordset object is used to execute SQL statements or stored procedures that return data to your application or receive recordsets created by executing Connection or Command objects that return recordsets. In this section we cover the most commonly used properties and methods of the Recordset object.

The BOF and EOF Properties   These properties indicate whether the record pointer of the Recordset object is positioned before the first record in the recordset (BOF, or beginning of file) or after the last record in the recordset (EOF, or end of file). If the recordset is empty, both BOF and EOF will be True. The following code example shows how to determine whether there is data in a recordset:

```
If Not rsData.EOF Then
    ' The Recordset contains data.
Else
    ' The Recordset is empty.
End If
```

You should always verify that a recordset contains data using the previous method prior to any attempt to access that data. Attempting to access data from an empty recordset causes a runtime error.

18. INTRODUCTION TO DATABASE DEVELOPMENT

The CursorLocation Property   This property allows you to specify whether the server-side cursor engine or the client-side cursor engine manages the records in the recordset. A cursor is the underlying object that manages the data in the recordset. This property must be set before the recordset is opened. If you do not specify a cursor location, the default is server side. You can set this property to one of the two `CursorLocationEnum` values: `adUseClient` or `adUseServer`. The following code sample demonstrates setting the cursor location to client-side:

```
rsData.CursorLocation = adUseClient
```

The most common reason to specify a client-side cursor in practice is to enable the use of disconnected recordsets. We cover these in more detail in Chapter 19.

The Filter Property   This property allows you to filter an open recordset so that only records that meet the specified condition are visible. The records that cannot be seen are not deleted, removed, or changed in any way, they are simply hidden from normal recordset operations. This property can be set to a string that specifies the filter you want to place on the records or to one of the `FilterGroupEnum` constants.

You can set multiple filters, and the records exposed by the filtered recordset are only those records that meet all of the conditions. To remove the filter from the recordset, set the Filter property to an empty string or the `adFilterNone` constant. The following code sample demonstrates filtering a recordset so that it displays only company names that begin with the letter B:

```
rsData.Filter = "Company LIKE 'B*'"
```

You can also use the logical AND, OR, and NOT operators to set multiple Filter property values:

```
rsData.Filter = "Company LIKE 'B*' AND Country = 'USA'"
```

Note that the use of wildcard characters is supported in a filter string. However, the specific wildcard characters supported differ depending on the database being used.

The Sort Property   The Sort property allows you to specify how the data in the recordset should be sorted once it has been retrieved. You can sort the data in the recordset in different orders as many times as you like by simply assigning different strings to the Sort property. In the following example we sort the recordset by the CompanyName field:

```
rsData.Sort = "CompanyName"
```

The Close Method   This method closes the Recordset object. This does not free any memory used by the recordset. To free the memory used by the Recordset object you must set the Recordset object variable to Nothing.

The Move Methods   When a recordset is first opened, the current record pointer is positioned on the first record in the recordset. The Move methods are used to navigate through the records in an open recordset. They do this by repositioning the Recordset object's current record pointer. The following Move methods are available:

- **MoveFirst**—Positions the current record pointer on the first record of the recordset
- **MoveNext**—Positions the current record pointer to the next record in the recordset
- **MovePrevious**—Positions the current record pointer to the previous record in the recordset
- **MoveLast**—Positions the current record pointer to the last record in the recordset

The code sample in Listing 18-5 demonstrates common recordset navigation techniques.

Listing 18-5   Recordset Navigation

```
' Verify that the Recordset contains data.
If Not rsData.EOF Then
    ' Loop until we reach the end of the Recordset.
    Do While Not rsData.EOF
        ' Perform some action on the current record's data.
        Debug.Print rsData.Fields(0).Value
        ' Move to the next record.
        rsData.MoveNext
    Loop
```

```
Else
    MsgBox "No records returned!", vbCritical, "Error"
End If
```

Pay particular attention to the use of the MoveNext method within the Do While loop. Omitting this is a common error and leads to an endless loop condition in your code. The very first line of code that you should place in the Do While loop in this case is a call to MoveNext.

The NextRecordset Method   Some providers allow you to execute commands that return multiple recordsets. The NextRecordset method is used to move through these recordsets. The NextRecordset method clears the current recordset from the Recordset object, loads the next recordset into the Recordset object, and sets the current record pointer to the first record in that recordset. If the NextRecordset method is called and there are no more recordsets to retrieve, the Recordset object is closed and set to Nothing. The code sample in Listing 18-6 demonstrates the use of the NextRecordset method.

Listing 18-6   The NextRecordset Method

```
' Verify that the Recordset contains more data.
Do While Not rsData Is Nothing
    ' Loop the records in the current recordset.
    Do While Not rsData.EOF
        ' Perform some action on the current record's data.
        Debug.Print rsData.Fields(0).Value
        ' Move to the next record.
        rsData.MoveNext
    Loop
    ' Return the next recordset
    Set rsData = rsData.NextRecordset
Loop
```

The Open Method   This method opens the Recordset object and retrieves the data specified by the Source argument. The Open method has the following syntax:

```
Recordset.Open Source, ActiveConnection, CursorType, LockType, Options
```

The Source argument tells the recordset what data it should retrieve. This is most commonly a SQL string or the name of a stored procedure, but it can also be the name of a table or even a Command object.

The ActiveConnection argument can be a connection string or a Connection object that identifies the connection to be used. If you assign a connection string to the ActiveConnection argument, the recordset creates a Connection object for itself.

The CursorType argument specifies the type of cursor to use when opening the recordset. This is set using one of the following `CursorTypeEnum` values:

- **`adOpenDynamic`**—All types of movement through the recordset are allowed. Modifications made by other users to the dataset referenced by the recordset are visible.
- **`adOpenForwardOnly`**—You can only scroll forward through the recordset. Modifications made by other users to the dataset referenced by the recordset are not visible. This is the fastest cursor type, so it should be used for accessing data wherever possible.
- **`adOpenKeyset`**—Similar to adOpenDynamic except that you can't see records other users add, and records that other users delete are no longer accessible. Modifications to existing data made by other users are still visible.
- **`adOpenStatic`**—All types of movement through the recordset are allowed. The recordset is a static copy of the data, so modifications made by other users are not visible.

The LockType argument specifies what type of locks the provider should place on the underlying data source when opening the recordset. This is set using one of the following `LockTypeEnum` values:

- **`adLockOptimistic`**—Specifies optimistic locking, record by record. The provider uses optimistic locking, locking records only when you call the Update method.
- **`adLockBatchOptimistic`**—Specifies optimistic batch locking. Required for batch update mode.
- **`adLockPessimistic`**—Specifies pessimistic locking, record by record. The provider does what is necessary to ensure successful editing of the records, usually by locking records at the data source immediately after editing has begun.
- **`adLockReadOnly`**—Specifies that the data in the recordset will be read-only. You cannot modify this data.

The Options argument here is the same as the Options argument covered in the Connection object's Execute method earlier in the chapter. It is used to tell the provider how to interpret and execute the contents of the Source argument.

The Fields Collection   The Fields collection contains the values, and information about those values, from the current record in a Recordset object. In Excel, the Fields collection is most commonly used to return the column names of each field in the recordset prior to accessing the contents of the recordset using the CopyFromRecordset method of the Range object. Listing 18-7 demonstrates how to read the field names from the Fields collection of a Recordset object.

Listing 18-7   Using the Fields Collection

```
With Sheet1.Range("A1")
    For Each objField In rsData.Fields
        .Offset(0, lOffset).Value = objField.Name
        lOffset = lOffset + 1
    Next objField
End With
```

Recordset Object Events   To trap Recordset object events, you must declare a module-level WithEvents Recordset object variable in a class module. Trapping these events is necessary whenever you are using a Recordset object asynchronously, because these events are what notify your application that the Recordset object has completed its task.

Covering asynchronous recordset usage is beyond the scope of this chapter; however, the topic is important enough to deserve mention so that you can pursue it further if you like. The two most commonly used Recordset object events are

- **FetchComplete**—This event is fired after all the records have been retrieved when opening an asynchronous recordset.
- **FetchProgress**—The provider fires this event periodically to report the number of records retrieved so far during an asynchronous open operation. It is typically used to provide a visual progress indicator to the user.

Further Reading

As we stated at the beginning of the chapter, the subjects covered here are all book-length topics in their own right. Therefore, we would be remiss if we didn't recommend some good books you could use to pursue the full breadth of these topics. The books recommended in this section have been found very useful by the authors of this book. We have no financial stake in any of them. These recommendations are based purely on quality.

Pro SQL Server 2005 Database Design and Optimization

Authored by Louis Davidson, Kevin Kline, and Kurt Windisch
ISBN# 1590595297—Apress
This book provides detailed coverage of data normalization and relational database design in a software-agnostic manner. If the first section of this chapter was unclear or left you wanting more information, this is the book for you.

ADO 2.6 Programmer's Reference

Authored by David Sussman
ISBN# 186100463X—Wrox

Professional ADO 2.5 Programming

Authored by David Sussman et al.
ISBN# 1861002750—Wrox
Unfortunately, there were never very many excellent books on "classic ADO" to begin with. Now that Microsoft has moved on to ADO.NET, what few good books there were are out of print. This is the case with both of these titles, although you should be able to locate used copies through Amazon.com.
The *ADO 2.6 Programmer's Reference* is exactly what its title would suggest: a comprehensive reference to the ADO object model. It is essentially a high-quality ADO dictionary. *Professional ADO 2.5 Programming* assumes that you understand all the basic concepts of ADO and goes on to show you how to apply them in a series of advanced application scenarios.

18. INTRODUCTION TO DATABASE DEVELOPMENT

Sams Teach Yourself SQL in 10 Minutes

Authored by Ben Forta
ISBN# 0672325675—Sams
Don't be fooled by the title, this is the gold standard for introductory SQL books. While the 10 minutes referenced in the title is a bit of an underestimate, you can easily digest one chapter per day in a small amount of spare time and within a few weeks come away with a solid understanding of basic SQL that can be applied to any database you are working with.

Summary

We covered a lot of ground in a very short space in this chapter. We explained what databases are and under what circumstances you should use them. We explained how to structure your data properly for storage in a relational database. We provided a brief introduction to SQL and ADO and demonstrated how you can use them to retrieve and manipulate data in a relational database. Since we can't possibly do justice to any of these topics in a single chapter we also provided you with pointers to some excellent resources for additional information.

PROGRAMMING WITH ACCESS AND SQL SERVER

The two specific database applications most commonly used in conjunction with Excel development are Access and SQL Server. In this chapter we demonstrate how to apply the database development building blocks introduced in Chapter 18, "Introduction to Database Development," to development with Access and SQL Server.

A Note on the Northwind Sample Database

All the examples in this chapter are based on the original version of the Northwind database supplied by Microsoft with Access and SQL Server. Beginning with SQL Server 2005, Microsoft stopped shipping a SQL Server version of Northwind, instead replacing it with a much more complex sample database called AdventureWorks. Beginning with Access 2007, Microsoft modified the Northwind sample database so there are significant differences between the original version and the Access 2007 version.

All the examples in this chapter are based on the original versions of the Northwind database, so for the best learning experience we recommend that you also use these versions, regardless of the versions of Access and SQL Server you have installed. The original versions of these databases work perfectly well in any current version of Access and SQL Server, and we have supplied them on the CD that accompanies this book in the \Concepts\Ch19 - Programming with Access and SQL Server\Northwind\ folder.

To use the Access version of the Northwind database, simply unzip the file NorthwindAccess.zip. The Northwind.mdb database file can then be used from anywhere on your computer. The SQL Server version of the Northwind database must be installed before it can be used. First unzip the file NorthwindSQLSever.zip. Next, open the instnwind.sql script file in SQL Sever Management Studio and run it by placing your cursor anywhere in the script and pressing the F5 key. Once the script has completed successfully, the Northwind database will be installed in the SQL Server data directory and you can safely delete the installation files.

Designing the Data Access Tier

As we saw in Chapter 3, "Excel and VBA Development Best Practices," the data access code in an application forms a unique logical tier that should be separated from the other application tiers. In this section we delve a bit more deeply into why the data access tier should be separated from the rest of the application and how this separation can be accomplished.

Why Have a Separate Data Access Tier

Over the lifetime of a non-trivial Excel application, the data storage mechanism is very likely to change. When data storage requirements are simple and limited, an Excel workbook may be a completely appropriate data container. As the amount and complexity of data stored increases and the number of users who need to access it grows, a file-based database may be required. Some applications grow so large and attract so many users that their data storage and access requirements can only be met by a client-server database.

If your data access tier is not physically and logically separated from the rest of your application you will very likely have to perform a significant rebuild any time the data storage container changes. By physically separate we mean that all data access code should be located in separate, dedicated code modules. By logically separate we mean that only data access code should have any dependencies on how the physical data is stored. If an application has a well-separated data access tier you should be able to move from one data storage system to another without having to modify any code in the business logic or presentation tiers.

The design of the data access tier interface should be driven by the needs of the business logic tier. The business logic tier should be able to call the data access tier to retrieve, input, update or delete data in a manner that reflects the application logic. The data access tier is responsible for translating application logic into specific actions required to accomplish the physical task with the data storage mechanism being used. Whenever possible, all data should be transferred between the business logic tier and the data access tier by way of plain variables, user-defined types, or a range of cells on a background worksheet specifically reserved for this purpose.

Physical Design of a Data Access Tier

One of the best ways of separating the data access tier from the rest of the application is to create a class module that encapsulates all the code required to perform the data access tasks required by the project. For simple data access requirements a single class can represent the entire data access tier. For more complicated data access requirements it may be worthwhile to link multiple class modules to create an internal data access object model for your application. See Chapter 7, "Using Class Modules to Create Objects," for a discussion on how to create classes and object models.

In this section we show a simple example of a data access class. Error handling and the storage and construction of the database connection string have been left out of this example so as not to obscure the primary features of the data access class design. A complete version of this design in the form of a small reporting application can be found on the CD that accompanies this book in the *\Concepts\Ch19 - Programming with Access and SQL Server* folder in the workbook named DataAccessClass.xls. This example uses the SQL Server version of the Northwind sample database. The code required for the simplest possible data access class is shown in Listing 19-1. This class module is named CDataAccess.

Listing 19-1 The CDataAccess Class

```
Option Explicit

' Set a reference to the Microsoft ActiveX Data Objects 2.X Library
Private mcnConnect As ADODB.Connection

Private Sub Class_Terminate()
    On Error Resume Next
    ' Close and destroy the connection object.
    mcnConnect.Close
    Set mcnConnect = Nothing
End Sub

Public Sub Initialize(ByRef sConnection As String)
    ' Create the connection to the database.
    Set mcnConnect = New ADODB.Connection
    mcnConnect.ConnectionString = sConnection
    mcnConnect.Open
```

```
End Sub

Public Sub GetCustomerData(ByRef rngDestination As Excel.Range)

    Dim rsData As ADODB.Recordset
    Dim sSQL As String

    sSQL = "SELECT * FROM Customers"

    Set rsData = New ADODB.Recordset
    rsData.Open sSQL, mcnConnect, adOpenForwardOnly, adLockReadOnly
    If Not rsData.EOF Then
        rngDestination.CopyFromRecordset rsData
    End If
    rsData.Close

End Sub
```

NOTE To use ADO from your Excel VBA project you must set a reference to the Microsoft ActiveX Data Objects 2.X Library, where X represents the highest numbered library available on your system.

The most fundamental task of the data access class is to declare and maintain the ADO connection to the external database. Because none of the other application tiers need to know how data is being stored and retrieved, this ADO connection object is private to the data access class.

The connection object is initialized within the public Initialize method of the class. When your code first runs it creates a new instance of the CDataAccess class and then calls the Initialize method and passes it a connection string. The reason we pass the connection string to the class when it is created is to enable us to store the connection string externally. This is because in a real-world application it is reasonably common for a connection string to change.

For example, a database may have to be relocated from one server to another. If you hard-code your connection string within your application, you will have to modify the application and distribute a new version of it to all your users. If you keep the connection string in an INI file instead, all you need to do is modify an entry in the INI file. You could even create a simple user interface within your application for this purpose.

Once the data access class has been created and initialized, the other tiers of the application call methods of the data access class to store and retrieve data. In this example our data access class has a single method that returns data from the Customers table. This method is designed to return the data to the calling procedure using an intermediate worksheet. The calling procedure passes the top-left cell of the range where the data should be placed, and the GetCustomerData method retrieves the data from the database and places it there. By structuring the data access method in this manner, the calling code has no dependency on how the data was stored or retrieved; it simply knows that once the call is successfully completed the data will be waiting in the specified range. Listing 19-2 shows how our CDataAccess class would be used within an application.

Listing 19-2   Using the CDataAccess Class

```
Option Explicit

Public gclsDataAccess As CDataAccess

Public Sub Auto_Open()

    Dim sConnection As String

    sConnection = "Provider=SQLOLEDB;" & _
                  "Data Source=MyServer;" & _
                  "Initial Catalog=Northwind;" & _
                  "Integrated Security=SSPI"

    Set gclsDataAccess = New CDataAccess
    gclsDataAccess.Initialize sConnection

End Sub

Public Sub TestDataAccess()
    gclsDataAccess.GetCustomerData Sheet1.Range("A1")
End Sub
```

Because the CDataAccess class represents a persistent logical and physical tier within the application, it must be assigned to a global object variable so that it is always available to other tiers in the application. The Auto_Open procedure constructs the database connection string and then creates and initializes the data access class. As we mentioned earlier, in a real-world application the specific elements of this connection string would be retrieved from some external container such as an INI file. We explain what each part of the connection string means later in the chapter.

Once the data access class is ready for use, our application retrieves data by simply calling the appropriate method of the class and passing it a Range object that specifies the destination for the data being returned. This is demonstrated by the TestDataAccess procedure. Passing the data by way of an intermediate range works best when retrieving a large table of data. For methods that store or retrieve a single record, a user-defined type would be a more appropriate method of passing data to or from the data access tier. You might also use arrays or individual argument variables according to your needs. The important thing is that whatever method you use does not create any dependency between the code that implements the application logic and the specific method used to physically store and retrieve data.

NOTE Because VBA doesn't support truly public classes in the way VB6 does, VBA doesn't provide any reasonable way to use user-defined types as arguments or return values for public class methods and properties. If you decided that user-defined types are the best method of passing data to the data access layer of your application, you will have to build that part of your data access layer using procedures in a standard code module. This is the approach we take in the PETRAS example at the end of this chapter.

Working with Microsoft Access Databases

The biggest advantage of using an Access database in your Excel application is that it is a very lightweight solution. Your clients don't even need to own a copy of Access for your application to use an Access database, and there are no installation or configuration requirements beyond copying the database file to the correct location on the client computer or network.

We use the section on Microsoft Access to demonstrate the basic techniques for storing and retrieving data using ADO and SQL. In the section on SQL Server that follows we demonstrate some of the more complex features of ADO. In most cases, however, everything we demonstrate in this chapter can be used with both Access and SQL Server.

Connecting to an Access Database

You connect to an Access database from ADO using the Microsoft Jet 4.0 OLE DB Provider (for Access 2003 and earlier) or the Microsoft Office 12

Access Database Engine OLE DB Provider (for Access 2007). The typical connection string syntax for an Access 2003 and 2007 database is shown in Listings 19-3 and 19-4, respectively.

Listing 19-3 A Connection String for Access 2003

```
Dim sConnect As String

sConnect = "Provider=Microsoft.Jet.OLEDB.4.0;" & _
           "Data Source=C:\Files\MyDatabase.mdb;" & _
           "User ID=UserName;" & _
           "Password=Password;"
```

Listing 19-4 A Connection String for Access 2007

```
Dim sConnect As String

sConnect = "Provider=Microsoft.ACE.OLEDB.12.0;" & _
           "Data Source=C:\Files\MyDatabase.accdb;" & _
           "User ID=UserName;" & _
           "Password=Password;"
```

NOTE Even though the Microsoft.ACE.OLEDB.12.0 provider can successfully read databases created in versions of Access earlier than 2007, it is not likely to be installed on the computers of users who are not running Office 2007. For this reason we recommend that you always use the Microsoft.Jet.OLEDB.4.0 provider unless you must connect to an Access 2007 database and you are sure your users have the 12.0 provider installed.

Once you have specified the Provider, the only other property that is always required is the Data Source property. This tells OLE DB where the Access database you want to connect to is located. If your Access database is password protected, you can provide the username and password required to open it using the User ID and Password properties. Otherwise these two properties can be removed from the connection string.

Using the Connection String

Once you have built your connection string, you can assign it to the ConnectionString property of the ADO Connection object or pass it directly to various properties and methods of other top-level ADO objects. Listing 19-5 demonstrates how to open a connection to an Access database using the Connection object.

Listing 19-5 Opening a Connection to an Access Database

```
Public Sub OpenAccessConnection()

    Dim cnAccess As ADODB.Connection
    Dim sConnect As String

    sConnect = "Provider=Microsoft.Jet.OLEDB.4.0;" & _
                "Data Source=C:\Files\Northwind.mdb;"

    Set cnAccess = New ADODB.Connection
    cnAccess.ConnectionString = sConnect
    cnAccess.Open

End Sub
```

Data Access Techniques with Microsoft Access

For the sake of clarity and simplicity, the following data access examples are completely self-contained. They assume there is a Sheet1 in the workbook from which they are run and that the Northwind.mdb database file is located in the same folder as the workbook from which the code is being run.

Retrieving Data

Listing 19-6 shows a plain text SQL query that retrieves a complete list of Beverages available to be sold by the fictional Northwind Trading Company.

Listing 19-6 Retrieving Data From Access

```
Public Sub SelectFromAccess()

    Dim rsData As ADODB.Recordset
```

```
Dim sPath As String
Dim sConnect As String
Dim sSQL As String

' Clear the destination worksheet.
Sheet1.UsedRange.Clear

' Get the database path (same as this workbook).
sPath = ThisWorkbook.Path
If Right$(sPath, 1) <> "\" Then sPath = sPath & "\"

' Create the connection string.
sConnect = "Provider=Microsoft.Jet.OLEDB.4.0;" & _
           "Data Source=" & sPath & "Northwind.mdb;"

' Build the SQL query.
sSQL = "SELECT P.ProductName " & _
       "FROM Products AS P " & _
       "INNER JOIN Categories AS C " & _
       "ON P.CategoryID = C.CategoryID " & _
       "WHERE C.CategoryName = 'Beverages'" & _
       "AND P.Discontinued = False;"

' Retrieve the data using ADO.
Set rsData = New ADODB.Recordset
rsData.Open sSQL, sConnect, _
            adOpenForwardOnly, adLockReadOnly, adCmdText
If Not rsData.EOF Then
    Sheet1.Range("A1").CopyFromRecordset rsData
Else
    MsgBox "No data located.", vbCritical, "Error!"
End If

rsData.Close
Set rsData = Nothing

End Sub
```

There are a few interesting techniques to point out in Listing 19-6. First, we join two tables in the FROM clause. We need to do this because even though the data we need is located in the Products table, the category name that we want to restrict our data to is located in the Categories table.

In the FROM clause we link the two tables on their common column, the CategoryID column. The CategoryID column is the primary key of the Categories table and a foreign key in the Products table.

Next, notice that we use multiple restriction conditions in the WHERE clause. We need to specify not only that the category we are looking for is Beverages, but also that the product has not been discontinued. To do this we simply link the two conditions with the SQL AND operator.

Finally, notice how we make use of the connection string in this example. Rather than creating an ADO Connection object, we simply pass the connection string directly to the ADO Recordset object's Open method. This is a useful technique when you are only performing a single query and you don't need advanced features of the ADO Connection object such as connection pooling.

Once we open the recordset, we check to see whether we have any data. This is accomplished by examining the recordset's EOF property. EOF stands for **end of file**. If no data was returned, the recordset's row pointer points to the end of the recordset and the EOF property is True; otherwise, the row pointer points to the first record in the recordset and the value of EOF is False.

If we successfully retrieved the data we asked for, we dump it onto Sheet1 using the CopyFromRecordset method of the Excel Range object. The CopyFromRecordset method provides an extremely fast method for extracting the data from a recordset onto a worksheet. Note that the CopyFromRecordset method returns only the data, not any associated column names. An alternative method that adds the column names and then adds the data by looping the recordset one row at a time is shown in the code fragment in Listing 19-7.

Listing 19-7 Looping a Recordset by Rows

```
If Not rsData.EOF Then
    ' Add the column headers.
    For lColumn = 0 To rsData.Fields.Count - 1
        With Sheet1.Range("A1")
            .Offset(0, lColumn).Value = _
                         rsData.Fields(lColumn).Name
        End With
    Next lColumn

    ' Add the data.
    lRow = 1
    Do While Not rsData.EOF
        For lColumn = 0 To rsData.Fields.Count - 1
            With Sheet1.Range("A1")
```

```
                    .Offset(lRow, lColumn).Value = _
                            rsData.Fields(lColumn).Value
            End With
        Next lColumn
        lRow = lRow + 1
        rsData.MoveNext
    Loop
Else
    MsgBox "No data located.", vbCritical, "Error!"
End If
```

Inserting Data

To illustrate the SQL INSERT statement we add a new shipper to the Northwind Shippers table. The code to accomplish this is shown in Listing 19-8.

Listing 19-8   Inserting Data into Access

```
Public Sub InsertIntoAccess()

    Dim cnAccess As ADODB.Connection
    Dim sPath As String
    Dim sConnect As String
    Dim sSQL As String

    ' Get the database path (same as this workbook).
    sPath = ThisWorkbook.Path
    If Right$(sPath, 1) <> "\" Then sPath = sPath & "\"

    ' Create the connection string.
    sConnect = "Provider=Microsoft.Jet.OLEDB.4.0;" & _
                "Data Source=" & sPath & "Northwind.mdb;"

    ' Build the SQL query.
    sSQL = "INSERT INTO Shippers (CompanyName, Phone)" & _
            "VALUES ('Excellent Shipping', '(555) 555-1212');"

    ' Use the Connection object to execute the SQL statement.
    Set cnAccess = New ADODB.Connection
    cnAccess.ConnectionString = sConnect
    cnAccess.Open
    cnAccess.Execute sSQL, , adCmdText + adExecuteNoRecords
```

```
cnAccess.Close
Set cnAccess = Nothing

End Sub
```

In this example, we demonstrate how to run SQL statements using the Execute method of the ADO Connection object. The first argument to the Execute method is the SQL statement to execute. The second argument is a return value equal to the number of records affected after the method has successfully completed. In this example we already know that our INSERT statement only affects a single record, so we don't use this argument. If the SQL statement fails to complete successfully a runtime error is generated by ADO.

The third argument tells the Execute method what type of command we are passing to its first argument and how that command should be processed. adCmdText is an enumeration member that tells the Execute method we are passing it a SQL text string. This is the same value we passed to the last argument of the Recordset.Open method in Listing 19-6. If this value is not specified, ADO has to figure out for itself what is being passed in the first argument, so giving it that information to begin with saves time. adExecuteNoRecords is an enumeration member that tells the Execute method how to process the call. In this case it means the Execute method should not return a recordset. The Execute method always returns a recordset unless told to do otherwise, even if a recordset is not logically required and is therefore empty. Telling the Execute method we don't need a recordset returned saves the time and resources required to create and return the unnecessary empty recordset.

Updating Data

To illustrate the SQL UPDATE statement we create and use an Access stored parameter query to modify the phone number of the shipper we inserted into the Shippers table in the previous section. Create a new query in the Northwind database, enter the SQL shown in Listing 19-9, and then save the query with the name UpdateShipper (we've already done this in the copy of the Northwind database supplied on the CD).

Listing 19-9 The UpdateShipper Parameter Query

```
UPDATE Shippers
SET Phone = [NewNumber]
WHERE ShipperID = [ID]
```

As you can see, this query takes two parameters. The `NewNumber` parameter is used to modify the phone number, and the `ID` parameter is used to uniquely identify the shipper whose phone number we want to update. The code to execute this query is shown in Listing 19-10.

Listing 19-10   Updating Access Data

```
Public Sub UpdateAccess()

    Dim cmAccess As ADODB.Command
    Dim objParams As ADODB.Parameters
    Dim lAffected As Long
    Dim sPath As String
    Dim sConnect As String

    ' Get the database path (same as this workbook).
    sPath = ThisWorkbook.Path
    If Right$(sPath, 1) <> "\" Then sPath = sPath & "\"

    ' Create the connection string.
    sConnect = "Provider=Microsoft.Jet.OLEDB.4.0;" & _
               "Data Source=" & sPath & "Northwind.mdb;"

    ' Create the Command object.
    Set cmAccess = New ADODB.Command
    cmAccess.ActiveConnection = sConnect
    cmAccess.CommandText = "UpdateShipper"
    cmAccess.CommandType = adCmdStoredProc

    ' Create and append the parameters.
    Set objParams = cmAccess.Parameters
    objParams.Append cmAccess.CreateParameter("NewNumber", _
                                adVarChar, adParamInput, 40)
    objParams.Append cmAccess.CreateParameter("ID", _
                                adInteger, adParamInput, 0)
    Set objParams = Nothing

    ' Load the parameters and execute the query.
    cmAccess.Parameters("NewNumber").Value = "(555) 555-5555"
    cmAccess.Parameters("ID").Value = 4
    cmAccess.Execute lAffected, , adExecuteNoRecords

    ' Verify the correct number of records updated.
    If lAffected <> 1 Then
```

```
        MsgBox "Error updating record.", vbCritical, "Error!"
    End If

    Set cmAccess = Nothing

End Sub
```

In this example, we bypass the ADO Connection object entirely by assigning the connection string directly to the Command object's ActiveConnection property. Instead of a plain text SQL statement we now use the name of the Access parameter query that we created in Listing 19-9. We tell ADO that we are running a stored query by setting the CommandType property of the Command object to adCmdStoredProc.

This example illustrates the use of the ADO Command object's Parameters collection. For each parameter in the Access parameter query we must create a Parameter object and add it to the Parameters collection. These parameters must be created and added to the collection in exactly the same order as they appear in the SQL of the Access parameter query. We create and store each parameter using a single line of code by passing the result of the Command object's CreateParameter method directly to the Parameters collection Append method. We use four arguments of the CreateParameter method:

- **Name**—This is the name of the parameter. It must be the same name that appears in the Access parameter query for the parameter.
- **Type**—This is an enumeration member specifying the data type of the parameter. adVarChar means a Text parameter, and adInteger means a Long Integer parameter.
- **Direction**—This is an enumeration member indicating which direction the parameter is used to pass data. adParamInput indicates the parameter is used to pass data from our code to the database.
- **Size**—This value indicates the size of the parameter. It is only required for Text data types. In the case of our NewNumber parameter, the column being updated has a maximum width of 40 characters. For numeric data types like the ID parameter you can simply pass zero to this argument.

Once we create the parameters and add them to our Command object's Parameters collection we load them with the values we want to send to the database and then execute the stored query. The first argument to the Command object's Execute method is a return value indicating the number of records affected. We use the `lAffected` variable to retrieve this value and check it to ensure that exactly one record was updated. As in our insert example, we do not require a recordset to be returned, so we're using the third argument of the Command object to prevent this from happening.

Deleting Data

To illustrate the SQL DELETE statement we remove the shipper that we added to the Shippers table with our insert example in Listing 19-8. The code to accomplish this is shown in Listing 19-11.

Listing 19-11   Deleting Access Data

```
Public Sub DeleteFromAccess()

    Dim cmAccess As ADODB.Command
    Dim lAffected As Long
    Dim sPath As String
    Dim sConnect As String
    Dim sSQL As String

    ' Get the database path (same as this workbook).
    sPath = ThisWorkbook.Path
    If Right$(sPath, 1) <> "\" Then sPath = sPath & "\"

    ' Create the connection string.
    sConnect = "Provider=Microsoft.Jet.OLEDB.4.0;" & _
               "Data Source=" & sPath & "Northwind.mdb;"

    ' Build the SQL query.
    sSQL = "DELETE FROM Shippers " & _
           "WHERE CompanyName = 'Excellent Shipping';"

    ' Create and execute the Command object.
    Set cmAccess = New ADODB.Command
    cmAccess.ActiveConnection = sConnect
    cmAccess.CommandText = sSQL
    cmAccess.CommandType = adCmdText
    cmAccess.Execute lAffected, , adExecuteNoRecords

    ' Verify the correct number of records deleted.
    If lAffected <> 1 Then
        MsgBox "Error deleting record.", vbCritical, "Error!"
    End If
```

```
    Set cmAccess = Nothing

End Sub
```

All the techniques used here should be familiar from previous examples, so we do not cover them in any detail.

Working with Microsoft SQL Server Databases

While the installation and maintenance requirements for SQL Server are more complex than for Access, these requirements are not typically the concern of the Excel developer. SQL Server is widely deployed, and you will often find yourself simply working with a preexisting installation.

SQL Server is also significantly more powerful than Access. It can support enormous databases and thousands of simultaneous users, and its security model is fully integrated with Windows network security, which vastly simplifies the task of providing user-based security in your database applications.

Beginning with SQL 2005 Express Edition, Microsoft also began offering a free version of SQL Server whose only significant limitation from an Excel development perspective is the 4GB maximum allowable size of the database. We have built a number of non-trivial applications using nothing but the Express Edition of SQL Server as our back-end database, and if the application outgrows the limitations of the Express Edition, upgrading to the full version of SQL Server is a completely transparent process.

Connecting to a SQL Server Database

The OLE DB Provider for SQL Server is used to connect to SQL Server databases. The base connection string syntax for this provider is shown in Listing 19-12.

Listing 19-12 Base Connection String Syntax for SQL Server

```
Dim sConnect As String

sConnect = "Provider=SQLOLEDB;" & _
            "Data Source=Server\Instance;" & _
            "Initial Catalog=DatabaseName;"
```

The Data Source property specifies the server and (optionally) instance you want to connect to. The Initial Catalog property is used to specify the database within the specified server that you want to connect to. SQL Server 2000 and later can have multiple server instances installed on a single computer, and each instance can contain multiple databases. If SQL Server has been installed as the default instance, then all you need to supply for the data source property is the server name. The server name is almost always the same as the machine name of the computer on which SQL Server is installed.

There are two common connection string variations you will encounter when connecting to a SQL Server database. Which variation you need depends on how you intend for your users to log in to SQL Server. Unlike Access, SQL Server always requires some sort of login credentials. The two types of SQL Server security are **standard security** and **Windows integrated security**. Standard security means that you log in to SQL Server with a username and password specific to SQL Server. Integrated security means that your Windows network login credentials are automatically used by SQL Server as your login credentials. The connection string variation for standard security is shown in Listing 19-13. The connection string variation for integrated security is shown in Listing 19-14.

Listing 19-13 Connection String for SQL Server with Standard Security

```
Dim sConnect As String

sConnect = "Provider=SQLOLEDB;" & _
           "Data Source=ServerName\InstanceName;" & _
           "Initial Catalog=DatabaseName;" & _
           "User ID=UserName;" & _
           "Password=Password;"
```

Listing 19-14 Connection String for SQL Server with Integrated Security

```
Dim sConnect As String

sConnect = "Provider=SQLOLEDB;" & _
           "Data Source=ServerName\InstanceName;" & _
           "Initial Catalog=DatabaseName;" & _
           "Integrated Security=SSPI"
```

Connection Pooling

Listing 19-15 shows how to create a connection to a SQL Server database using integrated security and support for ADO **connection pooling**.

Listing 19-15 Connecting to SQL Server with Integrated Security and Support for Connection Pooling

```
Private mcnSQLServer As ADODB.Connection

Public Sub ConnectToSQLServer()

    Dim sConnect As String

    ' Create the connection string.
    sConnect = "Provider=SQLOLEDB;" & _
                "Data Source=ServerName\InstanceName;" & _
                "Initial Catalog=DatabaseName;" & _
                "Integrated Security=SSPI"

    ' Attempt to open the connection.
    Set mcnSQLServer = New ADODB.Connection
    mcnSQLServer.ConnectionString = sConnect
    mcnSQLServer.Open

    ' Close connection to enable connection pooling.
    mcnSQLServer.Close

End Sub
```

Note that our ADO Connection object is declared at the module level so that it maintains its state throughout the lifetime of our application. This is required to enable an important ADO feature called connection pooling. Creating and tearing down a connection to a database is a resource-intensive process. If your application performs a large number of database operations you do not want ADO to have to create and destroy a connection for each one of them. To enable connection pooling you must do the following:

- Declare your ADO Connection object as a global or module-level variable.
- Create and open your ADO connection on application startup and then immediately close it.

- Each time a procedure needs to use the connection it can open the connection, use it, and then close it again.
- Do not set the Connection object to Nothing until your application is shutting down.

This technique allows ADO (or more accurately, the underlying OLE DB provider) to hold the database connection open behind the scenes and provide your procedures with an existing connection upon request, rather than forcing it to create a new connection each time one is needed.

Error Handling Connections

When talking about making database connections in theory, the connection attempts always succeed and you continue along your way. In the real world this is not always the case. When you attempt to access a database that is not located on the same computer as your code, any number of things can cause the connection attempt to fail.

The solution to this problem is to use your error handler to look for the error that is generated when a connection attempt fails and then handle it appropriately. Since congested network conditions or busy databases can both cause transient connection problems, the best strategy is to retry the connection attempt a few times before giving up and informing the user that a connection to the database could not be established.

The code required to accomplish this for an attempted connection to a SQL Server database is shown in Listing 19-16. For general details on the error handling technique used here, please refer back to Chapter 15, "VBA Error Handling."

Listing 19-16   Error Handling a Connection Attempt

```
Private mcnSQLServer As ADODB.Connection

Public Sub ConnectToSQLServer()

    Const sSOURCE As String = "ConnectToSQLServer"

    Dim lAttempt As Long
    Dim sConnect As String

    On Error GoTo ErrorHandler

    ' Create the connection string.
```

```
        sConnect = "Provider=SQLOLEDB;" & _
                   "Data Source=ServerName\InstanceName;" & _
                   "Initial Catalog=DatabaseName;" & _
                   "Integrated Security=SSPI"

    ' Attempt to open the connection.
    Application.StatusBar = "Attempting to connect..."
    Set mcnSQLServer = New ADODB.Connection
    mcnSQLServer.ConnectionString = sConnect
    mcnSQLServer.Open

    ' Close connection to enable connection pooling.
    mcnSQLServer.Close

ErrorExit:

    Application.StatusBar = False
    Exit Sub

ErrorHandler:

    ' We will try to make the connection three times before bailing out.
    If lAttempt < 3 And mcnSQLServer.Errors.Count > 0 Then
        If mcnSQLServer.Errors(0).NativeError = 17 Then
            Application.StatusBar = "Retrying connection..."
            lAttempt = lAttempt + 1
            Resume
        End If
    End If

    If bCentralErrorHandler(msMODULE, sSOURCE, , True) Then
        Stop
        Resume
    Else
        Resume ErrorExit
    End If

End Sub
```

The error indicating a connection failure is a provider error, so we must examine the Connection object's Errors collection to determine whether a connection attempt failed. The Errors collection may contain multiple errors, but the first item in the collection is almost always the one that describes the root cause of the error. Unlike many collections that you encounter in VBA, the Connection object Errors collection is indexed beginning with zero.

The process of retrying connection attempts can be lengthy. Therefore we add status bar messages to keep our users updated. Otherwise they may think the application is frozen and attempt to end it with Ctrl+Alt+Del.

Data Access with SQL Server

The primary advantage SQL Server has over Access is the ability to write **stored procedures**. These can be thought of as the SQL equivalent of functions and subroutines in VBA. Stored procedures can take arguments, return values, call other stored procedures, and execute very complex internal logic thanks to the power of Transact SQL, or T-SQL, which is the dialect of SQL supported by SQL Server.

Although you can execute plain text SQL queries against SQL Server just like you can against Access, the best practice for SQL Server development is to place all your SQL inside stored procedures on the server. This not only allows you to take advantage of the full power of T-SQL, it also centralizes the SQL for your application. If you need to modify your SQL logic at some point, you simply modify the stored procedure located in the SQL Server database, and the changes are immediately visible to all of your clients without any changes required to your application code. An example of the script required to create a simple stored procedure that returns information about suppliers in specific countries is shown in Listing 19-17.

Listing 19-17 A Simple Stored Procedure

```
CREATE PROC spGetSupplierInfo
    @Country nvarchar(15)
AS
    SELECT      CompanyName,
                ContactName,
                Phone
    FROM        Suppliers
    WHERE       Country = @Country
```

This stored procedure takes one argument, the country whose list of suppliers you want to return, and it returns a recordset containing the data specified by the SQL statement. In this case a list of company names, contact names, and phone numbers for all suppliers in the specified country.

Once this script has been run in the Northwind database, it can be called in a manner similar to an Access parameter query.

ADO provides a simple way to execute stored procedures using the Connection object. ADO treats all stored procedures in the currently connected database as dynamic methods of the Connection object. You can call a stored procedure exactly like any other Connection object method, passing any arguments to the stored procedure as method arguments and optionally passing a Recordset object as the last argument if the stored procedure returns a recordset. This method is best used for "one off" procedures rather than those you will execute multiple times since it isn't the most efficient method. However, it is significantly easier to code. Listing 19-18 shows how to execute the spGetSupplierInfo stored procedure as a method of the Connection object.

Listing 19-18 Executing a Stored Procedure as a Method of the Connection Object

```
Public Sub RunStoredProcAsMethod()

    Dim cnSQLServer As ADODB.Connection
    Dim rsData As ADODB.Recordset
    Dim sConnect As String

    ' Clear the destination worksheet.
    Sheet1.UsedRange.Clear

    ' Create the connection string.
    sConnect = "Provider=SQLOLEDB;Data Source=P2400;" & _
        "Initial Catalog=Northwind;Integrated Security=SSPI"

    ' Create the Connection and Recordset objects.
    Set cnSQLServer = New ADODB.Connection
    Set rsData = New ADODB.Recordset

    ' Open the connection and execute the stored procedure.
    cnSQLServer.Open sConnect
    cnSQLServer.spGetSupplierInfo "USA", rsData

    ' Make sure we got records back
    If Not rsData.EOF Then
        ' Dump the contents of the recordset onto the worksheet.
        Sheet1.Range("A1").CopyFromRecordset rsData
    Else
        MsgBox "Error: No records returned.", vbCritical
```

```
    End If

    ' Clean up our ADO objects.
    rsData.Close
    If CBool(cnSQLServer.State And adStateOpen) Then cnSQLServer.Close
    Set cnSQLServer = Nothing
    Set rsData = Nothing
End Sub
```

Parameter Refreshing

When working with SQL Server stored procedures it is a common practice to create a persistent ADO Command object for each one and populate its Parameters collection on startup. Once this has been done, the Command object can be used over and over again by simply assigning values to each of its parameters and executing it.

However, there are typically many stored procedures used by an application, and stored procedures often have many parameters. If you were to initialize each parameter of every Command object with individual lines of code you could easily create hundreds of lines of code that are difficult to debug and maintain.

The ADO Parameters collection gives you another option. You can initialize your Command object with its connection and command text information and then call the Refresh method of the Parameters collection of your Command object. This tells ADO to get all the information on the required parameters from the server and populate the entire Parameters collection automatically. Listing 19-19 shows a basic example of how this would work with the spGetSupplierInfo stored procedure from our previous example. Assume that the mcnSQLServer connection variable has been previously initialized.

Listing 19-19   Using the Parameters.Refresh Method

```
Private mcnSQLServer As ADODB.Connection
Private mcmGetSupplierInfo As ADODB.Command

Private Sub ParameterRefresh()

    ' Procedure from Listing 19-16
    ConnectToSQLServer
```

```
' Open the pooled connection
mcnSQLServer.Open

' Initialize the Command object and refresh its parameters
Set mcmGetSupplierInfo = New ADODB.Command
Set mcmGetSupplierInfo.ActiveConnection = mcnSQLServer
mcmGetSupplierInfo.CommandText = "spGetSupplierInfo"
mcmGetSupplierInfo.CommandType = adCmdStoredProc
mcmGetSupplierInfo.Parameters.Refresh

' Close the pooled connection
mcnSQLServer.Close

End Sub
```

With five lines of code each, your Command objects are populated and ready to use whether they have one parameter or one hundred parameters. Keep in mind that the Parameters.Refresh method does require a round-trip to the server to gather information for each Command object. However, our experience in practice has been that performing this once during startup for all the Command objects we intend to use during a session of our application has a minimal impact on performance.

Multiple Recordsets

One of the unique properties provided by the OLE DB provider for SQL Server is the ability to return multiple recordsets with a single ADO Recordset object. One example of where this feature can be useful is when you need to pull in a large number of similar lookup tables.

Let's say we had a worksheet user interface that would allow the user to specify Suppliers, Customers, and Shippers using worksheet cells containing data validation lists. To implement this user interface we would need to query the names and database ID numbers from our Northwind Suppliers, Customers, and Shippers tables. The stored procedure to do this is shown in Listing 19-20.

Listing 19-20 A Stored Procedure That Returns Multiple Recordsets

```
CREATE PROC spGetLookupTables
AS
    SELECT      CompanyName,
                SupplierID
    FROM        Suppliers
```

```
SELECT      CompanyName,
            CustomerID
FROM        Customers

SELECT      CompanyName,
            ShipperID
FROM        Shippers
```

Note that there are three separate SELECT statements in this stored procedure, each of which returns a separate recordset. ADO allows us to assign the results of this procedure to a single Recordset object and extract these individual recordsets one at a time. In the example shown in Listing 19-21 we place these lists in separate columns of Sheet1.

Listing 19-21 Extracting Multiple Recordsets from an ADO Recordset Object

```
Public Sub ExtractMultipleRecordsets()

    Dim rsData As ADODB.Recordset

    ' Clear the destination worksheet.
    Sheet1.UsedRange.Clear

    ' Procedure from Listing 19-16
    ConnectToSQLServer

    ' Open the pooled connection
    mcnSQLServer.Open

    ' Create and open the Recordset object.
    Set rsData = New ADODB.Recordset
    rsData.Open "spGetLookupTables", mcnSQLServer, _
            adOpenForwardOnly, adLockReadOnly, adCmdStoredProc

    If Not rsData.EOF Then

        ' The first recordset contains the Suppliers list.
        Sheet1.Range("A1").CopyFromRecordset rsData
        Set rsData = rsData.NextRecordset

        ' The second recordset contains the Customers list.
        Sheet1.Range("D1").CopyFromRecordset rsData
```

```
    Set rsData = rsData.NextRecordset

    ' The third recordset contains the Shippers list.
    Sheet1.Range("G1").CopyFromRecordset rsData
    Set rsData = rsData.NextRecordset

    ' There is no need to clean up the Recordset object at this
    ' point. It will be closed and set to Nothing automatically
    ' by ADO after the last call to the NextRecordset method.

Else
    MsgBox "No data located.", vbCritical, "Error!"
End If

    ' Close the pooled connection
    mcnSQLServer.Close

End Sub
```

Disconnected Recordsets

One of the primary goals when performing database access is to get in and out of the database as quickly as possible to prevent conflicts with other users who may be trying to access the same data. However, the ADO Recordset object has a number of useful features that may make you decide you want to hold it open for use within your application. For example, you may want to return a large chunk of data and then take advantage of the sorting and filtering features of the Recordset object to display this data to your users in a more flexible and interactive manner.

ADO lets you accomplish this without holding any locks in the database that might interfere with other users by allowing you to create a **disconnected recordset**. A disconnected recordset is a Recordset object that can remain open even after its connection to the database has been severed. The result is a fully functional Recordset object that does not hold any locks in the database. A disconnected recordset can remain open as long as you need it. You can also reconnect and synchronize the disconnected recordset with its source data and even persist its contents to disk for later retrieval. In Listing 19-22, we show how to create a disconnected recordset and demonstrate some of its features.

Listing 19-22 Creating and Using Disconnected Recordsets

```
Public Sub DisconnectedRecordset()

    Dim rsData As ADODB.Recordset
    Dim sSQL As String

    ' Clear the destination worksheet.
    Sheet1.UsedRange.Clear

    ' Procedure from Listing 19-16
    ConnectToSQLServer

    ' Open the pooled connection
    mcnSQLServer.Open

    ' Create the SQL Statement.
    sSQL = "SELECT CustomerID, CompanyName, ContactName, Country " & _
            "FROM Customers"

    ' Steps to create a disconnected recordset:
    ' 1) Create the Recordset object.
    Set rsData = New ADODB.Recordset
    ' 2) Set the cursor location to client side.
    rsData.CursorLocation = adUseClient
    ' 3) Set the cursor type to static.
    rsData.CursorType = adOpenStatic
    ' 4) Set the lock type to batch optimistic.
    rsData.LockType = adLockBatchOptimistic
    ' 5) Open the recordset.
    rsData.Open sSQL, mcnSQLServer, , , adCmdText
    ' 6) Set the Recordset's Connection object to Nothing.
    Set rsData.ActiveConnection = Nothing
    ' rsData is now a disconnected recordset.

    ' Close the pooled connection
    mcnSQLServer.Close

    ' Filter and Sort the recordset
    ' Display only records whose Country is USA.
    rsData.Filter = "Country = 'USA'"
    ' Sort the records by CompanyName.
    rsData.Sort = "CompanyName"
    ' Load the processed data onto Sheet1
    Sheet1.Range("A1").CopyFromRecordset rsData
```

```
' Reconnect and synchronize with any changes in the database
' Open the pooled connection
mcnSQLServer.Open
Set rsData.ActiveConnection = mcnSQLServer
' Rerun the Recordset object's underlying query,
rsData.Requery Options:=adCmdText
' Disconnect from the database
Set rsData.ActiveConnection = Nothing
' Close the pooled connection
mcnSQLServer.Close

End Sub
```

Upsizing from Access to SQL Server

When your database reaches the point where it needs to be upgraded from Access to SQL Server, Microsoft Access provides a handy tool called the Upsizing Wizard to automatically perform what would otherwise be a tedious process. Although we use Access as our database in the PETRAS application practical example for this chapter, we use a SQL Server version of the PETRAS database in Chapter 24, "Excel and VB.NET," so we quickly introduce you to the Access Upsizing Wizard now.

To begin the process, open the Access database you want to upsize and select *Tools > Database Utilities > Upsizing Wizard* from the Access menu. This displays the first step of the Upsizing Wizard shown in Figure 19-1.

Because we don't have an existing SQL Server database that we want to use as the target for our conversion we select the *Create new database* option and then click the *Next* button to display the second step, as shown in Figure 19-2.

The first piece of information we need to supply is the name of the SQL Server where we are creating our new database. This server does not have to be located on the same computer from which we are running the Upsizing Wizard, but the computer running the Upsizing Wizard must be able to connect to the SQL Server whose name you provide here.

In this case the name of the server is P2400. SQL Server names can vary depending on whether SQL Server was installed as the default instance or as a named instance (multiple instances of SQL Server can be installed on the same computer). In the case of a default instance, the

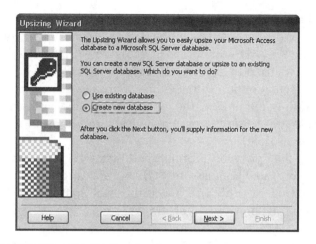

FIGURE 19-1 The first step of the Access Upsizing Wizard

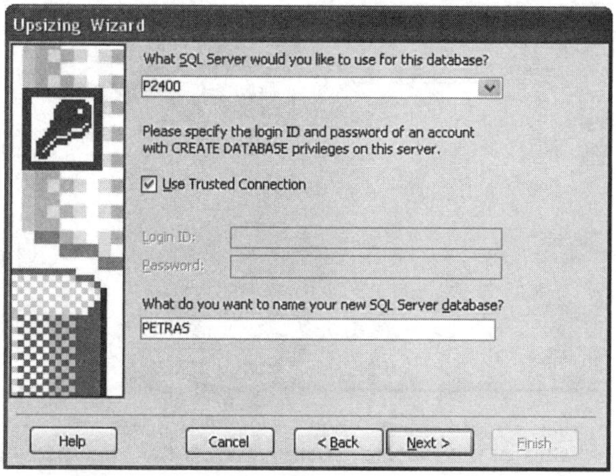

FIGURE 19-2 The second step of the Access Upsizing Wizard

name of SQL Server is the same as the machine name of the computer it is running on. In the case of a named instance the SQL Server name has the form

```
MachineName\InstanceName
```

where MachineName is the machine name of the computer where SQL Server is installed, and InstanceName can be any valid name. If you installed the Express Edition of SQL Server the instance name will usually be SQLExpress.

The next thing we need to tell this step is how it should connect to SQL Server. We selected the option *Use Trusted Connection*. This tells the Upsizing Wizard to connect to SQL Server with the Windows network credentials we used to log in to the computer. If you do not choose the trusted connection option you need to supply a valid SQL Server login ID and password. In either case, the login you use must have permission to create databases on the server (or in technical terms, must be assigned the dbcreator Server Role).

The final piece of information this step requires is the name we want to give our new database in SQL Server. In this case we call our SQL Server database PETRAS. Click the *Next* button to continue on to the third step, as shown in Figure 19-3.

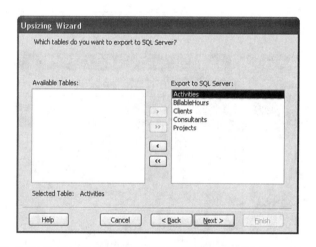

FIGURE 19-3 The third step of the Access Upsizing Wizard

In this step, we tell the Upsizing Wizard which tables we want to move from our Access database into SQL Server. As you can see from Figure 19-3 we moved all available tables from our Access database into the *Export to SQL Server* list. This is what you will want to do in the vast majority of upsizing situations. Click the *Next* button to continue on to the fourth step, as shown in Figure 19-4.

There are two groups of choices in this step. In the top group, labeled *What table attributes do you want to upsize?*, we select all four check boxes and the option *Use DRI* under the *Table relationships* check box. DRI stands for Declarative Referential Integrity, and it is the technology that you will almost always want to use to create relationships among your database tables. It is possible and sometimes useful to implement referen-

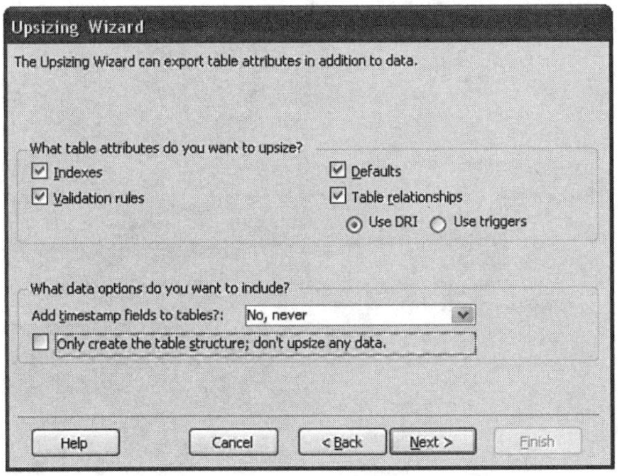

FIGURE 19-4 The fourth step of the Access Upsizing Wizard

tial integrity in SQL Server using triggers, but this is rare and beyond the scope of our discussion in this chapter.

In the second group of choices, labeled *What data options do you want to include?*, we want to instruct the Upsizing Wizard not to add timestamp fields to our tables, and we want to remove the check mark from the check box labeled *Only create the table structure; don't upsize any data.*

The first of these selections prevents the Upsizing Wizard from appending a new column to every table that contains a date/time value that automatically updates each time a row in the table changes. This option can be useful in certain advanced database scenarios, but not for ours. If we do not remove the check mark from the second selection, the Upsizing Wizard re-creates the entire structure of our Access database in SQL Server but does not transfer any of our data. This is not what we want. Click the *Next* button to continue on to the fifth step, as shown in Figure 19-5.

This step is designed to provide granular options for developers who are upsizing applications developed using the Access platform. Because we used Excel as our development platform, our Access database is a simple database, and we just want the Upsizing Wizard to convert our entire database into a new SQL Server database. We achieve this by selecting the *No application changes* option in this step. Click the *Next* button to proceed. This displays the final step of the Upsizing Wizard, as shown in Figure 19-6.

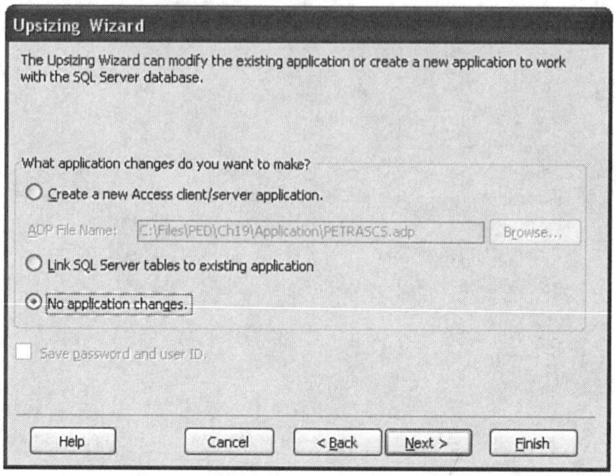

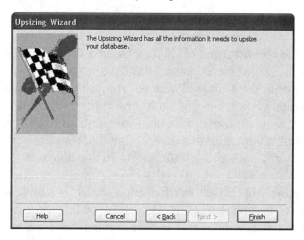

FIGURE 19-5   The fifth step of the Access Upsizing Wizard

FIGURE 19-6   The last step of the Access Upsizing Wizard

This step simply tells us the Upsizing Wizard has all the information it needs. Click the *Finish* button, and the Upsizing Wizard creates a new SQL Server database that is an exact copy of our Access database. When the Upsizing Wizard has completed its task it creates a report containing detailed information about the results of the upsizing process. Scan this report to make sure there are no obvious errors that might need to be addressed. The result of the upsizing process is a new PETRAS database in SQL Server, which is shown in the Object Explorer window of SQL Server Management Studio in Figure 19-7.

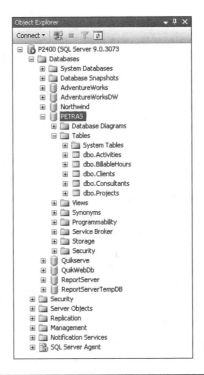

FIGURE 19-7   The new SQL Server PETRAS database

Further Reading

Access 2002 Developer's Handbook Set

Authored by Paul Litwin, Ken Getz, and Mike Gunderloy
ISBN# 0782140092—Sybex
This is the latest and sadly the last update of an ongoing series of first-class
Access development books that began with Access 95. This book touches on
all aspects of Access development, from running Access SQL directly against
an Access database to developing reports in the Access user interface. If you
want a comprehensive reference to Access development, this should be your
first choice. Virtually everything covered in this book is relevant to all later versions of Access, so don't be concerned about the title specifying Access 2002.

Professional SQL Server 2005 Programming

Authored by Robert Vieira
ISBN# 0764584340—Wrox

If you want to learn about SQL Server there is no better place to start than here. The best way to describe the scope of this book is that it starts where ADO ends. It is tightly focused on pure SQL Server topics. It provides excellent SQL Server-specific coverage of SQL, stored procedures, views, indexes, transactions, and the tools used to manage and program SQL Server, among many other topics.

Practical Example

In this section we move our data into an Access database. We provided a ready-made Access database for this project, PETRAS.mdb, in the *\Applications\Ch19 - Programming with Access and SQL Server* folder on the CD that accompanies this book. In Chapter 24 we introduce a new reporting application to the PETRAS suite that uses the SQL Server version of the PETRAS database we created in the "Upsizing from Access to SQL Server" section earlier in the chapter.

PETRAS Time Sheet

All the data access logic in our application has been isolated in a single module called MDataAccess. This makes it easy for us to change our back-end data store, to SQL Server for example, as our data access needs become more complex. We are also using the connection pooling feature of ADO to improve performance. Listing 19-23 shows the function in our MDataAccess module that is called from the Auto_Open procedure to initialize our Connection object.

Listing 19-23 Initializing the Connection Object

```
Private mcnConnection As ADODB.Connection

Public Function bCreateDBConnection( _
              ByRef szFullName As String) As Boolean

    Const sSOURCE As String = "bCreateDBConnection()"

    Dim bReturn As Boolean
    Dim sConnect As String

    On Error GoTo ErrorHandler
```

```
    ' Assume success until an error is encountered.
    bReturn = True

    ' Create the connection string.
    sConnect = "Provider=Microsoft.Jet.OLEDB.4.0;" & _
               "Data Source=" & szFullName & ";"

    Set mcnConnection = New ADODB.Connection
    mcnConnection.ConnectionString = sConnect
    mcnConnection.Open
    mcnConnection.Close

ErrorExit:

    bCreateDBConnection = bReturn
    Exit Function

ErrorHandler:
    bReturn = False
    If bCentralErrorHandler(msMODULE, sSOURCE) Then
        Stop
        Resume
    Else
        Resume ErrorExit
    End If
End Function
```

This function takes the full path and filename to our Access database file, which is passed in by the Auto_Open procedure, instantiates the module-level Connection object, and then opens and closes the connection to our database. This enables the ADO connection pooling feature. The Connection object remains active as long as the application is running; it is simply opened and closed as needed. When the application shuts down we destroy the connection object by calling the procedure shown in Listing 19-24.

Listing 19-24 Destroying the Connection Object

```
Public Sub DestroyConnection()
    Set mcnConnection = Nothing
End Sub
```

Modifying the Application to Load Data Validation Lists from the Database

In previous versions of our time entry workbook template, the data validation lists in the wksProgramData worksheet were hard-coded. If these lists changed you would need to distribute a new copy of the template to all your users. In this section we modify the application so it automatically loads the latest versions of these lists from our new database whenever a time entry workbook is opened.

The procedure that accomplishes this task is located in our MDataAccess module and called by our application event handler whenever a time entry workbook is created, opened, or detected on application startup. The entire procedure is long and repetitive, so we only show a representative sample of it in Listing 19-25.

Listing 19-25 Loading the Application Data

```
Public Function bLoadInitialData( _
            ByRef wkbTemplate As Workbook) As Boolean

    Const sSOURCE As String = "bLoadInitialData()"

    Dim rsData As ADODB.Recordset
    Dim bReturn As Boolean
    Dim lColOffset As Long
    Dim rngCell As Range
    Dim rngClients As Range
    Dim rngProjects As Range
    Dim sSQL As String
    Dim sSQLBase As String
    Dim wksProgData As Worksheet

    On Error GoTo ErrorHandler

    ' Assume success until an error is encountered.
    bReturn = True

    Application.StatusBar = gsSTATUS_LOADING_DATA

    ' Clear any existing data from the wksProgramData worksheet.
    Set wksProgData = wkbTemplate.Worksheets(gsSHEET_PROG_DATA)
    wksProgData.UsedRange.Offset(1, 0).ClearContents

    ' Create the Recordset object we'll use for all the queries.
    Set rsData = New ADODB.Recordset
```

```
    ' Get a connection from the pool.
    mcnConnection.Open

    ' Load each of the program data lists.
    ' Consultants
    sSQL = "SELECT FirstName + ' ' + LastName, ConsultantID" & _
            " FROM Consultants;"
    rsData.Open sSQL, mcnConnection, adOpenForwardOnly, _
            adLockReadOnly, adCmdText
    If Not rsData.EOF Then
        wksProgData.Range(gsRNG_CONSULT_TOP).Offset(1, 0) _
            .CopyFromRecordset rsData
    Else
        Err.Raise glHANDLED_ERROR, sSOURCE, _
            "Error retrieving consultant data."
    End If
    rsData.Close

    ' Load the rest of the lists here...

ErrorExit:

    Set rsData = Nothing
    ' Close the connection to return it to the pool.
    mcnConnection.Close

    Application.StatusBar = False
    bLoadInitialData = bReturn
    Exit Function

ErrorHandler:
    bReturn = False
    If bCentralErrorHandler(msMODULE, sSOURCE) Then
        Stop
        Resume
    Else
        Resume ErrorExit
    End If
End Function
```

The select operation using the recordset should look familiar. It is essentially identical to the operation we demonstrated in the "Retrieving Data" section earlier in the chapter. Notice how we open our module-level Connection object at the beginning of the procedure and close it at the end. This is the proper way to make use of a pooled connection.

You might wonder why we didn't take advantage of the multiple recordsets feature described in the previous section. Unfortunately, the Microsoft Jet 4.0 OLE DB Provider doesn't support this feature, so we must retrieve the lists one at a time.

Modifying the Application to Save Time Entries to the Database

In previous versions of our application, the entire completed time entry workbook was saved to a central consolidation location. In this section, we modify the application to save just the billable hours data to our new database. We added a new hidden section to our time entry worksheet that converts the data entered by the user into a format that can be loaded into the database.

The data from the visible UI is rearranged into a format identical to the BillableHours table in the database. All text column selections are converted to their ID numbers by looking them up in the appropriate wksProgramData worksheet table, and the total hours number is converted from Excel's date serial format into numeric format by multiplying by 24. The conversion section of the time entry worksheet is shown in Figure 19-8.

	J	K	L	M	N	O	P	Q
1					setHideCols			
2								
3			ptrNumEntries	ConsultantID				
4			5	1				
5				tblBillableHours				
6	Total Hours		EntryComplete	ConsultantID	DateWorked	ProjectID	ActivityID	Hours
7	8:00		TRUE	1	08/18/08	9	1	8
8	8:00		TRUE	1	08/19/08	9	1	8
9	8:00		TRUE	1	08/20/08	9	1	8
10	8:00		TRUE	1	08/21/08	9	1	8
11	8:00		TRUE	1	08/22/08	9	1	8
12			FALSE					
13			FALSE					
14			FALSE					
15			FALSE					
16			FALSE					
17			FALSE					
18			FALSE					
19			FALSE					
20			FALSE					
21								

FIGURE 19-8   Time entry data conversion section

For performing the insert operation on the time entry data we created a user-defined type structure to pass data between the business logic tier and the data access tier. The definition of this type structure is shown in Listing 19-26.

Listing 19-26   The BILLABLE_HOUR Type Structure

```
Public Type BILLABLE_HOUR
    lConsultantID As Long
    dteDateWorked As Date
    lProjectID As Long
    lActivityID As Long
    dHours As Double
End Type
```

The data access tier procedure that consumes this type structure and inserts its data into the database is shown in Listing 19-27.

Listing 19-27   The bInsertTimeEntry Function

```
Public Function bInsertTimeEntry( _
                        ByRef uData As BILLABLE_HOUR) As Boolean

    Const sSOURCE As String = "bInsertTimeEntry()"

    Dim cmInsert As ADODB.Command
    Dim bReturn As Boolean
    Dim sSQL As String

    On Error GoTo ErrorHandler

    ' Assume success until an error is encountered.
    bReturn = True

    ' Create the SQL statement to insert the data.
    sSQL = "INSERT INTO BillableHours (ConsultantID, " & _
        "DateWorked, ProjectID, ActivityID, Hours) " & _
        "VALUES (" & CStr(uData.lConsultantID) & ", " & _
        "#" & Format$(uData.dteDateWorked, "yyyy-mm-dd") & "#, " & _
        CStr(uData.lProjectID) & ", " & _
        CStr(uData.lActivityID) & ", " & _
        CStr(uData.dHours) & ");"

    ' Open the connection so we can use it.
    mcnConnection.Open

    Set cmInsert = New ADODB.Command
    Set cmInsert.ActiveConnection = mcnConnection
```

```
    mcnConnection.Execute sSQL, , adCmdText + adExecuteNoRecords

ErrorExit:

    Set cmInsert = Nothing
    ' Close the connection to return it to the pool.
    mcnConnection.Close

    bInsertTimeEntry = bReturn
    Exit Function

ErrorHandler:
    bReturn = False
    If bCentralErrorHandler(msMODULE, sSOURCE) Then
        Stop
        Resume
    Else
        Resume ErrorExit
    End If
End Function
```

Our new PostTimeEntriesToDatabase procedure, shown in Listing 19-28, simply loops the processed entries in the hidden section of the time entry worksheet, loads each of them into the BILLABLE_HOUR type structure one at a time, and passes them to the bInsertTimeEntry function to be inserted into the database.

Listing 19-28   The PostTimeEntriesToDatabase Procedure

```
Public Sub PostTimeEntriesToDatabase()

    Const sSOURCE As String = "PostTimeEntriesToDatabase"

    Dim uData As BILLABLE_HOUR
    Dim rngCell As Range
    Dim rngTable As Range
    Dim sSheetTab As String
    Dim wksSheet As Worksheet
    Dim wkbBook As Workbook

    On Error GoTo ErrorHandler

    If Not bInitGlobals() Then Err.Raise glHANDLED_ERROR
```

```
' We know the active workbook is a time entry workbook
' because our application event handling class would have
' disabled the menu that runs this procedure if it wasn't.
Set wkbBook = Application.ActiveWorkbook

' Make sure the TimeEntry worksheet does not have any
' data entry errors.
sSheetTab = sSheetTabName(wkbBook, gsSHEET_TIME_ENTRY)
Set wksSheet = wkbBook.Worksheets(sSheetTab)
If wksSheet.Range(gsRNG_HAS_ERRORS).Value Then
    Err.Raise glHANDLED_ERROR, sSOURCE, gsERR_DATA_ENTRY
End If

' Warn the user that this action cannot be reversed
' and give them a chance to bail out.
If MsgBox(gsMSG_WARN_POST, vbExclamation + vbYesNo, _
                          gsAPP_TITLE) = vbYes Then

    ' Loop each entry in the time sheet and save it to
    ' the database.
    Set rngTable = wksSheet.Range(gsRNG_BILLABLE_HOURS)
    For Each rngCell In rngTable

        uData.lConsultantID = rngCell.Value
        uData.dteDateWorked = rngCell.Offset(0, 1).Value
        uData.lProjectID = rngCell.Offset(0, 2).Value
        uData.lActivityID = rngCell.Offset(0, 3).Value
        uData.dHours = rngCell.Offset(0, 4).Value

        If Not bInsertTimeEntry(uData) Then
            Err.Raise glHANDLED_ERROR
        End If

    Next rngCell

    ' Clear the time entry worksheet and display a success
    ' message to the user.
    wksSheet.Range(gsRNG_CLEAR_INPUTS).ClearContents
    MsgBox gsMSG_POST_SUCCESS, vbInformation, gsAPP_TITLE

End If

ErrorExit:

Exit Sub
```

```
ErrorHandler:
    If bCentralErrorHandler(msMODULE, sSOURCE, , True) Then
        Stop
        Resume
    Else
        Resume ErrorExit
    End If
End Sub
```

Table 19-1 shows a summary of the changes made to the PETRAS time sheet application for this chapter.

Table 19-1 Changes to the PETRAS Time Sheet Application for Chapter 19

Module	Procedure	Change
CAppEventHandler	bInitializeWorkbook	Centralized workbook initialization code here.
	bLoadInitialData	Call this procedure to load initial time sheet data.
MDataAccess		New module to handle all the database connectivity.
MEntryPoints	PostTimeEntriesToNetwork	Converted to PostTimeEntriesToDatabase.
	SpecifyConsolidationFolder	Converted to SpecifyDatabaseLocation.
Auto_Open	bCreateDBConnection	Call this procedure to create pooled Connection object.
	ShutdownApplication	Destroy pooled Connection object on close.

PETRAS Reporting

The PETRAS reporting application has had a number of changes and additions, partly to demonstrate the database handling concepts introduced in this chapter, but also to demonstrate some of the more interesting concepts introduced in Chapter 13, "UserForm Design and Best Practices," and Chapter 14, "Interfaces."

The immediate result of using a database instead of workbooks to store our time sheet data is that we no longer need a (potentially time-consuming) procedure to consolidate the data. Instead of selecting the files to consolidate, the user now provides a start and end date, which the application uses to extract the required records from the database. The data extraction is done using code similar to Listing 19-25.

Using a central database also makes it much easier for us to maintain the static lists of consultants, activities, clients, and projects. The PETRAS time sheet add-in was modified to read these lists from the database whenever a new time sheet is created, which eliminates the requirement to distribute a new time sheet template any time this data has changed. A set of forms to maintain the lists was added to the PETRAS reporting application, demonstrating many of the concepts from Chapters 13 and 14, including

- All the forms have their code separated between a user interface layer (the form's module) and a separate user interface support (UIS) layer, implemented as a class module specific to each form.
- All the forms are resizable, implemented using the CFormResizer class from Chapter 13.
- The maintenance of the client and project lists has been implemented using a TreeView control to show the client/project hierarchy.
- All the forms have been implemented using the plug-in architecture from Chapter 14, allowing us to add new forms without changing any existing code.

The code changes required for these enhancements are detailed in Table 19-2.

Table 19-2   Changes to the PETRAS Reporting Application for Chapter 19

Module	Procedure	Change
General Changes for Database Handling		
MDataAccess		New module to handle all the database connectivity.
MEntryPoints	MenuSpecify DatabaseLocation	New procedure for the user to select the location of the central PETRAS database file.
MBrowseFor Folder		New module to show the standard "Browse for Folder" dialog.

Table 19-2 Changes to the PETRAS Reporting Application for Chapter 19

Module	Procedure	Change
Extracting Data Instead of Consolidating Workbooks		
MSystemCode	ImportData	Renamed from ConsolidateWorkbooks. Extracts data from the database instead of looping through workbooks.
FImportData		New UserForm to provide a range of dates for extracting time sheet records.
MDataAccess	GetTimesheetData	Retrieve the time sheet records for the given date range, writing the records to the results workbook.
FProgressBar, CProgressBar, IProgressBar		The three progress bar modules were removed, as they are no longer required to show the progress of the consolidation process.
UserForms to Maintain the Static Lists		
wksCommandBars		New menu structure created for the database interaction.
MEntryPoints		Added procedures called by the new menu items, one for each new form.
FActivities		New form to maintain the list of Activities. The code in the form concentrates on handling the user interaction.
CUISActivities		New class to support the FActivities form. The code in the class concentrates on managing the disconnected recordset, in response to the user actions.
FConsultants		New form to maintain the list of Consultants.
CUISConsultants		New class to support the FConsultants form.
FClients		New form to maintain the lists of Clients and Projects.
CUISClients		New class to support the FClients form.

Table 19-2 Changes to the PETRAS Reporting Application for Chapter 19

Module	Procedure	Change
MDataAccess		New procedures to create the disconnected recordsets for the Activities, Consultants, and Clients/Projects forms and to update the database with the changes to the recordsets.
CFormResizer		New class to handle the resizing of the new forms.
Implementing the Plug-in UserForm Architecture		
IPlugInForm		New class to define the IPlugInForm interface.
FActivities, FConsultants, FClients		The three new data-maintenance forms implement the IPlugInForm interface.
MSystemCode	ShowForm	A generic procedure to show any of the plug-in forms.

Summary

The ability to work with databases was once an optional skill for the professional Excel developer, but today it is an absolute requirement. As different types of applications converge, there are fewer and fewer non-trivial Excel applications that do not require interaction with a back-end database of some kind. If you need to be a true professional Excel developer you need to understand how to work with databases.

DATA MANIPULATION TECHNIQUES

In this chapter, we examine how to make the most of Excel's advanced data-manipulation features. While the user interface is usually the only part of our applications that our users will know (or care) about, it is the quality and efficiency of our data processing that provides the solid foundation on which a great user interface is built. Excel provides some powerful data manipulation features. The most difficult aspect of organizing our data processing is often deciding which features to use in each situation, and how they can be efficiently combined.

Excel's Data Structures

Excel's data handling features fall into two distinct groups. Most worksheet functions are designed to operate on individual items of data (usually stored in single cells), while features such as PivotTables, filtering, and so on operate on large sets of data, usually arranged in tables. There are comparatively few worksheet functions, such as VLOOKUP, MATCH, and the Dxxx functions that fill the gap between the two paradigms, operating on tables of data but returning single-value results. The way in which we arrange our data on the sheet can have a significant impact on the ease with which Excel's features can be used.

Most workbooks that we see are organized haphazardly. They often try to combine data entry, analysis, and reporting within the same area of the worksheet and are therefore a compromise between format and function. To design the best user interface we have to organize the worksheet to appeal to the user (such as including blank rows and/or columns around the data), ignoring the arrangement required by Excel's features (such as having to be in a single table). Conversely, to make the most efficient use of many of Excel's features we have to organize our data in specific ways, most of which probably are not the nicest to look at (such as having to leave a lot of white space around PivotTables to allow for their changing shape, or include artificial column and row labels).

Unstructured Ranges

Unstructured ranges are usually encountered in the parts of the workbook designed for data entry. The spatial arrangement of the data will probably have some meaning to the user, with labels and formatting used to identify the data to be typed into each input cell. When data is arranged in this unstructured manner we can only use worksheet functions for our analysis. We can't directly create PivotTables or charts from this data, nor can we consolidate, filter, or sort the items.

In practice, we probably wouldn't want to operate directly on this data anyway. These inputs are likely to be single, unrelated items of data, where the lack of structure is not a problem. Ideally, each data entry cell should be given an unambiguous name so we can tell at a glance where it's used by other functions.

The main problem with an unstructured arrangement of data is that every cell has to be treated individually, both by the user and through code, making it hard to copy and paste or import and export the data. The inability to import and export unstructured ranges can be overcome in Excel 2003 and higher by using XML to apply some structure to the cells, as we demonstrated in Chapter 9, "Introduction to XML."

Structured Ranges

Most of the features in Excel that are designed to operate on or with large sets of data require the data to be organized in a tabular arrangement, usually with a header row containing unique labels that Excel can use to identify each column. The most notable exceptions to this are the LOOKUP function and array formulas, both of which work better without a header row. The *Data > Consolidate* feature, which we cover in the "Data Consolidation" section later in this chapter, works best with an even stricter structure, where the contents of the first column in the data range can be used to identify each row.

The easiest way for us to arrange our data for analysis in Excel is to put it in a worksheet as a single table, with a header row and consistent data in each column, such as the list of customers shown in Figure 20-1. This data comes from the sample Northwind Access database supplied with Office, usually found at *C:\Program Files\Microsoft Office\OfficeXX\Samples\ Northwind.mdb*, where *XX* is the version number of Office that you have installed.

	A	B	C	D	E
1	CompanyName	Country	City	ContactName	Phone
2	Alfreds Futterkiste	Germany	Berlin	Maria Anders	030-0074321
3	Ana Trujillo Emparedados y helados	Mexico	México D.F.	Ana Trujillo	(5) 555-4729
4	Antonio Moreno Taquería	Mexico	México D.F.	Antonio Moreno	(5) 555-3932
5	Around the Horn	UK	London	Thomas Hardy	(171) 555-7788
6	Berglunds snabbköp	Sweden	Luleå	Christina Berglund	0921-12 34 65
7	Blauer See Delikatessen	Germany	Mannheim	Hanna Moos	0621-08460
8	Blondel père et fils	France	Strasbourg	Frédérique Citeaux	88.60.15.31
9	Bólido Comidas preparadas	Spain	Madrid	Martín Sommer	(91) 555 22 82
10	Bon app'	France	Marseille	Laurence Lebihan	91.24.45.40
11	Bottom-Dollar Markets	Canada	Tsawassen	Elizabeth Lincoln	(604) 555-4729
12	B's Beverages	UK	London	Victoria Ashworth	(171) 555-1212

FIGURE 20-1   A structured range of data

Using the techniques shown in Chapter 19, "Programming with Access and SQL Server," to retrieve data from a database, we can easily create a structured range by populating the sheet from an ADO recordset, as shown in Listing 20-1, where rsData is an object variable that refers to an ADO recordset:

Listing 20-1   Creating a Structured Range from an ADO Recordset

```
If Not rsData.EOF Then
    ' Clear the destination worksheet.
    Sheet1.UsedRange.Clear

    ' Add the column headers.
    For lField = 0 To rsData.Fields.Count - 1
        Sheet1.Cells(1, lField + 1).Value = _
                        rsData.Fields(lField).Name
    Next lField

    ' Make the column headers bold, for clarity
    Sheet1.Rows(1).Font.Bold = True

    ' Copy the data from the recordset
    Sheet1.Range("A2").CopyFromRecordset rsData

    ' Give the retrieved data range a name for later use
    Sheet1.Range("A1").CurrentRegion.Name = "Sheet1!MyData"
Else
    MsgBox "No data located.", vbCritical, "Error!"
End If
```

20. DATA MANIPULATION TECHNIQUES

Excel 2003 Lists

Working with a list of data is such a common use of Excel that Microsoft added the **List** feature in Excel 2003 to ease many of the tasks associated with them, such as sorting, filtering, and adding and removing rows. A range can be converted to a List using the *Data > List > Create List* menu item. Figure 20-2 shows the same table of customers converted to a List (with rows 8 to 90 hidden to save space). Notice the thick (blue) border, the automatic appearance of the autofilter drop-downs in the top row, and the "New Data" row in row 93. The List can also be set to automatically show a total row, using the same totaling options that are provided by the SUBTOTAL() function. Showing the total row makes sense only if the list contains numeric data, as the only option for textual data is to count the rows. It would have been more helpful to have a "count distinct" option, but perhaps that will be added in a future version of Excel.

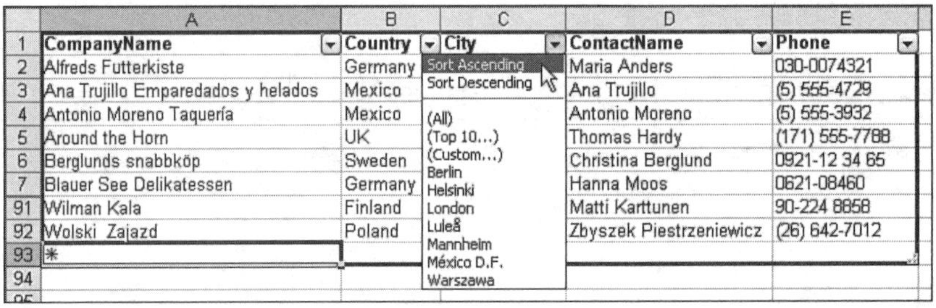

FIGURE 20-2   An Excel 2003 List range

The biggest benefit of using Lists is that any references to an entire column of the List are automatically updated as data is added or deleted, so we no longer need to worry about whether functions, charts, or defined names are referring to the full set of data.

The List object also provides some rudimentary consistency checking, such as ensuring the data in a row stays in sync. Excel mainly uses this under the covers to handle interaction with SharePoint and to enable the import and export of XML. SharePoint interaction is beyond the scope of this book. Using Lists for XML import and export was covered in Chapter 9.

QueryTables

Whenever we use one of the *Data > Import External Data* menu items to import a text file, a table from a Web page, or a database query, the result is a **QueryTable**. This is just a defined area of the worksheet that encompasses the retrieved data and (optionally) stores the connection information used to obtain the data. If the connection information is stored, the QueryTable can be configured to refresh the data when the file is opened, at regular intervals or when a cell containing a parameter value is changed. We can also tell the QueryTable how to handle different amounts of data, and whether to copy or delete any formulas in adjacent columns.

For anything other than the simplest database queries, Excel uses the MSQuery application to provide an interface for creating the SQL SELECT statement If you've used a UI for creating SQL statements before (such as MS Access), the MSQuery interface is easy to understand. Figure 20-3 shows the MSQuery screen with a query that retrieves some example data from the Northwind OrderDetails and associated tables.

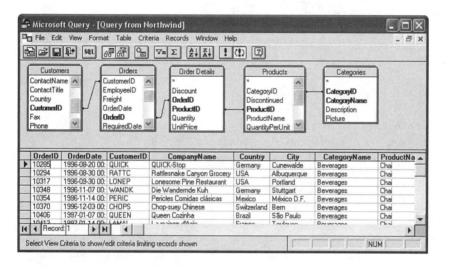

FIGURE 20-3   The MSQuery UI for creating SQL SELECT statements

The biggest problem with creating QueryTables is that the SQL produced by MSQuery is of poor quality and includes the full path to the database file being queried as a qualifier to each table referenced in the query. This makes it almost impossible to create a worksheet using a QueryTable to retrieve data from an Access database and expect it to work when installed at a client site. To create a robust solution, we always have to include some VBA code to set the QueryTable's `Connection` and `SQL` properties.

For example, we would rarely be able to use the built-in ability to refresh the query when the file was opened, because it would fail if the database were moved. Instead, we can use code similar to that shown in Listing 20-2, which sets the database location to the same directory as the workbook and updates the QueryTable's properties before doing the refresh. Note that for this example to work correctly, you need to copy the Northwind database to the folder containing your workbook. In practice, we would prompt the user to select the database location the first time the workbook is opened and store that choice for subsequent use.

Listing 20-2   Refreshing a QueryTable When Opening a Workbook

```
Private Sub Workbook_Open()

  Dim sDatabase As String
  Dim sConnect As String
  Dim sSQL As String

  'Where is the database to connect to?
  'This is the usual location of the Northwind database.
  'In practice, this should be a user-configurable option.
  sDatabase = Application.Path & "\Samples\Northwind.mdb"

  If Len(Dir(sDatabase)) > 0 Then

    'Create the connection string using ADO
    sConnect = "OLEDB;Provider=Microsoft.Jet.OLEDB.4.0;" & _
               "Data Source=" & sDatabase & ";"

    'Create a clean SQL statement, without the file paths
    sSQL = "SELECT O.OrderID, O.OrderDate, CUS.CustomerID, " & _
           "       CUS.CompanyName, CUS.Country, CUS.City, " & _
           "       CAT.CategoryName, P.ProductName, " & _
           "       OD.Quantity, OD.UnitPrice, OD.Discount " & _
           " FROM Categories CAT, Customers CUS, " & _
           "      'Order Details' OD, Orders O, Products P " & _
           " WHERE CUS.CustomerID = O.CustomerID AND " & _
           "       OD.OrderID = O.OrderID AND " & _
           "       P.ProductID = OD.ProductID AND " & _
           "       CAT.CategoryID = P.CategoryID"

    'Update and refresh the query table
    With wksData.QueryTables(1)
      .Connection = sConnect
      .CommandText = sSQL
      .Refresh False
```

```
    End With

  End If

End Sub
```

When creating a QueryTable using the Excel UI, the result is a table that uses ODBC to connect to the database, rather than the ADO connections that we covered in Chapter 19. We can easily switch to using an ADO connection if we want, by adding the OLEDB; prefix to the ADO connection string as we did in the previous example.

Even though we end up with similar code to connect to the database and run the query, QueryTables are often preferable for populating worksheets from ADO recordsets because the QueryTable automatically handles whether to insert new rows for additional data and whether to copy any formulas from adjacent columns.

The ability to create QueryTables is a useful feature, but QueryTables are limited in the amount of data they can efficiently handle. If your application must run in Excel 2003 or earlier, then you are limited to a maximum of 65535 rows of data. Large QueryTables also require Excel to devote significant resources (both display resources and drawing time) to show the data on the worksheet.

Data Processing Features

Once we arrange our data in a tabular form we can use Excel's data processing features to manipulate it. The specific manipulation required obviously depends on the problem being solved, so this section describes some of the techniques available and how they can be linked together. It is up to the reader to decide which techniques are most appropriate for their situation.

It Doesn't Have to Be Data

Even though we've only considered data so far, Excel is not a database; it's designed to manipulate numbers. We are not limited to include only raw data in our structured ranges. Some of the most powerful number crunching comes from organizing our *formulas* in a structured, tabular form, and then using Excel's data processing features on the results of those calculations. The only caveat with using formulas in our data tables is that the data processing (consolidation, pivot table, filter, and so on) is not updated or refreshed when the source formulas are recalculated. We can easily work

20. DATA MANIPULATION TECHNIQUES

around this by including some VBA code to trigger the processing from within the Worksheet_Calculate event (which conveniently occurs after the sheet has been calculated).

PivotCaches

When Microsoft introduced PivotTables in Excel 95, they realized that it would be much more efficient to store the source data for the PivotTables in a hidden form within the workbook file rather than within worksheet cells. These hidden data stores are called **PivotCaches**. They are just like QueryTables but without the visual representation; however, only PivotTables can use them as data sources. PivotCaches suffer from the same problem of including hard-coded paths to the database within their connection and SQL query information, and the same solution of using VBA to define the connection string and query text applies.

PivotTables

PivotTables are the premier data processing feature provided by Excel. Using either a table in a worksheet as the data source or a PivotCache for direct connection to a database, PivotTables allow us to filter, group, sort, total, count, and drill down into our data. Most books about using Excel include a section explaining how to set up and manipulate PivotTables, so we're assuming you already know the basics. Once the basics are understood, the skill is in knowing how to most efficiently use PivotTables to analyze our data and integrate them with the rest of our data processing.

The best way to use PivotTables for data processing in most applications is to create all the PivotTables in advance on individual worksheets. If the PivotTables need to connect directly to a database it is usually more efficient to have a single, large PivotCache that feeds multiple PivotTables than having separate PivotCaches for each pivot table.

The easiest way to do this is to create the first PivotTable using the external database as the data source, and then create subsequent PivotTables using the first PivotTable as the data source (in step one of the Pivot Table Wizard). By using the same PivotCache, Excel only needs to store one copy of the data within the workbook and all the PivotTables will be updated when that PivotCache is refreshed. While it is possible to use the Excel object model to create and modify PivotTables, this should be done sparingly because Excel refreshes and redraws the pivot table with every modification. With more than a trivial amount of data this can become very slow.

In the NWindOrders.xls example workbook, found on the CD in the \Concepts\Ch20 – Data Manipulation Techniques folder, the OrderData worksheet contains a QueryTable that retrieves information about each order from the Northwind sample Access database, as shown in Figure 20-4.

	A	B	C	D	E	F	G	H	I	J
1	OrderID	OrderDate	CustomerID	CompanyName	Country	City	CategoryName	ProductName	Quantity	UnitPrice
2	10285	8/20/1996	QUICK	QUICK-Stop	Germany	Cunewalde	Beverages	Chai	45	14.40
3	10294	8/30/1996	RATTC	Rattlesnake Canyon Grocery	USA	Albuquerque	Beverages	Chai	18	14.40
4	10317	9/30/1996	LONEP	Lonesome Pine Restaurant	USA	Portland	Beverages	Chai	20	14.40
5	10348	11/7/1996	WANDK	Die Wandernde Kuh	Germany	Stuttgart	Beverages	Chai	15	14.40
6	10354	11/14/1996	PERIC	Pericles Comidas clásicas	Mexico	México D.F.	Beverages	Chai	12	14.40
7	10370	12/3/1996	CHOPS	Chop-suey Chinese	Switzerland	Bern	Beverages	Chai	15	14.40
8	10406	1/7/1997	QUEEN	Queen Cozinha	Brazil	São Paulo	Beverages	Chai	10	14.40
9	10413	1/14/1997	LAMAI	La maison d'Asie	France	Toulouse	Beverages	Chai	24	14.40
10	10477	3/17/1997	PRINI	Princesa Isabel Vinhos	Portugal	Lisboa	Beverages	Chai	15	14.40
11	10522	4/30/1997	LEHMS	Lehmanns Marktstand	Germany	Frankfurt a.M.	Beverages	Chai	40	18.00
12	10526	5/5/1997	WARTH	Wartian Herkku	Finland	Oulu	Beverages	Chai	8	18.00
13	10576	6/23/1997	TORTU	Tortuga Restaurante	Mexico	México D.F.	Beverages	Chai	10	18.00
14	10590	7/7/1997	MEREP	Mère Paillarde	Canada	Montréal	Beverages	Chai	20	18.00
15	10609	7/24/1997	DUMON	Du monde entier	France	Nantes	Beverages	Chai	3	18.00
16	10611	7/25/1997	WOLZA	Wolski Zajazd	Poland	Warszawa	Beverages	Chai	6	18.00

FIGURE 20-4   The QueryTable for Northwind order details

As well as retrieving the specific data for the order information, we included extra information such as the company name, country, and product category. This additional data usually has little impact on query execution time or data storage requirements, and it allows us to perform more diverse analysis using the same raw data. For example, Figure 20-5 shows the *PivotTable* worksheet from the example workbook, which includes both a breakdown of order quantities by country and product category as well as a list of our UK customers.

	A	B	C	D	E	F	G
1	**Order Quantity Breakdown by Country and Product Category**						
2	Sum of Quantity	CategoryName					
3	Country	Beverages	Condiments	Confections	Dairy Products	Grains/Cereals	Meat/Poultry
4	Argentina	82	45	57	54	20	0
5	Austria	982	720	575	1027	580	362
22	UK	502	210	318	679	322	172
23	USA	1587	821	1617	1559	760	1157
24	Venezuela	533	166	504	555	244	192
25	Grand Total	9532	5298	7906	9149	4562	4199
26							
27							
28	**List of Customers for a Specific Country**						
29	Country	UK					
30							
31	Sum of Quantity						
32	CustomerID	CompanyName	Total				
33	AROUT	Around the Horn	650				
34	BSBEV	B's Beverages	293				
35	CONSH	Consolidated Holdin	87				
36	EASTC	Eastern Connection	569				
37	ISLAT	Island Trading	295				
38	NORTS	North/South	30				
39	SEVES	Seven Seas Imports	818				
40	Grand Total		2742				

FIGURE 20-5   Two PivotTables derived from the same PivotCache

Unfortunately, this technique is limited by the lack of a "distinct count" function to total the data. The "count" function gives the number of records, which in our case is the total number of order detail line items. If we had a "distinct count" function, we'd be able to identify the number of orders placed by each customer (by counting the number of distinct order IDs) or the number of customers in each country (by counting the number of distinct customer IDs).

Calculated PivotFields

Excel allows us to add extra fields and data to our PivotCaches, in the form of **calculated fields** and **calculated items**. A calculated field is an extra column, derived from one or more other fields, such as defining a calculated Profit field as Revenue – Cost, where Revenue and Cost are fields in the dataset. These are of limited use, because Excel always does the sum of the individual fields before performing the calculation, so we get

Sum of Profit = Sum of Revenue – Sum of Cost

This is acceptable and marginally useful for simple cases but useless and dangerous if a more complex formula is required. For example, in our Northwind dataset we have fields for the Quantity, UnitPrice, and Discount. We might be tempted to add a calculated Revenue field defined as Quantity * (UnitPrice – Discount). Unfortunately, because the PivotTable sums the individual fields before doing the calculation, we would end up multiplying the total quantity sold by the sum of all the prices minus the sum of all the discounts.

Because of this problem it is much safer to add the additional fields at the raw data level, either by including calculated fields in the SQL query itself, or by adding extra formula columns beside the QueryTable, as shown in Figure 20-6.

L2			*fx* =I2*(J2-K2)			
	G	H	I	J	K	L
1	CategoryName	ProductName	Quantity	UnitPrice	Discount	Revenue
2	Beverages	Chai	45	14.40	0.200	639
3	Beverages	Chai	18	14.40	0.000	259.2
4	Beverages	Chai	20	14.40	0.000	288
5	Beverages	Chai	15	14.40	0.150	213.75
6	Beverages	Chai	12	14.40	0.000	172.8
7	Beverages	Chai	15	14.40	0.150	213.75

FIGURE 20-6 Adding a calculated field beside a QueryTable

When creating formula columns beside the QueryTable, be sure to check the *Fill down formulas in columns adjacent to data* check box in the QueryTable properties dialog to make sure the formulas are copied to new rows. We should also use a defined name to link the PivotTable to the QueryTable. This name can then be adjusted to ensure the PivotTables always refer to the correct data range, including the additional formula columns. When creating the PivotTable we use this defined name instead of a direct range reference in Step 2 of the Pivot Table Wizard. The defined name can be updated using the QueryTable_AfterRefresh event shown in Listing 20-3, which also refreshes any PivotCaches that use it.

Listing 20-3 Updating Defined Names and Refreshing PivotCaches When a QueryTable Is Refreshed

```
'Code contained within the OrderData worksheet code module

'Variable to hook the Query Table events
Private WithEvents mqtData As QueryTable

'Called from the start of Workbook_Open()
Public Sub Initialize()

    'Set up the event hook for the query table
    Set mqtData = Me.QueryTables(1)

End Sub

'Update dependent data when the QueryTable is refreshed
Private Sub mqtData_AfterRefresh(ByVal Success As Boolean)

    Dim sRangeName As String
    Dim pcCache As PivotCache

    If Success Then
        'Update the defined name
        sRangeName = Me.Name & "!pdPivotDataRange"
        mqtData.ResultRange.CurrentRegion.Name = sRangeName

        'Refresh any dependent pivot caches
        For Each pcCache In ThisWorkbook.PivotCaches
            If pcCache.SourceData = sRangeName Then
                pcCache.Refresh
```

```
          End If
      Next
   End If

End Sub
```

Data Consolidation

Probably the least known of Excel's data processing features is its ability to consolidate numeric data from multiple ranges into a single table, matching the data using the labels in both the first row and first column of each range. If a single cell is selected, Excel creates a unique list of all the column headers and a unique list of all the row headers for the result table. If a range containing headers is already selected, Excel uses those row and column headers. It then adds (or counts, averages, max, min, and so on) all the items of data that share the same row and column header.

This is extremely useful when consolidating data and calculations that occur over a time series. For example, imagine a project to analyze whether to build and run a new theme park. You might have a workbook for the construction planning, another for the ongoing operations, another for concessions and retail planning, and so on. Each workbook contains a summary table showing the costs, revenue, and cash flow for each year. A greatly simplified version is shown in Figure 20-7, but imagine the *Construction Planning* and *Operations* tables actually exist in different workbooks and each has been given a defined name.

	A	B	C	D	E	F	G
1	**Construction Planning:**						
2	YEAR	2008	2009	2010	2011	2012	2013
3	Costs	50	100	200	200	40	0
4	CashFlow	-50	-100	-200	-200	-40	0
5							
6							
7	**Operations:**						
8	YEAR	2013	2014	2015	2016	2017	2018
9	Costs	50	10	10	10	10	10
10	Revenue	5	50	90	150	250	500
11	CashFlow	-45	40	80	140	240	490
12							
13							
14	**Consolidated Results:**						
15							
16							

FIGURE 20-7   Simplified project planning

To consolidate these ranges into a single table, select the top-left cell in the target consolidation area, A15 in this example, and click the *Data > Consolidate* menu to access the Consolidate dialog shown in Figure 20-8.

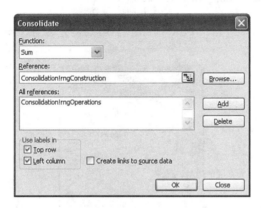

FIGURE 20-8 The data consolidation dialog

The *All references* list shows all the source data ranges that will be consolidated. The ranges can be from the same worksheet, a different worksheet, a different workbook, or even a closed workbook. Data consolidation is one of the few Excel features that work just as well with closed workbooks as with open ones. To add a source data range, type the reference in the *Reference* control and click the *Add* button. Make sure both of the *Use labels in* check boxes are checked to ensure Excel matches both row and column headers. If these options are not checked, Excel matches by position, which is rarely what we want.

When we click the OK button, Excel matches all the labels, adds up all the similar data, and creates the table shown in Figure 20-9.

14	**Consolidated Results:**										
15		2008	2009	2010	2011	2012	2013	2014	2015	2016	2017	2018
16	Costs	50	100	200	200	40	50	10	10	10	10	10
17	Revenue						5	50	90	150	250	500
18	CashFlow	-50	-100	-200	-200	-40	-45	40	80	140	240	490

FIGURE 20-9 The consolidated results

Advanced Filtering

The ability to extract specific records from a large dataset is often the key to successful and efficient data processing. PivotTables provide some rudimentary filtering capability, but only by hiding individual items of data. Excel's Advanced Filter feature allows us to filter the data using more complex expressions, either by hiding records in the original table, or more commonly by copying the resulting records to a new location for further processing. To access the Advanced Filter dialog select *Data > Filter > Advanced Filter* from the menu. This dialog is shown in Figure 20-10.

FIGURE 20-10   The Advanced Filter dialog

When used to copy the filtered data to a new location, an advanced filter requires three ranges:

- **List range**—The range containing the original data to be filtered.
- **Criteria range**—A worksheet range containing the criteria to use when filtering the data. Understanding how to get the most from the criteria range is the key to using advanced filtering and is the focus of the rest of this section.
- **Copy to**—The destination range where the filtered data should be copied.

When the OK button is clicked, Excel scans through the source data range, checks each record against the criteria specified in the criteria range, and copies the matching records to the next row in the *Copy to* range. The result is a subset of the original data, arranged as a simple structured data area—that is, not as a List or QueryTable.

Unfortunately, every time you return to the Advanced Filter dialog the *List range* is either empty or guessed, and the *Action* defaults to *Filter the list, in-place*. It would be much more helpful if Excel remembered the source range and action, which would be possible if Excel created the filter as a QueryTable. If that were the case, we'd also have a one-click Refresh option and be able to tell Excel to automatically copy down adjacent formulas. The best we can do in current versions of Excel is to give our ranges some specific names. If the worksheet contains the defined names *Database*, *Criteria*, and *Extract*, Excel populates the dialog using the ranges pointed to by those names.

To save you some frustration if you're working through these examples, we included the procedure shown in Listing 20-4 in the example workbook to refresh the filter without showing the Advanced Filter dialog.

Listing 20-4   Advanced Filtering with VBA

```
Private Sub cmdRefresh_Click()

    Static rngCriteria As Range
    Dim rngNewCriteria As Range

    'Provide a default initial selection
    If rngCriteria Is Nothing Then
        Set rngCriteria = Me.Range("A1")
    End If

    'Use error trapping to handle a cancel
    On Error GoTo ErrNoRangeSelected

    'Allow the user to select the criteria range to use
    'Type:=8 allows for selection of ranges.
    Set rngNewCriteria = Application.InputBox( _
        "Select the criteria range to use and click OK.", _
        "Refresh Advanced Filter Extract", _
        rngCriteria.Address, Type:=8)

    'Remember the criteria range for next time
    Set rngCriteria = rngNewCriteria

    'Perform the autofilter
    wksData.Range("pdPivotDataRange").AdvancedFilter _
        xlFilterCopy, rngCriteria, _
        Me.Range("rngAFExtract"), False

ErrNoRangeSelected:
    Exit Sub

End Sub
```

Note that in VBA we use the `AdvancedFilter` method on the *source* data range and specify the range to copy the filtered data to.

Criteria Ranges

The criteria range is used to specify the equivalent of a SQL WHERE clause, telling Excel which records to return. Figure 20-11 shows an example of a criteria range.

	A	B
1	Country	CategoryName
2	UK	
3	USA	Beverages

FIGURE 20-11 An advanced filter criteria range

The first row of the criteria range contains field names that must match field names used in the source data table but can be in any order. Subsequent rows contain the data to match for each field. All the items in a single row are joined with an AND operation, while separate rows are joined with an OR operation. Blank cells in the criteria range match anything.

The criteria range shown in Figure 20-11 should be read as `(Country="UK")` OR `(Country="USA"` AND `CategoryName="Beverages")`. It returns all orders of any kind from the UK and all orders for Beverages from the USA. If we only want Beverage orders from the UK or USA we have to include the Beverages filter in both lines, as shown in Figure 20-12. This criteria range should be read as `(Country="UK"` AND `CategoryName="Beverages")` OR `(Country="USA"` AND `CategoryName="Beverages")`.

	A	B
1	Country	CategoryName
2	UK	Beverages
3	USA	Beverages

FIGURE 20-12 Beverages from the UK or USA

By combining the AND and OR logic in this way, Excel allows us to create complex criteria.

We're not limited to filtering using "equals" relationships. In fact, the default filter for text items is "starts with," so the criteria range shown in Figure 20-12 would return Beverage orders from the Ukraine as well as the

UK. To specify an exact (case-insensitive) match we use an = sign, as shown in Figure 20-13. When typing these in, it's a good idea to add a leading single quote character (i.e. '=UK) to tell Excel this is text and not a formula. You can also format the criteria cells as text before entering the criteria.

	A	B
1	Country	CategoryName
2	=UK	=Beverages
3	=USA	=Beverages

FIGURE 20-13   Beverages from only the UK or USA, not the Ukraine

In addition to using the = sign to specify an exact match, we can include the ? and * wildcard characters to match any one character or any range of characters, respectively. We can also use the > and < symbols to match ranges of values. To specify both a lower and upper limit for the same field we can include the field name multiple times in the criteria range. For example, the criteria range shown in Figure 20-14 selects orders from UK customers whose names have first letters from G to N.

	A	B	C
1	Country	CompanyName	CompanyName
2	=UK	>=G	<O

FIGURE 20-14   Specifying a range of matches by repeating the field name

We can filter numeric and date fields in exactly the same way, although we have to be careful if our workbooks will be used in multiple countries with different date orders. For example, if you're American, you might expect the criteria range in Figure 20-15 to return all the records for 2008.

	A	B
1	OrderDate	OrderDate
2	>=1/1/2008	<=12/31/2008

FIGURE 20-15   Filtering between two dates in the USA

When this filter is applied in the UK, it doesn't return any records, because 12/31/2008 is not recognized as a date—it should be 31/12/2008 instead. To avoid these issues, we strongly recommend using formulas to construct date criteria. In this example we should replace the hard-coded date in B2 with the formula =`"<="&DATE(2008,12,31)`, which displays as the less readable date number <=38352, but works in all locales. Similarly, when filtering for a range of numbers you should create the criteria entry as a formula such as =`">="&1.23`, allowing Excel to use the correct decimal separators for the location.

In addition to specifying that individual fields must have certain values, we can also filter on relationships between data in multiple fields. To do this, we use a dummy field name that doesn't exist in the source data and create a formula that references cells in the first data row of the source data table (that is, not the header row). The formula must evaluate to TRUE or FALSE and must use relative referencing. As Excel scans through the source data table, it increments the relative row references in the formula, evaluates the formula for each row, and matches on a TRUE result. For example, the formula shown in Figure 20-16 returns any orders where the discount is more than 5% of the unit price. Note that this must be entered as an Excel formula, not as a text string, so you should see the result of the formula (TRUE or FALSE) displayed in the cell.

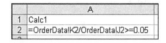

	A
1	Calc1
2	=OrderData!K2/OrderData!J2>=0.05

FIGURE 20-16   Filtering using a formula

Instead of using cell references, which can be hard to read when the referenced range is on a separate sheet, Excel allows us to use the field names in the formula, such as =`Discount/UnitPrice>=0.05` in this case. Doing so usually results in the cell displaying a #NAME! error, but that can be safely ignored.

Advanced Functions

The Database Functions

We often see advanced filtering used to select a subset of data, with the result of the filter being used by a few simple worksheet functions, such as SUM, AVERAGE, and so on. Depending on the complexity and number of the worksheet functions that refer to the filtered data, it can often be quicker and easier to use Excel's **database functions**. These are equivalent to the normal SUM, AVERAGE, MIN, MAX, COUNT, COUNTA, and others, but instead of providing a simple range to operate over, we provide a source database, a criteria range to filter the database by, and the field in the database to operate on.

For example, while AVERAGE(K2:K2156) would give us the overall average discount in our sample workbook, we could use the DAVERAGE function to calculate the average discount of our UK and USA Beverage sales, ignoring those with zero discount. The criteria range for the database functions follows exactly the same structure and rules as for advanced filtering, so we could use the range shown in Figure 20-17 in this case.

	A	B	C
1	Country	CategoryName	Discount
2	=UK	=Beverages	>0
3	=USA	=Beverages	>0

FIGURE 20-17 Criteria range for average of non-zero discount on UK and USA beverage sales

The average non-zero discount for our UK and USA Beverage sales could then be calculated using the following worksheet formula:

```
=DAVERAGE(OrderData!pdPivotDataRange,"Discount",$A$1:$C$3)
```

If we use these functions within the advanced filter criteria range, we can perform some powerful filtering. For example, the criteria range shown in formula view in Figure 20-18 extracts all the UK or USA Beverages sales that have a discount greater than the average discount for UK or USA Beverage sales, ignoring those sales where no discount was applied.

	A	B	C	D
1	Country	CategoryName	Discount	Discount
2	=UK	=Beverages	>0	=">"&DAVERAGE(OrderData!pdPivotDataRange,"Discount",$A$1:$C$3)
3	=USA	=Beverages	>0	=D2

FIGURE 20-18 Using a database function within an advanced filter criteria range

Here, the first three columns of the criteria range are being used by the DAVERAGE function to calculate the average discount. The average discount figure is then used to populate the fourth column in the criteria range, which is used by the Advanced Filter.

Array Formulas

The standard worksheet functions that we use every day typically accept one or more parameters and return a result. A few, such as SUM and AVERAGE accept ranges or arrays in their parameters and return the sum, average, and so forth of all the data they're given. Most worksheet functions and mathematical operators, however, are given a single number for each of their parameters and return a single number as the result.

Even though a function normally accepts single value parameters, we can usually give it a multicell range reference and enter the function using Ctrl+Shift+Enter instead of just pressing the Enter key. Doing this tells Excel to calculate the function as an **array formula**, whereby the function performs its calculation multiple times, iterating over each cell in the range. The result is an array of values, with each element in the array corresponding to one of the cells in the original reference. These results can in turn be fed into the parameters of other functions and so on until they are eventually aggregated to give a final answer. All of the array calculation is done inside Excel and does not usually appear on the worksheet.

The most common use of array formulas is to count and sum lists, using multiple criteria. Excel provides the COUNTIF and SUMIF functions that accept a single filter criterion, so we could sum our UK orders using the function

```
=SUMIF($E$1:$E$2156,"=UK",$I$1:$I$2156)
```

where column E contains the Country names and column I contains the order quantities. If we want the total of our UK Beverage sales, we can no longer use SUMIF, because we need two criteria. We could create a pivot table for it, or use DSUM with a criteria range, but both of those can be overkill if we only have a relatively small list and simple criteria, and can't be used if we don't have column headers.

Array formulas occupy the middle ground between the simplicity of a worksheet function and the complexity of criteria ranges. If we only have a series of conditions connected by a logical AND, we can use an array formula of the form

```
=SUM(ValueRange*(Criteria1)*(Criteria2)*(Criteria...))
```

To get the total orders of UK Beverages from our example data, we could use this formula:

```
=SUM($I$2:$I$2156*N($E$2:$E$2156="UK")*N($G$2:$G$2156="Beverages"))
```

and remember to enter it using Ctrl+Shift+Enter. Let's look at the sample data shown in Figure 20-19 to see how it works.

E	F	G	H	I
Country	City	CategoryName	ProductName	Quantity
Germany	Berlin	Beverages	Chartreuse verte	21
Germany	Berlin	Produce	Rössle Sauerkraut	15
UK	London	Beverages	Guaraná Fantástica	25
UK	London	Grains/Cereals	Ravioli Angelo	25
UK	London	Confections	Valkoinen suklaa	15
UK	London	Grains/Cereals	Gnocchi di nonna Alice	20
UK	London	Seafood	Konbu	20
UK	London	Beverages	Outback Lager	25
Germany	Berlin	Seafood	Spegesild	2
Germany	Berlin	Condiments	Vegie-spread	20

FIGURE 20-19 Sample data for an array formula

To explain how the array formula works, we need to break it up and explain each part of the formula, starting from the middle and working outwards:

- **`$E$2:$E$2156="UK"`**—Excel scans through each of the cells in the range E2:E2156 in turn, checking if each one is equal to the string `"UK"`. The result is an array of True or False values. In our case it is the array {F, F, T, T, T, T, T, T, F, F}.

- **`N($E$2:$E$2156="UK")`**—The `N()` function converts its parameter to a number. When given an array of True and False values, it converts each True to 1 and each False to 0. In our case, this is the array {0, 0, 1, 1, 1, 1, 1, 1, 0, 0}. You might see a double-minus being used instead of the `N()` function, such as `-($E$2:$E$2156="UK")`, which has the same effect and is preferred by some people. You might also see the `N()` function omitted because Excel often (but not always) does the conversion without being told.

- **`$G$2:$G$2156="Beverages"`**—Like the test for UK, Excel scans each cell in the range G2:G2156, checking if each one is equal to the string `"Beverages"`. In our case, the result is the array {T, F, T, F, F, F, F, T, F, F}.

- **`N($G$2:$G$2156="Beverages")`**—Converts the Beverages True/False array to 1s and 0s, giving the array {1, 0, 1, 0, 0, 0, 0, 1, 0, 0}.

- **`$I$2:$I$2156`**—A standard range reference, which is directly translated into the array {21, 15, 25, 25, 15, 20, 20, 25, 2, 20}.

- **`SUM($I$2:$I$2156*N($E$2:$E$2156="UK")*N($G$2:$G$2156="Beverages"))`**—Multiplies the matching elements from each of the intermediate arrays and totals the result, as shown in Figure 20-20.

$I$2:$I$2156		N($E$2:$E$2156="UK")		N($G$2:$G$2156="Beverages")		Result
21		0		1		0
15		0		0		0
25		1		1		25
25		1		0		0
15	X	1	X	0	=	0
20		1		0		0
20		1		0		0
25		1		1		25
2		0		0		0
20		0		0		0
SUM($I$2:$I$2156*N($E$2:$E$2156="UK")*N($G$2:$G$2156="Beverages"))=						50

FIGURE 20-20   The inner workings of an array formula

For these situations, the decision to use an array formula instead of a pivot table, advanced filter, or database function is largely dependent on the size of the dataset and the number of such formulas required. For one or two totals, array formulas are often the most efficient, but as the number of totals increases, it becomes more efficient to perform the filtering before calculating them.

Once you grasp the concept of array formulas, you will probably identify more and more situations where they can be used. A common requirement for many array formulas is to be able to generate a number sequence such as the array {1, 2, 3, 4, 5}. This can be achieved using the awkward-looking formula =ROW(INDIRECT("A1:A5")). The INDIRECT("A1:A5") part returns the range reference A1:A5, and is insensitive to rows being moved, added, or deleted. The ROW() part returns an array of the row number of each row in the range, being the array of rows 1 to 5, {1, 2, 3, 4, 5}.

The classic use of such a sequence is in the "sum of digits" calculation often used in checksum formulas. Given an arbitrary number, 672435, what is the sum of each of the digits in the number. In this case it's 6+7+2+4+3+5=27. To calculate it using a formula, we start off with a sequence from 1 to the number of digits, use the sequence in the MID() function to extract each digit in turn (as text), convert it to a number, and then sum the resultant array. The complete function is

```
=SUM(VALUE(MID(B7,ROW(INDIRECT("A1:A"&LEN(B7))),1)))
```

where B7 contains the number for which we want to calculate the sum of the digits. To understand how it works, let's break it down again:

■ **LEN(B7)**—Gives the length of the number, that is, the count of its digits, 6 in our case.

- `INDIRECT("A1:A"&LEN(B7))`—returns the range A1:A6.
- `ROW(INDIRECT("A1:A"&LEN(B7)))`—Returns the row of each cell in the range, giving the array {1, 2, 3, 4, 5, 6}.
- `MID(B7,ROW(INDIRECT("A1:A"&LEN(B7))),1)`—Applies the sequence to the startnum parameter of the MID() function, which returns the nth digit from the number as text. In this case, it's the array {"6", "7", "2", "4", "3", "5"}.
- `VALUE(MID(B7,ROW(INDIRECT("A1:A"&LEN(B7))),1))`—Converts the array of text items to numbers, giving the array {6, 7, 2, 4, 3, 5}.
- `SUM(VALUE(MID(B7,ROW(INDIRECT("A1:A"&LEN(B7))),1)))`— Sums the numbers in the array, giving 6+7+2+4+3+5=27.

Despite their definite power, array formulas have three main problems: They're relatively slow to calculate, particularly when operating on large datasets, they're relatively difficult to understand when compared to normal worksheet functions, and they're difficult to test, debug, and maintain. If you're using Excel 2002 or later, the *Tools > Auditing > Evaluate Formula* feature can be useful for analyzing and debugging array formulas.

Our advice is to use array formulas when absolutely necessary, but don't use them just to save a few cells. A calculation sequence is often faster to create and much easier to understand if intermediate cells are used for each step instead of trying to perform everything in a single array formula.

Circular References

Excel's online help file and most books mention circular references in terms of "circular reference errors," where you accidentally create a circular reference by mistyping a range reference in a formula. This is, indeed, one of many potential symptoms of spreadsheet errors, which can be difficult to track down. If you find yourself in that situation, the `findcirc.xla` add-in included on the CD in the *Tools* folder might come in handy. This add-in scans a workbook, trying to locate a circular reference chain, and provides the full list of cells involved in the circle. With any luck, you should be able to identify the erroneous references and break the chain.

Much more interesting, though, is the ***intentional*** use of circular references. A great many problems in the world of finance, for example, are circular in nature. One example is how to determine the repayments of a long-term loan. A company may have decided to devote 40% of its after-tax profits to repay a loan. The problem is that both the loan repayment and the interest charge can usually be offset against the tax liability, thereby increasing the after-tax profits and allowing the company to repay more of the loan. The problem can be expressed using the equation

```
R = (P - R - (B - R) * I) * (1 - T) * 0.4
```

where R is the amount of the loan to repay, P is the profit before financing and tax, B is the balance of the loan, I is the interest rate, and T is the tax rate. In this simple example it is possible to solve for R algebraically:

```
R = (P - I * B) / (1 - I + 1 / 0.4 / (1 - T))
```

In most real-life examples, though, the interest rate may be stepped depending on the outstanding balance, and the tax calculation is unlikely to be as simple as just multiplying by the tax rate. In these situations, we can intentionally use circular references to iterate to a solution. Figure 20-21 shows a worksheet to solve this simple problem using circular references.

	A	B	C
1	**Loan Repayment Calculation**		
2	Using Intentional Circular References		
3			
4			
5	Profit before finance and tax, P:	1,000,000	
6	Initial loan balance, B:	900,000	
7	Loan interest rate, I:	6%	
8	Tax rate, T:	42%	
9	Repayment rate (% of net profit):	40%	
10			
11			
12	Repayment (circ)	180,179	=B17
13	Loan Interest	43,189	=(B6-B12)*B7
14	Profit after financing	776,632	=B5-B12-B13
15	Tax	326,185	=B14*B8
16	Profit after tax	450,447	=B14-B15
17	Repayment (circ)	180,179	=B16*B9
18			

FIGURE 20-21   Using circular references to calculate loan repayments

When we created this worksheet, we initially put an estimated value in cell B12. After entering the remaining formulas we added a formula to B12, referencing B17.

By default, Excel disables the calculation of circular references. To enable them, put a check mark in the *Tools > Options > Calculation > Iteration* check box. The *Max Iterations* and *Max Change* settings can be left with their defaults; they have little impact on most circular reference problems. They come into play if the calculations are particularly slow at converging to a result. The *Max Change* determines when Excel considers a circular reference to have converged correctly (the new result must be within the given value of the previous iteration), while the *Max Iterations* provides a cut-off point to tell Excel to stop trying. In slowly converging calculations, the *Max Iterations* may need to be increased to allow the iterations to run until completion. Such situations should be examined to see whether the calculations can be reworked to give a solution that converges with fewer iterations.

The worksheet shown in Figure 20-21 adopts a number of best practices when designing worksheets in general and specifically when using circular references:

- The title of the worksheet makes it clear that intentional circular references exist on the sheet.
- The input ranges are clearly identified, with a light colored background.
- Each formula is clearly identified with a label stating what is being calculated.
- All the formulas except the circular reference refer to cells above them; the cell containing the circular reference is the only reference to a cell below it.
- The circular reference is clearly identified by including (circ) in the cell label.
- Both ends of the circular reference have the same label.
- The circular reference in cell B12 refers to the single cell holding the value to be fed back into the circular calculation, and only that cell.

Once you've used circular references for a while, you'll notice two common issues. First, if any of the functions within the circle results in an error value, it will propagate to every function in the circle. Second, the ability of the formulas to iterate to a solution can be sensitive to the initial estimate for the feedback value.

These issues can be resolved by adding a **kill switch** to control whether the circular reference is calculated and an extra cell to provide a seed value for the initial guess. When the kill switch is FALSE, the feedback cell(s) take on the seed value, which should also clear out any residual error values. When the kill switch is TRUE, the feedback cell(s) complete the circle. Figure 20-22 shows the loan repayment worksheet with these modifications. Changes are highlighted in bold.

20. DATA MANIPULATION TECHNIQUES

	A	B	C
1	**Loan Repayment Calculation**		
2	Using Intentional Circular References		
3			
4	Iterate?	TRUE	
5	Profit before finance and tax, P:	1,000,000	
6	Initial loan balance, B:	900,000	
7	Loan interest rate, I:	6%	
8	Tax rate, T:	42%	
9	Repayment rate (% of net profit):	40%	
10	**Initial repayment guess**	**100,000**	
11			
12	Repayment (circ)	180,179	=IF(B4,B17,B10)
13	Loan Interest	43,189	=(B6-B12)*B7
14	Profit after financing	776,632	=B5-B12-B13
15	Tax	326,185	=B14*B8
16	Profit after tax	450,447	=B14-B15
17	Repayment (circ)	180,179	=B16*B9

FIGURE 20-22 Using a kill switch to control the circular reference feedback

Unfortunately, including circular references in our worksheets prevents us from using a few of Excel's features. Specifically, the Goal Seek, Data Table, and Solver features only calculate a single iteration of the sheet for each step in their processing, and therefore never return correct results on a worksheet with intentional circular references.

Summary

In this chapter, we explained how to organize both our data and calculations so that Excel can readily use them, how to use QueryTables to access data in external databases, and how to efficiently link them to PivotTables. We also explained how to identify and perform calculations on subsets of our data, using advanced filters, database functions, and array formulas. Finally, we lifted the lid on the intentional use of circular references in our applications and explained how to remain in control when doing that.

Armed with these techniques, we can include efficient, robust, and scalable data processing in our Excel applications and can easily cope with the most complex data processing requirements.

ADVANCED CHARTING TECHNIQUES

Only a few minutes are required to learn the basics of Excel charting, but many frustrating hours are required to get a chart looking just right. Most people create charts using one of the built-in chart types, but are unable to modify them to meet their exact requirements. This chapter introduces and explains the fundamental techniques we can use to impose our will on the Excel charting engine to produce charts that look exactly how we want them to.

The chapter focuses solely on the technical aspects of working with the chart engine. We do not investigate which chart type should be used in any given situation, nor the pros and cons of whether 3D charts can be used to present data accurately, nor whether you should use few or many of the colorful formatting options that Excel supports. Because versions of Excel earlier than 2007 are still predominantly in use, we focus here on the earlier version of the charting engine. Most of the techniques presented here still work in the new Office-wide charting engine introduced with Office 2007.

Fundamental Techniques

Combining Chart Types

When most people create charts they start the Chart Wizard and browse through all the standard and custom chart types shown in Step 1, trying to find one that most closely resembles the look they're trying to achieve. More often than not, there isn't a close enough match, and they end up thinking that Excel doesn't support the chart they're trying to create.

In fact, we can include any number of column, bar, line, XY, and/or area series within the same chart. All the choices on the *Custom Types* tab of Step 1 of the Chart Wizard are no more than preformatted combinations of these basic styles. Instead of relying on these custom types, we can usually get better results (and a greater understanding of the chart engine) by creating these combination charts ourselves. Note that you can't combine the different 3D styles, pie charts, or bubble charts with other types.

Let's start by creating a simple column/line combination chart for the data shown in Figure 21-1, where we want the 2008 sales to be shown as columns, with the forecast shown as lines.

	A	B	C
1			
2		**2008 Fruit Sales**	
3		Sales	Forecast
4	Apples	1000	900
5	Oranges	1200	1400
6	Peaches	600	800
7	Pairs	700	1100
8	Bananas	1100	1000
9			

FIGURE 21-1 The sample data to plot as a combination column/line chart

The easiest way to start is by selecting the range A3:C8 and creating a simple column chart from it, as shown in Figure 21-2. We usually find it easiest to start with a column chart because it's the default selection in the Chart Wizard, so we can create the chart by selecting the source data, clicking the *Chart Wizard* toolbar button and then clicking the *Finish* button on the Chart Wizard.

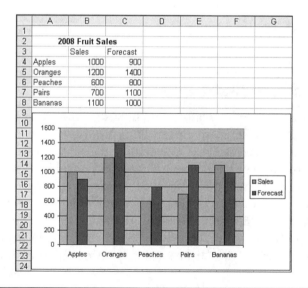

FIGURE 21-2 A standard chart created by the Chart Wizard

To change the Forecast series from a column to a line, right-click on the series and select *Chart Type* from the shortcut menu. In the Chart Type dialog select one of the 2D Line chart types and choose the option to apply the chart type to the selected series, as shown in Figure 21-3.

When you click OK, the Forecast series is displayed as a line, while the Sales series remains as the original column, as shown in Figure 21-4. (We modified the format of the Forecast line to make it stand out in the book.)

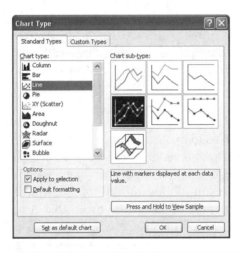

FIGURE 21-3   Selecting a new type for the series

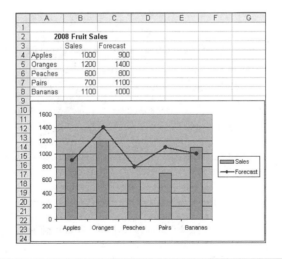

FIGURE 21-4   The resulting combination column/line chart

That's just about all there is to it. Start with a simple column chart with multiple series, select each series in turn, use the *Chart > Chart Type* menu to change its type, and then apply the required formatting. The possible combinations are limited only by your imagination and the legibility of the final chart.

Using Multiple Axes

When we create one of the standard 2D charts, the plot area can have two sets of axes. The primary axes are usually displayed on the bottom and left, while the secondary axes are usually displayed on the top and right. If we have more than one series on the chart, we can choose which set of axes to use for each series by double-clicking the series and making our choice on the *Axis* tab of the *Format Data Series* dialog.

When instructed to place a series on the secondary axis, Excel usually only displays a secondary y-axis on the chart. This can be changed using the *Chart > Chart Options* menu command, clicking the *Axes* tab, and choosing whatever combination of primary and secondary axes are desired. When two series are plotted on different axes, the axes are scaled independently. Care must be taken to ensure that it is obvious to the viewer which series is plotted on which axis, by adding relevant axis labels and matching them to the series labels, as shown in Figure 21-5.

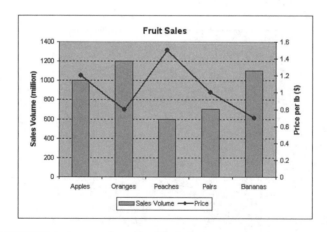

FIGURE 21-5   Using labels and axis titles to clearly identify which series applies to which axis

Using Defined Names to Link Charts to Data

The first thing to understand is that our charts do not have to refer directly to the cells containing their data. The source data for a chart series is provided by the =SERIES() function, which can be seen in the formula bar when a series is selected. The SERIES function has the following format:

```
=SERIES(Name, XValues, YValues, PlotOrder)
```

Each of the four parameters can be a constant or an array of constants, a direct range reference or a reference to a defined name. All the lines in Listing 21-1 are examples of valid SERIES functions.

Listing 21-1 Examples of Valid SERIES Functions

```
=SERIES(Sheet1!$B$1,Sheet1$A$2:$A$20,Sheet1!$B2:$B20,1)
=SERIES("Sales",Sheet1$A$2:$A$20,Sheet1!$B2:$B20,1)
=SERIES("Horizontal Line",{0,1},{123,123},1)
=SERIES("Book Names",Book1.xls!chtXName,Book1.xls!chtYName,1)
=SERIES("Sheet Names",Sheet1!chtXName,Sheet1!chtYName,1)
```

The last two examples of the SERIES formula use workbook-level and worksheet-level defined names, respectively, instead of direct cell references. This indirection allows us to use the defined names' definitions to modify the ranges or arrays passed to the chart, as shown in the following examples.

Setting Up the Defined Name Links

When you use a defined name in a SERIES formula, for best results you should begin with a name that references a worksheet range directly. Once you have this working correctly, you can modify the name to perform more complex operations. If the formula for the defined name is particularly complex or if we make an error in its definition, the charting module refuses to accept the name in the SERIES function. By starting with a very simple definition for the names, we are able to add them to the SERIES function without problem.

Figure 21-6 shows a simple line chart, with the series selected and the SERIES function displayed in the formula bar.

To change the chart to use defined names, we first create two defined names, one each for the Data and Value ranges. Select *Insert > Name > Define* from the menu and create the following two names:

Name: Sheet1!chtDates

Refers to: =Sheet1!$A$2:$A$9

Name: Sheet1!chtValues

Refers to: =Sheet1!$B$2:$B$9

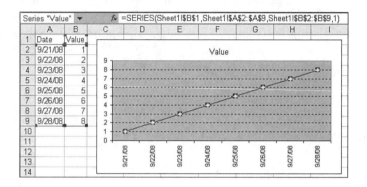

FIGURE 21-6   A simple line chart

Now select the chart series and edit the SERIES formula to read:

```
=SERIES("Value",Sheet1!chtDates,Sheet1!chtValues,1)
```

The chart series is now linked to the defined names, and the defined names refer to the source data ranges. Obviously, if we had more series in our chart we would have to create names for the values for each additional series. Now that we've created the links, we can modify the *Refers To:* formulas for the names to create some interesting and time-saving effects.

Auto-Expanding Charts

One of the most frequently asked questions in the microsoft.public.excel.charting newsgroup is how to get a chart to automatically include new data as it's typed in. In Excel 2003 and higher, if we create a List from the data range and set either the chart or the defined names to refer to an entire column of the List, the reference will automatically be adjusted to include any new data. In previous versions, or if we prefer not to convert the range to a List, we can use defined names to do the automatic updating.

The trick is to use a combination of the OFFSET and COUNTA functions in the definition of the name used for the X values, and then define the name used for the Y values as an offset from the X values range. Select a cell in the worksheet; then choose *Insert > Name > Define*. Change the definition of the chtDates range as follows by selecting the existing chtDates entry, typing the new definition, and clicking the Add button:

Name: `Sheet1!chtDates`

Refers to: `=OFFSET(Sheet1!$A$2,0,0,COUNTA(Sheet1!$A:$A)-1,1)`

The OFFSET function has the following parameters:

```
=OFFSET(SourceRange, RowsToMoveDown, ColumnsToMoveAcross,
        NumberOfRowsToInclude, NumberOfColumnsToInclude)
```

The COUNTA function returns the number of non-blank cells in the range, which in our case includes the header row. We therefore subtract one to get the number of data items. Putting the two together gives us a reference that starts in A2, moves down zero rows and across zero columns (so remains in A2), has a number of rows equal to the count of our data items, and is one column wide.

With the Define Name dialog open and the chtDates name selected, if we tab into the *Refers to* box Excel highlights the resulting range with its "dancing ants," as shown in Figure 21-7.

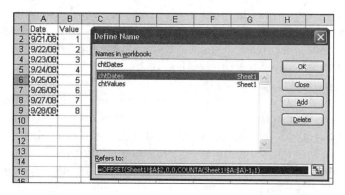

FIGURE 21-7   Excel's dancing ants showing the range referred to by the defined name

While we're in the Define Name dialog, we need to modify the definition of the chtValues name. The easiest way to do that is to again use the OFFSET function, but this time start at the range already referred to by the chtDates name and just move one column across, keeping the same height and width:

Name: `Sheet1!chtValues`

Refers to: `=OFFSET(Sheet1!chtDates,0,1)`

After clicking OK to apply those changes and return to the worksheet, the chart should appear exactly the same as before. The updated defined names resolve to the same ranges we started off with. The difference now is that if we type a new data point in row 10, it automatically appears on the chart (assuming calculation is set to Automatic).

To recap, it works because the COUNTA function contained within the definition of the chtDates range returns the number of items in column A, which now includes the new entry. That feeds into the OFFSET function, making it include the new entry in its resulting reference (now A2:A10). The chtValues range refers to an identically sized range one column to the right of the expanded chtDates range, and so becomes B2:B10. Both those names feed into the chart =SERIES() function, making the chart redraw to include the new data. The functions used in the defined name assume that the source data is contiguous, starting in cell A2. Blank cells result in an incorrectly calculated range. More precise formulas are beyond the scope of this chapter.

It is fundamental to the rest of this section that you fully understand the mechanism we're using. If anything is unclear, take some time to go through the example, perhaps trying to create an auto-expanding chart with two or three data series.

Scrolling and Zooming a Time Series

In the auto-expanding chart, we were only updating one of the OFFSET functions parameters. If we modify both the row offset and number of rows, we can provide a simple, codeless mechanism for our users to scroll and zoom through a time series. In the worksheet shown in Figure 21-8, we added two scrollbars from the Forms toolbar below the chart, set their Min and Max values to correspond to the number of data times, and linked their values to the cells in column D, using two defined names, ZoomVal and ScrollVal, to refer to cells D24 and D25, respectively.

In the definition for the chtDates name for this example, the ScrollVal figure is used for the row offset, and the ZoomVal figure provides the number of data points to include in the range:

Name: Sheet1!chtDates

Refers to: =OFFSET(Sheet1!$A$1,Sheet1!ScrollVal,0,Sheet1!ZoomVal,1)

The chtValues definition is the same as before, =OFFSET(chtDates,0,1).

Transforming Coordinate Systems

In the two previous examples we used the OFFSET function in the defined name to change the range of values drawn on the chart, while keeping the actual data intact. We can also use defined names to modify the data itself

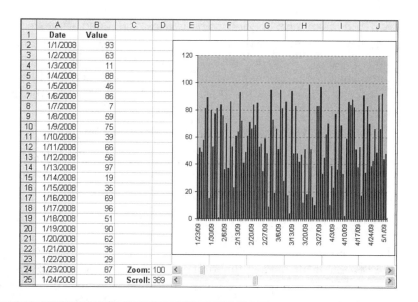

FIGURE 21-8 Allowing the user to zoom and scroll through time-series data

prior to plotting it, such as transforming between polar and x, y coordinate systems. In polar coordinates, a point's location is defined by its angle and distance from the origin, rather than its position along the X and Y axes.

Excel does not have a built-in chart type that plots data in polar coordinates, but we can use defined names to convert the (angle, length) polar coordinate to (x, y), which can then be drawn on a standard XY chart. We show you how to create the chart in Figure 21-9 from the data shown beside it by using defined names. In this example, the length figures are calculated from the angle using the formula `ABS(a*SIN(a))`.

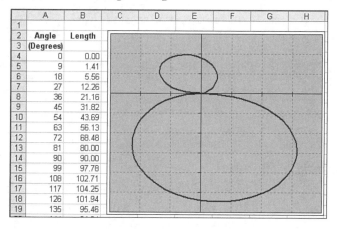

FIGURE 21-9 Plotting polar coordinates on an XY scatter chart

21. ADVANCED CHARTING TECHNIQUES

To demonstrate how the various uses of defined names can be combined, we implement two levels of indirection. The first level uses the technique from the "Auto-Expanding Charts" section earlier in the chapter to automatically handle changing datasets, while a second level performs the coordinate transformation. First, the names to handle the automatic updates are defined as

Name: Sheet1!datAngle

Refers to: =OFFSET(Sheet1!$A$3,1,0,COUNTA(Sheet1!$A$3:$A$5000)-1,1)

Name: Sheet1!datLength

Refers to: =OFFSET(Sheet1!datAngle,0,1)

The observant reader might have noticed that we're using a slightly different version of the OFFSET function in the definition for the datAngle name. The version shown here is slightly more robust because it counts within a specific range beginning at the data header cell. We previously demonstrated a variation on this technique in which the entire column address was used in the COUNTA function. By limiting the range the way we do here, it doesn't matter if the user changes the contents of the cells above the data range, such as adding extra titles to the sheet. With the datAngle and datLength names referring to our source data, we can define two more names to convert from polar to x, y coordinates.

Name: Sheet1!chtX

Refers to: =Sheet1!datLength*COS(Sheet1!datAngle*PI()/180)

Name: Sheet1!chtY

Refers to: =Sheet1!datLength*SIN(Sheet1!datAngle*PI()/180)

The chart series can then use the chtX and chtY names for the X and Y data:

=SERIES("Polar Plot",Sheet1!chtX,Sheet1!chtY,1)

Charting a Function

We used defined names to change the range of cells to plot and manipulate the data in that range before we plot it. In Chapter 20, "Data

Manipulation Techniques," we introduced array formulas and explained how they can be used to perform calculations on arrays of data. We also showed a specific array formula that is often used to generate a number sequence for use in other array formulas. What we didn't mention was that we can also use array formulas in our defined names and refer to them from charts. Figure 21-10 shows a worksheet that uses array formulas in defined names to plot a mathematical function over a range of x values, without needing to read any data from the worksheet.

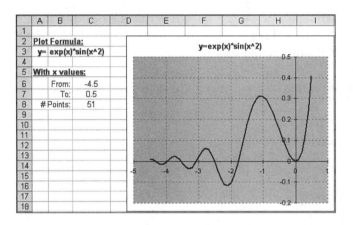

FIGURE 21-10   Using array formulas in defined names to generate and plot data

This worksheet combines a number of Excel tricks to generate the x axis values and use them to calculate the y axis values. First we create a defined named to generate the values for the x axis and give it the name x, for reasons that soon become clear.

Name: `Sheet1!x`

Refers to: `=$C$6+(ROW(OFFSET($A$1,0,0,$C$8,1))-1)*($C$7-$C$6)/($C$8-`
                `1)`

Working through the parts of this array formula

- `OFFSET($A$1,0,0, $C$8,1)` gives the range A1:A51.
- `ROW(OFFSET($A$1,0,0, $C$8,1))` converts the range to the array $\{1, 2, 3, ..., 50, 51\}$.
- `(ROW(OFFSET($A$1,0,0, $C$8,1))-1)` subtracts 1 from each item in the array, giving $\{0, 1, 2, ..., 49, 50\}$.

- `($C$7-$C$6)/($C$8-1)` calculates the x axis increment for each point, giving 0.1 in our example.
- `(ROW(OFFSET($A$1,0,0,$C$8,1))-1)*($C$7-$C$6)/($C$8-1)` multiplies each item in the array by the x axis increment, giving the array {0, 0.1, 0.2, ..., 4.9, 5.0}.
- `$C$6+(ROW(OFFSET($A$1,0,0,$C$8,1))-1)*($C$7-$C$6)/($C$8-1)` adds the array to the required x value start point, resulting in the range of x values to use in the chart {-4.5, -4.4, -4.3, ... 0.4, 0.5}.

Unfortunately, if we try to include Sheet1!x in the chart SERIES function, we get an error about an incorrect range reference. To create the chart, we use the workaround described at the start of this section, by creating two names, chtX and chtY, that point to worksheet cells, using them to create the chart, and then changing them to their real definitions:

Name:	`Sheet1!chtX`
Refers to:	`=Sheet1!x`
Name:	`Sheet1!chtY`
Refers to:	`=EVALUATE(Sheet1!$B$3&"+x*0")`

The definition for chtX is just a workaround for Excel not allowing us to use the x name in the chart itself. The definition for chtY needs some explaining. Cell B3 contains the equation to be plotted, `EXP(x)*SIN(x^2)`, as text. The EVALUATE function is an XLM macro function, equivalent to the VBA Application.Evaluate method, but which can be called from within a defined name.

XLM functions were the programming language for Excel 4. VBA replaced XLM in Excel 5, but XLM is still supported in all current versions of Excel. The documentation for the XLM functions can be downloaded from the Microsoft Web site at http://support.microsoft.com/kb/128185, or by searching for **macrofun.exe** or **xlmacro.exe**.

The EVALUATE function evaluates the expression it's given and returns a numeric result. In our case, when the expression is evaluated Excel replaces "x" in the formula with the array of values produced by our Sheet1!x defined name (which is why we called it "x") and returns an array containing the result of the function for each of our x axis values. These arrays are plotted on the chart to produce the line for the equation. The `&"+x*0"` part of the chtY definition works around an error in Excel that sometimes causes trig functions to not evaluate as array formulas, by forcing the entire formula to be evaluated as an array.

Faking It

A chart is designed to impart information to the viewer in a graphical manner. As such, we should mainly be interested in whether the final chart looks correct and performs its purpose of providing clear information. We should not be too bothered about whether the chart has been constructed according to a notional set of generally approved guidelines. In other words, we often need to cheat by using some of the chart engine's features in creative ways. This section explains a few of the ways in which we can get creative with Excel's chart engine by using some of its features in ways they were probably not designed to be used.

Error Bars

From a purely visual perspective, an error bar is a horizontal or vertical line originating from a data point, so if we ever have the need to draw horizontal or vertical lines around our data points, we may be able to use error bars to create those lines. A great example is the step chart shown in Figure 21-11, where the vertical lines show the change in an item's price during a day, and the horizontal lines connect the end price from one day to the start price for the next day.

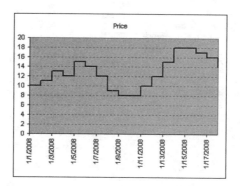

FIGURE 21-11   A step chart

Because Excel doesn't include a built-in Step Chart type, many people believe that Excel can't create them. There are quite a few ways in which it can be done, but the easiest is probably to use an XY chart with both vertical and horizontal error bars. The basic data for the chart consists of a list of dates and end-of-day prices, with a calculated field for the change in price from the end of the previous day. We start with a normal XY chart to plot the price against the date, as shown in Figure 21-12.

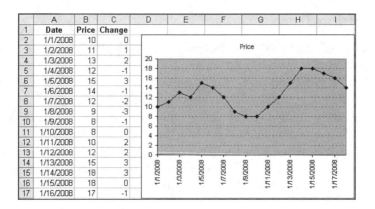

	A	B	C	D	E	F	G	H	I
1	Date	Price	Change						
2	1/1/2008	10	0						
3	1/2/2008	11	1						
4	1/3/2008	13	2						
5	1/4/2008	12	-1						
6	1/5/2008	15	3						
7	1/6/2008	14	-1						
8	1/7/2008	12	-2						
9	1/8/2008	9	-3						
10	1/9/2008	8	-1						
11	1/10/2008	8	0						
12	1/11/2008	10	2						
13	1/12/2008	12	2						
14	1/13/2008	15	3						
15	1/14/2008	18	3						
16	1/15/2008	18	0						
17	1/16/2008	17	-1						

FIGURE 21-12 Start with a normal XY (scatter) chart of price versus date.

Below each data point, we want to display a vertical line equal to the change in price for that day, which we do by specifying a custom minus error value in the *Y Error Bars* tab of the *Format Data Series* dialog, as shown in Figure 21-13.

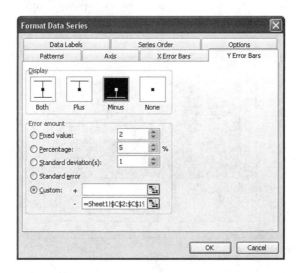

FIGURE 21-13 Add a custom minus Y error bar for the day's change in price.

The horizontal lines need to join each data point to the bottom of the subsequent point's error bar. That sounds difficult, but because these are daily prices all you need to do is add Plus markers to the X error bars with a fixed value setting of 1. With these error bars configured, you should see a chart something like that shown in Figure 21-14.

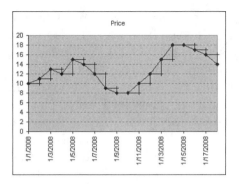

FIGURE 21-14   The chart with X and Y error bars

All that remains is to double-click the error bar lines and use the *Patterns* tab to change their color, thickness, and marker style; then double-click the original XY line and format that to have no line and no marker. The result is the step chart from Figure 21-11, but now you know it's only the error bars that are actually being drawn.

Dummy XY Series

Excel's value axes are either boringly linear or logarithmic. They do not support breaks in the axis nor scales that vary along the axis nor many other complex axis effects. Figure 21-15 shows a chart with a variable y axis, where the bottom half of the chart plots values from 0 to 100 in steps of 20, but the top half plots values from 100 to 1000 in steps of 200.

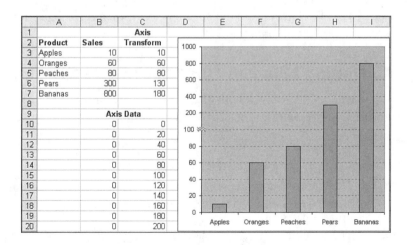

FIGURE 21-15   Chart with a complex axis scale

In this chart, the real y axis goes from 0 to 200, but we added a dummy XY series using the data from B10:C20, added data labels to the XY series, set them to display to the left of the point, and customized their text to that shown in the Figure 21-15. The result appears to be a complex axis scale that varies up the chart. The final step is to transform the real sales data in B3:B7 into the correct values for Excel to plot on its linear 0 to 200 scale. This is done using the simple mapping formula =IF(B3<=100,B3,100+ B3/10) in C3:C7, which is the data that Excel plots.

This effect can be misleading if it is not clearly shown that a break in the axis scale exists. The chart in Figure 21-15 looks linear along its entire range, but if plotted on a true linear scale, it would resemble a boomerang with a large angle in the middle. An easy way to indicate a break in the axis is to set an individual point's data marker using a custom image, as we have done. Draw the image using Paint or other graphics program, copy it to the Clipboard, select the data point, and paste the image.

We can use this technique to implement any axis scale of our choosing, such as including breaks in our axes; plotting using logarithmic, hyperbolic, or probability scales; or even including multiple dummy XY series to make the chart appear to have many axes (just be sure the user can determine which data is plotted against which scale).

VBA Techniques

So far, we've concentrated on the techniques we can use to get the most out of Excel's charting engine through the user interface. In this section, we examine how we can use VBA to manipulate charts.

Converting between Chart Coordinate Systems

When using VBA to work with charts, there are a number of different coordinate systems we often need to convert among:

- The chart series data displayed inside the plot area is in the axis coordinates if it's an XY Scatter chart.
- The mouse pointer coordinates provided by the various mouse events are measured in pixels, with the origin in the top-left corner of the ChartObject window.
- The coordinates of any drawing objects added to the chart are in points, with the origin being the top-left of the chart area, slightly inside the ChartObject window.

- The coordinates used by the GET.CHART.ITEM XLM function to locate the vertices of chart objects are in points, but with the origin in the bottom-left corner of the chart area. See the "Locating Chart Items" section later in the chapter for an example of its use.
- If the chart is embedded on a worksheet, the worksheet zoom factor affects the mouse pointer coordinates, but not the data nor location of any drawing objects on the chart.

Listing 21-2 shows the MouseMove event for a chart, within which we convert the x, y mouse coordinates given to the event into both data coordinates (displayed in the status bar) and drawing object coordinates (which we use to move an oval to follow the mouse pointer). Note that this code uses the PointsPerPixel function defined in Chapter 12, "Understanding and Using Windows API Calls."

Listing 21-2 Converting from Mouse Coordinates to Data and Drawing Object Coordinates

```
Private Sub mchtChart_MouseMove(ByVal Button As Long, _
    ByVal Shift As Long, ByVal X As Long, ByVal Y As Long)

  Dim dZoom As Double
  Dim dXVal As Double
  Dim dYVal As Double
  Dim dPixelSize As Double

  On Error Resume Next

  'The active window zoom factor
  dZoom = ActiveWindow.Zoom / 100

  'The pixel size, in points
  dPixelSize = PointsPerPixel

  'Mouse coordinates to (XY) Data coordinates
  With mchtChart
    dXVal = .Axes(xlCategory).MinimumScale + _
      (.Axes(xlCategory).MaximumScale - _
      .Axes(xlCategory).MinimumScale) * _
      (X * dPixelSize / dZoom - _
      (.PlotArea.InsideLeft + .ChartArea.Left)) / _
      .PlotArea.InsideWidth

    dYVal = .Axes(xlValue).MinimumScale + _
```

```
      (.Axes(xlValue).MaximumScale - _
        .Axes(xlValue).MinimumScale) * _
      (1 - (Y * dPixelSize / dZoom - _
            (.PlotArea.InsideTop + .ChartArea.Top)) / _
      .PlotArea.InsideHeight)
   End With


   Application.StatusBar = "(" & Application.Round(dXVal, 2) _
      & ", " & Application.Round(dYVal, 2) & ")"


   'Mouse coordinates to Drawing Object Points

   'We'll only move the oval if the Shift key is pressed
   If Shift = 1 Then
      With mchtChart
         dXVal = (X * dPixelSize / dZoom - .ChartArea.Left)
         dYVal = (Y * dPixelSize / dZoom - .ChartArea.Top)

         With .Shapes("ovlPointer")
            .Left = dXVal - .Width / 2
            .Top = dYVal - .Height / 2
         End With
      End With
   End If


End Sub
```

Locating Chart Items

Sometimes, however hard we try, the only way to get a chart looking exactly the way we want it is to add drawing objects, such as rectangles, lines, arrows, and so on, to it. As soon as we do this we encounter the problem of identifying where in the drawing object coordinate space an item on the chart is located—for example, the top-middle of a specific column in a column chart.

That level of positional information cannot be obtained through the Excel object model but can be obtained by calling the GET.CHART.ITEM XLM function. This function has the following parameters:

```
GET.CHART.ITEM(x_y_index, point_index, item_text)
```

where

- x_y_index is 1 to return the x position and 2 to return the y position.
- point_index depends on the item we're looking at, but is a number from 1 to 8 to identify a specific vertex within the item. For example, 2 is the upper-middle of any rectangular item, such as a column in a column chart.
- item_text identifies the item we're interested in, such as "Plot" for the plot area, or "S2P4" for the fourth data point in the second series in the chart.

The only caveat when using GET.CHART.ITEM is that the chart must be active for it to work. The code in Listing 21-3 moves an arrow on a chart to be from the top-left corner of the inside of the plot area (using normal VBA positioning) to the top-middle of the third column of a column chart, resulting in the chart shown in Figure 21-16.

Listing 21-3   Using GET.CHART.ITEM to Locate a Chart Item's Vertices

```
Private Sub cmdMoveArrow_Click()

  Dim rngActive As Range
  Dim dXVal As Double
  Dim dYVal As Double
  Dim chtChart As Chart

  Set rngActive = ActiveCell

  'We have to activate the chart to use GET.CHART.ITEM
  Me.ChartObjects(1).Activate

  'Find the XY position of the middle-top of the third
  'column in the data series,
  'returned in XLM coordinates
  dXVal = ExecuteExcel4Macro("GET.CHART.ITEM(1,2,""S1P3"")")
  dYVal = ExecuteExcel4Macro("GET.CHART.ITEM(2,2,""S1P3"")")

  'Get the Chart
  Set chtChart = Me.ChartObjects(1).Chart
  With chtChart

    'Convert the XLM coordinates to Drawing Object coordinates
    'The x values are the same, but the Y values need to be
    'flipped
    dYVal = .ChartArea.Height - dYVal
```

```
    'Move and size the Arrow
    .Shapes("linArrow").Left = .PlotArea.InsideLeft
    .Shapes("linArrow").Top = .PlotArea.InsideTop
    .Shapes("linArrow").Width = dXVal - .Shapes("linArrow").Left
    .Shapes("linArrow").Height = dYVal - .Shapes("linArrow").Top
  End With

  rngActive.Activate

End Sub
```

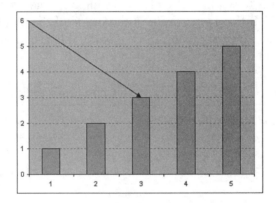

FIGURE 21-16 Moving an arrow to point to the top-middle of a column

Calculating Reasonable Axis Scales

Often when we're controlling charts through VBA we need to set our own values for the axis scales. The code in Listing 21-4 calculates reasonable Minimum, Maximum, and MajorUnit values. It is a different algorithm than the one Excel uses to determine chart axis scales, but is one that we have found to give better results.

Listing 21-4 Function to Calculate Reasonable Chart Axes Scales

```
Public Type CHART_SCALE
  dMin As Double
  dMax As Double
  dScale As Double
End Type
```

```
Public Function ChartScale(ByVal dMin As Double, _
        ByVal dMax As Double) As CHART_SCALE

    Dim dPower As Double, dScale As Double

    'Check if the max and min are the same
    If dMax = dMin Then
        dScale = dMax
        dMax = dMax * 1.01
        dMin = dMin * 0.99
    End If

    'Check if dMax is bigger than dMin - swap them if not
    If dMax < dMin Then
        dScale = dMax
        dMax = dMin
        dMin = dScale
    End If

    'Make dMax a little bigger and dMin a little smaller
    If dMax > 0 Then
        dMax = dMax + (dMax - dMin) * 0.01
    Else
        dMax = dMax - (dMax - dMin) * 0.01
    End If
    If dMin > 0 Then
        dMin = dMin - (dMax - dMin) * 0.01
    Else
        dMin = dMin + (dMax - dMin) * 0.01
    End If

    'What if they are both 0?
    If (dMax = 0) And (dMin = 0) Then dMax = 1

    'This bit rounds the maximum and minimum values to
    'reasonable values to chart.
    'Find the range of values covered
    dPower = Log(dMax - dMin) / Log(10)
    dScale = 10 ^ (dPower - Int(dPower))

    'Find the scaling factor
    Select Case dScale
    Case 0 To 2.5
        dScale = 0.2
```

```
Case 2.5 To 5
    dScale = 0.5
Case 5 To 7.5
    dScale = 1
Case Else
    dScale = 2
End Select

'Calculate the scaling factor (major unit)
dScale = dScale * 10 ^ Int(dPower)

'Round the axis values to the nearest scaling factor
ChartScale.dMin = dScale * Int(dMin / dScale)
ChartScale.dMax = dScale * (Int(dMax / dScale) + 1)
ChartScale.dScale = dScale

End Function
```

Summary

Although Excel's charting engine has a relatively poor reputation among users, most of that is due to a lack of knowledge about how to exploit the engine, rather than a lack of features. Yes, we would like to see a general overhaul of the user interface to make the advanced techniques shown in this chapter much more discoverable for the average user.

However, now that we've spent the time to explore the charting engine and fully understand the techniques introduced here, hopefully you can see that the limits of Excel's charting capabilities are to be found in our imagination and creativity, rather than in Excel.

CONTROLLING OTHER OFFICE APPLICATIONS

The primary purpose of Excel is to perform calculations. It has some database-like features, but it's not a relational database. It has some text editing and formatting features, but it's not a word processor. It has presentation-quality graphics, but it's not a presentation application. It can save worksheets as Web pages, but it's not a Web-authoring tool. It can send a workbook through e-mail, but it's neither an e-mail program nor personal information manager.

Excel's built-in database, word processing, presentation, e-mail, and Web features are sufficient for most applications, but there comes a time when we need to use a feature that is only provided by the Office application dedicated to the task. This chapter explains how to control those other Office applications from within Excel, suggests some best practices to use when controlling other applications, and provides an introductory overview of the major objects in each application's object model.

Fundamentals

Controlling another application is only a matter of knowing how to connect to the target application and efficiently use its object model. This part of the chapter discusses the fundamentals of connecting to other applications and best practices for using third-party object models.

Automation

Automation is Microsoft's generic term for technology that allows one application to manipulate another application's objects, including allowing VBA to manipulate Excel. Automation began with a technology called

Object Linking and Embedding (OLE) and has since evolved into other forms such as Component Object Model (COM), also known as ActiveX, and Distributed Component Object Model (DCOM).

The application that manipulates the objects is called the **automation client** or **host application**. Applications whose objects are manipulated are called **automation servers** or **target applications**. All the Office applications can be used as automation servers so long as they've been properly installed (registered) on our computer. Microsoft Office applications are automatically registered during installation but can be re-registered using the /regserver command-line switch.

Referencing

The easiest way to get started is to create a reference to the object library for the application that we want to automate using the *Tools > References* menu in the VBE. In Figure 22-1, we add a reference to the Word 2003 object library, as indicated by the 11.0 version number in the reference description.

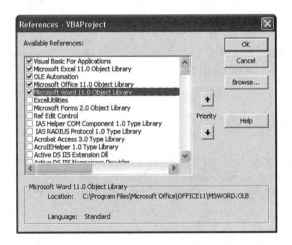

FIGURE 22-1   Adding a reference to the Word object library

With the reference set, we can use the objects in the Word object model as if they were classes in our project, as shown in Listing 22-1, which uses the New keyword to create a new instance of the Word application.

Listing 22-1   A Simple Procedure to Control Word

```
Sub ControlWord()

    'Declare an object variable to reference
    'the Word application
    Dim wrdApp As Word.Application

    'Start a new instance of Word
    Set wrdApp = New Word.Application

    'Do something

    'Close Word and tidy up
    wrdApp.Quit savechanges:=False
    Set wrdApp = Nothing

End Sub
```

Development Best Practices

In addition to the advice given in Chapter 3, "Excel and VBA Development Best Practices," there are some additional techniques that should always be used when automating other applications.

Always Include the Object Library in Variable Declarations

Whenever we declare a variable as a specific object type, such as Dim rngData As Range, the VBA interpreter scans through the object libraries referenced in the *Tools > References* list (in the order shown in that list) until it finds an object with the same name as specified in the variable declaration. In this case, the first object library to contain an object called Range is the Excel object library, so our variable is typed as an Excel Range object. In most cases, that's exactly what we want to happen.

Problems arise, though, if we reference multiple object libraries that use the same name for their own objects. For example, Excel and Word both have Range objects, but they're very different. To make sure the interpreter uses the Range object from the correct library, we should always include the object library name in the variable declaration, as shown in Listing 22-2.

Listing 22-2 Declaring Objects with the Correct Object Library

```
Sub GetRanges()

    'An Excel Range
    Dim rngData As Excel.Range

    'A Word Range
    Dim wrngTitle As Word.Range

End Sub
```

In addition to explicitly telling VBA which Range object we want a reference to, fully qualifying our object declarations also makes our code much easier to understand. When we see a variable declared `As Word.Range`, we have the mental prompt that the Word object library is being used. This prompt is carried through to the variable name, where we include a "w" prefix to indicate an object from the Word object library.

Always Fully Qualify Property and Method Calls

All the Office object libraries include some global properties that we often use as shortcuts into the object model, such as Excel's ActiveSheet, ActiveCell, Selection and Word's ActiveDocument, Selection, and so on. Whenever we use any such property in cross-application development, we must always provide a fully qualified object reference that can be traced back to the original variable we used to reference the target application. Listing 22-3 shows the correct way to get a reference to the ActiveDocument in a Word instance that we're controlling.

Listing 22-3 Referring to the ActiveDocument

```
Sub GetActiveDoc()

    'Declare an object variable to reference
    'the Word application
    Dim wrdApp As Word.Application
    Dim wrdDoc As Word.Document

    'Start a new instance of Word with a blank document
    Set wrdApp = New Word.Application
```

```
'Do something that opens or creates a document

'Get a reference to the active document
Set wrdDoc = wrdApp.ActiveDocument

'Close Word and clean up
wrdApp.Quit savechanges:=False
Set wrdDoc = Nothing
Set wrdApp = Nothing

End Sub
```

If we omitted the `wrdApp.` in the highlighted line of code in Listing 22-3, the VBA interpreter would try to find a Word document in any instance of Word the user might have open. This may not turn out to be the instance we're controlling. By providing the `wrdApp.` reference we're explicitly telling the interpreter to return the active document in the instance of Word we created.

Develop Using the Earliest Version You'll Support

For reasons explained later, references that we declare to Office object libraries are forward compatible but not backward compatible. This means that if we save our workbook with a reference to the Word 2003 object library, anyone opening the workbook on a PC with only Office 2000 installed receives a compile error "Can't find project or library" as soon as the code is run. If we save our workbook with a reference to the Word 2000 object library, it works correctly on any machine with Office 2000 or any later version.

Every version of Office adds more features to each application and correspondingly more objects, methods, properties, and optional parameters to each application's object library. By developing using the earliest version that we intend to support, we prevent ourselves from accidentally using any of the more recent features. If we were to develop using the latest version of the application, we might not discover our accidental use of the newer features until we were well into our testing, or even deployment.

Group Procedures in Application-Specific Modules

The VBA interpreter/compiler compiles our code on a module-by-module basis. A module is compiled when code contained in that module is first run. If we have a reference to an object library that isn't registered correctly, the compiler will not be able to compile any module that contains code that uses objects in that library, and we'll get a compile error. This issue can be partially mitigated by ensuring that all the code that controls another application is contained in a single module dedicated to that purpose.

If we're automating multiple applications, the procedures for each application should be in their own modules—one for Word, one for Access, one for PowerPoint, and so on, with each module having a descriptive name such as MWordCode. Once all the application-specific code is contained in a single module, we can check whether the target application is installed correctly and safely use or avoid that module, as shown later.

The vTable and Early Versus Late Binding

Every COM object has a structure called a **vTable**, or virtual function table, which lists all its properties and methods along with the memory addresses where their entry points are located and the parameters they take. When we declare a variable as a specific object data type, the compiler can look up the addresses of all the property and method calls for that object in its vTable at compile time. It can then store **jump to** instructions that identify the entry points of those property and method calls directly in our code. When the code is executed and VBA encounters one of these property or method calls, it simply runs the code at the memory location specified by the stored jump to instruction. This is known as **early binding**.

Early binding requires us to set a reference to the target object library through the *Tools > References* menu so VBA can include that object library's GUIDs and other type information in our project. (A GUID is a unique 128-bit number used to identify all COM objects.) When our project is run on a different computer, VBA verifies that an object with the same GUID as the one we originally referenced is available there. If so, it means this is the ***same object*** as the one we originally referenced, so it will have the same vTable, and all the direct memory jump instructions that were compiled into our application for that object can be trusted.

If the GUID is not found on the client computer, VBA knows the object we want to use is not available, and it gives us a compile error (and marks the reference as MISSING in the *Tools > References* list). This is why MISSING object library references caused by COM components not being installed on a user's computer stop a VBA application dead in its tracks.

When we declare a variable as the generic Object data type, the compiler doesn't know which vTable to use. Therefore, it can't determine the memory location of that object's properties and methods, and it can't compile jump to instructions for them into our code. Instead, once the generic object variable has been set to reference a specific object at runtime, VBA checks the vTable of that object every time it encounters one of the object's property or method calls to locate the memory address to jump to. This is known as **late binding**. The continual vTable lookups can have a significant impact on performance, but they don't require us to set a reference to the object library we're controlling. This results in any referencing problems (such as a missing object library) appearing as runtime errors (which we can handle gracefully) rather than compile errors.

The vTable also explains why Office object libraries are forward compatible, but not backward compatible. In each new version of an Office application the vTable is *extended* with new property and method entries, but the existing sections are not changed. This makes it safe to use an earlier version vTable entry to call into a later version of the same application, but not vice versa. The first section of the later version's vTable is identical to the earlier version's vTable, but it contains additional entries that do not appear in the earlier version. If VBA attempted to execute a property or method call identified by an entry late in the Word 2003 vTable while running under Word 2000, for example, that entry wouldn't exist in the Word 2000 executable and our application would crash.

As well as controlling whether we can use early binding, adding a reference to an object library also controls whether we can use the constants and parameter names defined in the library, as shown in Listing 22-4.

Listing 22-4 Early Versus Late Binding

```
'Early-Bound
'Requires a reference to the Word object library,
'but allows us to use specific object types,
'named parameters and defined constants
'and gives us IntelliSense information
Sub EarlyBound(wrdApp As Word.Application)
```

```
    'Open a text file
    wrdApp.Documents.Open FileName:="c:\myfile.txt", _
                        Format:=wdOpenFormatText

End Sub

'Late-Bound
'Have to use the generic Object type,
'can't use named parameters or defined constants,
'don't get IntelliSense information,
'but doesn't require a reference either.
Sub LateBound(wrdApp As Object)

    'Open a text file
    wrdApp.Documents.Open "c:\myfile.txt", , , , , , , , , 4

End Sub
```

The key factor in choosing between early or late binding is the likelihood that the applications we're controlling are available and installed correctly on the users' computers. We can ensure the applications are installed correctly on our computers, so we should always use early binding during development. That allows us to use the IntelliSense information, object types, constants, and named parameters, which together make early-bound code much easier to develop, read, debug, and maintain.

Before distributing our application to our users, we need to decide whether to switch to using late binding. This usually depends on both the likelihood that the applications are available and the amount of code that calls the application. The fundamental advantage of using late binding is that we can easily handle a failure to link to the object we want to control. (See the "Determining the Availability of an Application" section later in this chapter for an example.) In the case of Excel automating Word within a company environment, it's highly likely that anyone with Excel installed will have Word installed as well, so it's probably safe to use early binding. The same can't be said when automating FrontPage, so it would probably be best to switch to late binding for that.

If we only have a few lines of code, it's safest to always use late binding. With a lot of code, the inability to use named parameters and defined constants when using late binding can make our applications much harder to maintain.

Handling Instances

Before we can use an application's features we need to connect to an instance of the application. We can either hijack an instance the user might already have open or create a new instance for our dedicated use. Unless there is a specific need to link to the instance the user is working with, we should always create our own instances, use them, and close them when we're finished. This is mainly because the user may have left the instance they're using in a state that would cause errors in our application if we tried to use it, such as having a modal dialog displayed. This could either prevent our application from working correctly, or worse, result in our application damaging the work the user is doing in that instance.

Create a New Instance

We can use either the New keyword or CreateObject function to create a new instance of an application, as shown in Listing 22-5. The New keyword can only be used if we have set a reference to the **type library** (synonymous with object library), while the CreateObject function can be used either with or without a reference.

NOTE The manner in which an application is started does not determine whether we're using early or late binding. If we declared our object variables as specific class types we are early binding, and if we declared our object variables as the generic Object then we are late binding, regardless of how we start the application being automated.

While using the New keyword is slightly faster than CreateObject, it is our opinion that CreateObject should always be used because it is one less thing to change if we choose to switch between early and late binding.

Listing 22-5 Creating a New Instance of Word

```
Sub StartWord()

    'Early bound
    Dim wrdApp1 As Word.Application
    Set wrdApp1 = New Word.Application

    'Early bound
    Dim wrdApp2 As Word.Application
```

```
Set wrdApp2 = CreateObject("Word.Application")

'Late bound
Dim wrdApp3 As Object
Set wrdApp3 = CreateObject("Word.Application")

End Sub
```

Table 22-1 lists some of the Office application class names used by the CreateObject function.

Table 22-1 Class List for CreateObject

Application	Class
Access	Access.Application
Excel	Excel.Application
FrontPage	FrontPage.Application
Internet Explorer	InternetExplorer.Application
MapPoint	MapPoint.Application
Outlook	Outlook.Application
PowerPoint	PowerPoint.Application
Project	MSProject.Application
Publisher	Publisher.Application
Visio	Visio.Application
Word	Word.Application

Cleaning Up Properly

Whenever we create a new instance of an application, we must ensure that we close it correctly. In most cases, this is simply a matter of calling the application's Quit method and then destroying any variables that we may be using to reference it. We must be particularly careful with error handling, to ensure that the application we're controlling is shut down correctly in the case of an error, as shown in Listing 22-6. This error handling structure was explained in Chapter 15, "VBA Error Handling."

Listing 22-6   Starting and Closing Word, with Error Handling

```
Sub ControlWord()

    Const sSOURCE As String = "ControlWord"
    Dim wrdApp As Word.Application

    On Error GoTo ErrorHandler

    'Start Word
    Set wrdApp = CreateObject("Word.Application")

    'Do something here

ErrorExit:

    'The clean up code will be executed
    'whether or not we have an error.
    If Not wrdApp Is Nothing Then
        'Close Word, ignoring any errors
        'Without On Error Resume Next, an error would
        'cause an endless loop in the error handler.
        On Error Resume Next
        wrdApp.Quit savechanges:=False
        Set wrdApp = Nothing
    End If

    Exit Sub

ErrorHandler:
    If bCentralErrorHandler(msMODULE, sSOURCE) Then
        Stop
        Resume
    Else
        Resume ErrorExit
    End If
End Sub
```

Reference an Existing Instance

It is nearly always best to create a new instance of an application for our program to use. A notable exception is when controlling Outlook, because Outlook only allows a single instance to be running at any one time. Using either the New keyword or CreateObject function to create an instance of Outlook only creates a new instance if Outlook is not already running. If Outlook is already running, a reference to the running instance is returned instead.

This behavior can cause us problems when we finish using the instance we asked for, as we won't know whether we should shut Outlook down. If Outlook was already running when we asked for our instance, we should leave it running. If it wasn't already running, we should close it. We can use the GetObject function to obtain a reference to an existing instance of an application and then use CreateObject if the GetObject call fails, as shown in Listing 22-7. In either case, we set a Boolean variable that we use to determine whether we should close Outlook when cleaning up.

Listing 22-7 Checking for, Starting, and Closing Outlook, with Error Handling

```
Sub ControlOutlook()

    Const sSOURCE As String = "ControlOutlook"
    Const sOUTLOOK_APP As String = "Outlook.Application"

    Dim olkApp As Outlook.Application
    Dim bOutlookCreated As Boolean

    'Try to get a reference to Outlook
    On Error Resume Next
    Set olkApp = GetObject(, sOUTLOOK_APP)

    On Error GoTo ErrorHandler

    If olkApp Is Nothing Then
        'Start Outlook
        Set olkApp = CreateObject(sOUTLOOK_APP)
        bOutlookCreated = True
    End If
```

```
    'Do something here

ErrorExit:

    'The clean up code will be executed
    'whether or not we have an error.
    If Not olkApp Is Nothing Then

        If bOutlookCreated Then
            'Close Outlook, ignoring any errors
            On Error Resume Next
            olkApp.Quit
            On Error GoTo ErrorHandler
        End If

        'Clean up
        Set olkApp = Nothing
    End If

    Exit Sub

ErrorHandler:

    If bCentralErrorHandler(msMODULE, sSOURCE) Then
        Stop
        Resume
    Else
        Resume ErrorExit
    End If

End Sub
```

When we use CreateObject to start a new instance of PowerPoint, we actually get a reference to an existing instance if there is one already running. The Presentations collection includes all the open presentations from all the instances that have been created. This is similar to Outlook's behavior, but PowerPoint cleanly handles calls to `Application.Quit` by closing only the presentation and not the entire application. We can therefore safely use CreateObject to start PowerPoint and `Application.Quit` to close it.

Multiversion Support

It is a fact of Excel application development that we can expect our users to have a variety of Office versions, typically going back as far as Office 2000. We explained previously how the vTable allows object libraries to be forward compatible but not backward compatible. This means if we save our workbook containing a reference to Word 2003, it will give a compile error when run on a machine with only Office 2000 installed.

One solution to this problem is to save our workbook with a reference to the earliest version of the object library we intend to support. When a workbook saved with a reference to Word 2000 is run on a machine with Office 2003, the reference is automatically updated to Word 2003. Unfortunately, if that workbook is then saved, the reference to Word 2003 will remain. If the workbook is forwarded to our Office 2000 user, we get the compile error again. This technique is therefore only suitable for workbooks that our users won't need to save, such as add-ins and the code workbooks of dictator applications.

If we put our code and UI in separate workbooks, it is probably only the UI workbook that needs to be saved by our users, thereby avoiding this problem. The safest solution, though, is to use late binding and save our workbooks without any direct references. At runtime we can check the availability and version of the target application and run the code appropriately.

Determining the Availability of an Application

The function shown in Listing 22-8 checks whether an application is installed by simply trying to start it. If the application starts successfully, the function returns a reference to it via the objApp parameter. Note that this function can (and should) be used regardless of whether we're late binding or early binding. Even if an object library exists and is registered, there is no guarantee that the application will start correctly.

Listing 22-8 Checking for an Installed Application

```
Function bIsAppAvailable(ByVal sClass As String, _
                         ByRef objApp As Object) As Boolean
    On Error Resume Next
    Set objApp = CreateObject(sClass)
    bIsAppAvailable = (Not objApp Is Nothing)
End Function
```

Performance

VBA calls between applications (called cross-process calls), such as Excel controlling Word, are extremely slow, even if we use early binding. To improve performance we need to keep the number of cross-process calls to a minimum by using `With...End With` blocks and object variables to cache references to items deep in the object model. For best performance we should move the code into the target application.

For example, Listing 22-9 uses code contained in Excel to populate a number of Word bookmarks. In Listing 22-10 we move the code that populates the document into a Word template that is opened and called from our Excel code. Although this is a trivial example, the technique can result in a significant performance improvement in more complex situations. These examples can be found on the CD in the *Concepts\Ch22 - Controlling Other Office Applications* folder and consist of the following files:

- **PopulateWord.xls**—An Excel workbook containing both PopulateWordDoc procedures
- **Bookmarks.dot**—A simple Word template with some bookmarked text to update
- **FillDocument.dot**—A Word template containing the code from Listing 22-10

Listing 22-9   Populating a Word Document Entirely from Excel

```
'In an Excel module, with a reference to Word
Sub PopulateWordDoc1()

    Dim wrdApp As Word.Application
    Dim wrdDoc As Word.Document
    Dim sPath As String
    Dim vaBookmarks As Variant
    Dim lBookmark As Long

    'Fill the Bookmarks array from the sheet
    vaBookmarks = wksBookmarks.Range("rngBookmarkList").Value

    'Start Word
    Set wrdApp = CreateObject("Word.Application")

    'Open the template to populate
```

```
    sPath = ThisWorkbook.Path & "\"
    Set wrdDoc = wrdApp.Documents.Add(Template:=sPath & _
                "Bookmarks.dot")

    'Populate the bookmarks in the template from the array
    For lBookmark = LBound(vaBookmarks, 1) To _
                UBound(vaBookmarks, 1)
        wrdDoc.Bookmarks(vaBookmarks(lBookmark, _
            LBound(vaBookmarks, 2))).Range.Text = _
            vaBookmarks(lBookmark, UBound(vaBookmarks, 2))
    Next lBookmark

    'Save the filled document and close it
    wrdDoc.SaveAs sPath & "Filled1.doc"
    wrdDoc.Close
    Set wrdDoc = Nothing

    'Close Word
    wrdApp.Quit False
    Set wrdApp = Nothing

End Sub
```

Listing 22-10 Populating a Word Document Using Code in Word

```
'In a module in the Word template FillDocument.dot
Public Sub FillDocument(ByVal sTemplateName As String, _
                    ByVal sSaveName As String, _
                    ByVal vaBookmarks As Variant)

    Dim docToFill As Document
    Dim lBookmark As Long

    Set docToFill = Documents.Add(Template:=sTemplateName)

    For lBookmark = LBound(vaBookmarks, 1) To _
                UBound(vaBookmarks, 1)
        docToFill.Bookmarks(vaBookmarks(lBookmark, _
            LBound(vaBookmarks, 2))).Range.Text = _
            vaBookmarks(lBookmark, UBound(vaBookmarks, 2))
    Next lBookmark
```

```
        docToFill.SaveAs sSaveName
        docToFill.Close

End Sub

'In an Excel module, with a reference to Word
Sub PopulateWordDoc2()

        Dim wrdApp As Word.Application
        Dim wrdDoc As Word.Document
        Dim sPath As String
        Dim vaBookmarks As Variant

        'Fill the Bookmarks array from the sheet
        vaBookmarks = wksBookmarks.Range("rngBookmarkList").Value

        'Start Word
        Set wrdApp = CreateObject("Word.Application")

        'Open the template containing our controlling code
        sPath = ThisWorkbook.Path & "\"
        Set wrdDoc = wrdApp.Documents.Open(sPath & _
                    "FillDocument.dot")

        'Run the code within Word, passing all required information
        wrdApp.Run "FillDocument", sPath & "Bookmarks.dot", _
                    sPath & "Filled2.doc", vaBookmarks

        wrdDoc.Close
        Set wrdDoc = Nothing

        wrdApp.Quit False
        Set wrdApp = Nothing

End Sub
```

The Primary Office Application Object Models

Now that we can reliably detect, start, control, and shut down other Office applications, the final piece of the puzzle is to learn each application's object model. This section of the chapter provides an introduction to the primary objects within each Office application's object model and demonstrates some typical uses within Excel-based applications.

All the Office applications have a top-level Application object, which is the object we get a reference to when creating new instances of the application. From the Application object we drill down to the other objects that provide the application's functionality.

All the examples in this section can be found on the CD in the *\Concepts\Ch22 - Controlling Other Office Applications* folder. The workbook Ch22Examples.xls contains all the example code and a data sheet to represent the results of some analysis.

Access and Data Access Objects

It's actually rare to automate Access itself from an Excel application. We can easily manipulate the data in an Access (Jet) database from outside Access, as described in Chapter 19, "Programming with Access and SQL Server," and there's little reason to use Access forms instead of VBA UserForms in an Excel application. However, Access is much better than Excel for creating continuous data-driven reports, with its sorting and grouping capabilities and separate group, page, and report headers and footers.

Application

Each instance of Access has a single database, which we open using Application.OpenCurrentDatabase and close using Application.CloseCurrentDatabase (where "Application" in this case refers to an instance of the Access Application object). The CurrentDb object exposes a Data Access Objects (DAO) Database object, which we can use to manipulate the structure of the tables and queries in the database. Most of the other properties of the Application object provide information about the state of the application, such as which tables the user has open, and are rarely relevant when controlling Access from Excel.

DAO.Database

The DAO Database object that we get from Application.CurrentDb provides programmatic access to the structure of the database, via the TableDefs, QueryDefs, and Relations collections. The most commonly used of these is the TableDefs collection, through which we can access the properties of the database tables. In many situations, we may have an access table linked to a separate data source, such as an Excel workbook or SQL Server table and need to change the table's link information prior to running a report.

DoCmd

Most automation of Access is done through the DoCmd object, which provides programmatic access to most Access capabilities, including deleting tables, importing data, and running reports.

Example

The procedure in Listing 22-11 runs an Access report based on data in an Excel workbook. The Access database ReportOnExcelData.mdb contains a single table, tblExcelData, to link to the Excel workbook, a query to sort the data, and a report, rptExcelData, to run. The procedure creates an instance of Access, opens the database, updates the table's connection information, and runs the report, leaving it displayed onscreen.

This code can be found in the MAccess module of the Ch22Examples.xls workbook and the database containing the linked table and report is called ReportOnExcelData.mdb.

Listing 22-11   Running an Access Report Using Excel Data

```
Sub AccessRunReport()

    'Requires references to the Microsoft Access and
    'Microsoft DAO object libraries
    Dim objApp As Object
    Dim accApp As Access.Application
    Dim dbData As DAO.Database
    Dim tdExcelData As DAO.TableDef

    'Update the export range
    wksAccess.Range("tblExcelDataStart").CurrentRegion _
        .Name = "tblExcelData"

    'Save any changes to the workbook, so Access can read
    'the latest version from disk
    ThisWorkbook.Save
```

```
'Attempt to create a new instance of Access
Set accApp = Nothing
Set accApp = CreateObject("Access.Application")

With accApp
    'Set the access automation security,
    'so the database opens without prompts.
    'Use late binding and On Error Resume Next
    'to ignore version issues
    On Error Resume Next
    Set objApp = accApp
    objApp.AutomationSecurity = 1 'msoAutomationSecurityLow
    On Error GoTo 0

    'Open the database
    .OpenCurrentDatabase FilePath:=ThisWorkbook.Path & _
                                "\ReportOnExcelData.mdb"

    'Get a reference to the DAO TableDef for the
    'tblExcelData linked table
    Set dbData = .CurrentDb
    Set tdExcelData = dbData.TableDefs("tblExcelData")

    'Update the table link to point to this workbook
    tdExcelData.Connect = "Excel 8.0;HDR=YES;IMEX=2;" & _
        "DATABASE=" & ThisWorkbook.FullName
    tdExcelData.RefreshLink

    Set tdExcelData = Nothing
    Set dbData = Nothing

    'Open and preview the report
    .DoCmd.OpenReport ReportName:="rptExcelData", _
                    View:=acViewPreview
    'Make the App visible
    .Visible = True
    .DoCmd.Maximize

End With

ErrorExit:

    On Error Resume Next
    accApp.Quit acQuitSaveNone
```

```
    Set accApp = Nothing

    Exit Sub

ErrorHandler:
    'Display the error number and error description
    ' and note the routine in the title bar
    MsgBox "Error " & Err.Number & vbLf & Err.Description, _
          vbCritical, "Routine: AccessRunReport"
    Resume ErrorExit
End Sub
```

Word

Word is often automated from Excel when we need to populate a Word document from data in Excel—such as a monthly report that contains some data analyzed in Excel.

Application

As well as the usual properties to control the application itself, the Word Application object has a Documents collection that we use to create, open, and access Word documents.

Document

The Document object provides all the information about a Word document, akin to Excel's Workbook object.

Bookmark

Each bookmark within a document is included in the Document.Bookmarks collection and exposed as a Bookmark object. Bookmarks allow us to easily identify elements of text within a document.

Range

A Range is a contiguous area in a document, identified by its start and end points. Many Word objects (such as Paragraph and Bookmark) have a Range property that returns the area enclosed by the object. We can populate a bookmark by setting the text of its Range. One issue with doing this is that setting the text in a bookmark deletes the bookmark. To set a bookmark's text, we have to store the bookmark's range, set the text of the range, and then re-create the bookmark, as shown in Listing 22-12.

Example

Survey results are often analyzed in Excel and published as a Word document. This is usually achieved by creating a Word template for the survey results, identifying each insertion point as a bookmark, and then copying the data from the Excel workbook to the Word document using VBA. It is common in corporate surveys to create a document specific to each of the respondents, where each report is essentially the same, but with that respondent's results and rankings. Listing 22-12 shows a simple example of this, where we loop through all the divisions in a company, analyzing the data and producing a document for each. This code can be found in the MWord module of the Ch22Examples.xls workbook and the document template is called SalaryReport.dot.

Listing 22-12 Populating a Word Template from Excel Data

```
Sub GenerateDivisionSummaries()

    Dim wrdApp As Word.Application
    Dim wrdDoc As Word.Document
    Dim wrdrngBM As Word.Range
    Dim piDiv As Excel.PivotItem
    Dim rngBookmark As Excel.Range
    Dim sPath As String
    Dim sBookmarkName As String

    'Start Word
    Set wrdApp = CreateObject("Word.Application")

    sPath = ThisWorkbook.Path & "\"
    'Create a new document based on the template
    Set wrdDoc = wrdApp.Documents.Add(Template:= _
                    sPath & "SalaryReport.dot")

    'Loop through each division in the pivot table
    For Each piDiv In wksData.PivotTables(1) _
                        .PivotFields("Division").PivotItems

        'Populate the Division Name cell
        wksData.Range("ptrDivName") = piDiv.Value
```

```
    'Recalc the sheet to update the results
    'for the division
    wksData.Calculate

    'Populate the bookmarks from the sheet
    For Each rngBookmark In _
            wksData.Range("rngBookmarks").Rows

        'Get the name of the bookmark
        sBookmarkName = rngBookmark.Cells(1, 1).Value

        'Get the Word Range that the bookmark spans
        Set wrdrngBM = wrdDoc.Bookmarks(sBookmarkName) _
                        .Range

        'Set the text of the range
        '(which deletes the bookmark)
        wrdrngBM.Text = rngBookmark.Cells(1, 2).Text

        'Recreate the bookmark for the next iteration
        wrdDoc.Bookmarks.Add sBookmarkName, wrdrngBM
    Next rngBookmark

    'Update any fields linked to these bookmarks
    wrdDoc.Fields.Update

    'Save the filled document
    wrdDoc.SaveAs sPath & "Salary Results - " & _
                    piDiv.Value & ".doc"
    Next piDiv

    MsgBox "Division Summaries Generated OK."

ErrorExit:

    On Error Resume Next
    'Close the Word document
    wrdDoc.Close
    Set wrdDoc = Nothing

    'Close Word
    wrdApp.Quit False
    Set wrdApp = Nothing
```

```
    Exit Sub

ErrorHandler:
    'Display the error number and error description
    ' and note the routine in the title bar
    MsgBox "Error " & Err.Number & vbLf & Err.Description, _
            vbCritical, "Routine: WordGenerateDivisionSummaries"
    Resume ErrorExit
End Sub
```

PowerPoint and MSGraph

PowerPoint is usually used in a way similar to Word—populating pre-pre-pared presentations with data from Excel.

Application

As well as the usual properties to control the application itself, the PowerPoint Application object has a Presentations collection that we use to create, open, and access PowerPoint presentations.

Presentation

The Presentation object provides all the information about a PowerPoint presentation, akin to Excel's Workbook object.

Slide

The Slide object provides the information about a slide within a presentation, akin to Excel's Worksheet object. When automating PowerPoint, it helps to give each slide a meaningful name, which can be done by selecting the slide and running the following statement from the PowerPoint VBE's Immediate window:

```
ActiveWindow.Selection.SlideRange(1).Name = "NewSlideName"
```

Shape

The Shape object is the same as Excel's Shape object and is a drawing object on a Slide, which can be a container for text boxes, lines, pictures, or embedded objects such as charts. A shape can be given a meaningful name by selecting it and running the following statement from the PowerPoint VBE's Immediate window:

```
ActiveWindow.Selection.ShapeRange(1).Name = "NewShapeName"
```

Charts

PowerPoint charts are provided by the MSGraph object model, which is a version of Excel's charting engine, modified to remove the worksheet links. As such, most Excel charting code works on a PowerPoint chart. However, it is common to prepare the charts within Excel, copy them to the Clipboard, and paste them as pictures in PowerPoint.

Example

The procedure in Listing 22-13 updates a PowerPoint presentation with data from an Excel spreadsheet. It updates both text in a bulleted list and the source data for an embedded chart. This code can be found in the MPowerPoint module of the Ch22Examples.xls workbook and the presentation we're updating is called Salary Presentation.ppt.

Listing 22-13 Populating a PowerPoint Presentation from Excel Data

```
Sub PPTGenerateSalarySummary()

    'PowerPoint objects
    Dim pptApp As PowerPoint.Application
    Dim pptPres As PowerPoint.Presentation
    Dim pptSlide As PowerPoint.Slide
    Dim pptBullets As PowerPoint.Shape

    'MSGraph objects
    Dim gphChart As Graph.Chart
    Dim gphData As Graph.DataSheet

    'Excel objects
    Dim pfDiv As Excel.PivotField
    Dim rngDiv As Excel.Range

    'Other variables
    Dim sBulletText As String
    Dim lDiv As Long
```

```
'Start PowerPoint
Set pptApp = CreateObject("PowerPoint.Application")

'Switch back to Excel
AppActivate Application.Caption

'Open the presentation
Set pptPres = pptApp.Presentations.Open(Filename:= _
    ThisWorkbook.Path & "\Salary Presentation.ppt", _
    withwindow:=False)

'Get the 'Detail' slide
Set pptSlide = pptPres.Slides("sldDetail")

'Get the shape containing the bulleted list
Set pptBullets = pptSlide.Shapes("shpBullets")

'Get the text of the first bullet in the list
sBulletText = pptBullets.TextFrame.TextRange _
    .Paragraphs(1).Text

'Update the text with the calculated total
'from the worksheet
sBulletText = Replace(sBulletText, "#SalaryTotal#", _
    wksData.Range("ptrSalaryTotal").Text)

'Update the presentation with the correct text
pptBullets.TextFrame.TextRange.Paragraphs(1) _
    .Text = sBulletText

'Get the MSGraph Chart object embedded in the slide
Set gphChart = pptSlide.Shapes("shpChart").OLEFormat _
    .Object

'Get the graph's data sheet
Set gphData = gphChart.Application.DataSheet

'Get the 'Division' pivot field in the Data worksheet
Set pfDiv = wksData.PivotTables(1).PivotFields("Division")

'Loop through the range of Divisions in the pivot table
For Each rngDiv In pfDiv.DataRange
    lDiv = lDiv + 1

    'Write the division name and total salary to the
```

```
            'graph data sheet
            gphData.Cells(1, lDiv + 1).Value = rngDiv.Text
            gphData.Cells(2, lDiv + 1).Value = rngDiv _
                .Offset(0, 1).Value
        Next rngDiv

        'Apply the datasheet changes
        gphChart.Application.Update

        'Redraw the chart object
        gphChart.Refresh

        'Save the presentation with a new name
        pptPres.SaveAs ThisWorkbook.Path & "\Salaries 2008.ppt"

        'Display confirmation message
        MsgBox "Salary Summary Presentation Generated OK."

ErrorExit:

        On Error Resume Next
        'Clean up object variables
        Set pptSlide = Nothing
        Set pptBullets = Nothing
        Set gphChart = Nothing
        Set gphData = Nothing

        'Close the presentation
        pptPres.Close
        Set pptPres = Nothing

        'Close PowerPoint
        pptApp.Quit
        Set pptApp = Nothing

        Exit Sub

ErrorHandler:
        'Display the error number and error description
        ' and note the routine in the title bar
        MsgBox "Error " & Err.Number & vbLf & Err.Description, _
                vbCritical, "Routine: PPTGenerateSalarySummary"
        Resume ErrorExit
End Sub
```

Outlook

Outlook behaves quite differently from the rest of the Office applications. It only allows one instance to be open at any time and doesn't use the "document" concept. Instead, it stores all its data in a data store file, represented by a Namespace object. The data file is internally structured as multiple folders that each contain a specific category of information, such as e-mails, contacts, appointments, and so on.

Application

The Outlook Application object provides access to the data store through the GetNamespace property and allows us to easily create new data items (e-mails, contacts, appointments, and so on) using the `CreateItem` method.

NameSpace

The NameSpace object represents an Outlook data store. Outlook was originally designed to support multiple types of data store, but only one was ever implemented. That is called the MAPI data store and is retrieved using `Application.GetNamespace("MAPI")`. The NameSpace object acts as a container for all the Outlook folders, allowing us to navigate the entire folder hierarchy. It also provides the `GetDefaultFolder()` property to access each of the top-level folders.

MAPIFolder

The MAPIFolder object represents a single Outlook folder, such as the Inbox, Contacts, or Calendar folder. It has a Folders property that returns a collection of child folders, allowing us to drill down, and an Items property that returns a collection of all the individual items (e-mails, contacts, and others) contained in the folder.

AppointmentItem, ContactItem, DistributionListItem, JournalItem, MailItem, NoteItem, PostItItem, and TaskItem

These objects represent the individual items within an Outlook folder. We can access them through the Items collection of a MAPIFolder and create them by using either the `Add` method of an Items collection or the `CreateItem` method of the Application object. In either case, we get an empty object of the appropriate type that we populate and save to the data store.

Example

The procedure shown in Listing 22-14 retrieves all the holidays for a specified year from the default Outlook Calendar, displaying them in an Excel worksheet. The application can be initiated from the OutlookHolidays sheet of the Ch22Examples.xls workbook.

Listing 22-14   Retrieving Holiday Dates from the Outlook Calendar

```
Sub OutlookRetrieveHolidays()

    'Outlook objects
    Dim olApp As Outlook.Application
    Dim olNS As Outlook.Namespace
    Dim olItems As Outlook.Items
    Dim olAppt As Outlook.AppointmentItem

    Dim bCreated As Boolean
    Dim lYear As Long
    Dim lRow As Long

    'Obtain a reference to Outlook
    On Error Resume Next
    Set olApp = GetObject(, "Outlook.Application")
    On Error GoTo 0

    'If Outlook isn't running, start it and remember
    If olApp Is Nothing Then
        Set olApp = CreateObject("Outlook.Application")
        bCreated = True
    End If

    'Get the MAPI namespace
    Set olNS = olApp.GetNamespace("MAPI")

    'Get the items in the Calendar
    Set olItems = olNS.GetDefaultFolder(olFolderCalendar) _
        .Items

    'Clear the destination range if previously used
    wksOutlook.Range("tblStart").CurrentRegion.ClearContents

    'Get the year criteria
```

```
    lYear = wksOutlook.Range("Year").Value

    'Set the default row counter
    lRow = 1

    'Loop through the calendar entries
    For Each olAppt In olItems

       'We only want holidays...
       If olAppt.Categories = "Holiday" Then

          '... with a title ...
          If Len(olAppt.Subject) > 0 Then

             '... that start in the given year ...
             If Year(olAppt.Start) = lYear Then
               wksOutlook.Range("tblStart") _
                  .Cells(lRow, 1).Value = olAppt.Subject

               wksOutlook.Range("tblStart") _
                  .Cells(lRow, 2).Value = olAppt.Start
               lRow = lRow + 1
             End If
          End If
       End If
    Next olAppt

    'Sort the holidays by date
    With wksOutlook.Range("tblStart").CurrentRegion
       If .Rows.Count > 2 Then
          .Sort key1:=.Cells(1, 2), order1:=xlAscending, _
             Header:=xlNo
       End If
    End With

ErrorExit:

    On Error Resume Next
    'Clear intermediate Outlook object variables
    Set olAppt = Nothing
    Set olItems = Nothing
    Set olNS = Nothing

    'Close the Outlook window
    If bCreated Then olApp.Quit
```

```
    'Clear the Outlook application variable
    Set olApp = Nothing

    Exit Sub

ErrorHandler:
    'Display the error number and error description
    ' and note the routine in the title bar of the message box
    MsgBox "Error " & Err.Number & vbLf & Err.Description, _
           vbCritical, "Routine: OutlookRetrieveHolidays"
    Resume ErrorExit
End Sub
```

Further Reading

The Office Developer Center on the MSDN Web site should be your first point of call to learn about programming the Office applications: http://msdn.microsoft.com/en-us/office/default.aspx.

Numerous books have also been written for each application, of which the following are usually considered among the best:

Title:	*Access 2002 Desktop Developer's Handbook*
Author:	Paul Litwin, Ken Getz, Mike Gunderloy
Publisher:	Sybex Books
ISBN:	0782140092

Title:	*Powerful PowerPoint for Educators*
Author:	David M. Marcovitz
Publisher:	Libraries Unlimited
ISBN:	1591580951

Title:	*Microsoft Outlook Programming*
Author:	Sue Mosher
Publisher:	Digital Press
ISBN:	1555582869

It seems that the publishing community has decided that books about programming Word do not sell enough to be profitable, so we can't provide any recommended books for Word development. The best way to learn more about programming Word is to start at the Word MVP Web site at http://word.mvps.org/ and follow the links from there.

Practical Example

It would be too artificial to extend either the PETRAS time sheet add-in or the PETRAS reporting application to control one or more of the other Office applications. Excel's features are sufficient for our analysis and reporting requirements. If we were to do so, however, we would use the procedures shown in Listings 22-11 to 22-14, which should be considered the practical examples for this chapter.

Summary

Excel is only one part of the Office suite of applications. While its data handling, word processing, and presentation features are usually sufficient for many applications, we can often add a great deal of value to our applications by controlling some of the other components of the Office suite.

The easiest way to control the other Office applications is to have a pre-prepared template database, document, or presentation that we open, modify, and save; all the examples in this chapter do exactly that.

This chapter has barely scratched the surface of each application's object model, only describing them in sufficient detail for you to understand the sample code and get started using them. We can achieve some impressive results with only a little knowledge of the objects, so learning to automate the other Office applications is not as daunting a prospect as it first appears.

EXCEL AND VISUAL BASIC 6

Before we begin this chapter, we must make note of the fact that Visual Basic 6 is no longer sold by Microsoft. Its place has been taken by VB.NET, which is a very different programming language despite the similarity of its name to VB6. However, VB6 is still used by working programmers all over the world. VBA is the primary programming language for all current versions of Excel, and it will continue to be so for some time to come. VBA and VB6 are closely related and work well together, so the case for using VB6 to extend the powers of VBA is still a strong one.

If you do not already have a copy of VB6, it may be difficult to locate one. Check online auction sites such as eBay. Many used bookstores also sell used software, so those may be another good place to find a copy of VB6.

You can think of VB6 as the more powerful big brother to VBA. It has a number of capabilities that VBA does not, including the capability to generate truly compiled code in the form of DLLs or standalone executable files, a more powerful forms package, superior object oriented programming capabilities, support for resource libraries, and Clipboard, Printer, and Screen objects among others. All these features can be easily and tightly integrated with your VBA projects with no loss of performance. In fact you will see a gain in performance in some cases due to the fact that VB6 code is truly compiled, rather than being interpreted like VBA.

In this chapter, we show you how to get started combining VB6 and Excel and cover the most common reasons why you would want to extend your VBA projects with VB6. Keep in mind that VB6 is yet another topic that would require an entire book to cover properly, so we focus very narrowly on just the VB6 features you would be most likely to use in conjunction with your Excel applications.

A Hello World ActiveX DLL

VB6 can be used to create more than half a dozen different types of applications, but the only two that are typically used in conjunction with Excel are ActiveX DLLs and Standard EXEs. COM add-ins, which we cover later in the chapter, are a subset of ActiveX DLLs. In this section we introduce you to using VB6 ActiveX DLLs from Excel with a simple Hello World application.

The first iteration of our Hello World ActiveX DLL demonstrates one-way communication only, from Excel to the DLL. We then extend the example in the second iteration to demonstrate two-way communication. Excel communicates with the DLL and the DLL communicates back to Excel. In the third iteration we demonstrate how to show a VB6 Form in Excel as if it were a native UserForm. In this way, without complicating the example with any advanced features, you see just how easy it is to create and use all the basic features of a VB6 ActiveX DLL from Excel. Later sections of the chapter show how to add non-trivial VB6 features to the base that we build in our Hello World application. The complete set of files for this example is located on the CD in the \Concepts\Ch23 – Excel and Visual Basic 6\HelloWorld folder.

Creating an ActiveX DLL Project

When you first open VB6, you are presented with the New Project dialog shown in Figure 23-1. If you have used VB6 in the past and configured it not to display this dialog on startup you can access it from the File > New Project menu.

As shown in Figure 23-1, we select the ActiveX DLL project type. Once you have selected this project type, click the Open button and VB6 creates a new ActiveX DLL project for you.

In its simplest form, which is the form we use in the first iteration of our Hello World application, an ActiveX DLL consists of only two parts: a project and a class module. The project determines the application name of your DLL while the class module exposes the features of your DLL to other programs. Figure 23-2 shows the structure of a newly created ActiveX DLL project as seen in the Project window.

If this Project window appears familiar, it's no accident. You will find the VB6 development environment and the VBA development environment so similar that it's easy to confuse them. This also makes it easy to work with VB6 if you already have experience with VBA.

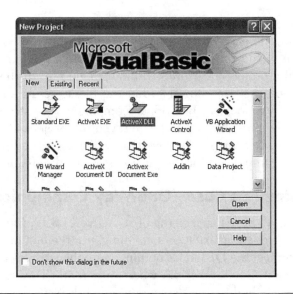

Figure 23-1 The VB6 New Project dialog

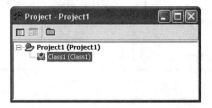

Figure 23-2 A newly created ActiveX DLL project

We use the Properties window in VB6 to provide friendly names for our project and class module in exactly the same way we would do it in VBA. Instead of Project1, we give our project the name AFirstProject. Instead of Class1 we give our class module the name CHelloWorld. We then save the project. The result is shown in Figure 23-3.

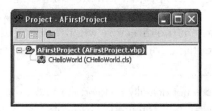

Figure 23-3 The component names for the Hello World project

Notice that once we save the VB6 project a filename appears in parentheses beside each of the friendly names of our components. This is one example of the difference between VBA and VB6. In VBA, all components of a project are stored within a single file. In the case of an Excel application they are stored within the file structure of the workbook in which they're located. In VB6, all components are stored as separate text files in the directory in which you saved the project. (Certain objects like Forms and Resource Files have binary files associated with them, but this detail isn't important for the purposes of our discussion.)

The Simplest Case—One-Way Communication

Now that we have the skeleton of an ActiveX DLL project completed, let's add some code to make it do something. For the first iteration of our Hello World project the DLL does nothing more than display a message box with the caption "Hello World!" when prompted. This is accomplished by adding a method to our class module that displays the message box when called. Adding a method to a VB6 class module is done in exactly the same way as adding a method to a VBA class module. Simply open the class module and add the code shown in Listing 23-1.

Listing 23-1   The ShowMessage Method

```
Public Sub ShowMessage()
    MsgBox "Hello World!"
End Sub
```

Now all we need to do is compile our ActiveX DLL and call it from an Excel application to display its message. Before you can use a VB6 project you must compile it. This is accomplished through the use of the *File > Make AFirstProject.dll* menu, as shown in Figure 23-4. The "AFirstProject.dll" portion of this menu name differs depending on the name and type of the project you are compiling.

Once you've compiled your DLL you will find a file named AFirstProject.dll in the directory where you saved your project. This is the compiled, executable form of all the files in the project combined.

NOTE   If you are not actually building the VB6 examples from this chapter on your own computer, you can use the example files provided on the CD. For this to work you need to copy these files onto your local hard disk and register the DLL manually (VB6 does this automatically when you compile the DLL).

To register the DLL, open a command prompt window, type the following command, and press Enter:

```
C:\>regsvr32 C:\MyPath\AFirstProject.dll
```

where C:\MyPath\AFirstProject.dll is the full path and filename of the DLL you
are trying to register on your computer.

FIGURE 23-4 Using the File > Make Menu to compile the DLL

So how do we use this from Excel? The first step is to create a new
workbook and save it as Book1.xls to the same directory as your VB6 project (Book1.xlsm if you are using Excel 2007). Saving the workbook to this
location is not a requirement; it just makes things simpler by keeping all
the files for the example in one place. In reality, the DLL could be used by
any Excel application anywhere on your computer.

Next, open the VBE from Excel and insert one standard code module. But before we can start adding code to call our DLL we need to tell
VBA where to find it. This is done using the *Tools > References* menu in
the VBE. As we mentioned earlier, the name of your VB6 project serves
as its application name. Therefore, the name of the reference you need to
add is the same as the name of your VB6 project, in this case
AFirstProject.

Figure 23-5 shows the VBA References dialog with the AFirstProject
DLL reference selected. Note that the path shown in the *Location* listing
at the bottom of the References dialog reflects the location where the DLL

was compiled on your computer, so it will be different from the path shown in the figure.

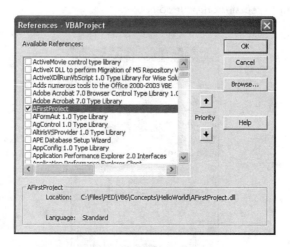

FIGURE 23-5 Referencing the AFirstProject DLL from Excel

One you've set a reference to the DLL you can use it exactly like you would use any other outside object referenced from Excel. To demonstrate our DLL we create a simple ShowDLLMessage procedure in the standard module of our Excel workbook. The complete code for this procedure is shown in Listing 23-2.

Listing 23-2 The ShowDLLMessage Procedure

```
Public Sub ShowDLLMessage()
    Dim clsHelloWorld As AFirstProject.CHelloWorld
    Set clsHelloWorld = New AFirstProject.CHelloWorld
    clsHelloWorld.ShowMessage
    Set clsHelloWorld = Nothing
End Sub
```

As originally suggested in Chapter 3, "Excel and VBA Development Best Practices," we referenced our DLL class using a two-part notation: ApplicationName.ClassName. This uniquely identifies the class we want to use and prevents any confusion that might arise from two referenced applications sharing the same class name. When you run the ShowDLLMessage procedure, the message box in Figure 23-6 is displayed.

FIGURE 23-6   The Hello World message from our ActiveX DLL

An interesting side note demonstrated by Figure 23-6 is the text displayed in the title bar of the message box. If you don't supply a title of your own, the text displayed in the title bar of a message box by default is the name of the application that displayed it. For example, if you displayed a message box from Excel without specifying a title, the title text would be set to "Microsoft Excel." Similarly, because we didn't specify a title for the message box shown by our ActiveX DLL, its title defaults to the application name of the DLL, which is "AFirstProject."

The More Complex Case—Two-Way Communication

The first iteration of our Hello World application demonstrated how to create an ActiveX DLL and a corresponding Excel project that could communicate with the DLL. But the example was significantly limited by the fact that all communication was one-way, Excel calling the DLL.

To take full advantage of the power afforded by combining Excel with a VB6 ActiveX DLL we must create a structure that allows communication to flow in both directions. In the second iteration of our Hello World application we extend the previous example to allow two-way communication.

A DLL is fundamentally a dependent component. A DLL cannot take any action by itself; it can only respond to requests from applications that are making use of its code. Once a request is made, however, a DLL can communicate directly with the application that called it. To enable two-way communication between Excel and the DLL we must provide the DLL with a way of knowing who called it.

The first step required to accomplish this is to set a reference from the DLL to the Excel object library, which provides the DLL with the all information about Excel that it needs to communicate directly with Excel. The process of setting a reference in VB6 is virtually identical to the process of setting a reference in VBA. The only difference is the location of the menu item. To set a reference to Excel from our VB6 ActiveX DLL we select *Project > References* from the VB6 menu. Figure 23-7 shows a reference created from our VB6 project to the Microsoft Excel 11.0 Object Library. This is the object library for Excel 2003.

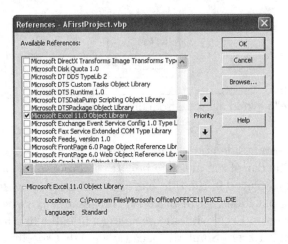

FIGURE 23-7 Setting a reference to Excel from VB6

As discussed in Chapter 22, "Controlling Other Office Applications," because of potential backward compatibility problems you should always set a reference to the earliest version of the application you expect to be using. In this case, the earliest version of Excel that we expect to use is Excel 2003.

Now that our DLL has a reference to the Excel object library, we add the code to allow the DLL to communicate with the instance of the Excel application that loaded it. Because a DLL is a fundamentally dependent component, it is up to the VBA code running in the Excel application to establish two-way communication by providing the DLL with a reference to the Excel Application object. The DLL must simply be prepared to accept and store this reference.

To demonstrate this process in our Hello World application, we create a second method that when called by Excel enters the string "Hello World!" into the currently selected cell on the active worksheet. As we implied earlier, the first thing our DLL needs to accomplish this is a reference to the Excel application that called it. We create a module-level variable to store the reference to the calling Excel Application object and a new Property procedure that Excel can use to pass a reference to itself into the DLL.

Because our DLL is now holding a reference to an outside application, we must also be sure this reference is destroyed when the DLL is unloaded from memory. We use the Class_Terminate event procedure to accomplish this. The complete code for the new version of our CHelloWorld class module is shown in Listing 23-3. Note that we use good code commenting techniques to visually separate the various sections of this new, more complex class module code.

Listing 23-3   The Complete Updated CHelloWorld Code Module

```
Option Explicit

'  *****************************************************
'  Class Variable Declarations Follow
'  *****************************************************
'  Object reference to the calling Excel Application.
Private mxlApp As Excel.Application


'  *****************************************************
'  Class Property Procedures Follow
'  *****************************************************
Public Property Set ExcelApp(ByRef xlApp As Excel.Application)
    Set mxlApp = xlApp
End Property


'  *****************************************************
'  Class Event Procedures Follow
'  *****************************************************
Private Sub Class_Terminate()
    Set mxlApp = Nothing
End Sub


'  *****************************************************
'  Class Method Procedures Follow
'  *****************************************************
Public Sub ShowMessage()
    MsgBox "Hello World!"
End Sub

Public Sub WriteMessage()
    mxlApp.ActiveCell.Value = "Hello World!"
End Sub
```

We added the following additional code to our DLL class module:

- An mxlApp module-level variable that holds a reference to the Excel Application object that called the DLL. The DLL communicates with Excel through this object reference.
- An ExcelApp property procedure that is used by the Excel Application calling the DLL to provide a reference to itself.
- A Class_Terminate event procedure that ensures the module-level reference to the Excel Application object is destroyed when the class is destroyed.
- A WriteMessage method that places the text string "Hello World!" into the currently selected cell in the currently active worksheet in the currently active workbook in the Excel Application that called the method.

It is now time to recompile our DLL. If you are following along on your own computer and you still have Excel open from testing the previous version of the DLL, you will notice that VB6 does not allow you to recompile the DLL until you close Excel. The symptoms of this are a "Permission denied:" error when you attempt to compile. Once Excel has loaded a DLL, the DLL will not be released from memory until Excel is closed. Closing the workbook that references the DLL will not do the trick. You must close Excel completely.

Once you've closed Excel you simply select the *File > Make AFirstProject.dll* menu, as in the previous example, to recompile your DLL so that it includes the features we've added in this section. Because you already have a previous version of AFirstProject.dll located in your project directory, VB6 warns you and asks if you want to replace it with a new version. Select yes and the new version of your DLL will be compiled.

Now that you have a newly compiled version of your DLL, you need to add a procedure to your Excel workbook that takes advantage of the new WriteMessage method. Open the Book1.xls workbook that you saved to the VB6 project directory and add the procedure shown in Listing 23-4 to its code module.

Listing 23-4 The WriteDLLMessage Procedure

```
Public Sub WriteDLLMessage()
    Dim clsHelloWorld As AFirstProject.CHelloWorld
    Set clsHelloWorld = New AFirstProject.CHelloWorld
    Set clsHelloWorld.ExcelApp = Application
    clsHelloWorld.WriteMessage
    Set clsHelloWorld = Nothing
End Sub
```

The only fundamental difference between the WriteDLLMessage procedure and the previous ShowDLLMessage procedure is that we use the new ExcelApp property of our CHelloWorld class to pass a reference to the Excel Application object into the class. This tells the class what application called it and therefore what application its communications should be directed back to.

Because the new WriteMessage method operates on a cell on the active worksheet, we add two Forms toolbar Button controls to the first (and only) worksheet in Book1.xls and assign their OnAction properties to each of the two procedures in Book1.xls. If you select a cell on the worksheet and click the *Write DLL Message* button, the WriteDLLMessage procedure assigned to that button will be run. This procedure asks the DLL to enter a message string into the currently selected cell of that Excel Application object. The DLL uses its reference to the Excel Application object to enter the string "Hello World!" into the currently selected cell. The result of this call is shown in our newly constructed Excel user interface in Figure 23-8.

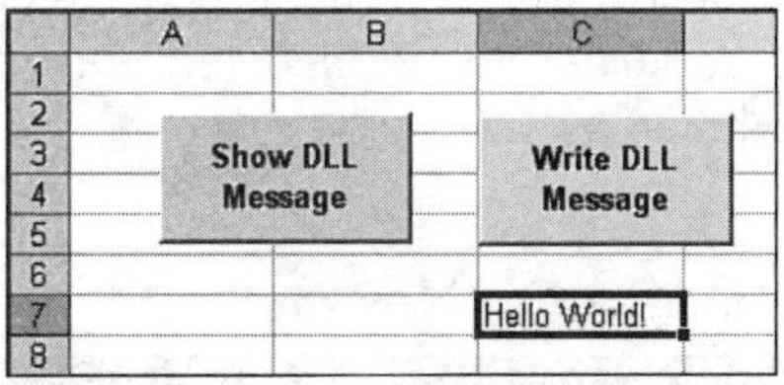

FIGURE 23-8   Two-way communication between Excel and an ActiveX DLL

Displaying a VB6 Form in Excel

For the next iteration of our VB6 Hello World application, we perform an even more complex task: displaying a VB6 Form object in Excel exactly as if it were a VBA UserForm. There are a number of reasons you might want to do this, and we discuss them at length in the "Taking Advantage of VB6 Forms" section later in the chapter. For now let's leave the complications aside and look at the minimum requirements for displaying a VB6 Form in Excel. The first step is to add a form to our Hello World project by choosing *Project > Add Form* from the VB6 menu. This displays the Add Form dialog shown in Figure 23-9.

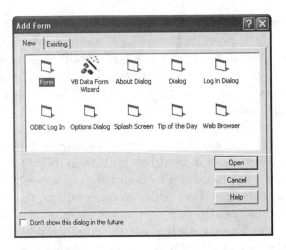

FIGURE 23-9 The Add Form dialog

Select the Form icon in the upper-left corner and click the Open button. A new Form object is added to your project. Before we save our project with the new Form object in it we need to change a few properties of the form. The properties to be changed and the values they should be changed to are shown in Table 23-1.

Table 23-1 The Property Settings for Our New Form

Property Name	Property Setting
(Name)	FHellowWorld
BorderStyle	3 – Fixed Dialog
Caption	Hello From VB6
Icon	(None) – Select and delete the default value
StartupPosition	1 – Center Owner

Once you've made these property changes, save your project. Because the form has never been saved before, VB6 prompts you with a Save File As dialog asking you where to save the form. Make sure you save it in the same directory where the rest of the project is saved. Your project should now look like the one shown in the Project window in Figure 23-10.

FIGURE 23-10   The project with a form added

Next we add a CommandButton and a Label control to our new form. Name the CommandButton cmdOK and give it the caption "OK." Give the Label the caption "Hello World!", change the Alignment property to 1 – Center, and increase the Font size to 24 points. Your completed form should resemble the one shown in Figure 23-11, but don't worry if yours looks a little different.

FIGURE 23-11   The VB6 Hello World! form

The only code that we need to put behind the form is a line in the cmdOK_Click event procedure that hides the form when the OK button is clicked. This event procedure is shown in Listing 23-5.

Listing 23-5   The cmdOK_Click Event Procedure

```
Private Sub cmdOK_Click()
    Me.Hide
End Sub
```

A Form object contained in a VB6 ActiveX DLL is not directly accessible to outside applications. Therefore, we need to add code to our class module that allows our Excel application to display the form. We also need to make one additional tweak to the form so that it behaves like a native Excel UserForm. The complete code for the new version of our CHelloWorld class is shown in Listing 23-6 with the new code for this version shaded.

Listing 23-6   The CHelloWorld Code Module Updated to Support the Form

```
Option Explicit

' ***************************************************************
' Class Constant Declarations Follow
' ***************************************************************
' SetWindowLongA API constant.
Private Const GWL_HWNDPARENT As Long = -8


' ***************************************************************
' Class Variable Declarations Follow
' ***************************************************************
' Object reference to the calling Excel Application.
Private mxlApp As Excel.Application
' Window handle of the calling Excel Application.
Private mlXLhWnd As Long
' ***************************************************************
' Class DLL Declaractions Follow
' ***************************************************************
Private Declare Function FindWindowA Lib "user32" _
                    (ByVal lpClassName As String, _
                    ByVal lpWindowName As String) As Long


Private Declare Function SetWindowLongA Lib "user32" _
                    (ByVal hWnd As Long, _
                    ByVal nIndex As Long, _
                    ByVal dwNewLong As Long) As Long


' ***************************************************************
' Class Property Procedures Follow

' ***************************************************************
Public Property Set ExcelApp(ByRef xlApp As Excel.Application)
    Set mxlApp = xlApp
```

```
    ' Get the window handle of the Excel Application object
    ' as soon as it is passed to us.
    If Val(Application.Version) > 9 Then
        ' Excel XP and higher expose the window handle directly.
        mlXLhWnd = Application.hWnd
    Else
        ' Excel 2000 requires an API call for the window handle.
        mlXLhWnd = FindWindowA(vbNullString, mxlApp.Caption)
    End If
End Property


' ***************************************************************
' Class Event Procedures Follow
' ***************************************************************
Private Sub Class_Terminate()
    Set mxlApp = Nothing
End Sub


' ***************************************************************
' Class Method Procedures Follow
' ***************************************************************
Public Sub ShowMessage()
    MsgBox "Hello World!"
End Sub


Public Sub WriteMessage()
    mxlApp.ActiveCell.Value = "Hello World!"
End Sub


Public Sub ShowVB6Form()
    Dim frmHelloWorld As FHelloWorld
    Set frmHelloWorld = New FHelloWorld
    Load frmHelloWorld
    ' Parent the Form window to the Excel Application window.
    SetWindowLongA frmHelloWorld.hWnd, GWL_HWNDPARENT, mlXLhWnd
    frmHelloWorld.Show vbModal
    Unload frmHelloWorld
    Set frmHelloWorld = Nothing
End Sub
```

A VB6 Form is a top-level window by default. That is to say it is a child window only of the Desktop. To make a VB6 Form behave like a native UserForm in Excel we need to use the Windows API to change the parent window of the VB6 Form from the Desktop to the window of the Excel Application object that called it. Changing the parent window of a form involves two steps:

1. Retrieving the window handle of the window we want to use as the form's parent window.
2. Changing the form's parent window by putting the window handle we retrieved into the storage area of the form's window structure that is used to specify the parent window of the form.

Implementing this in our code requires us to make a number of additions, all of which are highlighted in Listing 23-6. We declared a new module-level variable, mlXLhWnd, to hold the window handle of the Excel Application object that called our class. We added two Windows API function declarations: FindWindowA to locate the window handle of the Excel Application window and SetWindowLongA to change the parent window of our form. The new GWL_HWNDPARENT constant identifies the location in our form's window structure where the window handle of the new parent window will be placed. We added a line of code to the ExcelApp property procedure to determine the Excel Application object's window handle as soon as the property is set.

We also created a new ShowVB6Form method that is responsible for displaying the form in Excel in response to a call from the Excel application. This method uses the following steps to accomplish its task:

- It creates a new instance of the FHelloWorld form.
- It loads that instance of the FHelloWorld form into memory.
- It changes the form's parent window from the Desktop window to the Excel Application window using the SetWindowLongA API.
- It shows the form using the vbModal argument. Unlike UserForms, VB6 Forms show modeless by default. Since this is not what we want for this example we pass the vbModal argument to the form's Show method to force the form to be modal.

- When the user closes the form, the method unloads it from memory and destroys the object variable that refers to it.

Once you add the new code to your VB6 project, close Excel and recompile your DLL using the *File > Make AFirstProject* menu. On the Excel application side you simply need to add a new procedure in the code module to call the DLL and have it display the VB6 Form and add a new button on the worksheet assigned to this procedure. The code for the new DisplayDLLForm procedure is shown in Listing 23-7.

Listing 23-7 The DisplayDLLForm Procedure

```
Public Sub DisplayDLLForm()
    Dim clsHelloWorld As AFirstProject.CHelloWorld
    Set clsHelloWorld = New AFirstProject.CHelloWorld
    Set clsHelloWorld.ExcelApp = Application
    clsHelloWorld.ShowVB6Form
    Set clsHelloWorld = Nothing
End Sub
```

As you can see, the code for the DisplayDLLForm procedure is virtually identical to the code for the WriteDLLMessage procedure shown earlier in Listing 23-4. The only difference is that one calls the ShowVB6Form method of our CHelloWorld class while the other calls the WriteMessage method of our CHelloWorld class. The Excel user interface with the VB6 Form displayed over it is shown in Figure 23-12.

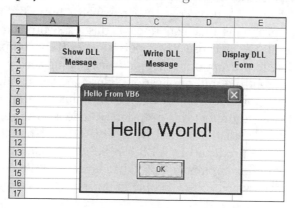

FIGURE 23-12   The VB6 Form displayed in Excel

23. EXCEL AND VISUAL BASIC 6

Notice how our VB6 Form looks and behaves exactly like a UserForm in Excel. You may be asking yourself why we would go through all this trouble when we could have spent 5 minutes creating an identical UserForm in VBA. In the "Taking Advantage of VB6 Forms" section later in this chapter we see that VB6 Forms have a number of features that UserForms don't, and the simple structure for displaying a VB6 Form in Excel that we developed here is the first step in allowing us to take advantage of these features.

Why Use VB6 ActiveX DLLs in Excel VBA Projects

Although the core VBA language contained in VB6 is exactly the same as that used by Excel, VB6 supports a number of additional features that are not available in a pure Excel application. These features include strong code protection due to its fully compiled nature and a more powerful forms package with the ability to use third-party ActiveX controls, control arrays, and with enhanced data binding capabilities. VB6 also provides better support for object oriented programming, the ability to create resource files, and other useful features, including the Clipboard, Printer, and Screen objects.

Code Protection

A frequent problem that arises in the context of Excel applications is the complete inability of VBA to protect your code from prying eyes. You can protect your VBA project with a password, but VBA project password breaking programs that can remove this password almost instantly are widely available. Because VBA code is never truly compiled, it will never be possible to prevent other people from gaining access to it.

For run-of-the-mill applications, this is not a significant problem. A number of applications, however, rely on valuable proprietary algorithms. The only way to protect this proprietary code is to store it in a truly compiled state like that provided by a VB6 DLL. Note that the compiled machine code produced by VB6 can be decompiled to a limited extent. The result of decompiling a VB6 DLL, however, is little more than assembly language, which so few people understand that code compiled in VB6 is effectively invulnerable.

Taking Advantage of VB6 Forms

The forms package used by VB6 is very different from the one used by VBA. As mentioned in Chapter 13, "UserForm Design and Best Practices," the forms package used to create UserForm objects in Excel applications is called MSForms. The forms package used to create Form objects in VB6 is known as Ruby Forms.

There are superficial similarities between the two. Both provide a blank canvas onto which you can drag and drop controls to visually construct your form. Both types of form have event models, and both allow you to program controls by responding to events raised by those controls.

There are also differences between the two forms packages, and those differences range from the subtle to the significant. For example, there are minor differences in the set of properties, methods, and events exposed by the two types of forms and their built-in controls. There are also significant differences in the capabilities of the two.

For example, in Chapter 13 we showed in detail how to modify the window styles of UserForms using API calls to achieve effects that were not directly supported by UserForms. All these window styles are directly supported by VB6 Forms, and it requires nothing more than setting the appropriate Form properties in the Properties window to implement them. VB6 Forms also provide a wide variety of built-in shapes and drawing methods that allow you to create sophisticated form designs without ever having to resort to the Windows API.

Where API techniques are still required to achieve a certain effect, they are much easier to implement in VB6 Forms because VB6 Forms expose their window handles and device contexts as a native properties, obviating the need for API calls to obtain them. And in contrast to the lightweight, windowless controls provided with VBA UserForms, VB6 Form controls all have windows, and they all expose their window handles as native properties. This allows them to be manipulated in ways that are simply impossible with windowless UserForm controls. We discuss additional differences between VBA UserForms and VB6 Forms that are of particular interest to the Excel programmer in the sections that follow.

Better ActiveX Control Support

Not only do VB6 Forms provide better support than UserForms for a wide variety of built-in Windows controls, they can also host hundreds of third-party ActiveX controls that are completely unavailable to UserForms. The reason for this is that almost all third-party ActiveX controls come in two versions. When building your project the version you use is called the **design-time version** of the control. When your project is distributed and running in a compiled state it uses the **runtime version** of the control.

When you purchase a third-party ActiveX control, what you are really buying is a license to build your VB6 Forms using the design-time version of the control. The runtime version of the control, required by your VB6 Form once it is compiled, can be redistributed without restrictions in most cases. This is because it cannot be used in the design-time environment and therefore cannot be used to build new projects.

By contrast, UserForms in VBA projects *always* exist in design mode, so runtime versions of ActiveX controls will not work with them. If you were to distribute the design-time version of a control to get it to run in an uncompiled VBA UserForm, you would essentially be giving that control away to other users for free. Anyone who has the design-time version of a control installed on their computer can use it in their own projects, whether they purchased it or not.

As you can imagine, very few ActiveX control vendors allow you to redistribute the design-time versions of their controls. This makes the use of those controls effectively off-limits to all VBA UserForm-based projects.

NOTE   It is possible to wrap a third-party ActiveX control inside a custom VB6 ActiveX control project. The wrapper project would need to duplicate all the required properties, methods, and events of the control it wraps. Once compiled, however, it uses the runtime version of the third-party control. UserForms can host custom VB6 ActiveX controls, so this is a way to get around the limitation described previously. However, this is difficult and time consuming to implement, probably a violation of the license agreements of most third-party controls and beyond the scope of this chapter.

Control Arrays

Control arrays are one of the most useful features provided by VB6 Forms. There is simply nothing like them supported by VBA UserForms. Using control arrays, you can declare a set of controls to be an array. Each control in the array is given the same name but a unique Index property value. VB6 then treats all the controls in the array almost as if they were a single control. For example, a single event procedure of each type is fired in response to activity from any of the controls within the array. This event procedure passes the Index value of the specific control that fired the event, allowing you to respond appropriately.

Not only are all controls in a control array treated as a single control, but you can easily add or remove controls dynamically from the array as required at runtime. Adding or removing controls from the array physically adds or removes actual controls on the form, a capability that greatly simplifies the creation of dynamically configured forms.

We demonstrate a simple example of a control array. This example is available on the CD in the \Concepts\Ch23 –Excel and Visual Basic 6\ControlArrays folder. The plumbing required to display the VB6 Form in Excel is identical to that shown in the third iteration of our Hello World example given previously, so we do not rehash any of that material. Instead we concentrate on how to create and program a control array on a VB6 Form.

Our control array demo consists of a VB6 Form that will eventually contain six OptionButton controls along with a ListBox control. The option button selected by the user determines the contents of the ListBox control. Rather than having to respond to a separate Click event from each option button, we create the six option buttons as a control array so that we can manage them from a single Click event.

The initial form containing a list box and a single non-array option button is displayed side-by-side with the Properties window showing the properties for the option button in Figure 23-13. The Properties window is shown with its Categorized tab active and all categories except Misc collapsed. The Misc properties are the ones we want to focus on when it comes to creating control arrays.

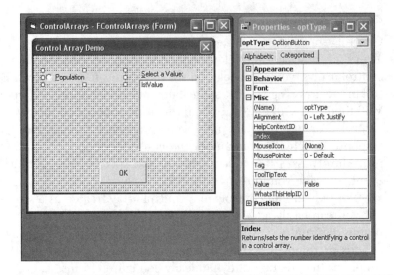

FIGURE 23-13   The initial Control Array Demo form

Note that we give our option button the name optType and that the Index property selected in the Properties window is empty. This identifies optType as a standard control. The next step is to add the five additional option buttons to our form. Since we've already drawn one OptionButton control on our form that we want to duplicate, there's no reason to add five more option buttons from scratch. Instead we just copy our first option button and paste new copies of it back onto the form.

To do this, we simply select our existing option button, right-click over it, and choose *Copy* from the shortcut menu. We then select an empty area on our form, right-click over it, and choose *Paste* from the shortcut menu. As soon as we attempt to paste a copy of our existing option button onto the same form where it originated VB6 displays the message shown in Figure 23-14.

When you attempt to paste a control that has the same name as an existing control onto a form, VB6 assumes you want to create a control array, and it offers to help you do so. Click the Yes button in the message box and let's see what happens. We re-selected our original option button and displayed the result in Figure 23-15.

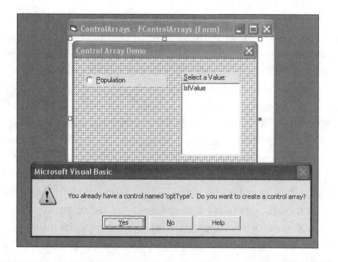

FIGURE 23-14   VB6 helps us create a control array

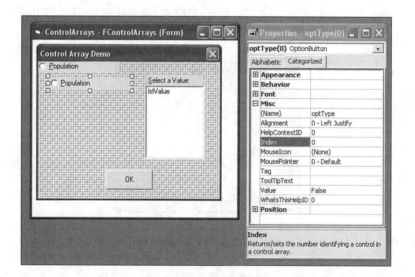

FIGURE 23-15   A control array created by the Copy/Paste method

The copy of the option button that we pasted appears in the upper-left corner of the form. It is intriguing to compare the previous property values for our first option button from Figure 23-13 with its new property values shown in Figure 23-15. The first thing to note is that the name shown in the Properties window selection drop-down for our original option button is now "optType(0) OptionButton" instead of "optType OptionButton." We allowed VB6 to create a control array for us when we pasted the copy of this option button onto our form, and the original option button is now the first element in the array. Control arrays begin at zero by default.

The second thing to notice is that the formerly empty Index property now also has a value of zero. This property is what really determines whether a control is part of an array. If the Index property is blank, the control is not part of an array. If the Index property contains a number, the control is part of an array and the Index property value is its position within the array.

We now position the copied option button control (which has an Index of 1) below the original option button and set its caption. Then we paste four more copies of the original option button onto the form and do the same. The results are shown in Figure 23-16.

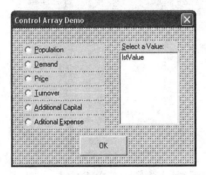

FIGURE 23-16   The completed control array demo form

Even though the option buttons have completely different captions, they have exactly the same name with a unique Index value to identify them. Therefore, we now have option buttons optType(0) through optType(5). Note that when you paste a control that is already part of a control array onto a form, VB6 no longer prompts you with the question shown in Figure 23-14. It simply adds the control to the next available index position within the existing control array.

Now that we've completed the visible part of our Control Array Demo form, let's have a look at the code required to manage it. Our form requires only two properties and three event procedures to perform all of its operations:

- One property to expose the option selected and another to expose the list item selected for that option
- A Click event procedure that handles all the option buttons in the control array
- A Click event procedure for the cmdOK button that validates the user's selections
- A QueryUnload event for the form that reroutes clicks on the x-close button to the cmdOK_Click event procedure

The code behind our Control Array Demo form is shown in Listing 23-8.

Listing 23-8 The Control Array Demo Form Specific Code

```
Option Explicit

' *************************************************************
' Form Property Procedures Follow
' *************************************************************
Public Property Get OptionSelected() As String
    Dim lIndex As Long
    For lIndex = optType.LBound To optType.UBound
        If optType(lIndex).Value Then
            OptionSelected = optType(lIndex).Caption
            Exit For
        End If
    Next lIndex
End Property

Public Property Get ListSelection() As Double
    ListSelection = CDbl(lstValue.Text)
End Property

' *************************************************************
' Form Event Procedures Follow
' *************************************************************
```

```vb
Private Sub optType_Click(Index As Integer)
    Dim vItem As Variant
    Dim vaList As Variant
    lstValue.Clear
    Select Case Index
        Case 0  ' Population
            vaList = Array(500, 1000, 100000, 100000)
        Case 1  ' Demand
            vaList = Array(50, 100, 1000, 10000)
        Case 2  ' Price
            vaList = Array(9.99, 19.99, 29.99, 39.99)
        Case 3  ' Turnover
            vaList = Array(0.01, 0.015, 0.02, 0.025, 0.03)
        Case 4  ' Additional Capital
            vaList = Array(1000, 2000, 3000, 4000)
        Case 5  ' Additional Expense
            vaList = Array(500, 1000, 1500, 2000)
    End Select
    For Each vItem In vaList
        lstValue.AddItem vItem
    Next vItem
    lstValue.ListIndex = -1
End Sub


Private Sub cmdOK_Click()
    Dim bOptionSelected As Boolean
    Dim lIndex As Long
    ' Do not allow the user to continue unless an option button
    ' has been selected and a list item has been selected
    For lIndex = optType.LBound To optType.UBound
        If optType(lIndex).Value Then
            bOptionSelected = True
            Exit For
        End If
    Next lIndex
    If Not bOptionSelected Or lstValue.ListIndex = -1 Then
        MsgBox "You must select an option and a list item."
    Else
        Me.Hide
    End If
End Sub


Private Sub Form_QueryUnload(Cancel As Integer, _
                                        UnloadMode As Integer)
```

```
' Route the x-close button through the
' cmdOK_Click event procedure.
If UnloadMode = vbFormControlMenu Then
    Cancel = True
    cmdOK_Click
End If
End Sub
```

The OptionSelected property procedure returns a string identifying the option button within the control array that the user selected. It does this by simply looping the control array until a control with a value of True is located. Once this control is located, the loop is exited and the index value converted into its corresponding string description. The ListSelection property does nothing more than return the Text property of the list box (whose values are constrained by the option button selection).

The optType_Click event procedure is something that we've never seen before. This event procedure behaves exactly like the Click event for any option button except that it fires when any option button in the control array is clicked. This is why it has an Index argument. The Index argument contains the value of the Index property of the option button that fired the event. We use this event procedure to load the list box with values that correspond to the options selected. Look at the structure of this procedure and imagine how easy it would be to add or remove options.

The cmdOK_Click event demonstrates some simple validation code. When the form is first displayed, no option button is selected and there is nothing in the list. If this were a real application we would write code to disable the cmdOK button until all of the appropriate selections had been made. For the purposes of this demo, however, we simply check the status of the option button array and the list when the cmdOK button is clicked. If everything is in order we hide the form and continue. Otherwise, we display a message to the user explaining what they need to do.

The Form_QueryUnload event is used to trap cases where the user tries to close the form with the x-close button rather than the OK button. In a real application we would have cancel logic coded into the form that would be activated by this button, but since the only route out of the form that we have provided for this example is through the cmdOK button, we cancel any clicks on the x-close button and reroute them through the cmdOK_Click event procedure.

As we mentioned in the final section of our Hello World example, VB6 Forms cannot be accessed directly by outside applications. Therefore we created a public CDialogHandler class module to expose the Control Array

Demo form and the selections the user has made in it to our Excel application. The method used to expose the form is shown in Listing 23-9.

Listing 23-9   The CDialogHandler ShowVB6Form Method

```
Public Sub ShowVB6Form(ByRef sOption As String, _
                                        ByRef dValue As Double)
    Dim frmCtrlArrays As FControlArrays
    Set frmCtrlArrays = New FControlArrays
    Load frmCtrlArrays
    ' Parent the Form window to the Excel Application window.
    SetWindowLongA frmCtrlArrays.hWnd, GWL_HWNDPARENT, mlXLhWnd
    frmCtrlArrays.Show vbModal
    sOption = frmCtrlArrays.OptionSelected
    dValue = frmCtrlArrays.ListSelection
    Unload frmCtrlArrays
    Set frmCtrlArrays = Nothing
End Sub
```

This ShowVB6Form method procedure is almost identical to the method we used to display the form in our Hello World application. The only difference is that in the Hello World application the form did not return any value to the calling procedure, while in this example the form returns the option selected by the user and the item the user selected in the list box. The additional code you see in this procedure is used to retrieve these two values and pass them back to the calling Excel application. This is accomplished by the two ByRef arguments to the ShowVB6FormMethod.

Once you have set a reference from an Excel workbook to the ControlArrays.dll you can display this form from Excel using the procedure shown in Listing 23-10.

Listing 23-10   The ShowControlArraysForm Procedure

```
Public Sub ShowControlArraysForm()
    Dim clsDialogHandler As ControlArrays.CDialogHandler
    Dim dValue As Double
    Dim sOption As String
    Set clsDialogHandler = New ControlArrays.CDialogHandler
    clsDialogHandler.ShowVB6Form sOption, dValue
    Set clsDialogHandler = Nothing
    MsgBox "You selected the option " & sOption & vbLf & _
        " and chose the value " & CStr(dValue) & "."
End Sub
```

In a real-world application, we would typically have much more data to transfer back to Excel and therefore we would design a much more efficient method for doing so, creating a global user-defined type to hold all the information transferred out of the form and passing this UDT directly from the DLL to the Excel application for example. We did not do so here so as not to draw attention away from the main point, which is to demonstrate the use of control arrays.

Better Support for Object Oriented Programming

More Class Instancing Types

The Instancing property of a class determines its visibility with respect to the application within which it is located. Excel VBA classes are limited to the Instancing types Private and PublicNotCreatable. A class with its Instancing property set to Private is invisible to all outside applications. A class with its Instancing property set to PublicNotCreatable can be seen by outside applications, but it can only be used by an outside application if your project creates and exposes an instance of the class through a publicly accessible property, method, or procedure first.

What this means for Excel VBA projects is that no outside applications (or even other VBA projects within the same instance of Excel) can create instances of classes that exist within an Excel VBA project. As shown in Figure 23-17, however, a VB6 ActiveX DLL has two additional Instancing types, both of which allow classes of those types to be created and used directly by other applications.

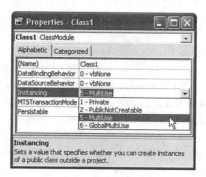

FIGURE 23-17   VB6 ActiveX DLL class types

MultiUse   MultiUse is the default instancing type for class modules added to a VB6 ActiveX DLL project. This is the instancing type used by all the class modules that we have created in this chapter so far. Once you create a class with the MultiUse instancing type, any application that references your DLL can create and use new instances of that class.

The MultiUse instancing type is the one you want to use in cases where it is important for you to require that your public classes are explicitly created before their features are used. This is most frequently the case when your VB6 ActiveX DLL contains an object model that implements the business logic layer of an application, for example.

GlobalMultiUse   Class modules with the instancing type GlobalMultiUse don't need to be explicitly created. Sometimes referred to as auto-instancing classes, this type of class module is instantiated automatically as soon as any reference is made to one of its publicly exposed components. This type of class is most frequently used for creating libraries of user-defined types, enumeration constants, and functions that will be used by multiple files in an application. They are also a good place to define interfaces that you will implement in multiple files.

For example, if the code for your data access tier resides in a VB6 ActiveX DLL and the code for your business logic tier resides in an Excel workbook but they both need to share the same user-defined type to pass data between them, you can define that UDT in a GlobalMultiUse class in a separate ActiveX DLL that both projects reference. Both projects then can "see" the declaration of the UDT and they can pass variables of that type between themselves even though the UDT is not declared in either one of them. This same technique can be used to expose common enumerations as well.

GlobalMultiUse classes also provide an excellent container for library procedures. Library procedures are generically designed custom subroutines and functions that you find yourself using in most of your projects. If you store these procedures in a GlobalMultiUse class compiled into an ActiveX DLL, all of them can be made available to any project by simply referencing that DLL. There is no need to create any object to use these library procedures, because public procedures of GlobalMultiUse classes effectively become part of the global namespace in any project that references their DLL. This means you can use your custom bSheetExists() function exactly the same way you use the built-in VBA Replace() function.

A working example of a VB6 ActiveX DLL containing a GlobalMultiUseClass can be found on the CD in the *Concepts**Ch23 –Excel and Visual Basic 6**GlobalMultiUse* folder.

Better Support for Custom Collections through Direct Support of NewEnum

As we explained in Chapter 7, "Using Class Modules to Create Objects," VB6 has two significant advantages over VBA when it comes to creating custom Collection objects. It supports default procedures, and it has a user interface that can give the required NewEnum method the "magic number" procedure attribute of –4. For example, the Item property and NewEnum method from the CCells collection introduced in Chapter 7 are shown in Listing 23-11.

Listing 23-11 The Item Property and NewEnum Method from the CCells Collection

```
Property Get Item(ByVal vID As Variant) As CCell
   Set Item = mcolCells(vID)
End Property


Public Function NewEnum() As IUnknown
    Set NewEnum = mcolCells.[_NewEnum]
End Function
```

If this code were located in a custom collection class in VB6, you would make the Item property the default procedure of the class by placing your mouse cursor anywhere within the procedure and selecting the *Tools > Procedure Attributes* menu. This displays the Procedure Attributes dialog. In the Procedure Attributes dialog click the Advanced button and select (Default) from the Procedure ID drop-down. This result of this is shown in Figure 23-18.

Similarly, to give the NewEnum procedure the magic number procedure attribute of –4, place your cursor anywhere inside the NewEnum procedure and select *Tools > Procedure Attributes* from the VB6 menu. Again, click the Advanced button, but instead of selecting a preexisting item from the Procedure ID drop-down, type in the number –4. The result of this is shown in Figure 23-19.

FIGURE 23-18 Creating a default procedure in VB6

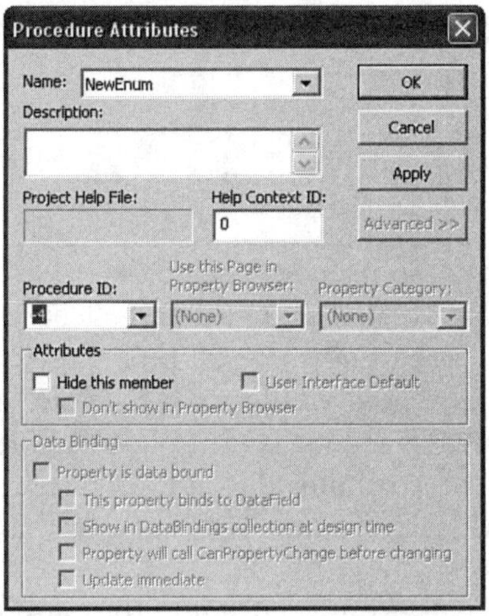

FIGURE 23-19 Adding the magic number to the NewEnum method

With VB6, it requires very little effort to create a custom collection object that behaves exactly like a built-in collection object. As described in Chapter 7, you can accomplish this in VBA, but it is a much more laborious process. Because custom collection objects are a fundamental building block in creating custom object models, the ease of creating them in VB6 is a significant advantage.

Resource Files

Resource files are a type of container provided by VB6 to store string tables and a wide variety of binary objects. These resources, as they are called, are compiled into your VB6 DLL and made available through the use of specialized VB6 functions. In traditional VB6 projects, the most common use of a resource file is to hold a string table that is used to translate the application into multiple languages. A separate string table is provided for each language under which the application needs to run, and all text displayed by the application is loaded dynamically from the string table that corresponds to the language setting on the user's computer.

Excel applications have the advantage of being able to use worksheets for this type of data storage. What Excel applications lack is an easy way to store binary resources like icons and bitmaps. You can store these types of resources on worksheets either directly as shapes or as picture objects within a large number of Image controls, or you can distribute them as separate files with the rest of the application. All these methods have significant problems associated with them that VB6 resource files do not. We show an example of how to use a resource file to store command bar control icons in the "Practical Examples" section later in the chapter.

Other VB6 Features

VB6 provides the following additional features not found in VBA. We have found them useful often enough to make them worth mentioning, but in-depth coverage of these features is beyond the scope of this chapter.

- **The ClipBoard object**—The MSForms object library provides text-only access to the Clipboard through the DataObject. VB6 has a Clipboard object that supports a complete range of operations for both text and graphics.
- **The Printer object**—The VB6 Printer object allows you to communicate directly with the printer installed on the user's computer. This in no way replaces the built-in printing capabilities of an application like Excel, but it opens up a wide variety of additional printing options that are not available from VBA.

- **The Screen object**—The VB6 Screen object, among other useful features, has two methods that allow you to convert from pixels to twips in both the horizontal and vertical directions, obviating the need for a series of API calls required to determine that information with VBA alone.

In-Process Versus Out-of-Process

When you connect two different applications, in this case an Excel VBA application and an application written in VB6, there are two different methods by which the two applications can communicate. These two methods are known as in-process and out-of-process communication.

In-Process Communication

In-process communication occurs when two applications run in the same virtual memory area allocated by Windows. ActiveX DLLs are the type of VB6 application that runs in process with Excel VBA applications. When an Excel VBA application calls a VB6 ActiveX DLL, Windows loads the DLL into the same memory area it has allocated for the Excel VBA application (all Excel VBA applications running within a given instance of Excel always run in the same memory area as each other and Excel).

This has important practical implications. When two applications share the same memory area, communication between them is very fast. In fact communication between an Excel VBA application and a VB6 ActiveX DLL operates at more or less exactly the same speed as communication within an Excel VBA application. Therefore, you do not sacrifice any performance due to communication overhead when using VB6 DLLs with Excel VBA applications, and you potentially gain performance due to the fact that unlike VBA, a VB6 DLL is truly compiled and runs more efficiently as a result.

Out-of-Process Communication

Out-of-process communication occurs when two applications run in different memory areas allocated by Windows. This is always the case for communications between two EXE applications. Windows loads all EXE applications into separate memory areas. It is not possible for two EXE applications to share the same memory area.

Therefore, when you use a VB6 EXE together with an Excel VBA application, the VB6 EXE and the Excel VBA application run in separate memory areas. This results in a significant performance degradation caused by the overhead of communicating between the two memory areas (technically termed interprocess communication). Out-of-process communication runs several orders of magnitude more slowly than in-process communication. One of the obvious implications of this is that you should not choose an out-of-process architecture for highly performance-intensive applications. If, for some reason, you must use an out-of-process architecture for a performance-intensive application, put as much code as possible in the Excel workbook so that it is run in-process by VBA.

Automating Excel from a VB6 EXE

In the most common types of applications that combine a VB6 EXE with Excel, the VB6 EXE is the initiating application. The VB6 EXE may either be the primary application automating Excel, or simply a front loader for an Excel application yet to be started. In this section we demonstrate a stripped-down example of a VB6 EXE application automating Excel. We then describe one of the most common real-world examples of a VB6 EXE combined with an Excel application, the front loader.

An Excel Automation Primer

Automating Excel from a VB6 EXE application is much simpler than using a VB6 ActiveX DLL from an Excel application. In fact we already covered all the points required to automate one application from another in Chapter 22. The process of controlling Excel from VB6 is no different than controlling an outside application from Excel.

We now demonstrate a basic example of a VB6 EXE that automates Excel. The files for this example can be found on the CD in the \Concepts\Ch23 –Excel and Visual Basic 6\AutomatingExcel folder. Creating an elaborate example using Excel would be time consuming and would tend to obscure the fundamentals. Instead we create a somewhat lighthearted example that uses an obscure function provided by Excel to convert whole numbers into Roman numerals. This is not as far from reality as it may seem at first. One of the primary reasons for automating Excel from VB6 is to utilize the powerful capabilities of Excel's calculation engine in a VB6 application.

To begin the project, start VB6 and select Standard EXE as the project type in the New Project dialog. In addition to the project itself, you get a single VB6 Form by default. This is all we need for this example. Rename

your project ConvertToRoman, rename your form FRoman, and then save
your project. In the VB6 Project window your project should now look like
Figure 23-20.

FIGURE 23-20 The ConvertToRoman project

The first step required in any project that intends to automate Excel is
to set a reference to the Excel object library. Choose *Project > References*
from the VB6 menu and select the Microsoft Excel X.0 Object Library, as
shown in Figure 23-21, where X is the version number of the earliest version of Excel that you expect to automate with your VB6 application.

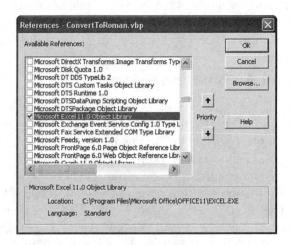

FIGURE 23-21 Referencing the Excel Object Library

The default form is the only VB6 class we use in this example. Add
three controls to the form: a TextBox control in which to enter the number to be converted to Roman numeral format, a CommandButton control
to run the code that performs the conversion, and a Label control in which
to display the results. Our completed form is shown in Figure 23-22.

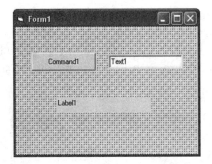

FIGURE 23-22   The initial FRoman form

We did not change any of the default properties of our form or its controls. For a change of pace we show how easy this is to do in code when the form loads. We do need to give our controls reasonable names, however, so we name the CommandButton cmdConvert, the TextBox txtConvert, and the Label lblResult.

Now let's look at the code behind our form. All this code consists of event procedures for the Form object and its controls. The first event procedure we examine is the Form_Load event shown in Listing 23-12.

Listing 23-12   The Form_Load Event Procedure

```
Private Sub Form_Load()
    ' Form properties
    Me.BorderStyle = vbFixedDouble
    Me.Caption = "Convert to Roman Numerals"
    ' CommandButton properties
    cmdConvert.Caption = "Convert To Roman"
    ' TextBox properties
    txtConvert.Alignment = vbRightJustify
    txtConvert.MaxLength = 4
    txtConvert.Text = ""
    ' Label properties
    lblResult.Alignment = vbCenter
    lblResult.BackColor = &HE0E0E0
    lblResult.BorderStyle = vbFixedSingle
    lblResult.Caption = ""
    lblResult.Font.Name = "Courier"
End Sub
```

In this procedure, we set all the properties of the form and its controls that are required to make the form user-friendly. The result of displaying the form with only this event procedure in place is shown in Figure 23-23. Compare this picture with the design-time version of the form shown in Figure 23-22.

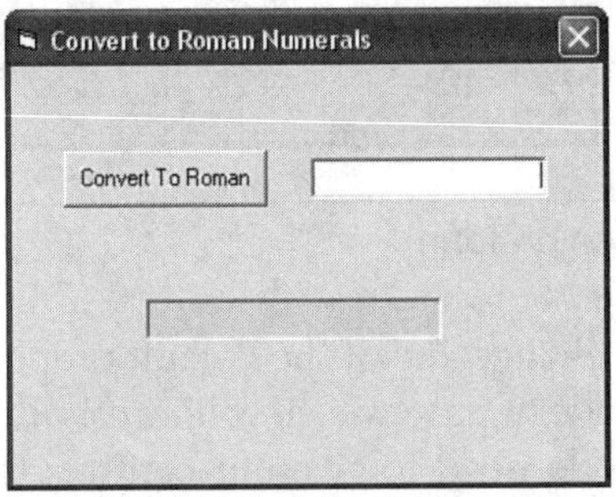

FIGURE 23-23 The display appearance of the form

The next thing we need to account for is the fact that we can only convert whole numbers to Roman numerals. This means we need to prevent the user from entering anything into the txtConvert TextBox control other than the numerals 0 through 9. We accomplish this using the txtConvert_KeyPress event.

The KeyPress event allows you to examine each character the user tries to enter into a control before it actually gets there. This allows you to alter the character, for example, by converting lowercase characters to uppercase characters, or cancel the character entirely, as we do for any character other than 0 through 9. The code for our txtConvert_KeyPress event is shown in Listing 23-13.

Listing 23-13 The txtConvert_KeyPress Event Procedure

```
Private Sub txtConvert_KeyPress(KeyAscii As Integer)
    Select Case KeyAscii
        Case 8, 48 To 57
            ' Backspace and numerals 0 through 9
            ' these are all OK. Take no action.
        Case Else
            ' No other characters are permitted.
            KeyAscii = 0
    End Select
End Sub
```

The KeyPress event passes us a KeyAscii argument that contains the ASCII value of the character the user is trying to enter. You can modify that character by changing the value of the KeyAscii argument inside the KeyPress event. To cancel a character you simply change the KeyAscii argument to zero, which is the equivalent of `Chr$(0)` or `vbNullChar`, and therefore has the effect of entering nothing.

In our txtConvert_KeyPress event, we use a `Select Case` statement to handle the incoming characters. We enable the Backspace character (to allow editing) and the numerals 0 through 9 by including their ASCII values in a Case expression that takes no action. All other characters are caught by the Case Else clause, which cancels them by setting the KeyAscii argument to 0. This ensures that the value in the txtConvert TextBox is always within the domain of values we are able to convert to Roman numerals.

We have now created everything required by our CommandButton's Click event procedure to use Excel to convert the contents of the txtConvert TextBox into an equivalent Roman numeral. The cmdConvert_Click event that accomplishes this feat is shown in Listing 23-14.

Listing 23-14   The cmdConvert_Click Event Procedure

```
Private Sub cmdConvert_Click()

    Dim bError As Boolean
    Dim xlApp As Excel.Application
    Dim lConvert As Long
    Dim sErrMsg As String

    ' Coerce the text box value into a long.
    ' Val is required in case it is empty.
    lConvert = CLng(Val(txtConvert.Text))

    ' Don't do anything unless txtConvert contains
    ' a number greater than zero.
    If lConvert > 0 Then

        ' The maximum number that can be converted
        ' to Roman numeral is 3999.
        If lConvert <= 3999 Then
```

```
            Set xlApp = New Excel.Application
            lblResult.Caption = _
                xlApp.WorksheetFunction.Roman(lConvert)
            xlApp.Quit
            Set xlApp = Nothing

        Else
            sErrMsg = "The maximum number that can be converted"
            sErrMsg = sErrMsg & " to a Roman numeral is 3999."
            bError = True
        End If

    Else
        sErrMsg = "The minimum number that can be converted"
        sErrMsg = sErrMsg & " to a Roman numeral is 1."
        bError = True
    End If

    If bError Then
        MsgBox sErrMsg, vbCritical, "Error"
        txtConvert.SetFocus
        txtConvert.SelStart = 0
        txtConvert.SelLength = Len(txtConvert.Text)
    End If

End Sub
```

Before we go into a detailed discussion of the cmdConvert_Click event procedure, we present a working example of the form in Figure 23-24. If you have been following along with the example in your own copy of VB6, simply press F5 to start the application. Because the form is the only object in the project it displays automatically. If you select the *File > Make ConvertToRoman.exe* menu you generate a standalone executable file that can be run by simply double-clicking it from Windows Explorer.

One of the first things you'll notice about the cmdConvert_Click event procedure is the vast majority of it has nothing to do with automating Excel. This is an important point. It often requires a significant amount of preparation on the part of the automating application to ensure Excel runs without error when it is finally started.

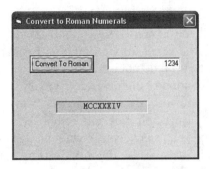

FIGURE 23-24 The completed convert to Roman Numerals dialog

The first thing the cmdConvert_Click event procedure does is to verify that the input from the txtConvert TextBox is within the bounds that can be handled by the Excel Roman function. The number to be converted to a Roman numeral must be greater than zero and less than or equal to 3999. If the number entered is out of bounds, an error message is displayed to the user, and the user is sent back to the txtConvert TextBox to try again.

If the number to be converted is within bounds, the event procedure creates an instance of Excel and goes to work. Using Excel to convert a whole number into a Roman numeral requires merely four lines of code (not counting variable declarations), but it illustrates several of the most important points to follow when automating Excel from VB6:

1. Wherever possible, start your own instance of Excel using the `Set xlApp = New Excel.Application` syntax. Hijacking an existing instance of Excel using `GetObject` should be avoided at all costs. You have no idea what the user is doing in any existing instance of Excel and therefore you can't be sure you won't cause them to lose data. Excel allows you to run multiple instances of itself on the same machine without any trouble at all, so design your applications to create and use their own private instance of Excel.

2. Always fully qualify all references to Excel objects you use, ultimately tying all of them back to the Excel Application object you created. If you don't do this you will often create separate implicit global references to objects within the instance of Excel you are automating. This makes it difficult or impossible to close your instance of Excel when you are finished with it.

3. When you are finished with your instance of Excel, be sure to explicitly call the `xlApp.Quit` method on the Excel Application object. Setting the Excel Application object variable to Nothing is not good enough. If you do not explicitly quit the instance of Excel you started, it may continue running even after your VB6 application has exited.

In addition, you can't help but notice that you never saw Excel when running this example. This is because when an instance of Excel is created via automation it is invisible by default. In the "Standard EXE—Creating a Front Loader for Your Excel Application" section later in the chapter, we demonstrate not only how to make an automated instance of Excel visible, but how to turn it over to the user and completely exit the VB6 application that started it, leaving that instance of Excel running for the user.

Finally, if you are expecting any add-ins or other auto-loaded files to be open when you create an instance of Excel via automation you will be disappointed. An instance of Excel created via automation does not load any add-ins selected in the *Tools > Add-Ins* list nor does it load any files located in auto-start directories like XLStart. If your application depends on these files being loaded along with Excel, you need to write the code to open them yourself.

Using a VB6 EXE Front Loader for Your Excel Application

A VB6 EXE front loader has the unique ability to examine the configuration of a user's computer without failing from the lack of any other program that your Excel application might depend on. If your Excel application will be distributed widely and/or run on hardware and software over which you have no control, the front loader can verify that everything required to run your application is in place prior to starting Excel, running your application, and exiting.

A VB6 EXE front loader can also create an instance of Excel and start your application in it without triggering any of Excel's macro security features. With a VB6 EXE front loader you never need to be concerned about the user disabling your application by setting macro security to high.

A VB6 EXE front loader can also be used as a security mechanism, for your application. The Excel *File > Open* password is the only truly strong password Excel has to offer. But you need to allow your users to open your Excel application to use it. A VB6 EXE front loader neatly solves this problem by allowing you to compile all of the *File > Open* passwords required to run your application into a VB6 EXE. This VB6 EXE can then open the

Excel files required by your application without ever exposing their passwords to VBA's weak project protection.

NOTE Any password stored as a literal string in any application is vulnerable to an experienced programmer with a Hex editor. Therefore, if you want your passwords to be truly secure, you must store them in an encrypted format and use a procedure to decrypt them just before they are required by your code. But keep in mind that simply compiling your passwords into a VB6 EXE front loader eliminates the ability of probably 99% of hackers to break into your application. Adding an encryption layer might increase this to 99.9%. For the vast majority of real-world applications, adding an encryption layer is simply not worth the effort.

COM Add-ins

Ever since VBA was added to Excel 5.0 we've been able to develop applications in Excel by creating add-in workbooks. Word, Access, and PowerPoint had their own application-specific add-in architectures. In Office 2000, Microsoft created a new add-in architecture, called a COM Add-in, common to all Office applications and the VBIDE. This section explains how to create COM add-ins using Visual Basic 6. Chapter 25, "Writing Managed COM Add-ins with VB.NET," explains how to achieve similar results using VB.NET.

A "Hello World" COM Add-in

An add-in architecture has four basic requirements:

- A mechanism for telling the host application the add-in exists.
- A mechanism for the host application to call a procedure in the add-in when the add-in is loaded, usually during the application's start-up processing. At this point, the add-in creates its menus, toolbar buttons, and/or shortcut keys.
- A mechanism for raising events that the add-in can respond to.
- A mechanism for the host application to call a procedure in the add-in when the add-in is unloaded, usually during the application's shutdown processing.

For Excel add-ins, we can either put the add-in file in the XLStart folder or use the *Tools > Add-Ins* dialog to select the add-in file and mark it as installed. When Excel starts up, it sees the add-in, opens the file, and runs the startup procedure. For workbook-based add-ins Excel calls the special Auto_Open procedure on startup, and prior to shutting down it calls the special Auto_Close procedure. Both procedures are placed in a standard VBA module. A workbook-based "Hello World" add-in looks like Listing 23-15.

Listing 23-15 A "Hello World" Add-in Using Auto_Open in a Standard Module

```
'Run when the addin is loaded
Sub Auto_Open()
    MsgBox "Hello World"
End Sub


'Run when the addin is closed
Sub Auto_Close()
    MsgBox "Goodbye World"
End Sub
```

When the VBIDE was introduced in Excel 97, every workbook was given a ThisWorkbook class module, within which we could write code to respond to a number of workbook-related events, including Workbook_Open and Workbook_BeforeClose. These event procedures are also called when Excel opens and closes an add-in workbook. Listing 23-16 shows a "Hello World" add-in that uses workbook events.

Listing 23-16 A "Hello World" Add-in Using Workbook Events in the ThisWorkbook Module

```
'Run when the addin is loaded
Private Sub Workbook_Open()
    MsgBox "Hello World"
End Sub


'Run when the addin is closed
Private Sub Workbook_BeforeClose(Cancel As Boolean)
    MsgBox "Goodbye World"
End Sub
```

Both the Auto_Open and Workbook_Open methods continue to work in all recent versions of Excel, and which one to use is a matter of personal preference.

COM add-ins work on a principle similar to workbook-based add-ins. The only additional complication is that they require VB6 (or VB.NET) to develop them and require you to implement an interface in your VB project that exposes the startup and shutdown procedures Excel calls.

To create a "Hello World" COM add-in in VB6, select the Addin project type from the New Project dialog. This creates a new COM Add-in project called MyAddin with a default form and a Designer class called Connect. Change the project name to HelloWorld, remove the default form, and delete all the existing code from the Connect class. The Add-in Designer is the COM add-in equivalent of Excel's ThisWorkbook class. It handles all the communication between Excel and the COM add-in. It has a simple UI that allows us to set the add-in's properties, such as its title, description, and which Office application it targets, as shown in Figure 23-25, where we've completed it for our Hello World example. We cover the dialog's options in more detail later.

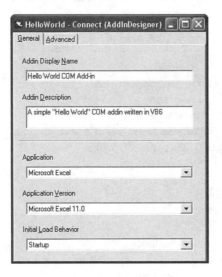

FIGURE 23-25 The completed add-in designer dialog

Excel's ThisWorkbook class gives us a Workbook object that has the Open and BeforeClose events that we use for our startup and shutdown code. The Add-in Designer class equivalents are the AddinInstance object and OnConnection and OnDisconnection events, shown in Figure 23-26.

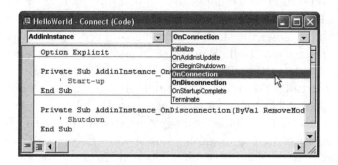

FIGURE 23-26   The AddinInstance object and events

Listing 23-17 uses these two events for our "Hello World" COM add-in.

Listing 23-17   A "Hello World" COM Add-in

```
'Run when the addin is loaded
Private Sub AddinInstance_OnConnection( _
        ByVal Application As Object, _
        ByVal ConnectMode As _
            AddInDesignerObjects.ext_ConnectMode, _
        ByVal AddInInst As Object, _
        custom() As Variant)

    MsgBox "Hello World"
End Sub


'Run when the addin is unloaded
Private Sub AddinInstance_OnDisconnection( _
        ByVal RemoveMode As _
            AddInDesignerObjects.ext_DisconnectMode, _
        custom() As Variant)

    MsgBox "Goodbye World"
End Sub
```

The only difference between these events and the events in a workbook-based add-in is that these two events have many more parameters, which we describe in the "The AddinInstance Events" section later in the chapter. To build the add-in, save all the project files and click *File > Make HelloWorld.DLL* from the VB6 menu. Now when you start Excel you should see the "Hello World" message box. Close Excel and the "Goodbye World" message box appears.

The first thing you want to do now is turn off this COM add-in. All the Office applications have a COM Add-Ins dialog to enable or disable COM add-ins, but it is not included on any of the default menus or toolbars. To add it, right-click anywhere over the toolbar area, choose *Customize*, select the *Commands* tab, and find *COM Add-Ins...* halfway down the list in the Tools category. Drag this command and drop it onto any of Excel's menus or toolbars. Figure 23-27 shows the COM Add-Ins dialog with our add-in selected. The add-in can be temporarily disabled by removing the check mark from beside its entry in this dialog, or it can be permanently disabled by selecting its entry and clicking the *Remove* button.

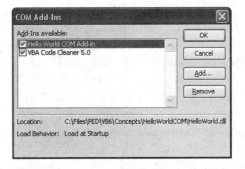

FIGURE 23-27   The COM Add-Ins dialog

If you are using Excel 2007, you can reach this dialog by choosing *Office Button > Excel Options > Add-Ins*. Next, select the *COM Add-Ins* entry from the *Manage* drop-down on the lower right side of the resulting Excel Options dialog and click the Go button.

The Add-in Designer

Excel's *Tools > Add-Ins* dialog is actually a simple UI for workbook-based add-ins that manages the following two registry keys (where the 11.0 indicates the version of Office):

- HKEY_CURRENT_USER\Software\Microsoft\Office\11.0\ Excel\Add-in Manager
- HKEY_CURRENT_USER\Software\Microsoft\Office\11.0\ Excel\Options

The first key lists the full path of any add-in workbooks that are not in Excel's Library folder (that is, where we've used the Browse button to locate the add-in) and are not installed—they just appear as unselected entries in the *Tools > Add-ins* list. The second key contains a number of OPENx values that contain the full path and filename for all add-in workbooks that are installed (selected in the *Tools > Add-ins* list). These registry entries are covered in more detail in Chapter 29, "Providing Help, Securing, Packaging, and Distributing." When Excel starts up, it looks for OPENx entries in the Excel\Options key, opens those workbooks and calls any Auto_Open and/or Workbook_Open procedures they contain.

To check for installed COM add-ins, Excel looks in the registry to see if there are any keys below HKEY_CURRENT_USER\Software\ Microsoft\Office\Excel\Addins. Each COM add-in creates a key below that with the ProgID of its Add-in Designer class, having the form <Project Name>.<Designer Name>. In our case, the key is called HelloWorld.Connect. Within that key are a number of registry entries that directly correspond to the options on the Designer form, shown in Figure 23-25 earlier. When the project is compiled and the DLL registered, the Designer writes its registry values into the HKEY_CURRENT_USER key (commonly referred to using its acronym HKCU) to install the add-in for the current user. The values within a COM add-in's registry key are described in the following sections.

General Tab

Add-in Display Name

This is the name displayed in Excel's *Tools > COM Add-ins* dialog box. It is stored in the registry in the *FriendlyName* value.

Add-in Description

Excel does not display the description anywhere. If writing a COM add-in that targets the VBIDE, the description is shown in the VBE's Add-in Manager dialog when the add-in in selected. It is stored in the registry in the *Description* value.

Application

This is a drop-down list of all the installed applications that can be extended using COM add-ins. The selection in this list determines which key is used for the registry entries, such as

- **Excel**—HKCU\Software\Microsoft\Office\Excel\Addins
- **Word**—HKCU \Software\Microsoft\Office\Word\Addins
- **VBIDE**—HKCU \Software\Microsoft\VBA\VBE\6.0\Addins

Application Version

This is a drop-down list of all the installed versions of the selected application. This setting determines which top-level registry key is used to store the settings for the COM add-in. The observant reader might have noticed that when we built our "Hello World" COM add-in previously, it was immediately working in all versions of Excel higher than Excel 2000. This is because the application version is ignored for COM add-ins that target Office applications. When writing COM add-ins that target the VBIDE, the version number (6.0) is included in the destination registry key. However, we have yet to see anything other than version 6.0 of the VBIDE, so this difference is probably academic.

Initial Load Behavior

This is a drop-down list containing four choices that control whether and how Excel loads our add-in. The choice is stored in the *LoadBehavior* value and can be one of the following:

- *Startup,* **value = 3**—The add-in is loaded every time Excel starts. This is the most common load behavior setting.
- *None,* **value = 0**—The add-in is not loaded and does not appear in the *Tools > COM Add-ins* dialog. This option would be selected if the COM Add-in is to be installed for all users. See "Installation Considerations" later in the chapter for more details.

- *Load on Demand*, **value = 9**—The add-in is loaded the first time one of its menu items is clicked. It is highly unusual for this value to be set within the Designer.
- *Load at Next Startup Only*, **value = 16**—The add-in is loaded the first time Excel is started after the add-in is installed, so it can add its menu items permanently to Excel's command bars. Once loaded, Excel changes this value to 9 (Load on Demand), so it is loaded the first time one of its menu items is clicked. See the "Command Bar Handling" section later in the chapter for more details.

Advanced Tab

Satellite DLL Name

The COM add-in architecture was designed to allow easy localization. This means that instead of storing the text of the add-in's name and description in the registry, we can store those strings in a resource table in a separate DLL. We can then use a standard Windows resource editor to translate the text into localized versions of the DLL. In the Designer form, we type in the resource IDs instead of the name and description and provide the name of the DLL containing the resource table in this field (stored as *SatelliteDLLName* in the registry). When Excel needs to show the Display Name in the *Tools > COM Add-ins* dialog, it should recognize that a resource DLL is being used and extract the display name from the resource table. Unfortunately, Excel doesn't check for the resource DLL and always displays the meaningless resource ID instead. A satellite DLL works correctly for add-ins targeting the VBIDE.

Registry Key for Additional Add-in Data and Add-in Specific Data

When a COM add-in is installed, we have the option of writing additional entries in the registry. These fields specify the entries to write and the registry key where those entries will be written. They are most often used if the COM add-in is to be installed for all users. See the "Installation Considerations" section next for more details.

Installation Considerations

A COM add-in is an ActiveX DLL that needs to be registered on the computer before it can be used. Registration is performed by a program called regsvr32.exe, usually found in the C:\Windows\System32 directory. The easiest way to register a COM add-in DLL manually is to right-click the DLL, choose *Open With...* from the shortcut menu, and browse to the regsvr32.exe file. You can also use the *Add...* button on Excel's COM Add-ins dialog and browse to the DLL. A final alternative is to use a setup program to automatically register any ActiveX DLLs it installs.

All these methods call a special function within the DLL, telling it to write whatever registry entries it requires to work. For COM add-ins, the Designer ensures this includes the registry entries required to get the COM add-in working with Excel. The Designer, however, only writes the entries required to install the add-in for the current user—that is, under the HKEY_CURRENT_USER section of the registry.

Excel also allows add-ins to be installed for all users of the machine. As well as looking within the HKCU section, it also looks in the same path of the HKEY_LOCAL_MACHINE section (often referred to as HKLM). If we want our add-in to be installed for all users, we have to set the Designer's *Initial Load Behavior* to None and use the Advanced tab to add our own registry entries, as shown in Figure 23-28. Note that the *LoadBehavior* value is a DWORD type, while the other two are strings.

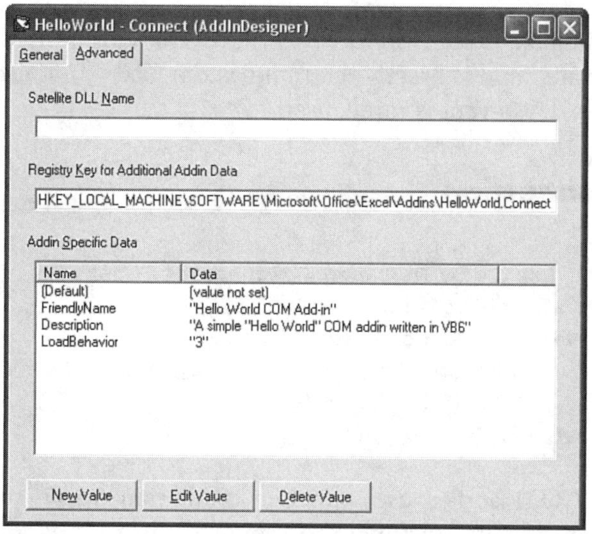

FIGURE 23-28   Advanced tab entries for an all-user installation

COM add-ins installed in this way do not appear in the COM Add-ins dialog and can only be uninstalled by deleting their registry entries. They also obviously require access to the HKLM section of the registry, which is usually only granted to people in the Power Users or Administrators network groups. Members of the basic Users group are not able to install (or uninstall) the add-in to this location.

The AddinInstance Events

Now that we've created, installed, and tested a simple "Hello World" COM add-in, it's time to take a more detailed look at how Excel interacts with the COM add-in using the Designer's code module. During the life of an Excel session, Excel communicates with us by raising events through the Designer's AddinInstance object in exactly the same way that it raises events through the Workbook object of a workbook's ThisWorkbook code module. These events are listed in the following sections in the order in which they're fired during a typical Excel session.

Initialize

```
Private Sub AddinInstance_Initialize()
```

The Initialize event is fired when the COM add-in's Designer class is first instantiated and is exactly the same as the Class_Initialize event of a class module. This event is rarely used.

OnConnection

```
Private Sub AddinInstance_OnConnection( _
    ByVal Application As Object, _
    ByVal ConnectMode As _
            AddInDesignerObjects.ext_ConnectMode, _
    ByVal AddInInst As Object, _
    custom() As Variant)
```

Every COM add-in uses the OnConnection event, which is raised by Excel during its startup processing, when a demand-loaded add-in is loaded or when the add-in is enabled in the COM Add-ins dialog. This is the equivalent of the VBA Auto_Open or Workbook_Open procedures and should be used to initialize the project, set up menu items, and so on. This event should not display any forms or show any message boxes.

The `Application` parameter is a reference to the host's Application object, that is, Excel.Application in our case. Most add-ins store this reference in a global variable to provide access to the application's properties, methods, and events.

The `ConnectMode` tells us when the add-in was started, either `ext_cm_Startup` (as Excel started) or `ext_cm_AfterStartup` (when a demand-loaded add-in is loaded, or from the COM Add-in dialog).

The `AddInInst` parameter is the Excel COMAddin object that refers to this COM add-in. We use this object to get the add-in's ProgID to use when setting up our menu items (see the "Command Bar Handling" section later in the chapter). The AddInInst object also allows us to expose the functions in our add-in to VBA, by including the line

```
AddInInst.Object = Me
```

in the OnConnection procedure. Any Public properties and methods we include in the Designer class can then be called from VBA using code like

```
'Run the SomeSub() procedure in the Hello World COM Addin
Application.COMAddins("HelloWorld.Connect").Object.SomeSub
```

The `custom()` parameter allows the COM add-in host application to send extra information to a COM add-in. For Excel, the first element of the `custom()` array is used to tell us how Excel was started: 1 = Opened from the user interface, 2 = Opened as an embedded object, 3 = Opened through automation.

OnStartupComplete

```
Private Sub AddinInstance_OnStartupComplete( _
    custom() As Variant)
```

Excel raises the OnConnection event within its startup processing when it encounters a COM add-in to load. The OnStartupComplete event is raised after Excel has completed its startup processing, just before returning control to the user. This is the place to display any forms you want to show on startup, such as "Thanks for Installing" or "Did You Know?" dialogs. In practice, it is rarely used.

OnAddInsUpdate

```
Private Sub AddinInstance_OnAddInsUpdate( _
    custom() As Variant)
```

The OnAddInsUpdate event is raised whenever another COM add-in is loaded or unloaded (though we're not told which, or whether it's just been loaded or unloaded). We've never seen it used.

OnBeginShutdown

```
Private Sub AddinInstance_OnBeginShutdown( _
    custom() As Variant)
```

The OnBeginShutdown event is raised when Excel starts its shutdown processing. It is not called if the add-in is unloaded using the COM Add-ins dialog. We've never seen it used.

OnDisconnection

```
Private Sub AddinInstance_OnDisconnection( _
    ByVal RemoveMode As _
        AddInDesignerObjects.ext_DisconnectMode, _
    custom() As Variant)
```

The OnDisconnection event is raised when Excel shuts down or when the add-in is unloaded using the COM Add-ins dialog. This procedure is where you should put your add-in's shutdown code, such as removing menus, for example.

The RemoveMode parameter tells us why the add-in is being unloaded, either ext_dm_UserClosed (unloaded using the COM Add-ins dialog) or ext_dm_HostShutdown (Excel is shutting down).

Terminate

```
Private Sub AddinInstance_Terminate()
```

The Terminate event is fired when the COM add-in Designer class is destroyed and is exactly the same as the Class_Terminate event of a class module. It's rare to see this event used.

Command Bar Handling

Using Command Bar Event Hooks

In Chapter 8, "Advanced Command Bar Handling," we explained the difference between using the CommandBarControl OnAction property to call our procedures and using class modules to hook the CommandBarButton Click event or the CommandBarComboBox Change event. When creating command bars for COM add-ins, we have to use the event-hook method for all our controls. It would be a good idea to reread that section of Chapter 8, but to summarize, we need to do the following:

- Give all our menu items the same Tag property, to uniquely identify them as belonging to our add-in.
- Give each menu item a unique Parameter property, to identify them in code.
- Have a class module containing a WithEvents declaration for a CommandBarButton (and/or CommandBarCombobox).
- In the class's CommandBarButton_Click event procedure, confirm that the Tag is set to ours and then call the procedure appropriate to the Parameter value.
- When setting up our menus, create a new instance of the class for each combination of ID and Tag that we use. If we're not using any built-in menu items, we would only need a single instance of the class.

CommandBar Architecture

In the OnConnection event, we always re-create our menus and set up the event hooks. In the OnDisconnection event, we always remove them. We need to store the visibility, docked state, and position of our command bars before removing them and make sure they're added back in the same state. Even though we're removing our menu items in the OnDisconnection event, it is good practice to add them with the `temporary` parameter set to True. The outline of the architecture for implementing COM add-in command bars is shown in Listing 23-18.

Listing 23-18   Implementing COM Add-In CommandBar Architecture

```
'Run when the addin is loaded
Private Sub AddinInstance_OnConnection( _
    ByVal Application As Object, _
```

23. EXCEL AND VISUAL BASIC 6

```
    ByVal ConnectMode As _
            AddInDesignerObjects.ext_ConnectMode, _
    ByVal AddInInst As Object, _
    custom() As Variant)

    'Store a reference to the application object
    Set gxlApp = Application

    'Always create our menu items
    CreateMenus

    'Set up our event hooks
    HookMenus

End Sub

'Run when the addin is unloaded
Private Sub AddinInstance_OnDisconnection( _
    ByVal RemoveMode As _
            AddInDesignerObjects.ext_DisconnectMode, _
    custom() As Variant)

    'Always remove our menus
    RemoveMenus

    'Tidy up our application reference
    Set gxlApp = Nothing

End Sub
```

Custom Toolbar Faces

A COM add-in does not have a worksheet handy to store the pictures and masks that we need for custom toolbar faces. Instead, we store the bitmaps in a resource file within the COM add-in project and use LoadResPicture to retrieve the image when needed. See the "Adding a Resource File to Your Project" section later in this chapter. For Excel 2002 and 2003, we set the Picture and Mask directly, but Excel 2000 gives us more of a problem. When stored in resource files, the bitmaps lose the transparency that we could give them when they were stored in a worksheet. When we Copy/PasteFace the picture onto an Excel 2000 toolbar and disable the button, the image usually turns into an unidentifiable gray blob. This can be worked around by using API calls to create a transparent bitmap during the Copy/Paste procedure and is documented in Microsoft KB article 288771 at http://support.microsoft.com/?kbid=288771.

The Paste Special Bar COM Add-in

In Chapter 8, we used a Paste Special command bar to demonstrate the concept of hooking command bar button events. The workbook is called PasteSpecialBar.xls and is located on the CD in the *Concepts\Ch08 – Advanced Command Bar Handling* folder. To demonstrate a working temporary menu architecture in a COM add-in and the use of custom toolbar faces, we converted the workbook to a COM add-in. The code for it can found in the *Concepts\Ch23 – Excel and Visual Basic 6\PasteSpecialBarVB6* folder. The READ_ME module lists the changes that were made to convert the Excel add-in to a COM add-in, while each module lists the changes required in the module header. The changes are summarized here:

- Use the Designer and OnConnection/OnDisconnection instead of Auto_Open / Auto_Close.
- Add a global variable to store a reference to the Excel.Application object and use that variable whenever referring to any of Excel's global objects.
- Remove all the code for the table-driven command bar builder, replacing it with a procedure to add the toolbar buttons individually.
- Copy the custom toolbar images to a resource file and use them instead of the PastePicture module.
- Add the MCopyTransparent module to handle copying transparent bitmaps for Excel 2000.
- Change the values of a few of the global variables so the Excel add-in and COM add-in can coexist in Excel.
- Modify a few minor references to ThisWorkbook.

It is interesting to note that the only change required to the add-in's payload of performing the Paste Special was to prefix `CommandBars` and `Selection` by our global Application object variable. If you're still unsure of the differences and similarities between Excel and COM add-ins, open both versions of the Paste Special Bar and compare them. Both add-ins do exactly the same things in exactly the same ways, using the same module and procedure names, except where noted in the comments.

Why Use a COM Add-in?

We already mentioned that while the details are slightly different between COM add-ins and Excel add-ins, the concepts are the same, and the code in them can be almost identical. That begs the question "Why bother?" In this section we discuss the primary reasons for building Excel applications as COM add-ins.

Improved Code Security

The code contained in Excel workbooks is notoriously easy to break into. Tools are readily available on the Internet that can crack (or simply remove) the VBProject protection password. If your add-in contains sensitive information or intellectual property that you'd prefer remained hidden, consider creating it as a COM add-in. Because COM add-ins are distributed as DLLs compiled to machine code, the source code is never included. While it is theoretically possible to decompile a VB6 DLL, it is extremely difficult and impractical to do.

Code security works in both directions. Workbook-based add-ins, especially those with unprotected VBA projects, are susceptible to code-injection by macro viruses or malicious users. Compiling your code into a COM add-in removes any possibility of this happening to your application.

Multi-Application Add-ins

A COM add-in can contain multiple Designer classes, each handling the connection to a different Office application. Imagine an Insert Customer Details add-in, which displayed a form allowing you to select a customer from a central database and then inserted the customer's name, address, and/or telephone number in the current place in the document. By including multiple Designer classes in the add-in, we could easily make the add-in available to all the Office applications. Each class's OnConnection event would be used to add a standard menu item to the host application's command bars, with the Click event handled by a single class. When clicked, it would display the form and would only branch into application-specific code when the Insert button was clicked to insert the selected details into the cell, paragraph, field, presentation, or Web page.

Exploiting Separate Threading

One of the more interesting things about COM add-ins is that each one is given its own execution thread. The vast majority of Excel and VBA is single-threaded, meaning that VBA code stops when Excel is working (such as showing one of its dialogs) and vice versa. COM add-ins don't have this limitation. A COM add-in can initialize a Windows timer callback, tell Excel to display a dialog (or Print Preview or whatever), and then continue processing (in the callback function) while Excel is still displaying the dialog. This allows us to prepopulate the dialog, watch what the user is doing within the dialog, respond to it, and even change the layout of the dialog itself.

It should be noted that Excel is not designed to be used like this, and these techniques are in no way supported by Microsoft. Attempting to call into Excel's object model while it is displaying a form may or may not work, often depending on whether we're simply reading properties (usually reliable) or trying to get Excel to do something (which usually fails), but if it works in one case, it will always work in that case.

As an example, the *\Concepts\Ch23 – Excel and Visual Basic 6\ToolsRefSize* folder on the CD contains a COM Add-in that uses this technique to modify the labels at the bottom of the VBE's *Tools > References* dialog to display the filename of the referenced project using two lines with word wrap.

Automation Add-ins

When initially introduced in Excel 2000, the functions contained in COM Add-ins could not be called directly from a worksheet. In Excel 2002, Microsoft added **Automation Add-ins** to solve that problem. An automation add-in is nothing more than an ActiveX DLL that contains at least one public function.

Creating the IfError Automation Add-in

Chapter 5, "Function, General, and Application-Specific Add-ins," introduced the IFERROR() function, written as a VBA user-defined function. In Chapter 27, "XLLs and the C API," it is rewritten in C, for best performance. We can re-create this as an automation add-in to improve on the performance of the VBA version, though not as much as the C version. This can be thought of as a compromise; improving the performance but keeping the simplicity of the Visual Basic code. Automation add-ins can only be used in Excel 2002 or higher. To create the add-in, start a new empty ActiveX DLL project in VB6, change the project name to ProExcel and the class name to Functions, and then copy in the code shown in Listing 23-19.

Listing 23-19   The IFERROR User-Defined Function

```
Public Function IFERROR(ByRef ToEvaluate As Variant, _
                        ByRef Default As Variant) As Variant
    If IsError(ToEvaluate) Then
        IFERROR = Default
    Else
        IFERROR = ToEvaluate
    End If
End Function
```

Note that this is **exactly** the same code as Listing 5-3 in Chapter 5. Click on *File > Make ProExcel.DLL* to build the DLL.

Using the IfError Automation Add-in

Open Excel 2002 or higher, click the *Tools > Add-ins* menu and click the *Automation...* button. The Automation Servers dialog lists every registered ActiveX DLL on the PC, including the one we just created. Select the entry for ProExcel.Functions and click OK. It should now appear selected in the *Tools > Add-ins* dialog list. Click OK to return to the worksheet. The function can now be called directly from the worksheet just like any other function:

```
=IFERROR(A1/B1,0)
```

Accessing the Excel Application Object from an Automation Add-in

When creating anything more than a trivial function, we usually want to use some of Excel's worksheet functions within the procedure. Alternatively, we may need to mark our function as volatile, so it is called every time the sheet is recalculated. Both of these situations require us to interact with the Excel Application object.

If we add one of the same Add-in Designer classes to our project that we used for COM Add-ins, Excel calls the OnConnection event when the DLL is first loaded, giving us the opportunity to store a reference to the Application object. We can then use that object within our functions. The following steps explain how to set it up:

1. Within the ProExcel project, click on *Project > Add Add-in Class* to add a new Add-in Designer to the project. If that menu isn't

available, click on *Project* > *Components* and put a tick next to the *Add-in Class* item on the *Designers* tab to make it available.

2. In the Designer dialog, set the *Application* to Microsoft Excel and the *Initial Load Behavior* to None.

3. We don't need to provide a name or description, but change the Designer's class name in the Properties window from AddInDesigner1 to AppFunctions and set *Public* to True (ignoring the warning).

4. Click on *Project* > *References*, select Microsoft Excel from the list to create a reference to the Excel object library, and then copy in the code shown in Listing 23-20.

Listing 23-20   The AppFunctions Code, Using the Excel Application within Automation Addins

```
Option Explicit

'Reference to the Excel application
Dim mxlApp As Excel.Application

'Called when the automation addin is loaded
Private Sub AddinInstance_OnConnection( _
    ByVal Application As Object, _
    ByVal ConnectMode As _
          AddInDesignerObjects.ext_ConnectMode, _
    ByVal AddInInst As Object, _
    custom() As Variant)

    'Store away a reference to the Application object
    Set mxlApp = Application
End Sub

'Volatile function to return VB's Timer value
Public Function VBTimer() As Double
    mxlApp.Volatile True
    VBTimer = Timer
End Function

'Function to count how many items in Source lie between
'Min and Max
Public Function CountBetween(ByRef Source As Range, _
      ByVal Min As Double, ByVal Max As Double) As Double

    'If we get an error, return zero
```

```
On Error GoTo ErrHandler

'Count the items bigger than Min
CountBetween = mxlApp.WorksheetFunction _
               .CountIf(Source, ">" & Min)

'Subtract the items bigger than Max, giving the number
'of items in between
CountBetween = CountBetween - mxlApp.WorksheetFunction _
               .CountIf(Source, ">" & Max)

Exit Function

ErrHandler:
    CountBetween = 0
End Function
```

5. Close Excel, compile the DLL, and install the ProExcel.AppFunctions add-in by selecting it from the *Tools > Add-ins > Automation* list.

The first time any of the functions in the add-in is used, Excel loads the add-in, calls the OnConnection procedure, and then calls the function. In the OnConnection procedure, we store a reference to the Excel Application object, which we use within the functions contained in the class.

Practical Examples

ActiveX DLL—Using a Resource File to Load Icons

Adding a Resource File to Your Project

To use resource files in VB6, you must have the **VB6 Resource Editor** add-in loaded in the VB6 IDE. If this add-in is loaded you see a *Project > Add New Resource File* menu item on the VB6 menu bar. If you do not see this menu, choose *Add-Ins > Add-In Manager* from the VB6 menu. This displays the Add-In Manager dialog shown in Figure 23-29.

The list of available add-ins likely is different on your system, but locate and select the VB6 Resource Editor add-in and then check the *Loaded/Unloaded* and *Load on Startup* check boxes under the *Load Behavior* section of the Add-In Manager dialog. Once the Resource Editor add-in is installed, make sure your project has been saved and then choose

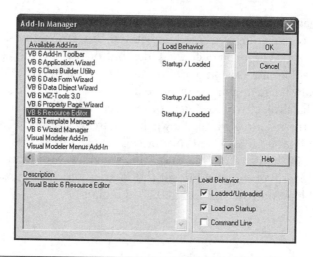

FIGURE 23-29   The Add-In Manager dialog

Project > Add New Resource File from the VB6 menu to add a resource file to your project. You are prompted with the rather confusingly named Open a Resource File dialog shown in Figure 23-30.

This dialog can be used to either add an existing resource file to your application or create a new resource file. We'll create a new resource file.

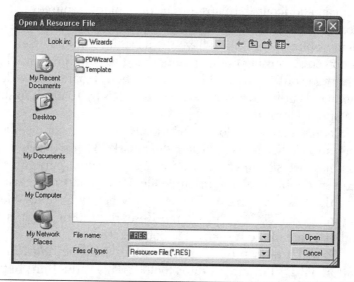

FIGURE 23-30   The Open a Resource File dialog

23. EXCEL AND VISUAL BASIC 6

Navigate to the folder where your project is saved and type the name you want to give your resource file, without the .RES extension, into the File name box. When you click the Open button, the Resource Editor tells you the file does not exist and ask whether you want to create the file. Click the Yes button and an empty resource file is created and added to your project.

The Project window view of our ActiveX DLL project containing the Icons.res resource file is shown in Figure 23-31. As we see later in this example, the CResourceProvider class is used to expose the bitmaps contained in the resource file to outside callers as StdPicture objects. This is the object type required to set the Picture and Mask properties for command bar controls in Excel 2002 and higher.

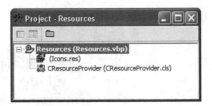

FIGURE 23-31   The Resources ActiveX DLL project

Adding Bitmaps to the Resource File

You can add icons, bitmaps, or custom binary resources to your resource file. Since our resources will be used as command bar button icons we load them as bitmaps. Bitmaps have the advantage of being very simple. They can be created using nothing more than the Paint program that ships with every copy of Windows. The only restriction is that bitmaps designed to be command bar button icons must be 16 pixels by 16 pixels in size to provide the optimal appearance.

In this section, we load two bitmaps into our resource file: a command bar button icon and its corresponding mask. We use the custom arrow icon and mask we saw in Chapter 8 for demonstration purposes. To begin the process, double-click the resource file in the VB6 Project window to open it in the Resource Editor. The currently empty resource file is shown in Figure 23-32. The top line in the Resource Editor displays the full path and filename of the resource file being edited.

To add a bitmap to the resource file, click the *Add Bitmap...* toolbar button on the Resource Editor toolbar. This is the third button from the right in Figure 23-32. The Resource Editor displays the Open a Bitmap File dialog shown in Figure 23-33.

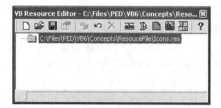

FIGURE 23-32   The empty Icons.res file opened in the Resource Editor

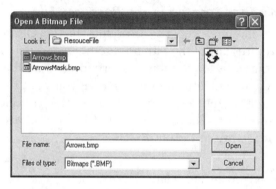

FIGURE 23-33   The Open a Bitmap File dialog

We already navigated to the folder containing the two bitmaps we want to load and selected the first one. As you can see, the Open a Bitmap File dialog displays a preview of the selected bitmap in its right pane. Click the Open button to add the selected Arrows.bmp bitmap to the resource file. The result is shown in Figure 23-34.

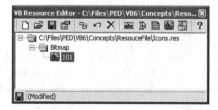

FIGURE 23-34   The Icons.res resource file containing one bitmap

The Resource Editor has given our bitmap the default ID property value 101. You can modify this value by selecting the bitmap resource and clicking the *Edit Properties...* toolbar button. In the next section we use an enumeration to map these numeric IDs onto something more recognizable.

Repeat the previous steps to load the ArrowsMask.bmp resource into the resource file. This is given the default ID property value 102. Click the *Save* icon to save the resource file and then close the Resource Editor using the x-close button in the upper-right corner. An important point to note is that adding bitmaps to your resource file copies them into it. The original bitmap files you selected are still in their original location, and they are not connected to the copies contained in the resource file in any way.

Using Bitmaps Located in the Resource File

A simple, one-line property procedure in the CResourceProvider class module returns any of the bitmap resources stored in our resource file. All that is required is to pass this property procedure the enumeration value (discussed later) identifying the resource you want to retrieve. The property procedure returns a reference to the specified resource as an StdPicture object. The entire contents of the CResourceProvider class module are shown in Listing 23-21.

Listing 23-21 The Icon Property Procedure

```
Public Enum resIcon
    resIconArrows = 101
    resIconArrowsMask = 102
End Enum

Public Property Get Icon(ByVal uName As resIcon) As StdPicture
    Set Icon = LoadResPicture(uName, vbResBitmap)
End Property
```

As you can see, we used an enumeration to provide human readable names for the numeric ID property values that identify the bitmap resources in our resource file. Inside the property procedure the VB6 LoadResPicture function is used to retrieve the specified resource from the resource file. The first argument to this function specifies which resource should be returned. The second argument specifies the type of the resource to be returned using a built-in VB6 constant, in this case vbResBitmap.

Once you compile the Resources ActiveX DLL, any program capable of consuming an StdPicture object can use the resources it contains. To demonstrate the use of this DLL we rework the Load Picture and Mask example from Chapter 8 to retrieve its icons from the Resource DLL rather than loading them from individual bitmap files on disk. The procedures shown in Listing 23-22 build a command bar with a single button that uses our custom arrow icon and mask loaded from the Resources DLL.

Listing 23-22   Loading a Custom Icon from a Resource File into a Command Bar Button

```
Public Sub CreateBar()

    Dim cbrBar As CommandBar
    Dim ctlControl As CommandBarButton
    Dim objRes As Resources.CResourceProvider

    ' Make sure any previously created version of our demo
    ' command bar is deleted.
    RemoveBar

    ' Create an instance of the resource provider.
    Set objRes = New Resources.CResourceProvider

    ' Create a toolbar-type command bar.
    Set cbrBar = CommandBars.Add("Demo", msoBarTop, False, True)
    cbrBar.Visible = True

    ' Add the command bar button control.
    Set ctlControl = cbrBar.Controls.Add(msoControlButton)
    ' Load the foreground bitmap file.
    ctlControl.Picture = objRes.Icon(resIconArrows)
    ' Load the mask bitmap file.
    ctlControl.Mask = objRes.Icon(resIconArrowsMask)

End Sub

Public Sub RemoveBar()
    On Error Resume Next
    CommandBars("Demo").Delete
End Sub
```

The complete code for this example can be found in the LoadPictureAndMask.xls workbook located on the CD in the \Concepts\Ch23 –Excel and Visual Basic 6 folder. Note that this example only works in Excel 2002 or later, and you must have registered the Resources ActiveX DLL on your computer. Notice how the Picture and Mask properties of our command bar button in this example are now retrieving their contents from the custom resource file in our DLL rather than from bitmap files stored on disk.

23. EXCEL AND VISUAL BASIC 6

Standard EXE—Creating a Front Loader for Your Excel Application

An Excel application that utilizes a VB6 front loader begins with the execution of a VB6 EXE file rather than Excel. Excel will be run only if the conditions verified by the front loader application are met by the system on which the application is executing.

We covered the reasons for using a VB6 EXE front loader in your Excel application in the "Using a VB6 EXE Front Loader for Your Excel Application" section earlier in the chapter. In this section, we focus on how to build a VB6 EXE front loader. In this example, we assume the task of our front loader is to verify that Word and Outlook are correctly installed on the user's computer before running our PETRAS time sheet application.

Start by opening VB6 and choosing Standard EXE as the project type in the New Project dialog. In addition to the default Form object that VB6 provides with this project type, add one standard code module to your project using the *Project > Add Module* menu. Rename your default objects to the names shown in Table 23-2.

Table 23-2 Front Loader Application Object Names

Default Object Name	New Object Name
Project1	FrontLoader
Form1	FWarning
Module1	MEntryPoints

Next, set a reference to the Microsoft Excel Object Library using the *Project > References* menu. Finally, save your project's files to a common folder.

When you create a Standard EXE project, the default startup object is the Form object added by default when the project is first created. This is not how we want our front loader application to work. Instead, we add a special procedure to the MEntryPoints module called Sub Main. We then modify our project's properties so that Sub Main is run on startup rather than the default form. Open the MEntryPoints module and create the Sub Main stub procedure shown in Listing 23-23.

Listing 23-23 The Sub Main Stub Procedure

```
Public Sub Main()
    ' Code goes here later.
End Sub
```

We must now tell the project that we want our Sub Main procedure to be executed when our VB6 EXE is first run. This is accomplished using the *Project > FrontLoader Properties...* menu. As shown in Figure 23-35, we changed the *Startup Object* setting in the upper-right corner of the Project Properties dialog *General* tab from FWarning (the default) to Sub Main.

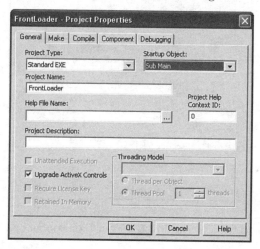

FIGURE 23-35 Changing the Startup Object to Sub Main

Next, we build the FWarning form. This form is relatively uncomplicated. Its only purpose is to notify the user that the validation check failed prior to the front loader exiting without starting the Excel application. First we set the properties of the Form object itself as shown in Table 23-3.

Table 23-3 FWarning Property Settings

Property Name	Setting
BorderStyle	3 – Fixed Dialog
Caption	Startup Validation Failed
Icon	PetrasIcon.ico (supplied on the CD)
StartupPosition	2 – Center Screen

23. EXCEL AND VISUAL BASIC 6

Rather than displaying the bland, default VB6 icon for our final FrontLoader.exe file, we want to use the same branded PETRAS icon that we used in our FWarning form. To accomplish this, select the *Project > FrontLoader Properties...* menu and then select the *Make* tab in the Project Properties dialog. As shown in Figure 23-36, select FWarning from the *Icon* drop-down in the upper-right corner. This makes the icon defined for the FWarning dialog be the icon displayed for our FrontLoader.exe file in Windows Explorer and by any shortcuts we create to it.

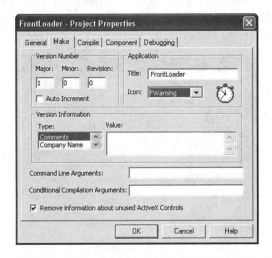

FIGURE 23-36   Modifying the icon displayed by our FrontLoader.exe file

The FWarning form itself contains only two controls: a cmdOK CommandButton to dismiss the form and a static Label control to display the validation failure message to the user. The form should look similar to the one displayed in Figure 23-37.

FIGURE 23-37   The layout of the FWarning dialog

The Click event of the cmdOK button is displayed in Listing 23-24. It simply unloads the form once the user has read the message.

Listing 23-24 The cmdOK_Click Event Procedure

```
Private Sub cmdOK_Click()
    Unload Me
End Sub
```

The decision whether to run the Excel application or display the FWarning message is made by the code logic controlled by the Sub Main procedure. Our Word and Outlook validation logic is encapsulated in two separate functions. One determines whether Word is installed and operating correctly and the other does the same for Outlook.

Two functions are required because the two applications behave differently when automated. When your application creates an instance of Word via automation you always get a brand new hidden instance of Word, regardless of whether the user is currently running Word. With Outlook, the result of creating an instance via automation depends on whether the user already has Outlook open. If Outlook is already open, you get a reference to the currently open instance. If Outlook is not open, you get a new hidden instance.

For our validation logic, we use the most rigorous test possible, whether or not we can actually get a reference to running instances of Word and Outlook. The functions that perform the validation for the status of Word and Outlook are shown in Listing 23-25.

Listing 23-25 The bWordAvailable and bOutlookAvailable Functions

```
Private Function bWordAvailable() As Boolean
    Dim wdApp As Object
    ' Attempt to start an instance of Word.
    On Error Resume Next
        Set wdApp = CreateObject("Word.Application")
    On Error GoTo 0
    ' Return the result of the test.
    If Not wdApp Is Nothing Then
        ' If we started Word we need to close it.
        wdApp.Quit
        Set wdApp = Nothing
        bWordAvailable = True
    Else
        bWordAvailable = False
```

23. EXCEL AND VISUAL BASIC 6

```
        End If
End Function

Private Function bOutlookAvailable() As Boolean
      Dim bWasRunning As Boolean
      Dim olApp As Object
      On Error Resume Next
          ' Attempt to get a reference to a currently open
          ' instance of Outlook.
          Set olApp = GetObject(, "Outlook.Application")
          If olApp Is Nothing Then
              ' If this fails, attempt to start a new instance.
              Set olApp = CreateObject("Outlook.Application")
          Else
              ' Otherwise flag that Outlook was already running
              ' so that we don't try to close it.
              bWasRunning = True
          End If
      On Error GoTo 0
      ' Return the result of the test.
      If Not olApp Is Nothing Then
          ' If we started Outlook we need to close it.
          If Not bWasRunning Then olApp.Quit
          Set olApp = Nothing
          bOutlookAvailable = True
      Else
          bOutlookAvailable = False
      End If
End Function
```

The first thing to notice is that we use late binding in both of these validation functions. If we didn't use late binding and tried to run our front loader on a computer that didn't have Word or Outlook installed, the front loader would fail before it ever got the chance to run the validation functions. This is the result of using a compiled versus an interpreted programming language. When you run an Excel VBA application, its code is validated by the VBA runtime on a module-by-module basis. The code in any given module is only validated when some code in that module is called or referenced by the application. Therefore, if you had a reference to an invalid component in your Excel VBA project, but the code making use of this reference was confined to one module and no code in that module was ever called or referenced by your application, that module would never be loaded by the VBA runtime, its code would never be validated, and your application would not experience a runtime error. In a fully compiled application, all references are validated on startup. Therefore, if you reference a component that doesn't exist on the machine where your fully compiled application is run, the application fails immediately.

The second thing to notice is the difference between the bWordAvailable() and bOutlookAvailable() functions. Since automating Word is straightforward, we simply attempt to create a new instance of Word, and the result of the function is determined by whether we succeed or fail. The logic of the Outlook validation function is exactly the same, but due to the different behavior of Outlook the implementation is different.

Rather than simply attempting to create a new instance of Outlook, we first need to try the GetObject function. This returns a reference to any instance of Outlook the user is currently running. If this succeeds, it satisfies our validation test. If the user can successfully run Outlook we can be reasonably sure that our application can as well. If we are not able to locate a currently running instance of Outlook, we then try to create a new one using the CreateObject function. If this succeeds we have validated the availability of Outlook, but we have also started a new instance of Outlook that needs to be closed before our function exits.

This is the point where the logic of the bWordAvailable() and bOutlookAvailable() functions diverge. If the bWordAvailable() function succeeds, then we know we have started a new instance of Word that we must close before the function exits. If the bOutlookAvailable() function succeeds, whether we need to close Outlook on exit depends on whether our function actually started the instance of Outlook that validated its availability or whether we simply attached to an instance of Outlook the user was already running. If the GetObject function retrieved our reference to Outlook, then we leave it alone. If CreateObject retrieved our reference to Outlook, then we must close that instance of Outlook before we exit. This is the purpose of the bWasRunning variable in the bOutlookAvailable() function. It tells us whether we need to close Outlook at the end of the function.

Now that we've seen all the pieces of the front loader application, let's look at the procedure that brings them all together. As we stated earlier, the Sub Main procedure is the controlling procedure in our front loader application. It calls the validation functions and examines their results. Based on those results it determines whether to run our Excel application or display a warning message and exit. The Sub Main procedure is shown in Listing 23-26.

Listing 23-26   The Sub Main Procedure

```
Public Sub Main()

    Dim bHasWord As Boolean
    Dim bHasOutlook As Boolean
    Dim xlApp As Excel.Application
    Dim wkbPetras As Excel.Workbook
    Dim frmWarning As FWarning

    ' Verify that we can automate both Word and Outlook on this
    ' computer.
    bHasWord = bWordAvailable()
    bHasOutlook = bOutlookAvailable()

    If bHasWord And bHasOutlook Then
        ' If we successfully automated both Word and Outlook,
        ' load our Excel app and turn it over to the user.
        Set xlApp = New Excel.Application
        xlApp.Visible = True
        xlApp.UserControl = True
        Set wkbPetras = xlApp.Workbooks.Open(App.Path & _
                                        "\PetrasAddin.xla")
        wkbPetras.RunAutoMacros xlAutoOpen
        Set wkbPetras = Nothing
        Set xlApp = Nothing
    Else
        ' If we failed to get a reference to either Word or
        ' Outlook, display a warning message to the user and
        ' exit without taking further action.
        Set frmWarning = New FWarning
        frmWarning.Show
        Set frmWarning = Nothing
    End If

End Sub
```

There are two things in particular to note about the way the Sub Main procedure handles Excel. First, after creating an instance of Excel and making it Visible, it sets the Excel Application object's UserControl property to True. This makes the Excel Application behave as if it had been started directly by the user rather than via automation.

Second, after opening the PETRAS application workbook, it runs the RunAutoMacros method of the Workbook object. This is because the Auto_Open procedure does not run automatically when an Excel workbook is opened via automation. Therefore, we need to run it ourselves.

As mentioned previously in the "An Excel Automation Primer" section, an Excel Application object created via automation will also not open any add-ins specified in the *Tools > Add-Ins* list nor any workbooks located in startup folders like XLStart. If your application relies on any secondary workbooks of this nature you have to add code to your front loader to open these workbooks (and run their startup procedures if required).

Summary

There are many good reasons to take advantage of the additional power afforded by VB6 in your Excel VBA applications. VB6 ActiveX DLLs provide code protection, the ability to use the more powerful VB6 Forms in your Excel projects, excellent support for object oriented programming, support for resource files, and a number of miscellaneous features not available in VBA, including the ClipBoard, Printer, and Screen objects. VB6 EXE applications allow you to automate Excel, initiating your application from VB6 rather than Excel. This allows you to create components such as front loaders. These can scan the operating environment for you prior to startup to ensure that your application has the required resources available, allow you an extra level of VBA code protection by compiling your *File > Open* passwords in an EXE file, and let you start Excel and run your VBA application without triggering any VBA macro security features.

The COM add-in architecture allows you to create a single add-in that can target any (or many or all) of the applications in the Office suite. The code contained in a COM add-in is virtually impossible to decompile, making it a much more secure medium than standard Excel add-ins, in terms of protecting intellectual property.

There is very little difference between the code contained in a COM add-in and an Excel add-in. In many cases, the code can be copied from Excel and run virtually unchanged in the COM add-in. Both the Paste Special Bar and the PETRAS time sheet add-in examples demonstrated that an Excel add-in can be converted to a COM add-in relatively easily.

EXCEL AND VB.NET

In 2002, Microsoft released the first version of its development suite **Visual Studio.NET (VS.NET)** together with the **.NET Framework**. Since then, Microsoft has released new versions of the Framework and development suite in quick succession. Microsoft has strongly indicated that .NET is the flagship development platform now and for the foreseeable future.

Visual Basic.NET (VB.NET) is part of VS.NET, and despite its similarity in the name with **Classic VB** (VB6), the two have little in common. VB.NET is the successor to Classic VB and as such it provides the ability to create more technically modern solutions, a large group of new and updated controls, and a new advanced IDE. Moving from Classic VB to VB.NET is a non-trivial process, primarily because VB.NET is based on a new and completely different technology platform.

Excel developers also face the situation where applications created with the new .NET technology need to communicate with applications based on the older COM technology, for example, VB.NET applications communicating with Excel. Because Excel is a COM-based application it cannot communicate directly with code written in .NET. All .NET code that communicates with Excel must cross the .NET → COM boundary. This is important to keep in mind because it is a challenge to manage and can have significant performance implications.

In the first part of this chapter, VB.NET is introduced along with the .NET Framework. The second part of this chapter focuses on how we can automate Excel with VB.NET. Finally we cover ADO.NET, which is used to connect to and retrieve data from various data sources. ADO.NET is the successor to classic ADO on the .NET platform.

To provide a better understanding of VB.NET, we develop a practical solution, the **PETRAS Report Tool.NET**. This solution is a fully functional Windows Forms based reporting tool. It retrieves data from the PETRAS SQL Server database and uses Excel templates to present the reports.

VB.NET, ADO.NET, and the .NET Framework are book-length topics in their own right; what we examine here and in the two following chapters merely scratches the surface. At the end of this chapter you find some recommended books and online resources that provide additional detail on these subjects.

.NET Framework Fundamentals

The .NET Framework is the core of .NET. Before we can develop or run any .NET-based solutions, the Framework must be installed and available. The Framework provides the foundation for all .NET software development. The .NET Framework is also responsible for interoperability between .NET solutions and COM servers and components. This topic is covered later in the chapter. For the purposes of our discussion, we can think of the .NET Framework architecture as consisting of two major parts:

- **A huge collection of base class libraries and interfaces**—This collection contains all the class libraries and interfaces required for .NET solutions. **Namespaces** are used to organize these class libraries and interfaces into a hierarchical structure. The namespaces are usually organized by function, and each namespace usually has several child namespaces. Namespaces make it easy to access and use different classes and simplify object references. We discuss namespaces in more detail when presenting VB.NET later in this chapter.
- **Common Language Runtime (CLR)**—This is the engine of the .NET Framework, and it is responsible for all .NET base services. It controls and monitors all activities of .NET applications, including memory management, thread management, **structured exception handling (SEH)**, **garbage collection**, and security. It also provides a **common data type system (CTS)** that defines all .NET data types.

The rapid evolution of the .NET Framework is reflected in the large number of versions available. Different Framework versions can coexist on one computer, and multiple versions of the Framework can be run side-by-side simultaneously on the same computer. However, an application can only use one version of the .NET Framework at any one time. The Framework version that becomes active is determined by which version is required by the .NET-based program that is loaded first. A general recommendation is to only have one version of the Framework installed on a target computer.

Because there are several different Framework versions in common use and we may not be able to control the version available on the computers we target, we need to apply the same strategy to the .NET Framework as we do when targeting multiple Excel versions: Develop against the lowest Framework version we plan to target. Of course there will also be situations that dictate the Framework version we need to target, such as corporate clients who have standardized on a specific version.

As of this writing, the two most common Framework versions are 2.0 and 3.0. Both versions can be used on Windows XP, and version 3.0 is included with Windows Vista and Windows Server 2008. Visual Studio 2008 (VS 2008) includes both of these Framework versions as well as version 3.5. By providing all current Framework versions, VS 2008 makes it easy to select the most appropriate version to use when building our solutions. Versions 3.0 and 3.5 of the .NET Framework are backward compatible in a similar manner as the latest versions of the Excel object libraries.

The .NET Framework can run on all versions of Windows from Windows 98 forward, but to develop .NET-based solutions we need to have Windows 2000 or later. If we plan to target Windows XP or earlier we need to make sure the desired version of the .NET Framework is installed on the target computer, because these Windows versions do not include the Framework preinstalled. All versions of the Framework are available for download from the Microsoft Web site and can be redistributed easily. To avoid confusion, we only use version 2.0 of the .NET Framework in this chapter and the next.

NOTE The standard version 3.5 .NET Framework distribution is around 197MB in size. Microsoft provided a lighter edition of about 25MB in size that can be installed on the target computers instead. To find out more about this edition, search for the phrase ".NET Framework Client Profile Deployment Guide" at www.microsoft.com.

Visual Basic.NET

With VS.NET we can create Web applications, server applications, database applications, console applications, Windows desktop applications, setup and deployment projects, and much more. VS.NET ships with the following programming languages: Visual C#, VB.NET, and Visual C++.

VB.NET is distributed in all VS.NET packages as well as in a standalone version. However, not all capabilities are present in all distributions.

You need to select the version of VB.NET that fits your requirements best. Table 24-1 shows the capabilities related to Excel development and the distributions in which they are available.

Table 24-1 Available Tools in Different Versions of VS.NET

	VB.NET Express	VS.NET Standard	VS.NET Professional
Automate Excel	✓	✓	✓
Shared Add-in Template (To create managed COM add-ins with.)		✓	✓
Office templates			✓
Visual Studio Tools for Office System (VSTO)			✓

For a full comparison among the versions, see http://msdn.microsoft.com/en-us/vs2008/products/cc149003.aspx. If you just want to try out VB.NET you can download the free Express Edition from Microsoft's Web site. VS.NET Professional is required if you plan to develop **managed COM add-ins** and VSTO solutions. It is also required to follow the discussions here and in the next two chapters.

VB.NET was the first version of VB that broke backward compatibility badly enough that you could not even open a project created in an earlier version of VB. If you have non-trivial Classic VB projects that you would like to transfer to VB.NET, the best choice is to create them from scratch in VB.NET. Microsoft has some tools to ease the transition, but for larger VB projects they cannot do all the work. On the other hand, you may also consider keeping your Classic VB solutions for as long as it is still possible to run them on the Windows versions your solution targets. VB.NET is the first BASIC language version that fully supports object oriented programming (OOP). It means that with VB.NET we can fully utilize encapsulation, inheritance, and polymorphism.

Code that targets the .NET runtime is described as **managed code** while code that cannot be hosted by the .NET runtime is described as **unmanaged code**. **Assemblies** are the binary units (*.DLL or *.EXE) that contain the managed code. Since it is common that one .NET assembly contains only one binary unit, it is safe to refer to .NET-based DLL files as assemblies.

The Visual Studio IDE

The **Visual Studio IDE (VS IDE)** is shared by all .NET programming languages. The VS IDE is a complex development environment, even for developers who are very familiar with the Classic VB IDE. Figure 24-1 shows the VS IDE with a simple VB.NET Windows Forms project open.

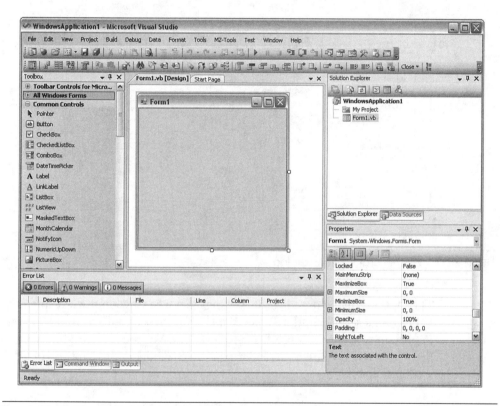

FIGURE 24-1 The Visual Studio .NET IDE

When you first run VS.NET, you are prompted to select a development category for VS.NET to use in customizing the environment. If your previous experience is with Classic VB or VBA, you will probably want to allow VB.NET to be your first choice of programming language. In this case, choose the **Visual Basic Development Settings**. The VS IDE is also highly customizable by the user, but before beginning to customize it you should learn the basics using the default configuration.

General Configuration of the VS IDE

After launching the VS IDE, you should change some general configuration settings for the development environment. Start by selecting *Tools > Options...* from the menu. This displays the Options dialog shown in Figure 24-2.

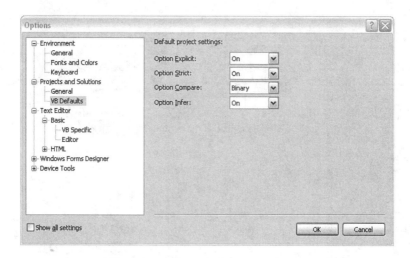

FIGURE 24-2 The general Options dialog

The Options dialog organizes its settings in a tree view on the left side. The *VB Defaults* section under *Projects and Solutions* contains four of the more important settings for VB.NET development. We recommend that you set them exactly as shown in Figure 24-2. A detailed description of each setting follows:

- **Option Explicit**—Determines whether VB.NET requires us to declare all variables before using them.
- **Option Strict**—Turning on this setting disallows late binding (to improve performance), implicit data type conversion, and provides **strong typing** (strict use of type rules with no exceptions).
- **Option Compare**—Specifies the default method used for string comparisons. It can either be Binary (case-sensitive) or Text (case-insensitive). The default value is Binary, which provides the same text comparison behavior as Classic VB. See Chapter 3, "Excel and VBA Development Best Practices," for more information.
- **Option Infer**—When this setting is turned on it allows us to omit the data type when declaring a variable and instead let VB.NET

identify ("infer") the data type. Listing 24-1 shows a simple example. The right-hand value tells the compiler the data type is an Integer. Declaring a variable and giving it a value at the same time in this manner is fully supported in VB.NET.

Listing 24-1   Omitting the Data Type When Declaring a Variable

```
Dim iCountRows = 225
```

When working with **VB.NET solutions** (a solution can contain one or more projects), these settings can be overridden at the code module level. This means, for example, that if we really need to use late binding in one code module we can modify the Option Strict setting at the top of that code module. Listing 24-2 shows how to turn off the Option Strict setting and also change comparisons to Text.

Listing 24-2   Changing Settings at the Code Module Level

```
Option Compare Text
Option Strict Off
```

Adding line numbers to your code can make many development tasks easier, the debugging process in particular. To activate this option, expand the *Text Editor* section in the Options dialog and select the *Basic* section below it. Check the option *Line numbers* and then close the dialog.

Next we make screentips and keyboard shortcuts available in the IDE. Choose *Tools > Customize...* from the menu. This displays the Customize dialog shown in Figure 24-3. Check the two options *Show ScreenTips on toolbars* and *Show shortcut keys in ScreenTips* and then close the dialog.

The final setting is to make various docked windows in the IDE hide themselves when they are not being used. This provides us with a workspace that is not cluttered with open windows not relevant to the current context.

1. Click on the window you want to hide so it gets the focus.
2. On the *Window* menu click on the option *Auto Hide* or click on the pushpin icon on the title bar for the window.
3. Repeat these steps for every window that you want to auto hide.

When an auto-hidden window loses focus, it automatically slides back to its tab on the edge of the IDE.

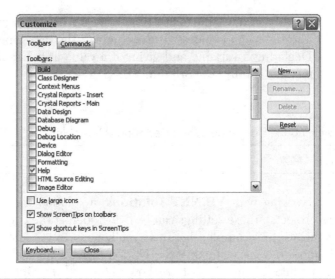

FIGURE 24-3 The Customize dialog

Creating a VB.NET Solution

We create a new VB.NET project by selecting the *File > New Project...* from the menu. This displays the New Project dialog shown in Figure 24-4.

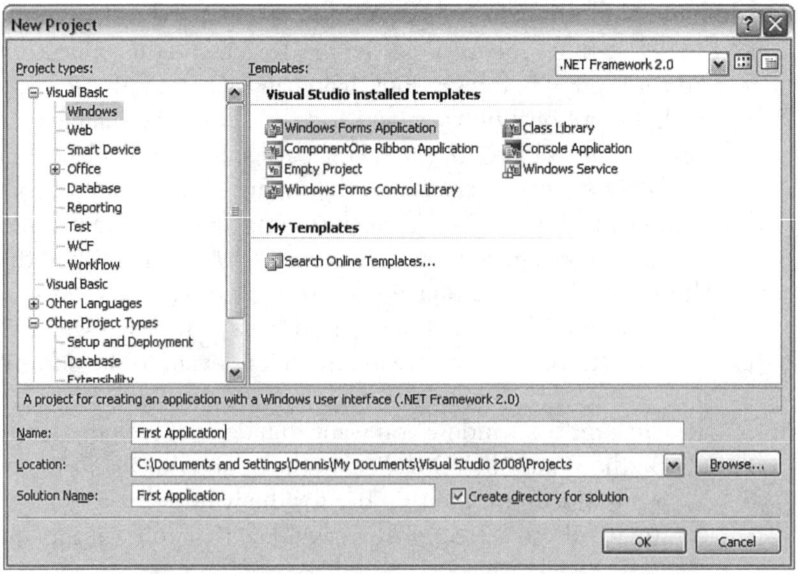

FIGURE 24-4 The New Project dialog

Since we are creating a Windows based-solution, select *Windows* in the *Project types* section and then select the *Windows Forms Application* template. We also select the version of .NET Framework to target using the combo box in the upper-right corner. Next, enter the name "First Application" in the *Name* box. By default, the solution name is the same as the name entered in the *Name* box, as shown in Figure 24-4. The solution name is also used to name the main folder of the project. Finally, click the OK button to create the solution.

The **Solution Explorer** window provides the workspace for working with files and projects inside VB.NET solutions. Figure 24-5 shows the workspace for our solution. A single Windows Form has been added to the solution and we have right-clicked on the form to display the shortcut menu containing the various actions available to perform on that object.

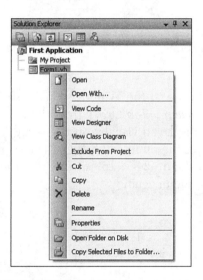

FIGURE 24-5 The Solution Explorer window

Windows Forms are the basic building block of many solutions. They provide us with a graphical user interface to which we can add controls. Windows Forms and all other Windows controls are contained in the `System.Windows.Forms` namespace. Windows Forms are in many ways identical to their counterpart Forms in Classic VB but are more modern and offer more properties to work with.VB.NET provides a large number of Windows controls for various purposes. However, use the new controls with good judgment. They exist to create a friendly user interface, not confuse the user.

Although VB.NET is designed to use Windows Forms controls, we can still use ActiveX controls. Therefore, if we own expensive third-party ActiveX controls, we can still use them in VB.NET. To add a control to a Windows Form, click the control's icon in the Toolbox and then drag and drop over the area on the form where you want the control to be placed. For our solution we add a label control, combo box, and two buttons to the Windows Form and resize the form itself. Figure 24-6 shows how the final Windows Form looks.

FIGURE 24-6 The Windows Form

Before we add code to the Windows Form, we set the tab order for the controls. Select *View > Tab Order* from the menu. The tab order for each control is now displayed visually on the form. Clicking on a control's tab number increases the number. Change the tab order so that it matches the order shown in Figure 24-7. To exit the tab order view, select *View > Tab Order* from the menu again.

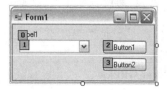

FIGURE 24-7 The tab order for the form

As a final step, we add code to the solution. Select *View > Code* from the menu. This opens the class module for the Windows Form. The first event we use is the Load event of the Windows Form. This is created by first selecting *(Form1 Events)* from the combo box in the upper-left corner of the module and then selecting *Load* from the combo box in the upper-right corner of the module. Listing 24-3 shows the code in the Load event.

Listing 24-3 The Code for the Load Event of the Windows Form

```
Private Sub Form1_Load(ByVal sender As Object, _
                       ByVal e As System.EventArgs) _
                       Handles Me.Load

      'Create and populate the array with names.
      Dim sArrNames() As String = {"Rob Bovey", _
                                   "Stephen Bullen", _
                                   "John Green", _
                                   "Dennis Wallentin"}
      With Me
          'The caption of the Form.
          .Text = "First Application"

          'The captions of the label and button controls.
          .Label1.Text = "Select the name:"
          .Button1.Text = "&Show value"
          .Button2.Text = "&Close"

          'Populate the combobox control with the list
          'of names.
          With .ComboBox1
              .DataSource = sArrNames
              .SelectedIndex = -1
          End With

      End With
End Sub
```

In this code, we create a string array, set values for various control properties, and then add the array as a data source for the combo box control. We use a single dimension array to populate the combo box with the list of names. It is a perfectly accepted practice to declare and initialize an array at the same time in VB.NET, as shown in Listing 24-3. When using this approach we do not need to specify the size of the array because this is inferred from the number of items within the scope of the curly brackets.

The next step is to get the selected value from the combo box and display it in a message box. Before doing that we need to import the namespace System.Windows.Forms into the code module, which gives us a shortcut to the .NET MessageBox class. Importing namespaces saves keystrokes each time we refer to objects that are part of the imported namespaces. It also makes our code easier to read and maintain by making it less verbose.

The `Imports` statements tell the compiler which namespaces the code uses. Usually we first set a reference to a namespace and then we import it to one or more code modules. Here we only do the latter because the `System` namespace is referenced by default in all new VB.NET solutions. This is because Visual Studio automatically adds a reference to the `System` namespace when a new VB.NET project is created. At the top of the Form's class module we add the `Imports` statement shown in Listing 24-4.

Listing 24-4   The Imports Statement

```
'To use the messagebox object.
Imports System.Windows.Forms
```

The namespace `Microsoft.VisualBasic` also belongs to the namespaces that are referenced by default in all new VB.NET solutions. This namespace is also globally imported, which means we do not need to import it into individual code modules to use it. From a practical standpoint this means we can use the well-known `MsgBox` function instead of its .NET variant. However, in Listing 24-5 we use .NET `MessageBox` class in the Click event for Button1, which displays the selected name in a message box.

Listing 24-5   Show Selected Name

```
Private Sub Button1_Click(ByVal sender As System.Object, _
                          ByVal e As System.EventArgs) _
                          Handles Button1.Click

    'Make sure that a name has been selected.
    If Me.ComboBox1.SelectedIndex <> -1 Then

        'Show the selected value.
        MessageBox.Show( _
            text:=Me.ComboBox1.SelectedValue.ToString(), _
            caption:="First Application")
    End If

End Sub
```

The final piece of the puzzle is to add a command to close (unload) the Windows Form in the Button2 Click event. Listing 24-6 shows the required code.

Listing 24-6   Unload the Windows Form

```
Private Sub Button2_Click(ByVal sender As System.Object, _
                          ByVal e As System.EventArgs) _
                          Handles Button2.Click
        Me.Close()
End Sub
```

To begin testing the application, we just have to press the F5 key. Figure 24-8 shows the First Application in action after we select a value in the combo box and then click the Show value button.

FIGURE 24-8   Our first application in action

Whenever we execute the application in the debugger, the VS IDE creates a number of new files, including an executable file for our application. These files are located in the ..*First Application\bin\Debug* folder. A working example of this solution can be found on the companion CD in the *Concepts\Ch24 - Excel & VB.NET\First Application* folder. If you just want to run the application without opening it in Visual Studio, the First Application executable file can be found in the *Concepts\Ch24 - Excel & VB.NET\First Application\First Application\bin\Debug* folder on the CD.

Structured Exception Handling

When an unexpected condition occurs in managed code, the CLR creates a special object called an **exception**. The exception object contains properties and methods that give detailed information about the unexpected condition. Because we deal with exceptions rather than errors in .NET development, we use the expression exception handling rather than error handling.

Exception handling covers the techniques used to detect exceptions and take appropriate actions after they are detected. **Structured exception handling (SEH)**, is the term used to describe how we implement exception handling in managed code. Although it is possible to use the Classic VB error handling approach in VB.NET, we strongly encourage the use of SEH because it gives us much better options for dealing with exceptions. SEH consists of the following building blocks:

- **Try**—We place the code we want to execute in this block. This code may create one or more exceptions.
- **Catch**—In this block we place the code that handles the exceptions. It is possible to place several Catch blocks within the same structure to handle different types of exceptions. Catch blocks are optional.
- **Finally**—Code placed in this block always is executed, which makes this block a perfect place for code to clean up and release references to objects like COM objects and ADO.NET objects. This block is also optional.
- **End Try**—Ends the SEH structure.

Listing 24-7 shows the skeleton structure of SEH in code. When we enter a Try statement in a code module, the VS IDE automatically adds the Catch block and End Try statement. The Finally block must be typed manually.

Listing 24-7 The Building Blocks of SEH

```
Private Function iDiscount(ByVal iPrice As Integer) As Integer

        Try
            'Do the calculation here.

        Catch ex As Exception
            'In case of any unexpected scenarios take
            'some action here, like a message to the user.

        End Try
End Function
```

Most of the namespaces in the .NET Framework class library include their own specific exception classes, which make it possible to catch them in separate `Catch` blocks. All built-in exception classes extend the built-in `System.Exception` class. `Catch` blocks are executed (or tested for execution) in the order in which they are coded. .NET works its way through the `Catch` blocks trying to find a matching exception type. Therefore the preferred approach is to implement the `Catch` blocks with more specific exception types first, followed by the `Catch` blocks with the more generic exception types. Listing 24-8 shows an example using two `Catch` blocks.

Listing 24-8   Using Several Catch Blocks and the Finally Block

```
Try
      frmSaveFile = New SaveFileDialog

      With frmSaveFile
          .Filter = "XML File|*.xml"
          .Title = "Save report to XML file"
          .FileName = sFileName
      End With

      dtTable.WriteXml(fileName:=sFileName)

      dtTable.WriteXmlSchema( _
            fileName:=Strings.Left(sFileName, _
          Len(sFileName) - 4) & ".xsd")

Catch XMLexc As Xml.XmlException

      MessageBox.Show(text:=sMESSAGENOTSAVEDXML, _
                      caption:=swsCaption, _
                      buttons:=MessageBoxButtons.OK, _
                      icon:=MessageBoxIcon.Stop)

Catch COMExc As COMException

      MessageBox.Show(text:= _
                      sERROR_MESSAGE & _
                      sERROR_MESSAGE_EXCEL, _
                      caption:=swsCaption, _
                      buttons:=MessageBoxButtons.OK, _
                      icon:=MessageBoxIcon.Stop)

Catch Generalexc As Exception
```

```
MessageBox.Show(text:=sMESSAGENOTSAVEDGENERAL, _
                caption:=swsCaption, _
                buttons:=MessageBoxButtons.OK, _
                icon:=MessageBoxIcon.Stop)

Finally

    frmSaveFile.Dispose()
    frmSaveFile = Nothing

End Try
```

The first `Catch` block handles any `XmlException` exceptions. The second block catches COM exceptions that might occur when working with COM servers like Excel. The final `Catch` block is generic and handles all other exceptions. The example also shows how we can use the `Finally` block to release an object. Listing 24-8 also shows how to use custom error messages to respond to each exception type.

During development we need to see the underlying technical details for all exceptions. In Listing 24-9 the previously customized end user messages have been replaced with the exception object and its method `ToString` in each `Catch` block. The `ToString` method gives a textual summary of the exception. You can also use the `GetBaseException` method to return the first exception in the chain.

Listing 24-9 Displaying Exception Descriptions

```
Catch XMLexc As Xml.XmlException

    MessageBox.Show(XMLexc.ToString())

Catch COMExc As COMException

    MessageBox.Show(COMExc.ToString())
    MessageBox.Show(COMExc.ErrorCode.ToString())

Catch Generalexc As Exception

    MessageBox.Show(Generalexc.ToString())
```

When VB.NET receives an exception from a COM server like Excel, it checks the **COM exception** code and tries to map that code to one of the

.NET exceptions classes. If this fails, which is the most common outcome, VB.NET throws a large and mostly unhelpful HRESULT message like the one shown in Figure 24-9.

System.Runtime.InteropServices.COMException (0x800A03EC): Exception from HRESULT: 0x800A03EC
at System.RuntimeType.ForwardCallToInvokeMember(String memberName, BindingFlags flags, Object target, Int32[] aWrapperTypes, MessageData& msgData)
at Excel.Names.Item(Object Index, Object IndexLocal, Object RefersTo)
at PETRAS_Report_Tool.NET.MExportExcel.bExport_Excel(DataTable dtTable, String sClient, String sProject, String sStartDate, String sEndDate) in C:\Documents and Settings\Dennis\My Documents\Visual Studio 2008\Projects\PETRAS Report Tool .NET\PETRAS Report Tool .NET\MExportExcel.vb:line 314

OK

FIGURE 24-9   The COM exception message

The line of code that generates this message is the first `MessageBox.Show` line under the COM exception block in Listing 24-9. COM exceptions are wrapped into generic `COMException` objects when .NET does not have a matching exception class for the HRESULT error generated by a COM component.

In SEH, it is possible to exit a `Try` block with the `Exit Try` statement. This statement can be placed either in the `Try` block or in any `Catch` block. Any code in a `Finally` block is still executed after the `Exit Try` statement.

Another option is to use nested `Try` structures. A nested SEH can be added either to the `Try` block or to a `Catch` block. When using nested exception handlers the **InnerException** property of the exception object becomes very important. It helps us determine the cause of the nested exception and allows us to obtain the chain of exceptions that led to that exception.

We can use the **Throw** statement to communicate exceptions to the calling code. `Throw` is usually used within a `Catch` block only if the exception is to be bubbled up the call stack. A `Throw` statement causes code execution to be intentionally interrupted. The `Throw` statement also allows us to create our own exceptions, but this topic is beyond the scope of this chapter.

Modules and Methods, Scope and Visibility

When we make a declaration at the module level (module here stands for module, class, or structure), the access level we choose determines the scope of the thing being declared. In VB.NET we can use the keywords `Public` and `Private`, which have the same scopes as in Classic VB, but VB.NET also provides the following additional keywords to specify module scope and visibility:

- **Friend**—A data member or **method** (function or subroutine) declared with the Friend modifier can be accessed from any part of the program containing the declaration. This is not a new keyword, as it is also available in Classic VB. However, if we do not explicitly include a scope in our declaration, then the default scope is Friend in VB.NET, while in Classic VB the default scope is Public.
- **Protected**—Data members or methods declared with Protected scope are only accessible from the module itself or from derived classes.
- **Protected Friend**—This scope is equivalent to the union of Protected and Friend access. A data member or method declared as Protected Friend is accessible from anywhere in the program in which the declaration occurs, or from any derived class containing the declaration.

Declare Variables and Assign Values

In VB.NET, we declare local variables using the keyword Dim, module-level variables using the keyword Private, solution-level variables using the keyword Friend, and public variables using the keyword Public. All .NET programming languages provide the option to declare variables and assign values to them at the same time.

The first two lines in Listing 24-10 show how we can declare variables and initialize them with values using one line of code. The third line creates three String variables without assigning any values to them. Since they don't have assigned values, these String objects are marked as unused local variables by the VS IDE. This is a result of the Option Strict setting being on. Good coding practice in .NET says that we should always assign known values to variables, even if they initially will not have any "real" values. Lines 4 through 6 show how we can achieve this in practice.

Listing 24-10 Declare Variables and Assign Values to Them

```
1   Dim sTitle As String = "PETRAS Report Tool"
2   Dim iPrice As Integer = 100
3   Dim sAddress, sCity, sCountry As String
4   Dim sName = String.Empty
5   Dim bReportStatus = Nothing
6   Dim iNumberOfRecords As Integer = Nothing
7   Dim iNumberOfColumns As Integer = dtTable.Columns.Count - 5
8   Dim iNumberOfRows As Integer = dtTable.Rows.Count - 1
9   Dim obDataArr(iNumberOfRows, iNumberOfColumns) As Object
```

Lines 7 and 8 in Listing 24-10 contain two variables that hold the number of columns and rows of a **DataTable** (an ADO.NET object covered later in this chapter). These two variables are then used as parameters to dimension the array of data type Object in line 9. The data type Object is the VB.NET counterpart to the data type Variant in Classic VB. An Object array behaves in roughly the same manner as a Variant array.

VB.NET also offers the ability to declare variables anywhere in the code. Listing 24-11 shows an example where we have declared a variable within a `Try` block in conjunction with a `For...Next` loop.

Listing 24-11 Block Scope Variable Declaration

```
Try

    For iCountRows As Integer = 0 To 9
        'Do the iteration.
    Next iCountRows


Catch ex As Exception

    MessageBox.Show(ex.ToString())


End Try
```

Block scope can also be achieved by declaring variables within `With...End With` blocks, `For...Next` blocks, and `Do...Loop` blocks. In Listing 24-12 we show a variable that is declared in a `Do...Loop`.

Listing 24-12 Block Scope within a Do...Loop

```
'Declaration of a variable with
'a block scope of Do...Loop.
Do
    Dim iMonth As Integer = 1
    'Other code goes here...
Loop
```

However, declaring variables using this method may cause unexpected problems. This is because the scope of variables declared in this manner is limited to the block in which they are declared. This means we cannot access these variables or use them outside that block. Code that uses this method can also be more difficult to debug and maintain. In general we should avoid this approach. Good coding practice suggests that all variables used within a method should be declared at the beginning of that method.

Creating New Instances of Objects

We can create new instances of objects in VB.NET using the same techniques as in Classic VB. The only difference is that we do not use the Set keyword in VB.NET. Listing 24-13 shows two methods of creating objects in VB.NET. The Nothing keyword is a way of telling the system that the variable does not currently have any value but still may use memory.

Listing 24-13   Declare and Instantiate Objects

```
'The classic approach.
Dim frmSaveDialog As SaveFileDialog = Nothing
frmSaveDialog = New SaveFileDialog

'.NET approach.
Dim frmSaveDialog As New SaveFileDialog
```

The .NET approach is singled out in the second example in Listing 24-13, which shows that we declare and set the variable to a new instance of the SaveFileDialog class with one line of code. Although the .NET approach may look attractive, we still recommend using the classic approach. This is also outlined as the best practice in Chapter 3.

Using the .NET approach can cause unwanted exceptions because of the block scoping of variables. For example, if we create a new instance of the SaveFileDialog component and we want to trap any exceptions that may occur (or we want to throw an exception), block scoping of the variable itself causes an exception. This is demonstrated in Listing 24-14, where we have declared and instantiated the frmSaveDialog object variable in the Try block. However, because the scope of this variable is limited to the Try block, the VS.IDE displays a compile error for the two lines of code inside the Finally block.

Listing 24-14   Using the .NET Approach

```
Sub Show_Save_Dialog()

    Try
```

```
        Dim frmSaveDialog As New SaveFileDialog
        frmSaveDialog.ShowDialog()


    Catch ex As Exception

    Finally

        frmSaveDialog.Dispose()
        frmSaveDialog = Nothing

    End Try

End Sub
```

To correct this problem, we modify the code to use the classic approach as shown in Listing 24-15. The `frmSaveDialog` variable can now be seen throughout the `Try` block, and it traps any exceptions that may occur.

Listing 24-15 Using the Classic Approach

```
Sub Show_Save_Dialog()

    Dim frmSaveDialog As SaveFileDialog = Nothing

    Try

        frmSaveDialog = New SaveFileDialog
        frmSaveDialog.ShowDialog()


    Catch ex As Exception

        MessageBox.Show(ex.ToString())

    Finally

        frmSaveDialog.Dispose()
        frmSaveDialog = Nothing

    End Try

End Sub
```

Using ByVal or ByRef

Unlike Classic VB, procedure arguments in VB.NET are passed ByVal by default **not** ByRef. If we do not explicitly specify procedure arguments as either ByVal or ByRef, the VB.NET default is ByVal. However, good practice states that we should always explicitly specify the keyword we want to use.

Using Wizards in VB.NET

Compared to the wizards in Classic VB, the wizards in VB.NET have been significantly improved. New wizards have also been added to the VS IDE. The advantage of using a wizard is that we get the desired result in a fast and reliable way without needing to have a deep understanding of the process. The wizard takes care of the details. The disadvantage of using a wizard is that the wizard works in "black box" mode, which means we do not have much control over the process. Developing real-world applications requires you to be in control and to understand your solutions inside and out. You can explore the wizards in the VS IDE, but for any non-trivial solution you should avoid them.

Data Types in VB.NET

Compared with Classic VB, some data types are new in VB.NET. Table 24-2 shows most of the VB.NET data types but not all of them.

Table 24-2 Data Types in VB.NET

Data Type	Size	Values
Boolean	2 bytes	True or False.
Short	2 bytes	-32,768 to 32,768.
Integer	4 bytes	-2,147,483,648 to 2,147,483,648.
Long	8 bytes	-9,223,372,036,854,775,808 to 9,223,372,036,854,775,808.
Decimal	16 bytes	It provides the greatest number of significant digits for a number.
Double	8 bytes	It provides the largest and smallest possible magnitudes for a number.

Table 24-2   Data Types in VB.NET

Data Type	Size	Values
String	Variable	A string can hold 0 to 2 billion Unicode characters.
Date	8 bytes	January 1, 0001 0:0:00 to December 31,9999 11:59:59.
Object	4 bytes	Point to any type of data.

As we can see in Table 24-2, the data type **Short** includes the interval -32,768 to 32,768, and the **Integer** data type now covers a much greater interval than it does in Classic VB. The Currency data type is no longer available in VB.NET. It has been replaced by the new **Decimal** data type, which can handle more digits on both sides of the decimal point. The Byte data type from Classic VB has no counterpart in VB.NET. The data type **Object** is the universal data type in VB.NET, taking the place of the Variant data type in Classic VB.

String Manipulation

As previously mentioned, whenever a new .NET solution is created the namespace `Microsoft.VisualBasic` is included by default. This provides access to the .NET versions of the well-known string functions in Classic VB. The .NET Framework also provides us with a `System.String` class to manipulate strings. However, using the old functions has no negative impact on solution performance, so using the old familiar functions is completely acceptable.

Using Arrays in VB.NET

The .NET Framework provides us with powerful new options for creating and using arrays and collections in VB.NET. There are two basic kinds of VB.NET arrays. Arrays that we declare as array variables of a specific data type by using parentheses after the variable name are normal arrays. We can also use the Array class, which provides us with a new array data type that offers methods for managing items in arrays as well manipulating arrays. Arrays in VB.NET inherit from the Array class in the System namespace, so methods of the Array class can also be used with normal arrays.

In this section, we discuss normal arrays along with some methods of the Array class. In VB.NET, all arrays are zero-based. This is important to keep in mind, especially when working with Excel objects or Classic VB code that may have 1-based arrays. We already showed one way to use an array in Listing 24-3, where we used an array to populate a combo box control. In Listing 24-16 we use the same approach to populate a list box control and then add the selected items to an array.

Listing 24-16 Populate an Array with Selected Items from a List Box

```
Private Sub Button1_Click(ByVal sender As System.Object, _
                          ByVal e As System.EventArgs) _
                          Handles Button1.Click

'Make sure that at least one item is selected.
If Me.ListBox1.SelectedIndex <> -1 Then

    'Grab the number of selected items.
    Dim iCountSelectedItems As Integer = _
        Me.ListBox1.SelectedItems.Count - 1

    'Declare and dimension the one-dimensional array.
    Dim sArrSelectedItems(iCountSelectedItems) As String

    'Populate the array.
    For iCountSelectedItems = 0 To iCountSelectedItems
        sArrSelectedItems(iCountSelectedItems) = _
        Me.ListBox1.SelectedItems(iCountSelectedItems).ToString()
    Next iCountSelectedItems

   'Show the number of items in the array.
    MessageBox.Show(CStr(sArrSelectedItems.GetLength(0)))

    'Show the lower bound of the array.
    MessageBox.Show(CStr(sArrSelectedItems.GetLowerBound(0)))

    'Show the upper bound of the array.
    MessageBox.Show(CStr(sArrSelectedItems.GetUpperBound(0)))

    'Iterate through the array and display each value.
    For iCountSelectedItems = sArrSelectedItems.GetLowerBound(0) _
                        To sArrSelectedItems.GetUpperBound(0)
        MessageBox.Show(text:= _
                  sArrSelectedItems(iCountSelectedItems).ToString())
    Next iCountSelectedItems

End If

End Sub
```

When working with arrays we should always specify which dimension we are targeting. Since we are working with a one-dimensional array in this example, the dimension we are targeting is zero.

One of the more resource-intensive processes in VB development is redimensioning arrays, so we should always look for ways to reduce or eliminate this process. Listing 24-16 shows how VB.NET allows us to do this easily. We first retrieve the number of selected list items and then declare and dimension the array all at once. Note that in Listing 24-16 we use the **GetLowerBound** and **GetUpperBound** methods to return the lower bound and upper bound index values for the array. Both these methods are part of the Array class. In some scenarios we may not know the bounds for an array initially, but we can get the necessary information later. Listing 24-17 shows how we can initialize an array after declaring it.

Listing 24-17 Declare an Array and Initialize It Later

```
Dim iNumberOfHouses() As Integer
...
...
iNumberOfHouses = New Integer() {10, 15, 20}
```

Listing 24-16 shows one way to iterate an array, but we could actually enumerate it as shown in Listing 24-18.

Listing 24-18 Enumerating an Array

```
Dim iNumberOfHouses() As Integer = {10, 15, 20}
Dim iItem As Integer

For Each iItem In iNumberOfHouses
    Debug.WriteLine(iItem)
Next iItem
```

The Array class also provides methods that allow us to manipulate the items in different ways. Among the more common actions we might want to perform on an array are reversing the order of items in the array, sorting the array, removing items from the array, returning specific array items, and copying items from one array to another. Listing 24-19 shows how to perform these operations using methods of the Array class.

Listing 24-19 Methods of the Array Object

```
Dim sArrProjects() As String = _
                {"Upgrade","Investment", "Maintenance"}

Array.Reverse(sArrProjects)

Array.Sort(sArrProjects)

Array.Clear(sArrProjects, 0, 1)

Dim sItem As String = sArrProjects.GetValue(1).ToString()

Dim sArrProjectsCopy(sArrProjects.GetLength(0)) As String

Array.Copy(sArrProjects, sArrProjectsCopy, _
                sArrProjects.GetLength(0))
```

The first example shows how to reverse the order of the items in an array. The second example sorts the array in ascending order. The third example shows how to delete the first item from an array. Note that deleting an item from an array in this manner does not resize the array or move any of the other items into new positions in the array.

To get a specific item value from an array you use the **GetValue** method, as shown in the fourth example. And as the final example shows, we can even copy one array to another using the Copy method. The last argument of this method allows us to specify the number of items to be copied. This can be a good alternative to the redimension approach when resizing an array. In this example we copy all items from the first array into the second array.

Next we demonstrate how to search for a value in an array using the **BinarySearch** method. This method is useful when you want to determine whether a specific value exists in an array. To use this method the items in the array must be sorted. The result of executing the BinarySearch method is an integer that represents the index number of the value you are searching for within the array. If the result is -1 the value you are searching for does not exist. If the value you are searching for exists more than once within the array, the index number of the last occurrence is returned.

Listing 24-20 shows how to use the BinarySearch method to locate the index number of an item in an array. There are also several other methods of the array object that allow us to find specific items and work with them in various ways.

Listing 24-20 The BinarySearch Method

```
Dim sArrProjects() As String = _
    {"Upgrade", "Investment", "Maintenance"}

Dim sSearchedValue As String = "Investment"

Array.Sort(sArrProjects)

Dim iSearchedIndex As Integer = _
    Array.BinarySearch(sArrProjects, sSearchedValue)

MessageBox.Show(CStr(iSearchedIndex))
```

A good alternative to the normal array is the **ArrayList** class, which is part of the System.Collection namespace. By using this class we can dynamically increase a list, hold several different data types in one list, manipulate the elements in a list, and manipulate ranges of elements in one operation. The ArrayList is something of a hybrid between the Array and Collection objects. In Listing 24-21 we demonstrate the use of an ArrayList object.

Listing 24-21 Working with the ArrayList Object

```
Dim Arrlst As New ArrayList(7)
Dim oArrlstObject As Object = Nothing

Debug.Print(Arrlst.Capacity.ToString())

With Arrlst
    .Add("Dennis")
    .Add(True)
    .Add(12)
End With

Debug.Print(Arrlst(1).GetType.ToString())

Dim sNames() As String = {"Rob Bovey", _
                          "Stephen Bullen", _
                          "John Green", _
                          "Dennis Wallentin"}

Arrlst.AddRange(sNames)
```

```
Arrlst.RemoveRange(0, 3)

Arrlst.TrimToSize()

Debug.Print(Arrlst.Capacity.ToString())

For Each oArrlstObject In Arrlst
     Debug.Print(oArrlstObject.ToString())
Next oArrlstObject

Me.CheckedListBox1.DataSource = Arrlst
```

We first create a new ArrayList object and dimension it to hold seven items. Expanding an ArrayList is a resource-intensive process, so we want to try and create it with the capacity to hold as many items as we will need. The first debug print command gives us the current capacity of the ArrayList. We then populate the ArrayList object with items that represent different data types, in this case a string value, a boolean value, and an integer value. To verify that the ArrayList actually holds different data types we print the data type of the second item to the Immediate window using the **GetType** method.

Next we add a range of values to the ArrayList using the **AddRange** method. Our ArrayList already has the capacity to hold these new items, but if an ArrayList does not have sufficient capacity to hold the number of items being added it automatically expands itself. The **RemoveRange** method enables us to remove several items at once, so next we use this method to remove the first three items we added to it. At this stage the ArrayList object still has a capacity of seven items, but since we no longer need them all we resize it by using the **TrimToSize** method. Using the debug print command to check the capacity of the ArrayList after resizing it should show a capacity of four items. Just to check which values the ArrayList now holds we iterate over all its items using a For...Each loop. Finally, the collection of items in the ArrayList is added to a **CheckedBoxList** control.

In addition to the ArrayList, the .NET Framework provides additional data structures like **Stack** and **Queue**. The Stack class is a data structure that allows adding and removing objects from one position only. This position is referred to as the "Top" of the stack. The last object placed on the stack is the first one to be removed. This is a **Last In First Out** (**LIFO**) data access method. The Queue class is a data structure that allows us to add objects to the back and remove objects from the front. This is a **First in First Out** (**FIFO**) data access method.

Debugging

The most important task in development is to debug non-trivial solutions. The VS IDE offers a large number of tools to assist you in this task. Depending on the complexity of the solution, debugging can be quite difficult and time consuming. One of the best features of the VS IDE is that we can interact with it during debugging sessions.

Selecting the *Debug* menu reveals the available tools and options. As we can see, most of the commands and windows are familiar from Classic VB. During the debugging process, and while in break mode, additional tools become available as shown in Figure 24-10. Although a detailed walk-through is beyond the scope of this chapter, we focus on the most important new and updated debugging tools that the VS IDE provides. See the Chapter 16, "VBA Debugging," for a more detailed discussion of the debugging process.

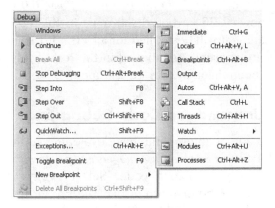

FIGURE 24-10   Debugging tools available in break mode

Set Keyboard Shortcuts

Before we start to explore the many tools for debugging, we customize our keyboard shortcuts. Select *Tools > Options...* from the menu to display the

Options dialog. In the Options dialog tree view, select the *Keyboard* section under *Environment*, as shown in Figure 24-11.

This section allows us to set the mapping scheme for keyboard shortcuts. Changing the mapping scheme to *Visual Basic 6.0* provides access to all the well-known VB6 keyboard shortcuts in the VS IDE. This change is global, meaning it will be applied for all VB.NET solutions in the VS IDE. The keyboard shortcuts mentioned in the rest of this chapter assume this setting has been made in your environment.

Enable Unmanaged Code Debugging

If we do a lot of interoperability development, that is, calls to COM objects, the option *Enable unmanaged code debugging* gives us the possibility to debug the native code. Select *Project > [Solution Name] Properties...* from the menu to display the Properties window; then select the *Debug* tab and check this option.

The Exception Assistant

Whenever a runtime exception is thrown, the Exception Assistant highlights the line of code that caused the exception and displays a dialog with suggestions on how to solve the problem. Figure 24-12 shows the Exception Assistant in action.

The Exception Assistant attempts to provide context-sensitive help related to the exception, and it allows the developer to perform certain

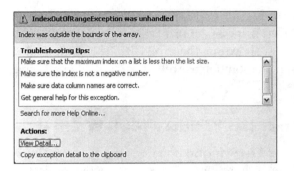

FIGURE 24-12 The Exception Assistant

actions, such as viewing details of the exception and copying exception information to the Clipboard. For COM exceptions, however, the information provided by the Exception Assistant is of limited value.

We can provide troubleshooting tips for our own exception types by creating an XML file containing the information in the correct ExceptionAssistantContent directory under C:\Program Files\Microsoft Visual Studio 9.0\Common7\IDE\ExceptionAssistantContent.

The Object Browser (F2)

The Object Browser is one of the most valuable development resources. The VS IDE ships with a modern Object Browser that can be customized by selecting the *Object Browser Settings* icon on its toolbar, as shown in Figure 24-13. We can also add components to the *Custom Component Set Browsing scope* by selecting the *Edit Custom Component Set* button directly to the right of the *Browse* drop-down in the Object Browser toolbar.

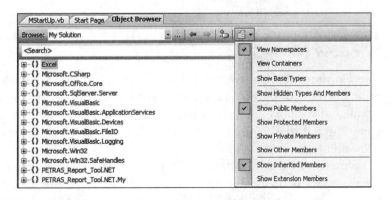

FIGURE 24-13 The Object Browser

The *Browse* drop-down is used to limit the scope of items displayed in the Object Browser. One of the selections available is to browse *My Solution*, as shown in Figure 24-13. This option allows us to browse the objects in our solution as well as any outside namespaces the solution references.

The Error List Window (Ctrl+W Ctrl+E)

The **Error List window** shows errors, warnings and other messages that result from attempting to compile the active project. It detects most common syntax and deployment errors. Figure 24-14 shows an example Error List window displaying some errors. Double-clicking on an item in the list takes you to the module and line of code it refers to.

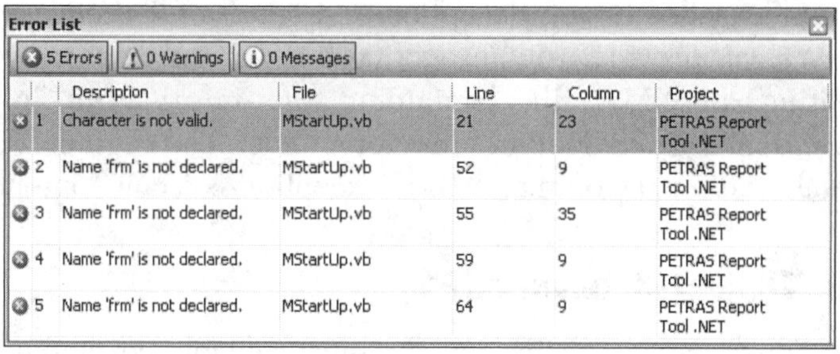

	Description	File	Line	Column	Project
1	Character is not valid.	MStartUp.vb	21	23	PETRAS Report Tool .NET
2	Name 'frm' is not declared.	MStartUp.vb	52	9	PETRAS Report Tool .NET
3	Name 'frm' is not declared.	MStartUp.vb	55	35	PETRAS Report Tool .NET
4	Name 'frm' is not declared.	MStartUp.vb	59	9	PETRAS Report Tool .NET
5	Name 'frm' is not declared.	MStartUp.vb	64	9	PETRAS Report Tool .NET

(Error List — 5 Errors, 0 Warnings, 0 Messages)

FIGURE 24-14 The Error List window

The keyboard shortcut to display the Error List window requires two steps, Ctrl+W followed by Ctrl+E. It may feel a bit odd to use two instructions to access a feature, but this reflects how many features the VS IDE contains.

The Command Window (Ctrl+Alt+A) and Immediate Window (Ctrl+G)

The **Command window** and Immediate window overlap each other to some degree, but they actually have two different tasks to accomplish. The Command window allows you to execute VS IDE commands instead of going through the menus and toolbars. It can also execute commands to open other windows.

Suppose we have started a debugging session and we are running in break mode. If we enter the command shown in Listing 24-22 into the Command window the variable bExport will be added to the Watch window.

Listing 24-22   Add a Watch Using the Command Window

```
>Debug.AddWatch bExport
```

If we want to see all the command aliases, or command shortcuts, defined by the VS IDE, we can run the command >*Alias* in the Command window to produce a list.

The Immediate window in the VS IDE behaves much like its counterpart in Classic VB. We can assign variables, run procedures, and invoke methods in standard VB.NET syntax in the Immediate window.

The Output Window (Ctrl+Alt+O)

The **Output window** displays compilation results and the text output from several tools such as Debug and Trace. The *Show output from:* drop-down in the toolbar allows you to show the output from either the debug or the build process. It is also possible to save the output to a text file by clicking anywhere inside the Output window and then using the keyboard shortcut Ctrl+S.

Break Points (Ctrl+Alt+B)

To insert a new break point, use the keyboard shortcut Ctrl+B. Compared with its older sibling in Classic VB, the break points feature has been improved significantly in VS.NET. First, VS.NET provides a **Breakpoints window** that displays the location and settings for all break points in the solution, as shown in Figure 24-15.

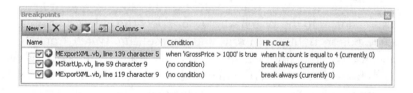

Figure 24-15   The Breakpoints window

Second, we can set conditions for a break point by right-clicking on that break point and selecting *Condition...* from the shortcut menu. In Figure 24-15 we set a condition for the first break point. When the break point is reached, this condition is evaluated to determine whether it is true or false.

If the condition is true the break point is triggered; otherwise, the break point is skipped.

Third, we can add a **hit count** for a break point by right-clicking on that break point and selecting *Hit Count...* from the shortcut menu. This provides us with an additional parameter to control whether code execution should stop at break points. Figure 24-16 shows us defining a hit count for our first break point in the Breakpoint Hit Count dialog.

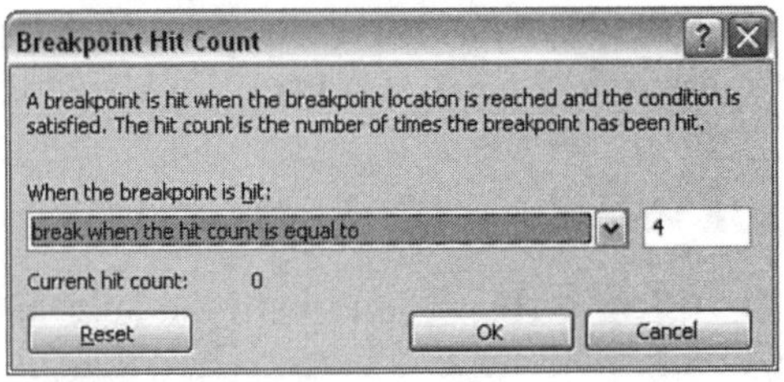

FIGURE 24-16 Defining a break point hit count

The Call Stack (Ctrl+L)

The Call Stack window displays the method calls that are currently on the stack. It is a useful debugging tool because it allows you to see the specific execution path that led to the current position in your code.

The Quick Watch and Watch Windows

Once our code is in break mode we have access to the Quick Watch and Watch windows. The Watch window, accessed by selecting the *Debug > Windows > Watch* menu while in break mode, provides four different Watch tabs. It is easy to add watches. You can drag and drop an object or expression onto the Watch window or select the object or expression in the code editor, right-click on it, and choose *Add Watch* from the shortcut menu. To delete a watch, select it in the Watch window, right-click on it, and choose *Delete Watch* from the shortcut menu. You can add as many different watches as you want. To access one of the Watch windows during a debugging session, press Ctrl+Alt+W followed by a digit between 1 and 4.

Quick Watch works the same way as the Watch window except that it can only handle one watch variable at the time.

Exceptions (Ctrl+Alt+E)

The Exceptions dialog is an advanced debugging tool that allows us to specify what types of exceptions we want VS.NET to throw during debugging.

The debugger stops whenever the selected type of exception occurs. Figure 24-17 shows this dialog.

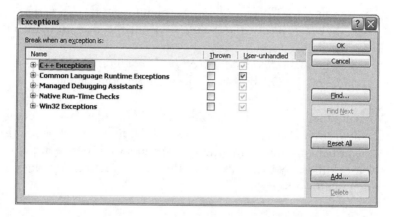

FIGURE 24-17 The Exceptions dialog

The *Thrown* option causes the debugger to break unconditionally when the specified exception type occurs. If we check the *Thrown* option for the **Common Language Runtime Exceptions**, we ensure that when a Common Language Runtime exception is thrown it breaks into the debugger, overriding any custom SEH we may have defined. The *User-unhandled* option causes the debugger to stop for the specified exception type only if no error handler is active when the exception occurs.

We can also configure specific exception types below the top-level namespaces by clicking on the plus sign (+) to the left of a namespace. This expands the namespace node to show all exceptions within the namespace that can be configured.

Conditional Compilation Constants

Chapter 16 introduced the concept of conditional compilation constants, so in this section we only cover conditional compilation topics that are specific to the .NET platform.

VB.NET provides several predefined conditional compilation constants, including the Boolean constant DEBUG. When DEBUG is set to true we have a **debug build**, and when it is set to false we have a **release build**. When compiling a release build we do not need to manually remove any debugging information. VS.NET handles this automatically when the DEBUG constant is set to false. Debugging information is also ignored when running a release build in the VS IDE. To compile a release build we need to use the Configuration Manager. Verify that the Configuration Manager is available in the following manner:

1. Select the *Tools > Options...* menu from the VS IDE.
2. Select *Projects and Solutions* from the tree view in the Options dialog.
3. Check the *Show advanced build configurations* check box.
4. Click the OK button to close the Options dialog.

We can then access the Configuration Manager by selecting *Build > Configuration Manager...* from the VS IDE menu, as shown in Figure 24-18. By changing the configuration we can switch between debug and the release builds. We can also use the Configuration Manager to specify which platform to target.

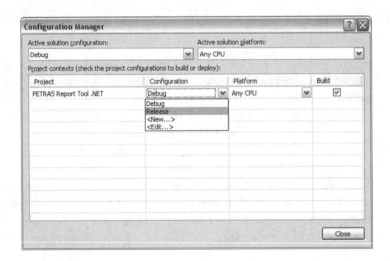

FIGURE 24-18 The Configuration Manager

We can execute code conditionally based on the value of the DEBUG constant as shown in Listing 24-23.

Listing 24-23 Using DEBUG in Code

```
#If DEBUG then
'Do some evaluation.
#End If
```

Using Assertions

The Debug.Assert method is used exactly the same way in the VS IDE as it is in Classic VB. Chapter 16 already covered the use of this method, so we do not discuss it further here.

Useful Development Tools

The VS IDE ships with a large number of useful development tools. Although it is beyond the scope of this chapter to discuss them all, we cover some of the most important tools in this section.

Code Region

The **Code Region** feature allows us to expand and collapse different sections, or regions, in our code modules. We can use this feature to create logical groups of methods that expand and collapse together. We can then collapse all regions in a code module that are unrelated to the one we are working with.

To create a region, we enter #Region followed by the name of the region in double quotes on a blank line above where the region should start. We then move to the next blank line below the code we want included in the region and enter #End Region (or select it from the IntelliSense list when we are prompted). Listing 24-24 shows an example of a code region.

Listing 24-24 A Code Region

```
#Region "Export data to Excel"
'Many lines of code here
#End Region
```

The Code Snippets Manager (Ctrl+K Ctrl+B)

Code snippets are small, reusable pieces of code. They are stored in a snippet library and managed using the **Code Snippets Manager**. The VS IDE includes a large number of code snippets already written and stored in the Code Snippets Manager. Code snippets are particularly easy to use because they are exposed as part of the VS IDE IntelliSense feature. Code snippets are stored in text files in XML format. This makes it easy to use them on other computers as well as to share them with other developers.

You can insert a code snippet into your code module in the following manner:

1. Place the cursor at the position where you want to insert the code snippet.
2. Right-click and select *Insert Snippet...* from the shortcut menu.
3. Select the desired category.
4. Select the desired code snippet.

Figure 24-19 shows the Insert Snippet command in action.

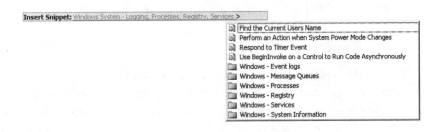

FIGURE 24-19   Inserting a code snippet

Instead of using the menu to insert code snippets, we can use **code shortcuts**. First we need to find out which code shortcuts are available in the Code Snippets Manager. The Code Snippets Manager can be accessed from the *Tools > Code Snippets Manager...* menu. Next we type the shortcut text, for instance ForEach, in the code editor and press the Tab key to execute it. Listing 24-25 first shows the shortcut text and then the result after we press the Tab key.

Listing 24-25   Using a Shortcut to Insert a Code Snippet

```
'The shortcut.
ForEach

'The result.
For Each Item As String In CollectionObject

Next Item
```

As we can see in Listing 24-25, we need to fix the code snippet before it can be properly used. On first consideration it may seem like too much effort to remember all the shortcuts as well as correct the code that is actually inserted into the code editor. However, the code snippets are completely customizable, so it is worth your effort to spend some time and make the changes required to suit your needs.

The built-in Code Snippets tool is rather primitive and doesn't provide a very user-friendly interface. If you find yourself working extensively with code snippets the free **Snippet Editor** may be a better tool. As of this writing, it is available at www.codeplex.com/SnippetEditor.

Insert File as Text

Insert File as Text is not a standalone tool but rather a built-in function of the VS IDE. It can be used to import code from plain text files. To display the Insert File dialog select *Edit > Insert File as Text...* from the menu. The default file extension is *.vb* so we need to change the file extension to *.txt* before we can select a text file. The code in the selected text file is imported into the active code module at the current cursor position. Using text files to manage complete and reusable class modules, standard modules, and methods requires only a simple text editor, making it a portable, light-weight solution.

Task List (Ctrl+Alt+K)

The **Task List** is a simple but handy tool for managing the To-Do list for a solution. Using the only button on its toolbar we can create different tasks and set flags indicating their priority. By right-clicking on the list we can also sort, copy, and delete tasks.

Automating Excel

At the most fundamental level, automating Excel from .NET solutions does not differ from automating Excel from Classic VB. What must be taken into consideration is that the .NET Framework cannot communicate directly with Excel because of differences between .NET technology and the COM technology Excel is built on. It is necessary to create a bridge between these two technologies for us to be able to automate Excel from the .NET platform. The bridge between .NET and COM is mostly provided by features contained in two .NET Framework namespaces: **System.Runtime.InteropServices** and **System.EnterpriseServices**.

24. EXCEL AND VB.NET

However, there are additional components required to allow interoperability that we need to discuss further.

Primary Interop Assembly (PIA)

When we set a reference to a COM type library in a .NET solution, the VS IDE automatically creates a default **Interop Assembly (IA)**. The auto-generated IA is a .NET-based assembly that acts as a wrapper for the COM type library. The IA provides us with basic access to the COM type library, and it contains type definitions (as metadata) of types implemented by COM. A **Primary Interop Assembly (PIA)** is a prebuilt, vendor-supplied assembly. The difference between an IA and a PIA is more or less semantic.

Microsoft has released PIAs for all Excel versions beginning with Excel 2002 as part of the Microsoft Office PIAs. The PIAs have **strong names** and are digitally signed by Microsoft. The use of strong names makes it possible to install PIAs in the **Global Assembly Cache (GAC)**. The GAC is a machinewide .NET assembly cache for the CLR. Assemblies that should have only one version on the system should be installed in the GAC.

One important point to understand is that only one version of the PIAs can be used on a system, although multiple versions can be installed side by side in the GAC. In addition, PIAs are registered in the Windows registry. If multiple versions of the PIAs are installed, only the latest version is registered, and the entries for any previous version are overwritten.

When we set a reference to Excel in a .NET solution the VS IDE reads the registry and adds a reference to the PIA instead of generating a new IA. This guarantees that we always use the PIAs if they are available. As a practical matter, when we are automating Excel from .NET we are always developing against the PIA and not the Excel COM type library.

The PIAs are optimized for Excel and you should always use the official Microsoft versions. The PIAs are also Excel version-specific. This means you cannot automate Excel 2002 using the PIA for Excel 2003. Therefore, you must be sure the correct version of the PIA is installed on your development computer. Whether or not the PIA is already installed on a computer depends on the following:

- For Excel 2002 on Windows XP or Windows Vista you need to manually download and install the redistributable PIA package from the

Microsoft Web site. If you run Windows XP, then the .NET Framework must be installed prior to installing the PIA package.

- For Excel 2003 or Excel 2007 on Windows XP, if Microsoft Office has been installed *before* the .NET Framework, then you must install the PIA package manually. You can either download the redistributable PIA package from the Microsoft Web site or install it from the Office CD.

- For Excel 2003 or Excel 2007 on Windows Vista you do not need to take any action at all. Because version 3.0 of the .NET Framework is shipped with Windows Vista, the PIAs are automatically installed when Office is installed.

Since no official PIA exists for Excel 2000, we must compile our own IA using the **TlbImp.exe** tool that is shipped as part of the .NET Framework SDK. It takes the Excel9.olb file as its input and generates a .NET assembly as its output. When automating Excel from .NET you should always develop against the earliest versions of the PIA and Excel that you plan to target and the earliest version of the .NET Framework you intend to use.

You need to be aware of the code execution overhead for all kinds of .NET solutions, especially when it comes to interaction between .NET and COM. Compared with Classic VB, .NET solutions require more components and therefore require more overhead to run. These components include

- The COM interop layer (PIA)
- The CLR
- The .NET Framework

As we see in the next section, there are additional aspects we need to consider to maintain acceptable performance for .NET solutions that automate Excel. If high performance is critical to your solution you may even consider using Classic VB if it is available and is an acceptable development platform.

Using Excel Objects in .NET Solutions

Create a Windows Forms solution and name it "Automate Excel." Add a button to the form and name it "Automate Excel." Next, add a reference to the Excel 2003 PIA or later. Choose *Project > Add Reference...* from the VS IDE menu to display the Add Reference dialog. Select the *COM* tab and scroll down to locate the Microsoft Excel 11.0 Object Library as shown in Figure 24-20. The reference is added when you close the dialog by clicking the OK button.

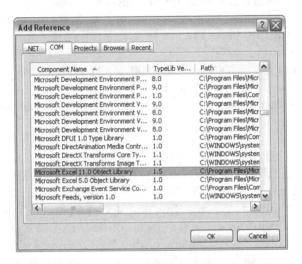

FIGURE 24-20   Adding a reference to the Excel Object Library

Choose *Project > Automate Excel Properties...* from the VS IDE menu. Select the *References* tab, and you see that three new Excel-related references have been added: the Excel Object Library, the Office Object Library, and the VBA Extensibility Object Library. Figure 24-21 shows the current list of references in the solution.

The System references are added by default. These give us access to the most commonly used .NET Framework class libraries. The imported namespaces are automatically included in all new .NET solutions. These are globally available in a solution. Open the Windows Form class module. When working with namespaces like Excel it is a good development practice to create a **namespace alias** for it at the top of the code module. We also add another Imports statement that is required as shown in Listing 24-26.

Listing 24-26   Namespace Alias and Imports Statements

```
'Namespace alias for Excel.
Imports Excel = Microsoft.Office.Interop.Excel


'To release COM objects and catch COM errors.
Imports System.Runtime.InteropServices
```

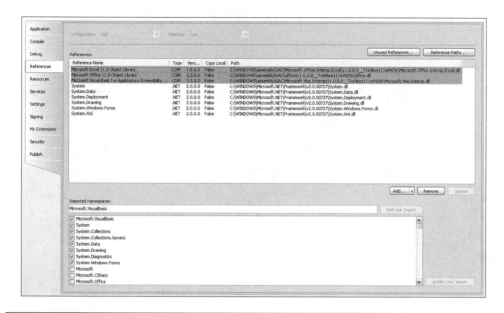

FIGURE 24-21   References in the automate Excel solution

Declaring and instantiating some Excel COM objects, like Workbook and Range objects, requires that we **cast** the object reference to the precise type using the **CType** function. This is because the Option Strict setting prevents us from using code that might fail at runtime due to type conversion errors. The VS IDE actually helps us with this task by visually marking the objects that need to be cast.

Next, add a Click event handler for the button. Listing 24-27 shows the code required to get the Excel automation started. Put this code in the button's Click event. As you can see, we implemented an SEH but intentionally left out any exception handling code. At this stage we also did not add the code required to release any of the Excel objects we used.

Listing 24-27   Declare and Instantiate Excel Objects

```
Dim xlApp As Excel.Application = Nothing
Dim xlWkbNew As Excel.Workbook = Nothing
Dim xlWksMain As Excel.Worksheet = Nothing
Dim xlRngData As Excel.Range = Nothing
Dim sData() As String = {"Hello", "World", "!"}
```

```
Try

    'Instantiate a new Excel session.
    xlApp = New Excel.Application

    'Add a new workbook.
    xlWkbNew = xlApp.Workbooks.Add

    'Reference the first worksheet in the workbook.
    xlWksMain = CType(xlWkbNew.Worksheets(Index:=1), _
                    Excel.Worksheet)

    'Reference the range to which we will write some
     data to.
    xlRngData = CType(xlWksMain.Range("A1:C1"),   _
                    Excel.Range)

    'Write the data to the range.
    xlRngData.Value = sData

    'Save the workbook.
    xlWkbNew.SaveAs(Filename:="c:\Test\New.xls")

    'Make Excel visible for the user.
    With xlApp
        .UserControl = True
        .Visible = True
    End With

Catch COMex As COMException

Catch ex As Exception

End Try
```

As shown in Listing 24-27, we must explicitly use the Value property of the Excel Range object in VB.NET. This is because VB.NET does not recognize default properties.

Whenever Excel objects are instantiated at runtime the CLR creates so called **Runtime Callable Wrapper (RCW)** for each underlying COM object in the memory. It is the group of RCWs that constitute the runtime proxies, or bridges, between a .NET solution and the COM type libraries it references. This is important to keep in mind because the more Excel COM objects we use, the more memory our solution consumes at runtime. It is a good development practice to clean up the RCW reference counts so we don't end up with a large number orphaned RCWs.

Let's take a closer look at the code in Listing 24-27. Initially it looks like we are only using four objects: the Application object, the Workbook object, the Worksheet object, and the Range object. But we indirectly reference the Workbooks collection, the Worksheets collection, and the Range collection, so we actually use seven objects. The objects used indirectly are out of our control but must be managed anyway.

On the .NET platform the **Garbage Collector (GC)**, is responsible for all memory management. The GC uses a managed memory scheme that periodically traces live references. When the trace is complete, all unreachable objects are released, and the GC reclaims the memory they previously used. The GC operates in a nondeterministic manner, so we never know exactly when it will perform its memory management tasks.

For pure .NET solutions this is not a problem, but it becomes an issue when trying to release COM objects properly. When releasing Excel objects we must be sure to release **all** the objects we have used. Otherwise, we may end up in a situation where Excel remains in memory and continues to consume resources even after our application has ended.

The first step in a practical solution is to explicitly call the GC from our .NET code. Calling the GC is a time-consuming process, but one that may be necessary when automating Excel because it is the only way to release all the Excel COM objects referenced indirectly. Each RCW has a **finalizer** that is responsible for releasing its COM object from memory. This finalizer needs to be called twice to fully remove the COM object from memory. Therefore, if we call the GC twice it releases our three indirectly referenced Excel objects.

The second step in a practical solution is to call the `Marshal.FinalReleaseComObject` method for every Excel COM object. Note that Excel objects must be released in the reverse order in which they were created, with the Excel Application object released last. Listing 24-28 shows the code in our solution used to release all the Excel COM objects. This should normally be performed when we are closing the application.

Listing 24-28 Releasing Excel COM Objects with a Function

```
'In the calling sub procedure.
'...
    Finally

        'Calling the Garbage Collector twice.
        GC.Collect()
        GC.WaitForPendingFinalizers()
        GC.Collect()
        GC.WaitForPendingFinalizers()

        'Releasing the Excel objects.
        ReleaseCOMObject(xlRngData)
        ReleaseCOMObject(xlWksMain)
        ReleaseCOMObject(xlWkbNew)
        ReleaseCOMObject(xlApp)

    End Try

End Sub

Private Sub ReleaseCOMObject(ByVal oxlObject As Object)
    Try
        Marshal.ReleaseComObject(oxlObject)
        oxlObject = Nothing
    Catch ex As Exception
        oxlObject = Nothing
    End Try

End Sub
```

Note how we use the custom ReleaseCOMObject function to release the
Excel objects and set them to Nothing. This example also shows why the
Finally block is so useful; it ensures that the code required to clean up our
Excel objects will always run.

The Automate Excel example can be found on the companion CD in
\Concepts\Ch24 - Excel & VB.NET\Automate Excel folder. If you just want
to run the example, the Automate Excel executable file can be found in the
\Concepts\Ch24 - Excel & VB.NET\Excel Automate\Excel Automate\bin\
Debug folder on the CD.

Using Late Binding

Whenever possible, we should use early binding and declare all variables as specific types. The reasons for this are simple:

- Our .NET solutions run faster because it is not necessary to perform type conversion on any variables.
- The compiler can detect and display exceptions and therefore prevent runtime exceptions.
- We get IntelliSense support and dynamic help during the development process.

Unfortunately, it is common for developers to have the latest version of an application such as Microsoft Office while end users have earlier versions. However, given access to desktop virtualization software such as **WMware** (commercial software) and **Microsoft Virtual PC** (free tool) it is now much easier for developers to use the same versions of software as the end users they develop for. This makes it possible for developers to use early binding in their applications.

Resources in .NET Solutions

On the .NET platform we can add images, icons, strings, and text files as resources to our solutions. To add resources we select the *Resources* tab from the .NET solution Properties window and click the *Add Resource* button on its toolbar. All resources associated with a solution become part of the EXE or DLL file upon compilation of the solution.

NOTE VS 2008 ships with a large group of images and icons. These are contained in the file VS2008ImageLibrary.zip that is located in the folder *Program Files\Microsoft Visual Studio 9.0\Common7\VS2008ImageLibrary\1033*.

To work with resources in code, we use `My.Resources` together with the name of the resource file. Listing 24-29 shows how we use an icon resource in code.

Listing 24-29   Associate an Icon Resource File to a Windows Form

```
Me.Icon = My.Resources.PetrasIcon
```

In this example, the `Me` keyword refers to a Windows Form, and `PetrasIcon` refers to an icon resource file. The `My` keyword refers to the My namespace that the .NET Framework makes available for all VB.NET solutions. This namespace exposes seven objects that allow us to work with various resources and features. Table 24-3 lists the `My` namespace objects along with the purpose of each.

Table 24-3   Objects in the My Namespace

Object	Purpose
`My.Application`	Provides information about the application such as path, assembly information, and environment variables.
`My.Computer`	Provides features for manipulating computer components such as audio, the clock, the keyboard, the file system, and so on.
`My.Forms`	Provides access to all Windows Forms in the solution.
`My.Resources`	Provides access to resources used by the solution.
`My.Settings`	Allows reading and storing application configuration settings.
`My.User`	Provides access to information about the current user, including whether or not the user belongs to a special user group.
`My.WebServices`	Provides features for creating and accessing a single instance of each XML Web service referenced by the solution.

Retrieving Data with ADO.NET

Despite the similarity in the name, ADO.NET is something totally different from classic ADO on the unmanaged platform. For instance, it does not include a Recordset object, and the Excel `CopyFromRecordset` method is not supported. This is covered in more detail in Chapter 25, "Writing Managed COM Add-ins with VB.NET." Another major difference is that ADO.NET has strong support for XML data representation. VS 2008 ships with version 3.5 of the ADO.NET class library.

ADO.NET is one of the default namespaces included in all Windows Forms based solutions, so to use it we just need to add `Imports` statements to the top of code modules from which ADO.NET will be called. However, to complicate things ADO.NET can be used in two different ways: **connected mode** and **disconnected mode**.

Before we can examine these two different approaches we need to first discuss **.NET Data Providers**. Data providers are used to connect to databases, execute commands, and provide us with the results. Each database, like SQL Server, Oracle, MySQL, and so on requires its own unique data provider. Some data providers are available by default in the .NET Framework, including SQL Server, Oracle, and OLE DB. Other data providers can be obtained from specific database vendors. For Microsoft Access and other databases that support ODBC, the OLE DB Data Provider can be used.

Connected mode means that we work with an open connection to the database. In this mode we explicitly use command objects and the **DataReader** object. A DataReader object retrieves a read-only, forward-only stream of data from a database. It can also handle multiple result sets. To do this, the connection must be open during the whole data retrieval process. Connected mode provides a performance advantage if we need to work with database records one at a time because the DataReader object retrieves and stores them in memory. However, the drawback is that connected mode creates more network traffic and requires having an active connection open during the whole database operation.

In Listing 24-30, we use a SQL Server database and therefore we import the namespace `System.Data.SqlClient`, which gives us access to the .NET Data Provider for SQL Server. We also use the ADO.NET class library and therefore we import the namespace `System.Data`.

Listing 24-30   Using a DataReader Object

```
'At the top of the code module.
Imports System.Data
Imports System.Data.SqlClient

Friend Function Retrieve_Data_With_DataReader() As ArrayList

        'SQL query in use.
        Const sSqlQuery As String = _
            "SELECT CompanyName AS Company " & _
            "FROM Customers " & _
```

```
                "ORDER BY CompanyName;"

        'Connection string in use.
        Const sConnection As String = _
            "Data Source=PED\SQLEXPRESS;" & _
            "Initial Catalog=Northwind;" & _
            "Integrated Security=True"

        'Declare and initialize the connection.
        Dim sqlCon As New SqlConnection(connectionString:= _
                                        sConnection)
        'Declare and initialize the command.
        Dim sqlCmd As New SqlCommand(cmdText:=sSqlQuery, _
                                     connection:=sqlCon)
        'Define the command type.
        sqlCmd.CommandType = CommandType.Text

        'Explicitly open the connection.
        sqlCon.Open()

        'Populate the DataReader with data and
        'explicit close the connection.
        Dim sqlDataReader As SqlDataReader = _
        sqlCmd.ExecuteReader(behavior:= _
                        CommandBehavior.CloseConnection)

        'Variable for keeping track of number of rows in the
        'DataReader.
        Dim iRecordCounter As Integer = Nothing

        'Get the number of columns in the DataReader.
        Dim iColumnsCount As Integer = sqlDataReader.FieldCount

        'Declare and instantiate the ArrayList.
        Dim DataArrLst As New ArrayList

        'Check to see that it has at least one
        'record included.
        If sqlDataReader.HasRows Then

            'Iterate through the collection of records.
            While sqlDataReader.Read

                For iRecordCounter = 0 To iColumnsCount - 1
```

```
                     'Add data to the ArrayList's variable.
                     DataArrLst.Add(sqlDataReader.Item _
                                  (iRecordCounter).ToString())

             Next iRecordCounter

        End While
   End If

   'Clean up by disposing objects, closing and
   'releasing variables.
   sqlCmd.Dispose()
   sqlCmd = Nothing

   sqlDataReader.Close()
   sqlDataReader = Nothing

   sqlCon.Close()
   sqlCon.Dispose()
   sqlCon = Nothing

   'Send the list to the calling method.
   Return DataArrLst

End Function
```

We first create a SqlConnection object and then a SqlCommand object. Next we explicitly open the connection, create the DataReader object, and iterate through the collection of records in the DataReader object by using its Read method. Within the loop we populate an ArrayList object with the data from the DataReader object. Finally, we close and clean up the objects we've used and return the data in the ArrayList to the calling method. The Northwind database used in this example can be found on the companion CD in \Applications\Ch24 - Excel & VB.NET \Northwind.

When working in disconnected mode we make use of the DataAdapter, DataSet, and DataTable objects, which are supported by all .NET Data Providers. A DataAdapter acquires the data from the database and populates the DataTable(s) in a DataSet. The DataAdapter object includes commands to automatically connect to and disconnect from the database. It also includes commands to select, insert, update, and delete data. The DataAdapter object runs these commands automatically. The DataSet is an in-memory representation of the data, and like the DataReader object it can handle multiple SQL queries at the same time.

The advantages of using disconnected mode are that it creates less network traffic because it acquires the data in one go, and it does not require an open connection to the database once the data has been retrieved. It also allows us to first update the retrieved data and then return the updated data to the database.

Listing 24-31 shows a complete function, including SEH, which first creates the Connection object together with the DataAdapter object. It then creates and initializes a new DataSet. Next it initializes the DataAdapter object, which automatically establishes a connection, retrieves the data, and closes the connection. The DataSet is filled with the retrieved data and finally the function returns the first DataTable in the DataSet.

Listing 24-31   Using DataAdapter and DataSet Objects

```
'On top of the code module.
Imports System.Data
Imports System.Data.SqlClient


    Friend Function Retrieve_Data_With_DataAdapter() As DataTable

        'SQL query in use.
        Const sSqlQuery As String = _
            "SELECT CompanyName AS Company " & _
            "FROM Customers " & _
            "ORDER BY CompanyName;"

        'Connection string in use.
        Const sConnection As String = _
            "Data Source=PED\SQLEXPRESS;" & _
            "Initial Catalog=Northwind;" & _
            "Integrated Security=True"

        'Declare the connection variable.
        Dim SqlCon As SqlConnection = Nothing

        'Declare the DataAdapter variable.
        Dim SqlAdp As SqlDataAdapter = Nothing

        'Declare and initialize a new empty DataSet.
        Dim SqlDataSet As New DataSet

        Try
            'Initialize the connection.
            SqlCon = New SqlConnection(connectionString:= _
```

```
                                        sConnection)
        'Initialize the DataAdapter.
        SqlAdp = New SqlDataAdapter(selectCommandText:= _
                                    sSqlQuery, _
                                    selectConnection:= _
                                    SqlCon)

        'Fill the DataSet.
        SqlAdp.Fill(dataSet:=SqlDataSet, srcTable:="PED")

        'Return the datatable.
        Return SqlDataSet.Tables(0)

    Catch Sqlex As SqlException
        'Exception handling for the communication with
        'the SQL Server Database.

        'Tell it to the calling method.
        Return Nothing

    Finally

        'Releases all resources the variable has consumed from
        'the memory.
        SqlDataSet.Dispose()

        'Release the reference the variable holds and
        'prepare it to be collected by the Garbage Collector
        '(GC) when it comes around.
        SqlDataSet = Nothing

        SqlCon.Dispose()
        SqlCon = Nothing

        SqlAdp.Dispose()
        SqlAdp = Nothing

    End Try

End Function
```

The function returns a DataTable object from the ADO.NET class, but we do not need to cast it into a DataTable object from the DataSet class before returning it. The exception handler catches any exceptions that occur in the SQL Server Data Provider. In the Finally block we dispose all object variables and set them to nothing. A working example of this solution can be found on the companion CD in *\Concepts\Ch24 - Excel & VB.NET\Northwind* folder.

ADO.NET may be a new technology for developers who are working with the .NET platform for the first time. But for Microsoft, the latest technology is **.NET Language Integrated Query (LINQ)**, which is part of the .NET Framework 3.5 and was released with VS 2008. LINQ is a set of .NET technologies that provide built-in language querying functionality similar to SQL for accessing data from any data source. Instead of using string expressions that represent SQL queries, we can use a rich SQL-like syntax directly in our VB.NET code to query databases, collections of objects, XML documents, and more.

The future will tell us more about how well LINQ will succeed. Developers who are coming from classic ADO are more likely to first adopt ADO.NET and later perhaps also begin to use LINQ.

Further Reading

When it comes to the .NET Framework, VB.NET, and ADO.NET we have only scratched the surface. These technologies are all book-length topics in their own right. The following books are sources that we have found to be useful for a general introduction to VB.NET and to ADO.NET.

Programming Microsoft Visual Basic .NET Version 2003

Authored by Francesco Balena
ISBN# 0735620598—Microsoft Press
Unfortunately, this book has not been updated since VB.NET 2003 was released. However, it provides an excellent introduction to the .NET Framework and to VB.NET, as well as to other related technologies such as ADO.NET. It explicitly targets Classic VB developers who are moving to the .NET platform.

Visual Basic 2008 Programmer's Reference

Authored by Rod Stephens
ISBN# 0470182628—Wrox

This book offers a light introduction to VB.NET that explicitly targets beginning to intermediate level developers. This is a practical book about the .NET Framework, VS IDE, and VB.NET, written well in plain English. The only thing that may be annoying is that some screen shots are oversized. Hopefully this will be corrected in later editions of the book.

Additional Development Tools

The authors have no financial interest in these tools and are not connected to their vendors. The recommendations are based on our own daily use of these tools as .NET developers.

MZ-Tools

MZ-Tools 6.0 is an add-in to the VS IDE. It works with all current versions of VS.NET except for the Express edition. It adds many tools and functions to the VS IDE that are designed to simplify development work and increase productivity. For more information see www.mztools.com.

VSNETCodePrint

VSNETCodePrint 2008 is an add-in to the VS IDE that helps developers document their solutions. With this tool we can print, preview, and export a complete solution, selected projects, project items, classes, modules, and procedures in several file formats. It can save you a significant amount of time when you need to document solutions and inspect code. For more information see www.starprint2000.com.

It should be noted that MZ-Tools provides features to generate documentation using either HTML or XML file formats that overlap the features in VSNETCodePrint to some degree but are less advanced.

Q&A Forums

There are many general public VB.NET Q&A forums, but the Microsoft MSDN section for VB.NET is one of the best at http://forums.msdn. microsoft.com/en-US/tag/visualbasic/forums/. The VB.NET section at Xtreme VB Talk is also good, and it includes a subforum for .NET Office automation at www.xtremevbtalk.com/forumdisplay.php?f=97.

24. EXCEL AND VB.NET

Practical Example—PETRAS Report Tool .NET

PETRAS Report Tool .NET is a practical case study that demonstrates a more complex VB.NET application than is possible to cover in a single chapter. In Chapter 25, the tool is converted into a managed COM add-in for Excel. The tool is a standalone, fully functional reporting solution. It retrieves data from a SQL Server database (created in Chapter 19, "Programming with Access and SQL Server") based on the user selection in the main Windows Form. It then populates predefined Excel report templates with the data. It can export reports either to Excel or to XML files. The solution can be found on the companion CD in \Applications\Ch24 - Excel & VB.NET\PETRAS Report Tool.NET. Please read the Read Me First.txt file located in the \Applications\Ch24 - Excel & VB.NET\ folder. You will find it helpful to open this solution in the VB IDE so that you can reference it while reading this section.

When the tool starts up, it first tries to establish a connection to the database. A custom Windows Form is displayed while the tool is trying to connect. If the connection attempt is successful, the main Windows Form shown in Figure 24-22 is displayed. If the connection attempt fails, an error message is displayed.

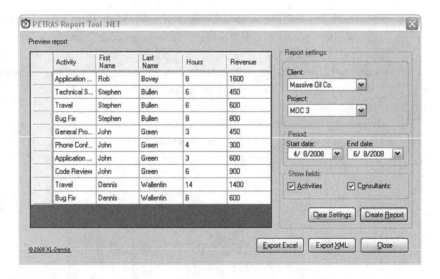

FIGURE 24-22 PETRAS Report Tool .NET user interface

Use the following steps to create a report in the main form:

1. Select a *Client*.
2. Select a *Project*.
3. Select the reporting time period by entering a *Start date* and an *End date*.
4. Uncheck or keep the fields *Activities* and *Consultants*.
5. Click on the *Create Report* button to preview the report in the DataGrid.
6. Click the appropriate button to export to an Excel report or to an XML file.
7. If export to Excel is selected, Excel is launched and a copy of one of the four predefined report templates is created.
8. If export to XML is selected, a Save File dialog is displayed so you can specify a filename and location where the XML file should be saved.
9. If the export is successful, the selections you made become the new default values for all controls on the Windows Form. It is possible to clear these settings by selecting the *Clear Settings* button.
10. To close the Windows Form, click the *Close* button.

The .NET Solution

Although we only use one main Windows Form, our .NET solution includes some additional modules and files. Table 24-4 shows a summary of what the solution contains.

Table 24-4 Contents for the PETRAS Report Tool.NET Solution

Module Name	Type and Function
app.config	XML configuration file containing the connection string
frmConnecting.vb	Windows Form displayed while connecting to the database
frmMain.vb	Windows Form that is the main form for the solution
MCommonFunctions.vb	Standard module containing general functions for the tool
MDataReports.vb	Standard module containing all database functions
MExportExcel.vb	Standard module containing all the functions required to export data to Excel
MExportXML.vb	Standard module containing all the functions required to export data to XML files

Table 24-4 Contents for the PETRAS Report Tool.NET Solution

Module Name	Type and Function
MSolutions Enumerations Variables.vb	Standard module containing all the enumerations used in the solution
MStartUp.vb	Standard module containing the Main procedure for the solution

As you can see in Table 24-4, the solution does not include any class modules. Creating well-designed class modules is covered in Chapter 25. In addition to the components shown in Table 24-4, the solution uses four different Excel report templates. Depending on the user selections, one of them is used to create the requested report:

- **PETRAS Report Activities.xlt**—Used when only the Activities control is checked
- **PETRAS Report Activities Consultants.xlt**—Used when both the Activities and Consultants controls are checked
- **PETRAS Report Consultants.xlt**—Used when only the Consultants control is checked
- **PETRAS Report Summary.xlt**—Used when neither the Activities nor the Consultants controls are unchecked

If we click the *Show All Files* button in the Solution Explorer toolbar, it displays an expanded tree view. If we then expand the References item in the tree view we can see all references for the solution, as shown in Figure 24-23. Most hidden files are system files that we rarely need to work with, but it's a good exercise to explore all the files included in the solution.

In any non-trivial real-world application where we initially load a Windows Form, we usually need to ensure that certain conditions are met before loading it. In VB.NET we can use the same approach as with Classic VB. We create a Main subroutine in a standard code module that is used as the startup subroutine.

But in VB.NET, we need to change some additional settings in the solution before this will work correctly. After creating the new Windows Forms application, open the solution Properties window, and select the *Application* tab. Figure 24-24 shows the original startup settings for the PETRAS Report Tool.NET solution.

We add a standard code module to the solution that we name MStartup.vb. We add the Main subroutine and its code to this module, as shown in Listing 24-32.

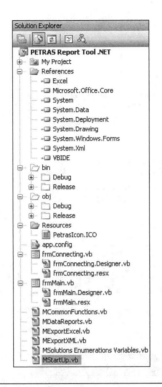

FIGURE 24-23   The tree view in Solution Explorer

FIGURE 24-24   Default settings for the solution

Listing 24-32   Code for the Main Subroutine

```vb
Sub Main()
        'Enable Windows XP's style.
        Application.EnableVisualStyles()

        'Declare and instantiate the Windows Form.
        Dim frm As New frmMain

        'Set the position of the main Windows Form.
```

```
      frm.StartPosition = FormStartPosition.CenterScreen

      'Show the main Windows Form.
      Application.Run(mainForm:=frm)

      'Releases all resources the variable has consumed from
      'the memory.
      frm.Dispose()

      'Release the reference the variable holds and prepare it
      'to be collected by the Garbage Collector when it
      'comes around.
      frm = Nothing
End Sub
```

Now we return to the *Application* tab of the solution Properties window, where we uncheck the option *Enable application framework* and change the *Startup object* to the Main subroutine as shown in Figure 24-25.

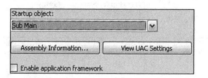

FIGURE 24-25 Modified startup settings

Unchecking the *Enable application framework* option implicitly removes the option to use **Windows XP styles**. Therefore, we need enable this option manually in the startup code, which is done in the first line of our `Main` procedure in Listing 24-32.

The `Main` subroutine is also a good place to put code to position the Windows Form before it is loaded. The `Main` subroutine is also an acceptable place to put code for connecting to a database, but in the PETRAS Report Tool.NET we use a different approach that is covered soon. When the user closes the main Windows Form we dispose its class and set the variable to nothing.

Windows Forms Extender Providers

The .NET Framework provides so-called **extender providers** to Windows Forms. These components can only be used with visual controls.

By adding them to our Windows Forms we get additional properties to work with. Extender providers are added to a Windows Form in exactly the same way as regular controls. However, the extender providers appear in the form's **Component Tray** rather than on the surface of the form itself.

Figure 24-26 shows the Component Tray for the main form of the PETRAS Report Tool.NET. The components used are the **ErrorProvider**, **HelpProvider**, and **ToolTip** components, for the main Windows Form, the **BackgroundWorker** component, which we cover later, and the SaveFileDialog component that was introduced earlier in the chapter.

FIGURE 24-26   Extender providers in the PETRAS Report Tool.NET

The first extender provider in use is the ErrorProvider, which provides us with the option to set validation errors. It can be used with one or more controls on the Windows Form as each of them have the **Validating** event.

When a control's input is not valid the ErrorProvider places an error icon next to the control and displays an error message when the user hovers the mouse over the icon. Listing 24-33 shows how this is implemented in the PETRAS Report Tool.NET solution. As the code shows, we can create a single event that hooks the `Validating` events of all the targeted controls on the form.

Listing 24-33   The Validating Event Subroutine for Several Controls

```
Private Sub Client_Project_Validating(ByVal sender As Object, _
        ByVal e As System.ComponentModel.CancelEventArgs) _
        Handles cboClients.Validating, _
        cboProjects.Validating


Const sMESSAGECLIENTERROR As String = _
    "You need to select a client."

Const sMESSAGEPROJECTERROR As String = _
    "You need to select a project."

Dim Ctrl As Control = CType(sender, Control)

   If Ctrl.Text = "" Then
```

```
    Select Case Ctrl.Name

    Case "cboClients"
    Me.ErrorProvider1.SetError(control:=Ctrl, _
                        value:=sMESSAGECLIENTERROR)

    Case Else
    Me.ErrorProvider1.SetError(control:=Ctrl, _
                        value:=sMESSAGEPROJECTERROR)

    End Select

  Else

    Me.ErrorProvider1.SetError(control:=Ctrl, value:="")

  End If

End Sub
```

If one of the controls being validated has the focus when the user clicks the *Clear Settings* button, the validation handling code is executed. To prevent this we must add one line of code to the load event of the main Windows Form. This is shown in Listing 24-34.

Listing 24-34   Code to Prevent Validation when the Clear Settings Button Is Clicked

```
Me.cmdClearSettings.CausesValidation = False
```

We can prevent the entry of bad data into a control by writing handlers for the key press event as well.

Looking more closely at the code in Listing 24-33 may raise the question of why we do not use a control array as we would in Classic VB. This is because VB.NET does not currently support control arrays, and it does not appear as if this feature will be implemented in any future version. The solution shown is the closest workaround in VB.NET. The second extender provider, HelpProvider, is used to associate a help file (either a .chm or .htm file) with our application. Whenever our application is running and has focus, the HelpProvider associates the F1 button with our application's help file. For the PETRAS Report Tool.NET we use a simple **form-based help** system, meaning that we associate the help file with our main Windows Form. It is much easier to set this up using Windows Form properties manually at design time than to do it at runtime with code. The design-time property settings required to create a form-based help system are the following:

- Set the HelpKeyword property on HelpProvider1 to the value About.htm.
- Set the HelpNavigator property on HelpProvider1 to the value Topic.

One property of the HelpProvider that should be set in code is the HelpNameSpace property. Doing this provides us with a more flexible solution because we can change the location of the help file dynamically. Listing 24-35 shows the code in the main Windows Form load event required to set the HelpNameSpace property.

Listing 24-35   Setting the Path and Name to the Help File

```
'The help file in use.
Const sHELPNAMESPACE As String = "PETRAS_Report_Tool.chm"

'Setting the helpfile to the HelpProvider component.
Me.HelpProvider1.HelpNamespace = swsPath + sHELPNAMESPACE
```

The swsPath is a global enumeration member that holds the path to the application EXE file for the PETRAS Report Tool.NET.

The third extender provider is the ToolTip component. It provides us with the option to add a Tooltip to each control in a Windows Form. Whenever the user hovers over a control with the mouse the control's Tooltip is displayed.

Threading

With .NET we can leverage multithreading to create more powerful solutions. It is beyond the scope of this chapter to cover multithreading in detail, but we demonstrate a simple example. The .NET Framework includes an extender provider, BackgroundWorker, which allows us to run code on a separate, dedicated thread, meaning we can run our project in multithreading mode. This extender provider is normally used for time-consuming operations, but as this case shows, we can use it for other tasks as well.

24. EXCEL AND VB.NET

In the PETRAS Report Tool.NET, we use the BackgroundWorker component to run the code that connects to the database. By using two of its events, `BackgroundWorker1_DoWork` and `BackgroundWorker1_RunWorkerCompleted`, we attempt to connect to the database in the background and be notified about the outcome. Listing 24-36 shows the code for the load event of the main Windows Form followed by the code for the two events of the BackgroundWorker component.

Listing 24-36 Code in Use for the BackgroundWorker

```
Private Sub Form1_Load(ByVal sender As System.Object, _
                       ByVal e As System.EventArgs) _
                       Handles MyBase.Load


'...


'Settings for the BackgroundWorker component.
With Me.BackgroundWorker1
          'Makes it possible to cancel the operation.
          .WorkerSupportsCancellation = True
          'Start the background execution.
          .RunWorkerAsync()
End With


'Change the cursor while waiting to BackgroundWorker
'component has been finished.
Me.Cursor = Cursors.WaitCursor


End Sub


Private Sub BackgroundWorker1_DoWork(ByVal sender As Object, _
          ByVal e As System.ComponentModel.DoWorkEventArgs) _
          Handles BackgroundWorker1.DoWork

     'Instantiate a new instance of the connecting
     'Windows Form.
     mfrmConnecting = New frmConnecting

     'Position the Windows Form and display it.
     With mfrmConnecting
         .StartPosition = FormStartPosition.CenterScreen
         .Show()
     End With
```

```vb
        'Can we connect to the database?
        If MDataReports.bConnect_Database() = False Then

            'OK, we cannot establish a connection to the
            'database so we cancel the background operation.
            Me.BackgroundWorker1.CancelAsync()

            'Let us tell it for the other backgroundWorker
            'event - the RunWorkerCompleted.
            mbIsConnected = False

        Else

            'Let us tell it for the other backgroundWorker
            'event - the RunWorkerCompleted.
            mbIsConnected = True

        End If

        'Close the connecting Windows Form.
        mfrmConnecting.Close()

        'Releases all resources the variable has consumed
        'from the memory.
        mfrmConnecting.Dispose()

        'Release the reference the variable holds and prepare
        'it to be collected by the Garbage Collector (GC) when
        'it next time comes around.
        mfrmConnecting = Nothing

End Sub

Private Sub BackgroundWorker1_RunWorkerCompleted _
        (ByVal sender As Object, _
        ByVal e As System.ComponentModel. _
        RunWorkerCompletedEventArgs) _
        Handles BackgroundWorker1.RunWorkerCompleted

    'If we have managed to connect to the database then we can continue.
    If mbIsConnected Then

        '...
```

```
    End If

    'Restore the cursor.
    Me.Cursor = Cursors.Default

End Sub
```

On its surface, the use of the BackgroundWorker component may look attractive. However, multithreaded application development is complex and easy to get wrong, so it should only be used in situations where it is absolutely necessary to run code outside the main process.

Retrieving the Data

A database connection string can be created using several different methods. For the PETRAS Report Tool.NET we create a solutionwide connection string using an application setting. This is accomplished in the *Settings* tab of the solution Properties windows, as shown in Figure 24-27.

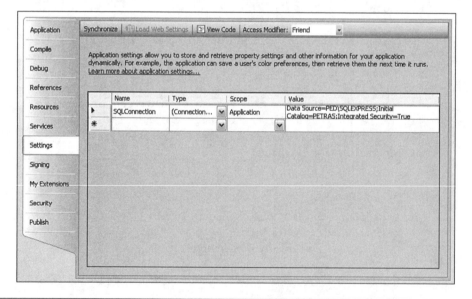

FIGURE 24-27   A solutionwide connection string

We first create a name for the setting and then select the type (*Connection string*). The scope is now automatically set to Application. After placing the cursor in the *Value* field a button appears on the right side. Clicking this button displays a very useful built-in wizard for creating connection strings.

If we look in the Solution Explorer window, we notice that a new app.config XML file has been created and added to the solution. The app.config file will not be compiled into the executable file when we develop standalone applications like the PETRAS Report Tool.NET. Instead, it is a separate XML file that is installed alongside the PETRAS Report Tool.NET executable. This allows us to easily update the connection string by simply opening and editing the XML file. When we compile the solution the VS IDE creates an XML file based on the solution name, PETRAS Report Tool .NET.exe.xml, for example, instead of using the name app.config.

When creating a DLL, the app.config file is compiled into the DLL, which makes it more difficult to update the connection string. This is addressed in Chapter 25. Listing 24-37 shows how to read the connection string setting from within our application code.

Listing 24-37   Reading the Application Setting for the Connection String

```
'Read the connection string into a module variable.
Private ReadOnly msConnection As String = _
My.Settings.SQLConnection.ToString()
```

Next we use it to initialize a new SqlConnection object, as shown in Listing 24-38.

Listing 24-38   Function to Create New SqlConnection

```
Friend Function sqlCreate_Connection() As SqlConnection

    Return New SqlConnection(connectionString:=msConnection)

End Function
```

All functions that retrieve data using disconnected mode expect the DataSet object to contain one DataTable at the time. We use a module-level DataTable variable to populate the DataGridView control. If the user decides to either create an Excel report or export the data to an XML file, the same DataTable is used as an argument to one of the export functions.

Exporting Data

The MExportExcel.vb module contains all the functions required to export data to Excel using one of the four predefined Excel templates described earlier. The main export function, shown in Listing 24-39, takes several arguments. Since the query has already been executed we can get the results as a DataTable from the DataGridView control on the main Windows Form. The other arguments provide information about the options specified by the user when the data was retrieved from the database.

Listing 24-39 The Main Export to Excel Function

```
Friend Function bExport_Excel(_
            ByVal dtTable As DataTable, _
            ByVal sClient As String, _
            ByVal sProject As String, _
            ByVal sStartDate As String, _
            ByVal sEndDate As String) As Boolean
```

Because the PETRAS Report Tool.NET is a standalone application not related to Excel, we first need to determine whether Excel exists and if so, determine which version of Excel is available. To accomplish this we examine the value of a critical Excel-related registry entry and use it to determine the current Excel version.

The lowest version of Excel that we can support is version 2002, meaning the tool cannot be used if version 2000 is installed. The function uses an enumeration of Excel versions, which is defined in the MSolutions Enumerations Variables.vb code module. To provide access to the .NET Framework functions that allow us to read the Windows registry, we import the namespace Microsoft.Win32. We also use regular expressions to complete this task, so the namespace System.Text. RegularExpressions also is imported into the code module. Listing 24-40 shows the code for the function.

Listing 24-40 Determine Which Version of Excel Is Available

```
'At the top of the module.
'To read the Windows Registry subkey.
Imports Microsoft.Win32
'To use regular expressions.
Imports System.Text.RegularExpressions
```

```
Friend Function shCheck_Excel_Version_Installed() As Short

Const sERROR_MESSAGE As String = _
                    "An unexpected error has occurred " + _
                    "when trying to read the registry."

 'The subkey we are interested in is located in the
 'HKEY_CLASSES_ROOT Class.
 'The subkey's value looks like the following:
 'Excel.Application.10
Const sXL_SUBKEY As String = "\Excel.Application\CurVer"

Dim rkVersionkey As RegistryKey = Nothing
Dim sVersion As String = String.Empty
Dim sXLVersion As String = String.Empty

'The regular expression which is interpreted as:
'Look for integer values in the interval 8-9
'in the end of the retrieved subkey's string value.
Dim sRegExpr As String = "[8-9]$"

Dim shStatus As Short = Nothing

Try
    'Open the subkey.
    rkVersionkey = Registry.ClassesRoot.OpenSubKey _
                    (name:=sXL_SUBKEY, writable:=False)

    'If we cannot open the subkey then Excel is not available.
    If rkVersionkey Is Nothing Then
        shStatus = xlVersion.NoVersion
    End If

    'Excel is installed and we can retrieve the wanted
    'information.
    sXLVersion = CStr(rkVersionkey.GetValue(name:=sVersion))

    'Compare the retrieved value with our defined regular
    'expression.
    If Regex.IsMatch(input:=sXLVersion, pattern:=sRegExpr) Then
        'Excel 97 or Excel 2000 is installed.
        shStatus = xlVersion.WrongVersion
    Else
```

```
        'Excel 2002 or later is available.
        shStatus = xlVersion.RightVersion
    End If

Catch Generalexc As Exception

    'Show the customized message.
    MessageBox.Show(text:=sERROR_MESSAGE, _
                    caption:=swsCaption, _
                    buttons:=MessageBoxButtons.OK, _
                    icon:=MessageBoxIcon.Stop)


    'Things didn't worked out as we expected so we set the
    'return variable to nothing.
    shStatus = Nothing

Finally

    If rkVersionkey IsNot Nothing Then

        'We need to close the opened subkey.
        rkVersionkey.Close()

        'Release the reference the variable holds and prepare it
        'to be collected by the Garbage Collector (GC) when it
        'comes around.
        rkVersionkey = Nothing
    End If

End Try

'Inform the calling procedure about the outcome.
Return shStatus

End Function
```

The module `MExportExcel.vb` also contains a function to verify that the Excel templates exist in the same folder as the executable file.

The function that exports data to an XML file also creates the Schema file for it. Listing 24-41 shows the two lines of code required to generate these files. We actually use the methods of the DataTable object to generate the XML files. This is because ADO.NET uses XML as its underlying data representation scheme. Both of these XML files can be opened and studied in more detail.

Listing 24-41   Creating XML and Schema Files

```
...
'Write the data to the XML file.
dtTable.WriteXml(fileName:=sFileName)

'Create the Schema file for the XML file.
dtTable.WriteXmlSchema(fileName:=Strings.Left( _
        sFileName, Len(sFileName) - 4) & ".xsd")
...
```

Summary

In this chapter, we provided a brief introduction to the .NET Framework, VB.NET, data access using ADO.NET, and Excel automation from VB.NET. Compared to Classic VB, the .NET Framework is a completely new and different platform. It is also a modern, advanced development platform with a great set of tools for creating user-friendly solutions. To fully utilize the .NET platform you must be prepared to invest significant time exploring and learning it. As we all know, there are no real shortcuts to learning new technology. Only hard work can accomplish the task. But the reward, in addition to the new knowledge itself, is that we can leverage all the knowledge from this chapter in the two chapters that follow.

24. EXCEL AND VB.NET

WRITING MANAGED COM ADD-INS WITH VB.NET

Chapter 23, "Excel and Visual Basic 6," demonstrated how to create **unmanaged COM add-ins** using the add-in designer. In this chapter we perform the same task using VB.NET and its **Shared Add-in Template**. This template is the natural successor to the add-in designer in Classic VB. To use the code examples presented in this chapter you need Visual Studio 2008 Standard or higher and Excel 2003 or later. The Ribbon user interface examples require Excel 2007.

A cornerstone of modern, object oriented programming is the use of classes. Class modules were intentionally ignored in the preceding chapter, but we introduce them here. We also briefly discuss setup packages, which are automatically created when creating managed COM add-ins. With VB.NET we can also create Automation add-ins, which we introduce here as well. On the .NET platform we should **isolate** our COM add-ins so they will run independent of each other. This is achieved by using a dedicated **shim** for each of them. The shims are built using the **COM Shim Wizard**, also discussed in this chapter.

Issues surrounding security have become more and more important in recent years, especially when using managed code that targets the Windows platform. In this chapter we demonstrate how to digitally sign **managed COM add-ins**, so they will continue to operate even when macro security is set to the highest level in Excel, as well as to leverage some of the built-in security features in .NET.

For our practical example, the PETRAS Report Tool.NET application is transformed into a managed shimmed COM add-in. Keep in mind that a complete exploration of this topic would require a book of its own. What we attempt to do here is provide a solid introduction to working with managed COM add-ins using VB.NET.

Choosing a Development Toolset

With VS 2008, we can create managed COM add-ins based on the Shared Add-in Template in a manner similar to how we would do it in Classic VB. VS 2008 ships with the latest version of VSTO, version 3.0, which also offers the ability to create managed COM add-ins based on VSTO technology. We therefore need to decide which toolset to use when creating a managed COM add-in.

With a shared add-in, it is possible to target multiple Office applications at the same time and target versions of Office from 2000 through 2007. But this flexibility comes with a price. The IDTExtensibility2 interface is not strongly typed—that is, it uses generic objects or late binding—and code redundancy may exist. However, both of these issues can be easily resolved, especially if we only target Excel.

A shared add-in requires version 2.0 or later of the .NET Framework, and if we want to isolate the shared add-ins from each other we need to use a custom COM shim "runtime." However, using COM shims adds an extra layer to shared add-ins solutions. If we need our shared add-in to work with the Excel 2007 Ribbon user interface we will have to write the code by hand. VSTO automates this process. The deployment of shared add-ins can be less complicated than with VSTO solutions, but for simpler solutions VSTO can offer a smooth deployment model. As for security, we cannot set strict security rules for shared add-ins, which it is possible to do with VSTO solutions.

VSTO is covered in more detail in Chapter 26, "Developing Excel Solutions with Visual Studio Tools for Office System (VSTO)," so in this chapter we discuss it only as a tool for writing managed COM add-ins. VSTO is part of the professional version of VS 2008 and higher and is also a standalone development platform. VSTO is built on top of the same interfaces that shared add-ins use. Unlike the Shared Add-in Template, VSTO offers application-specific and version-specific managed COM add-ins. VSTO explicitly targets the Professional and Standalone versions of Excel 2003, along with all versions of Excel 2007. This means we can only create VSTO add-ins for Excel 2003 or Excel 2007.

The .NET Framework version 3.5 or later must be installed for VSTO to target Excel 2007. We do not need to use a COM shim with VSTO because VSTO provides its own runtime. However, the VSTO runtime creates more overhead than the COM shim does. If we target Excel 2007 we can use the **Ribbon designer tool** in VSTO to customize the Ribbon user interface instead of writing all the required code ourselves. And with VSTO-based managed COM add-ins it is possible to control the security settings for each COM add-in individually.

If you need to support multiple versions of Excel, or versions of Excel prior to 2003, the only workable choice is to create managed COM add-ins based on the Shared Add-in Template. If you only need to support the versions of Excel supported by VSTO, then it is possible to create VSTO solutions with only Excel 2003 Professional. VSTO is in many ways an attractive technology with excellent tools, but it is also still under rapid development and has not yet reached a mature stage. By contrast, the Shared Add-in Template has been available since the first version of VS.NET.

Creating a Managed COM Add-in

The architecture for COM add-ins is straightforward. We have one or more Office host applications and we have the add-in, which is an in-process COM server. For managed COM add-ins we also need to consider the interop layer. The .NET Framework is required along with the PIAs for each of the Office host applications the add-in targets.

The elements of the COM add-in model consist of the **IDTExtensibility2** interface, which allows us to establish communication with the host applications, entries in the Window Registry that expose the COM add-in to the host applications, and finally references to the host application that make it possible to access the methods and properties in the host from the COM add-in. These basic elements are the same for both managed and unmanaged COM add-ins. But if we also want our managed COM add-ins to be isolated and secured, in the same way unmanaged COM add-ins are, shimming and digital signing are required. Later in this chapter we cover these two aspects of managed COM add-in development in more detail.

In VB.NET, we can easily create the Connect class for a managed COM add-in, a class that connects the managed COM add-in to the host, using the Shared Add-in Template. Create a new project by selecting *File > New Project...* from the VS menu. Expand the *Other Project Types* node in the New Project dialog and select the subgroup *Extensibility*. Finally, select *Shared Add-in* from the *Templates* list as shown in Figure 25-1.

In the *Name* field, enter the name FirstAddin and then click the OK button. This launches the **Shared Add-in Wizard**. This wizard gathers information from the developer and creates a skeleton for the add-in based on that information. The wizard consists of five steps. The following list explains the selections and entries you should make in each step for this first add-in:

- **Page 1**—Select the option *Create an Add-in using Visual Basic*.
- **Page 2**—*Uncheck all host applications* except Microsoft Excel.

- **Page 3**—*Name* the add-in *First Addin* and add the following *description* for the add-in Chapter 25 - Writing Managed COM Add-ins with VB.NET. The name will be used in the COM Add-ins dialog while both the name and the description will be added to the Windows Registry entries for the add-in.
- **Page 4**—Select the option *I would like my Add-in to load when the host application loads*.
- **Page 5**—This step displays a summary of our selections as shown in Figure 25-2.

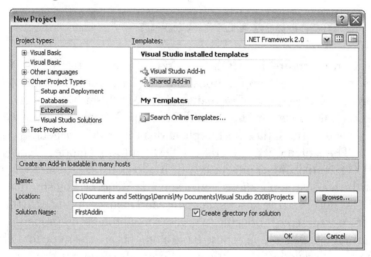

FIGURE 25-1   Creating a managed COM add-in project

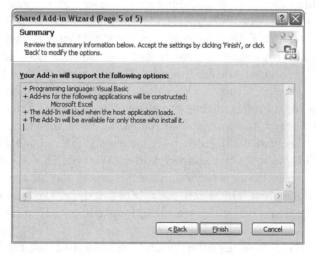

FIGURE 25-2   Summary of selections for our first add-in

Anatomy of a Managed COM Add-in

The Shared Add-in Wizard creates a skeleton for our COM add-in that consists of several parts, including

- A Connection class module containing the code framework required to connect to and disconnect from the host application, in this case Excel 2003.
- References to required system files and the Excel 2003 PIA.
- Entries in the Windows Registry on the development computer.
- A basic **setup solution** project that creates an MSI installer for the add-in.

The Connection Class

The code in the Connection class module traps the same events that we trapped when we created an unmanaged COM add-in with Classic VB. This should not come as a surprise, because all COM add-ins implement the IDTExtensibility2 class. The information provided in Chapter 23 about the AddinInstance events and other general aspects of COM add-ins is also relevant to managed COM add-in development.

The Shared Add-in Wizard creates two `imports` statements at the top of the Connection class module to import the `Extensibility` namespace and the `System.Runtime.InteropServices` namespace. The `Extensibility` namespace includes the IDTExtensibility2 interface that provides access to COM add-in events and is included in the Extensibility assembly. The System.Runtime.InteropServices allows us to work with COM Interop. The wizard also adds the code to implement the IDTExtensibility2 interface, enabling us to use its methods and events. Listing 25-1 shows these three statements and the two most important IDTExtensibility2 event procedures, `OnConnection` and `OnDisconnection`. The other IDTExtensibility2 events are rarely used but are required when implementing this interface. We also make the following additional customizations to the Connection class code for our add-in:

- Since the Extensibility namespace is imported to the class module we can safely remove its qualifier from the line of code that implements the IDTExtensibility2 interface.
- We remove the two generic module objects, `applicationObject` and `addInInstance`, because we only plan to target one host application.
- A constant module-level string is added to hold the title used by the message boxes in our event procedures.

- We add a "Hello World" message that is shown when the add-in is loaded, in this case when Excel is loaded.
- We add a "Goodbye World" message that is shown when the add-in is unloaded, in this case when Excel is unloaded.

Listing 25-1   Generated Code in the Connection Class

```
imports Extensibility
imports System.Runtime.InteropServices

Implements IDTExtensibility2

Const msTITLE As String = "Our first add-in"

Public Sub OnConnection(ByVal application As Object, _
                        ByVal connectMode As   _
                        ext_ConnectMode, _
                        ByVal addInInst As Object, _
                        ByRef custom As System.Array) _
                        Implements IDTExtensibility2.OnConnection

    MessageBox.Show(text:="Hello World", _
            caption:=msTITLE)

End Sub

Public Sub OnDisconnection(ByVal RemoveMode As _
                           ext_DisconnectMode, _
                           ByRef custom As System.Array) _
                           Implements _
                           IDTExtensibility2.OnDisconnection

    MessageBox.Show(text:="Goodbye World", _
            caption:=msTITLE)

End Sub
```

As we can see in Listing 25-1, no explicit references are made to the Excel object model, meaning we are using late binding. We demonstrate the use of early binding later in the chapter.

Before we can debug our add-in we need to set a pointer from our solution to the Excel.exe file on our development computer. This allows

Visual Studio to launch Excel and load our add-in for debugging purposes. This is accomplished in the following manner.

1. Select the *Project > FirstAddin Properties...* from the Visual Studio menu, and then in the Properties windows select the *Debug* tab.
2. Under the *Start Action* section select the *Start External Program* option. Next, click the button directly to the right of this option.
3. In the File dialog navigate to the folder where Exce.exe is located. The default location for Excel.exe in Excel 2003 is *C:\Program Files\Microsoft Office\OFFICE11*. Select the Excel.exe file and click the OK button.

The *Start External Program* option in the *Debug* tab should now look similar to Figure 25-3.

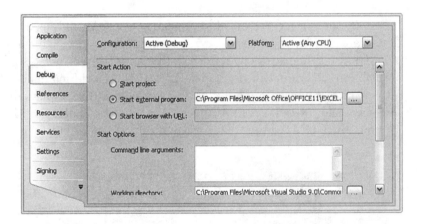

FIGURE 25-3 The Start External Program setting in the Debug tab of the Properties window

If this is the first time we have attempted to run the add-in solution we must also run our installer once to create the registry entries to notify Excel that our solution is a COM add-in. To do this, right-click the *FirstAddinSetup* node in the Solution Explorer window and choose *Install* from the shortcut menu. To test the add-in solution, press the F5 button. Visual Studio starts Excel and loads the COM add-in. When the COM add-in is loaded the "Hello World" message box shown in Figure 25-4 should be displayed. When Excel is closed, the "Goodbye World" message box should also be displayed.

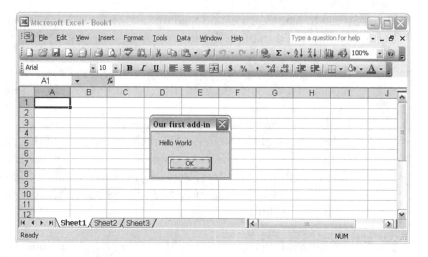

FIGURE 25-4 The "Hello World" message box in Excel

Just like unmanaged COM add-ins, managed COM add-ins available to Excel are displayed in the COM Add-ins dialog. Also like unmanaged COM add-ins, managed COM add-ins that have been installed so they are available to all users will not appear in the COM Add-ins dialog. For an explanation of how to add a button to your toolbar that displays the COM Add-ins dialog, see the "COM Add-ins" section of Chapter 23. Figure 25-5 shows the COM Add-ins dialog with our first COM add-in selected.

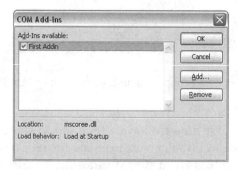

FIGURE 25-5 The COM Add-ins dialog with our managed COM add-in selected

If we look closely at Figure 25-5, we see that the location refers to **mscoree.dll** rather than to the full path and filename of the COM add-in. This is an important point that we address later in the chapter. Another subject we discuss later in the chapter is how to install and remove COM add-ins on the development computer.

Auto-Generated References

Whenever we create a managed COM add-in, Visual Studio creates all the required default references for the solution. Figure 25-6 shows the list of auto-generated references for our COM add-in solution.

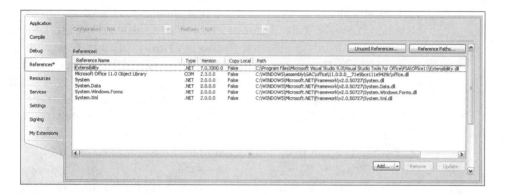

FIGURE 25-6   Auto-generated reference list for the COM add-in

The column entries for each reference shown in Figure 25-6 provide the following information:

- **Reference Name**—The name of the referenced assembly.
- **Type**—The type can either be COM or .NET depending on whether the reference is to a COM class or a .NET namespace.
- **Version**—The version of the referenced assembly. This information can be important if we want to compare the versions of the classes in the solution with the versions available on the target computers. However, during installation we can easily check which versions are available and compare them with the required **prerequisites**. This is covered in more detail later in the chapter. As Figure 25-6 shows, the version information on its own does not give any indication of which version of the Office Library is actually referenced. For .NET namespaces references it indicates that version 2.0 is in use.
- **Copy Local**—This is the only editable property and it can be set to either *True* or *False*. If set to *True*, the referenced class should be included as part of the solution installation and deployed to the main

folder of the solution. For customized assemblies, that is, third-party components, the default value of Copy Local is always *True*. Changing this property to *True* changes the path associated with the assembly. Instead of using the path to the referenced assembly's location on the development computer, the solution creates a sub-directory based on the reference's name and places all files required by the reference into that subdirectory. This may or may be not a good idea.

The advantage is that we can avoid "DLL hell" by keeping certain versions of assemblies private so that version conflict does not occur when new versions of the assemblies are installed on the system. The disadvantage is that future versions of these assemblies installed by the user will be system versions and not private versions that are part of our solutions. If the Copy Local property is set to *False*, it is assumed the target computers already have the required assemblies or that the required assemblies will be installed when our solution is installed.

- **Path**—The full path and filename to the referenced assembly.

Also note in Figure 25-6 that no reference exists to the Microsoft Excel 11.0 Object Library. To use early binding with Excel in our managed COM add-in we must add a reference to this object library. To do this, click the *Add...* button in the *References* tab and select the object library under the *COM* tab in the Add Reference dialog. Figure 25-7 shows the updated list of references for our managed COM add-in solution.

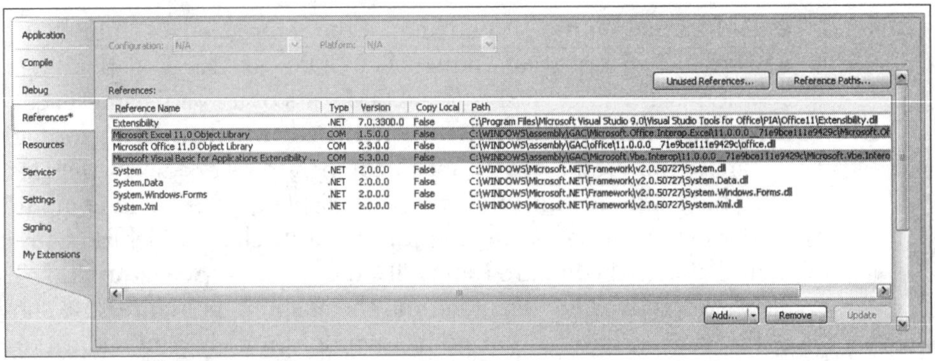

Figure 25-7 Updated references for our managed COM add-in solution

When we add a reference to the Microsoft Excel 11.0 Object Library, Visual Studio automatically adds a reference to the Microsoft Visual Basic for Applications Extensibility 5.3 object library as well. We can easily remove this reference from our solution if we will not be using it by selecting it in the list and clicking the *Remove* button.

Entries in the Windows Registry

When we create a managed COM add-in using the Shared Add-in Wizard, the wizard creates all required entries in the Windows Registry on the development computer. The registry settings for managed COM add-ins are similar to the registry settings for unmanaged COM add-ins. Listing 25-2 shows the two auto-generated class-level attributes at the top of the Connect module in our solution.

Listing 25-2 Auto-Generated Attributes in the Connect Class

```
<GuidAttribute("B7B5D1ED-8528-4C11-B70A-EE1BD7E4D1BD"), _
ProgIdAttribute("FirstAddin.Connect")> _
```

The first attribute in Listing 25-2 contains the GUID of the 'FirstAddin' Connect class. This GUID is also a subkey in the Windows Registry under the `HKEY_CLASSES_ROOT\CLSID\` key. This subkey contains the main settings for our solution, as shown in Figure 25-8. Note that the default value of the **InprocServer32** key for managed COM add-ins based on the Shared Add-in Template is mscoree.dll rather than the full path and filename of the COM add-in assembly.

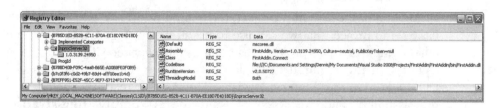

FIGURE 25-8 Settings in the HKEY_CLASSES_ROOT\CLSID\ section of the Windows Registry

All managed code execution is handled by the CLR. If the registry pointed directly to the location of our assembly, all calls to COM servers would fail because these calls must be executed by the CLR. This is achieved by placing the execution engine DLL, mscoree.dll, as the default value of InprocServer32.

Using mscoree.dll solves some problems but creates other problems as well. The shortcoming of using mscoree.dll is fully explored when we discuss **shimming** in more detail later in the chapter.

The second attribute in Listing 25-2 contains the ProgID for the solution. In addition to other locations, the ProgID refers to a subkey in the Windows Registry under the `HKEY_CURRENT_USER\Software\Microsoft\Office\Excel\AddIns\` key. This subkey contains the settings required to notify Excel that our managed DLL is a COM add-in. The contents of this subkey are shown in Figure 25-9. These settings are identical to the settings for a similar unmanaged COM add-in.

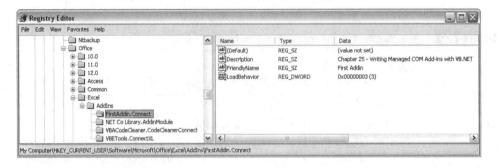

FIGURE 25-9   Settings in HKEY_CURRENT_USER\Software\Microsoft\Office\Excel\AddIns\

The Setup Project

In addition to the assembly project, the Shared Add-in Wizard generates a basic setup project that we can use to install the manage COM add-in on other computers. This project creates an installer for the COM add-in that includes all the required dependencies and that registers the managed COM add-in in the Windows Registry. The installer reads the metadata in the assembly and registers it using the **Assembly Registration** (**regasm.exe**) tool. This creates a COM registration for the managed COM add-in. Figure 25-10 shows the two projects in our solution. Note the list of **detected dependency** files below the setup project.

Always be sure that dependency files like Microsoft.Office.Interop.Excel.dll, Microsoft.Vbe.Interop.dll, and Office.dll are all excluded from the setup project. You do not want to install these with your COM add-in, because they will overwrite the existing files without any version checking. Under the *Detected Dependencies* root node, click on the file to be excluded and set the *Exclude* property of the file to True in the Properties

FIGURE 25-10 The two projects in our solution

window. Repeat this for all files that should be excluded. As shown in Figure 25-10, Solution Explorer displays a visual confirmation icon (a red circle with a red diagonal line) next to any files that have been excluded.

You can customize properties of the setup project by selecting the *FirstAddinSetup* node in the Solution Explorer window and pressing the F4 key. This activates the Properties window for the setup project as shown in Figure 25-11.

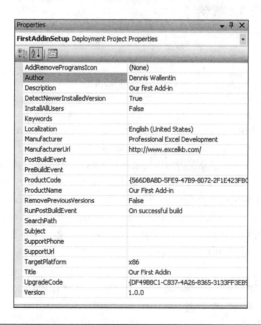

FIGURE 25-11 Customizing the properties of the setup project

We can also customize the assembly metadata. The Assembly Information dialog is used to specify the values for various .NET Framework global assembly attributes. These are stored in the **AssemblyInfo.vb** file created automatically by Visual Studio within our solution. To display the Assembly Information dialog, select the *Project > FirstAddin Properties...* from the Visual Studio menu. Next, select the *Application* tab in the property window and then click the *Assembly Information...* button. Figure 25-12 shows the assembly information for our solution.

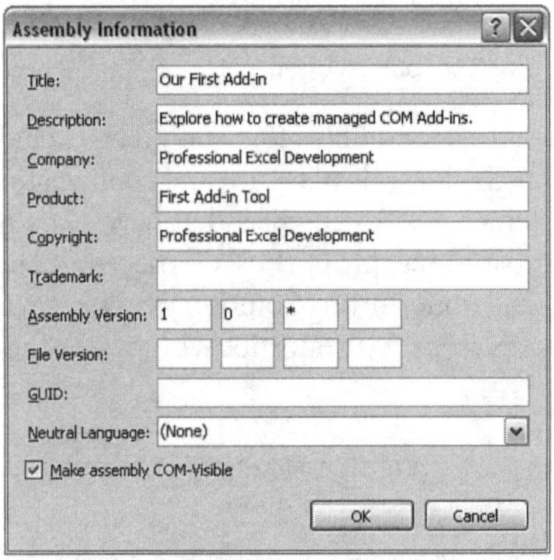

FIGURE 25-12 Assembly information for our solution

The assembly version numbers for all .NET applications are auto-generated by default. The assembly version number has four parts: *<major version><minor version><build number><revision>*. As we can see in Figure 25-12 there is an asterisk inside the build number field that indicates we accept the default build and revision numbers. Note that two assemblies with identical names but different version numbers are treated by the CLR as different assemblies. The option *Make assembly COM-Visible* is checked by default.

Setup Prerequisites Packages Setup prerequisites are standard components that may be required to run an application but are not part of the application itself. To access the Prerequisites dialog for our setup project we right-click the *FirstAddinSetup* node in Solution Explorer, which displays the shortcut menu shown in Figure 25-13.

Next we select the *Properties* menu, which displays the Property Pages dialog for our setup package. Finally, we click the *Prerequisites...* button on

FIGURE 25-13   The shortcut menu for the FirstAddinSetup solution in Solution Explorer

the Property Pages dialog to display the setup Prerequisites dialog shown in Figure 25-14.

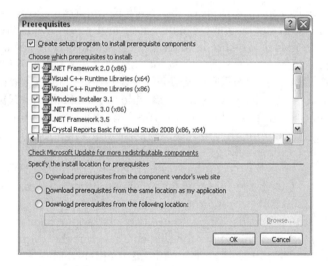

FIGURE 25-14   The setup Prerequisites dialog

By default, the Windows Installer 3.1 and .NET Framework 3.5 prerequisites are checked in the list. Since we target version 2.0 of the .NET Framework we need to uncheck the .NET Framework 3.5 prerequisite and check .NET Framework 2.0 prerequisite, which we have already done in Figure 25-14. Because Windows Installer 3.1 is available by default in Windows XP SP-2 and higher, it may not be necessary to include it.

When the installation process is executed, it automatically checks for the presence of the prerequisites and installs them if required. As Figure 25-14 shows, we can choose one of three options for the installation (or source) location of the prerequisites. This option applies to all prerequisites; we cannot select individual locations for each prerequisite. For each situation, we should evaluate whether to use prerequisites. It's not possible to give one general guideline that covers all scenarios, but the following recommendations apply in most cases:

- If all computers in the target environment run the same versions of Windows and Office with the same service packs, then it is safe to simply include all the prerequisites in the setup package.
- If the computers in the target environment run a mix of Windows and Office versions, then the prerequisites should be installed as separate components.

Eventually, older versions of the .NET Framework and other system components will no longer be maintained and made available by Microsoft. For this reason we should always have backup copies of all system components that we use in our solutions, including the .NET Framework, Office PIAs, and VSTO components. We should also keep our licenses for older versions of VS.NET because older versions of the .NET Framework may not be supported by future versions of Visual Studio.

If you examine the prerequisites list, you will notice it does not include **bootstrapper packages** for the Office 2003 PIAs. The PIAs for Office 2007 are included if you have VS 2008 SP1 or higher. When we develop managed COM add-ins as well as VSTO solutions we may need to include Office 2003 PIAs among the prerequisites.

Creation and use of customized bootstrapper packages for the Office PIAs is beyond the scope for this chapter, but the required packages for the Office 2003 PIA together with instructions on how to use them can be found on the companion CD in the *\Applications\Ch25 – Writing Managed COM Add-ins with VB.NET \Office2003PIA* folder.

Create a Launch Condition   **Launch conditions** are a set of defined conditions that the target computers must meet before the installation will run. It is beyond the scope of this chapter to cover launch conditions in detail. However, because we explicitly target the .NET Framework 2.0 and later for our solution, we need to make an important launch condition change in the setup. To do so we first need to open the **Launch Condition**

Editor by right-clicking the *FirstAddinSetup* node in Solution Explorer and selecting *View > Launch Conditions* from the shortcut menu. Next we select the launch condition *.NET Framework* to display its properties in the Properties window. Finally, we change the *Version* property to 2.0.50727 as shown in Figure 25-15.

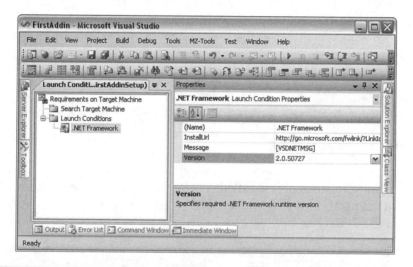

FIGURE 25-15   The Launch Condition Editor

Create an Entry in the Windows Registry   It is good practice to let Excel know that our managed COM add-in is not command-line safe and may display a User Interface (UI). To do this, we must add a name and value to the Windows Registry under

```
HKEY_CURRENT_USER
\Software\Microsoft\Office\Excel\AddIns\FirstAddin.Connect
```

We can do this with the **Registry Editor** in the VS IDE. Right-click the *FirstAddinSetup* node in Solution Explorer and select *View >Registry* from the shortcut menu to display the Registry Editor. Next, expand the HKEY_CURRENT_USER node in the tree inside the left window so it looks like Figure 25-16. Right-click inside the right window and select the *New > DWORD Value* from the shortcut menu. Name the value **CommandLineSafe** and make sure its value is set to 0.

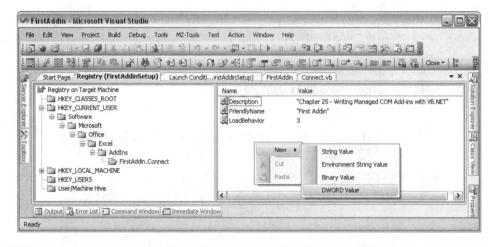

FIGURE 25-16 The Registry Editor

When our solution is installed on a target computer, the entries for it under its ProgID in the HKEY_CURRENT_USER section should look like Figure 25-17.

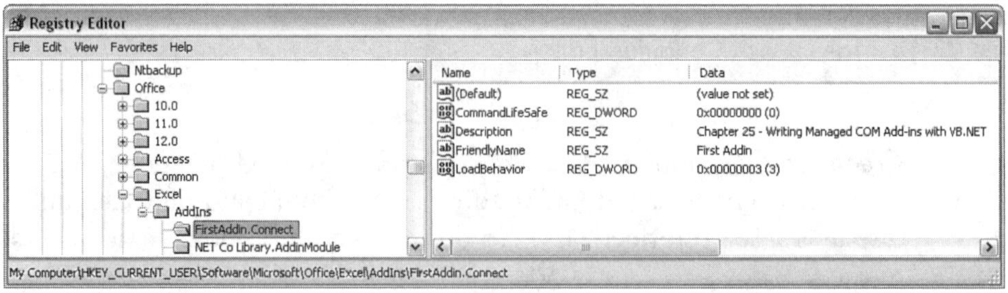

FIGURE 25-17 Entries in the Windows Registry

If the solution is designed to target all users who use the computer, then you should create these entries under the HKEY_LOCAL_MACHINE\Software\ Microsoft\Office\Excel\AddIns\ key instead.

Build the Setup In this chapter, we focus on creating MSI packages. In Chapter 26, we cover the ClickOnce deployment model. We can build the setup project by selecting the project's node in Solution Explorer and then selecting *Build > Build FirstAddinSetup* from the menu. This process creates two files, FirstAddinSetup.msi and Setup.exe, in the Debug folder under the main folder *FirstAddinSetup*. These two files should always be available for the installation of the solution. You should normally install solutions with Setup.exe because it verifies that the prerequisites exist and the launch conditions are met.

If we want to build both the solution and the setup project at the same time, we can configure our solution to do this. Select *Build > Configuration Manager...* from the menu. In the Configuration Manager dialog place a check mark in the *Build* column next to the *FirstAddinSetup* project, as shown in Figure 25-18. Now, whenever we build the solution the setup project will also be built automatically.

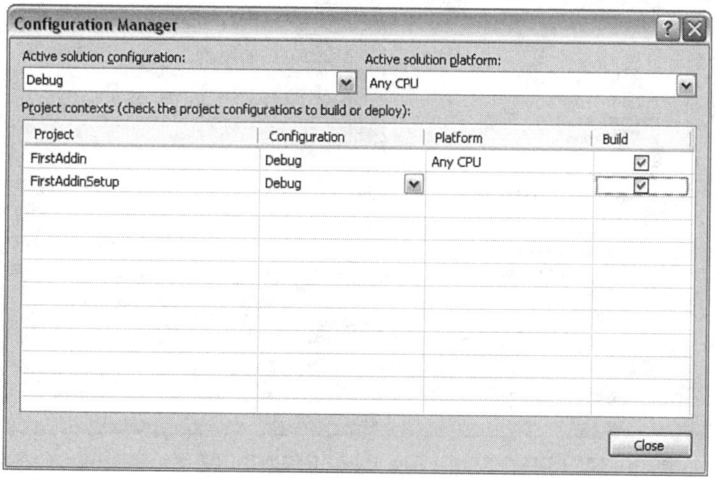

FIGURE 25-18 The Configuration Manager

After we build the setup package, we can right-click the root node of the setup package in Solution Explorer to access the *Install* and *Uninstall* commands. As we mentioned earlier, you must install the solution on the development computer at least once before you will be able to test and debug it.

The last aspect of the setup project is to specify whether the managed COM add-in should be installed for all users of a computer or only for the user performing the installation. This is controlled by two properties. The first one, *InstallAllUsers*, is located in the property page of the setup project, shown previously in Figure 25-11. The default value of this property is False, which indicates the solution should only be installed for the current user.

But we need to make an additional setting in the **User Interface Editor**. Right-click the *FirstAddinSetup* node in Solution Explorer and select *View > User Interface* from the shortcut menu. In the User Interface Editor, right-click *Installation Folder* under the *Start* node and select *Properties Window* from the shortcut menu. Set the *InstallAllUsersVisible* property to *False*, as shown in Figure 25-19.

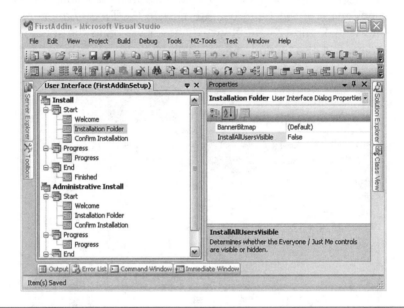

FIGURE 25-19 Changing a property of the setup project in the User Interface Editor

Additional tools are available to customize the setup project further, including the **File System Editor**, the **File Types Editor**, and the **Custom Actions Editor**. However, these are beyond the scope of this chapter, so we leave it up to you to explore them in more detail. A working example of this solution can be found on the companion CD in the *\Concepts\Ch25 - Writing Managed COM Add-ins with VB.NET\FirstAddin* folder.

Building the User Interface

Most managed COM add-ins have a user interface that allows the user to interact with the features provided by the add-in. For Excel 2003 we create toolbar buttons and menu items using the CommandBars object model. With Excel 2007 we have the Ribbon user interface, which requires a different approach. If we need to provide a Ribbon user interface for a project that must also support Excel 2003 we face the following problems:

- The **IRibbonExtensibility** interface required to implement a Ribbon user interface is not included in the Microsoft Office 11.0 Object Library shipped with Excel 2003.
- We cannot use Microsoft Office 12.0 Object Library shipped with Excel 2007, which does include the IRibbonExtensibility interface, in a project that must support Excel 2003.

The Microsoft Office 12.0 Object Library does support the CommandBars object model, which means we can develop with Excel 2007 even when targeting Excel 2003. When writing managed COM add-ins we face one of the three following user interface scenarios:

- **Targeting only Excel 2003**—We can develop a command bars user interface with either Excel 2003 or Excel 2007.
- **Targeting only Excel 2007**—If we want to customize the Ribbon UI, then we can only develop with Excel 2007.
- **Targeting both Excel 2003 and 2007**—The best solution is to develop a command bars user interface with Excel 2003. This user interface will appear in the Add-Ins tab of the Excel 2007 Ribbon.

Using Excel 2003 together with VS 2008 provides the most flexible development platform for creating managed COM add-ins based on the shared add-in template.

Command Bar User Interface Handling

In this section, we create a toolbar for our COM add-in. The first step is to add two more Imports statements to the Connection class as shown in Listing 25-3.

Listing 25-3 Imports Statements Required for CommandBar Handling

```
Imports Excel = Microsoft.Office.Interop.Excel
Imports Office = Microsoft.Office.Core
```

Next we create the module-level variables and constants for the Connection class shown in Listing 25-4. We have a variable in which to store a reference to the Excel Application object, a command bar button variable declared WithEvents to hook our toolbar button clicks, and a CommandBar variable to hold a reference to the toolbar itself. Because we have three command bar button controls, we need to create module-level string constants to identify each one.

Listing 25-4   Module-Level Variables in the Connection Class

```
'The variable for the main Excel application object.
Private mxlApp As Excel.Application = Nothing

'The hooking command bar control event.
Private WithEvents mcmdFirstAddinButton As     _
                  Office.CommandBarButton = Nothing

'The command bar variable.
Private mcbrFirstAddin As Office.CommandBar = Nothing

'Constant string variables.
Private Const msTITLE As String = "Our First Add-in"
Private Const msTAG As String = "OFA"

Private Const msBUTTON1 As String = "Button 1"
Private Const msBUTTON2 As String = "Button 2"
Private Const msBUTTON3 As String = "Button 3
```

The OnConnection event procedure requires the following modifications:

- Add a structured exception handler (SEH) to eliminate the risk that Excel will disable the COM add-in if anything goes wrong with it during the loading process. (Disabled items can be found by clicking the *Help > About Microsoft Excel* menu from the *Worksheet Menu Bar* and then clicking the *Disabled Items...* button in the About dialog.)
- Call a procedure to delete any previous instance of the COM add-in's toolbar that may have been left by Excel terminating unexpectedly.
- Call a procedure to create a new toolbar for the COM add-in.
- Hook our three custom command bar button controls to one Click event.

Listing 25-5 shows all these modifications. As Listing 25-5 also shows, we must cast the Excel object retrieved through COM interop to its typed equivalent.

Listing 25-5 Modifications to the OnConnection Event Procedure

```
Public Sub OnConnection(ByVal application As Object, _
                        ByVal connectMode As   _
                        ext_ConnectMode, _
                        ByVal addInInst As Object, _
                        ByRef custom As System.Array) _
                        Implements IDTExtensibility2.OnConnection


    'Customized error message.
    Const sERROR_MESSAGE As String = _
                        "An unexpected error has occurred."

    Try

        'Instantiate the Excel Application's variable.
        mxlApp = CType(application, Excel.Application)

        'Make sure that the command bar does not exists.
        Delete_Commandbar()

        'Create the command bar.
        Create_New_Commandbar()

        'Find and hook one of our customs buttons which will hook
        'all our customs buttons to the Click event.
        mcmdFirstAddinButton = _
            CType(mxlApp.CommandBars.FindControl(Tag:=msTAG),   _
                                        Office.CommandBarButton)

    'The following lines may be necessary to add in order to
    'support Windows XP visual style.
    System.Windows.Forms.Application.EnableVisualStyles()
    System.Windows.Forms.Application.DoEvents()

    Catch GeneralEx As Exception

    Show the customized message.
    MessageBox.Show(text:=sERROR_MESSAGE, _
                    caption:=msTITLE, _
                    buttons:=MessageBoxButtons.OK, _
                    icon:=MessageBoxIcon.Stop)

    End Try

End Sub
```

The OnDisconnection event procedure requires the following modifications:

- Call a procedure to delete the toolbar.
- Release all COM objects we have used. We do not always need to do this, but if we experience any problem with COM objects not being released that prevent Excel from shutting down properly, calling ReleaseComObject will solve it.

Listing 25-6 shows the modified OnDisconnection event procedure, together with a new procedure for releasing all the COM objects.

Listing 25-6 Modifications to the OnDisconnection Event Procedure

```
Public Sub OnDisconnection(ByVal RemoveMode As _
                           ext_DisconnectMode, _
                           ByRef custom As System.Array) _
                           Implements _
                           IDTExtensibility2.OnDisconnection

    Try

        Delete_Commandbar()

        Release_All_COMObjects(mcmdFirstAddinButton)
        Release_All_COMObjects(mcbrFirstAddin)
        Release_All_COMObjects(mxlApp)

    Catch GeneralEx As Exception
        'An error message during the debug process
        'should be added."

    End Try

End Sub


Private Sub Release_All_COMObjects(ByVal oxlObject As Object)

    Try
        Marshal.ReleaseComObject(oxlObject)
        oxlObject = Nothing
    Catch ex As Exception
        oxlObject = Nothing
    End Try

End Sub
```

In this example, we hard-code creation of the toolbar, as shown in Listing 25-7. We also use built-in Face IDs for the three command bar button controls.

Listing 25-7   Creating the Toolbar

```
Private Sub Create_New_Commandbar()

    'The button control variable.
    Dim ctlFirstAddin As Office.CommandBarButton = Nothing

    'Create the temporarily commandbar.
    mcbrFirstAddin = _
            CType(mxlApp.CommandBars.Add(Name:=msTITLE, _
            Position:=Office.MsoBarPosition.msoBarTop, _
            Temporary:=True), Office.CommandBar)

    With mcbrFirstAddin

        'Add a new button.
        ctlFirstAddin = CType(.Controls.Add( _
                Office.MsoControlType.msoControlButton), _
                Office.CommandBarButton)

        'Configure the created new button.
        With ctlFirstAddin
            .Caption = msBUTTON1
            .FaceId = 71
            .Parameter = msBUTTON1
            .Style = _
             Office.MsoButtonStyle.msoButtonIconAndCaption
            .Tag = msTAG
            .TooltipText = msBUTTON1
        End With

        'Add an additional new button.
        ctlFirstAddin = CType(.Controls.Add( _
                Office.MsoControlType.msoControlButton), _
                Office.CommandBarButton)

        'Configure the created new button.
        With ctlFirstAddin
            .BeginGroup = True
            .Caption = msBUTTON2
```

```
                        .FaceId = 72
                        .Parameter = msBUTTON2
                        .Style = _
                         Office.MsoButtonStyle.msoButtonIconAndCaption
                        .Tag = msTAG
                        .TooltipText = msBUTTON2
                    End With

                    'Add an additional new button.
                    ctlFirstAddin = CType(.Controls.Add( _
                            Office.MsoControlType.msoControlButton),  _
                            Office.CommandBarButton)

                    'Configure the created new button.
                    With ctlFirstAddin
                        .BeginGroup = True
                        .FaceId = 73
                        .Caption = msBUTTON3
                        .Parameter = msBUTTON3
                        .Style = _
                         Office.MsoButtonStyle.msoButtonIconAndCaption
                        .Tag = msTAG
                        .TooltipText = msBUTTON3
                    End With

                    'Position of the command bar.
                    .Position = Office.MsoBarPosition.msoBarTop
                    'Make the command bar visible.
                    .Visible = True
                End With

        'Set the WithEvents to hook the created buttons, all
        'controls that have the same Tag property will fire the
        'mcmdPetrasButton_Click event.
        mcmdFirstAddinButton = ctlFirstAddin

        'Release of the button control object.
        If (ctlFirstAddin IsNot Nothing) Then ctlFirstAddin = Nothing

End Sub
```

The procedure for deleting the toolbar is shown in Listing 25-8. As you can see, it attempts to get a reference to the first control on the toolbar and then evaluate if the control exists. If the control exists then the procedure deletes the toolbar.

Listing 25-8   Deleting the Toolbar

```
Private Sub Delete_Commandbar()

    'The check button control variable.
    Dim ctlCheck As Office.CommandBarButton = Nothing

    'If the command bar exists then get the first control
    'from the command bar.
    ctlCheck = _
            CType(mxlApp.CommandBars.FindControl(Tag:=msTAG), _
            Office.CommandBarButton)

    'If the command bar exists then delete it.
    If (ctlCheck IsNot Nothing) Then
        mxlApp.CommandBars(msTITLE).Delete()
    End If

End Sub
```

We test the COM add-in by pressing the F5 key. Visual Studio loads Excel and then Excel loads our COM add-in and displays our customized toolbar as shown in Figure 25-20.

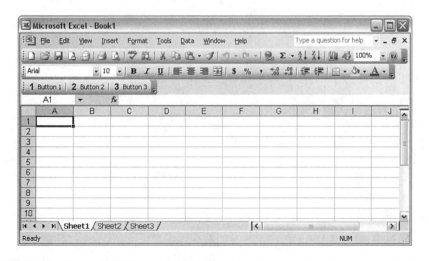

FIGURE 25-20   The toolbar for our COM add-in

Up to this point, we have only created the framework for our COM add-in's toolbar. The final piece is to put some code into the Click event for the toolbar buttons. Listing 25-9 shows how we hook the Click event and use it to display a message box when the user clicks one of the toolbar buttons.

Listing 25-9   Hooking the Command Bar Control Click Event

```vb
Private Sub cmdFirstAddinButton_Click( _
                    ByVal Ctrl As Office.CommandBarButton, _
                    ByRef CancelDefault As Boolean) _
                    Handles mcmdFirstAddinButton.Click

    'Customized error message.
    Const sERROR_MESSAGE As String = _
            "Cannot execute the wanted action."

    Dim sTEXT As String = "You clicked on "

    Try
        'Make sure it is one of ours controls.
        If Ctrl.Tag = msTAG Then

            'Run the appropriate message.
            Select Case Ctrl.Parameter
                Case msBUTTON1
                    MessageBox.Show(text:=sTEXT & msBUTTON1, _
                                    caption:=msTITLE)
                Case msBUTTON2
                    MessageBox.Show(text:=sTEXT & msBUTTON2, _
                                    caption:=msTITLE)
                Case msBUTTON3
                    MessageBox.Show(text:=sTEXT & msBUTTON3, _
                                    caption:=msTITLE)
            End Select

        End If

        'We handled the event, so cancel its default behavior.
        CancelDefault = True
```

```
Catch Generalex As Exception

    'Show the customized message.
    MessageBox.Show(text:=sERROR_MESSAGE, _
                    caption:=msTITLE, _
                    buttons:=MessageBoxButtons.OK, _
                    icon:=MessageBoxIcon.Stop)

    End Try

End Sub
```

When we click one of the command bar controls on our toolbar, a message box displays the caption of the control we clicked, as shown in Figure 25-21.

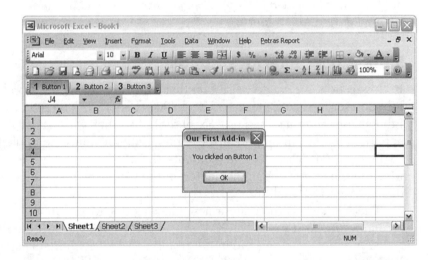

FIGURE 25-21 A message box is displayed after clicking one of the toolbar buttons.

Finally, Figure 25-22 shows how our managed COM add-in toolbar appears when the add-in is run under Excel 2007. Note that Excel 2007 dumps all command bar-based toolbars into the same Add-Ins Ribbon group, and we cannot control where our toolbar appears in relation to other command bar-based toolbars. This is one disadvantage of using command bars in Excel 2007.

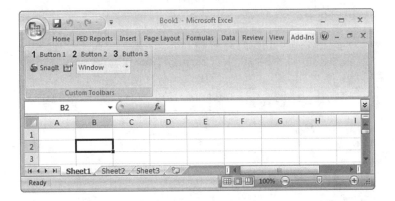

FIGURE 25-22 The classic toolbar solution running in the Excel 2007 Ribbon user interface

A working example of this solution can be found on the companion CD in the *\Concepts\Ch25 - Writing Managed COM Add-ins with VB.NET\FirstAddin* folder.

Ribbon User Interface Handling

In this section, we create a solution that explicitly targets the Excel 2007 Ribbon user interface. Because Excel 2003 cannot work directly with the Ribbon user interface, we use Excel 2007 together with VS 2008. It is important to keep in mind that the Ribbon interface must be implemented in the same class that implements the IDTextensibility2 interface, which means it must be implemented in the Connection Class module of the managed COM add-in.

The first step is to create a new managed COM add-in and name it *SecondAddin*. Next we add an XML file to the assembly. Select the *Project > Add New Item...* menu and in the resulting Add New Item dialog select *XML File* from the *Templates* list. Enter the name RibbonCustom.xml for the XML file and click the *Add* button.

The next step is to change the build action for the XML file. Right-click the RibbonCustom.xml file in Solution Explorer and choose *Properties* from the shortcut menu. In the Properties window change the *Build Action* property to *Embedded Resource*. This means the XML file will be part of the compiled assembly instead of being a separate file. Figure 25-23 shows the property settings for the RibbonCustom.xml file.

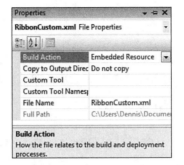

FIGURE 25-23 The properties of the customized XML file

For the content of the XML file, first remove the default line of XML markup and replace it with the XML markup shown in Listing 25-10.

Listing 25-10 The XML for the Ribbon User Interface

```
<customUI
  xmlns="http://schemas.microsoft.com/office/2006/01/customui">

    <ribbon startFromScratch="false">

    <tabs>

        <tab id="rxPED.Tab"
             label="PED Reports"
             keytip="Z"
             insertAfterMso="TabHome"
             visible="true">

            <group id="rxReport.Group"
                   label="Reports"
                   visible="true">

                <button id="rxbtnTime"
                        label="Time Report"
                        screentip="Create a Time report."
                        keytip="T"
                        imageMso="DateAndTimeInsert"
                        size="large"
                        onAction="PED_Reports_Click" />

                <button id="rxbtnChart"
                        label="Chart Report"
```

```
                            screentip="Create Chart report."
                            keytip="C"
                            imageMso="ChartInsert"
                            size="large"
                            onAction="PED_Reports_Click" />

                 <button id="rxbtnData"
                            label="Data Report"
                            screentip="Create Data report."
                            keytip="D"
                            imageMso="ExportExcel"
                            size="large"
                            onAction="PED_Reports_Click" />

          </group>

       </tab>

     </tabs>

   </ribbon>

 </customUI>
```

The XML shown in Listing 25-10 creates a new tab with the name *PED Reports*, a group for our controls, and three button controls inside the group. In this solution we use some of the built-in icon images in Excel 2007. The button controls share the same callback handler, so the same subroutine catches the Click event for all three of them. For the tab and for the three button controls we use keytips, which enable us to navigate our custom Ribbon using the keyboard.

The **XML Editor** in the VS IDE provides both IntelliSense and validation when working with Ribbon customization. The XML Editor is invoked for some well-known file extensions such as .xml, .xsd, .xsl, and .config.

To see which schema the Ribbon customization is validated against, open the RibbonCustom.xml file. With the XML file open, the Properties window shows that the active schema is the customUI.xsd file shown in Figure 25-24. It should be noted that customUI.xsd is the default schema for the Ribbon user interface.

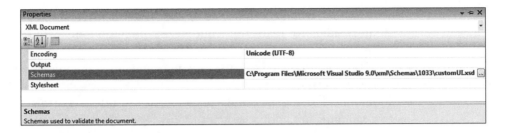

FIGURE 25-24   Properties windows for the RibbonCustom.xml file

By default, no line numbers are displayed in the XML Editor. You can change this by selecting *Tools* > *Options...* from the VS menu. In the Options dialog tree view, locate and expand the *Text Editor* > *XML* > *General* node. Make sure the *Line Numbers* check box is checked as shown in Figure 25-25.

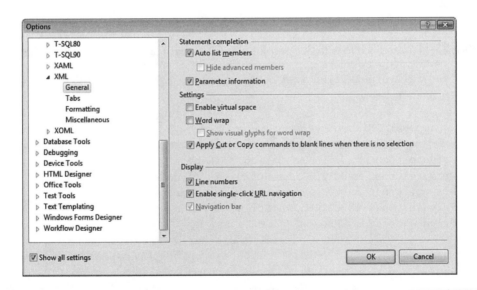

FIGURE 25-25   Settings for the XML Editor in VS IDE

To get the Ribbon customization up and running, we need to modify the Connection class as described here and shown in Listing 25-11:

■ Two new namespaces are imported and placed at the top of the module. The namespace `System.Reflection` is used to work with the assembly, while the namespace System.IO is used to create a StreamReader to read the content of the RibbonCustom.xml document.

- The IRibbonExtensibility interface must be implemented in the Connection class.
- Module-level string constants related to the button controls and error handling are added.
- The public function GetCustomUI is required by the IRibbonExtensibility interface. It loads the XML markup from the RibbonCustom.xml file and passes it to the Ribbon user interface. This function is called immediately after the OnConnection event has been executed.
- We create the shared callback handler named PED_Reports_Click. Inside it we use a Select Case statement to determine which button triggered the handler and display a message box with the name of this button.

Listing 25-11   Modifications to Support Ribbon Customization in the Connection Class

```
Imports System.Reflection
Imports System.IO

Implements IRibbonExtensibility

Private Const msTITLE As String = "Ribbon Handling"
Private Const msBUTTON1 As String = "Time Report"
Private Const msBUTTON2 As String = "Chart Report"
Private Const msBUTTON3 As String = "Data Report"
Private Const msERROR_MESSAGE As String = _
            "Cannot execute the desired action."

Public Function GetCustomUI(ByVal ribbonID As String) As String _
                Implements IRibbonExtensibility.GetCustomUI

    'The resource we want to retrieve the XML markup from.
    Const sResourceName As String = "RibbonCustom.xml"

    'Variable for iterating the collection of resources.
    Dim sName As String = Nothing

    'Set a reference to this assembly during runtime.
    Dim asm As Assembly = Assembly.GetExecutingAssembly()
```

```vbnet
        'Get the collection of resource names in this assembly.
        Dim ResourceNames() As String = _
                        asm.GetManifestResourceNames()

        'Iterate through the collection until it finds the
        'resource named RibbonCustom.xml.
        For Each sName In ResourceNames

            If sName.EndsWith(sResourceName) Then
                'Create an instance of the StremReader object that
                'reads the embedded file containing the XML markup.
                Dim srResourceReader As StreamReader = _
                New StreamReader( _
                    asm.GetManifestResourceStream(sName))

                'Reads the content of the resource file.
                Dim sResource As String = _
                    srResourceReader.ReadToEnd()

                'Close the StreamReader.
                srResourceReader.Close()

                'Returns the XML to the Ribbon user interface.
                Return sResource

            End If

        Next

        Return Nothing

End Function

Public Sub PED_Reports_Click(ByVal control As IRibbonControl)

    Try
        'Run the appropriate message.
        Select Case control.Id
            Case "rxbtnTime"
                MessageBox.Show(text:=msTEXT & msBUTTON1, _
                                caption:=msTITLE)
            Case "rxbtnChart"
                MessageBox.Show(text:=msTEXT & msBUTTON2, _
```

```
                                caption:=msTITLE)
            Case "rxbtnData"
                MessageBox.Show(text:=msTEXT & msBUTTON3, _
                               caption:=msTITLE)
        End Select

    Catch Generalex As Exception

        'Show the customized message.
        MessageBox.Show(text:=msERROR_MESSAGE, _
                       caption:=msTITLE, _
                       buttons:=MessageBoxButtons.OK, _
                       icon:=MessageBoxIcon.Stop)
    End Try
End Sub
```

Figure 25-26 shows our solution running in Excel 2007 with keytips activated (by pressing the Alt key).

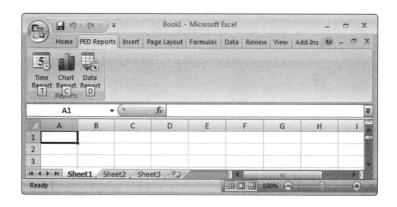

Figure 25-26 The Ribbon customization with keytips activated

When one of the button controls is clicked, the `PED_Reports_Click` handler is executed and a message box with the name of the button is displayed, as shown in Figure 25-27.

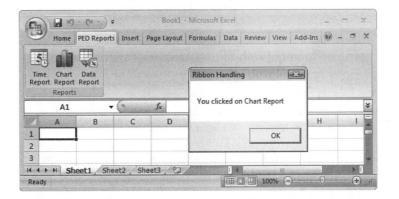

FIGURE 25-27   Our Ribbon customization in action

A working example of this solution can be found on the companion CD in the *\Concepts\Ch25 - Writing Managed COM Add-ins with VB.NET \SecondAddin* folder.

Using Custom Icon Images

It is easy to add and use custom icon images in VB.NET solutions. The VS IDE provides a tool to create custom icon images, but it is a primitive and time-consuming activity. The better option is to use icon images shipped in commercial packages. These packages usually include icons in several image file formats such as .bmp, .gif, .jpeg, and .png.

The preferred image file format for Ribbon customization is the .png file format. This is because the .png format natively supports full transparency for the image background. It is technically possible to get the same transparency with other file formats, but this requires more advanced solutions that are beyond the scope of this chapter. Figure 25-28 shows a Ribbon customization using the .bmp image format as compared to the customization using the .png image format shown in Figure 25-29. You can easily see the difference in background transparency between them.

FIGURE 25-28   Using custom icon images with the .bmp file format

FIGURE 25-29 Using custom icon images with the .png file format

The XML markup previously shown in Listing 25-10 requires only minor modifications to support custom icon images. Listing 25-12 shows an updated XML markup for the first button control. Note that we have specified a callback in the `getImage` attribute instead of specifying a button image with the `imageMso` attribute. We soon see how this callback is used to apply the image to the button.

Listing 25-12 Revised XML Markup for Using Custom Icon Images

```
<button id="rxbtnTime"
    label="Time Report"
    screentip="Create a Time report."
    keytip="T"
    getImage="bmpGetImage"
    size="large"
    onAction="PED_Reports_Click" />
```

Next we add our custom icon image files as resources to the solution. Select the *Project > [Projectname] Properties...* menu and then select the *Resources* tab. If this is the first time we have added a resource then we need to click on the link *This project does not contain a default resource file. Click here to create one*. Next click on the down arrow at the right side of the *Add Resource* button and select the *Add Existing File...* option from the drop-down menu. Use the Add Existing File to Resources dialog to navigate to the folder that contains the custom icon image files and select them. Figure 25-30 shows the Resources window and the Solution Explorer window of an example solution with icon resources.

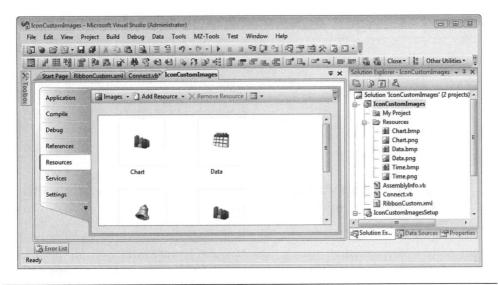

FIGURE 25-30 Resources added to a solution

In Listing 25-12, we specified the custom callback function bmpGetImage to apply the custom icon images. This function is placed in the Connection class and is executed when the XML markup in RibbonCustom.xml is passed to the Ribbon user interface. Listing 25-13 shows the additional code required to implement the bmpGetImage function.

Listing 25-13 The Callback Function for the Custom Icon Images

```vbnet
Imports System.Drawing

Public Function bmpGetImage(ByVal control As _
                            IRibbonControl) _
                            As Bitmap

    Select Case control.Id
        Case "rxbtnTime" : Return New Bitmap(My.Resources.Time)
        Case "rxbtnChart" : Return New Bitmap(My.Resources.Chart)
        Case "rxbtnData" : Return New Bitmap(My.Resources.Data)
    End Select

    Return Nothing

End Function
```

Creating Managed Automation Add-ins

In Chapter 23, we described how to create Automation add-ins with Classic VB. Here we describe how to do it with VB.NET and how to make the UDFs available in Excel. Although we demonstrate the ability to create Automation add-ins using VB.NET, we actually discourage the use of VB.NET for this purpose due to several limitations that we also cover in more detail.

Creating an Automation Add-in That Interacts with the Excel Application Object

Any real-world application needs to interact with the Excel Application object, so we demonstrate how to create a solution based on the Shared Add-in Template. Since the add-in implements the IDTextensibility2 interface, it can be loaded as both a COM add-in and an Automation add-in. However, it is loaded in two separate and independent instances, where the COM add-in is loaded on startup and the Automation add-in loads on demand.

Using VS 2008 create a new project based on the Shared Add-in Template under *Other Project Types* > *Extensibility* and name it FirstAutoAddin. Then make the following selections in the Shared Add-in Wizard:

- **Page 1**—Select the option *Create an Add-in using Visual Basic*.
- **Page 2**—Uncheck all host applications except *Microsoft Excel*.
- **Page 3**—Name the add-in Our first UDFs Add-in and add the description Chapter 25 - Writing Managed COM Add-ins with VB.NET.
- **Page 4**—Leave both check boxes unselected.
- **Page 5**—Verify that the selections are what you intended and click the *Finish* button.

Next, select the *Project* > *FirstAutoAddin Properties...* menu and make the following settings:

- Select the *Application* tab and enter AutoAddin as the Assembly name.
- Select the *Compile* tab and make sure the *Register for COM Interop* check box is checked.
- Select the *Debug* tab and set a pointer to the Excel.exe file for the *Start external program* option.

- Select the *References* tab and add a reference to *Microsoft Excel 11.0 Object Library* from the COM references list.

Next, open the *Registry Editor* by right-clicking the *FirstAutoAddinSetup* node in Solution Explorer and selecting *View > Registry* from the shortcut menu. In the Registry Editor, right-click the *HKEY_CLASSES_ROOT* node and select *New Key* from the shortcut menu. Name the new key CLSID. Right-click the new CLSID key and select *New > Key* from the shortcut menu. The name of this key will be the GUID for our solution, which can be found in the `GuidAttribute` in the Connect class module. In our example the generated GUID is `29EA6584-871E-438A-ADA8-8EBA0A7BCC5A`, and we surround it with curly brackets so the key name will actually be `{29EA6584-871E-438A-ADA8-8EBA0A7BCC5A}`. Select the new key and in the Properties window change the value of the *AlwaysCreate* property to *True* and the value of the *DeleteAtUninstall* property to *True*.

Finally, create a new key under the GUID key and name it Programmable. Make sure that its *AlwaysCreate* and *DeleteAtUninstall* property values are set to *True* as well. These keys contain entries that are used to register the add-in as an **Automation Server** in the Windows Registry when the COM add-in is installed. Figure 25-31 shows the new keys in the Registry Editor. It also shows the keys that were automatically created when we created the solution.

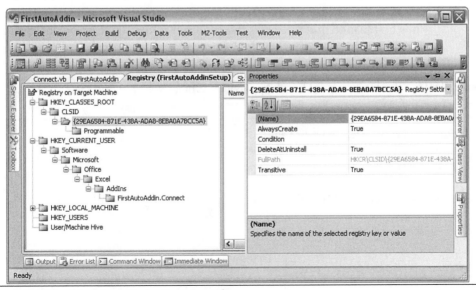

FIGURE 25-31 New keys in the Registry Editor

The next step is to add the code to the Connect class to make our UDFs available for Excel and visible to it. The imports statements are shown in Listing 25-14.

Listing 25-14 Imports Statements

```
Imports Extensibility
Imports System.Runtime.InteropServices
Imports Excel = Microsoft.Office.Interop.Excel
```

We also need to add an additional attribute for **ClassInterface**, specifying **AutoDual** as the type, as shown in Listing 25-15.

Listing 25-15 The ClassInterface Attribute

```
<GuidAttribute("29EA6584-871E-438A-ADA8-8EBA0A7BCC5A"), _
ProgIdAttribute("FirstAutoAddin.Connect"), _
ClassInterface(ClassInterfaceType.AutoDual)> _
Public Class Connect
```

To interact with Excel, the solution needs to retrieve and store a reference to the Excel Application object. Here we use the same mechanism to retrieve the reference as described in Chapter 23 in the section "Automation Add-ins." Excel calls the OnConnection event when the add-in is first loaded and passes us the required reference. Listing 25-16 shows how this is implemented in the Connect class.

Listing 25-16 The Module-Level Excel Application Object Variable and the OnConnection/OnDisconnection Events

```
#Region "Module-level variables."

    Dim mxlApp As Excel.Application

    Private Const mSTITLE As String = "Automation Add-in"

#End Region

#Region "Connect and Disconnect"

    Public Sub OnConnection(ByVal application As Object, _
                    ByVal connectMode As ext_ConnectMode, _
```

```
                                ByVal addInInst As Object, _
                                ByRef custom As System.Array) _
                                Implements IDTExtensibility2.OnConnection

        Const sERROR_MESSAGE As String = _
                "An unexpected error has occurred."

        Try
                mxlApp = CType(application, Excel.Application)

        Catch GeneralEx As Exception

                MessageBox.Show(text:=sERROR_MESSAGE, _
                                caption:=msTITLE, _
                                buttons:=MessageBoxButtons.OK, _
                                icon:=MessageBoxIcon.Stop)

        End Try

    End Sub

    Public Sub OnDisconnection(ByVal RemoveMode As _
                                ext_DisconnectMode, _
                                ByRef custom As System.Array) _
                                Implements _
                                IDTExtensibility2.OnDisconnection
        Marshal.ReleaseComObject(mxlApp)
        mxlApp = Nothing
    End Sub

#End Region
```

Next, we add the code for the UDFs to the Connect class as shown in Listing 25-17.

Listing 25-17   The User-Defined Function in Our Automation Add-in

```
#Region "User Defined Functions."

    Public Function IFERROR(ByVal ToEvaluate As Object, _
                            ByVal UseDefault As Object) As Object

        Dim objOutput As Object = Nothing
```

```vb.net
        If IsError(ToEvaluate) Then
            objOutput = UseDefault
        Else
            objOutput = ToEvaluate
        End If


        Return objOutput

    End Function


    Public Function VBTIMER() As Double

        Dim dTime As Double = Nothing

        mxlApp.Volatile(True)

        dTime = Microsoft.VisualBasic.Timer

        Return dTime

    End Function

    Public Function COUNTBETWEEN(ByRef Source As Excel.Range, _
                                 ByVal Min As Double, _
                                 ByRef Max As Double) As Double

        Dim dCountBetween As Double = Nothing

        Try

            dCountBetween =  _
             mxlApp.WorksheetFunction.CountIf(Source, ">" & Min)

            dCountBetween = dCountBetween - _
             mxlApp.WorksheetFunction.CountIf(Source, ">=" & Max)

        Catch GeneralEx As Exception

            dCountBetween = 0

        End Try

        Return dCountBetween
```

```
End Function

#End Region
```

Before we can run the solution, we need to perform two final steps: Build the solution and create the setup. First select the *Build > Build Solution* menu; then save the solution and select the *Build > Build FirstAutoAddin* menu. To test the solution on the development computer we first need to install it. Right-click the *FirstAutoAddinSetup* node in Solution Explorer and select *Install* from the shortcut menu. Complete the steps required by the Installation Wizard and then press the F5 key to test the solution.

Because this is the first time we have run our solution, we also need to load the Automation add-in in Excel. Once Excel has started select the *Tools > Add-ins...* menu. In the Excel Add-Ins dialog click on the *Automation...* button. In the Automation Servers dialog browse until you see the `FirstAutoAddin.Connect` entry in the list. Select this entry and click OK. The add-in should now be listed and checked in the Add-Ins dialog. The ProgId for the solution is used as the name for the add-in. Click OK in the Add-Ins dialog to return to Excel. Now the functions in the Automation add-in are available, and we can use them just like any other functions in a worksheet:

- =IFERROR(A1/B1,0)
- =VBTIMER()
- =COUNTBETWEEN(A10:A20,2,10)

A working example of the FirstAutoAddin solution can be found on the companion CD in the *\Concepts\Ch25 - Writing Managed COM Add-ins with VB.NET\FirstAutoAddin* folder.

Why We Should Not Create Automation Add-ins with .NET

Trying to integrate .NET with COM does not always produce acceptable results. Using VB.NET to create managed Automation add-ins is a case where we should consider using another development tool. This is due to a number of limitations.

CVErr Values Not Implemented in .NET

Built-in worksheet functions and UDFs created in VBA or Classic VB can return **CVErr values** like #DIV0! or #VALUE!. Instead of CVErr values, in .NET we get Int32 values like -2146826273. This can be resolved but requires a complex solution that includes all possible scenarios and all CVErr values. For more information please see the following URLs:

- http://xldennis.wordpress.com/2006/11/22/dealing-with-cverr-values-in-net-%e2%80%93-part-i-the-problem/
- http://xldennis.wordpress.com/2006/11/29/dealing-with-cverr-values-in-net-part-ii-solutions/

Insert Function Wizard

We cannot create new function categories for our Automation add-in UDFs. Each add-in is listed in its own function category, where the ProgId name is used as the function category name. We cannot change the name of this function category. In addition, we cannot specify function descriptions, argument descriptions, or help for our Automation add-in functions. Also, various .NET typeinfo functions are displayed in the function list for our Automation add-in as if they were worksheet functions, as shown in Figure 25-32.

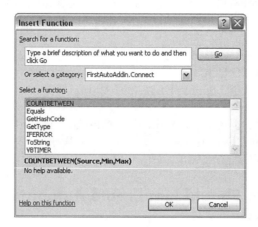

FIGURE 25-32 Typeinfo for the add-in in the function list

Three of these functions can be hidden using the code shown in Listing 25-18. The last one, GetType, can only be hidden if we avoid using a class interface. To interact with the Excel Application object and shim the Automation add-in we must implement the IDTExtensibility2 interface, so it might appear that there is no way to hide the GetType function.

Listing 25-18   Code to Hide Typeinfo in the Function List

```
#Region "Hide unwanted options in the function category."
    <ComVisible(False)> _
    Public Overrides Function Equals(ByVal obj As Object) As Boolean

        Return MyBase.Equals(obj)

    End Function

    <ComVisible(False)> _
    Public Overrides Function GetHashCode() As Integer

        Return MyBase.GetHashCode()

    End Function

    <ComVisible(False)> _
    Public Overrides Function ToString() As String

        Return MyBase.ToString()

    End Function
#End Region
```

By eliminating the Connect class interface, we can solve this problem entirely. However, this creates a new problem. Without the Connect class interface the default interface for the add-in class is the first interface implemented by the Connect class. If we want to implement additional interfaces, for instance for a new set of UDFs, they will not be visible in Excel. The solution is to create only one interface per class.

To demonstrate this solution we create a new automation add-in project identical to the first project and name it SecondAutoAddin. Next we need to create a GUID for the Connect class. This is done with a special-purpose utility supplied with Visual Studio. Open a Visual Studio command window by selecting *Start > All Programs > Microsoft Visual Studio 2008 > Visual Studio Tools > Visual Studio 2008 Command Prompt*. At the command prompt type guidgen.exe and press Enter. This displays the Create GUID dialog shown in Figure 25-33.

FIGURE 25-33 The Create GUID dialog

In the Create GUID dialog, select the *4 Registry Format* option, as shown in Figure 25-33 and click the *Copy* button. Paste the GUID to a temporary location in the Connect.vb class module. We use it in a moment.

At the top of the Connect.vb class module just below the Imports statements, we create a custom Public interface for our UDFs called IPEDFunctions. Within the definition for this interface we add declarations for all the functions we will expose as Excel worksheet functions. We then add a GuidAttribute to this interface and assign it the GUID we created earlier. All this is shown in Listing 25-19.

Listing 25-19 The Custom UDF Interface IPEDFunctions

```
Imports statements go here.

<GuidAttribute("203C934D-B76C-42da-932C-E0ECF8815AEC")> _
Public Interface IPEDFunctions

    Function IFERROR(ByVal ToEvaluate As Object, _
                   ByVal UseDefault As Object) As Object

    Function VBTIMER() As Double

    Function COUNTBETWEEN(ByRef Source As Excel.Range, _
                   ByVal Min As Double, _
                   ByRef Max As Double) As Double
End Interface
```

Next, we change the `ClassInterface` attribute of our Connect class to `ClassInterfaceType.None` and implement the `IPEDFunctions` interface as its first interface, as shown in Listing 25-20.

Listing 25-20 Updated ClassInterface Attribute

```
<GuidAttribute("FE553451-81D5-4DC8-9896-B5019D6A2AF4"), _
ProgIdAttribute("SecondAutoAddin.Connect")> _
<ClassInterface(ClassInterfaceType.None)> _
Public Class Connect

    Implements IPEDFunctions
    Implements IDTExtensibility2
```

Finally, we use the Registry Editor to create a new entry for the custom GUID in the same way as we did for the FirstAutoAddin project. Under the GUID key we add an additional key and name it Programmable. Make sure the values for the properties *AlwaysCreate* and *DeleteAtUnInstall* are set to True for both of these registry keys. Now, after installing our automation add-in and loading it in Excel, only our UDFs are visible in the Insert Function dialog, as shown in Figure 25-34.

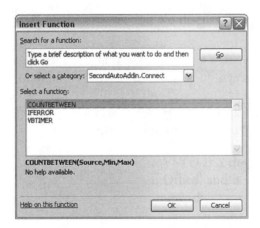

FIGURE 25-34 Only the UDFs are available in the Insert Function dialog.

A working example of the SecondAutoAddin solution can be found on the companion CD in the *\Concepts\Ch25 - Writing Managed COM Add-ins with VB.NET\SecondAutoAddin* folder.

ProgId Limitations

The maximum length of a ProgId is 39 characters. If we exceed this limit no explicit error message is given. The only error we get is that the add-in is not a valid add-in.

Selecting a Managed Automation Add-in in the Add-in Manager Generates an Error Message

Whenever we open the Add-in manager in Excel and select a managed Automation add-in from the list, the error message shown in Figure 25-35 is displayed. Selecting *Yes* in the dialog removes our managed Automation add-in from the Excel add-ins list.

FIGURE 25-35   Error message when selecting a managed automation add-in in the Add-in Manager

However, it is possible to resolve this issue by adding the full path to the mscoree.dll file in the Windows Registry under HKEY_CLASSES_ROOT. To do so we add the ComRegisterFunctionAttribute and ComUnregister-FunctionAttribute to the class that connects the automation add-in to Excel as shown in Listing 25-21. The method inside ComRegister-FunctionAttribute is executed during COM registration of the assembly. The method inside ComUnregisterFunctionAttribute is executed in a similar way when the assembly is unregistered.

Listing 25-21   Register and Unregister the Assembly for Use by COM

```
'On top of the module.
Imports Microsoft.Win32

    <ComRegisterFunctionAttribute()> _
    Public Shared Sub RegisterFunction(ByVal type As Type)
```

```
    'Create the sub-key Programmable.
    Registry.ClassesRoot.CreateSubKey(GetSubKeyName(type, _
                                    "Programmable"))

    'Get access to the sub-key InprocServer32.
    Dim rkKey As RegistryKey = Registry.ClassesRoot.OpenSubKey _
                (GetSubKeyName(type, "InprocServer32"), True)

    'Add a String value under the sub-key InprocServer32.
    rkKey.SetValue("", System.Environment.SystemDirectory + _
                "\mscoree.dll", RegistryValueKind.String)

End Sub

<ComUnregisterFunctionAttribute()> _
Public Shared Sub UnregisterFunction(ByVal type As Type)

    'Delete the created sub-key Programmable.
    Registry.ClassesRoot.DeleteSubKey(GetSubKeyName(type, :
                                    "Programmable"), False)

End Sub

Private Shared Function GetSubKeyName(ByVal type As Type, _
                ByVal subKeyName As String) As String

    Dim sBuilder As New System.Text.StringBuilder()

    sBuilder.Append("CLSID\{")

    sBuilder.Append(type.GUID.ToString().ToUpper())

    sBuilder.Append("}\")

    sBuilder.Append(subKeyName)

    Return sBuilder.ToString()

End Function
```

Because of the limitations discussed in this section, we do not recommend VB.NET as a tool for creating Automation add-ins. But what are the alternatives? VBA is a possibility, but VBA project protection is rather weak. Classic VB is a good candidate, but it may be difficult to find if you don't already own it. A third option is to write XLLs in C++. XLLs provide speed, security, and ease of deployment but also a high degree of complexity. Writing XLLs in C++ is covered in Chapter 27, "XLLs and the C API."

Manually Register and Unregister COM Add-ins

Up to this point, we have relied on the auto-generated setup projects to automatically register and unregister our COM add-ins. In this section, we take a closer look at how this is done so we can do it manually if necessary.

We use the regasm.exe command-line utility to register and unregister managed add-ins. This utility serves the same purpose for .NET solutions as regsvr32.exe serves for unmanaged DLLs. You use regasm.exe from the Visual Studio 2008 command prompt. A shortcut to open this command prompt can be found in the *Microsoft Visual Studio 2008 > Visual Studio Tools* folder under *Start Menu > All Programs*. To register a COM add-in on Windows XP use the following command:

```
regasm c:\<path>\NameOfTheAddin.dll
```

To unregister a COM add-in we add the /u switch to the command as in the following example:

```
regasm /u c:\<path>\NameOfTheAddin.dll
```

It is also possible to retrieve all the settings that are created when registering a managed add-in with regasm.exe. The following command from the Visual Studio 2008 Command Prompt creates a file named Test.reg, which then can be opened in a text editor like NotePad to view its content.

```
regasm c:\<path>\NameOfTheAddin.dll /regfile;<path>\Test.reg
```

Using Classes in VB.NET

Although we have not focused on classes until now, they play a central role in the .NET platform and provide VB.NET with object oriented programming capabilities. In this section we provide an introduction to classes and discuss how to work with them in VB.NET. Chapter 7, "Using Class

Modules to Create Objects," provided a basic overview of classes that can also be applied to classes in the .NET platform, although there are differences in the coding techniques required.

To add a class module to a VB.NET solution, select the *Project > Add Class...* menu. In the Add New Item dialog give the class module a name and click the *Add* button.

Creating Well-Designed Classes

A class can be described as a template for objects that we can create copies of whenever we want to use them. In VB.NET we define a class by using the keyword `Class` within a `Class...End Class` block. Classes can contain data, or **Fields** (the name for variables on the .NET platform), properties, events, methods, and function members like **constructors** and **destructors**. The data and functions are important, but it is also important to create a robust framework for the class.

The first decision to make when designing a class is to what degree the object defined by the class should be visible to other objects within the same solution as well as other solutions. The general strategy is to make classes invisible as much as possible. In the following example we make the class available within the solution where it resides. We accomplish this by declaring its visibility as `Friend`.

When we write the implementation of a class interface, the VS IDE autocompletes it by adding code statements to the class. For this example we can delete all this automatically generated code because we enter the required code manually. In this example we use a customized process to release both managed and unmanaged resources in the class. This is typical when we use unmanaged resources like the Excel object model in a class. For classes that use only managed resources it is not necessary to implement a custom cleanup process. Listing 25-22 shows the initial class framework that we build upon in this section.

Listing 25-22 A Framework for Well-Designed Classes

```
Friend Class CFirstClass

    Implements IDisposable

    'A solution-wide field.
    Friend swiStatus As Integer

    'A flag which indicates the status of the disposal.
```

```vbnet
Private mbDisposed As Boolean = False

'The constructor.
Sub New()

    swiStatus = 10

End Sub

'The disposal of the class.
Public Sub Dispose() Implements IDisposable.Dispose

    CleanUp(True)
    GC.SuppressFinalize(Me)

End Sub

'The custom clean-up method.
Private Sub CleanUp(ByVal bDisposing as Boolean)

    If Not Me.mbDisposed Then

        If bDisposing Then

            'Here we dispose managed resources.

        End If

        'Here we clean up unmanaged resources.

    End If

    mbDisposed = True

End Sub

'The destructor.
Protected Overrides Sub Finalize()

    Try

        CleanUp(bDisposing:=False)

    Catch ex As Exception
```

```
            'No error message should be shown.

        Finally

            MyBase.Finalize()

        End Try

    End Sub

End Class
```

In VB.NET, we use constructors and destructors similarly to the way we use the `Class_Initialize` and `Class_Terminate` events in VBA and VB6. The constructor in a VB.NET class only runs once, when the class is first created, and the code in the constructor always runs before any other code in a class. The constructor cannot be called explicitly anywhere other than in the first line of code of another constructor in either the same class or a derived class.

The name of the constructor is always `Sub New`. When invoked, the constructor can initialize objects in the class, as shown in Listing 25-22. The constructor can also take user-defined parameters, which make it more flexible. In Listing 25-23 we show how to create a new instance of a class where we also pass a value to the constructor.

The class in Listing 25-22 also has a destructor, the `Finalize` method. A custom `Finalize` method comes with a performance penalty and should only be used when we need to explicitly release managed and unmanaged objects. The Finalize destructor is a protected method that can only be called from the class it belongs to or from derived classes. When you override the `Finalize` method, .NET assumes that a custom cleanup process will actually take place.

The `Finalize` method is automatically called by the CLR when it determines the object is no longer required. The .NET garbage collector (GC) is responsible for releasing objects. In the .NET environment we do not know when garbage collection will be performed, because the process is nondeterministic. Another problem is that the GC cannot dispose unmanaged objects because they are outside the CLR, so the CLR is not aware of them. To overcome this lack of control and to supplement the GC we can implement the **IDisposable** interface, which includes only one method, the `Dispose` method. Unlike the `Finalize` method we must call the `Dispose` method explicitly when we want to dispose objects.

To summarize, we have two destructors, `Finalize` and `Dispose`, which complement each other so that both managed and unmanaged resources can be disposed when necessary.

We create a helper method that actually performs the cleanup process. This method, called CleanUp, is also shown in Listing 25-22. To ensure that the `Dispose` method can be called several times we use a module-level Boolean field that we initially set to `True`. Executing `GC.SuppressFinalize(Me)` sets a flag that indicates to the GC that the specified object should not have its `Finalize` method called. Even if the calling code does not call the `Dispose` method the GC will eventually finalize the object.

Listing 25-23 A Constructor with Arguments

```
'In the source that create a new instance of the class.

Dim iGroups As Integer = CInt(Me.TextBox1.Text)
Dim clsStart As New CFirstClass(iNumberOfGroups:=iGroups)

'In the class module.
'The constructor with an argument.
Sub New(ByVal iNumberOfGroups As Integer)

    If iNumberOfGroups > 5 Then
        'Do something.
    Else
        'Do something else.
    End If

End Sub
```

Listing 25-24 shows how we create a new instance of a class, use the instance, and dispose the instance when we are finished with it.

Listing 25-24 Create a New Instance and Dispose the Instance of a Class

```
'Instantiate a new instance of the class.
Dim clsStart As New CFirstClass

'Do the work...
MessageBox.Show(clsStart.swiStatus.ToString())
```

```
'Dispose the instance.
clsStart.Dispose()

'Prepare the object for the GC.
clsStart = Nothing
```

It is also possible to automatically call the `Dispose` method by using the **Using** keyword, as shown in Listing 25-25. Within the scope of the `Using` block we can work with all objects in the class as well as implement SEH logic to handle errors.

Listing 25-25 Using the Using Keyword to Automatically Call the Dispose Method

```
Using clsStart As New CFirstClass

    MessageBox.Show(clsStart.swiStatus.ToString())

End Using
```

Although it is possible to create several classes in one code module, it is preferable to let each class reside in its own file. This provides a better structure and allows us to use the **Class View** window in the VS IDE to get a detailed overview of all the classes in the solution. If the *Class View* tab is not visible you can select *View > Other Windows > Class View* from the VS menu to make it available. Figure 25-36 shows the Class View window.

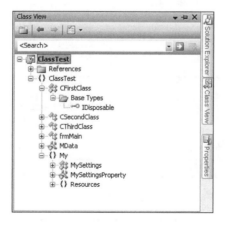

FIGURE 25-36 The Class View Window

Properties

Properties in .NET classes have the same function as in VBA and Classic VB, but we implement them differently in VB.NET. In VB.NET we use the single property declaration. Although a Property is a single structure it is divided into two parts: a Get and a Set block.

In Listing 25-26, we create a single value read-write Property. The class has a field called i_Numbers declared as Private. The Property is called iNumbers, and it acts as a wrapper for the i_Number field. The property is declared as Friend, which makes it available within the solution only. The parameter for Set must have the same data type as the Property and must be defined as ByVal. By default the parameter is named value; we can change this to a more relevant name if we want.

Listing 25-26 A Read-Write Property

```
Private i_Numbers As Integer

Friend Property iNumbers() As Integer

    Get
        Return i_Numbers
    End Get

    Set(ByVal value As Integer)

        'Before we assign the value to i_Numbers we can
        'validate here.
        i_Numbers = value

    End Set

End Property
```

Listing 25-27 shows how we use the iNumbers Property in code.

Listing 25-27 Using the Property

```
Dim clsStart As New CFirstClass

clsStart.iNumbers = 200
```

A read-only property is one that contains only the Get block, as shown in Listing 25-28. In this case we use the property to retrieve the database connection string from the solution's app.config.xml file. Similarly, a write-only property is one that contains only the `Set` block.

Listing 25-28 A Read-Only Property

```
Friend ReadOnly Property sConnection() As String

    Get
        Return My.Settings.Connection
    End Get

End Property
```

It is also possible to declare the `Get` and `Set` blocks of a property with different scopes. Listing 25-29 shows a property that is declared as `Public` while the `Set` block is declared as `Protected`. The `Get` block has the same visibility as the `Property`. If the scope of the `Get` or `Set` block is different from the scope of the property, it must be more restrictive than the scope of the property. We can restrict the scope of either the `Get` or the `Set` block but not both at the same time.

Listing 25-29 Get and Set Blocks with Different Scopes

```
Private s_Department As String

Public Property sDepartment() As String
    Get
        Return s_Department
    End Get
    Protected Set(ByVal value As String)
        s_Department = value
    End Set
End Property
```

Debugging Properties

When trying to debug properties, we may get the message "Your step-into request resulted in an automatic step-over of a property or operator." To prevent this we need to change a setting in the VS IDE. Select *Tools > Options* from the menu and in the Options dialog select the *Debugging* node. In the list of debugging options uncheck *Step over properties and operators (Managed only)*. This change takes effect immediately.

Using Classic ADO to Export Data to Excel

When working with large datasets, we need a fast way of placing large amounts of data onto a worksheet. The Excel object model provides the CopyFromRecordset method, but it only supports DAO and Classic ADO recordset objects. This is one of the main reasons for using Classic ADO in VB.NET.

To use Classic ADO we first need to add a reference to the *Microsoft ActiveX Data Objects Library 2.6* or later in the solution. Open the *Properties* window of the solution, select the *References* tab, and click the *Add* button. In the Add Reference dialog select the *COM* tab, scroll down the list, and select the desired version of the Classic ADO object library. See Chapter 18, "Introduction to Database Development," for a detailed discussion of Classic ADO. Listing 25-30 shows a solution that uses Classic ADO to retrieve data and populate a worksheet. In this example we use a module-level Recordset variable to retrieve data from the PETRAS database.

Listing 25-30   Class Module to Export Data to an Excel Worksheet

```
'Namespace alias for Excel.
Imports Excel = Microsoft.Office.Interop.Excel

Friend Class CDataExcel

#Region "Variables."

    'A module-level variable for the recordset.
    Private mrsData As New ADODB.Recordset

#End Region

#Region "Data acquisition."

    Friend Function bAdd_Data_Excel() As Boolean

        'Excel variables.
        Dim xlWkbTarget As Excel.Workbook = Nothing
        Dim xlWksData As Excel.Worksheet = Nothing
        Dim xlRngFields As Excel.Range = Nothing
        Dim xlRngData As Excel.Range = Nothing
```

```
'ADODB Connection, SQL query and recordset variables.
Dim sConnection As String = "Provider=SQLNCLI.1;" & _
                            "Integrated Security=SSPI;" & _
                            "Persist Security Info=False;" & _
                            "Initial Catalog=PETRAS;" & _
                            "Data Source=PED\SQLEXPRESS"

Dim sSQL As String = "SELECT FirstName + ' ' " & _
                     "+ Lastname AS Consultant, " & _
                     "DateWorked AS Date, " & _
                     "Hours FROM BillableHours AS b " & _
                     "INNER JOIN Consultants AS c " & _
                     "ON b.ConsultantID =c.ConsultantID " & _
                     "WHERE FirstName = 'Dennis' " & _
                     "AND LastName = 'Wallentin';"

Dim fldField As ADODB.Field = Nothing
Dim iColumnsCount As Integer = Nothing

If Me.bGet_Data(sConnection, sSQL) Then
    'Get the number of columns in the retrieved recordset.
    iColumnsCount = mrsData.Fields.Count

    'An array to hold the field names.
    Dim arrFieldNames(0, iColumnsCount) As String

    Dim iNameCounter As Integer = 0

    'Populate the array with the field names.
    For Each fldField In mrsData.Fields
        arrFieldNames(0, iNameCounter) = fldField.Name
        iNameCounter = iNameCounter + 1
    Next fldField

    'Add a new workbook.
    xlWkbTarget = swXLApp.Workbooks.Add()
    xlWksData = CType(xlWkbTarget.Worksheets(1), _
                Microsoft.Office.Interop.Excel.Worksheet)

    With xlWksData
        'Resize the range for the field names.
        xlRngFields = _
          .Range(.Cells(2, 2), .Cells(2, iColumnsCount + 1))
```

```vb.net
            'Startcell for the data range to be populated.
            xlRngData = .Range("B3")
    End With

    'Dump the data into the worksheet.
    If Not mrsData.EOF Then

            'To avoid flickering during the operation.
            swXLApp.ScreenUpdating = False

            'Add the field names.
            With xlRngFields
                .Value = arrFieldNames
                .Font.Bold = True
                '.AutoFit()
            End With

            'Dump the data into the worksheet.
            xlRngData.CopyFromRecordset(mrsData)

            'Restore the setting.
            swXLApp.ScreenUpdating = True

    Else

            MessageBox.Show("No data located.", "Report", _
                        MessageBoxButtons.OK, _
                        MessageBoxIcon.Warning)
    End If

    'Prepare the object to be released from memory
    'next time the GC comes around.
    mrsData.Close()
    mrsData = Nothing

    xlRngData = Nothing
    xlWksData = Nothing
    xlWkbTarget = Nothing

    End If


End Function
```

```vbnet
Private Function bGet_Data(ByVal sConnect As String, _
                         ByVal sSQLExpression As String) _
                                        As Boolean

    'Variable for database connection.
    Dim cnConnect As New ADODB.Connection

    Dim bFlag As Boolean = False

    Try
        'Open a connection to the SQL Server.
        cnConnect.Open(sConnect)

        'Open the recordset.
        With mrsData
            .CursorLocation = _
                    ADODB.CursorLocationEnum.adUseClient
            .Open(sSQLExpression, cnConnect, _
                    ADODB.CursorTypeEnum.adOpenForwardOnly, _
                    ADODB.LockTypeEnum.adLockReadOnly, _
                    ADODB.CommandTypeEnum.adCmdText)

            'Disconnect the Recordset.
            .ActiveConnection = Nothing
        End With

        'Close the connection
        cnConnect.Close()

        'OK so we set the flag to true.
        bFlag = True

    Catch ADODBex As Exception

        MessageBox.Show(ADODBex.Message.ToString, _
                    "Error", _
                    MessageBoxButtons.OK, _
                    MessageBoxIcon.Error)
        bFlag = False

    Finally
```

```
        'Prepare the object to be released from memory
        'next time the GC comes around.
        cnConnect = Nothing

    End Try

    Return bFlag

End Function

#End Region

End Class
```

Shimming COM Add-ins

MSCoree.DLL Hell

When you have multiple managed COM add-ins installed on a single computer, you will notice that all of them actually refer to the .NET runtime engine mscoree.dll. This can be seen in the COM add-ins dialog, where the Load Behavior for managed COM add-ins refers to mscoree.dll, and in the Windows Registry, where the subkey value for InprocServer32 refers to mscoree.dll.

If all of the managed COM add-ins work perfectly, then we will never face a problem with the reference to mscoree.dll. However, if even one of them fails to operate as expected, all of the managed COM add-ins will stop working due to mscoree.dll being blacklisted by Excel. Microsoft has provided a tool called the COM Shim Wizard to resolve this problem. The COM Shim Wizard allows us to create a COM shim for our managed COM add-ins. It is possible to write our own shim, but this is beyond the scope of this chapter. We cover the COM Shim Wizard in more detail shortly.

Isolation

One of the cornerstones of the .NET platform is that all applications should be isolated so they do not affect each other. To achieve this, each application is loaded by the CLR in its own unique memory address space, or **Application Domain** (**AppDomain**). The CLR can load one or more solutions (DLLs or EXEs) into each AppDomain. It is also possible to create and run several AppDomains in a single process.

If any managed COM add-ins are loaded when Excel is loaded, the CLR creates a default AppDomain for Excel. All unshimmed managed COM add-ins are loaded into Excel's default AppDomain. Therefore, if one COM add-in crashes then the default AppDomain is released from memory together with all the other unshimmed COM add-ins it contains. By shimming managed COM add-ins we isolate them in separate AppDomains so that the failure of one will not affect all the rest. This is only applicable when creating managed COM add-ins with the Shared Add-in Template. As we see in the next chapter, VSTO-based managed COM add-ins do not require a customized COM shim.

Security

Another cornerstone of the .NET platform is security, and with Windows Vista we get even better support for it than with Windows XP. This topic is too broad for us to cover in any significant detail here, but we briefly cover one of the most frequently encountered security topics for Excel developers; digital signatures.

Digital signatures are used to verify the integrity of data being passed from the originator, or signer, to a recipient, or verifier. In the case of an Excel solution, a digital signature provides our clients with the assurance that our code has not been altered after we signed it. Digitally signing a solution can also allow it to run in Excel even when macro security is set to the highest level, but this requires a commercial digital certificate. A commercial digital certificate can be obtained from companies such as Veritas, Thawte, and COMDO. Digital certificates are discussed more in detail in Chapter 29, "Providing Help, Securing, Packaging, and Distributing

Authenticode Certificates

By digitally signing managed COM add-ins with an **Authenticode certificate** we can support desktop environments where the security level in Excel is set to the highest level. If we create a COM shim for our managed COM add-in we can digitally sign the COM shim DLL files. We cannot digitally sign the mscoree.dll file because it is a system file.

Strong Names

Digitally signing solutions with **strong names** does not require a certificate. By using strongly named files we can create unique identities for our solutions and at the same time prevent any unauthorized changes to the code in the solution. We create a strong name when we build the solution. Before loading the solution the .NET Framework tries to verify the strong name signature. Only if the signature can be verified will the solution be loaded.

Good .NET practice says that we should always use strong names. In addition, if we create a COM shim solution without a strong name then a warning message is displayed when the solution is run that no strong name exists. In the next section we describe how to create a strong name.

The COM Shim Wizard

The COM Shim Wizard is a tool provided by Microsoft to create COM shims for Office applications, including Excel. The tool itself is a set of several wizards that collect information from the developer and use this information to create a COM shim solution. The output of the shimming process is an unmanaged COM shim DLL file that loads and unloads the managed solution in its own AppDomain within the Excel.exe process memory area. It also acts as a bridge between Excel and the managed add-in during runtime.

The COM Shim Wizard can be downloaded from the Microsoft Web site. The best way to find it is to use Google to search for *COM Shim Wizard*. There is also documentation from Microsoft that can be located by searching for *Isolating Microsoft Office Extensions with the COM Shim Wizard*. This documentation gives more detailed technical information about the tool than we discuss here. Note that Microsoft does not provide official support for this tool.

Creating a COM Shim DLL

A COM shim for a solution should be created after work on a solution is finished but before the solution is deployed. This reduces the number of times you need to rebuild the setup package. Before we create a COM shim for our FirstAddin solution we should give the solution a strong name key. This is accomplished in the following manner.

1. In the VS IDE select *Project > FirstAddin Properties...* from the menu and then select the *Signing* tab in the Properties window.
2. Check the option *Sign the assembly* and select *<new>* from the combo box below it.

3. In the Create Strong Name Key dialog add a filename. If we enter a password we create a **Personal Information Exchange (.pfx)** file. Without a password a **Strong Name Key** (**.snk**) file is created. The .pfx file is more secure because it requires other users to provide the password to open the solution in the VS IDE. For our solution we use a password, as shown in Figure 25-37.

FIGURE 25-37 Creating a strong name key

4. A new file, <name>.pfx has now been added to the solution. This file is visible in the Solution Explorer window. Be sure to save the solution before closing it.

It is also possible to use an existing .pfx or .snk file, which you can browse for using the combo box associated with the *Sign the assembly* option described previously.

A COM shim can either be created as a standalone solution or added to an existing managed COM add-in solution. In this example we create a standalone COM shim solution:

1. In the VS IDE select *File > New > Project...* from the menu.
2. In the New Project dialog, expand the *Visual C++* node and select the COMShim subgroup.
3. Select the *Addin Shim* template and name it FirstAddinShim. Figure 25-38 shows how the dialog should look at this point.
4. Click the OK button and the COM Shim Wizard starts.
5. In the first wizard step, *Specify the Managed Add-in Assembly*, use the find file button to locate the FirstAddin.dll file. This is located in a folder similar to *<path>\FirstAddin\FirstAddin\bin*. Accept the default settings to use the *GUID* and *ProgID* from the source solution and apply it to the COM shim.

FIGURE 25-38 Creating a new COM shim solution

6. Skip the next wizard step, *Secondary Extensibility Interfaces*.
7. In the next wizard step, *Shared Add-in Detail*, enter the description *Chapter 25 - Writing Managed COM Add-ins with VB.NET* and the friendly name *First Shimmed Add-in*. These entries will be available in the Windows registry. Make sure the option *Load the add-in when the Office application starts* is checked and the option *Add-in available to all users, not just the person that installs it* is unchecked. Also make sure that *Microsoft Excel* is checked in the list of host applications.
8. A summary of your selections is displayed in the final wizard step. If everything looks okay, click on the *Finish* button.

The COM Shim Wizard generates two Visual C++ projects and builds a COM shim DLL. It also unregisters our managed COM add-in DLL and instead registers the unmanaged COM shim DLL. The unmanaged COM shim DLL replaces mscoree.dll as the runtime for the managed COM add-in.

Adding a COM shim project to an existing solution is accomplished in a manner identical to the preceding steps. We simply open the solution to which we want to add the COM shim project, select *File > Add > New Project...* from the VS IDE menu, and complete the wizard steps as described previously.

We do not need to make any changes to the two Visual C++ projects generated by the COM Shim Wizard. The COM shim should be correctly implemented at this point. What we need to do next is add a setup project to the solution:

1. Select *File > Add > New Project...* from the VS IDE menu. In the Add New Project dialog select the *Other Project Types* node in the *Project Types* list; then select the subgroup *Setup and Deployment*.
2. Select *Setup Project* from the Templates list and name the project FirstAddinShimSetup. Click on the OK button to add it to the solution.

At this stage, we have only added an empty setup project to the solution. In the following steps we add content to it:

1. The first file we must add to the setup project is the managed COM add-in itself: FirstAddin.dll. Right-click the *FirstAddinShimSetup* node in Solution Explorer and select *Add > Assembly...* from the shortcut menu. Browse to the folder that contains FirstAddin.dll, select it, and add it to the setup project. Make sure all the dependency files are excluded from the setup project.
2. Right-click again on the *FirstAddinShimSetup* node in Solution Explorer and select the *Add > Project Output...* from the shortcut menu. In the Add Project Output Group dialog select *FirstAddinShim* from the combo box, select the list option *Primary Output*, and then click on the OK button.
   Figure 25-39 shows the Add Project Output Group dialog at this point. A *Project Output* contains all the files that must be included in a deployment project. The only file from the *FirstAddinShim* project that needs to be included in our setup project is the COM shim file itself, FirstAddinShim.dll.

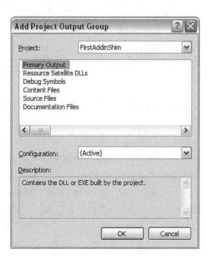

FIGURE 25-39 The Add Project Output Group dialog

3. Repeat the previous step, but this time select the *Project Output for ManagedAggregator*. The only file from this project that must be added to the setup project is the ManagedAggregator.dll file.

Figure 25-40 shows the three projects that now make up our complete standalone COM Shim solution.

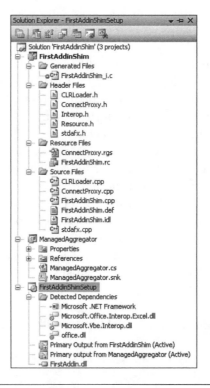

FIGURE 25-40 The COM shim standalone solution with three projects

So far we have not discussed the **User/Machine Hive** registry section in the Registry Editor. By putting the appropriate registry entries in this section the setup project automatically detects whether the option Just me or Everyone has been selected and then writes the settings to the appropriate section in the Windows Registry. Interestingly, when selecting the Everyone option during the installation process on Windows Vista the COM shim DLL will actually be available in the COM Add-in dialog in Excel.

Figure 25-41 shows the settings for our COM shim DLL. We should also make sure that these entries are always created when our solution is installed and always deleted when our solution is uninstalled. To do this, right-click the *FirstAddin.Connect* node and choose *Property Window* from the shortcut menu. In the Properties window set the options *AlwaysCreate* and *DeleteAtUninstall* to *True*.

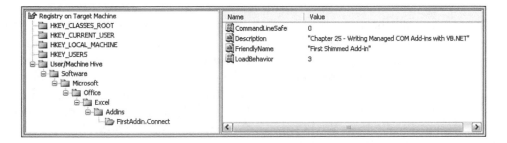

FIGURE 25-41 The User/Machine Hive section in the Registry Editor

Before we continue, make sure that version 2.0 of .NET Framework is selected under the *.NET Framework launch condition* in the Launch Condition Editor and that the prerequisites have been updated accordingly. We also need to set the Register status for each of the added files.

- Right-click on FirstAddin.dll in Solution Explorer and select *Properties* from the shortcut menu. Confirm that the *Register* status is *vsdraDoNotRegister*.
- Right click on the *Primary output from ManagedAggregator (Active)* node in Solution Explorer and select *Properties* from the shortcut menu. Confirm that the *Register* status is *vsdrpDoNotRegister*.
- Right-click on the *Primary output from FirstAddinShim (Active)* node in Solution Explorer and select *Properties* from the shortcut menu. Change the *Register* status to *vsdrpCOMSelfReg*. This setting causes the DLL to be called at install time to register itself and requires all dependent DLLs to be present.

NOTE The documentation for the COM Shim Wizard recommends setting the Register property to *vsdrpCOM* instead. This runs the registration at the time the MSI-package is built and places the registration data into the MSI-package itself.

At install time it then copies the files, and Windows writes the appropriate registry entries, which should provide a smoother installation process. However, we were not able to get it to work properly using that setting.

Before building the setup project we need to customize it. Select the *FirstAddinShimSetup* node in Solution Explorer and press the F4 key to activate the Properties window. Here we can enter general information about the setup that will be seen by the user during installation. To build the setup project we right-click the *FirstAddinShimSetup* node in Solution Explorer and select *Build* from the shortcut menu. The build command generates two files, Setup.exe and FirstAddinShimSetup.MSI, which are placed in the Debug folder (unless we changed the output to the Release folder).

Finally, if we need to unregister or re-register the COM shim DLL file, FirstAddinShim.dll, during the build process, we can use the well-known *regsvr32* command from a Command Prompt. This is because the COM Shim DLL is an unmanaged native DLL file. A working example of this solution can be found on the companion CD in the \Concepts\Ch25 - Writing Managed COM Add-ins with VB.NET\ FirstAddinShim folder.

Digitally Signing Files

Signing files with an Authenticode certificate provides two primary benefits. It allows the signed add-in to run when Excel's macro security level is set to either High or Very High, and it guarantees that the setup package was actually created by the signer.

To allow our users to run our managed COM add-in even when Excel's macro security level is set to the highest level, we must sign the unmanaged COM shim DLL. To sign this file we need the **Sign Tool** that is included in the Windows SDK for Windows Server 2008 and .NET Framework 3.5 (in addition to an Authenticode certificate). The Windows SDK can be downloaded from the Microsoft Web site. The Sign Tool is a command-line utility, but we can get it to run as a visual wizard too.

1. Open a new Command Prompt window by executing the command *cmd* from the Run dialog in Windows.
2. Change the directory to *C:\Program Files\Microsoft SDKs\Windows\v6.0A\bin*, which is the default directory for the Sign Tool.
3. From the Command Prompt enter `signtool signwizard`.

4. The **Digital Signature Wizard** now starts. In the first step we point to our COM shim DLL file, FirstAddinShim.dll. In the second step we accept the default to make a *typical signing*, and in the third step we select the certificate to use for the signing. Figure 25-42 shows a valid certificate selected in the Digital Signature Wizard.

FIGURE 25-42   A valid certificate selected in the Digital Signature Wizard

The fourth step in the wizard, *Data Description*, is optional. In the fifth step we **timestamp** the data. Figure 25-43 shows one common URL to timestamp the data with.

The final step displays a summary of the actions taken in the wizard. Click the *Finish* button here to perform the signature process. Any time we need to rebuild the signed DLL we must also redo the signing process. The process for signing package files, such as MSI and EXE files, is identical to the process we just stepped through.

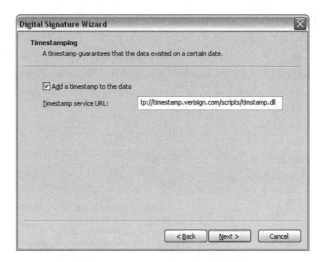

FIGURE 25-43 Adding a timestamp to the data using the Digital Signature Wizard

Related Blogs

XL-Dennis—VSTO & .NET & Excel

The author makes frequent posts to this blog about managed COM add-ins and related technologies: http://xldennis.wordpress.com/.

Andrew Whitechapel

Andrew is one of the creators of the COM Shim Wizard. In his blog you find the latest news about the tool together with other interesting posts concerning the technology behind managed COM add-ins and VSTO: http://blogs.msdn.com/andreww/.

Additional Development Tools

Add-in Express for Microsoft Office and .NET

This toolset provides a fast and a robust way to develop managed COM add-ins, Automation add-ins, Smart Tags, and Excel Real-Time Data (RTD) servers. Some of its key features are

- **Target Excel 2000 to 2007**—With this tool we can easily target all current versions of Excel with one solution.
- **Create version-neutral PIA solutions**—We can create solutions that target Excel 2000 to 2007 without the need to use version-specific PIAs.

- **Provides its own shim**—A shim is automatically added to the solutions when they are created so there is no need to manually shim the solutions.
- **Visual designers for creating custom menus**—We can easily create customized menus for both the Classic Commandbar UI and for the Ribbon UI with visual designers.
- **Keyboard shortcut commands**—We can easily implement keyboard shortcut commands at the application level using visual components together with a few lines of code.
- **Deployment**—A configured setup package is created for each solution that supports the ClickOnce deployment model.

For more information, see http://www.add-in-express.com/add-in-net/. The authors have no financial interest in this tool and are not connected to its vendor. The recommendations are based on our own daily use of this tool as .NET developers.

AddinSpy

AddinSpy is a free but unsupported diagnostic tool from Microsoft that reports as much information as possible about all registered Office add-ins on a computer. It can be useful when troubleshooting issues with deployed add-ins. For more information see http://msdn.microsoft.com/en-us/library/cc984533.aspx.

Practical Example—PETRAS Report Tool.NET

Introduction

For our practical example, we converted the PETRAS Report Tool.NET into a managed COM add-in for Excel. We also created a COM shim for it. Table 25-1 provides a summary of the contents of the new solution.

Table 25-1 Updated Contents for the PETRAS Report Tool.NET Solution

Module Name	Type and Function
app.config	XML configuration file containing the connection string
AssemblyInfo.vb	General information about the solution
CCommonMethods.vb	Class module that contains general methods
CDataReports.vb	Class module containing all the database methods

Table 25-1 Updated Contents for the PETRAS Report Tool.NET Solution

Module Name	Type and Function
CExportExcel.vb	Class module that contains all the methods required to export data to Excel
CExportXML.vb	Class module containing all the methods required to export data to XML files
Connect.VB	Class module that connects and disconnects the add-in together with functions to build and delete the custom menu
frmAbout	Windows Form that shows information about the add-in
frmConnecting.vb	Windows Form displayed while connecting to the database
frmMain.vb	Windows Form that is the main form for the solution
MSolutions Enumerations Variables.vb	Standard module containing all the enumerations used in the solution
PED.snk	Strong name file
RibbonCustom.xml	XML file that holds the XML markup for the Ribbon user interface customization (exists only in the version for Excel 2007)

The PETRAS Report Tool.NET exists in two versions on the companion CD, one for Excel 2003 and earlier and one for Excel 2007 and later. The difference between the two versions is that the first uses the Classic CommandBar UI, and the second uses the Ribbon UI. These solutions can be found on the companion CD in the folders *\Application\Ch25 - Writing Managed COM Add-ins with VB.NET\PETRAS ReportTool.NET Excel 2003* and *\PETRAS ReportTool.NET Excel 2007*, respectively.

Load and Unload the COM Add-in

Listing 25-31 shows the two primary COM add-in events, OnConnection and OnDisconnection. It may be necessary to add support for Windows XP style via the EnableVisualStyles method, which we do when the add-in is connected to Excel at startup. The Create_Tool_Menu procedure builds a custom menu when the add-in is loaded, and the Delete_Tool_Menu procedure destroys the custom menu when the add-in is unloaded.

Listing 25-31 OnConnection and OnDisconnection Events

```vbnet
#Region "Connection and Disconnection"

    Public Sub OnConnection(ByVal application As Object, _
                            ByVal connectMode As ext_ConnectMode, _
                            ByVal addInInst As Object, _
                            ByRef custom As System.Array) _
                                Implements
                                IDTExtensibility2.OnConnection

        'Customized error message when wrong Excel version is
        'detected.
        Const sMESSAGEWRONGVERSION As String = _
            "Version 2002 and later of Excel must" + vbNewLine + _
            "be installed in order to proceed."

        'Customized error message.
        Const sERROR_MESSAGE As String = _
                "An unexpected error has occurred."

        'Create and instantiate a new instance of the class.
        Dim cMethods As New CCommonMethods()


        Try
            'Get a reference to Excel.
            swXLApp = (CType(application, Excel.Application))

            'Check to see that Excel 2002 or later is installed
            'on the computer.
            Dim shInstalled As Short = _
                        cMethods.shCheck_Excel_Version_Installed

            If shInstalled = xlVersion.WrongVersion Then

                'Customized message that the wrong Excel version
                'is installed.
                MessageBox.Show(text:=sMESSAGEWRONGVERSION, _
                                caption:=swsCaption, _
                                buttons:=MessageBoxButtons.OK, _
                                icon:=MessageBoxIcon.Stop)

                Exit Try
```

```
            End If

            'Create the custom menu.
            Create_Tool_Menu()

            'The following lines may be necessary to
            'add in order to support
            'Windows XP visual style.
            System.Windows.Forms.Application.EnableVisualStyles()
            System.Windows.Forms.Application.DoEvents()

        Catch Generalex As Exception

            'Show the customized message.
            MessageBox.Show(text:=sERROR_MESSAGE, _
                            caption:=swsCaption, _
                            buttons:=MessageBoxButtons.OK, _
                            icon:=MessageBoxIcon.Stop)

        Finally

            If Not IsNothing(Expression:=cMethods) Then _
                                cMethods = Nothing

        End Try

    End Sub

    Public Sub OnDisconnection(ByVal RemoveMode As _
                                ext_DisconnectMode, _
                                ByRef custom As System.Array) _
                                Implements
                                IDTExtensibility2.OnDisconnection

        'Delete the custom menu.
        Delete_Tool_Menu()

        'Release and prepare the objects for GC.
        If Not IsNothing(Expression:=mcmdPetrasButton) Then _
                                mcmdPetrasButton = Nothing
        swXLApp = Nothing

    End Sub

#End Region
```

The Custom Menu

The two subroutines that build and delete the custom menu are located in the Connect.vb class and shown in Listing 25-32. When Excel is loaded the custom menu is added to the Worksheet Menu Bar. The custom menu for the PETRAS Report Tool.NET is shown in Figure 25-44.

FIGURE 25-44   The PETRAS Report Tool.NET menu

Listing 25-32   Subroutines to Create and Delete the Custom Menu

```
#Region "Module-level variables"

    'The hooking command bar control event.
    Private WithEvents mcmdPetrasButton As _
                    Office.CommandBarButton = Nothing

    'The tag variable for our control.
    Private Const msTAG As String = "PETRASNET"

    'Parameter variables for the two buttons on the
    'custom menu.
    Private Const msABOUT As String = "&About"
    Private Const msREPORT As String = "&Report"

#End Region

#Region "Build and tear down the custom menu."

    Friend Sub Create_Tool_Menu()

        Const sPETRASREPORT As String = "&Petras Report Tool.NET"
        Const sREPORTTOOLTIP As String = _
                            "Create a report for PETRAS."
        Const sABOUTTOOLTIP As String = _
                            "About PETRAS Report Tool.NET"
```

```vb.net
'The commandbar variable.
Dim cbrPetras As Office.CommandBar = Nothing

'The Popup control variable.
Dim ctlPetras As Office.CommandBarPopup = Nothing

'The button control variable.
Dim ctlReport As Office.CommandBarButton = Nothing

'Grab the worksheet menu commandbar.
cbrPetras = CType(swXLApp.CommandBars(1), Office.CommandBar)

'Can we find our control?
ctlPetras = CType(cbrPetras.FindControl(Tag:=msTAG), _
                  Microsoft.Office.Core.CommandBarPopup)

'If the custom menu does not exist create it.
If ctlPetras Is Nothing Then
    With cbrPetras

        'Add the popup control to the worksheet menu.
        ctlPetras = CType(.Controls.Add( _
                Office.MsoControlType.msoControlPopup), _
                Office.CommandBarPopup)

    With ctlPetras

        'Configure the created popup control.
        .Caption = sPETRASREPORT
        .Tag = msTAG

        'Add a new button control.
        ctlReport = CType(.Controls.Add( _
                Office.MsoControlType.msoControlButton), _
                Office.CommandBarButton)

        'Configure the added button control.
        With ctlReport
            .Caption = msREPORT
            .FaceId = 162
            .Parameter = msREPORT
            .Style = _
            Office.MsoButtonStyle.msoButtonIconAndCaption
            .Tag = msTAG
            .TooltipText = sREPORTTOOLTIP
```

```vb.net
        End With

        'Add a new button control.
        ctlReport = CType(.Controls.Add( _
                Office.MsoControlType.msoControlButton),  _
                Office.CommandBarButton)

        'Configure the added button control.
        With ctlReport
            .BeginGroup = True
            .Caption = msABOUT
            .FaceId = 487
            .Parameter = msABOUT
            .Style = _
            Office.MsoButtonStyle.msoButtonIconAndCaption
            .Tag = msTAG
            .TooltipText = sABOUTTOOLTIP
        End With
      End With

    End With

    'Set the WithEvents to hook the created buttons,
    'all controls that have the same Tag property will fire
    'the mcmdPetrasButton_Click event.
    mcmdPetrasButton = ctlReport

  Else

    'Re-hooking the custom buttons to the WithEvents.
    mcmdPetrasButton = CType(swXLApp.CommandBars. _
            FindControls(Tag:=msTAG).Item(2),  _
            Microsoft.Office.Core.CommandBarButton)

  End If

  'Release of objects.
  If (ctlReport IsNot Nothing) Then ctlReport = Nothing
  If (ctlPetras IsNot Nothing) Then ctlPetras = Nothing
  If (cbrPetras IsNot Nothing) Then cbrPetras = Nothing

End Sub


Friend Sub Delete_Tool_Menu()
```

```vb.net
        Dim octlItem As Office.CommandBarControl = Nothing

        'Find and delete our controls.
        For Each octlItem In swXLApp.CommandBars. _
                          FindControls(Tag:=msTAG)
            octlItem.Delete()
        Next

        'Release object.
        If (octlItem IsNot Nothing) Then octlItem = Nothing

    End Sub

    Private Sub mcmdPetrasButton_Click(ByVal Ctrl As _
                          Office.CommandBarButton, _
                          ByRef CancelDefault As Boolean) _
                          Handles mcmdPetrasButton.Click

        'Create and instantiate a new instance of the class.
        Dim cCMethods As New CCommonMethods

        Select Case Ctrl.Parameter

            'User selected to show the Report form.
            Case msREPORT : cCMethods.Load_Form(sForm:=msREPORT)

            'User select to show the About form.
            Case msABOUT : cCMethods.Load_Form(sForm:=msABOUT)

        End Select

        'Release object.
        If (cCMethods IsNot Nothing) Then cCMethods = Nothing

    End Sub

#End Region
```

Display Windows Forms in Excel

Windows Forms are displayed in Excel using methods similar to those described for VB6 Forms in Chapter 23. Listing 25-33 shows the subroutine that displays one of two Windows Forms in PETRAS Report Tool.NET. We use the **NativeWindow** class to assign a handle to Excel's main window and then we let the main window become the owner of the Windows Form to be displayed. To release the handle we need to get back the DialogResult using the Windows Form's DialogResult property. The NativeWindow class is included in the `System.Windows.Forms` namespace. A global reference to this namespace is set for the solution and therefore we do not need to explicitly import it.

Listing 25-33   Subroutine to Display a Windows Form in Excel

```
Friend Sub Load_Form(ByVal sForm As String)

    'Customized error message.
    Const sERROR_MESSAGE As String = _
         "An unexpected error has occurred."

    'Instantiate a new instance of the NativeWindow class.
    Dim appWindow As New NativeWindow()

    'A Windows Form variable.
    Dim frm As Form = Nothing

    Try
        'Which form to load?
        If sForm = "&Report" Then
            frm = New frmMain
        Else
            frm = New frmAbout
        End If

        'Assign a handle to Excel's Main Window.
        appWindow.AssignHandle(Process.GetCurrentProcess(). _
                                        MainWindowHandle)

        'Show the Windows Form and let Excel's Main Window be the
        'owner of the form.
        If frm.ShowDialog(appWindow) = _
                        DialogResult.OK Then Exit Try
```

```vbnet
        'Release the handle.
        appWindow.ReleaseHandle()
        appWindow = Nothing

    Catch Generalex As Exception

        'Show the customized message.
        MessageBox.Show(text:=sERROR_MESSAGE, _
                    caption:=swsCaption, _
                    buttons:=MessageBoxButtons.OK, _
                    icon:=MessageBoxIcon.Stop)

    Finally

        If (appWindow IsNot Nothing) Then

            'If the handle still exists then destroy it.
            appWindow.DestroyHandle()

        End If

        If (frm IsNot Nothing) Then

            'Dispose the Windows Form class.
            frm.Dispose()
            frm = Nothing

        End If

    End Try

End Sub
```

Summary

VB.NET is an advanced and flexible development tool that provides us with many opportunities to master the development process. The downside is a rather high level of complexity and a steep learning curve. The complexity is not necessarily limited to writing the code itself but includes putting all the pieces together so the outcome becomes a professional product. If we have experience developing unmanaged COM add-ins with Classic VB, however, we notice that developing managed COM add-ins in VB.NET shares many aspects with its predecessor. This is not surprising because Excel is still a COM server and expects that any extensions follow the specifications of that communication protocol.

DEVELOPING EXCEL SOLUTIONS WITH VISUAL STUDIO TOOLS FOR OFFICE SYSTEM (VSTO)

Visual Studio Tools for Office (VSTO) had a bad start with version 1.0. It was difficult to use, lacked significant capabilities, and suffered from major bugs. To make things worse, very few developers even understood what VSTO was really designed for. The next version, VSTO 2005, addressed many of the problems with version 1.0 and added more features to the toolset. A major update, called VS2005 Second Edition (SE), was later released. This update enabled developers to target Office 2007 and create application-level solutions.

As of this writing, the latest version—VSTO 2008 (also known as version 3.0)—is included in Visual Studio 2008 Professional and above. VSTO 2008 has finally reached a level of maturity that makes it an attractive toolset for developing Office solutions on the .NET platform.

To gain a better understanding of VSTO we begin the chapter by answering two questions: What is VSTO and when would we want to use VSTO as opposed to some other development tool? Understanding the answers to these questions is just as important as coding techniques and deployment. Next we discuss VSTO 2008 development in detail, with a strong focus on Excel solutions. Finally, we discuss **ClickOnce** deployment technology for VSTO solutions and the related VSTO security model.

All the examples in this chapter use VSTO 2008 and Excel 2007. You need Excel 2007 to fully follow these examples. If you are going to use Excel 2003 with VSTO then you must be using Office 2003 Professional edition with the latest service pack. VSTO can only work with Office 2003 Professional edition and higher because this was the first version of Office to recognize and understand the .NET runtime. VSTO development for Excel is yet another subject that could easily fill an entire book on its own. In this chapter, we provide an introduction to the core functions and most important aspects of Excel development with VSTO.

What Is VSTO?

Before we move on, we need to take off our Excel developer hat and step back so we can examine VSTO from a broader perspective. If we define VSTO in strictly technical terms, we will lose sight of the larger context that VSTO was designed for. This context is the **Office System**. The Office System consists of two major parts: **Office Application Clients** and **Office Servers**.

The Office Application clients, also known as the Office product suite, usually include applications such as Excel, Outlook, Word, and PowerPoint. These clients are primarily used as presentation layers, but Excel and InfoPath can also be used as development tools. The Office System has evolved over time to include more server platforms. Office Servers include the following applications:

- **Exchange Server**—The e-mail server to which Outlook is connected.
- **Office SharePoint Server (also known as MOSS)**—MOSS includes a large number of services such as **Excel Services** (Excel Web Access, Excel Web Services, and Excel Calculation) and **Business Data Catalog (BDC)**, which is used to present business data from back-end server applications. MOSS offers the ability to create **Document Libraries** to which it is possible to add VSTO solutions along with native Office solutions and documents. MOSS also includes tools to create **Business Intelligence (BI)** solutions as well as advanced enterprise search solutions with Office Forms Service (also available as a standalone Office Forms Server). **Windows Workflow Foundation (WF)** provides tools to create system and human workflows using MOSS, and, finally, **Windows SharePoint Services** sits at the base of MOSS, providing administrative and management services.
- **Office PerformancePoint Server**—This server is built on SQL Server and allows the business to monitor, analyze, and plan its business activities. Excel is commonly used to present information from it. This server can also be integrated with MOSS.

The data that supports the Office Servers is stored in and retrieved from various **business systems** (SAP, PeopleSoft, and so on), **Enterprise**

Resource Planning (ERP) systems, **relation database management systems (RDBMS)**, and **Data Warehouses**.

VSTO is a toolset for creating managed solutions that target the Office System. Since VSTO is part of VS we can also say that VS fully supports the creation of solutions for the Office System. Figure 26-1 shows how all these applications, servers, and development tools interact. On the surface it may look simple, but it is a complex and advanced environment for building managed solutions.

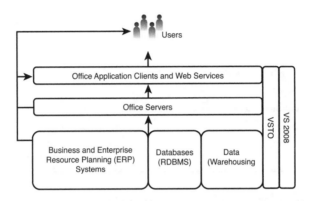

FIGURE 26-1 The Office System and VSTO

We can use either C# or VB.NET to develop solutions with VSTO in the VS IDE, just as we can with standalone managed solutions and managed COM add-ins. The VSTO toolset consists of Office and MOSS project templates for various purposes. The specific project templates available depend on whether we are targeting Office 2003 Professional or any version of Office 2007. If we are using Office 2007, the project templates available to us are shown in Figure 26-2.

When using Office 2003 Professional we have access to fewer project templates, as shown in Figure 26-3. When comparing the project templates available between the two versions of Office we notice that with Office 2007 we have project templates for MOSS 2007 and InfoPath.

With the exception of the SharePoint templates, the project templates shown in Figure 26-2 are usually categorized into one of two groups.

- **Application-centric project templates**—Excel 2007 Add-in, InfoPath 2007 Add-in, Outlook 2007 Add-in, PowerPoint 2007 Add-in, Project 2007 Add-in, Visio 2007 Add-in, and Word 2007 Add-in

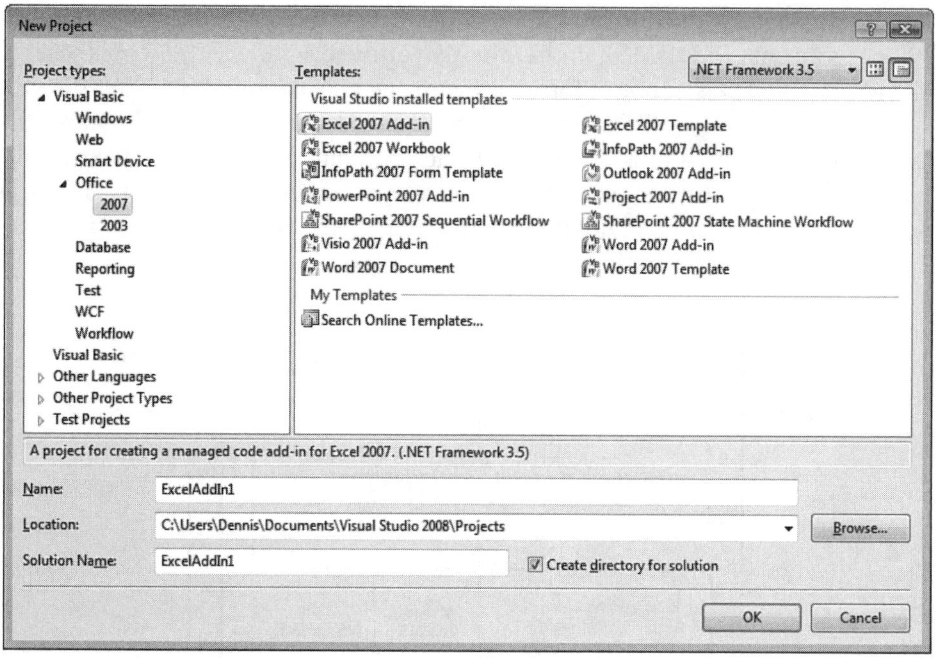

FIGURE 26-2 Templates for Office 2007 and MOSS 2007

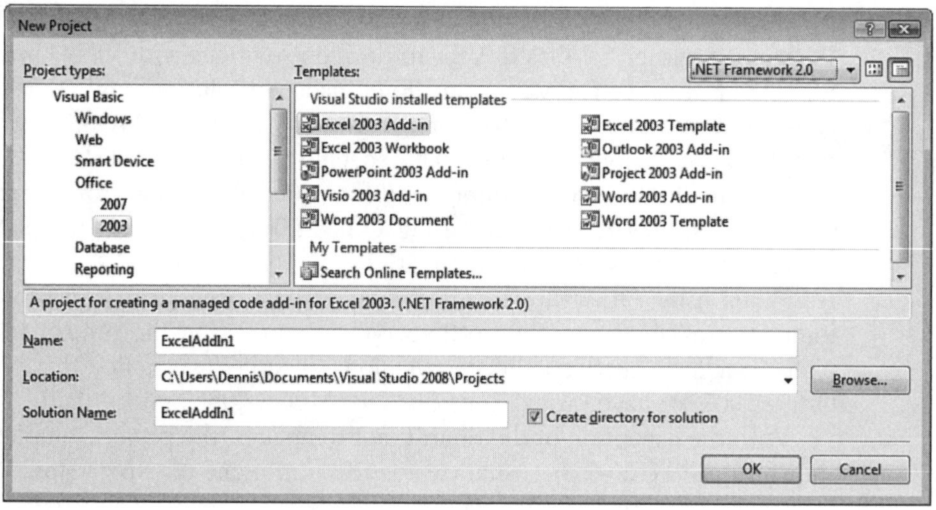

FIGURE 26-3 Templates for Office 2003

- **Document-centric project templates**—Excel 2007 Template, Excel 2007 Workbook, InfoPath 2007 Form Template, Word 2007 Template, and Word 2007 Document

Next, we take a closer look at these two categories of templates.

VSTO Project Templates

Application-Centric Project Templates

These project templates are used to create managed **VSTO add-ins**. Unlike managed COM add-ins, they only target the specific host application they are designed for.

Document-Centric Project Templates

There are two types of solutions included in this category: **VSTO template** and **VSTO document** project templates. VSTO templates work exactly the same way as native templates do. When using VSTO templates we create new copies of the templates. We also work with a VSTO document solution in exactly the same way as we use individual native Word documents or Excel workbooks. From the perspective of the end user there is no difference between document-centric solutions, native templates, or individual documents.

The templates and documents used in VSTO are actually native Excel and Word files. The difference is that we hook up .NET assemblies, known as **code-behind assemblies**, to the templates and documents in VSTO. In Figure 26-4 we show a graphical representation of the structure of a VSTO workbook solution.

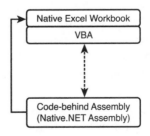

FIGURE 26-4 Workbook-centric VSTO solution

The code-behind assemblies can communicate with VBA and vice versa. If we only use code-behind assemblies in VSTO solutions and we do not interact with VBA, the data is completely separate from the code. The advantage of this arrangement is that the document or workbook files can be hosted in one place, like a file share on a file server, and the code-behind assemblies in another location, for instance on a SharePoint server.

When opening a VSTO solution in the host application, only the VBA part is accessible from within the VBE, and when opening the solution in the VS IDE only the VSTO part is accessible.

When creating VSTO solutions, both the Excel and Word objects are hosted within the VS IDE as design surfaces. This gives us access to most objects, methods, properties, and functionality in Excel and Word, including the document or workbook itself. Technically, this is accomplished using **OLE in-place activation**. In-place activation is a user interface standard by which an object provided by one application can be selected, modified, and generally manipulated by the developer from within another application that contains it.

A link to the code-behind assembly is added to the document or workbook file as a custom document property (**_AssemblyLocation**) that can be updated if necessary. Another custom document property (**_AssemblyName**) holds the name of the code-behind assembly. When the document or workbook is opened it reads the assembly location from the document property.

We can also use these document properties to associate a code-behind assembly to an unrelated document or workbook file as well as associate several unrelated document or workbook files to one code-behind assembly.

When creating VSTO solutions, we have access to all the tools the VS IDE provides as well as third-party Windows Forms controls. A visual designer tool for creating customized Ribbon UI solutions is also available. It can generate the basic code required to interact with the custom Ribbon UI solution. Interoperability between VSTO solutions and VBA has not yet reach a high level of sophistication, but it continues to improve with each new version of VSTO.

Many companies have generated server-side Excel reports by having the Office suite installed on a Web server. In many cases it works, even though Excel was never intended to be used on a server platform, but it is not a reliable solution, and Microsoft officially discourages server-side use of Office.

Beginning with VSTO 2005, true Office server-side programming is available. VSTO 2005 includes a **ServerDocument** class that can manipulate the data in workbooks without having to open them. The ServerDocument class requires that the workbooks it operates on have a property called an **XML data island** to contain the data. We can populate data islands with data in XML format from a central database. This allows us to create distributed data applications with a centralized data source and also allows us to separate the source data from its visual representation in our workbooks.

Suppose we have an Excel application that is distributed among a group of users. When they are connected to the central data source the data is automatically updated, and when they are offline they can work with the locally cached data.

Choosing Project Templates

The following guidelines help you decide which project templates to choose depending on which version of Office you want to target:

- If you are targeting Office 2003 Professional, then use Office 2003 Professional together with VSTO and the specific application <version 2003> project template.
- If you are targeting Office 2007, then use Office 2007 together with VSTO and the specific application <version 2007> project template.
- When targeting both Office 2003 and 2007, you can either create one solution or two separate solutions. If you decide to create one solution then you must apply the lowest common denominator strategy. Use Office 2003 Professional with VSTO and the specific application <version 2003> project template. In this scenario you can only use version 2.0 of the .NET Framework, and you cannot leverage any new features introduced in Office 2007, VSTO, or version 3.5 of .NET Framework. In addition, the ClickOnce deployment model cannot be used. Creating one solution per version may be a better alternative, but it requires more time to develop, deploy, and maintain.

The Layers of a VSTO Solution

If we compare VSTO add-ins with managed COM add-ins, we discover they are similar. The major differences are

- VSTO add-ins use a generic VSTO loader instead of COM shims for each managed COM add-in. More specifically, the loading components for VSTO 3.0 add-ins are the unmanaged VSTOEE.DLL and VSTOLoader.DLL files. The host application loads VSTOEE.DLL, which then loads VSTOLoader.DLL, which in turn loads the assemblies for the VSTO add-in. We discuss the loading sequence in more detail later in this chapter.
- In the connection class of a VSTO add-in, only the `ThisAddIn_Startup` and `ThisAddIn_Shutdown` events are available. The VSTO runtime implements the **IStartup** interface and forwards these two events to the connection class.
- In a VSTO solution, we do not need to explicitly set any references to the host application like we do in a managed COM add-in. Subsequently, it is not necessary to release any references.

Document-centric solutions also use the generic VSTO runtime. For Excel solutions, the ThisWorkbook class includes the `ThisWorkbook_Startup` and `ThisWorkbook_Shutdown` event handlers.

All VSTO solutions operate through the same number of layers as managed COM add-ins, with the only difference being that VSTO solutions use the VSTO runtime. The layers for VSTO solutions are shown in Figure 26-5.

FIGURE 26-5   The layers of a VSTO solution

Installing and Running VSTO Solutions

VSTO solutions can use either the **ClickOnce** deployment model or the Windows Installer deployment model. Both models require us to work with the .NET Framework security model to grant the solutions full trust on the target computers. Security is a major component of the .NET platform, and it is complex to work with. We discuss ClickOnce in more detail and compare it with the Windows Installer model later in this chapter.

Running Multiple Office Versions with VSTO

Developing VSTO solutions on a computer that is running multiple versions of Office is difficult at best and produces arbitrary results. It is also unsupported by Microsoft. We strongly encourage you to only develop VSTO solutions on computers that have a single target version of Office installed. In the past this would have required multiple physical computers or complicated multiple OS installations. However, virtualization technology is now so cheap and sophisticated that you can easily support many combinations of Windows, Office, and Visual Studio on a single computer.

When Should You Use VSTO?

VSTO is an interesting development platform with a modern IDE, access to Windows Forms controls, and access to the huge library of namespaces in the .NET Framework. It would be easy to simply begin showing what we can do with VSTO, but we need to stop and ask ourselves when we should use VSTO as opposed to some other development tool.

Bear in mind that VSTO is still under rapid development and has not yet reached a mature stage. New features are being added frequently. For example, SP1 for VS 2008 got the option to use the document-centric features in VSTO add-ins. This situation creates a degree of instability in the VSTO platform and is one reason why you might not want to use it for a client's solution.

Another detail to keep in mind is that different groups within Microsoft control VSTO and Office. The practical implication of this is that the two products' release cycles are not synchronized. When a new version of Office is released the current version of VSTO does not initially support it. If we create solutions using VSTO, we face the situation where we must work with interim versions of VSTO and may be forced to ship interim Office solutions between new versions of VS.NET.

Enterprises have installed and used Office on servers for years despite the fact that Microsoft discourages it. Office was designed to be a client-side application suite, not a server program. The reason enterprises do this is to use Office to generate reports as native Excel workbooks. VSTO is a good candidate to replace these unsupported Office solutions because we can use it to build solutions that can generate the same reports but without having Office installed on the server. If we also use the VSTO data island option then even more flexible reporting solutions can be developed.

The major difference between managed COM add-ins and VSTO add-ins is that the latter are optimized for Office by design. As a practical matter, any solution that we create with VSTO can also be created as a managed COM add-in. It simply requires more coding and more manual configuration.

For document-centric solutions, business requirements can almost always be met with native Word and Excel solutions, but not necessarily with the same attractive UI as VSTO offers. In our experience VSTO is used primarily in response to a client's request. One reason for this is that within the enterprise the designated or preferred development platform is VS.NET.

One very important aspect to consider is the desktop environment the solution will be used in. The development tool we choose dictates the requirements for the desktop infrastructure. For native Office solutions, including add-ins, templates, and individual documents and workbooks, the requirements are simple. With managed COM add-ins the complexity of the requirements increases, and for VSTO the complexity of the requirements increases even further. A summary of the requirements for these scenarios is shown in Table 26-1.

Table 26-1   Desktop Environment Requirements for Different Office Solutions

Requirements	Native Office Solutions	Managed COM Add-ins Solutions	VSTO Solutions
Windows XP or Windows Vista	✓	✓	✓
Office 2000 through 2007	✓	✓	
Office 2003 Professional SP-1 and later			✓
.NET Framework 2.0 and higher		✓	✓
PIAs		✓	✓
VSTO Runtime 3.0 and higher			✓
Code Access Security (CAS)			✓

In our experience, it is large enterprises that request VSTO solutions, not only because they already work with .NET but also because they can meet the desktop requirements dictated by VSTO. Large enterprises usually have centralized IT and development departments that control the desktop environment throughout the organization. These departments have the experience necessary to deploy .NET solutions and work with security on the .NET platform.

Many small and medium-sized businesses (SMB) lack a centralized IT department and commonly have multiple versions of Office deployed throughout their desktop environment. Given the specific requirements for VSTO it is not economically feasible to implement VSTO solutions in these companies.

Finally, while it easy to get started with VSTO because the VS IDE offers wizards to automate the most common tasks, VSTO is by design a far more complex development tool than VBA. To create professional VSTO solutions you need a high level of knowledge and understanding of the VSTO development platform.

At present, the answer to the question of when we want to use VSTO is more a matter of client preference than technical requirements for a specific situation. But as more companies move to newer Office versions and Microsoft continues to improve VSTO, some of the present requirements will be eliminated and VSTO will be more attractive to use. We can create VSTO solutions that target the Office application clients directly or MOSS directly. In the next section we discuss how to create VSTO solutions that target Excel 2007.

Working with VSTO Add-Ins

Working with VSTO add-ins is in many ways identical to working with managed COM add-ins. But from a technical point of view there are major differences between them. Because VSTO is a development platform on its own, it is optimized to work with Office, and it also uses and leverages the security model of the .NET Framework.

Creating Our First VSTO Add-In

In VSTO add-ins, we use the `IStartup` interface, which forwards two event handlers, `ThisAddIn_Startup` and `ThisAdd-in_Shutdown`. We put the initialization code in the startup event and the cleanup code in the shutdown event. To create a basic VSTO add-in, select *File > New Project...* from the

VS menu. Next, select the *Excel 2007 Add-in* project template in the New Project dialog and name it FirstVSTOAddin. At this stage the VS IDE creates the VSTO add-in and we get access to the ThisAddin class, ThisAddin.vb, which is equivalent to a connection class in a managed COM add-in. This class includes two event handlers, the startup and shutdown events described previously for the VSTO add-in. We add a "Hello World" message when the VSTO add-in is loaded and a "Goodbye World" message when it is shut down as shown in Listing 26-1.

Listing 26-1 Hello World and Goodbye World Messages

```vb
Imports System.Windows.Forms

Public Class ThisAddIn

    Private Sub ThisAddIn_Startup(ByVal sender As Object, _
                            ByVal e As System.EventArgs) _
                            Handles Me.Startup


        MessageBox.Show("Hello World")


    End Sub

    Private Sub ThisAddIn_Shutdown(ByVal sender As Object, _
                            ByVal e As System.EventArgs) _
                            Handles Me.Shutdown


        MessageBox.Show("Goodbye World")
    End Sub

End Class
```

To use the .NET `MessageBox` class, we imported the `System.Windows.Forms` namespace, as shown at the top of Listing 26-1. To start the debugging session for our VSTO add-in we just have to press the F5 button.

Because VSTO add-ins directly reference the Interop Excel Application object (that is, `Microsoft.Office.Interop.Excel.Application`), we can easily access the Excel Application object in our code. We access it through the ThisAddin class, and we need to use it in two different ways depending on where we want to work with it in the solution. If we are working with it in the ThisAddin class we access the Excel Application object as shown in Listing 26-2.

Listing 26-2 Accessing the Excel Application Object from the ThisAddin Module

```
Private Sub ThisAddIn_Startup(ByVal sender As Object, _
                              ByVal e As System.EventArgs) _
                              Handles Me.Startup

    'Add a workbook with one worksheet.
    Me.Application.Workbooks.Add(Excel.XlWBATemplate.xlWBATWorksheet)

End Sub
```

If we want to access the Excel Application object in other class modules, we access it using the Globals class as shown in Listing 26-3.

Listing 26-3 Accessing the Excel Application Object from a Class Module

```
Friend Function bAdd_Workbook() As Boolean

    Globals.ThisAddIn.Application. _
    Workbooks.Add(Excel.XlWBATemplate.xlWBATWorksheet)

End Function
```

The direct reference to the Excel Application object makes it easy to also access its events in the ThisAddin class. Select the *Application* entry in the left-side combo box at the top of the code module window and then select the desired event from the right-side combo box at the top of the code module, as shown in Figure 26-6.

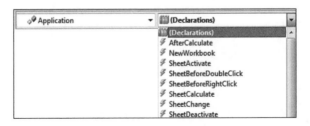

FIGURE 26-6 Accessing Excel Application object events in the ThisAddin class module

Loading and Unloading XLAs

In Excel applications development, it is a common task to control the availability of other add-ins in Excel. For example, if a user opens a

specific workbook we can make a specific XLA that corresponds to that
workbook available, and when the user closes the workbook the
corresponding XLA is unloaded. The code for this scenario is shown in
Listing 26-4.

Listing 26-4 Loading and Unloading an XLA

```vbnet
Private Const m_sXLWBUDGET As String = "Budget.xlsx"
Private Const m_sXLABUDGET As String = "C:\Budget\Budget.xlam"
Private Const m_sXLABUDGET_DISPLAYNAME As String = "Budget"


    Private Sub Application_WorkbookBeforeClose( _
            ByVal Wb As Microsoft.Office.Interop.Excel.Workbook, _
            ByRef Cancel As Boolean) _
            Handles Application.WorkbookBeforeClose

        Dim xlAddin As Excel.AddIn = Nothing

        Try

            If Wb.Name.ToString = m_sXLWBUDGET Then

                For Each xlAddin In _
                    Globals.ThisAddIn.Application.AddIns
                    If xlAddin.FullName = m_sXLABUDGET Then
                        xlAddin.Installed = False
                        Exit For
                    End If
                Next

            End If

        Catch ex As Exception

            MsgBox(ex.Message.ToString())

        End Try

    End Sub


    Private Sub Application_WorkbookOpen( _
        ByVal Wb As Microsoft.Office.Interop.Excel.Workbook) _
```

```
        Handles Application.WorkbookOpen

    Try


        If Wb.Name.ToString() = m_sXLWBUDGET Then

            With Globals.ThisAddIn.Application
                .AddIns.Add(Filename:=m_sXLABUDGET)
                .AddIns(m_sXLABUDGET_DISPLAYNAME).Installed = True
            End With

        End If


    Catch ex As Exception

        MsgBox(ex.Message.ToString())

    End Try

End Sub
```

Loading and Unloading VSTO and COM Add-Ins

Although there are technical differences among VSTO add-ins, unmanaged COM add-ins, and managed COM add-ins, we can control them in the same way. So if we have the same scenario as the previous case with an XLA, Listing 26-5 shows how we can resolve it for VSTO and COM add-ins.

Listing 26-5   Loading and Unloading VSTO and COM Add-Ins

```
Private Const m_sXLWBUDGET As String = "Budget.xlsx"

'Name of the add-in as listed in the COM Add-ins dialog.
Private Const m_sXLABUDGET As String = "BudgetReport"

Private m_xlCOMAddins As Office.COMAddIns
Private m_xlCOMBudget As Office.COMAddIn

    Private Sub Application_WorkbookBeforeClose( _
            ByVal Wb As Microsoft.Office.Interop.Excel.Workbook, _
            ByRef Cancel As Boolean) _
```

26. DEVELOPING EXCEL SOLUTIONS

```vb
        Handles Application.WorkbookBeforeClose

    m_xlCOMAddins = Globals.ThisAddIn.Application.COMAddIns
    m_xlCOMBudget = m_xlCOMAddins.Item(m_sXLABUDGET)

    Try

        If Wb.Name.ToString = m_sXLWBUDGET Then

            If m_xlCOMBudget.Connect Then _
                m_xlCOMBudget.Connect = False

        End If

    Catch ex As Exception

        MsgBox(ex.Message.ToString())

    End Try

End Sub


Private Sub Application_WorkbookOpen( _
            ByVal Wb As Microsoft.Office.Interop.Excel.Workbook) _
            Handles Application.WorkbookOpen

    m_xlCOMAddins = Globals.ThisAddIn.Application.COMAddIns
    m_xlCOMBudget = m_xlCOMAddins.Item(m_sXLABUDGET)

    Try


        If Wb.Name.ToString() = m_sXLWBUDGET Then

            If m_xlCOMBudget.Connect = False Then _
                m_xlCOMBudget.Connect = True
            End If


    Catch ex As Exception

        MsgBox(ex.Message.ToString ())

    End Try

End Sub
```

References in VSTO Add-ins

Before moving on, we should explore the referenced assemblies in our first VSTO add-in as well as the globally imported namespaces. Select *Project > FirstVSTOAddin Properties...* from the menu, followed by the *References* tab on the left to display the referenced assemblies together with the globally imported namespaces, as shown in Figure 26-7.

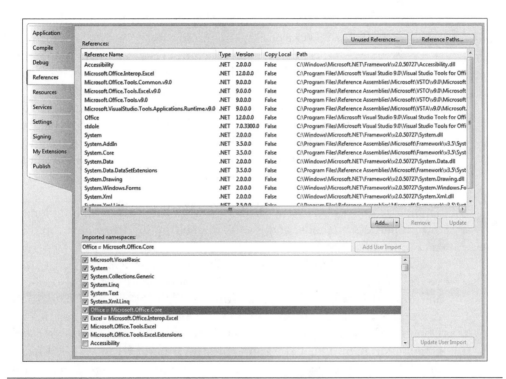

FIGURE 26-7 Referenced assemblies and globally imported namespaces

As we can see in Figure 26-7, the PIAs for Excel and Office (`Microsoft.Office.Interop.Excel` and `Office`) are included among the references. These give us access to the objects and methods of Office and Excel in a way similar way to how they are exposed in VBA. But we also have four new VSTO-specific references in the list of assemblies. These assemblies include classes that together provide the communication layer between VSTO solutions and Excel and are part of the VSTO runtime.

- `Microsoft.Office.Tools.Common.v9.0`—Includes classes that provide the ability to customize the Ribbon UI, create custom task panes in VSTO add-ins, and create action panes for VSTO workbook solutions.
- `Microsoft.Office.Tools.Excel.v9.0`—Provides host items and host controls for VSTO workbook solutions.
- `Microsoft.Office.Tools.v9.0`—Includes classes for data binding for host controls in VSTO workbook solutions and also nonaccessible classes that are part of the VSTO runtime infrastructure.
- `Microsoft.VisualStudio.Tools.Applications.Runtime.v9.0`— Includes the ServerDocument class, which enables us to attach and detach code-behind assemblies and to work with data islands in VSTO workbook solutions. It also includes nonaccessible classes that are part of the VSTO runtime infrastructure.

These assemblies also extend many of Excel's base classes and implement the properties, methods, and events defined by the `Microsoft.Office.Interop.Excel` interface.

One of the globally imported namespaces is `Microsoft.Office.Tools.Excel`. This namespace contains a set of classes that also extend and support Excel's object model. Another globally imported namespace is `Office = Microsoft.Office.Core`, which gives us access to the DocumentProperty objects. This namespace also allows us to work with CommandBars in Excel 2003 and with the Ribbon UI in VSTO. Finally, the PIA namespace `Excel = Microsoft.Office.Interop.Excel` is also globally imported into the solution.

Entries in the Windows Registry

When examining the entries in the `HKEY_CURRENT_USER\Software\Microsoft\Office\Excel\AddIns\` hive for our first VSTO add-in we can see that they look similar to the entries for a managed COM add-in. The first notable difference is that the subkey name for our VSTO add-in excludes the "Connect" class as part of the ProgID, as shown in Figure 26-8.

A new entry also exists, the **Manifest**, which specifies the full path of the **deployment manifest**. What the deployment manifest actually does is point to the current **application manifest**, which in return points to the

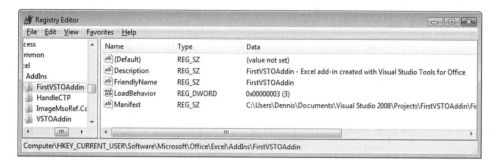

FIGURE 26-8   Entries in the Windows Registry

add-in assembly. The application manifest also specifies the entry point class to execute in the assembly. The manifest is discussed in more detail later in this chapter. The LoadBehavior values in the Windows Registry for VSTO add-ins are identical to the group of values that can be applied to managed and unmanaged COM add-ins.

The full path and filename for the deployment manifest is displayed when we select *Office Button > Excel Options > Add-ins* and select the VSTO add-in from the list in the dialog. This information is also available when we select the add-in in the COM Add-ins dialog.

Because VSTO add-ins use the generic VSTO loader, no entries for a VSTO add-in are created under the HKEY_CLASSES_ROOT hive. Also note that Excel only recognizes VSTO add-ins that are registered under the HKEY_CURRENT_USER hive. If you need to install and register VSTO add-ins for all users under the HKEY_LOCAL_MACHINE hive you must use the Windows Installer deployment model. This technique is beyond of the scope of this chapter, but further information is available in the article "Deploying your VSTO 2008 Add-In to All Users (Part III)" at http://blogs.msdn.com/mshneer/.

Running VSTO Add-Ins

To run a VSTO add-in, the generic VSTO loader must be available on the computer. The VSTO loader is part of the VSTO runtime and includes unmanaged components that actually load the add-in. The VSTO loader serves the same purpose COM shims do for managed COM add-ins, loading each VSTO add-in into its own application domain. Figure 26-9 shows how a VSTO add-in is loaded into Excel and how the communication between Excel and the VSTO add-in assembly is implemented.

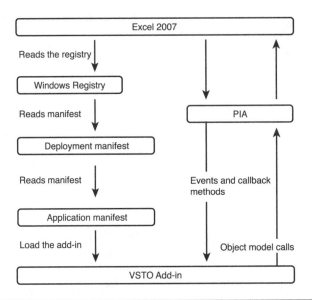

FIGURE 26-9   Add-in architecture for Excel 2007

The loading process consists of the following steps:

1. Excel checks the Windows Registry for VSTO add-in entries.
2. If Excel finds any entries it loads the VSTO loader. The VSTO loader loads the .NET Framework, unless it is already running, and then loads the VSTO runtime.
3. The VSTO runtime performs security checks and also verifies that the latest versions of the deployment and application manifests are being used.
4. The VSTO runtime creates a new application domain and loads the VSTO add-in assembly into it.
5. The VSTO runtime calls the ThisAddIn_Startup method in the VSTO add-in.

On shut down, we would expect the VSTO runtime to perform all necessary cleanup for us. It does enough to be acceptable under normal circumstances. However, when debugging you may find that the Excel process is not terminated properly. In this case you can add the custom cleanup code shown in Listing 26-6 to fix the problem.

Listing 26-6 Custom Cleanup Code

```
Private Sub ThisAddIn_Shutdown(ByVal sender As Object, _
                                ByVal e As System.EventArgs) _
                                Handles Me.Shutdown

    'Other code...

    GC.Collect()
    GC.WaitForPendingFinalizers()
    GC.Collect()

End Sub
```

The Ribbon Visual Designer

The **Ribbon Visual Designer** is a new tool shipped with VS 2008. It is available when working with VSTO solutions. The tool allows us to design and develop custom Ribbon UI solutions easily. With this tool, we can

- Add custom or built-in tabs to a Ribbon.
- Add custom groups to a custom or built-in tab.
- Add Office Ribbon controls to a custom group.
- Add Office Ribbon controls to the Microsoft Office menu.

It is available for both VSTO add-ins and for VSTO workbook solutions. In this section we use it to create a custom tab for our first VSTO add-in. First we need to add the Ribbon Visual Designer item to the VSTO solution in the following manner:

1. Select *Project > Add Component...* from the menu.
2. In the Add New Item dialog, first select the *Office* category and then select the *Ribbon (Visual Designer)* template, as shown in Figure 26-10.
3. Name the template CustomRibbonUI.vb and then click the *Add* button.

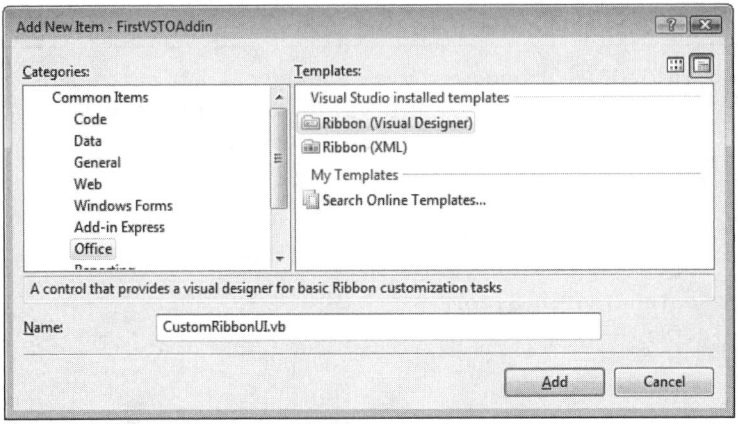

FIGURE 26-10   Adding a Ribbon Visual Designer

As we can see in Figure 26-10, it is also possible to use an XML file instead of the Ribbon Visual Designer. The process for creating a Ribbon UI with an XML file in a VSTO add-in is exactly the same as the process for doing so in a managed COM add-in, as described in Chapter 25, "Writing Managed COM Add-ins with VB.NET." Continuing with our Ribbon Visual Designer, in the next steps we

1. Remove the built-in *Add-Ins* tab from the Ribbon component. We add a custom tab rather than using the *Add-Ins* tab. Drag a *Tab* control from the Toolbox and drop it onto the Ribbon component. Open the Tab control's properties window and change its *Label* property to First VSTO Add-in.
2. Drag a *Group* control from the Toolbox and drop it onto the *FirstVSTO Add-in* tab. Open the Group control's properties window and change its *Label* property to First Group.
3. Drag a *Button* control from the Toolbox and drop it onto the *First Group* group. Open the Button control's properties window and change its *Label* property to Message.

If you have been following the steps so far, the result should appear similar to Figure 26-11.

The current version of the Ribbon Visual Designer offers only the basic set of controls shown in Figure 26-11. In addition to the visual design environment, the Ribbon Visual Designer also offers the ability to generate a basic configured setup of our customized Ribbon UI solution, including a Ribbon class and an XML file. Right-click on the Ribbon component and select *Export Ribbon to XML* from the shortcut menu. A Ribbon class

FIGURE 26-11 The Ribbon Visual Designer in action

is created in the Ribbon.vb file. This file also contains detailed instruction on how to complete the setup for the custom Ribbon UI.

The only callback function we need to create is the `Button1_Click` event. This is placed in the "Ribbon Callbacks" region of the Ribbon class, as shown in Listing 26-7.

Listing 26-7 The Callback for the Button in the Ribbon Class Module

```
'At the top of the class module.
Imports System.Windows.Forms

Sub Button1_Click(ByVal control As Office.IRibbonControl)
    MessageBox.Show("Hello World")
End Sub
```

We also need to add the *OnAction* attribute for the Button control to the XML markup in the Ribbon.xml file, as shown in Listing 26-8.

Listing 26-8 The OnAction Attribute Added to the Button Control

```
<button
    id="Button1"
    label="Message"
    onAction="Button1_Click"
    showImage="false"
/>
```

The final step is to test the solution, which we do by pressing the F5 key. When Excel loads our VSTO add-in, we click the Message button on our custom Ribbon UI and the message shown in Figure 26-12 is displayed.

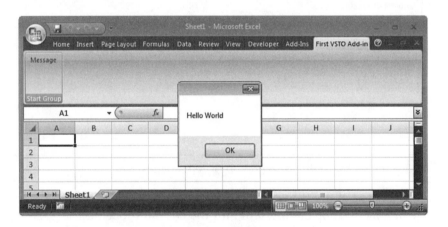

FIGURE 26-12 The message displayed by the Message button

The VSTO add-in project, FirstVSTOAddin, can be found in the *\Concepts\Ch26 – Developing Excel Solutions with Visual Studio Tools for Office System (VSTO)* folder on the CD that accompanies this book.

Custom Task Panes

Task panes were first introduced to Excel with Office XP. These panes display within the Excel application window, usually to the right side of the worksheet. Task panes can have one of two scopes: workbook level, which means they apply only to a specific workbook, or application level, which means they are available to all open workbooks. Excel uses the task pane interface for several tasks, including help, search, and browsing for clip art. Task panes in Excel also work well with SharePoint lists.

When task panes are scoped to the application level we name them **custom task panes (CTPs)**, and when they are scoped to single workbooks we refer to them as **action panes**. VSTO allows us to create custom task panes by implementing the **ICustomTaskPaneConsumer** interface in the add-ins template for Excel. We can create CTPs in managed COM add-ins as well, but we would need to implement this interface manually.

CTPs are similar to Windows Forms, and we use the Windows Forms controls when building them. This means that we can work with CTPs and their controls in exactly the same way we work with Windows Forms. For VSTO solutions we use a **user control**, which provides the user interface for each CTP (there is no visual designer for CTPs). In code, the user control is added to the Custom Task Panes collection.

The most important consideration is to decide when it is truly appropriate to use a custom task pane. The VS IDE makes them easy to create and use, even when they are not the best choice for implementing our user interface. As a general rule CTPs are best used for performing tasks external to the workbook, such as processing data from external data sources.

To add a CTP to a VSTO add-in, select *Project > Add User Control...* from the menu and in the *Add New Item* dialog give the control an appropriated name. For this example we use the name Cctp.vb. In the designer window we can drag and drop the desired controls onto the CTP user control. Figure 26-13 shows the result of customizing our CTP user control.

Be sure to test your CTP carefully to ensure that all its controls are sized correctly under various conditions. Some controls, like the DateTimePicker, require more space than other controls do. To work with the CTP in our code, we need to import the namespace `Microsoft.Office.Tools` into the ThisAddin class module. To make the CTP available when the add-in is loaded, we add the appropriate code to the `ThisAddin_StartUp` event, as shown in Listing 26-9.

Listing 26-9 Code to Make the CTP Available When the Add-In Is Loaded

```
Imports Tools = Microsoft.Office.Tools

Public Class ThisAddIn

    'Declare an instance of the class.
    Private cReport As Cctp
```

```vb
'Make the CTP available in the solution.
Private m_ctpTaskPane As Tools.CustomTaskPane

Friend Property ctpTaskPane() As Tools.CustomTaskPane
    Get
        Return m_ctpTaskPane
    End Get
    Set(ByVal value As Tools.CustomTaskPane)
        m_ctpTaskPane = value
    End Set
End Property

Private Sub ThisAddIn_Startup(ByVal sender As Object, _
                             ByVal e As System.EventArgs) _
                             Handles Me.Startup
    'Instantiate a new instance of the class.
    cReport = New Cctp

    'Add the CTP to Excel's collection of Custom Task Panes.
    ctpTaskPane = Me.CustomTaskPanes.Add(cReport, "Report")

    'Manipulate some main properties of the CTP.
    With CtpTaskPane
        .Width = 225
        .DockPosition = _
        Office.MsoCTPDockPosition.msoCTPDockPositionRight
        .DockPositionRestrict = _
        Office.MsoCTPDockPositionRestrict. _
        msoCTPDockPositionRestrictNoChange
        'By default all CTPs are invisible so we explicit need to
        'make the CTP visible.
        .Visible = True
    End With

    cReport = Nothing

End Sub
End Class
```

Like Windows Forms, the CTP class has a Load event that we use to populate the controls with data, as shown in Listing 26-10.

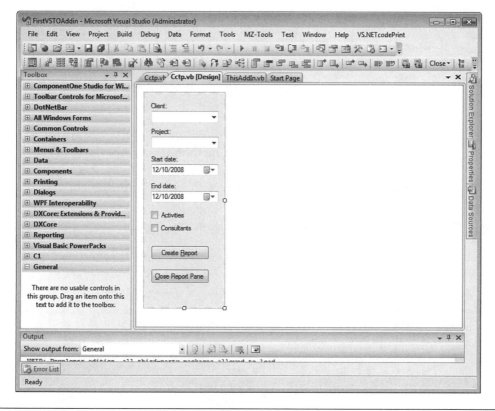

FIGURE 26-13 A customized CTP in design view

Listing 26-10 Code in the Load Event for the CTP

```vb
'At the top of the class module.
Imports System.Windows.Forms

Private Sub Cctp_Load(ByVal sender As System.Object, _
                      ByVal e As System.EventArgs) _
                      Handles MyBase.Load

    'Manipulate the two DateTime Picker Controls.
    With Me.dtpStartDate
        .Format = DateTimePickerFormat.Short
        .Value = DateTime.Now.AddDays(-10)
        .MinDate = DateTime.Now.AddMonths(-10)
        .MaxDate = DateTime.Now.AddMonths(-1)
    End With

    With Me.dtpEndDate
```

```
    .Format = DateTimePickerFormat.Short
    .Value = Today
    .MinDate = DateTime.Now.AddDays(-10)
    .MaxDate = Today
End With

End Sub
```

In the CTP class, we need to have a method that writes the data specified by the user to the active worksheet. For our CTP solution we use the Click event of the "Create Report" button as shown in Listing 26-11.

Listing 26-11   Code to Write Selected Data to the Active Worksheet

```
Private Sub cmdCreate_Report_Click(ByVal sender As System.Object, _
                                   ByVal e As System.EventArgs) _
                                   Handles cmdCreate_Report.Click

    'Write data from the Report CTP to the active worksheet.
    If (Globals.ThisAddIn.Application.ActiveSheet IsNot Nothing) Then

        Dim wsTarget As Excel.Worksheet = _
        CType(Globals.ThisAddIn.Application. _
            ActiveSheet, Excel.Worksheet)

        With Me.
            wsTarget.Range("D7").Value = .cboClient.Text
            wsTarget.Range("D8").Value = .cboProject.Text
            wsTarget.Range("D9").Value = CDate(.dtpStartDate.Text)
            wsTarget.Range("D10").Value = CDate(.dtpEndDate.Text)
        End With

        wsTarget = Nothing

    End If

End Sub
```

In some solutions, it may be best to close the CTP when all data has been written to a worksheet. Under other circumstance it may be better to provide a button that closes the CTP and allow the user to decide when to close it. We used the second approach with the task pane we built in Figure 26-13. The code to implement the close button is shown in Listing 26-12.

Listing 26-12   Code to Close the CTP

```
Private Sub cmdClose_Pane_Click(ByVal sender As System.Object, _
                                ByVal e As System.EventArgs) _
                                Handles cmdClose_Pane.Click

    Globals.ThisAddIn.ctpTaskPane.Visible = False

End Sub
```

A third approach is to provide a ToggleButton in a custom Ribbon UI solution. When the user clicks the ToggleButton it can show or hide the CTP. This way the user has full control over the CTP. We demonstrate an example of this method. In this example, we use the Ribbon Visual Designer but not together with an XML file and callback functions. This is because we want to trap when the user closes the CTP by clicking the x-close button and update the state of the ToggleButton in response so that the visibility of the CTP and the state of the ToggleButton remain synchronized. To create this example (result shown in Figure 26-14), follow these steps:

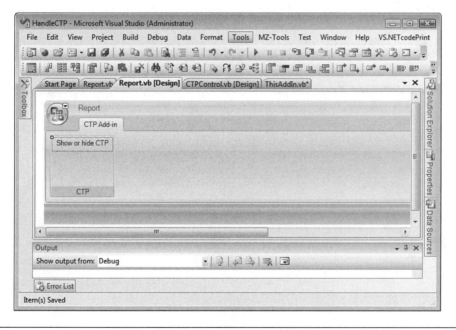

FIGURE 26-14   The custom Ribbon UI for the HandleCTP example

1. Create a new VSTO add-in solution and name it HandleCTP.
2. Add a user control to the solution and name it CTPControl.
3. Add a Ribbon Visual Designer item to the solution and name it Report.
4. Remove the built-in Add-In tab from the Ribbon component. Drag the *Tab* control from the Toolbox and drop it onto the Report component. Set the *Label* property of the Tab control to CTP Add-in.
5. Drag the *Group* control from the Toolbox and drop it onto the *CTP Add-in* tab. Set the *Label* property of the Group control to CTP.
6. Drag the *ToggleButton* control from the Toolbox and drop it onto the CTP group. Set the *Label* property of the ToggleButton to Show or Hide CTP.

Next, we add the code to implement the example in the ThisAddin class as shown in Listing 26-13.

Listing 26-13   The ThisAddin Class for the HandleCTP Example

```
Imports Tools = Microsoft.Office.Tools

Public Class ThisAddIn

    'Declare an instance.
    Private CTP As CTPControl

    'To use the VisibleChanged event of the CTP
    Private WithEvents CTPVisible As Tools.CustomTaskPane

    Private m_ctpTaskPane As Tools.CustomTaskPane

    'Make the CTP available in the solution.
    Public ReadOnly Property CtpTaskPane() As Tools.CustomTaskPane
        Get
            Return CTPVisible
        End Get

    End Property

    Private Sub ThisAddIn_Startup(ByVal sender As Object, _
                                  ByVal e As System.EventArgs) _
                                  Handles Me.Startup
```

```
        'Instantiate a new instance of the class.
        CTP = New CTPControl()
        'Add the CTP to the collection of CTPs.
        CTPVisible = Me.CustomTaskPanes.Add(CTP, "Report")

        CTP = Nothing

    End Sub

    Private Sub CTPVisible_VisibleChanged(ByVal sender As Object, _
                            ByVal e As System.EventArgs) _
                            Handles CTPVisible.VisibleChanged

        'Synchronize the ToggleButton state (to not pressed)
        'when users close the CTP via the Close button (x).
        Globals.Ribbons.Report.ToggleButton1.Checked = _
                                    CTPVisible.Visible

    End Sub

End Class
```

Finally, we add code to the ToggleButton_Click event in the Report class. Activate the Ribbon Visual Designer and double-click the Show or Hide CTP ToggleButton; then add the code shown in Listing 26-14 to the ToggleButton_Click event.

Listing 26-14 The ToggleButton_Click Event Code

```
Imports Tools = Microsoft.Office.Tools

Public Class Report

    Private Sub ToggleButton1_Click(ByVal sender As System.Object, _
    ByVal e As Microsoft.Office.Tools.Ribbon.RibbonControlEventArgs) _
    Handles ToggleButton1.Click

        'Show or hide the CTP.
        Globals.ThisAddIn.CtpTaskPane.Visible = _
        CType(sender, Tools.Ribbon.RibbonToggleButton).Checked
    End Sub

End Class
```

Now we can test the VSTO add-in by pressing the F5 key. Keep in mind that we can either use an XML file with callback functions or use this approach, which is identical to how we add code to controls on Windows Forms, but we cannot combine them in a single solution. The VSTO add-in project, HandleCTP, can be found in the \Concepts\Ch26 – Developing Excel Solutions with Visual Studio Tools for Office System (VSTO) folder on the CD that accompanies this book.

VSTO Automation Add-ins

So far, we have not mentioned VSTO automation add-ins, and the reason for this is simple; we cannot directly call managed UDFs from worksheet cells. To use managed UDFs in a worksheet we would have to create VBA wrappers for them. The performance penalty caused by this solution makes the creation of automation add-ins in VSTO impractical. This means we either develop UDFs in VBA, or if we need high performance UDFs we create XLLs. XLLs are discussed in more detail in Chapter 27, "XLLs and the C API."

Working with VSTO Templates and Workbook Solutions

If we disregard the technology and architecture differences between creating workbooks with Excel and with VSTO, the process itself is identical. VSTO provides us with a feature rich IDE where we can work directly with the Excel UI, as shown in Figure 26-15.

We can use all of Excel's features as well as the large group of additional features provided by VSTO workbook solutions. Since VSTO uses the .NET Framework we can also use all the facilities provided by the VS IDE and .NET Framework.

Individual VSTO workbooks and workbook templates behave identically to workbooks created in Excel. We do not explicitly discuss workbook template solutions in the sections that follow, but unless otherwise stated, everything we cover applies to both workbooks and workbook templates.

Host Items and Host Controls

VSTO gives us access to **host items** and **host controls** that extend Excel objects for interaction with managed code. Host items consist of the workbook and worksheet objects, and they are required to add and use host controls on worksheets. Host controls are based on the native COM controls (interop controls) and behave like them as well. These host controls are accessible via the `Microsoft.Office.Tools.Excel` namespace.

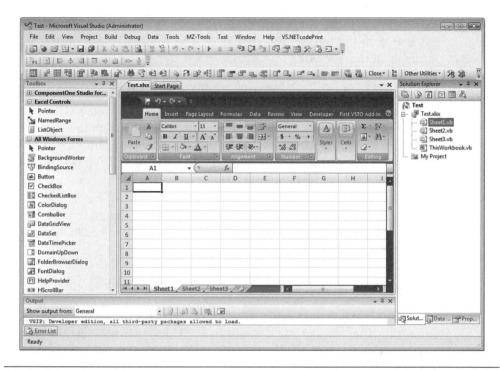

FIGURE 26-15 The VSTO IDE

In general, the host controls extend Excel objects to allow data binding with ADO.NET. The host controls also expose events of the objects enabling us to code against them in VSTO. The managed extensions are added on top of the interop objects. Some objects, like the Chart and the ListObject, can be accessed via both the Interop namespace and through VSTO code directly.

We can easily drag a ListObject control onto a worksheet from the Toolbox. It is also possible to add a ListObject control via Excel's user interface, but then it is labeled as Table in Excel 2007 and List in Excel 2003. We do not have access to the Chart control from the Toolbox. Instead we create one by clicking on the *Insert* tab and then selecting the desired chart type. VSTO automatically creates a host Chart control when the chart is added to the worksheet.

VSTO also provides us with some host controls that cannot be accessed via the Interop namespace. These include the **NamedRange** and **XMLMappedRange** objects. These host controls are also accessible through the `Microsoft.Office.Tools.Excel` namespace.

The NamedRange control contains a range that has a unique name. It supports managed data binding and exposes events. The control allows us to code directly against the range's events, which is not possible to do when working with the interop range objects. The NamedRange control is also available in the Toolbox.

The XMLMappedRange control contains a range that has an XML schema mapped against it. This control also supports managed data binding, and we can import XML data to the range based on the XML schema. Like the Chart control, this control must be added through the Excel user interface. Select the *Developer* tab, click on the *Import* button, and in the Import XML dialog select the XML file to be imported. VSTO automatically creates a host XMLMappedRange control when it is added to the worksheet.

Host controls can be added to worksheets during design time or at runtime. We take a closer look at the NamedRange and the ListObject controls later on.

Windows Forms Controls

We can use Windows Forms controls in a worksheet by dragging them from the Toolbox onto the worksheet. These controls reside in the `System.Windows.Forms` namespace, but in this context we use them from the `Microsoft.Office.Tool.Excel.Controls` namespace.

Managed Windows Forms controls cannot be placed directly on a worksheet as COM objects. The worksheet object is not aware of managed controls. The solution is to place an ActiveX control on the worksheet, place a **ContainerControl** inside the ActiveX control, and finally place Windows Forms controls inside the ContainerControl. The ContainerControl object is part of the `System.Windows.Forms` namespace. We do not need to work directly with the ActiveX control or the ContainerControl, only with the Windows Forms controls and the worksheet.

Working with Windows Forms controls on a worksheet is identical to working with them on Windows Forms. It should be noted that we cannot set the tab order between the controls, and we cannot set the positioning properties such as Left, Top, Height, and Width. The controls can be added during design time or at runtime. If we add them at runtime we need to be aware that the Windows Forms controls added in this manner are not persisted—that is, they are not saved when the workbook is saved.

Server-Side VSTO Solutions

Before VSTO 2005, Microsoft only offered the ability to create client-side solutions with Excel. Beginning with VSTO 2005 it is possible to create server-side solutions without having Excel installed on the server. This is a complex process that is beyond the scope of this chapter, but we briefly describe it in this section.

Since its introduction in Office 2002, Microsoft's commitment to the XML file format has grown stronger with each new release of Office. The latest and most advanced iteration of the XML file format was introduced in Office 2007 and is called Open XML. This XML file format allows us to create and manipulate fully formatted workbooks without the use of the Excel application. These workbooks look and behave exactly like workbooks created natively in Excel.

In Excel applications, it is common to store data we retrieve from external sources in hidden worksheets. With VSTO this is no longer necessary. We can use the XML data island document property of the workbook to store, access, and manipulate this data directly. Because the data is XML-based we can create so-called typed datasets to access the underlying data schema by name, and by doing so we do not need to go through the Excel user interface. In this manner, VSTO separates business logic from the user interface. More specifically, VSTO is based on the **Mode-view-controller (MVC)** architectural pattern, which results in solutions where we can modify the visual appearance of the solution or the underlying business rules without affecting the other.

The ServerDocument class makes it possible to access cached data. It also provides access to the application manifest without the need to start Excel. This class also provides us with the ability to programmatically attach or remove code-behind assemblies. This means we can create a workbook solution, including a code-behind assembly, execute the code, remove the assembly, and then distribute the workbook without any code. The ServerDocument class resides in the `Microsoft.VisualStudio.Tools.Applications.Runtime` namespace. One important limitation is that we cannot use the Excel calculation engine in these types of solutions.

Creating Our First VSTO Workbook Solution

Creating a VSTO workbook solution is as easy creating a VSTO add-in solution. Select *File > New Project* from the menu. In the *Project types* window expand the *Office* node and select the *2007* node. Select the *Excel 2007 Workbook* template in the *Templates* window and name it FirstVSTOWorkbook.

In the next dialog, *Select a Document for Your Application*, we can either create a new workbook or make a copy of an existing workbook. In our case we want to start with a new workbook so we accept the default selection and name the workbook FirstWorkbook. For new workbooks we can specify which file format should be used. Since we are targeting Excel 2007 and will not be using VBA we accept the default setting of *.xlsx.

Next, open Windows Explorer and drill down to the solution folder, which in Vista is ...\Documents\Visual Studio 2008\Projects\ FirstVSTOWorkbook\FirstVSTOWorkbook as shown in Figure 26-16. As we can see in Figure 26-16, the workbook created for our solution is listed among the rest of the files for the solution. If we need to work with it in Excel we can just double-click the file and it will then be opened in Excel.

Name	Date modified	Type	Size	Tags
bin	12/18/2008 10:35 ...	File Folder		
My Project	12/18/2008 10:35 ...	File Folder		
obj	12/18/2008 10:35 ...	File Folder		
FirstVSTOWorkbook	12/18/2008 10:35 ...	Visual Basic Project file	11 KB	
FirstWorkbook	12/18/2008 10:35 ...	Microsoft Office Excel Worksheet	8 KB	
Sheet1.Designer.vb	12/18/2008 10:35 ...	Visual Basic Source file	8 KB	
Sheet1.Designer	12/18/2008 10:35 ...	XML Document	1 KB	
Sheet1.vb	12/18/2008 10:40 ...	Visual Basic Source file	1 KB	
Sheet2.Designer.vb	12/18/2008 10:35 ...	Visual Basic Source file	8 KB	
Sheet2.Designer	12/18/2008 10:35 ...	XML Document	1 KB	
Sheet2.vb	12/18/2008 10:35 ...	Visual Basic Source file	1 KB	
Sheet3.Designer.vb	12/18/2008 10:35 ...	Visual Basic Source file	8 KB	
Sheet3.Designer	12/18/2008 10:35 ...	XML Document	1 KB	
Sheet3.vb	12/18/2008 10:35 ...	Visual Basic Source file	1 KB	
ThisWorkbook.Design...	12/18/2008 10:35 ...	Visual Basic Source file	10 KB	
ThisWorkbook.Designer	12/18/2008 10:35 ...	XML Document	1 KB	
ThisWorkbook.vb	12/18/2008 10:35 ...	Visual Basic Source file	1 KB	

FIGURE 26-16 The contents of the VSTO workbook solution's main folder

VSTO workbook solutions have the same namespace references and imported namespaces as VSTO add-ins. When we examine the Solution Explorer we see that it contains one class for the workbook and one class per worksheet. The number of available worksheets in a new workbook solution is controlled by the *Include this many sheets* setting in Excel.

VSTO workbook solutions also implement the IStartup interface, but the Startup and Shutdown events are associated with the ThisWorkbook class. Because VSTO workbook solutions also directly reference the Interop Excel Application object, Microsoft.Office.Interop.Excel.Application, we can easily access the Excel Application object. If we work in the ThisWorkbook class then we access it in a similar way as we do in VBA, which Listing 26-15 also lists.

Listing 26-15 Startup Events in VSTO Workbook Solutions

```
Private Sub ThisWorkbook_Startup(ByVal sender As Object, _
                        ByVal e As System.EventArgs) _
                        Handles Me.Startup
```

```
    Me.Application.Workbooks.Add()

End Sub
```

If we work with the Application object from a worksheet class, then we also use the ThisWorkbook class as shown in Listing 26-16.

Listing 26-16 Startup and Shutdown Events for a Worksheet

```
Private Sub Sheet1_Startup(ByVal sender As Object, _
                           ByVal e As System.EventArgs) _
                           Handles Me.Startup

    Globals.ThisWorkbook.Application.Workbooks.Add()

End Sub
```

It is possible to add worksheets at design time. Activate the FirstVSTOWorkbook.xlsx tab, select the *Home* tab, and on the *Cells* group click *Insert* followed by *Insert Sheet*. It is also possible to add worksheets at runtime, but only native worksheets.

Working with a NamedRange Host Control

To add a NamedRange control to a worksheet, just drag it from the Toolbox and drop it onto the worksheet Sheet1. A dialog appears that prompts us to select the NamedRange cell area, as shown in Figure 26-17.

VSTO automatically creates a name for the range, NamedRange1. If we want to change the name we need to do it using the *Formulas* tab *Name Manager* button. It would have been nice if we could specify the name for our range in the same dialog used to select the range.

Next, we use the NamedRange control to track the values entered into cells within its range. Open the code window for the Sheet1 class and select the object NamedRange1 in the upper-left combo box. In the upper-right combo box select the Change event and add the code shown in Listing 26-17.

Listing 26-17 The Change Event of the NamedRange1 Control

```
Private Sub NamedRange1_Change(ByVal _
        Target As Microsoft.Office.Interop.Excel.Range) _
        Handles NamedRange1.Change
```

```
Dim sMessage As String = "The value "

sMessage = sMessage + Target.Value.ToString()
sMessage = sMessage + " has been entered into cell "
sMessage = sMessage + Target.Address.ToString()

MessageBox.Show(sMessage)
```

End Sub

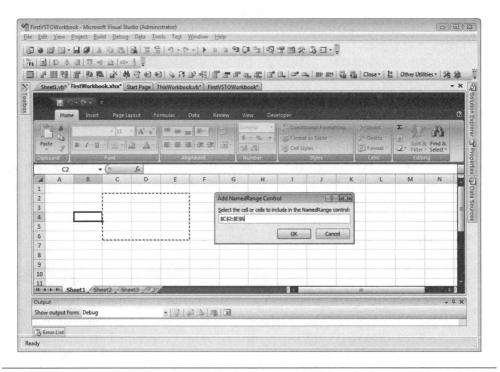

Figure 26-17   Adding a NamedRange control to a worksheet

When the code in Listing 26-17 is executed, we receive information about the value entered and which cell it has been entered in, as shown in Figure 26-18.

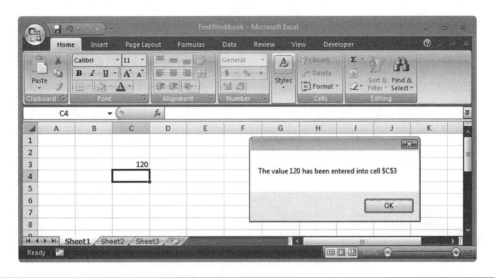

FIGURE 26-18   Trapping the NamedRange control Change event

Using the ListObject Host Control

We now programmatically create a ListObject host control and populate it with data. We start by adding a new class module to the FirstVSTOWorkbook solution and name it CDataReport. Next, we add two functions, which are shown in Listing 26-18.

Listing 26-18   Functions to Create a ListObject Host Control and Populate it with Data

```
Imports System.Data.SqlClient
Imports Tools = Microsoft.Office.Tools.Excel

Public Class CDataReport

    Friend Function Create_ListObject() As Boolean

        Dim dtTable As DataTable = Create_DataTable()

        'Get a reference to the host item
        Dim wsTargetSheet As Tools.Worksheet = Globals.Sheet2

        'Create a new ListObject control.
        Dim MyList As Tools.ListObject = _
        wsTargetSheet.Controls.AddListObject( _
        wsTargetSheet.Range("B4"), "Report")

        Try
```

26. Developing Excel Solutions

```vb
            Globals.ThisWorkbook.Application.ScreenUpdating = False

        With MyList
            'Add the field names from the data source to the first
            'row of the ListObject.
            .AutoSetDataBoundColumnHeaders = True
            'Bind the ListObject to the data source and populate
            'it with the datatable's data.
            .DataSource = dtTable
            'Disconnect the ListObject from its data source.
            .Disconnect()
            .DataBoundFormat = _
              Excel.XlRangeAutoFormat.xlRangeAutoFormatClassic1
            .HeaderRowRange.Columns.AutoFit()
            'If we want to convert the ListObject to a plain range
            'then it's done by using the Unlist method.
            '.Unlist
        End With

            Globals.ThisWorkbook.Application.ScreenUpdating = True

    Catch ex As Exception

        MessageBox.Show(ex.ToString())

    End Try

    If (MyList IsNot Nothing) Then MyList = Nothing
    If (wsTargetSheet IsNot Nothing) Then wsTargetSheet = Nothing
    If (dtTable IsNot Nothing) Then dtTable = Nothing


End Function

Private Function Create_DataTable() As DataTable

    Dim sqlCon As New SqlConnection( _
    connectionString:=My.Settings.sDBConnection)

    'Select only clients that have running projects.
    Dim sSqlQuestion As String = _
        "SELECT ClientID, ClientName FROM Clients " + _
        "WHERE ClientID IN _
        (SELECT DISTINCT ClientID FROM Projects) " + _
```

```
        "ORDER BY ClientName;"


    'The variable for the SQL adapter in use.
    Dim adpSql As SqlDataAdapter = Nothing

    'Declare and instantiate a new dataset.
    Dim dsData As New DataSet

    Try
        'Instantiate a new SQL adapter.
        adpSql = New _
         SqlDataAdapter(selectCommandText:=sSqlQuestion, _
                    selectConnection:=sqlCon)
        'Fill the dataset with data.
        adpSql.Fill(dataSet:=dsData, srcTable:="PETRA")

        'Name the retrieved datatable.
        dsData.Tables(0).TableName = "Clients"

        'Return the datatable.
        Return dsData.Tables("Clients")


    Catch SqlExc As SqlException

        MessageBox.Show(SqlExc.ToString())
        Return Nothing

    Finally

        dsData.Dispose()
        dsData = Nothing

        adpSql.Dispose()
        adpSql = Nothing

        sqlCon.Dispose()
        sqlCon = Nothing

    End Try

End Function

End Class
```

The second function, `Create_Datatable`, retrieves the desired data from the database and adds it to a DataTable. The ListObject host control is then bound to the DataTable. Both when creating a reference to the target worksheet and when creating the ListObject host control we use Excel objects in the namespace `Microsoft.Office.Tools.Excel`.

Deployment and Security

We have two alternatives for deploying VSTO solutions: Windows Installer or the ClickOnce deployment technology. Using Windows Installer we can customize deployment to a much higher degree than with ClickOnce, because it is not possible to customize the UI for ClickOnce solutions. On the other hand it is much easier to deploy VSTO solutions with ClickOnce than with Windows Installer. In this section we focus on the ClickOnce deployment technology.

NOTE   For more information about Windows Installer, see parts 1 and 2 of the article series "Deploying a Visual Studio Tools for the Office System 3.0 Solution for the 2007 Microsoft Office System Using Windows Installer," beginning on the Microsoft Web site at http://msdn.microsoft.com/en-us/library/cc563937.aspx.

Security plays a critical role when we deploy and run VSTO solutions. The Office security model is generally not involved because VSTO has its own security model. As a practical matter this means we can set Office security to the highest level and still be able to run VSTO solutions. However, the Trust Center in Office may be involved because the deployment location must be added to the Trusted Locations list when using a network file share as the deployment location.

An Introduction to Using ClickOnce Deployment with VSTO Solutions

The ClickOnce deployment technology has been available ever since the first version of VS was released but was not made available for VSTO until VSTO 2008. ClickOnce allows us to create self-updating Windows-based applications that can be installed and run with minimal user interaction. It allows us to make solutions available for download and installation via Web servers, FTP sites, and network file shares. It is also possible to use ClickOnce for local installation from CD/DVD, USB sticks, or the local hard drive. In our experience, using ClickOnce with VSTO solutions is much easier than creating MSI installation packages.

The VSTO Security Model

The security model of VSTO involves several technologies, including the VSTO runtime, ClickOnce, the Trust Center in Office, digital certificates, security zones, the deployment manifest, and the application manifest. At its core it is about modifying the security policy of each target computer to trust VSTO-based Office solutions.

In previous versions of VSTO, the security was based on **Code Access Security (CAS)**, but starting with VSTO 2008 it is based on **inclusion lists**. Inclusion lists enable us to grant trust to VSTO solutions that are signed with a digital certificate. Inclusion lists are user-specific. An entry in an inclusion list consists of two parts: a path to the deployment manifest and the public key used to sign the VSTO solution. When a VSTO solution has been added to the inclusion list it is considered to be trusted. When a VSTO solution is uninstalled it is removed from the inclusion list. The ClickOnce deployment technology automatically updates the inclusion list.

The VSTO runtime is responsible for all the security checks that take place during installation, updating, and loading of VSTO solutions. What the VSTO runtime looks for in these processes is **evidence** of

- The digital certificate used to sign the deployment manifest
- The location of the deployment manifest

A deployment manifest describes the VSTO solution deployment and the current version of the solution. The VSTO runtime queries the deployment manifest to determine which version of the application manifest to download. The application manifest, which is also an XML file, describes the VSTO solution's assemblies and dependent libraries. The application manifest provides the VSTO runtime with information required to load and update the VSTO solution.

The Trust Center in Office plays an important role in the security model. If we deploy the VSTO solution from a network file share then the full path, such as `\\servername\fileshare\`, of the network file share must be added to the Trusted Locations list. Any required subdirectories must also be added. When using a Web server or an FTP site as the deployment location it is not necessary to include the URL in the Trusted Locations list.

Before a digital certificate can take part in VSTO security, it must be installed on the target computer in one of the following ways:

- If the certificate authority that issued the digital certificate has been added to the **Trusted Root Certification Authority certificate store** it provides proof of identity.
- If the digital certificate has been installed to the **Trusted Publishers certificate store** it provides proof of trust.

The use of digital certificates has an impact on how to configure the installation prompts, that is, for trust decision and for download. These settings are grouped into different security zones, and we can change the settings in one zone independently from the other. To change these settings we need to work with the Windows Registry.

On computers that will run our VSTO solutions we need to add the following key in the Windows Registry (if it does not already exist) to control user prompting and the requirement for trusted certificates:

```
HKEY_LOCAL_MACHINE\SOFTWARE\Microsoft\.NETFramework\Security\
TrustManager\PromptingLevel
```

The **TrustManager** registry key and its subkey **PromptingLevel** with the default settings are shown in Figure 26-19.

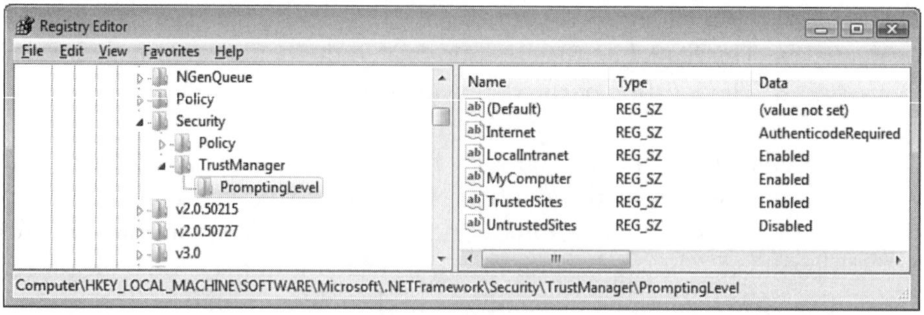

FIGURE 26-19 Trust Manager settings in the Windows Registry

The names shown in Figure 26-19 refer to the available security zones. These security zones can have different values, which result in different prompting behavior during installation, as listed in Table 26-2.

Table 26-2 PromptLevel Values and Their Corresponding Prompts

Data Value	Installation Prompt
Enabled	If the solution is not signed with a trusted certificate the installation prompts the user to decide whether to trust the solution, as shown later in Figure 26-21.
Disabled	If the solution is signed with a trusted certificate it will be installed silently.
Authenticode Required	If the solution is signed with a trusted certificate the user will not be prompted. Instead the user sees the message shown in Figure 26-22.

The configuration of the digital certificate and of the Windows Registry settings on the target computers is done one time. When the digital certificate expires and is replaced with a new certificate the target computers must be updated accordingly.

VBA in VSTO Workbook Solutions If we need to use VBA in a VSTO workbook solution then the VBA part will be part of the Office security model. This means it should be signed with the same digital certificate that is used to sign the deployment manifest.

Working with the Internet Security Zone

Here we assume that we have a signed VSTO workbook solution that can only be made available via a Web server and where the target computers only have the digital certificate installed in the Trusted Publishers certificate store. To make the VSTO workbook solution accessible we must change the Internet security zone's value from `AuthenticodeRequired` to `Enabled` on every target computer. The installation process includes two steps:

1. Download the workbook and save it to the local hard drive.
2. Trust the code-behind assembly.

We open Internet Explorer and in the address bar type the full URL path to the workbook. For example: www.excelkb.com/vsto/Installation/FirstWorkbook.xlsx.

Next, we are prompted to either open or save the workbook as shown in Figure 26-20. The workbook must be downloaded and then opened in Excel. It cannot be opened directly from the Web browser.

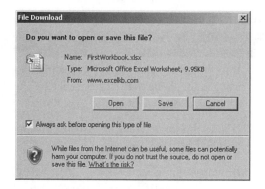

FIGURE 26-20   The File Download prompt

When we have saved the workbook to the local hard drive we open it in
Excel. During the opening of the workbook we are prompted whether to
trust the publisher of the certificate as shown in Figure 26-21. If the publisher's root certificate is installed on our computer then this prompt is not
displayed. By accepting the publisher the prompt will not reappear when
updating the solution in the future.

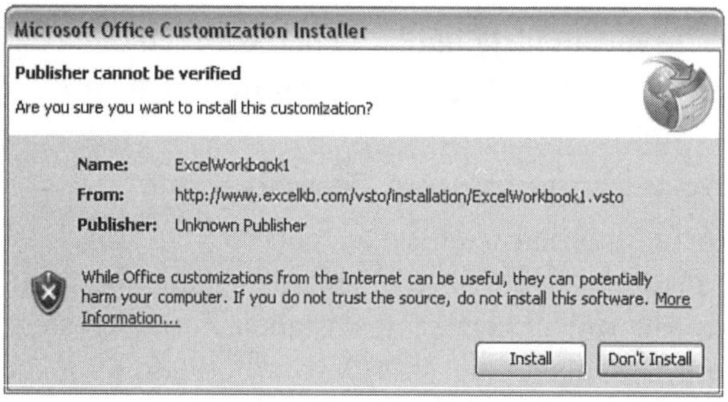

FIGURE 26-21   The installation prompt to trust the VSTO workbook solution

Finally, we see the installation message for the code-behind assembly as
shown in Figure 26-22.

When this is complete, the workbook and the code-behind assembly
are loaded in Excel, and we can start to work with the solution.

To summarize, we downloaded the workbook and made one installation of the code-behind assembly where we first trusted the publisher and
then the code-behind assembly was installed. During this process the
VSTO runtime made several security checks.

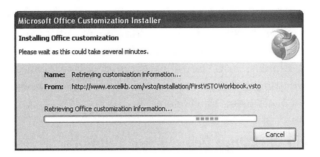

Figure 26-22 The installation message for the code-behind assembly

If we open the Windows Control Panel and choose *Program and Features* (in Vista) or *Add/Remove Programs* (under Windows XP) it shows that the code-behind assembly is installed. Removing the VSTO solution requires two steps:

1. Remove the code-behind assembly via *Program and Features* or *Add/Remove Programs*.
2. Delete the workbook from the local hard disk

Every time our VSTO workbook solution is opened in Excel the VSTO runtime performs a security check. If the security check fails the workbook will be loaded but without the code-behind assembly.

To use a Web server we need to make sure the Web server is configured correctly. The Web server must recognize the **MIME types** shown in Table 26-3. If they are not already configured they must be added.

Table 26-3 Filename Extensions and Their MIME Types

Filename Extension	MIME Type
.application	Application/x-ms-application
.manifest	Application/x-ms-application
.deploy	Application/octet stream
.msp	Application/microsoftpatch
.msu	Application/microsoftupdate
.vsto	Application/x-ms-vsto

26. Developing Excel Solutions

The first three extensions in Table 26-3 are required to run ClickOnce deployment solutions. The extensions .msp and .msu must exist to allow prerequisites that will be downloaded from the Web, such as the .NET Framework. The last extension is required to execute deployment manifests, which have the extension .vsto. These settings also allow us to automatically update our VSTO solutions via the Web server.

Creating ClickOnce Deployment Solutions

Creating a ClickOnce deployment solution is simple. Sign the deployment manifest, specify where to save the deployment solution, specify the location from which users will download the VSTO solution, and finally publish it. Signing a deployment manifest is done under the *Signing* tab in the VSTO solution Properties window, as shown in Figure 26-23. Note that we also use a strong name for the code-behind assembly.

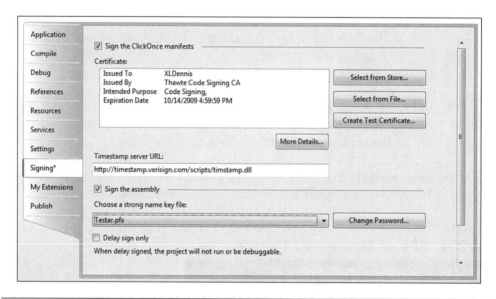

FIGURE 26-23 The deployment manifest signing tab in the VS IDE

Publishing the VSTO workbook solution is done under the *Publish* tab in the VSTO solution Properties window, as shown in Figure 26-24.

The first decision to make is where to publish the VSTO workbook solution, that is, where to place the ClickOnce files and the files from the VSTO workbook solution. The default is to place these files in a new publisher subfolder below the main folder of the VSTO solution. We recommend that you always use this location so the whole project is located in one main folder.

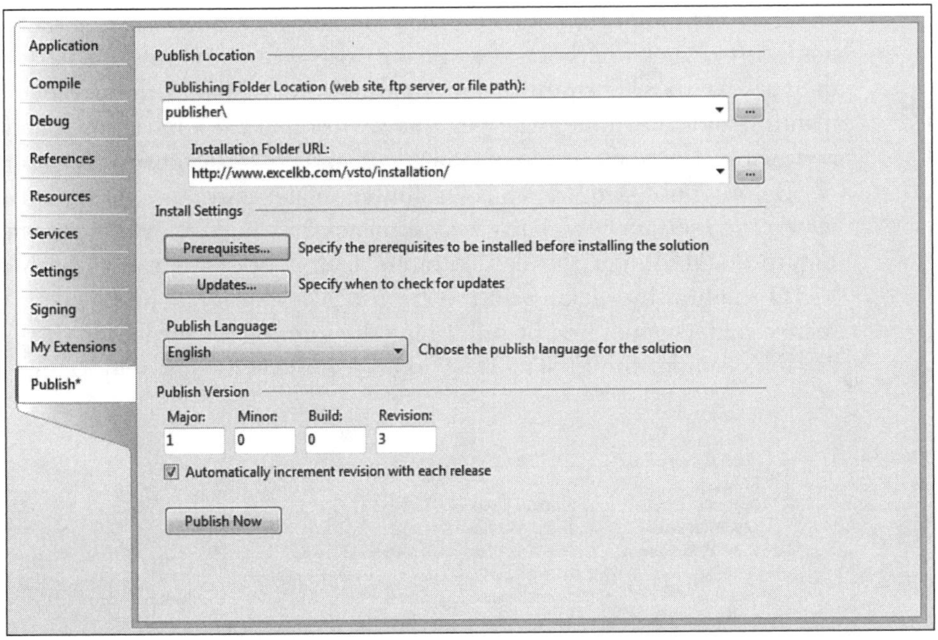

FIGURE 26-24   The Publish tab for the VSTO workbook solution

The next decision is to choose a location from which the users will download the VSTO solution. This is the installation folder. If possible, try to use a corporate network file share for ease of administration. As Figure 26-24 also shows we can administer the prerequisites, the publish language to use, updates, and an incremental publish version.

The third decision to make is when to check for updates for the VSTO solution. This can be carried out any time the target computers are connected to the Internet. To configure updates we click the *Updates...* button in Figure 26-24. This displays the Customization Updates dialog shown in Figure 26-25.

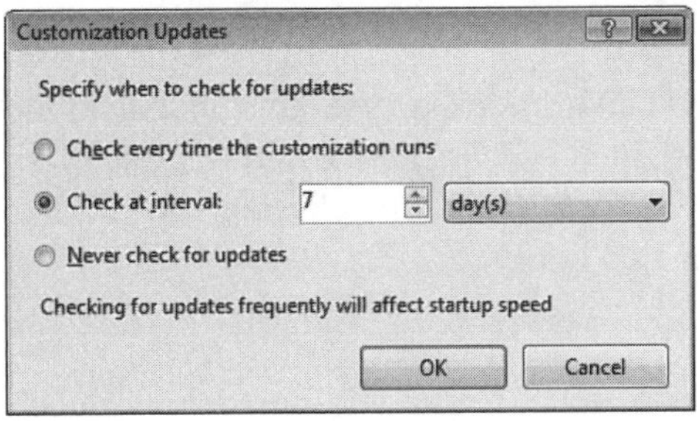

FIGURE 26-25   The dialog to configure when to check for updates

If the computer running the VSTO solution is connected to Internet and it is time to check whether a new version exists, the VSTO runtime performs the task. The VSTO runtime downloads a new version of the deployment manifest and determines whether a new version of the application manifest is available. If a new version is available it starts the download process.

Before publishing a VSTO solution, make sure the *Automatically increment revision with each release* check box is checked, as shown in Figure 26-24. When the configuration is complete we can publish the VSTO solution by clicking on the *Publish Now* button. The files and the related folders generated by publishing the solution are located in the publish folder under the FirstVSTOWorkbook project, as shown in Figure 26-26.

Name	Date modified	Type	Size
Application Files	12/23/2008 5:49 PM	File Folder	
Office2007PIARedist	12/23/2008 5:49 PM	File Folder	
FirstVSTOWorkbook	12/23/2008 5:49 PM	VSTO Deployment Manifest	8 KB
FirstWorkbook	12/23/2008 5:49 PM	Microsoft Office Excel Worksheet	11 KB
setup	12/23/2008 5:49 PM	Application	689 KB

Figure 26-26   Files and subfolders for the ClickOnce solution

Whenever we update a VSTO solution by publishing it, ClickOnce stores the previous version in a separate folder with all previous versions, as shown in Figure 26-27. By storing previous versions it is possible to roll back any update.

Name	Date modified	Type
FirstVSTOWorkbook_1_0_0_0	12/19/2008 3:53 AM	File Folder
FirstVSTOWorkbook_1_0_0_1	12/19/2008 3:55 AM	File Folder
FirstVSTOWorkbook_1_0_0_2	12/22/2008 4:14 PM	File Folder
FirstVSTOWorkbook_1_0_0_3	12/23/2008 5:49 PM	File Folder

Figure 26-27   All published versions of the VSTO solution

The FirstVSTOWorkbook project and its ClickOnce deployment solution can be found in the \Concepts\Ch26 – Developing Excel Solutions with Visual Studio Tools for Office System (VSTO) folder on the CD that accompanies this book.

Installing VSTO Solutions

As mentioned earlier, for workbook and workbook template solutions the easiest approach is to type the full URL into the Web browser address bar like this: www.excelkb.com/vsto/installation/FirstWorkbook.xlsx. For VSTO add-ins we have two other options:

■ The name of the deployment manifest, such as http://www.excelkb.com/vsto/installation/Addin.vsto

■ The complete setup package if we want to be sure that all prerequisites are available: http://www.excelkb.com/vsto/installation/setup.exe

Location of Installed VSTO Solutions

All VSTO solutions that are deployed with ClickOnce are stored on the client computer in a **ClickOnce application cache**. A ClickOnce cache is a group of hidden directories under the Local Settings directory of the current user's Documents and Settings folder. The cache holds all the files for VSTO solutions including assemblies, configuration files, user settings, and any data directory.

On target computers that run Windows XP, VSTO solution files are located under *C:\Documents and Settings\<UserName>\Local Settings\Apps\2.0*, while on Windows Vista they are located under *C:\Users\<UserName>\AppData\Local\Apps\2.0*.

Limitations of the ClickOnce Deployment Technology

The simplicity of ClickOnce deployment comes with a price in terms of limitations. The two most important limitations are

■ We cannot customize the UI.

■ For VSTO add-ins we can only write to the HKEY_CURRENT_USER\Software\Microsoft\Office\Excel\AddIns section of Windows Registry during the installation process.

If we need to control the UI or make other entries to the Windows Registry, then we need to use the Windows Installer technology.

Further Reading

Visual Studio Tools for Office: Using Visual Basic 2005 with Excel, Word, Outlook, and InfoPath

Authored by Eric Carter and Eric Lippert
ISBN# 0321411757—Addison-Wesley
As of this writing, there are no books available that target only VSTO development for Excel. This book covers VSTO development for several Office applications at a high level of detail. It covers all the events for each of the Office applications. If you know the Excel object model and its events then the detailed walkthrough is of little interest. Hopefully, by the time this is written the next edition that targets VSTO 2008 and Office 2007 will be available.

Related Portal and Blogs

Microsoft's VSTO Portal

The VSTO portal is a good starting point for information about VSTO from Microsoft: http://msdn.com/vsto.

Office Development with Visual Studio

The VSTO team at Microsoft has an interesting blog where they frequently post VSTO-related information: http://blogs.msdn.com/vsto/default. aspx.

Additional Development Tools

Microsoft Visual Studio Tools for the Office System Power Tools

This is a free toolkit that developers can use for both VSTO development and for other .NET based Office development. The download URL from the Microsoft Web site is very long and likely to change by the time you read this, so use Google to search for the title above to find the latest download URL. Included in these tools are

- **VSTO Developer Cleaner**—A tool to list and remove Windows Registry entries, temporary certificates in the current user's personal store, and the current user's inclusion list entries created for debugging purposes
- **VSTO Troubleshooter**—A diagnostic tool that can determine whether target computers have the required prerequisites installed
- **Open XML Package Editor**—An add-in to the VS IDE with which we can view and edit Open XML Package files
- **Ribbon IDs Toolwindow**—An add-in to VS IDE that displays all built-in Office Ribbon IDs

Summary

In this chapter, we introduced VSTO but barely scratched the surface of the subject. In many ways, VSTO is an attractive modern platform for developing Excel solutions. At the same time, it is advanced and complex. VSTO is also still under development and subsequently it has not yet reached a mature state.

To use VSTO, certain requirements, such as a unified desktop environment, must be met. This may be easier to achieve within large corporations with dedicated centralized IT departments rather than in small and medium sized companies. VSTO is a perfect companion for corporate .NET developers, because they can leverage all their .NET experience when developing Office solutions. For independent professional Excel developers, VSTO may still be a complement to the native Excel development platform and to managed COM add-ins.

26. DEVELOPING EXCEL SOLUTIONS

XLLs AND THE C API

This chapter in no way attempts to provide a complete guide to programming Excel using the C API. That would be a book-length topic in its own right. A skilled C++ programmer with an in-depth knowledge of the Excel C API can create add-ins that can do anything a VBA add-in can do.

Instead, this chapter focuses on the core strength of the C API, and what is arguably the most common use for it in Excel development, programming custom worksheet functions. Even this topic is too large to be covered in a single chapter, so we get you started with solid fundamentals and then point you to additional resources at the end of the chapter.

Please note that this chapter only demonstrates XLL development using the small grid data types that are compatible with all current versions of Excel. For Excel 2007 big grid development, multithreading, and other new features specific to Excel 2007 XLL development, see one of the resources mentioned at the end of this chapter.

All the examples discussed in this chapter assume that you are running Microsoft Visual C++.NET 2008. The accompanying CD contains complete versions of the sample project discussed in this chapter for both VC++ 6.0 and VC++.NET 2008 in the \Concepts\Chapter 27 – XLLs and the C API folder. If you are unfamiliar with C programming, you are strongly advised to open the sample files and follow along as you read. C is a verbose programming language compared to VB/VBA and so we only have room to show the most important code contained in the sample.

Why Create an XLL-Based Worksheet Function

An XLL is a Windows DLL that is structured so Excel can recognize and open it directly. Because worksheet functions built into XLLs are compiled to machine code and treated by Excel as if they were native worksheet functions, they are extremely fast. You can create custom versions of worksheet functions that Excel doesn't get quite right as well as creating worksheet functions that Excel doesn't provide at all. Also, Excel doesn't store hard-coded paths to XLL-based worksheet functions, so they don't suffer from broken links when files are relocated like VBA add-in based functions do.

Creating an XLL Project in Visual Studio

An XLL is simply a Windows DLL with an XLL file extension and an internal structure that Excel recognizes. Prior to creating your XLL project you need to copy **xlcall.h** and **xlcall32.lib** from the Microsoft Excel 2007 SDK into your Visual Studio include and lib directories, respectively. The Excel 2007 SDK can be downloaded from www.microsoft.com/downloads/details.aspx?FamilyID=5272e1d1-93ab-4bd4-af18-cb6bb487e1c4.

To create your XLL project, choose *File > New > Project* from the Visual Studio menu. In the New Project dialog, expand the *Visual C++* folder on the left-hand side and select the *Win32* folder below it. From the *Templates* list select *Win32 Console Project*. Enter the name for your XLL in the *Name* text box and select the location where you want the project to be saved. This is shown in Figure 27-1.

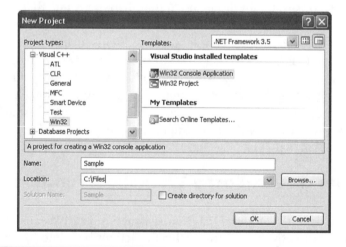

FIGURE 27-1 Creating the initial XLL project

Click the OK button and Visual Studio displays the Application Wizard dialog box shown in Figure 27-2. Select *Application Settings* on the left-hand side and choose *DLL* as your Application type. Place a check mark in the

Empty project check box under *Additional options* and click the Finish button. You now have an empty Win32 DLL project.

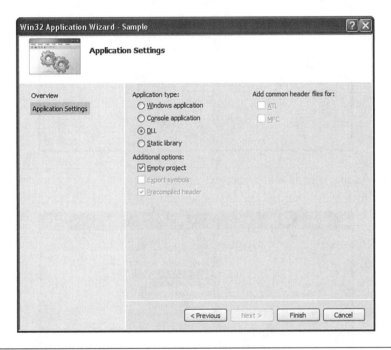

FIGURE 27-2 Choosing the correct Application Wizard settings

Next, add two files to your project. Select *Project > Add New Item* from the Visual Studio menu. In the Add New Item dialog select *C++ File* (.cpp) from the *Templates* list. This will be the file that contains your code. Because we are creating a C project you need to explicitly give your file a .c extension, as shown in Figure 27-3. The *Location* setting should already be pointing to your project folder. Leave this as is.

The next file you need to add to your project is a module definition file. This allows you to export function names from your XLL that Excel can recognize. Select *Project > Add New Item* from the Visual Studio menu again, but this time choose *Module-Definition File (.def)* from the list of templates. Give your module definition file the same name as the .c code file you added earlier but with a .def file extension, as shown in Figure 27-4.

There are several project-level settings that you need to make before you're ready to start writing code. Choose *Project > Sample Properties* from the Visual Studio menu (where "Sample" is the actual name you

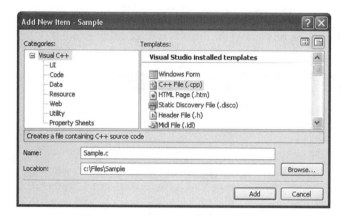

FIGURE 27-3   Adding a code file to your XLL project

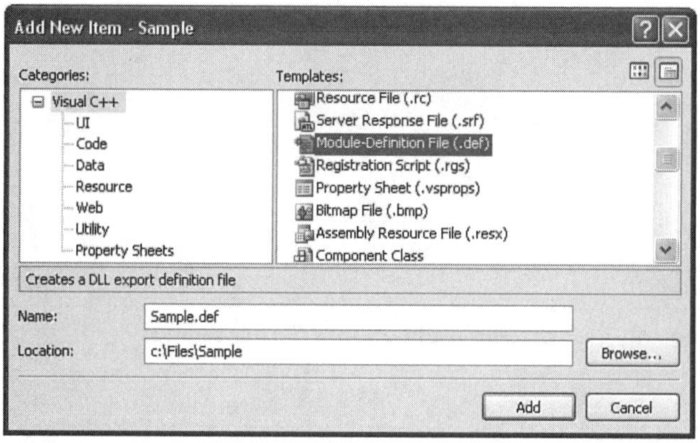

FIGURE 27-4   Adding a module definition file to your XLL project

selected for your project). In the Sample Property Pages dialog shown in Figure 27-5, expand *Configuration Properties* from the tree view and select the *Debugging* folder. Next, select the *Command* option from the list of settings on the right-hand side and browse to the location of Excel.exe on your computer. This tells Visual Studio what program to use when debugging your XLL.

Next, select the *C/C++* folder, followed by the *General* subfolder from the tree view. The first setting you need to change is the *Debug Information Format* setting. The default value for this setting is *Program Database for Edit and Continue*. This value adds debug symbols to the XLL that causes Excel not to recognize it. Change this setting to *Program Database* instead. This setting is demonstrated in Figure 27-6.

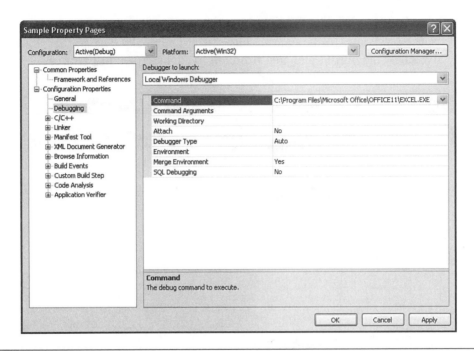

FIGURE 27-5 Specifying Excel.exe as the debugging program for your XLL project

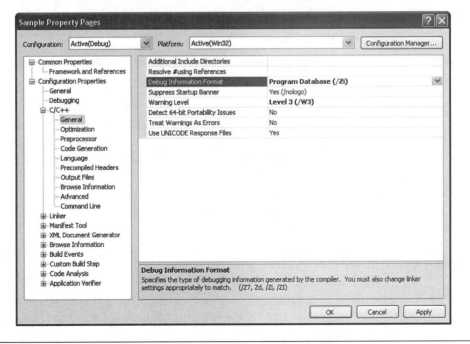

FIGURE 27-6 Specifying the correct debug information format setting

Next, select the *Linker* folder, followed by the *General* subfolder from the tree view. In the *Output File* setting, manually change the file extension of the output filename from .dll to .xll as shown in Figure 27-7.

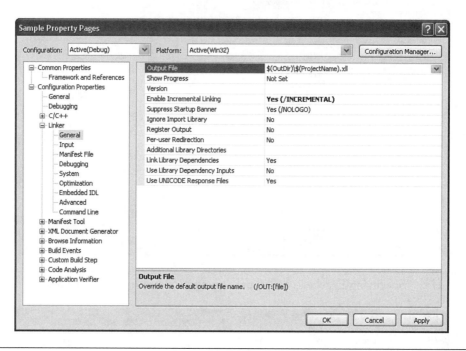

FIGURE 27-7   Changing the output filename extension

Select the *Release* entry from the *Configuration* drop-down and repeat the file extension change for the release build. Finally, choose the *Input* folder from the Linker section of the tree view. Choose the *All Configurations* entry from the *Configurations* drop-down. Type the filename xlcall32.lib into the *Additional Dependencies* setting as shown in Figure 27-8.

We've made all the necessary settings now, so click the OK button and we'll start writing the code for our XLL.

The Structure of an XLL

We start our discussion by creating an XLL that contains two trivial custom worksheet functions. This allows us to concentrate on the structure required to create an XLL independent of whatever worksheet functions it

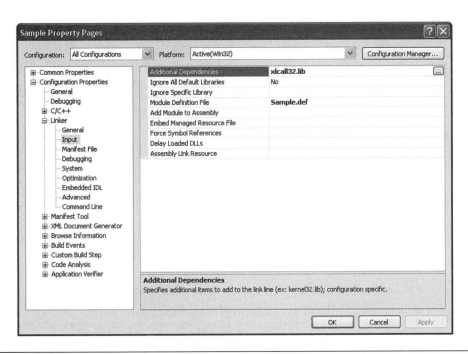

FIGURE 27-8   Adding xlcall32.lib to the additional dependencies for your project

happens to contain. We look at an example of a real-world function later in the chapter. Listing 27-1 shows the two custom worksheet functions our first XLL provides.

Listing 27-1   Sample Custom Worksheet Functions

```
double WINAPI AddTwo(double d1, double d2)
{
    return d1 + d2;
}

double WINAPI MultiplyTwo(double d1, double d2)
{
    return d1 * d2;
}
```

The Function Table

The first thing you need to do when creating your XLL is build a function table. This is a three-dimensional string array holding detailed descriptions of each custom worksheet function your XLL contains. The function table is used to register your custom worksheet functions with Excel when the XLL is opened. The first dimension of the table holds an entry for each custom worksheet function in the XLL. The second dimension of the table holds all the arguments passed to the Register function for a given custom worksheet function. The third dimension of the table holds the string values for each argument.

The maximum allowable length of a Register function argument string is 255 characters. You must leave a blank space at the first character position of each string in the table (even unused strings). This is because Excel does not use null-terminated C-strings but rather byte-counted Pascal strings. Later we insert a byte count for each string in its first character position.

Listing 27-2 shows the function table that describes our two custom worksheet functions. Note that the NUM_REGISTER_ARGS constant must be large enough so the function table can hold all the descriptions required for the custom worksheet function in the XLL that contains the most arguments. For custom worksheet functions with fewer than the maximum number of arguments, the unused argument help topic entries at the end of the table can be left empty and Excel ignores them. Adjustments to the NUM_REGISTER_ARGS constant must also be reflected in the HandleRegistration function described in the "Registering and Unregistering Custom Worksheet Functions" section later in the chapter.

Listing 27-2   The Sample XLL Function Table

```
#define NUM_FUNCTIONS           2
#define NUM_REGISTER_ARGS       11
#define MAX_LENGTH              255

static char
gszWorksheetFuncs[NUM_FUNCTIONS][NUM_REGISTER_ARGS][MAX_LENGTH] =
{
    {" AddTwo",                     // procedure
     " BBB",                        // type_text
     " AddTwo",                     // function_text
     " d1, d2",                     // argument_text
     " 1",                          // macro_type
     " Sample Add-In",              // category
     " ",                           // shortcut_text
     " ",                           // help_topic
     " Adds the two arguments.",    // function_help
     " The first number to add.",   // argument_help1
     " The second number to add."   // argument_help2
```

```
        },
        {" MultiplyTwo",
         " BBB",
         " MultiplyTwo",
         " d1, d2",
         " 1",
         " Sample Add-In",
         " ",
         " ",
         " Multiplies the two arguments.",
         " The first number to multiply.",
         " The second number to multiply."
        }
};
```

The following are brief descriptions of the purpose and usage of each entry in the function table in the order in which they appear. We describe how to actually register your functions with Excel based on this information in the "Registering and Unregistering Custom Worksheet Functions" section.

- **procedure**—This is the name of your custom worksheet function. It should be exactly the same as the name that appears in your function definition.
- **type_text**—This is a coded string that specifies the data types of all the function's arguments as well as its return value. The first letter specifies the return type of the function, and all following letters specify the data types expected by each of the function's arguments, from left to right. Table 27-1 lists the codes for the most commonly used data types. For a complete list of data types, see the Microsoft Excel 97 SDK, referenced in the "Additional Resources" section at the end of the chapter.

Table 27-1   The Most Commonly Used type_text Data Types

Code	Description	Data Type
A	Boolean (TRUE = 1, FALSE = 0)	`short int`
B	Floating point number	`Double`
D	Byte-counted string (max length = 255 characters)	`unsigned char *`
I	Signed 2-byte integer	`short int`

Table 27-1 The Most Commonly Used type_text Data Types

Code	Description	Data Type
J	Signed 4-byte integer	`int`
K	Array	`FP *` (see Listing 27-3)
P	Excel OPER struct	`OPER *`
R	Excel XLOPER struct	`XLOPER *`

Excel normally recalculates worksheet functions only when they are first entered into a worksheet cell or when one of their dependencies changes. You can make a custom worksheet function volatile by appending an exclamation point character (!) to the end of that function's type_text string. Volatile functions are recalculated whenever any worksheet cell is recalculated. Therefore, you must be very careful with them, as they can cause extreme degradation in recalculation performance.

- **`function_text`**—This is the name of the function as it appears in the Excel Function Wizard.
- **`argument_text`**—This text string allows you to display a list of arguments that your function accepts in the Excel Function Wizard.
- **`macro_type`**—This is a numeric value indicating the type of the function. Excel worksheet functions always have a macro type of 1. We make use of the hidden function macro type 0 to overcome a bug in unregistering custom worksheet functions. The last macro type is 2, which defines a function that can only be called from an XLM macro sheet. This function type is beyond the scope of this chapter.
- **`category`**—Allows you to specify the category that your function appears in when viewed in the Function Wizard. You should always create a separate category for custom worksheet functions so you do not confuse the user about which functions are built in and which functions require your XLL to be loaded to be used.
- **`shortcut_text`**—This is used to assign a shortcut key to command-type functions. This function type is not covered here, so this entry can be left empty.
- **`help_topic`**—If you have a custom help file associated with your XLL, this is the help topic ID for this worksheet function.
- **`function_help`**—This is a short descriptive help text string that appears in the Excel Function Wizard when the user selects your function.

- **argument_help1 ... 20**—This is a short descriptive help text string that appears in the Function Wizard when the user is entering data for each of your arguments. An Excel worksheet function can take up to 29 arguments. Unfortunately, the Register function, which we discuss later, uses the first nine of its arguments for other purposes. Therefore, you can only document the first 20 arguments of any custom worksheet function. All arguments beyond the twentieth will have an argument help string that is a duplicate of that used for the twentieth argument.

Note again that every function must have exactly the same number of entries in the function table, so the function with the maximum number of arguments determines the number of function table entries for all the functions in your XLL. If an argument_helpX string is not used by a function, leave it empty and Excel will ignore it.

The K data type is most frequently used as a custom worksheet function argument type because it is the nearest thing in the Excel C API to a strongly typed array data type. To use K data type arguments in your XLL you need to add the definition for the FP struct shown in Listing 27-3 to your code.

Listing 27-3 The FP Struct

```
typedef struct _FP
{
    unsigned short int rows;
    unsigned short int columns;
    double array[1];
} FP;
```

When received as an argument, the `array[]` member of the FP struct is sized such that it contains `rows*columns` elements.

The DLLMain Function

Since an XLL is just a variation on a standard Windows DLL, Windows expects to find a DLLMain function to call when it loads the XLL. In most XLLs, this function doesn't have to do anything other than return TRUE. You may use the DLLMain function for any normal initialization operations if you want, but in an XLL it is more customary to use the xlAutoOpen callback function for this purpose.

There is one situation where use of the DLLMain function makes more sense than xlAutoOpen. This is when your XLL requires some critical internal initialization to succeed, and if that initialization fails you want to prevent Excel from loading the XLL. By returning FALSE from DLLMain you can prevent Excel from loading your XLL. In our sample XLL, DLLMain is empty except for a `return TRUE;` statement, as shown in Listing 27-4.

Listing 27-4   The DllMain Function

```
BOOL WINAPI DllMain(HINSTANCE hInstance, DWORD fdwReason, PVOID
pvReserved)
{
    return TRUE;
}
```

Standard XLL Callback Functions

Excel calls the following three functions at various times during its use of an XLL. Only the xlAutoOpen function is strictly required, but most XLLs will make use of all three of these callback functions.

xlAutoOpen

The xlAutoOpen function is the startup function of your XLL. xlAutoOpen is called whenever

- You open the XLL file from the Excel *File > Open* menu.
- You load the XLL as an add-in using the *Tools > Add-Ins* menu.
- The XLL is in the XLSTART directory and is automatically opened when Excel starts.
- Excel opens the XLL for any other reason.
- A macro calls the XLM REGISTER() function with only one argument, which is the name of the XLL.

Note that the xlAutoOpen function is not called if your XLL is opened from a VBA macro using the Workbooks.Open method. This is consistent with the behavior of VBA add-ins. If you want to load your XLL from VBA, use the `Application.RegisterXLL` method instead.

xlAutoOpen should register all the custom worksheet functions in the XLL and perform any other initialization your XLL requires. Listing 27-5 shows the xlAutoOpen code for our sample XLL. We defer discussion of

how the HandleRegistration function works until we've covered the
XLOPER data type and the Excel4 function.

Listing 27-5 The xlAutoOpen Function

```
EXPORT int WINAPI xlAutoOpen(void)
{
    static XLOPER xDLL;
    int i, j;

    // In the following loop, the strings in
    // gszFunctionTable are byte-counted.
    for (i = 0; i < NUM_FUNCTIONS; ++i)
        for (j = 0; j < NUM_REGISTER_ARGS; ++j)
            gszFunctionTable[i][j][0] =
                (BYTE) lstrlen(gszFunctionTable[i][j] + 1);

    // Register the functions using our custom procedure.
    HandleRegistration(TRUE);

    return 1;
}
```

xlAutoClose

The xlAutoClose function is the shutdown function of your XLL.
xlAutoClose is called whenever

- You quit Excel.
- You unselect the XLL from the add-ins list under the *Tools > Add-ins* menu.

xlAutoClose should perform any cleanup operations required by your XLL
as well as unregister the worksheet functions it contains so they no longer
appear in the Function Wizard or the paste functions list. Note that if the
user attempts to exit Excel when an unsaved workbook is open, Excel calls
the xlAutoClose function of any open XLLs before prompting the user to
save changes to the unsaved workbook. If the user cancels the save
prompt, Excel and your XLL remain open. This may constrain the amount

of cleanup you can safely do in the xlAutoClose function in some circumstances. Listing 27-6 shows the xlAutoClose function for our sample XLL. Again, we defer discussion of how the HandleRegistration function works until later in the chapter.

Listing 27-6   The xlAutoClose Function

```
EXPORT int WINAPI xlAutoClose(void)
{
    // Unregister the worksheet functions
    // using our custom procedure.
    HandleRegistration(FALSE);
    return 1;
}
```

xlAddInManagerInfo

The Excel Add-in Manager calls the xlAddinManagerInfo function when it loads your XLL to determine the descriptive string that it should display for your XLL in the list of add-ins. This function is not strictly required. If you don't provide it, the Add-In Manager uses the filename of the XLL as the descriptive text. However, providing a descriptive name for your XLL makes it much easier for users to locate. Listing 27-7 shows the xlAddinManagerInfo code for our sample XLL. We describe what most of this code is doing in the sections on the XLOPER data type and the Excel4 function.

Listing 27-7   The xlAddInManagerInfo Function

```
EXPORT LPXLOPER WINAPI xlAddInManagerInfo(LPXLOPER xlAction)
{
    static XLOPER xlReturn, xlLongName, xlTemp;

    // Coerce the argument XLOPER to an integer.
    xlTemp.xltype = xltypeInt;
    xlTemp.val.w = xltypeInt;
    Excel4(xlCoerce, &xlReturn, 2, xlAction, &xlTemp);

    // The only valid argument value is 1. In this case we
```

```
// return the long name for the XLL. Any other value should
// result in the return of a #VALUE! error.
if(1 == xlReturn.val.w)
{
    xlLongName.xltype = xltypeStr;
    xlLongName.val.str = "\021Sample XLL Add-In";
}
else
{
    xlLongName.xltype = xltypeErr;
    xlLongName.val.err = xlerrValue;
}

    return &xlLongName;
}
```

Note how we manually byte-counted the descriptive text string for our XLL using an octal length prefix, \021. This is the format in which Excel expects to receive all string values. Rather than using the C convention of relying on the position of a null character within a string to determine its length, Excel uses the Pascal convention of a numeric prefix specifying the length of a string.

Additional XLL Callback Functions

The following functions are optional and are not covered in detail in this chapter.

xlAutoRegister

Excel calls the xlAutoRegister function if an XLM macro tries to register one of the custom worksheet functions contained in the XLL without specifying the type_text argument. In that case, Excel passes the name of the function the XLM macro tried to register to the xlAutoRegister function, and the xlAutoRegister function should fully register the function it was passed. If the function name passed by Excel is not recognized, xlAutoRegister should return a #VALUE! error. The prototype for the xlAutoRegister function is

```
LPXLOPER WINAPI xlAutoRegister(LPXLOPER);
```

xlAutoAdd

The xlAutoAdd function works exactly like the xlAutoOpen function except Excel only calls xlAutoAdd when the Excel Add-In Manager loads the XLL. The prototype for the xlAutoAdd function is

```
int WINAPI xlAutoAdd(void);
```

xlAutoRemove

The xlAutoRemove function works exactly like the xlAutoClose function except Excel only calls xlAutoRemove when the Excel Add-In Manager unloads the XLL. The prototype for the xlAutoRemove function is

```
int WINAPI xlAutoRemove(void);
```

xlAutoFree

We discuss this function in a bit more detail in the upcoming section on the XLOPER data type. Briefly, when your XLL passes an XLOPER containing a pointer to a large amount of memory that is managed by the XLL, you can tell Excel to call the xlAutoFree function as soon as it is finished with that XLOPER so the memory it uses can be freed as soon as possible. The prototype for the xlAutoFree function is

```
void WINAPI xlAutoFree(LPXLOPER xlToFree);
```

The XLOPER and OPER Data Types

As you can see from the definitions of our two sample functions in Listing 27-1, you can write a custom Excel worksheet function using nothing but fundamental C data types. However, any time you need to communicate with Excel through its C API or create custom worksheet functions that support multiple return data types or use optional arguments you need to make use of the special Excel XLOPER data type and its subset OPER. An XLOPER is a struct that provides all the storage permutations required to implement the polymorphic behavior you experience when working with cells on an Excel worksheet. The definition of

the XLOPER data type is located in the xlcall.h file and is reproduced in
Listing 27-8.

Listing 27-8   The XLOPER Data Type

```
typedef struct xloper
{
    union
    {
        double num;                      /* xltypeNum */
        LPSTR str;                       /* xltypeStr */
        WORD bool;                       /* xltypeBool */
        WORD err;                        /* xltypeErr */
        short int w;                     /* xltypeInt */
        struct
        {
            WORD count;                  /* always = 1 */
            XLREF ref;
        } sref;                          /* xltypeSRef */
        struct
        {
            XLMREF far *lpmref;
            DWORD idSheet;
        } mref;                          /* xltypeRef */
        struct
        {
            struct xloper far *lparray;
            WORD rows;
            WORD columns;
        } array;                         /* xltypeMulti */
        struct
        {
            union
            {
                short int level;         /* xlflowRestart */
                short int tbctrl;        /* xlflowPause */
                DWORD idSheet;           /* xlflowGoto */
            } valflow;
            WORD rw;                     /* xlflowGoto */
            BYTE col;                    /* xlflowGoto */
            BYTE xlflow;
        } flow;                          /* xltypeFlow */
        struct
```

```
    {
        union
        {
            BYTE far *lpbData;          /* data passed to XL */
            HANDLE hdata;               /* data returned from XL */
        } h;
        long cbData;
    } bigdata;                          /* xltypeBigData */
    } val;
    WORD xltype;
} XLOPER, FAR *LPXLOPER;

// The following additional structs are used to implement
// the SRef and Ref XLOPER sub-types.

// Describes a single rectangular reference
typedef struct xlref
{
    WORD rwFirst;
    WORD rwLast;
    BYTE colFirst;
    BYTE colLast;
} XLREF, FAR *LPXLREF;

// Describes multiple rectangular references.
// This is a variable size structure.
// Its default size is 1 reference.
typedef struct xlmref
{
    WORD count;
    XLREF reftbl[1];            // actually reftbl[count]
} XLMREF, FAR *LPXLMREF;
```

At its simplest level, an XLOPER contains two pieces of information: some kind of data and a flag indicating what type of data that is. There are 12 possible data types an XLOPER can hold. These are represented by the following constants defined in the xlcall.h header file:

- **xltypeNum**—Used for both integer and floating point numeric data
- **xltypeStr**—A byte-counted string
- **xltypeBool**—A boolean value
- **xltypeRef**—An external cell reference or multiple area reference
- **xltypeErr**—An error value

- **xltypeFlow**—An XLM macro flow control command
- **xltypeMulti**—An array of values
- **xltypeMissing**—A missing worksheet function argument
- **xltypeNil**—An empty XLOPER
- **xltypeSRef**—A single rectangular cell reference on the current sheet
- **xltypeInt**—A short int; not commonly used
- **xltypeBigData**—Used for persistent data storage

Due to space limitations, we only discuss the most frequently used XLOPER types. When you receive an XLOPER from Excel, either as an argument to a custom worksheet function or as the return value from an Excel4 function call (discussed later), you query the xltype member of the XLOPER struct to determine what type of data you are receiving. When you create an XLOPER you set the xltype member to indicate what type of data your XLOPER holds. The following are some examples of XLOPERs you might create.

Numeric Data

Although the XLOPER data type has two fields that could potentially contain numeric data, only one is commonly used: xltypeNum. This is equivalent to the double data type in C. Because xltypeInt is a short int data type, its size constraints rule it out for many purposes.

```
XLOPER xlNum;
xlNum.xltype = xltypeNum;
xlNum.val.num = 5.5;
```

String Data

The key thing to remember when using string data with Excel is that Excel does not use null-terminated C strings. Rather it uses byte-counted Pascal strings. Therefore, you *must* byte-count any string you pass to Excel and be sure not to treat any string returned from Excel as if it were a C string. For string literals the byte count must be provided in octal format as shown in the following example:

```
XLOPER xlString;
xlString.xltype = xltypeStr;
xlString.val.str = "\035This is a byte-counted string";
```

Error Values

One important use of XLOPERs is to provide your function with the ability to return a normal value when the function is used correctly and an error value when the function is used outside its expected parameters. An error value is indicated by the type xltypeErr, and the `err` field is set to one of the following error value constants supplied in xlcall.h:

- **xlerrNull** (#NULL!)—Refers to the intersection of two ranges that don't intersect
- **xlerrDiv0** (#DIV/0!)—Indicates an attempt to divide by zero or by a blank cell
- **xlerrValue** (#VALUE!)—Indicates an argument of the wrong type
- **xlerrRef** (#REF!)—Indicates an invalid cell reference
- **xlerrName** (#NAME?)—Indicates a string value that cannot be recognized as a function or defined name
- **xlerrNum** (#NUM!)—Indicates that an argument value is out of bounds
- **xlerrNA** (#N/A)—Indicates that the function cannot calculate a valid return value based on the arguments passed to it

In the following example, we return a #VALUE! error:

```
XLOPER xlError;
xlError.xltype = xltypeErr;
xlError.val.err = xlerrValue;
```

Arrays

These are somewhat more complex XLOPERs that allow you to return arrays from your custom worksheet functions, thereby creating custom array formulas. In Listing 27-9 we create an XLOPER containing the array {1, 2, 3, 4}.

Listing 27-9 An XLOPER Containing an Array

```
XLOPER xlArray, xlValues[4];
int i;
for (i = 0; i < 4; ++i)
{
```

```
    xlValues[i].xltype = xltypeNum;
    xlValues[i].val.num = i + 1;
}
xlArray.xltype = xltypeMulti;
xlArray.val.array.lparray = &xlValues[0];
xlArray.val.array.rows = 1;
xlArray.val.array.columns = 4;
```

The most difficult part of using XLOPERs is deciding whether the XLL or Excel is responsible for the memory allocated to the XLOPER and any data it points to, as well as determining when and how this memory should be freed. The OPER data type is a struct that is a subset of an XLOPER containing only value data types, not reference data types. This makes it much simpler to work with because there is never any memory allocated to an OPER that needs to be freed by either the XLL or EXCEL. As a general rule, if your worksheet function accepts OPER data types as arguments and uses XLOPER data types as return values, your memory management chores will be much simplified.

The definition of the OPER struct is not included in the xlcall.h file, and you are not required to define it in your application in order to accept OPER arguments to or return an OPER data type from your custom worksheet functions. You can simply declare your arguments and return values as LPXLOPER (an alias for XLOPER *) and then register your function with the code P at the appropriate positions within the type_text argument in your function table. Excel then passes and accepts OPER structs even though XLOPER structs were specified in your function definition. If you want to declare and use OPER variables in your XLL you need to add the OPER struct definition shown in Listing 27-10 to your project.

Listing 27-10 The OPER Data Type

```
typedef struct _oper
{
    union
    {
        double num;
        unsigned char *str;
        unsigned short int bool;
```

```
        unsigned short int err;
        struct
        {
            struct _oper *lparray;
            unsigned short int rows;
            unsigned short int columns;
        } array;
    } val;
    unsigned short int type;
} OPER;
```

The Excel4 Function

The entire breadth of the Excel C API is accessed through a single function called Excel4. This function is declared in xlcall.h as follows:

```
int far _cdecl Excel4(int xlfn,
            LPXLOPER operRes, int count,... );
```

As you can see, the Excel4 function has three required parameters followed by a variable argument list. The required parameters and their meanings are as follows:

- **xlfn**—This is a constant that identifies the Excel function you are trying to call. The values for this parameter are defined in xlcall.h. Three types of functions can be called by the Excel4 function. C API-only functions are identified by a constant with a prefix of xl. These are discussed in the next section. Excel4 can also call all valid Excel worksheet functions. These are identified by a constant with an xlf prefix. Finally, all valid XLM macro commands can be called from Excel4. These command-equivalent functions are identified by a constant with the prefix xlc. We do not cover command-equivalent functions in this chapter.

- **operRes**—This argument takes either the address of an XLOPER variable in which the Excel4 function will place the result of the function being called, or zero if the function being called does not have a return value. We address memory management issues related to Excel4 XLOPER return values in the "XLOPERs and Memory Management" section later in the chapter.

- **count**—This argument is used to tell Excel4 how many optional arguments follow. The number of optional arguments varies depending on the specific function being called and can vary from 0 to 30. All optional arguments passed to Excel4 must be either XLOPER or OPER data types.

You must always remember to make a distinction between the result of the function being called by Excel4 and the result of the Excel4 function call itself. The former is contained in the operRes parameter of the Excel4 function, while the latter is the int return value of the Excel4 function. All possible return values from Excel4 are represented by constants defined in xlcall.h. Most of these return values will not be encountered once you've debugged your XLL. Some of them are outside the scope of this chapter. A brief description of the Excel4 function return value constants follows:

- **xlretSuccess**—The Excel4 function call succeeded. This does not mean the function being called by Excel4 succeeded. You determine that by checking the operRes argument for an error data type.
- **xlretAbort**—An internal abort occurred. A discussion of this return value is outside the scope of this chapter.
- **xlretInvXlfn**—The function number supplied as an argument to the xlfn parameter was an invalid function number. If you use only the predefined function constants supplied by xlcall.h you should not encounter this error.
- **xlretInvCount**—Your Excel4 function call did not supply the correct number of arguments for the function it specified in the xlfn argument.
- **xlretInvXloper**—An invalid XLOPER was passed to one of the Excel4 function arguments or a valid XLOPER containing an incorrect data type was passed.
- **xlretStackOvfl**—A stack overflow occurred. A discussion of this return value is outside the scope of this chapter.
- **xlretFailed**—An XLM command-equivalent function call failed. A discussion of this return value is outside the scope of this chapter.
- **xlretUncalced**—An attempt was made to dereference a cell that has not been calculated yet. If you ever encounter this error, your function must exit immediately. Excel calls your function again when the cell in question has been calculated.

Commonly Used C API Functions

The functions discussed in the following sections can only be called from within an XLL using the Excel4 function. They are not available from within Excel. This is not a complete list of these functions, only those that apply most commonly to custom worksheet function projects.

xlFree

The xlFree function is used to tell Excel you are finished with the contents of an XLOPER variable Excel has allocated the memory for and that Excel is now free to reclaim that memory. The xlFree function takes one or more XLOPER variables as parameters to be freed and does not return a value to the operRes parameter of the Excel4 function. We discuss XLOPER memory management in the next section, but for now, here's the basic syntax of an xlFree function call:

```
XLOPER xlToBeFreed;
// Do something here that causes Excel to allocate
// the xlToBeFreed variable.
Excel4(xlFree, 0, 1, xlToBeFreed);
```

xlCoerce

The xlCoerce function is used to convert XLOPER structs from one data type to another. For example, you can make a custom worksheet function more robust by using xlCoerce to explicitly convert to a numeric value whatever is passed to an XLOPER parameter that expects a numeric value. The need for this would arise if the user entered something similar to the following for a function whose parameter expected a numeric data type:

```
=MYFUNC("100")
```

The default behavior of xlCoerce is to convert a cell reference to any non-reference type, in effect looking up the value of a cell that an XLOPER points to. The syntax of an xlCoerce call looks like the following:

```
XLOPER xlResult, xlType;
xlType.xltype = xltypeInt;
xlType.val.w = xltypeNum;
Excel4(xlCoerce, &xlResult, 2, pxlInput, &xlType);
```

The xlCoerce function takes two arguments:

- **pxlInput**—A pointer to an XLOPER (LPXLOPER) that contains the value or reference to be converted.
- **xlType**—A pointer to an XLOPER of type xltypeInt whose val.w member contains a bitmask of types you are willing to accept. This argument is optional. If it is not provided, xlCoerce converts the pxlInput reference argument into the closest possible data type associated with the value in the referenced cell.

xlGetName

The xlGetName function returns the full path and filename of your XLL. As we see in the "Registering and Unregistering Custom Worksheet Functions" section, this information is required to register and unregister the custom worksheet functions in an XLL.

XLOPERs and Memory Management

Excel allocates and frees any arguments passed to a custom worksheet function. For most XLOPER return values, you pass Excel a static XLOPER variable. Your XLL must allocate any arguments passed to the Excel4 function. When a call to the Excel4 function returns an XLOPER containing a pointer, that memory is allocated and managed by Excel. You must call the xlFree function on that XLOPER so Excel can free its memory. You can safely call xlFree on every return value from the Excel4 function. Calling xlFree on an XLOPER that does not contain a pointer does nothing, and if xlFree is called twice on the same XLOPER Excel ignores the second call.

Excel supports two special memory management bits in the xltype field of the XLOPER data type. If you need to use an XLOPER as the return value of a worksheet function, but that XLOPER itself was returned from Excel via the Excel4 function, you set the xlbitXLFree bit in the xltype field of the XLOPER. When you do this, Excel copies out the data it needs and then frees the XLOPER for you, relieving you of the requirement to call xlFree on the XLOPER.

Similarly, if you set the xlbitDLLFree bit in the xltype field of an XLOP-ER, Excel copies the data it requires out of the XLOPER and then calls the xlAutoFree function in your XLL, passing it a pointer to the XLOPER. Your XLL can then free any memory it allocated for this XLOPER. This is useful for returning large amounts of data to Excel without being required to have the memory for it remain allocated indefinitely.

NOTE   Do not modify any XLOPER managed by Excel. This includes worksheet function arguments and return values from the Excel4 function. Copy the data into your own memory area if you need to work with it. Remember that Excel does not use null-terminated C-strings, so if you copy a string value from an XLOPER returned by Excel you must copy it character by character into a new char array for the number of characters specified in the first byte of the XLOPER string.

Registering and Unregistering Custom Worksheet Functions

For Excel to recognize the custom worksheet functions in your XLL, you must register them. This is accomplished by using the aptly named Register function. Conversely, when your XLL is unloaded it must remove its function registrations so that Excel no longer displays them in the list of available functions.

As you saw in the xlAutoOpen and xlAuto_Close functions, we created a special-purpose function called HandleRegistration to manage the registering and unregistering of our custom worksheet functions. Pass TRUE to the function and it registers all the custom worksheet functions specified in the function table with Excel. Pass FALSE to the function and it unregisters all the custom worksheet functions. The definition of the HandleRegistration function is shown in Listing 27-11.

Listing 27-11   The HandleRegistration Function

```
//////////////////////////////////////////////////////////////
// Comments:     This function handles registering and
//               unregistering all of the custom worksheet
```

```
//                functions specified in our function table.
//
// Parameters:  bRegister   [in] Pass TRUE to register all the
//                               custom worksheet functions or FALSE
//                               to unregister them.
//
// Returns:     No return.
//
static void HandleRegistration(BOOL bRegister)
{
    XLOPER   xlXLLName, xlRegID, xlRegArgs[NUM_REGISTER_ARGS];
    int      i, j;

    // Get the filename of the XLL by calling xlGetName.
    Excel4(xlGetName, &xlXLLName, 0);

    // All of the XLOPER arguments passed to the Register
    // function will have the type xltypeStr.
    for (i = 0; i < NUM_REGISTER_ARGS; ++i)
        xlRegArgs[i].xltype = xltypeStr;

    for (i = 0; i < NUM_FUNCTIONS; ++i)
    {
        // Load the XLOPER arguments to the Register function.
        for(j = 0; j < NUM_REGISTER_ARGS; ++j)
            xlRegArgs[j].val.str = gszFunctionTable[i][j];

        if (TRUE == bRegister)
        {
            // Register each function.
            // NOTE: The number of xlRegArgs[] arguments passed
            // here must be equal to NUM_REGISTER_ARGS - 1.
            Excel4(xlfRegister, 0, NUM_REGISTER_ARGS + 1,
                &xlXLLName,
                &xlRegArgs[0], &xlRegArgs[1], &xlRegArgs[2],
                &xlRegArgs[3], &xlRegArgs[4], &xlRegArgs[5],
                &xlRegArgs[6], &xlRegArgs[7], &xlRegArgs[8],
                &xlRegArgs[9], &xlRegArgs[10]);
        }
        else
        {
            // Unregister each function.
            // Due to a bug in Excel's C API this is a 3-step
            // process. Thanks to Laurent Longre for discovering
            // the workaround described here.
```

27. XLLs AND THE C API

```
        // Step 1: Redefine each custom worksheet function
        // as a hidden function (change the macro_type
        // argument to 0).
        xlRegArgs[4].val.str = "\0010";
        // Step 2: Re-register each function as a hidden
        // function.
        // NOTE: The number of xlRegArgs[] arguments passed
        // here must be equal to NUM_REGISTER_ARGS - 1.
        Excel4(xlfRegister, 0, NUM_REGISTER_ARGS + 1,
            &xlXLLName,
            &xlRegArgs[0], &xlRegArgs[1], &xlRegArgs[2],
            &xlRegArgs[3], &xlRegArgs[4], &xlRegArgs[5],
            &xlRegArgs[6], &xlRegArgs[7], &xlRegArgs[8],
            &xlRegArgs[9], &xlRegArgs[10]);
        // Step 3: Unregister the now hidden function.
        // Get the Register ID for the function.
        // Since xlfRegisterId will return a non-pointer
        // type to the xlRegID XLOPER, we do not need to
        // call xlFree on it.
        Excel4(xlfRegisterId, &xlRegID, 2, &xlXLLName,
                                        &xlRegArgs[0]);
        // Unregister the function using its Register ID.
        Excel4(xlfUnregister, 0, 1, &xlRegID);
    }
}

// Since xlXLLName holds a pointer that is managed by Excel,
// we must call xlFree on it.
Excel4(xlFree, 0, 1, &xlXLLName);
}
```

Registering a custom worksheet function with Excel is straightforward. You simply get the name of your XLL by calling the xlGetName function; then loop the functions in the function table and call the xlfRegister function for each one, passing the XLL name as the first argument and all the function table entries as successive arguments.

Unregistering your functions requires a bit more work. Theoretically, you should simply be able to call the xlfUnregister function, passing it the Register ID of each worksheet function you want to unregister. Due to a bug in the xlfUnregister function, however, this does not remove the names of your functions from the Excel function table. They continue to be displayed in the Function Wizard even though they are no longer available.

XLL guru Laurent Longre (see Web site reference at the end of this chapter) discovered a workaround for this bug. It involves changing the macro_type of each function to 0, or hidden, reregistering each function as a hidden function, and then unregistering the hidden functions. Since hidden functions are not displayed in the Excel UI, this has the effect of correctly removing them when your XLL exits.

Sample Application Function

For our real-world example function, we create a new worksheet function called IFERROR. As we noted in Chapter 5, "Function, General, and Application-Specific Add-Ins," we often encounter the following worksheet function construct:

```
=IF(ISERROR(<some_long_function>), 0, <some_long_function>)
```

This is tedious and unwieldy, so we created a user-defined function in VBA that allowed us to accomplish exactly the same thing with the following:

```
=IFERROR(<some_long_function>, 0)
```

In this section, we rewrite our IFERROR function in C. This dramatically improves its performance because it will be compiled to native code and be able to communicate directly with Excel through the Excel C API. Our C IFERROR function has the definition shown in Listing 27-12.

Listing 27-12 The IFERROR Function

```
//////////////////////////////////////////////////////////////////
// Comments:     This function provides a short-cut replacement
//               for the common worksheet function construct:
//               =IF(ISERROR(<some_function>),0,<some_function>)
//
// Arguments:    ToEvaluate   [in] A value, expression or cell
//                            reference to be evaluated.
//               Default      [in] A value, expression or cell
```

```
//                              reference to be returned if the
//                              ToEvaluate argument evaluates to an
//                              error condition.
//
// Returns:     ToEvaluate if not an error, Default otherwise.
//
EXPORT LPXLOPER IFERROR(LPXLOPER ToEvaluate, LPXLOPER Default)
{
    int             IsError = 0;
    XLOPER          xlResult;
    static XLOPER   xlBadArgErr;

    // This is the return value for bad or missing arguments.
    xlBadArgErr.xltype = xltypeErr;
    xlBadArgErr.val.err = xlerrValue;

    // Check for missing arguments.
    if ((xltypeMissing == ToEvaluate->xltype) ||
        (xltypeMissing == Default->xltype))
        return &xlBadArgErr;

    switch (ToEvaluate->xltype)
    {
        // The first four all indicate valid ToEvaluate types.
        // Drop out and use ToEvaluate as the return value.
        case xltypeNum:
        case xltypeStr:
        case xltypeBool:
        case xltypeInt:
            break;
        // A cell reference must be dereferenced to see what it
        // contains.
        case xltypeSRef:
        case xltypeRef:
            if (xlretUncalced == Excel4(xlCoerce, &xlResult, 1,
                                                    ToEvaluate))
                // If we're looking at an uncalculated cell,
                // return immediately. Excel will call this
                // function again once the dependency has been
                // calculated.
                return 0;
            else
            {
                if (xltypeMulti == xlResult.xltype)
                    // Multi-cell arguments are not permitted.
```

```
                    return &xlBadArgErr;
            else if (xltypeErr == xlResult.xltype)
                // ToEvaluate is a single cell containing an
                // error. Return Default instead.
                IsError = 1;
        }
        // ToEvaluate is returned for all other types.
        // Always call xlFree on the return value from
        // Excel4.
        Excel4(xlFree, 0, 1, &xlResult);
        break;
    case xltypeMulti:
        // This function does not accept array arguments.
        return &xlBadArgErr;
        break;
    case xltypeErr:
        // ToEvaluate is an error. Return Default instead.
        IsError = 1;
        break;
    default:
        return &xlBadArgErr;
        break;
    }

    if (IsError)
        return Default;
    else
        return ToEvaluate;
}
```

The additional function table entry required to register this function with Excel is shown in Listing 27-13.

Listing 27-13 Function Table Entry for the IFERROR Function

```
{" IFERROR",
 " RRR",
 " IFERROR",
 " ToEvaluate, Default",
 " 1",
 " Sample Add-In",
 " ",
 " ",
```

```
" If the first argument is an error value, the second "
    "argument is returned. Otherwise the first argument "
    "is returned.",
" The argument to be checked for an error condition.",
" The value to return if the first argument is an error."
}
```

Debugging the Worksheet Functions

In the course of writing custom worksheet functions, you need to do some debugging to fix errors and prove that your function is operating as intended. This is easy to do. Since we already specified Excel.exe as our debug executable, all that's required is to compile your XLL using the *Build > Build Solution* menu, put a break point somewhere in your function, and press F5 to start debugging. Visual Studio starts Excel for you. The first time you do this you are prompted with the warning dialog shown in Figure 27-9.

FIGURE 27-9   The first-time Excel.exe debug warning dialog

This is just telling you that you won't be able to debug Excel itself because no debugging information is available. Since that's not what we're trying to do here, you can safely check the *Do not prompt in the future* check box and click OK to continue.

Once Excel is open, make sure your XLL is also open inside Excel. This does not happen automatically. You can open your XLL in one of two ways. Either use the *File > Open* menu to open the XLL directly, or add the XLL to the list of add-ins that Excel loads automatically on startup. The second method is the preferred method for use over multiple debugging sessions. To do this, choose *Tools > Add-Ins* from the Excel menu to display the Add-Ins dialog. Click the *Browse* button on the Add-Ins dialog and use the Browse window to point Excel at your XLL. If you have both debug and release versions of your XLL, be sure to point Excel at the debug version. Click OK twice and your XLL is loaded.

Now all you need to do is enter your custom worksheet function into a worksheet cell. As soon as code execution reaches your break point it stops, and you can begin debugging your code.

Miscellaneous Topics

A Caution for Users of COM Automation

A function defined in an XLL can be called in three situations:

1. During the recalculation of a workbook
2. As a result of Excel's Function Wizard being called to help with the XLL function
3. As a result of a VBA macro calling Excel's Application.Run method

Under the first two circumstances, Excel's object model does not expect and is not prepared for incoming Automation calls. Unexpected results or crashes may occur if you use COM Automation under these circumstances.

C++ Keyword Clash with the XLOPER Definition

To compile xlcall.h in a C++ project (as opposed to the C project demonstrated here) using a standards-compliant C++ compiler (such as VC.NET), you must add the following wrapper around the xlcall.h include. This is because the bool variable name used in the XLOPER struct definition is now a C++ keyword.

```
#define bool boolean
#include "xlcall.h"
#undef bool
```

Additional Resources

The Excel 2007 SDK on MSDN

An extensive resource on creating XLLs using plain C code, the Excel 2007 SDK covers a much wider variety of topics than this chapter. In addition, the source files that go with it include a handy framework for easing some of the repetitive chores involved in building an XLL. The documentation for the Excel 2007 SDK can be found in the MSDN library at http://msdn2.microsoft.com/en-us/library/bb687883.aspx.

Financial Applications Using Excel Add-in Development in C/C++

Authored by Steve Dalton
ISBN# 0470027975—Wiley
An excellent book-length discussion on creating XLLs in C and C++, this title is highly recommended for anyone who wants to pursue this topic further.

Laurent Longre's Web Site (French-Only)

This Web site (http://xcell05.free.fr/) provides an excellent discussion of XLL creation for those who can read French.

The Microsoft Excel Public Newsgroups

Point your newsreader to msnews.microsoft.com. You'll find experts in a wide array of topics willing to answer your questions for no charge. Most discussions related to XLL development are found in the microsoft.public.excel.sdk newsgroups. The microsoft.public.vc.language newsgroup is the best choice for C/C++ specific questions.

Planatech XLL+

If you develop any significant number of XLLs, then you owe it to yourself to buy a copy of XLL+ (www.as-ltd.co.uk/main/). This is absolutely the best object oriented XLL development framework available. It eliminates all the grunt work involved in creating XLLs as well as provides many advanced features in an easily accessible format. In addition, the help file for XLL+, although specific to the XLL+ development framework, is probably the best basic XLL development tutorial available. (Note: The authors have no financial incentive for this recommendation; it is based purely on the merits of the product.)

Keith Lewis's Freeware Object Oriented C++ Wrapper for the Excel C API

This is an open source implementation of an object oriented wrapper for the Excel C API. Go to http://sourceforge.net/projects/xll.

Managed XLL

Managed XLL (www.managedxll.com/) is similar to Planatech XLL+ but designed to work specifically with the .NET programming languages.

Summary

Once you've written a few user-defined functions in VBA, you can't help but notice that they do awful things to your calculation performance. Converting your VBA user-defined functions into C or C++ based XLLs solves this performance problem. Well-written XLL functions exhibit calculation performance that is indistinguishable from native Excel worksheet functions. If you need user-defined functions and calculation speed is important, take the time to learn how to program XLLs. The results are well worth the effort.

EXCEL AND WEB SERVICES

Web Services is a term you've probably heard about with mild curiosity but ultimately rejected as being irrelevant to Excel. This chapter aims to explain what Web Services are, how to create them (using Visual Basic.NET), and how they can play an important role in our applications. What we do *not* do in this chapter is go into any detailed explanation of how they work, as that *is* largely irrelevant to us as Excel developers.

Web Services

A Web Service is a piece of code running on a server computer that we can locate, connect to, and use from anywhere in the world (as long as we have an Internet connection). The server on which the Web Service is running can be tightly controlled, monitored, and secured, forcing the clients to treat the code as a black box. The user of the Web Service can see its inputs and outputs but can't access the program itself. This makes Web Services ideal for providing information in a controlled and regulated manner. The use of Web Services can help avoid the necessity of distributing applications that include sensitive information (such as database IDs and passwords) or intellectual property (such as a proprietary financial model). Additionally, we only need to manage one copy of the Web Services code, running on the server, so as soon as we modify the code and copy it to the server, all users immediately start using the new version.

Any application that exposes its functionality to such a wide audience is going to have the problem of how to specify and validate the data it accepts and the results it produces. This is accomplished through the use of XML. All communication between the Web Service and its client is done with XML.

In this chapter, we explain how to create a simple Web Service for a financial model and connect to it from VBA, so we can call it directly from the worksheet. In the "Practical Example" section, we modify the PETRAS time sheet add-in to retrieve data from and send data to a Web Service. Instead of the time sheet add-in connecting directly to a database on the network, the Web Service handles the database connection. In both cases, we focus on **using** a simple Web Service. Implementing the scalability and security requirements of a professional quality Web Service is a task that is beyond the scope of this chapter.

Creating a Web Service with VB.NET

For this example, we use the local Web server (http://localhost) to run the Web Service. To run the examples in this chapter you need a computer running Internet Information Services (IIS), and you need Visual Studio 2008 to create the Web Services. The Excel side of the Web Services example will work in any version of Excel from 2000 forward.

To demonstrate how to connect to and use a Web Service from Excel, we create a simple Web Service to reproduce the AddTwo and MultiplyTwo functions seen in Chapter 27, "XLLs and the C API." Start Visual Studio 2008, create a new project, choose the *ASP.NET Web Service Application* Visual Basic project template, name it ProExcelDev, and specify a location for it on your local hard drive, as shown in Figure 28-1.

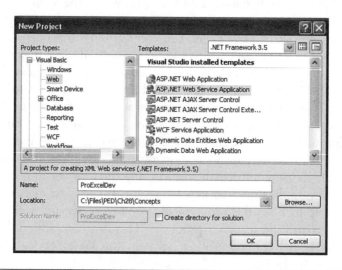

FIGURE 28-1   Creating a new Visual Basic Web Service

Click OK to let Visual Studio create the new Web Service project. This project includes a class called Service1 that we want to rename to Maths. The name needs to be changed in three places: the filename (by editing the filename in the Solution Explorer tree), the class name (by editing the code module), and the name stored in the XML markup behind the .asmx file.

First rename the class and filename, then right-click the Maths.asmx entry in the Solution Explorer window, and select *View Markup* from the shortcut menu. A file containing the following line is displayed:

```
<%@ WebService Language="VB" CodeBehind="Maths.asmx.vb"
Class="ProExcelDev.Service1" %>
```

Edit the Class attribute so it contains "`ProExcelDev.Maths`" instead of "`ProExcelDev.Service1`"; then save and close this file.

In Listing 28-1, we change the class name, give the Web Service a unique namespace, and add the two functions we want to make available to users of our Web Service. These functions replace the default HelloWorld function generated by Visual Studio. To simplify the code we also remove some additional imports and attributes added by Visual Studio that are not required for this discussion.

Listing 28-1   The ProExcelDev Maths Web Service

```
'The Professional Excel Development Maths Web Service
Imports System.Web.Services

<System.Web.Services.WebService( _
    Namespace:="http://tempuri.org/ProExcelDev/Maths", _
    Description:="Pro Excel Dev Maths Functions")> _
Public Class Maths
    Inherits System.Web.Services.WebService

    'Add two numbers
    <WebMethod(Description:="Adds two numbers")> _
    Public Function AddTwo(ByVal d1 As Double, _
            ByVal d2 As Double) As Double
        Return d1 + d2
    End Function

    'Multiply two numbers
    <WebMethod(Description:="Multiplies two numbers")> _
    Public Function MultiplyTwo(ByVal d1 As Double, _
            ByVal d2 As Double) As Double
        Return d1 * d2
    End Function

End Class
```

That's all there is to it; we created a Web Service. The key part is the <WebMethod()> attribute that we add to any functions we want to expose. In this example we're only passing simple data types—doubles—but in the PETRAS Web Service in the "Practical Example" section later in the chapter we pass and return more complex datasets using XML.

To use the new Web Service you first need to build the solution by selecting *Build > Build Solution* from the Visual Studio menu. Next, you need to publish the Web Service to IIS by selecting *Build > Publish ProExcelDev* from the Visual Studio menu. This displays the Publish Web dialog shown in Figure 28-2.

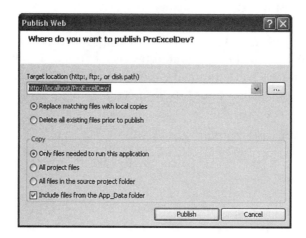

FIGURE 28-2   Publishing a Web Service

In the Target Location combo box, you need to enter http://localhost/ProExcelDev/ as we have done here. You can accept all the other setting defaults and click the *Publish* button. Visual Studio then creates all the files, folders, and settings in IIS to expose the Web Service for use from your computer.

Using a Web Service from Excel

The Microsoft Office Soap Type Library, mssoap30.dll, is used to provide Excel with Web Service connectivity. This type library is included in the Microsoft Office 2003 Web Services Toolkit, which can be downloaded by following the *Microsoft Office 2003 Web Services Toolkit 2.01* link at the top of the following Web page: http://msdn.microsoft.com/en-us/library/aa192537(office.11).aspx.

To use Web Services in our Excel applications, our users need to have the Web Services Toolkit installed to provide them with the Soap type library DLL and its dependencies. In addition to the Soap type library, the toolkit includes an add-in to the VB IDE that allows us to locate Web Services and automatically adds the code required to use them to a VBA project. This code is in the form of one or more classes that wrap the calls into the Soap Type Library. Despite its name, the Web Services Toolkit works in all versions of Excel from 2000 forward.

NOTE The setup package for the Web Services Toolkit that Microsoft offers on its Web site will not install under Office 2007 or higher. There is no practical reason for this because the Web Services Toolkit is a COM add-in that targets the Visual Basic Editor, and the Visual Basic Editor has not changed since Office 2000. To resolve this problem we provide a version of the Web Services Toolkit installer on the accompanying CD that will install under all current versions of Office. This file can be found in the *\Concepts\Ch28 - Excel and Web Services\Web Services Toolkit* folder.

Download and install the toolkit, switch to the Excel VBE and click on the *Tools > Web Service References...* menu to display the Microsoft Office 2003 Web Services Toolkit dialog shown in Figure 28-3. This dialog provides the capability to search for a Web Service by keyword, by linking to a Microsoft Web site for that information, but we provide it with the location of the ProExcelDev Maths Web Service that we created earlier.

When we built the Web Service, Visual Studio compiled our source code into a file called Maths.asmx, which is the Web Service equivalent of an EXE or DLL. When we published the Web Service, Visual Studio created a ProExcelDev folder within the IIS folder structure and copied this file into it. Because we know the complete URL of the file to connect to, we can tell the Web Services Toolkit to connect directly to this file and search for the Web Services it contains. We have done this in Figure 28-3 by selecting the *Web Service URL* option, entering the complete URL to our Maths.asmx file, and clicking the *Search* button.

The Web Services Toolkit then connects to our Maths.asmx file and determines what Web Services it contains. These are displayed in the *Search Results* tree view on the right. When we place a check mark next to the Maths entry and click the *Add* button, the toolkit creates the class modules required to call our Web Services from VBA. The class module generated by the toolkit is called clsws_Maths. An extract of the generated code is shown in Listing 28-2.

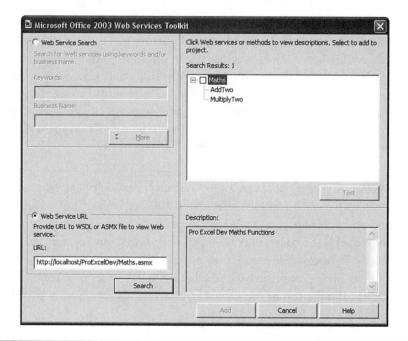

FIGURE 28-3   Connecting to the ProExcelDev Maths Web Service

Listing 28-2   The Generated Class to Connect to the Maths Web Service

```
'Dimensioning private class variables.

'The sc_Maths object handles all the communication
Private sc_Maths As SoapClient30

'These constants reflect the selections in the dialog,
'and tell the class where to connect to
Private Const c_WSDL_URL As String = _
    "http://localhost/ProExcelDev/Maths.asmx?wsdl"

Private Const c_SERVICE As String = "Maths"
Private Const c_PORT As String = "MathsSoap"
Private Const c_SERVICE_NAMESPACE As String = _
    "http://tempuri.org/ProExcelDev/Maths"

Private Sub Class_Initialize()

  Dim str_WSML As String
```

```vb
    str_WSML = ""

    Set sc_Maths = New SoapClient30

    'Initialize the connection to the web service
    sc_Maths.MSSoapInit2 c_WSDL_URL, str_WSML, c_SERVICE, _
        c_PORT, c_SERVICE_NAMESPACE

    sc_Maths.ConnectorProperty("ProxyServer") = "<CURRENT_USER>"
    sc_Maths.ConnectorProperty("EnableAutoProxy") = True

End Sub

Private Sub Class_Terminate()
  Set sc_Maths = Nothing
End Sub

'Wrapper for the AddTwo function in our web service
Public Function wsm_AddTwo(ByVal dbl_d1 As Double, _
    ByVal dbl_d2 As Double) As Double

  wsm_AddTwo = sc_Maths.AddTwo(dbl_d1, dbl_d2)

End Function

'Wrapper for the MultiplyTwo function in our web service
Public Function wsm_MultiplyTwo(ByVal dbl_d1 As Double, _
    ByVal dbl_d2 As Double) As Double

  wsm_MultiplyTwo = sc_Maths.MultiplyTwo(dbl_d1, dbl_d2)

End Function
```

Note that we removed the error handling and changed a few comments to improve the clarity of the code. In general, the code generated by the Web Services Toolkit is fully functional but requires significant cleanup before it is suitable for distribution in a professional application.

The class uses a module-level variable called sc_Maths to hold a reference to a SoapClient30 object, which handles all the communication with the Web Service for us. The constants at the top of the module specify the location of the Web Service, its name, and so on. These are used in the Class_Initialize event to connect to the Web Service.

The rest of class contains wrappers for each function exposed by our Web Service, each of them having the prefix wsm_, for Web Service method. This class module is no different from any other VBA class module, so we can change the names of these methods to anything we want, add more properties, and so on. To use the Web Service from our VBA code, we create an instance of the class and call the wrapper functions as shown in Listing 28-3.

Listing 28-3   Using the Maths Web Service from VBA

```
Sub Add1And2()

    Dim clsMaths As clsws_Maths

    Set clsMaths = New clsws_Maths

    MsgBox "1 + 2 = " & clsMaths.wsm_AddTwo(1, 2)

End Sub
```

We could, of course, put the same code in a standard VBA user-defined function and call it from a worksheet formula. So, for example, if a proprietary pricing function has been exposed as a Web Service we can now use it within our worksheets.

Practical Example

In the practical example for this chapter, we create a rather more complex Web Service to act as an interface between our PETRAS time sheet add-in and the central database used to store the static lists of consultants, clients, and projects as well as submitted time sheet data. By using the Web Service our consultants can now access the time sheet information over the Internet, allowing them to submit their time sheets from anywhere in the world.

The data sent between the Web Service and the add-in is done using XML, which makes it extremely easy to connect to the database and allows us to validate the data structure at each end of the communication channel. Specifically, the following data is passed between the Web Service and the add-in:

- At startup the add-in retrieves XML containing the static lists of consultants, clients, projects, and activities by calling the Web Service's GetStaticData function.

- When the user clicks the *Post Timesheet Data* button the add-in generates XML to contain the time sheet data and send it to the Web Service, which stores it in the central database.

VBA is used to transfer the static list into the wksProgramData worksheet. This is because the structure of the XML data is too complex to be handled by Excel's fairly simplistic XML mapping capabilities. In particular, our PETRAS time sheet data includes a table of clients and projects with the client names across the top and the projects listed below each client (to feed the data validation drop-downs). It is not possible to map an XML schema to that layout, so the import of that section of the XML data file has to be done with VBA in all versions of Excel.

PETRAS Web Service

The new PETRAS Web Service has been written in Visual Basic.NET. It connects to the same Access database we introduced in Chapter 19, "Programming with Access and SQL Server," but this time using ADO.NET instead of ADO. Visual Studio.NET creates numerous files for a Web Service. The interesting files are

- **StaticData.XSD**—Containing the XSD file for the XML returned by the GetStaticData function
- **TimeSheet.XSD**—Containing the XSD file for the XML passed to the StoreTimeSheet function
- **PETRAS.asmx**—Containing the code for the Web Service

The Web Service provides the following two functions:

- **GetStaticData**—Returns an XML dataset containing all the lists of consultants, activities, clients, and projects. An example of the XML returned is shown in Listing 28-4. Notice that the Project elements for a client are nested inside the Client element.
- **StoreTimeSheet**—Is passed as an XML dataset containing the time sheet data entered into the Excel worksheet, writes the data to the BillableHours table of the Access database, and returns a confirmation message that includes the number of rows inserted. An example of the XML passed is shown in Listing 28-5.

Listing 28-4   Example XML Output from the GetStaticData Function

```xml
<StaticData xmlns="http://www.appspro.com/PETRASWeb/StaticData">
  <Consultant>
    <ID>1</ID>
    <Name>Rob Bovey</Name>
  </Consultant>
  <Consultant>
    <ID>2</ID>
    <Name>Stephen Bullen</Name>
  </Consultant>
  <Activity>
    <ID>1</ID>
    <Name>General Programming</Name>
  </Activity>
  <Activity>
    <ID>2</ID>
    <Name>Phone Conference</Name>
  </Activity>
  <Client>
    <ID>1</ID>
    <Name>Big Auto Corp.</Name>
    <Project>
      <ID>1</ID>
      <Name>BAC 1</Name>
    </Project>
    <Project>
      <ID>2</ID>
      <Name>BAC 2</Name>
    </Project>
  </Client>
</StaticData>
```

Listing 28-5   Example XML Passed to the StoreTimeSheet Function

```xml
<TimeSheet xmlns="http://www.appspro.com/PETRASWeb/TimeSheet">
  <Consultant>
    <ID>2</ID>
    <Name>Rob Bovey</Name>
  </Consultant>
  <WeekEnding>2008-07-04</WeekEnding>
  <BillableHours>
    <DateWorked>2008-07-01</DateWorked>
```

```
      <ProjectID>2</ProjectID>
      <ActivityID>1</ActivityID>
      <Hours>6.75</Hours>
   </BillableHours>
   <BillableHours>
      <DateWorked>2008-07-02</DateWorked>
      <ProjectID>2</ProjectID>
      <ActivityID>1</ActivityID>
      <Hours>7.5</Hours>
   </BillableHours>
</TimeSheet>
```

All the data connectivity for the Web Service is set up using Visual Studio wizards, resulting in the following objects that can be seen on the Web Service's Design page:

- **conPETRASDbConnection**—An OleDbConnection used to define the connection to the Access database
- **daConsultants, daActivities, daClients, and daProjects**—OleDbDataAdapters, used to retrieve the list of consultants, activities, clients, and projects from the database
- **cmDeleteTime**—An OleDbCommand to delete time sheet records from the database. When a time sheet is submitted, any previous records for the same consultant and period are deleted
- **cmInsertTime**—An OleDbCommand to insert time sheet records into the database

When we include an XSD file in a Visual Studio project, we have the option of automatically creating a DataSet from the schema. Once we've done that, we can map the elements in our schema to fields in a DataAdapter, in much the same way that Excel 2003 allows us to map elements to worksheet cells.

In our Web Service, each section of the schema is mapped to its own DataAdapter (for example, the <ID> and <Name> in the <Consultant> elements in the XSD are mapped to the ConsultantID and Name fields in the daConsultants DataAdapter). Having mapped everything in our StaticData schema to the DataAdapters, we can retrieve the XML for all our static lists by telling each of the DataAdapters to fill their part of the schema, and then read the XML from the dataset, as shown in the code for the GetStaticData function in Listing 28-6.

Listing 28-6 The GetStaticText Function

```
<WebMethod(Description:="Provides all the static data " & _
    for the PETRAS Time Sheet")> _
Public Function GetStaticData() As String

  'Declare an instance of our StaticData data set,
  'which was generated by .NET from the XSD
  Dim dsStatic As New StaticData

  'Set the connection string of our connection object
  Me.conPETRASDbConnection.ConnectionString = _
    "Provider=""Microsoft.Jet.OLEDB.4.0"";Data Source=""" & _
    msDATABASE & """;"

  'Clear the data set
  dsStatic.Clear()

  'Fill each section of the data set
  daConsultants.Fill(dsStatic)
  daActivities.Fill(dsStatic)
  daClients.Fill(dsStatic)
  daProjects.Fill(dsStatic)

  'Return the resulting XML
  Return dsStatic.GetXML

End Function
```

The DataSet created from our XSD is a strongly typed object that allows us to treat our data as if it were a full object model. Each of our XML complexType elements become objects, our repeating elements become collections, and our simple element types become properties. We are then able to use the names of our data types directly in our code, such as iterating through all the <BillableHours> elements of the time sheet table as shown in Listing 28-7.

Listing 28-7 Using Objects Created from Our XSD

```
Dim bhRow As PETRASTimeSheet.BillableHoursRow

For Each bhRow In dsTimeSheet.BillableHours.Rows
    ' Code here
Next bhRow
```

Listing 28-8 shows the code for the StoreTimeSheet function, with the error handling removed for clarity.

Listing 28-8   The StoreTimeSheet Function

```
<WebMethod(Description:="Writes time sheet data to the " & _
    "central database")> _
Public Function StoreTimeSheet(ByVal sTimesheet As String) _
    As String

  Dim dsTimeSheet As New PETRASTimeSheet
  Dim iConsultant As Integer
  Dim dtWeekEnd As Date
  Dim bhRow As PETRASTimeSheet.BillableHoursRow

  'Read the text into the data set and validate it
  dsTimeSheet.ReadXML(New System.IO.StringReader(sTimesheet))

  'Get the consultant ID and week ending
  iConsultant = dsTimeSheet.Consultant(0).ID
  dtWeekEnd = dsTimeSheet.TimeSheet(0).WeekEnding

  'Open the database connection
  conPETRASDbConnection.ConnectionString = _
      "Provider=""Microsoft.Jet.OLEDB.4.0"";Data Source=""" _
      & msDATABASE & """;"

  conPETRASDbConnection.Open()

  'Clear any existing data for this consultant and week
  With cmDeleteTime
    .Parameters("prmConsultantID").Value = iConsultant
    .Parameters("prmWeekStart").Value = dtWeekEnd.AddDays(-6)
    .Parameters("prmWeekEnd").Value = dtWeekEnd
    .ExecuteNonQuery()
  End With

  'Loop through the billable hours, adding them to the table
  With cmInsertTime

    .Parameters("prmConsultantID").Value = iConsultant
```

```
'We can treat our data like objects!
For Each bhRow In dsTimeSheet.BillableHours.Rows
   .Parameters("prmDateWorked").Value = bhRow.DateWorked
   .Parameters("prmProjectID").Value = bhRow.ProjectID
   .Parameters("prmActivityID").Value = bhRow.ActivityID
   .Parameters("prmHours").Value = bhRow.Hours
   .ExecuteNonQuery()
Next bhRow

End With


'Close the connection when we're done
conPETRASDbConnection.Close()


'Return an OK message, with the number of rows inserted
Return "OK:" & dsTimeSheet.BillableHours.Rows.Count & _
   " row(s) inserted for " & dsTimeSheet.Consultant(0).Name

End Function
```

It must be noted that the Web Service we created for this book is for demonstration purposes only and should not be used in a production environment. We have not included any security checks in our connectivity or any data validation checks (other than that provided by the XML schema), so anyone who can connect to the Web Service could insert records into our time sheet database (assuming they can work out the XML schema we're using).

PETRAS Time Sheet

The PETRAS time sheet add-in has been changed for this chapter to receive data from and send data to the new Web Service, instead of connecting directly to the central database across the network. To maintain compatibility with Excel 2000 onwards, we do not use Excel 2003's XML handling features, instead we use the MSXML object library to do the validating and parsing of the XML data we receive from the Web Service directly. Similarly, we construct the XML containing our time sheet information using VBA. The communication between the add-in and the Web Service is done using classes generated with the Web Services Toolkit.

Because we no longer connect directly to the database, we no longer need the Browse for Database feature, which has been replaced by a simple input box to provide the URL of the PETRAS Web Service (in case we have to deploy it to a different server). Table 28-1 details the changes required to use the Web Service.

Table 28-1 Changes to the PETRAS Time Sheet Add-in for Chapter 28

Module	Procedure	Change
wksCommandBars		Renamed menu items to refer to the Web Service instead of the database.
MEntryPoints	PostTimeEntriesToWebService	Renamed to refer to Web Service. Modified to create XML string instead of UDT and submit to Web Service.
MEntryPoints	SpecifyWebServiceLocation	Renamed to refer to Web Service. Modified to use an input box to specify the Web Service URL instead of a folder.
MBrowseForFolder		Removed module as it is no longer required.
CPetrasWeb (new class)		Class created by the Web Service Toolkit to handle the connection to the PETRAS Web Service.
MOpenClose		Removed calls to create and destroy the database connection.
MDataAccess		Modified to communicate with the Web Service (via the CPetrasWeb class) instead of the database, importing the XML using VBA.
MDataAccess	bLoadInitialData	Rewritten to retrieve the data from the XML obtained from the Web Service and populate the static data worksheet.

The most interesting changes to the PETRAS time sheet add-in are in the MDataAccess.bLoadInitialData and MEntryPoints.PostTimeEntries-ToWebService procedures. Part of the bLoadInitialData procedure is shown in Listing 28-9, showing the VBA used to extract the Consultant data from the XML and populate the static data sheet. Using the MSXML library to parse the XML allows us to navigate through our data using syntax similar to navigating an object library.

Listing 28-9   *Populating the Consultant List from GetStaticData*

```
'An object to parse the XML from GetStaticData
Dim xmlParser As MSXML2.DOMDocument40

'Objects use to navigate around the XML
Dim xeParent As MSXML2.IXMLDOMElement

'Create an instance of the web service connection
Set clsPetrasWeb = New CPetrasWeb

'Initialize the URL
clsPetrasWeb.WebServiceURL = GetSetting(gsREG_APP, _
    gsREG_SECTION, gsREG_KEY, clsPetrasWeb.WebServiceURL)

'Connect to the web service
clsPetrasWeb.Connect

'Get the XML representing the static lists
sXML = clsPetrasWeb.GetStaticData

'Load the XML into the MSXML parser
Set xmlParser = New MSXML2.DOMDocument30
xmlParser.LoadXml sXML

'Use XPath expressions to find our elements
xmlParser.SetProperty "SelectionLanguage", "XPath"

'Specify the default namespace to look for, giving it
'the alias 'sd' to use in our element names
xmlParser.SetProperty "SelectionNamespaces", _
    "xmlns:sd=""http://www.appspro.com/PETRASWeb/StaticData"""

' Load each of the program data lists.
' Consultants
With wksProgData.Range(gsRNG_CONSULT_TOP)
```

```
'Remove any existing consultants
.CurrentRegion.Offset(1, 0).ClearContents
lItem = 1

'Loop through all the Consultant elements in the XML
'Equivalent to:  For Each oConsultant in Consultants
For Each xeParent In xmlParser.selectNodes( _
    "sd:StaticData/sd:Consultant")

  lItem = lItem + 1

  'Store the consultant name and ID
  'Equivalent to:  Cell.Value = oConsultant.Name
  .Cells(lItem, 1).Value = xeParent.selectSingleNode( _
      "sd:Name").nodeTypedValue

  .Cells(lItem, 2).Value = CLng(xeParent.selectSingleNode( _
      "sd:ID").nodeTypedValue)

Next xeParent

End With
```

We also use the MSXML library to create our XML in the PostTimeEntriesToWebService procedure, as shown in Listing 28-10.

Listing 28-10   Building the XML to Submit to the Web Service

```
Public Sub PostTimeEntriesToWebService()

  Dim rngCell As Range
  Dim rngTable As Range
  Dim domXML As MSXML2.DOMDocument

  Set rngTable = wksSheet.Range(gsRNG_BILLABLE_HOURS)

  'Create a new XML document
  Set domXML = New MSXML2.DOMDocument

  'Create the root element <TimeSheet>
  Set domXML.documentElement = _
      NewElement(domXML, "TimeSheet")
```

```
With domXML.documentElement

   'Add the <Consultant> element
   With .appendChild(NewElement(domXML, "Consultant"))

      'Add the Consultant's ID and Name elements and values
      .appendChild(NewElement(domXML, "ID")) _
         .nodeTypedValue = rngTable.Cells(1, 1).Value

      .appendChild(NewElement(domXML, "Name")) _
         .nodeTypedValue = wksSheet.Range("inpEmployee").Value

   End With

   'Add the WeekEnding element and value
   .appendChild(NewElement(domXML, "WeekEnding")) _
      .nodeTypedValue = Format( _
      wksSheet.Range("inpWeekEnding").Value, "yyyy-mm-dd")

   ' Loop each entry in the time sheet and add it to the XML
   For Each rngCell In rngTable

      'Add a <BillableHours> element
      With .appendChild(NewElement(domXML, "BillableHours"))

         'Add the elements for a BillableHours record
         .appendChild(NewElement(domXML, "DateWorked")) _
            .nodeTypedValue = Format(_
            rngCell.Offset(0, 1).Value, "yyyy-mm-dd")

         .appendChild(NewElement(domXML, "ProjectID")) _
            .nodeTypedValue = rngCell.Offset(0, 2).Value

         .appendChild(NewElement(domXML, "ActivityID")) _
            .nodeTypedValue = rngCell.Offset(0, 3).Value

         .appendChild(NewElement(domXML, "Hours")) _
            .nodeTypedValue = _
            Trim$(Str$(rngCell.Offset(0, 4).Value))
      End With

   Next rngCell
```

```
End With

    'Submit the XML to the web service
    bSubmitXML domXML.XML

    'etc.

End Sub


' Create a new element with our namespace
Public Function NewElement( _
    ByRef domXML As MSXML2.DOMDocument, _
    ByVal sElementName As String) As IXMLDOMNode

    Const sNS As String = _
        "http://www.appspro.com/PETRASWeb/TimeSheet"

    Set NewElement = domXML.createNode(NODE_ELEMENT, _
        sElementName, sNS)

End Function
```

Summary

Web Services are programs running on Web servers that expose the functions they contain for use over the Internet. They can be used to provide access to proprietary financial models, company data, and other information without having to expose the code for the model, the database connection information, or any other details that should be kept secret. By using the Office Web Services Toolkit we can use the features provided by Web Services from within our VBA code and from within our worksheets (via VBA user-defined functions).

We can combine Excel 2003's use of XML with the ability to connect to Web Services to create an entirely new breed of Excel application: the rich client of a distributed, Web-based application, such as this final iteration of our Professional Excel Timesheet Reporting and Analysis System.

PROVIDING HELP, SECURING, PACKAGING, AND DISTRIBUTING

The final step in developing an Excel-based application is preparing it for release to our users. This includes creating a help file and incorporating it into our application, securing the application to prevent accidental or malicious changes, limiting access to features by checking the user's network group memberships, and avoiding the display of the Macro Security warning dialogs. Finally, we need to decide on a mechanism for installing the application on our users' computers. We might also want to include features within our application to easily deploy updates.

Providing Help

From the very start of a project we should be thinking about how to provide assistance to our users. For simple add-ins this can take the form of a set of instructions displayed at the bottom of an About dialog, or in a separate text file or a Word document distributed with the add-in. For more complex add-ins and dictator applications, we should consider providing a dedicated help file. Doing so requires us to add code throughout the application to display pages from the help file as well as writing the help text.

To demonstrate how to create a help file and display it from our application, we use the Microsoft HTML Help Workshop to create a simple help file for our PETRAS reporting application. The HTML Help Workshop is a fairly rudimentary tool, best used for simple help files. For large or complex help files we recommend you use a third-party application, such as Adobe Systems RoboHelp (www.adobe.com/products/robohelp/) or Component One's Doc-to-Help (www.doctohelp.com).

Overview

We create each page of an HTML Help file as a separate HTML file and give it a name known as a **topic**. We can use any string we want for the topic name, but it's good practice to use a naming convention to help us quickly and easily identify each topic. For example, we might use the name `htFrmActivities` to denote the help topic for a UserForm used to maintain a list of activities.

The HTML Help Workshop is used to create and maintain a **help project** file, which contains configuration information and a list of the topics to include in the help file. Once all the help content has been written, the HTML Help Workshop is used to compile the individual HTML files into a single HTML Help file (with a **chm** file extension) that we distribute with our application. To display help pages from Excel, we have to give each topic a unique number. The mapping between topic names and numbers is also stored in the help project file.

Getting Started

If you don't already have the HTML Help Workshop installed, you can download it from http://go.microsoft.com/fwlink/?LinkId=14188. We also include this file in the *Concepts\Ch29 - Providing Help, Securing, Packaging and Distributing* folder on the accompanying CD. Upon installing the Help Workshop you will likely receive a message stating that you already have a later version of HTML Help installed on your computer. This refers to the HTML Help runtime, not the Help Workshop application. There are a number of steps that need to be followed to produce a compiled skeleton help file:

1. Create a help project file.
2. Update the project options.
3. Create an introductory HTML file.
4. Create a simple HTML file to display "Sorry, there is no help available for this topic."
5. Create a list of topics, with each topic initially referring to the file created in step 4.
6. Create a list that maps each topic to a numeric ID.
7. Compile the project.

Create a Help Project File

To create a new help project, start the HTML Help Workshop. Click *File > New*, select *Project* from the list, and click OK to launch the New Project Wizard. We're not converting an old help project, so skip over step 1. In step

2, enter or select a location and name for the help project file, such as C:\PETRAS\Help\PETRAS.hhp (where the C:\PETRAS\Help directory must already exist). Ideally, the location should be an empty directory because we'll add a lot of files to it. The name we give to the help project file is used as the name for the compiled help file by default, but we can change it later if we want. We don't have any existing files to include, so skip step 3 and click Finish. We end up with a help project similar to Figure 29-1.

FIGURE 29-1 The HTML help project window

Update the Project Options

Click the *Change project options* button shown in Figure 29-2 to set the initial project options.

FIGURE 29-2 The Change Project Options button

In the *General* tab of the Options dialog, give our help file the title of PETRAS Reporting Application. In the *Files* tab, enter a Contents filename of Contents.hhc, an Index file name of Index.hhk, and select the check boxes below each entry. This instructs the Help Workshop to automatically populate a Table of Contents and an Index file for us when the project is compiled. Set the *Maximum head level* to 1, which tells the compiler to create Table of Contents entries from all the <H1> header tags in our HTML files. In the *Compiler* tab, select *Compile full-text search information* to add a *Search* tab to the help file. Click OK to close the Options dialog.

To create the Table of Contents and index files, click on the *Contents* and *Index* tabs. With each tab, ignore the error message that the file can't be found and let the Help Workshop create new files. Give them the names Contents.hhc and Index.hhk.

Create an Introductory HTML File

To create the pages of the help file, we can use any application that generates HTML files, such as FrontPage, Word, Notepad, or the HTML Workshop itself. In this case, create a simple introductory page within the HTML Workshop by selecting *File > New > HTML File* from the menu. Give this file the title Introduction. Just below the <BODY> tag enter the following text:

<H1>Introduction</H1>
This is the Help file for the PETRAS Reporting application.

Save the file as *C:\PETRAS\Help\htIntro.htm*. After creating the file, we need to include it in our help project. Click the *Add/Remove topic files* button shown in Figure 29-3; then click the *Add...* button in the *Topic Files* dialog and select the htIntro.htm file.

Create a "No Help Available" Topic File

When we first set up the help file we point every topic to the same help page, which displays a simple "No Help Available" message. To create this page, add a new HTML file and type the following text after the <BODY> tag:

Sorry, there is no help available for this topic.

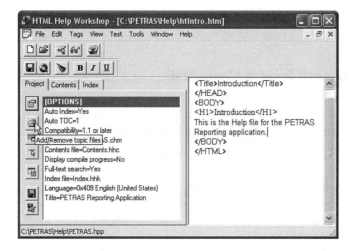

FIGURE 29-3   The Add/Remove Topic Files button

Save the file as htNoHelp.htm and use the *Add/Remove topic files* button to add it to our project.

Create a List of Topics

We can create a skeleton help file containing just a few topics and add to it as we develop our application. Click *File > New > Text* to create a blank text file and type in the list of topics shown in Listing 29-1. Note that each one refers to the htNoHelp.htm file.

Listing 29-1   The PETRAS Help File Topic List

```
htNoHelp=htNoHelp.htm          ;The No Help page
htFrmActivities=htNoHelp.htm   ;The Activities userform
htFrmConsultants=htNoHelp.htm  ;The Consultants userform
htFrmClients=htNoHelp.htm      ;The Clients/Projects userform
htFrmExtractData=htNoHelp.htm  ;The Extract Data userform
```

Save the file as *C:\PETRAS\Help\TopicToFile.h*. Each time we add a form to our application, we should give it a topic name and add the topic to this list. When the time comes to write the help file content, we can edit this list to point each topic to the correct HTML file. To include the list of topics in our help project, click on the *HtmlHelp API information* button (the fourth of the Project buttons), select the *Alias* tab, click the *Include...* button, and enter the filename TopicToFile.h.

Give Each Topic a Numeric ID

When we display a help file from Excel, we have to use numeric IDs to identify our help topics. We map each topic to an ID in the same way we map them to HTML files. Click *File > New > Text* to create another text file and type in the list of mappings shown in Listing 29-2.

Listing 29-2 The PETRAS Help File Topic IDs

```
#define htNoHelp          100   //The No Help page
#define htFrmActivities   101   //The Activities userform
#define htFrmConsultants  102   //The Consultants userform
#define htFrmClients      103   //The Clients/Projects userform
#define htFrmExtractData  104   //The Extract Data userform
```

We're actually creating a C-style header file that defines these topic names as constants using the #define directive. The // is used to indicate the start of a comment. Save the file as *C:\PETRAS\Help\TopicToID.h*. We also need to include this file in our help project by clicking the *HtmlHelp API information* button, selecting the *Map* tab, clicking the *Header file...* button, and entering the filename TopicToID.h. Again, each time we add a new feature to our application we should give it a topic ID and add the topic name and ID to this list.

Compile the Project

Click *File > Compile...* to create the PETRAS.chm help file; then click *View > Compiled File...* to display it. If all goes well, you should see a window similar to Figure 29-4.

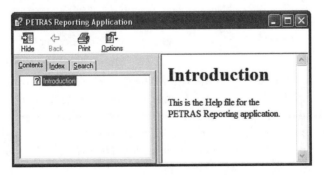

FIGURE 29-4 The PETRAS reporting skeleton help file

Writing Content

The best recommendation we can give about writing help content is: ***Don't write it yourself***. As the developer of the application you know far too much about its inner workings to be able to explain it at the level required by the average user. The best person to write the help content is a user representative, if you have one. This person will be able to explain the application in business terms, including how it should be used within the business environment. When writing the content, there are two things a writer needs to do to allow the Help Workshop to automatically generate the Table of Contents and Index files.

Table of Contents

In the *Files* tab of the project's Options dialog, we can specify the *Maximum head level* to use when automatically creating the Table of Contents. That number corresponds to the <Hn> heading styles used in the HTML files. If Word is being used to write the help content, this number corresponds to Word's Heading styles. If these tags are used consistently throughout all the help files the Table of Contents can be generated without any effort on our part.

Index

In the *Files* tab of the project's Options dialog, we can select the *Include keywords from HTML files* box. The content author can then include the keywords for the index within the source HTML file. To do so, the content author needs to include the <OBJECT> tag shown in Listing 29-3 inside the <BODY> tag of the HTML file, replacing Keyword1, Keyword2, and so on with his own keywords for that file.

Listing 29-3   Adding Index Keywords to an HTML File

```
<OBJECT type="application/x-oleobject"
        classid="clsid:1e2a7bd0-dab9-11d0-b93a-00c04fc99f9e">
    <param name="Keyword" value="Keyword1">
    <param name="Keyword" value="Keyword2">
</OBJECT>
```

Displaying Help from VBA

When we display a help topic from VBA, we have to use the numeric topic IDs rather than the names. Instead of scattering these "magic numbers" throughout our code it is a good idea to expose them in an enumeration such as the one shown in Listing 29-4.

Listing 29-4 Enumeration for the Help Topic IDs

```
Public Enum pxlHelpTopics
    htNoHelp = 100              'Generic 'No Help Available'
    htFrmActivities = 101       'The Activities UserForm
    htFrmConsultants = 102      'The Consultants UserForm
    htFrmClients = 103          'The Clients/Projects UserForm
    htFrmExtractData = 104      'The Extract Data UserForm
End Enum
```

We can then use the enumeration members instead of the topic IDs. For example, the code in Listing 29-5 can be used to display a message box with a Help button that displays our help file when clicked.

Listing 29-5 Displaying a Help File from a Message Box

```
Sub ShowAMessage()

    Dim sMessage As String
    Dim sHelpFile As String

    sHelpFile = ThisWorkbook.Path & "\PETRAS.chm"
    sMessage = "The activity name is already being used."

    MsgBox sMessage, vbExclamation + vbMsgBoxHelpButton, _
           "Add Activity", sHelpFile, htFrmActivities

End Sub
```

Other than using the additional arguments of the MsgBox function, the best way to display a help file from VBA is to call directly into the HHCtrl.ocx file using the HtmlHelp API function. While it is possible to use Application.Help to display a custom help file it usually mixes our help file with Excel's. In Listing 29-6 we wrap the call to the HtmlHelp API in a generic ShowHelp procedure. This procedure verifies that the help file exists and handles missing topic IDs.

Listing 29-6   Displaying a Help File with the HtmlHelp API Function

```
Declare Function HtmlHelp Lib "HHCtrl.ocx" _
    Alias "HtmlHelpA" (ByVal hwndCaller As Long, _
    ByVal pszFile As String, ByVal uCommand As Long, _
    ByVal dwData As Long) As Long


Const HH_DISPLAY_TOPIC = &H0
Const HH_HELP_CONTEXT = &HF


'Show a topic of a help file
Public Sub ShowHelp(ByVal uTopicID As pxlHelpTopics)

    Dim sHelpFile As String
    Dim sCheckFile As String
    Dim lResult As Long

    'Locate the help file
    sHelpFile = ThisWorkbook.Path & "\PETRAS.chm"

    'Check the help file exists
    On Error Resume Next
        sCheckFile = Dir$(sHelpFile)
    On Error GoTo 0

    If Len(sCheckFile) > 0 Then

        'Try to show the requested help topic
        lResult = HtmlHelp(0, sHelpFile, HH_HELP_CONTEXT, _
                        uTopicID)

        If lResult = 0 Then
            'If it failed, try to show the 'No Help' topic
            lResult = HtmlHelp(0, sHelpFile, HH_HELP_CONTEXT, _
                            htNoHelp)
        End If
    End If

    'If we couldn't find the help file, or failed to show it,
    'display a message in VBA.
    If lResult = 0 Then
        MsgBox "No help is available at this time.", _
                vbInformation, "PETRAS Reporting"
    End If

End Sub
```

29. PROVIDING HELP, SECURING, PACKAGING, AND DISTRIBUTING

We call this procedure from within our application wherever we want to display a help topic, such as in the Click event handler of a form's Help button as shown in Listing 29-7. Passing the enumeration member as the argument helps to ensure that we show the correct topic for the form.

Listing 29-7   Using the ShowHelp Procedure from a Form's Help Button

```
Private Sub cmdHelp_Click()
    ShowHelp htFrmActivities
End Sub
```

Securing

Securing an application can mean several different things. We may need to prevent users from seeing how the application works to protect intellectual property. We may need to limit certain application features to certain users. We may also need to guarantee that our application code has not been modified by anyone else for potentially malicious purposes.

Excel Security

Excel was not designed to be a secure development platform, and therefore Excel applications cannot be made totally secure. There is no way to prevent a determined hacker from gaining access to our worksheets, formulas, and VBA code. Workbook, Worksheet, and VBProject passwords are weak and can be easily broken.

The only aspect of Excel's security that can be considered secure is the Workbook file open password, but that is little help because we can't run an Excel application without opening its workbooks. At this point, the determined hacker can use GetObject to get a reference to the instance of Excel running our application and use automation to save all our workbooks without passwords. The best we can achieve using Excel's security is to prevent accidental damage and discourage the casual hacker.

The only way to really secure our code is to move it out of Excel workbooks and into a compiled DLL, using either Visual Basic 6, as described in Chapter 23, "Excel and Visual Basic 6," or VB.NET, as described in Chapters 24 through 26. We can use DLLs for most of our application's features, so our workbooks contain only enough VBA to instantiate the DLL and call its procedures.

Checking Network Groups

It's a common requirement for us to restrict access to parts of our applications depending on the user's network group membership. For example, we might want to allow only people in the Auditors group to be able to run certain reports. We can find this information from the Windows Script Networking and Active Directory Service Interfaces object libraries, as shown in Listing 29-8. We need to set references to these object libraries, which are listed in the *Tools > References* dialog as Windows Script Host Object Model and Active DS Type Library.

Listing 29-8   Checking Network Group Membership

```
'Define a UDT to hold user login information
Public Type LOGON_INFO
  ComputerName As String
  UserName As String
  Domain As String
  Groups As String
End Type

'Retrieve user's login information
Public Function GetUserInfo() As LOGON_INFO

  'Use a static variable, so we only retrieve the
  'information once
  Static uLogonInfo As LOGON_INFO

  'Requires a reference to
  '"Windows Script Host Object Model"
  Dim wshNetwork As IWshRuntimeLibrary.wshNetwork

  'Requires a reference to "Active DS Type Library"
  Dim adsUser As ActiveDs.IADsUser
  Dim adsGroup As ActiveDs.IADsGroup

  'Fill the logon info UDT if not already set
  If Len(uLogonInfo.UserName) = 0 Then

    'Get the username and domain from Windows Scripting
    Set wshNetwork = New IWshRuntimeLibrary.wshNetwork
```

```
    With wshNetwork
      uLogonInfo.ComputerName = .ComputerName
      uLogonInfo.UserName = .UserName
      uLogonInfo.Domain = .UserDomain
    End With

    'Use the domain/username to get a list of groups from
    'Windows Active Directory Services
    Set adsUser = GetObject("WinNT://" & uLogonInfo.Domain & _
                   "/" & uLogonInfo.UserName & ",user")

    'Create a concatenated string of groups,
    'separated by commas
    For Each adsGroup In adsUser.Groups
      uLogonInfo.Groups = uLogonInfo.Groups & _
                          adsGroup.ADsPath & ","
    Next adsGroup

  End If

  'Return the login information
  GetUserInfo = uLogonInfo

End Function

'Function to check if the current user is in the
'Auditors group
Function IsAuditor() As Boolean
  IsAuditor = InStr(1, GetUserInfo().Groups, _
    "/Domain/Auditors,", vbTextCompare) > 0
End Function
```

Note that we store the fully qualified `ADsPath` for the group, which includes both the domain name and the group name, and then check for the domain and group in the IsAuditor function. This prevents a malicious user from creating a bogus Auditors group on his machine, which would have passed a test based on the group name alone. Even using the domain/group style leaves a possible security hole, as our user could rename his computer to be the same as the domain name. To be totally sure, we could store and check the groups' GUIDs instead of their names.

Macro Security and Digital Signatures

When we open a workbook that contains VBA code, Excel checks the macro security settings and either enables or disables any VBA code contained within the workbook depending on the security level, the way in which the file is opened, whether the VBA code has been digitally signed, and whether the signature has been trusted. The behavior of Excel for each of the various macro security settings is summarized in Table 29-1.

Table 29-1   Summary of Excel's Macro Security Behavior

Security Level	Unsigned	Signed, but Untrusted	Signed and Trusted
Low	Allows code to run without prompting	Allows code to run without prompting	Allows code to run without prompting
Medium	Prompts us whether to run the code	Prompts us whether to run the code and allows us to trust the signature	Allows code to run without prompting
High	Does not run the code	Prompts us whether to trust the signature and only runs the code if we choose to trust it	Allows code to run without prompting
Very High (new to Excel 2003)	Does not run the code	Does not run the code	Only runs code in installed add-ins and templates, and only if that option is enabled

Some of the details are a little different if the code is signed but the signature is invalid or expired, or if the add-in is being opened using *Tools > Add-ins* instead of *File > Open* and the *Trust all installed add-ins and templates* option in the Macro Security dialog is selected. The specific details can be found by searching for "Macro security levels" in Excel's help.

If we want our code to run even under the strictest macro security settings, we have to sign it with a digital signature purchased from a Certificate Authority such as VeriSign (www.verisign.com) or Thawte (www.thawte.com). Digital certificates are expensive and have to be renewed annually or biennially.

If our workbook is opened after the certificate has expired (usually one year), Excel treats it as if it were unsigned (though the prompts will be slightly different). This can be avoided by telling Excel to timestamp the signing of the file. When a signed and timestamped file is opened, Excel can see that the file was signed while the digital signature was still valid and therefore it will allow the code to run. We tell Excel to timestamp the signature by adding the following registry entries to HKEY_CURRENT_USER\Software\Microsoft\VBA\Security (creating that key if it doesn't exist):

```
TimeStampURL =
http://timestamp.verisign.com/scripts/timstamp.dll
TimeStampRetryCount = 1
TimeStampRetryDelay = 2
```

The digital signature is applied whenever the VBA code is changed and the file is saved. If the digital signature private key is not installed, the signature will be removed from the file. This gives us a foolproof way of identifying whether our code has been tampered with—it won't be signed with our digital signature.

Alternatives to Digital Signatures

In practice, very few Excel developers digitally sign their workbooks. Most users have the *Trust all installed add-ins and templates* check box selected in the Macro Security dialog, which means that add-ins opened using the *Tools > Add-ins* dialog run without being signed (unless Macro Security is set to Very High in Excel 2003). Workbooks and add-ins opened using *File > Open* still display the macro security warnings.

For dictator applications we can make use of the fact that the macro security checks are not done when workbooks are opened through the object model. Chapter 23 shows how to create and use a front-loader EXE to start Excel and open our workbooks without triggering the macro security checks.

Ultimately, the need to digitally sign our code depends on the users' security settings, the client's security policies, and our own professionalism. Using a digital signature is the only sure way to have our code run without displaying a macro security prompt.

Packaging

For simple single-workbook applications, we can just e-mail the workbook to our users and ask them to open it. For more complex applications, we may need to install templates, add-ins, or other files in specific directories and write specific registry entries to ensure our add-ins are listed and installed correctly.

Installation Location

When thinking about how to install our application, we need to consider how the user will start it, create new files, and so on. Dictator applications are almost always started by opening a workbook or running an EXE front-loader. As such, all the files for a dictator application are typically installed to a single folder and run from there.

Add-ins can be installed either by copying them to one of two specific locations or by writing registry entries that tell Excel to include them in the *Tools > Add-ins* list. (See the "Installation Requirements" section for details.) Copying the xla to the user's AddIns folder is the easiest way to manually install add-ins but is only appropriate for single-file add-ins. If our add-in uses other supporting files (such as templates, databases, and so on), all the files for our add-in should be installed to a dedicated folder, with the appropriate registry entries created so that our add-in appears in the *Tools > Add-Ins* list.

When installing application-specific add-ins, we need to consider whether the user should be able to use the *File > New* menu to create new instances of our data entry workbooks. If we want to allow this mechanism, the template workbook needs to be copied to the user's Templates folder. For this to work properly, the corresponding add-in must be installed and must use Application events to detect when the user creates a new data entry workbook (see Chapter 7, "Using Class Modules to Create Objects").

The main problem with this approach is that the only way to ensure the corresponding add-in is installed is to include code in the template file to verify it. This breaks the principle of not including code in our templates. Instead, we can use the AddIn_Install event to copy the template file to the user's templates folder and the AddIn_Uninstall event to remove it.

Many application-specific add-ins (including our PETRAS example)
ignore the *File > New* menu and provide their own menu or toolbar button for creating new instances of their data entry workbooks. By doing this,
we don't need to copy files to different locations for Excel to use them. We
can simply install all our files to a single folder and write registry entries to
install our add-ins.

Installation Requirements

Templates

Templates intended to appear in the *File > New* dialog are installed on a
per-user basis by copying them to the folder C:\Documents and
Settings\<UserName>\Application Data\Microsoft\Templates. If templates are opened under program control (such as the New Timesheet button in our PETRAS time sheet example) they should be installed to the
same folder as their associated add-in file.

Add-ins

Single-file, general purpose add-ins can be installed on a per-user basis by
copying them to the C:\Documents and Settings\<UserName>\Application
Data\Microsoft\AddIns folder, or for all users by copying them to the
C:\Program Files\Microsoft Office\OfficeXX\Library folder, where XX is
the version number of Office that is installed.

Add-ins located in either of these folders automatically appear in the
Tools > Add-ins list but are not loaded by default. To have them automatically loaded as well requires us to write some registry entries.

Complex add-ins that have additional support files are better installed
to their own directory. To get these add-ins to appear in the *Tools > Add-
ins* list we add a string value in the registry key:

```
HKEY_CURRENT_USER\Software\Microsoft\Office\11.0\Excel\Add-in
Manager
```

where the name of the value is the full path and filename of the add-in.
The 11.0 in the registry key in the preceding line refers to the version of
Excel, as described in the following list:

- 9.0 = Excel 2000
- 10.0 = Excel 2002

- 11.0 = Excel 2003
- 12.0 = Excel 2007

When we add a value to the Add-in Manager registry key the add-in specified by that entry is listed in the *Tools > Add-ins* dialog but is not loaded (that is, not run when Excel starts up). To have the add-in load automatically we have to write an entry to the registry key:

```
HKEY_CURRENT_USER\Software\Microsoft\Office\11.0\Excel\Options
```

instead of the Add-in Manager key. The entry must be a string value where the name is the next available item in the sequence OPEN, OPEN1, OPEN2, OPEN3, and so on, and the value is the full path and filename of the add-in, surrounded in quotation marks. This means we have to first check if there is a value called "OPEN", then check if there is a value called "OPEN1", then check for "OPEN2", and so on until we find the next entry in the sequence that isn't being used. If we precede the add-in name with a /R switch, Excel opens the add-in read-only. Figure 29-5 shows two OPEN registry entries, the first for the analysis toolpack and the second for the IfError automation add-in from Chapter 23.

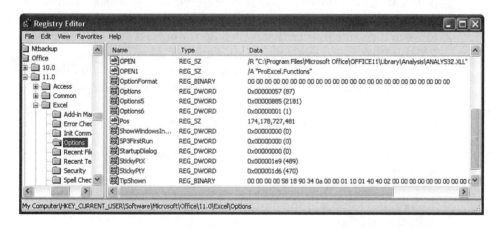

FIGURE 29-5   The OPEN registry entries for an Excel add-in and an automation add-in

29. PROVIDING HELP, SECURING, PACKAGING, AND DISTRIBUTING

COM Add-ins

The registry entries required to install COM add-ins are covered in detail in Chapter 23. These registry entries can be written by the Add-in Designer object under either

```
HKEY_CURRENT_USER\Software\Microsoft\Office\Excel\Addins
```

for per-user installation or

```
HKEY_LOCAL_MACHINE\SOFTWARE\Microsoft\Office\Excel\Addins
```

to install the COM add-in for all users. The Designer writes the registry entries when the COM add-in DLL is registered on the user's machine, which is done using the regsvr32.exe program with a command line similar to the following:

```
regsvr32 c:\mypath\myCOMAddin.dll
```

Automation Add-ins

Automation add-ins must also be registered on the user's machine using regsvr32, but they do not write their own registry entries. Instead, we have to write the same entries that we would for normal add-ins, but using the ProgID (that is, ProjectName.ClassName) of the automation add-in class that exposes the worksheet functions instead of the path and filename.

For example, to install the IfError function from Chapter 23 so it is listed in the *Tools > Add*-ins list but not loaded on startup, we would add a new string value with the name ProExcel.Functions within the registry key

```
HKEY_CURRENT_USER\Software\Microsoft\Office\10.0\Excel\Add-in
Manager
```

To have the same add-in automatically load on startup, we would instead write a new value in

```
HKEY_CURRENT_USER\Software\Microsoft\Office\10.0\Excel\Options
```

where the name is OPEN, OPEN1, OPEN2, and so on, and the value is

```
/A "ProExcel.Functions"
```

The /A prefix identifies it as an automation add-in, while ProExcel.Functions is the ProgID of the class containing the IfError function.

Installation Mechanisms

Manual

If our application consists of just a template and associated add-in we could provide instructions telling the user where to copy the files to and hope they do it correctly. But as the number of files increases, so does the likelihood of failure.

An Installation Workbook

A common method of installing Excel-based applications is to zip all our files together and tell our users to unzip the file to a new directory and open the Setup.xls workbook. The Setup.xls workbook performs the following tasks and then closes itself:

- Registers any DLLs, using

```
Shell "regsvr32 /s """ & ThisWorkbook.Path & "\MyDLL.DLL"""
```

- Copies add-ins and templates to the correct directories using properties such as `Application.LibraryPath` and `Application.TemplatesPath` to identify where to copy them
- Uses the Excel object model to install add-ins (instead of writing registry entries) as shown in Listing 29-9

Listing 29-9 Installing Add-ins Using the Object Model

```
Sub InstallAddins()

    'Install an Excel Addin
    Application.AddIns.Add(ThisWorkbook.Path & _
        "\MyAddin.xla").Installed = True

    'Silently register an Automation Addin
    Shell "regsvr32 /s """ & ThisWorkbook.Path & _
        "\ProExcel.dll"""

    'Install an Automation Addin
    Application.AddIns.Add("ProExcel.Functions") _
        .Installed = True

End Sub
```

Windows Installer

The biggest problems with the Manual or Workbook installs is that they do not provide an easy uninstall mechanism and they aren't really professional. Doing it properly requires us to write an installation routine using InstallShield, WISE or a similar application for writing dedicated application installers. Each program has advantages, disadvantages, and usage quirks, and it is beyond the scope of this book to describe how to create installation routines with them. If you intend to use one of these packages we suggest you refer to the product documentation.

Distributing

Originals

Simple Excel-based applications are usually easy to distribute—just zip up the files and e-mail them to the users. There are no runtimes that must be installed before our application can work, other than Excel itself, so the user can just unzip and go.

Some companies prefer to administer the installation of applications centrally, rolling them out as part of the user's login scripts. For those cases we need to create a proper installation package that installs our application without displaying any prompts (such as asking for file locations).

Updates

When distributing updates, we need to take a little more care to preserve our users' data and application settings. If we followed the advice to always physically separate the code from the data, the only thing we need to be careful about is to not overwrite the users' data files with the empty templates we might include. If we didn't follow the advice to separate data from code, this is the time that we realize why we should have.

We should never distribute patches that attempt to modify the VBA code contained within another workbook. For us to be able to do this, the user must have selected the *Trust Access to Visual Basic Project* check box in the *Tools > Macro > Security* dialog, the project can't be protected, and saving the modified project removes any digital signature we've applied. If the separation between data and code has been observed, however, we can always simply overwrite code files with new versions.

Phone Home

If we included a front-loader workbook or VB6 EXE to start our application, we could include "phone home" distribution of updates. Every time the application starts, it connects to a central Web site (or Web Service) to see whether any of the application files have been updated. If they have, the new files are downloaded, opened, and run. This mechanism is built into the Visual Studio Tools for Office but can easily be built into a front-loader workbook by using a Web Service to check for updates (see Chapter 28, "Excel and Web Services"), and then using `Workbooks.Open` and `Workbook.SaveAs` to open the new file from the server and save it to the local machine.

Summary

As developers of applications, it's all too easy for us to assume our user interfaces are so intuitive that there's no need to provide a help file. In reality, we can only achieve that level of simplicity with the most trivial features. Including a well-written help file with our application can provide the explanations our users require to effectively use the features we provide. The increase in confidence that brings often leads to a more positive perception of the entire application.

During the process of developing Excel applications we usually don't include any security restrictions because they tend to get in the way of our work. We must, however, consider the security implications of everything we do, both in terms of whether our application could be misused and whether our application can be broken into. Excel is not a secure environment. A malicious hacker can access any worksheet or VBProject in any workbook using tools readily available on the Internet. If we want to protect our code from a determined hacker we must move it outside Excel VBA and into a fully compiled DLL environment.

When distributing our applications to end users, we usually need to provide an installation routine that ensures all our files are copied to the correct folders and writes any registry entries that may be required. This is most often done using a separate setup.xls workbook that can use the Excel object model to copy the files, install add-ins, and so on. For a professional look, though, we should create proper installation packages using a commercial installer application such as WISE or InstallShield that can also be used to uninstall our applications.

INDEX

Symbols

character prefix (conditional compilation constants), 512

(:) colon character in Immediate window, 520

. (dot operator), performance and, 571

= (equal sign) in criteria ranges, 677

<, > (greater than/less than symbols) in criteria ranges, 677

\ (integer division operator), 570

? (question mark character) in Immediate window, 519

3D effects, simulating, 84

A

accelerator keys. *See also* keyboard shortcuts
  creating, 205
  for UserForm controls, 386

Access 2002 Desktop Developer's Handbook (Litwin, Getz, Gunderloy), 739

Access 2002 Developer's Handbook Set (Litwin, Getz, Gunderloy), 647

Access databases
  adding data (time sheet example application), 652-656
  advantages of, 620
  connecting to, 620-622
    time sheet example application, 648-649
  deleting data, 629-630
  inserting data, 625-626
  modifying data, 626-629

Northwind sample database, installing, 615
  retrieving data, 622-625
  time sheet example application, 650-652
  upsizing to SQL Server, 642-646

Access object library, 726-729
  Application object, 726
  DAO.Database object, 726
  DoCmd object, 727
  example application, 727-729

access restrictions, checking network group membership, 1095-1096

accessing Application object from automation add-ins, 800-802

action panes, 999

Activate event, error handling, 489

activating error handlers, 468

active, error handlers as, 468

Active Directory Service Interfaces object library, 1095

ActiveConnection property (ADO Command object), 605, 628

ActiveDocument (Word), referencing, 712

ActiveSheet property, performance and, 573

ActiveX, 710

ActiveX controls
  adding to Windows Forms, 826
  advantages of, 100
  forms (VB6) support for, 760

ActiveX Data Objects. *See* ADO

ActiveX DLLs, 742
  advantages of using, 758-774
    ClipBoard object, 773
    code protection, 758
    forms (VB6) versus UserForms, 759-762, 764-769
    object oriented programming support, 769-772
    Printer object, 773
    resource files, 773
    Screen object, 774
  COM add-ins. *See* COM add-ins
  compiling, 744, 750
  form display example, 751-758
  in-process communication, 774
  loading icons with resource file, 802-807
  one-way communication example, 744-747
  projects, creating, 742-744
  referencing, 745-746
  registering, 744
  setting references, 747
  two-way communication example, 747-751

adAsyncExecute (ExecuteOptionEnum constant value), 603

adCmdStoredProc (CommandTypeEnum constant value), 603

adCmdTable (CommandTypeEnum constant value), 603

adCmdTableDirect (CommandTypeEnum constant value), 603

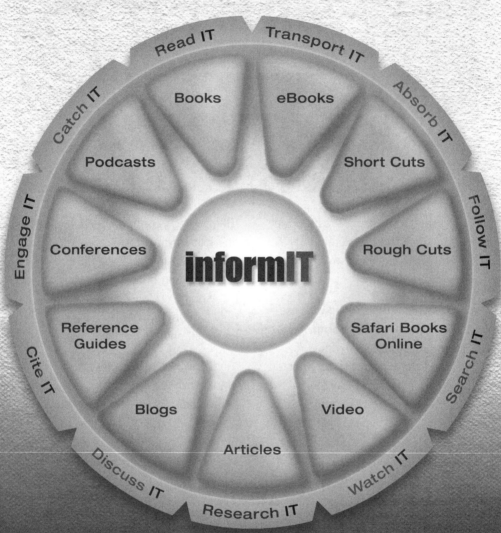

FREE Online Edition

Your purchase of **Professional Excel Development, Second Edition** includes access to a free online edition for 120 days through the Safari Books Online subscription service. Nearly every Addison-Wesley Professional book is available online through Safari Books Online, along with more than 5,000 other technical books and videos from publishers such as Cisco Press, Exam Cram, IBM Press, O'Reilly, Prentice Hall, Que, and Sams.

SAFARI BOOKS ONLINE allows you to search for a specific answer, cut and paste code, download chapters, and stay current with emerging technologies.

Activate your FREE Online Edition at
www.informit.com/safarifree

> **STEP 1:** Enter the coupon code: XMIPGBI.

> **STEP 2:** New Safari users, complete the brief registration form.
> Safari subscribers, just log in.

If you have difficulty registering on Safari or accessing the online edition, please e-mail customer-service@safaribooksonline.com